*NEW PERSPECTIVES*

# COMPUTER CONCEPTS

JUNE JAMRICH PARSONS • DAN OJA

EDITION
**10**

## INTRODUCTORY

Includes access to an integrated Web site and an interactive BookOnCD. The Web site offers audio clips, labs, games, relevant links, practice tests, and more. The BookOnCD contains the entire contents of the textbook with figures that come to life as videos, software tours, and animations. See the Preface for more information!

**THOMSON**
COURSE TECHNOLOGY ™

Australia • Canada • Denmark • Japan • Mexico • New Zealand • Philippines • Puerto Rico • Singapore • South Africa • Spain • United Kingdom • United States

**ACQUISITIONS EDITOR**
Kristina Matthews

**DEVELOPMENTAL EDITOR**
Deb Kaufmann

**PRODUCT MANAGER**
Donna Gridley

**TECHNOLOGY PROJECT MANAGER**
Jeffrey Joubert

**ASSOCIATE PRODUCT MANAGER**
Brandi Henson

**SENIOR CONTENT PRODUCT MANAGER**
Jennifer Goguen McGrail

**EDITORIAL ASSISTANT**
Rebecca Padrick

**COMPOSITION**
GEX Publishing Services

**MARKETING MANAGER**
Joy Stark-Vancs

**INTERIOR DESIGNER**
Joel Sadagursky

# TABLE OF CONTENTS

## NEW PERSPECTIVES LABS

**CHAPTER 1** Operating a Personal Computer;
Working with Binary Numbers

**CHAPTER 2** Benchmarking

**CHAPTER 3** Installing and Uninstalling Software

**CHAPTER 4** Working with Windows Explorer;
Backing Up Your Computer

**CHAPTER 5** Local Area Networks

**CHAPTER 6** Tracking Packets;  Securing Your Connection

**CHAPTER 7** Browser Security Settings; Working with Cookies

**CHAPTER 8** Working with Bitmap Graphics; Video Editing

## STUDENT EDITION LABS

**CHAPTER 1** Binary Numbers;
Understanding the Motherboard

**CHAPTER 2** Peripheral Devices; Using Input Devices

**CHAPTER 3** Word Processing; Spreadsheets; Installing
and Uninstalling Software; Databases; Presentation
Software; Keeping Your Computer Virus Free

**CHAPTER 4** Maintaining a Hard Drive; Managing Files
and Folders; Backing Up Your Computer

**CHAPTER 5** Networking Basics; Wireless Networking

**CHAPTER 6** Connecting to the Internet;
Protecting Your Privacy Online;
Getting the Most Out of the Internet

**CHAPTER 7** Creating Web Pages; E-mail;
E-commerce; Web Design Principles

**CHAPTER 8** Working with Graphics;
Working with Video; Working with Audio

# Study Smarter: The NP10 Experience

## You have purchased more than just a book.

*New Perspectives on Computer Concepts, 10th Edition* includes a printed book, an integrated Web site, and an interactive BookOnCD designed to be used together to provide a cutting-edge learning experience.

Want to study smarter? The NP10 Web site offers tools to help you understand the material from all angles and to thoroughly prepare you for exams. Want to see the concepts in the book in action? The BookOnCD and other BookOn products bring concepts to life through figures that become videos, animations, and software tours.

The NP Computer Concepts pedagogy is like no other. Chapters are divided into three essential learning components: preparatory activities, chapter activities, and review activities. This model helps students focus their learning, study more efficiently, and retain information better. Web-based, book-based, and CD-based activities work together for an interactive, hands-on, and engaging learning experience.

## CREATE YOUR OWN LEARNING PLAN

Use the book, the NP10 Web site, the BookOnCD, BookOnFlashDrive, or other BookOn technology in **ANY WAY THAT'S RIGHT FOR YOU**. The Orientation helps you get acquainted with the wide array of NP10 technology that's at your command.

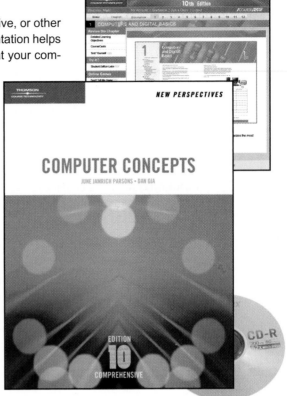

### Your BookOn Plan

Use the BookOnCD, BookOnFlashDrive, or other BookOn product to take the **PRE-ASSESSMENT** and gauge what you already know.

Work on the Chapter opener **TRY IT ACTIVITY** for a hands-on introduction to the chapter topics.

Read a chapter, completing the **QUICKCHECKS** at the end of each section.

Work with **NEW PERSPECTIVES LABS** to apply your knowledge.

Complete **REVIEW ACTIVITIES** using your BookOnCD, BookOnFlashDrive, or other BookOn product.

Take a **PRACTICE TEST** to see if you're ready for the exam.

Transmit your results to your instructor on **WEBTRACK**.

### Your Web Plan

Listen to a **COURSECAST OVERVIEW** of chapter highlights.

Read a chapter, completing **QUICKCHECKS** at the end of each section.

Work with the **STUDENT EDITION LABS** to apply your knowledge.

Have some fun reviewing with **ONLINE GAMES**.

Use **COURSECAST FLASHCARDS** to review key terms from the chapter.

Check the **DETAILED LEARNING OBJECTIVES** to make sure you've mastered the material.

**TEST YOURSELF** to see if you are ready for the exam.

Store your results in the online **UNIVERSAL GRADEBOOK**.

### Your Own Plan

**MIX AND MATCH** any of your favorite activities from the book, electronic textbook, or Web site.

## THE BOOK

New Perspectives on Computer Concepts gives you the straight story on today's technology. Now in its 10th edition, the style has been carefully honed to be clear, concise, and visual.

### Easy to read

A chapter is divided into five **SECTIONS**, each offering a chunk of information that's easy to assimilate in one session. **FAQS** answer commonly asked questions about technology topics and help you follow the flow of the presentation.

### Keeps you on track

**QUICKCHECKS** at the end of each section help you find out if you understood the most important concepts. Extensive review activities at the end of each chapter include **INTERACTIVE CHAPTER SUMMARIES**, **KEY TERMS**, **INTERACTIVE SITUATION QUESTIONS**, and **CONCEPT MAPS**.

### Helps you explore

**ISSUE** sections in each chapter highlight controversial aspects of technology. In the **COMPUTERS IN CONTEXT** section, you'll discover how technology plays a role in careers such as film-making, architecture, banking, and fashion. **INFOWEBLINKS** lead you to Web-based information on chapter topics. Work with **NP10 PROJECTS** to apply the concepts you learned, explore technology, consider globalization, build your resume, work with a team, and experiment with multimedia.

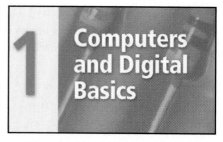

**NEW!** Chapter 1 guides you through the digital revolution and gives you the scoop on the bits and bytes that are the foundation for all things digital.

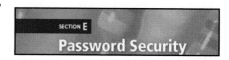

**NEW!** Section E of every chapter focuses on security to help you keep your data safe and maintain your privacy.

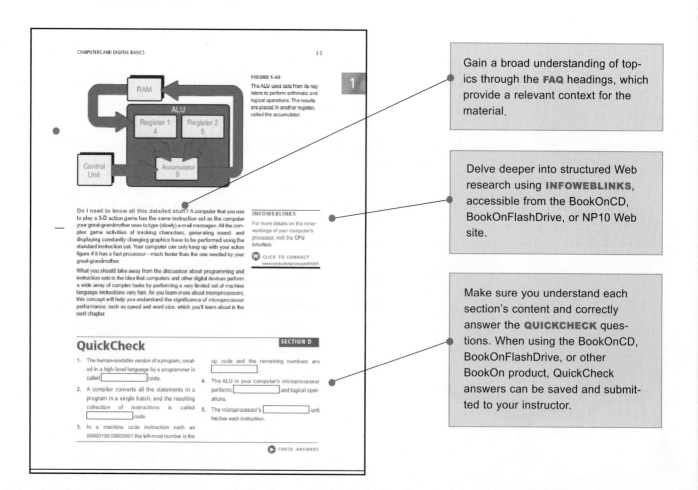

Gain a broad understanding of topics through the **FAQ** headings, which provide a relevant context for the material.

Delve deeper into structured Web research using **INFOWEBLINKS**, accessible from the BookOnCD, BookOnFlashDrive, or NP10 Web site.

Make sure you understand each section's content and correctly answer the **QUICKCHECK** questions. When using the BookOnCD, BookOnFlashDrive, or other BookOn product, QuickCheck answers can be saved and submitted to your instructor.

## THE TECHNOLOGY

The **BOOKONCD**, **BOOKONFLASHDRIVE**, and other BookOn products offer an electronic version of your textbook with multimedia and interactive activities designed to enhance your learning experience.

### Works alone or with the book

Every page of the electronic textbook **MIRRORS THE PRINTED TEXTBOOK**, so use the tool that's most convenient and that best suits your learning style.

**NEW!** NP10 is available as a portable application on a flash drive. No installation is required, so you can plug your textbook into any computer, read chapters, watch multimedia figures, work on labs, and review. After you complete computer-scored review activities, you can save your scores right on the flash drive!

### Brings concepts to life

In the electronic textbook, many photos turn into **VIDEOS**. Illustrations become **ANIMATED DIAGRAMS**. Screen shots activate guided **SOFTWARE TOURS**, so you can see how applications and operating systems like **WINDOWS VISTA** work even if they aren't installed on your computer.

### Makes learning interactive

Before you read a chapter, take the **PRE-ASSESSMENT** to find out how to best focus your study time. You can master hundreds of computer concepts using the **NEW PERSPECTIVES LABS**. When you complete a chapter, try your hand at interactive, **COMPUTER-SCORED ACTIVITIES**. Take some **PRACTICE TESTS** to gauge how well you'll perform on exams. Easily transmit your scores to your instructor on **WEBTRACK**.

The electronic textbook is easy to use, packed with **MULTIMEDIA** and offers plenty of **COMPUTER-SCORED ACTIVITIES**.

Interactive **NEW PERSPECTIVES LABS** give you hands-on experience with concepts and software.

## THE NP10 WEB SITE

The NP10 Web site is packed full of information and activities to accompany each chapter. Follow the directions on the inside front cover of this book to create your CoursePort account for access to the NP10 Web site.

### Gives you options

Want to have fun while you review? Try an **ONLINE GAME** that packages chapter concepts into an entertaining quiz show or action game. When you're ready for some serious exam preparation, work with the **TEST YOURSELF** activity to see how well you can answer questions similar to those on your upcoming test. Need some last minute review? Load up your portable music player with a **CHAPTER OVERVIEW COURSECAST** and a **KEY TERM FLASHCARD COURSECAST**.

### Reinforces your understanding

**STUDENT EDITION LABS** give you hands-on experience with key concepts and skills. **DETAILED LEARNING OBJECTIVES** help you determine if you've mastered all the requirements for completing a chapter. **CNET VIDEOS** highlight popular technologies and **TECHBUZZ** gives you the scoop on emerging technology trends.

### Keeps track of your progress

CoursePort allows you to save your results from Web site activities and share them with your instructor through the **UNIVERSAL GRADEBOOK**.

**NEW!** Now you can listen to NP10 CourseCasts on your computer or download them to your portable music player. Audio chapter overviews and flashcards help you study while you're out and about.

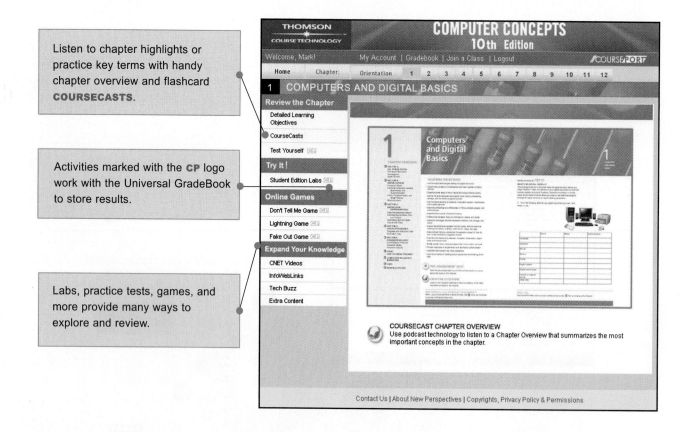

Listen to chapter highlights or practice key terms with handy chapter overview and flashcard **COURSECASTS**.

Activities marked with the **CP** logo work with the Universal GradeBook to store results.

Labs, practice tests, games, and more provide many ways to explore and review.

## INSTRUCTOR RESOURCES

New Perspectives instructional resources and technology provide instructors with a wide range of tools that enhance teaching and learning. These tools can be accessed from the Instructor Resources CD or at *www.course.com*.

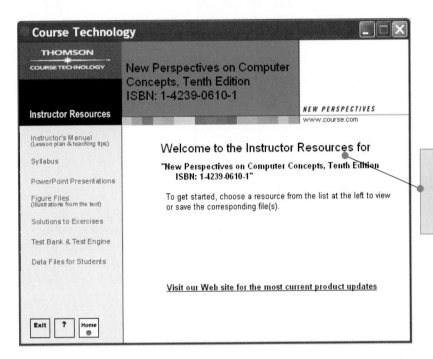

Instructors can find a full collection of **SYLLABUS**, **PRESENTATION**, **GRADING**, and **TESTING** tools in the electronic Instructor's manual.

### Instructor's Manual: Help is Only a Few Keystrokes Away

The special Instructor's Manual offers bullet point lecture notes for each chapter, plus classroom activities and teaching tips, including how to effectively use and integrate the Web site content, BookOnCD content, and labs.

### Instructor Edition

The Instructor Edition provides an in-depth description of everything this textbook has to offer, and includes resources and tools to help instructors teach the course in the way that makes the most sense for them. It also provides suggestions on how to use New Perspectives on Computer Concepts technology in the classroom.

### Course Presenter

Instructors can deliver engaging and visually impressive lectures for each chapter with the professionally-designed Course Presenter. Course Presenter is a PowerPoint presentation enhanced with screentours, animations, and videos.

### WebTrack

Monitoring student progress is easy by tracking scores from BookOnCD, BookOnFlashDrive, or other BookOn products. Using the WebTrack store-and-forward system, a student can transmit scores to an instuctor, who can download them at any time. Newly downloaded scores are consolidated with previous scores and can be displayed, printed, or exported in a variety of report formats.

**ANNOTATIONS!** Instructors can create their own text, graphical, or video annotations that students will see as they read the BookOnCD or BookOnFlashDrive. Find out more about this innovative feature in the Instructor Edition.

## Universal Gradebook

For courses that take advantage of the activities at the NP10 Web site, the Universal Gradebook allows students to send results to instructors.

## BlackBoard Learning System™ Content

We offer a full range of content for use with the BlackBoard Learning System to simplify the use of New Perspectives in distance education settings.

## ExamView: Our Powerful Testing Software Package

With ExamView, instructors can generate printed tests, create LAN-based tests, or test over the Internet.

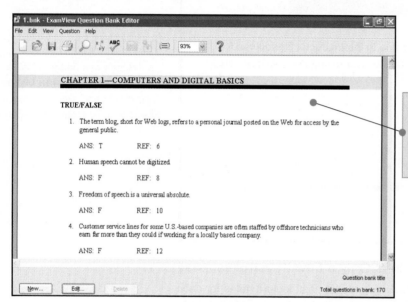

ExamView test banks for New Perspectives on Computer Concepts 10th Edition make test creation a snap.

## SAM

SAM Software helps instructors teach, test, and train. It can be used to reinforce the lessons presented in this textbook and to create realistic hands-on exams. For a total teaching solution to introductory computer courses, SAM for Computer Concepts is available with SAM for Office 2003. This integrated offering provides seamless training, testing, and reporting for concepts and software skills covered in introductory computer courses. For more information about SAM Computer Concepts Training and Assessment, please visit *www.course.com/sam*.

## FROM THE AUTHORS

Many of today's students have substantially more practical experience with computers than their counterparts of 10 years ago, and yet other students enter college with inadequate technology preparation. The goal of New Perspectives on Computer Concepts is to bring every student up to speed with computer basics, and then go beyond basic computer literacy to provide students with technical information that a college-educated person would be expected to know.

In producing the 10th edition of this very popular textbook, we incorporated significant technology trends that affect computing and everyday life. Concerns for data security and personal privacy, controversy over digital rights management, interest in open source software and portable applications, the release of Windows Vista, and the emerging Intel Mac platform are just some of the trends that we've included in this edition of the book.

Whether you are an instructor or a student, we hope that you enjoy the learning experience provided by our text-based and technology-based materials.

## ACKNOWLEDGEMENTS

The book would not exist—and certainly wouldn't arrive on schedule—were it not for the efforts of our media, editorial, and production teams. We thank Deb Kaufmann for her tireless work on every detail of the project; Donna Gridley for handling all the administrative tasks; Rachel Goldberg for many years of guiding the New Perspectives series; Kristina Matthews for her executive leadership; Jennifer Goguen McGrail for managing production; artist Joel Sadagursky for a stunning book design; Abigail Reip for photo research; and Brandi Henson for managing the supplements.

The MediaTechnics team worked tirelessly and we can't offer enough thanks to Tensi Parsons for her extraordinary devotion to desktop publishing; Keefe Crowley for his versatile skills in producing the BookOnCD, creating videos, taking photos, and maintaining the InfoWebLinks site; Donna Mulder for creating screentours and animations; Marilou Potter for her invaluable contributions to research and writing; Chris Robbert for his clear narrations; and Sue Oja, Debora Elam, Deana Martinson, Karen Kangas, Jaclyn Kangas, and Kevin Lappi for checking and double-checking the alpha and beta CDs. We want to thank you all!

We also want to give special thanks to Officer David Zittlow of the City of Fond du Lac Police Department for providing photos of computer technology used in law enforcement; Bob Metcalf for giving us permission to use his original sketch of Ethernet; The University of Illinois for supplying photos of PLATO; Rob Flickenger for providing the photo of his Pringles can antenna; Jonathan Atwell for permission to use the photo of his computer mod; and Joe Bush for his distinctive photo work.

June Parsons and Dan Oja

**NEW PERSPECTIVES ON COMPUTER CONCEPTS ADVISORY COMMITTEE**

**Ione Good**
Southeastern
Community College

**Heith Hennel**
Valencia Community
College

**Ann Rowlette**
Liberty University

**Dorothy Harman**
Tarrant County College

**Robert Moore**
Laredo Community
College

**Ella Strong**
Hazard Community
College

**ACADEMIC, TECHNICAL, AND STUDENT REVIEWERS**

We would also like to thank the reviewers and members of past Advisory Committees who helped provide valuable feedback that is still an influence on the 10th Edition:

Dr. Nazih Abdallah, University of Central Florida; Beverly Amer, Northern Arizona University; Ken Baldauf, Florida State University; Dottie Baumeister, Harford Community College; Paula Bell, Lock Haven University of Pennsylvania; Barbara Burns, St. Johns River Community College; Mary Caldwell, Rollins College; Chuck Calvin, Computer Learning Centers; Wendy Chisholm, Barstow College; Linda Cooper, Macon State College; Dave Courtaway, Devry University, Ponoma; Becky Curtin, William Rainey Harper College; Eric Daley, University of New Brunswick; Sallie Dodson, Radford University; Robert Erickson, University of Vermont; Mark Feiler, Merritt College; Pat Frederick, Del Mar College; Phil Funk, Southern New Hampshire University; Michael Gaffney, Century College; John Gammell, St. Cloud State University; Ernest Gines, Tarrant Count College SE; Tom Gorecki, College of Southern Maryland; Steve Gramlich, Pasco-Hernando Community College; Michael Hanna, Colorado State University; Dorothy Harman, Tarrant County College Northeast; Bobbye Haupt, Cecil Community College; Heith Hennel, Valencia Community College; Gerald Hensel, Valencia Community College; Patti Impink, Macon State College; Bob Irvine, American River College; Stan Leja, Del Mar College; Martha Lindberg, Minnesota State University; Richard Linge, Arizona Western College; Terry Long, Valencia Community College; Karl Smart Lyman, Central Michigan University; Dr. W. Benjamin Martz, University of Colorado, Colorado Springs; Deann McMullen, Western Kentucky Community and Technical College; Dori McPherson, Schoolcraft College; Saeed Molki, South Texas College; Robert Moore, Laredo Community College; Ed Mott, Central Texas College; Dr. Rodney Pearson, Mississippi State University; Catherine Perlich, St. Thomas; David Primeaux, Virginia Commonwealth University; Ann Rowlette, Liberty University; Lana Shyrock, Monroe County Community College; Betty Sinowitz, Rockland Community College; Martin Skolnik, Florida Atlantic University; Jerome Spencer, Rowan University; Ella Strong, Hazard Community and Technical College; Gregory Stefanelli, Carroll Community College; Martha J. Tilmann, College of San Mateo; Michael Wiemann, Blue River Community College; Kathy Winters, University of Tennessee, Chattanooga; Mary Zayac, University of the Virgin Islands; Student Reviewers Kitty Edwards and Heather House; Technical Reviewers Jeff Harrow, Barbra D. Letts, John Lucas, Ramachandran Bharath, and Karl Mulder.

*NEW PERSPECTIVES*

# COMPUTER CONCEPTS

JUNE JAMRICH PARSONS • DAN OJA

EDITION
**10**

# Orientation

## LEARNING OBJECTIVES

- Identify the basic components of your computer system
- Identify the major components of the Windows desktop
- Use the mouse and keyboard
- Start and exit a software program
- Use the menu bar, toolbar, and sizing buttons
- Create, save, and print documents using Microsoft Word
- Use a browser
- Use a search engine to find specific information on the Web
- Create, read, and reply to e-mail messages
- Secure your computer for working online
- Take steps to protect your online privacy
- Start the BookOnCD, explore its features, and create a Tracking file
- Work with a New Perspectives Lab
- Use the Internet to connect to the New Perspectives NP10 Web site
- Explore the NP10 Web site
- Work with a Student Edition Lab

**MULTIMEDIA and INTERACTIVE ELEMENTS**
⌨ Keyboard icons indicate hands-on activities. When using the BookOnCD, or other BookOn product, the ▶ icons are clickable to access multimedia resources.

BEFORE YOU READ ON, **TRY IT**

## WHAT DO I NEED TO GET STARTED?

To complete the activities in the Orientation, you'll need access to a computer, the BookOnCD packaged with your textbook (or other electronic versions of the textbook), Internet access, an e-mail address for yourself, and your instructor's e-mail address.

To make sure you have what you need, use the following check-list. Check off the boxes for each item that you have.

☐ Access to a computer. If you're using your own computer, you might need a user ID and password to log into Windows. Don't write your password down, but make sure you know what it is.

☐ Access to a school computer network. You might need a user ID and password if you'll be using a lab computer or accessing your school's network. Check with your instructor or lab manager to learn how your school handles network access.

☐ BookOnCD or other BookOn product. The BookOnCD should be packaged with your textbook and requires a computer CD or DVD drive to run. If your computer does not have this type of drive, check with your instructor. The BookOnFlashDrive requires a USB port. Your school network might provide access to the BookOnCD or BookOnFlashDrive from lab computers.

☐ E-mail address. Your instructor should explain how you can obtain an e-mail address if you don't already have one. Write your e-mail address here:

_____

☐ Instructor e-mail address. To mail in assignments, you'll need your instructor's e-mail address. Write it here:

_____

☐ Instructor WebTrack address. If your instructor will be collecting your scores with WebTrack, make sure you have your instructor's WebTrack address. Write it here:

_____

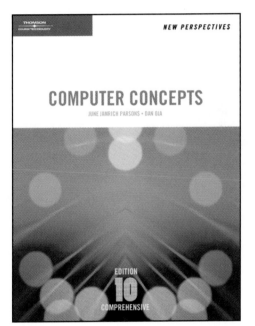

## WEB SITE

Visit the NP10 Web site to access additional resources Ⓦ that accompany this chapter.

SECTION **A**

# Getting Started

**WHEN YOU USE** the *New Perspectives on Computer Concepts* textbook, you not only learn about computers, you also use computers as learning tools. Therefore, it is a good idea to have a basic understanding of how to use your computer. Section A is designed to get computer novices quickly up to speed with computing basics, such as turning on computer equipment, working with Windows, using a mouse and computer keyboard, and accessing Help. Work through this section next to a computer so that you can do the TRY IT! activities.

## COMPUTER EQUIPMENT

**What do I need to know about my computer?** Your computer—the one you own, the one you use in a school lab, or the one provided to you at work—is technically classified as a microcomputer and sometimes referred to as a personal computer. A computer runs software (also called programs) that help you accomplish a variety of tasks. A typical computer system consists of several devices—you must be able to identify these devices to use them.

**What are the important components of my computer system?** The system unit contains your computer's circuitry, such as the microprocessor that is the "brain" of your computer and memory chips that temporarily store information. It also contains storage devices, such as a hard disk drive.

Your computer system includes basic hardware devices that allow you to enter information and commands, view work, and store information for later retrieval. Devices for entering information include a keyboard and mouse. A display device, such as a TV-like monitor, allows you to view your work, a printer produces "hard copy" on paper, and speakers produce beeps and chimes that help you pay attention to what happens on the screen.

**Where are the important components of a desktop computer system?** A desktop computer is designed for stationary use on a desk or table. Figure 1 shows the key components of a desktop computer system.

**FIGURE 1**

A desktop computer system includes several components, usually connected by cables.

**Where are the important components of a notebook computer system?** Notebook computers (sometimes called laptops) are small, light-weight computers designed to be carried from place to place. The components of a notebook computer system, except the printer, are housed in a single unit, as shown in Figure 2.

LCD screen

Speakers

Keyboard

Touchpad

Storage devices

**FIGURE 2**

A notebook computer includes a flat-panel LCD screen, key-board, speakers, and touchpad in the same unit that contains the microprocessor, memory, and storage devices. An exter-nal mouse is sometimes used instead of the touchpad.

**FIGURE 3**

You should use the hard disk to store most of your data, but to transport or back up data, you can use floppy disks, CDs, DVDs, or USB flash drives.

**How do I identify my computer's storage devices?** Your computer contains a hard disk, housed inside the system unit. It is also likely to have some type of drive that works with CDs. Figure 3 can help you identify your computer's storage devices and their uses.

**Floppy disk drive**

Low-capacity storage, but an inexpensive way of transporting small files from one computer to another.

**CD drive**

CD drives can play CD-ROMs, but can't change the data they contain. CD drives can store data on CD-Rs, CD+Rs, or CD-RWs.

**DVD drive**

DVD drives read CD-ROMs and DVD-ROMs, but can't change the data on them. Most of today's DVD drives can write data on CD-Rs, CD-RWs, DVD-Rs, and DVD-RWs.

**USB flash drive**

A USB flash drive is about the size of a high-lighter and plugs directly into the computer system unit. Capacity ranges from 32 million to 8 billion characters.

## HOW TO TURN YOUR COMPUTER ON AND OFF

**How do I turn it on?** A notebook computer typically has one switch that turns on the entire system. Look for the switch along the sides of the computer or above the keyboard. When using a desktop computer, turn on the monitor, printer, and speakers before you flip the switch on the system unit.

Most computers take a minute or two to power up, and you might be required to log in by entering a user ID and password. Your computer is ready to use when the Windows desktop (Figure 4 on the next page) appears on the computer screen and you can move the arrow-shaped pointer with your mouse.

**How do I turn it off?** Your computer is designed to turn itself off after you initiate a shutdown sequence by clicking the onscreen Start button, selecting Shut Down or Turn Off Computer, and following the instructions on the screen. After the computer shuts itself off, you can turn off the monitor, speakers, and printer. When using computers in a school lab, ask about the shutdown procedure. Your lab manager might ask that you log out but do not turn the computer off.

**TRY IT!**

**Turn your computer on**

**1.** Locate the power switch for any devices connected to your computer and turn them on.

**2.** Locate the power switch for your computer and turn it on.

**3.** If a message asks for your user ID and/or password, type them in, and then press the **Enter** key on your computer's keyboard.

**4.** Wait for the Windows desktop to appear.

## WINDOWS BASICS

**What is Windows?** Microsoft Windows is an example of a type of software called an operating system. The operating system controls all the basic tasks your computer performs, such as running application software, manipulating files on storage devices, and transferring data to and from printers, digital cameras, and other devices. The operating system also controls the user interface—the way software appears on the screen and the way you control what it does.

**What is the Windows desktop?** The Windows desktop is your base of operations for using your computer. It displays small pictures called *icons* that help you access software, documents, and the components of your computer system. The design of the Windows desktop depends on the version of Windows you're using. Figure 4 shows the important elements of Windows XP and Windows Vista.

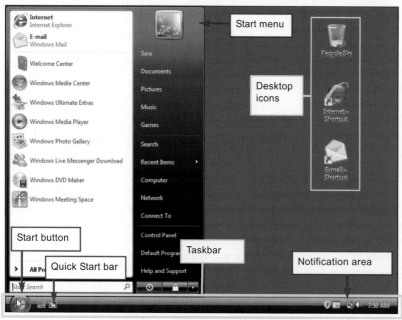

**FIGURE 4**

Windows desktop components as they appear in Windows XP (top) and Windows Vista (bottom).

**Desktop icons** can represent programs, documents, folders, or other electronic tools.

The **taskbar** contains the Start button, Quick Start bar, and Notification area. In this book, screens with a blue taskbar are Windows XP and those with a black taskbar are Windows Vista.

The **Start button** is used to display the Start menu, which lists all the programs installed on your computer.

The **Start menu** lists application and utility programs installed on your computer.

The **Quick Start bar** is always visible, making it a good place for icons that represent the programs you frequently use.

The **Notification area** displays the current time and the status of programs, devices, and Internet connections.

## MOUSE BASICS

**What is a mouse?** A mouse is a device used to manipulate items on the screen, such as the buttons and icons displayed on the Windows desktop. The mouse controls an on-screen pointer. The pointer is usually shaped like an arrow ⌖, but it can change to a different shape, depending on the task you're doing. For example, when the computer is busy, the arrow shape turns into an hourglass ⧗, signifying that you should wait for the computer to finish its current task before attempting to start a new task.

PC-compatible mice have at least two buttons, typically located on top of the mouse. Some mice also include a scroll wheel mounted between the left and right mouse buttons. Other mice include additional buttons on the top or sides (Figure 5).

**How do I use a mouse?** Hold the mouse in your right hand as shown in Figure 6. When you drag the mouse from left to right over your mousepad or desk, the arrow-shaped pointer on the screen moves from left to right. If you run out of room to move the mouse, simply pick it up and reposition it. The pointer does not move when the mouse is not in contact with a flat surface.

**FIGURE 5**

For basic mousing, you need use only the left and right mouse buttons.

Scroll wheel

Left mouse button

Additional buttons

Right mouse button

There are several ways you can manipulate on-screen objects. Although you might not be able to manipulate every object in all possible ways, you'll soon learn which mouse actions are allowed for each type of control. The following list describes your repertoire of mouse actions.

**FIGURE 6**

Rest the palm of your right hand on the mouse. Position your index finger over the left mouse button and your middle finger over the right mouse button.

### ⌨ TRY IT!

**Use your mouse**

**1.** With your computer on and the Windows desktop showing on the screen, move your mouse around on the desk and notice how the mouse movements correspond to the movement of the arrow-shaped pointer.

**2.** Move the mouse to position the pointer on the Start button.

**3.** Click the left mouse button to open the Start menu.

**4.** Click the **Start** button again to close the Start menu.

| Action | How to | Result |
|---|---|---|
| Click | Press the left mouse button once, and then immediately release it. | Select an object |
| Double-click | Press the left mouse button twice in rapid succession without moving the body of the mouse. | Activate an object |
| Right-click | Press the right mouse button once, and then immediately release it. | Display a shortcut menu |
| Drag | Hold the left mouse button down while you move the mouse. | Move an object |

## KEYBOARD BASICS

**What are the important features of a computer keyboard?** You use the computer keyboard to input commands, respond to prompts, and type the text of documents. An insertion point that looks like a flashing vertical bar indicates where the characters you type will appear. You can change the location of the insertion point by using the mouse or the arrow keys. Study Figure 7 for an overview of important computer keys and their functions.

**FIGURE 7**

Computer Keyboard

[A] The **Esc** (Escape) key cancels an operation.

[B] **Function keys** activate commands, such as Save, Help, and Print. The command associated with each key depends on the software you are using.

[C] The **Print Screen** key prints the contents of the screen or stores a copy of the screen in memory that you can print or manipulate with graphics software.

[D] The **Scroll Lock** key's function depends on the software you're using. This key is rarely used with today's software.

[E] **Indicator Lights** show you the status of three toggle keys: Num Lock, Caps Lock, and Scroll Lock. The Power light indicates whether the computer is on or off.

[F] The **Backspace** key deletes one character to the left of the insertion point.

[G] The **Insert** key switches between insert mode and type-over mode.

[H] The **Home** key takes you to the beginning of a line or the beginning of a document, depending on the software you are using.

[I] The **Tab** key can move your current typing location to the next tab stop or the next text-entry box.

[J] The **Caps Lock** key capitalizes all the letters you type when it is engaged, but does not produce the top symbol on keys that contain two symbols. This key is a toggle key, which means that each time you press it, you switch between uppercase and lowercase modes.

[K] The **Shift** key capitalizes letters and produces the top symbol on keys that contain two symbols.

[L] You hold down the **Ctrl** key while pressing another key. The result of Ctrl or Alt key combinations depends on the software you are using.

[M] You hold down the **Alt** key while you press another key.

[N] The **Enter** key is used to indicate that you have completed a command or want to move your typing position down to the next line.

[O] The **Delete** key deletes the character to the right of the insertion point.

[P] The **End** key takes you to the end of a line or the end of a document, depending on the software you are using.

[Q] The **Page Up** key displays the previous screen of information. The **Page Down** key displays the next screen of information.

[R] The up, down, right, and left **arrow keys** move the insertion point.

[S] The **numeric keypad** produces numbers or moves the insertion point, depending on the status of the Num Lock key shown by the status lights.

**What do Alt and Ctrl mean?** The Alt and Ctrl keys work with the letter keys. If you see <Ctrl X>, Ctrl+X, [Ctrl X], Ctrl-X, or Ctrl X on the screen or in an instruction manual, it means to hold down the Ctrl key while you press X. For example, Ctrl+X is a keyboard shortcut for clicking the Edit menu, and then clicking the Cut option. A keyboard shortcut allows you to use the keyboard rather than the mouse to select menu commands.

**What if I make a mistake?** Everyone makes mistakes. The first rule is don't panic! Most mistakes are reversible. The hints and tips in Figure 8 should help you recover from mistakes.

**FIGURE 8**

Most mistakes are easy to fix.

| What Happened | What To Do |
|---|---|
| Typed the wrong thing | Use the Backspace key to delete the last characters you typed. |
| Selected the wrong menu | Press the Esc key to close the menu. |
| Opened a window you didn't mean to | Click the X button in the upper-right corner of the window. |
| Computer has "hung up" and no longer responds to mouse clicks or typed commands | Hold down the Ctrl, Alt, and Delete keys, and then follow instructions to close the program. |
| Pressed the Enter Key in the middle of a sentence | Press the Backspace key to paste the sentence back together. |

## HOW TO START SOFTWARE

**How do I start programs?** You can use the Start button to launch just about any software that's installed on your computer. Clicking the Start menu displays a list of recently accessed programs. Clicking the All Programs option displays a list of every program installed on your computer. You can run a program from this list simply by clicking it. Follow the instructions in the TRY IT! box to start Microsoft Word (assuming it is installed on your computer).

### TRY IT!

**Start Microsoft Word**

**1.** Make sure your computer is on and it is displaying the Windows desktop.

**2.** Click the **Start** button to display the Start menu.

**3.** Click **All Programs** to display a list of all software installed on your computer.

**4.** Click **Microsoft Word**.

**5.** Wait a few seconds for your computer to display the main screen for Microsoft Word, shown below. Leave Word open for use with the next TRY IT!.

## WINDOWS CONTROLS

**How do I tell the software what I want to do?** Word processing, photo editing, and other software designed for use on computers running the Windows operating system is referred to as *Windows software*. Most Windows software works in a fairly uniform way and uses a similar set of controls.

Each software application appears within a rectangular area called a *window*, which includes a title bar, a menu bar, and various controls shown in Figure 9.

**FIGURE 9**

The **title bar** displays the title of the software, the name of the current data file, and the window sizing buttons.

The **Minimize button** shrinks the window to a button at the bottom of the screen.

The **Maximize button** stretches the window to fill the screen.

The **Close button** closes the window and exits the program.

The **menu bar** displays the titles of menus you can click to select commands.

The **toolbar** displays a series of tools for accomplishing various tasks.

The **scroll bar** can be clicked or dragged to see any material that does not fit in the displayed window.

The **workspace** is the area in which your document is displayed.

If you're unfamiliar with Windows controls, take a few minutes to complete the steps in the TRY IT! box below.

## TRY IT!

### Use the menu bar

**1.** Click **Insert** on the menu bar.

**2.** Click **Date and Time**.

**3.** Select the first option.

**4.** Click the **OK** button. The current date is inserted at the top of the workspace.

### Use the toolbar

**1.** As shown below, click the **Spelling and Grammar** button on the Word toolbar.

**2.** The computer checks the spelling in your document.

**3.** You didn't have any misspelled words, so click the **OK** button to end the spell check.

### Use the sizing buttons

**1.** Click the ⬜ Minimize button.

**2.** The Microsoft Word window shrinks down to a button on the taskbar at the bottom of the screen.

🔲 Document1 - Micro...

**3.** Click the taskbar button to make the Word window reappear. Leave Word open for the next TRY IT!.

## HELP

**How can I get help using software?** If you've had problems using software, you're not alone! Everyone has questions at one time or another. Most software offers several sources of help, such as the following:

● **Message boxes.** When using software, it is important to pay attention to any message boxes displayed on the screen. Make sure you carefully read the options they present. If the box doesn't seem to apply to what you want to do, click its Cancel button to close it. Otherwise, set the options the way you want them, and then click the OK button to continue.

● **User manual.** Whether you're a beginner or a power user, the manual that comes with software can be an excellent resource. User manuals can contain quick-start guides, tutorials, detailed descriptions of menu options, and tips for using features effectively. Many manuals are offered online along with tools you can use to browse through them or look for the answer to a specific question.

● **Help menu.** The Help menu provides access to on-screen documentation. Most Windows software offers a standard method for searching through its Help files. Documentation can be accessed through a table of contents, by consulting the index, or by searching for particular words or phrases (Figure 10).

● **Office Assistant.** Some software includes animated assistants that prompt you to type in simple questions. After you've entered a question, the assistant might ask you additional questions to refine your search, or it might display a list of documents that answer your question.

**FIGURE 10**

Clicking Help on the software menu bar produces a menu of help options, such as the office assistant (below left) or a Help window (below right), where you can use the Contents, Index, or Find tabs to search the Help file for information.

---

# QuickCheck

1. When turning on the components of a desktop computer system, the computer's system _____ should be switched on last.

2. Instead of using the on/off switch to turn off your computer, you should use the _____ button to initiate a shutdown.

3. Ctrl+X means to hold down the Ctrl key, then press +, then press X. True or false? _____

4. The _____ key can be used to delete the last character you typed.

5. Most Windows software displays a(n) _____ bar that includes options, such as File and Help.

▶ CHECK ANSWERS

# Documents, Browsers, and E-mail

**TO COMPLETE ASSIGNMENTS** for your course, you should be able to work with documents, browsers, and e-mail. Section B walks you through the basics.

## CREATING DOCUMENTS

**How do I create and save a document?** To create a document, simply type text in the workspace provided by word processing software such as Microsoft Word or OpenOffice. The flashing vertical insertion point (Figure 11) indicates your place in the document. Figure 12 explains how to save a document.

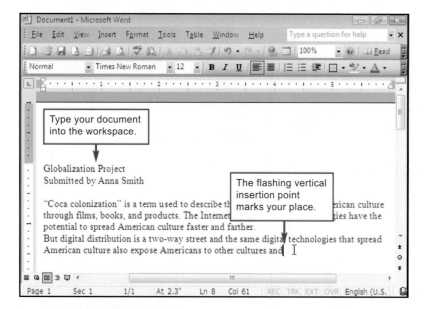

**FIGURE 11**

When typing text, you can use the following keys to move within a document and make revisions:

- **Backspace**: Delete the character to the left of the insertion point.

- **Delete:** Delete the character to the right of the insertion point.

- **Enter:** End a paragraph and begin a new line.

- **Arrow keys:** Move the insertion point up, down, right, or left.

**FIGURE 12**

It is a good idea to save your document every few minutes, even if it is not finished. When you save a document, use the Save option on the File menu. Your computer is probably configured to save documents on the hard disk in a folder called Documents or My Documents. No need to change that until you gain more experience. Make sure to enter a descriptive name for the document in the *File name* box. File names can be several words long; just do not use the * / \ " ' : symbols in the file name.

**How do I print a document?** To print a document, simply click the File menu, and then select Print. Your computer displays a window containing a series of print options. If you want to print a single copy of your document, these settings should be correct, so you can click the OK button at the bottom of the window to send your document to the printer.

**Can I send a document to my instructor?** You can e-mail a document by using the Send To option on the File menu (Figure 13). To do so, you must know your instructor's e-mail address. You'll learn more about e-mail later in the Orientation, but keep this option in mind because it is a handy way to submit assignments, such as projects and term papers.

**How do I find my documents again in the future?** If you want to revise a document sometime in the future, simply start Microsoft Word, click File on the menu bar, and then click Open. Your computer should display a list of documents stored in the Documents or My Documents folder. Locate the one you want to revise and click it.

**What should I do when I'm done?** When you're ready to quit, you can close the document by clicking the Close option from the File menu. When you want to close Microsoft Word, you can click the ☒ Close button in the upper-right corner of the screen.

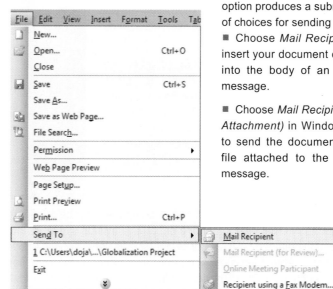

**FIGURE 13**

The File menu's Send To option produces a submenu of choices for sending mail.

■ Choose *Mail Recipient* to insert your document directly into the body of an e-mail message.

■ Choose *Mail Recipient (as Attachment)* in Windows XP to send the document as a file attached to the e-mail message.

## ⌨ TRY IT!

### Create a document

**1.** Make sure that Microsoft Word is open. (See page O-9 to review how to open Microsoft Word.)

**2.** Click the workspace to position the insertion point in the upper-left corner, just under the date.

**3.** Type a paragraph. Refer to Figure 11 for keys to use while typing and revising your work.

**4.** When the first paragraph is complete, press the **Enter** key to begin a new paragraph.

**5.** Type a second paragraph of text.

### Save a document

**1.** Click **File** on the Word menu bar.

**2.** Click **Save**.

**3.** Make sure the *Save in* box lists the Documents or My Documents folder. If not, click the ▾ button and then click the correct folder from the list.

**4.** In the *File name* box, type a name for your document.

**5.** Click the **Save** button.

**6.** When the Save As dialog box closes, your document is saved.

### Print a document, close it, and exit Word

**1.** Click **File** on the Word menu bar, and then click **Print**.

**2.** Make sure the *Page Range* is set to **All**.

**3.** Make sure *Number of copies* is set to **1**.

**4.** Click the **OK** button and wait a few seconds for the printer to produce your document.

**5.** Close the document by clicking **File**, then clicking **Close**. The workspace should become blank.

**6.** Exit Microsoft Word by clicking the ☒ Close button.

## INTERNET AND WEB BASICS

**What is the Internet?** The Internet is the largest computer network in the world, carrying information from one continent to another in the blink of an eye (Figure 14). The computers connected to this network offer many types of resources, such as e-mail, instant messaging, popular music downloads, and online shopping.

**What is the Web?** Although some people use the terms *Internet* and *Web* interchangeably, the two are not the same. The Internet refers to a communications network that connects computers all around the globe. The Web—short for World Wide Web—is just one of the many resources available over this communications network.

The World Wide Web is a collection of linked and cross-referenced information available for public access. This information is accessible from Web sites located on millions of computers. The information is displayed as a series of screens called Web pages. You'll use the Web for general research and for specific activities designed to accompany this textbook. To use the Web, your computer must have access to the Internet.

**FIGURE 14**

The Internet communications network stretches around the globe.

**How do I access the Internet?** Most computers can be configured to connect to the Internet over telephone or cable television systems. Internet access can be obtained from school computer labs, local service providers, such as your cable television company, and national Internet service providers, such as AOL (America Online), AT&T Worldnet, and MSN (Microsoft Network).

To expedite your orientation, it is assumed that your computer has Internet access. If it does not, consult your instructor, or ask an experienced computer user to help you get set up.

**How do I know if my computer has Internet access?** The easiest way to find out if your computer can access the Internet is to try it. You can quickly find out if you have Internet access by starting software called a browser that's designed to display Web pages.

Browser software called Internet Explorer is supplied with Microsoft Windows. Other browsers, such as Netscape, Firefox, and Opera, are also available. Follow the steps in the TRY IT! box to start Internet Explorer.

## HOW TO USE A WEB BROWSER AND SEARCH ENGINE

**How do I use a browser?** A browser lets you enter a unique Web page address called a URL and jump from one Web page to another by using links. Links are usually underlined, and when you position the arrow-shaped mouse pointer over a link, it changes to a hand shape.

### ⌨ TRY IT!

**Start your browser**

**1.** Click the 🖝 icon located near the Start button.

**2.** Your computer should soon display a window containing "Microsoft Internet Explorer" in the title bar. (Refer to the next page.)

If your computer displays a *Connect to* box, click the **Dial** button to establish a dial-up connection over your telephone line.

You'll need to cancel the browser command and consult an experienced computer user if:

- Your computer displays a "working off line" message.
- Your computer displays an Internet Connection Wizard box.

Although browsers offer many features, you can get along quite well using the basic controls shown in Figure 15.

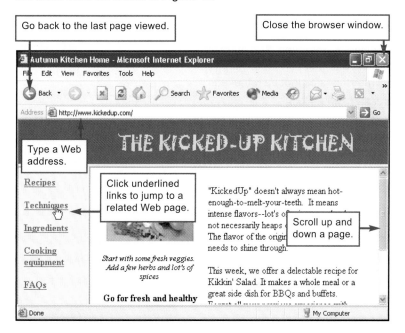

**FIGURE 15**

Using a Browser

A full Web address might look like this:
**http://www.kickedup.com**
It is not necessary to type the http://, so to access the Kicked-Up Kitchen page shown here, you would type:
**www.kickedup.com**
When typing a Web address, do not use any spaces and copy upper- and lowercase letters exactly.

**How do I find specific information on the Web?** If you're looking for information and don't know the Web site where it might be located, you can use a search engine to find it. Follow the steps in the TRY IT! box to "Google it" by using the Google search engine.

**TRY IT!**

**Use a search engine**

1. Make sure the browser window is open.

2. Click the Address box and type:

www.google.com

3. Press the **Enter** key. Your browser displays the Web page for the Google search engine.

4. Click the blank search box and then type **national parks**.

5. Press the **Enter** key. Google displays a list of Web pages that relate to national parks.

6. Click the underlined **National Park Service** link. Your browser displays the Park Service's home page.

7. To close the browser, click the Close button.

## WORKING WITH E-MAIL

**What is e-mail?** E-mail is a form of communication that relies on computer networks, such as the Internet, to transmit messages from one computer to another. Like regular mail, e-mail messages are sent to a mailbox where they are kept until the recipient retrieves the message. Messages might arrive at their destination within seconds, or might not arrive for a few hours. Once sent, e-mail messages cannot be retrieved.

**What do I need to use e-mail?** To send and receive e-mail, you need an Internet connection, an e-mail account, and software that enables you to compose, read, and delete e-mail messages. An e-mail account consists of an e-mail address (Figure 16), a password, and a mailbox. You can usually obtain an e-mail account from your Internet service provider, your school, or a Web-based e-mail provider, such as Hotmail, Yahoo! Mail, or Gmail.

**How do I create and send an e-mail message?** Many e-mail systems are available, and each uses slightly different software, making it impossible to cover all options in this short orientation. You might want to enlist the aid of an experienced computer user to help you get started. The steps in the TRY IT! box are designed for students who use e-mail software supplied with Windows XP or Vista.

**FIGURE 16**

E-mail Addresses

An e-mail address consists of a user ID followed by an @ symbol and the name of a computer that handles e-mail accounts. Ask your instructor for his or her e-mail address. It is likely similar to the following:

**instructor@school.edu**

When typing an e-mail address, use all lowercase letters and do not use any spaces.

### TRY IT!

**Create and send e-mail**

**1.** Click the **Start** button and look for an e-mail program, such as Outlook, Outlook Express, or Microsoft Mail.

**2.** Click the **Create** button to display a form like the one below.

**3.** Follow steps 4-6 as shown below.

**7.** When your message is complete, click the **Send** button. With most computers, this button places the e-mail in your Outbox.

**8.** Click the **Send/Receive** button on the toolbar to ship the message over the network to your instructor.

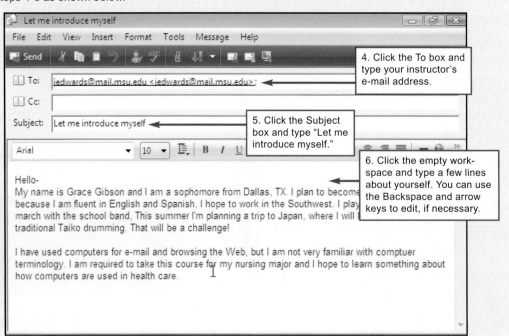

4. Click the To box and type your instructor's e-mail address.

5. Click the Subject box and type "Let me introduce myself."

6. Click the empty workspace and type a few lines about yourself. You can use the Backspace and arrow keys to edit, if necessary.

**How do I get my e-mail?** As with sending mail, the way you get mail depends on your e-mail system. In general, clicking the Send/Receive button collects your mail from the network and stores it in your Inbox. Your e-mail software displays a list of your messages. The new ones are usually shown highlighted or in bold type. You can click any message to open it, read it, and reply to it, as shown in Figure 17.

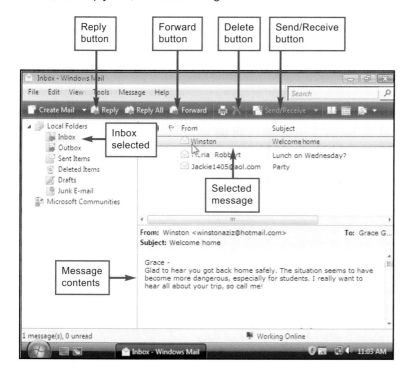

**FIGURE 17**

Most e-mail software displays a list of your messages. You can:

■ Open a message and read it.

■ Reply to a message.

■ Delete unwanted messages (a good idea to minimize the size of your mailbox).

■ Forward a message to someone else.

# QuickCheck

1.  It is a good idea to [＿＿＿＿＿＿] your work every few minutes, even if you are not finished with it.

2.  Software called a(n) [＿＿＿＿＿＿] helps you access Web pages.

3.  If you don't know where to find information, you can use a(n) [＿＿＿＿＿＿] engine to pro-

    duce a list of links to Web pages that might contain the information you seek.

4.  The special symbol used in e-mail addresses is [＿＿＿＿＿＿].

5.  An e-mail [＿＿＿＿＿＿] consists of an e-mail address, a password, and a mailbox.

● CHECK ANSWERS

# Security and Privacy

**AS WITH MOST OTHER** facets of modern life, computing has its share of troublemakers, scam artists, and identity thieves. Section C offers some tips on navigating through the sometimes rough neighborhoods of cyberspace, while keeping your data safe and your identity private.

## SECURING YOUR COMPUTER AND DATA

**What's at risk if my computer is stolen?** A computer can be an attractive target for thieves, but the value of a stolen computer is not so much in the hardware as in the data it contains. With stolen data such as your bank account numbers and PINs, a thief can wipe out your checking and savings accounts. With your credit card numbers, a thief can go on a spending spree. Even worse, a criminal can use stolen data to assume your identity, run up debts, get into legal difficulties, ruin your credit rating, and cause you no end of trouble.

**How can I protect my computer data from theft?** When you carry a notebook computer, never leave it unattended. To thwart a thief who breaks into your home or dorm room, anchor your computer to your desk with a specially designed lock you can buy at most electronics stores.

If a thief steals your computer, you can make it difficult to access your data by setting up a password. Until the password is entered, your data is off limits. A thief might be able to boot up the Windows desktop, but should not be able to easily look at the data in your folders.

Many new computers are shipped with a standard administrator password that everyone knows. If you are the only person using your computer, you can use the administrator account for your day-to-day computing, but create a secure password (Figure 18) for this account as soon as you can.

Your computer might also include a preset guest account with a nonsecure password such as "guest." You should disable this guest account or assign it a secure password.

**FIGURE 18**

To create a secure password:

■ Use at least five characters, mixing numbers with letters, as in 2by4s.

■ Do not use your name, the name of a family member, or pet's name.

■ Do not use a word that can be found in the dictionary.

■ Do not forget your password!

### TRY IT!

**Check the accounts on your computer**

**1.** Click the **Start** button, then select **Control Panel**.

**2.** For Windows XP, select **User Accounts**; for Windows Vista, select **Add or remove user accounts.** (You might be required to enter an administrator password.)

**3.** Check the password protection on all accounts. If you are working on a school lab computer, close the User Accounts window without making any changes. If you are using your own computer, click the Administrator account and make sure it has a secure password.

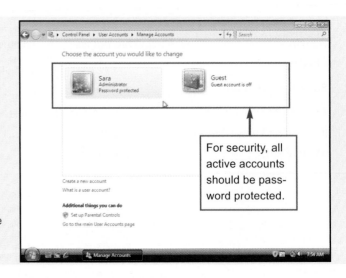

For security, all active accounts should be password protected.

Orientation

## AVOIDING VIRUSES

**What's so bad about computer viruses?** The term *virus* has a technical meaning, but many people use the term loosely when referring to malicious programs that circulate on disks, in e-mail attachments, and on the Internet. This malware, as it is sometimes called, can steal your data, destroy files, or create network traffic jams. It might display an irritating message to announce its presence, or it might work quietly behind the scenes to spread itself to various files on your computer or mail itself out to everyone in your e-mail address book.

After a virus takes up residence in your computer, it is often difficult to disinfect all your files. Rather than wait for a virus attack, you should take steps to keep your computer virus free.

**How can I keep viruses out of my computer?** Back when viruses were less sophisticated, computer users were commonly warned not to download pirated software or open e-mail attachments from unknown senders. These two common sources of viruses still exist, but virus creators have found ways to make pirated software look legitimate and to affix your friends' names to e-mails that carry infected attachments.

Although it is a good idea to avoid pirated software and stay alert when opening e-mail attachments, the best defense against viruses is to install antivirus software such as the packages listed in Figure 19, and configure it to run continuously whenever your computer is on. You should make sure your antivirus software is set up to scan for viruses in incoming files and e-mail messages. At least once a week your antivirus software should run a full system check to make sure every file on your computer is virus free.

As new viruses emerge, your antivirus software needs to update its virus definition file. It gets this update as a Web download. If you've selected the auto update option, your computer should automatically receive updates as they become available.

**FIGURE 19**

Popular Antivirus Software

| Norton AntiVirus |
| McAfee VirusScan |
| Kaspersky Anti-Virus |
| F-Prot |
| Softwin BitDefender |
| Panda Antivirus |
| Trend Micro PC-cillin |

### TRY IT!

**Get familiar with your antivirus software**

**1.** Click the **Start** button, and then select **All Programs**. Look for antivirus software (refer to Figure 19 for a list). Open your antivirus software by clicking it.

**Can't find any?** If you are using your own computer and it doesn't seem to have antivirus software, you can connect to an antivirus Web site and download it.

**2.** Each antivirus program has unique features. The figure on the right shows the main screen for Norton AntiVirus software. Explore your antivirus software to make sure it is configured to do the following:

■ Scan incoming e-mail

■ Run continuously in the background—a feature sometimes called Auto Protect

■ Block malicious scripts

**3.** Check the date of your last full system scan. If it was more than one week ago, you should check the settings that schedule antivirus scans.

**4.** Check the date when your computer last received virus definitions. If it was more than two weeks ago, you should make sure your antivirus software is configured to receive automatic live updates.

## PREVENTING INTRUSIONS

**Is it risky to go online?** The Internet offers lots of cool stuff—music downloads, movie reviews and trailers, online shopping and banking, consumer information, chat groups, news, sports, weather, and much more. Most Internet offerings are legitimate, but some downloads contain viruses, and shady characters called hackers control programs that lurk about waiting to snatch your personal data or infiltrate your computer. The longer your computer remains connected to the Internet, the more vulnerable it is to a hacker's infiltration attempts.

If a hacker gains access to your computer, he or she can look through your files, use your computer as a launching platform for viruses and network-jamming attacks, or turn your computer into a server for pornography and other unsavory material. Hackers have even found ways to turn thousands of infiltrated computers into "zombies," link them together, and carry out coordinated attacks to disrupt online access to Microsoft, Bank of America, and other Internet businesses.

**How do hackers gain access to my computer?** Intruders gain access by exploiting security flaws in your computer's operating system, browser, and e-mail software. Software publishers are constantly creating patches to fix these flaws. As part of your overall security plan, you should download and install security patches as they become available.

**How can I block hackers from infiltrating my computer?** Firewall software, such as the packages listed in Figure 20, provides a protective barrier between a computer and the Internet. If your computer is directly connected to the Internet, it should have active firewall software. If your computer connects to a local area network for Internet access, the network should have a device called a router to block infiltration attempts.

When a firewall is active, it watches for potentially disruptive incoming data called *probes*. When a probe is discovered, your firewall displays a warning and asks what to do. If the source looks legitimate, you can let it through; if not, you should block it (Figure 21).

**Where do I get a firewall?** Windows XP and Vista include built-in firewalls. If your computer uses an earlier version of Windows, you can download a third-party firewall.

**TRY IT!**

**FIGURE 20**

Popular Firewall Software

Tiny Personal Firewall
McAfee Personal Firewall
ZoneAlarm Pro
Sygate Firewall Pro
Norton Personal Firewall
BlackICE Defender
Mac OS Firewall
Outpost Firewall
Windows Firewall

**FIGURE 21**

When your firewall software encounters new or unusual activity, it asks you what to do.

**Check your computer's firewall**

Finding out if your computer has an active firewall requires a little detective work. Try one or more of these two methods. If your computer doesn't seem to have a firewall, you might want to download one and install it.

**For Windows XP and Vista users:**

Click the **Start** button, then click **Control Panel**. Click the **Security** link or double-click the **Security Center** icon and then make sure the Firewall is on.

**For users with earlier versions of Windows:**

Click the **Start** button, click **All Programs**, and then look through the program list for firewalls such as those in Figure 20. If you find a firewall listed, start it and explore to see if it has been activated.

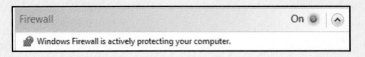

## BLOCKING SPYWARE AND POP-UP ADS

**Are some Web sites dangerous?** When you access Web sites, data is transferred to your computer and displayed by your browser. Most of this data is harmless, but malicious HTML scripts, rogue ActiveX components, and spyware have the potential to search your computer for passwords and credit card numbers, monitor your Web-browsing habits for marketing purposes, block your access to legitimate Web sites, or surreptitiously use your computer as a staging area for illicit activities.

Spyware is the most insidious threat. It often piggybacks on pop-up ads and activates if you click the ad window. Some spyware can begin its dirty work when you try to click the Close button to get rid of an ad.

**How can I block spyware?** The first line of defense is to never click pop-up ads—especially those with dire warnings about your computer being infected by a virus or spyware! (See Figure 22.) To close an ad, right-click its button on the taskbar at the bottom of your screen, and then select the Close option from the menu that appears. Some browsers can be configured to block spyware and pop-up ads. Your antivirus software might offer similar options. You can also install software specially designed to block spyware and pop-up ads. Figure 23 lists some popular titles.

**What other steps can I take to browse the Web safely?** Most browsers include security features. You should take some time to become familiar with them. For example, Internet Explorer allows you to specify how you want it to deal with ActiveX components. You can also specify how to deal with HTML scripts, cookies, security certificates, and other Web-based data. If you don't want to be bothered by these details, however, Internet Explorer offers several predefined configurations for Low, Medium, and High security. Most Internet Explorer users set security and privacy options to Medium.

**FIGURE 22**

Some pop-up ads contain fake warnings about viruses, spyware, and intrusion attempts.

**FIGURE 23**

Popular Antispyware and Ad-Blocking Software

| |
|---|
| Webroot Spy Sweeper |
| Ad-Aware |
| Spybot S&D |
| SpyHunter |
| SpyRemover |
| Pest Patrol |
| SpyKiller |
| Pop-up Defender |

### ⌨ TRY IT!

**Check Internet Explorer security and privacy options**

**1.** Start Internet Explorer. Click **Tools** on the menu bar, then select **Internet Options**.

**2.** Click the **Security** tab. Typically, your security setting should be Medium.

**3.** Click the **Privacy** tab. Typically, your privacy setting should be Medium.

**4.** Check the bottom of the window for a Pop-up Blocker option. If your version of Internet Explorer offers this feature, make sure its box contains a check mark so that it is activated.

**5.** If your version of Internet Explorer does not offer a pop-up blocker, check your antivirus software to see if it can provide protection. Otherwise, you can use the Start button to see if any of the software listed in Figure 23 has been installed. If your computer seems to have no antispyware or ad-blocking software, you might want to download some and install it.

## PROTECTING E-COMMERCE TRANSACTIONS

**Is online shopping safe?** Online shopping is generally safe. From time to time, shoppers encounter fake storefronts designed to look like legitimate merchants but that are actually set up to steal credit card information. You can avoid these fakes by making sure you enter correctly spelled URLs when connecting to your favorite shopping sites.

**How safe is my credit card information when I'm shopping online?** Online shopping is not much more dangerous than using your credit card for a telephone order or giving it to a server when you've finished eating in a restaurant. Anyone who handles your card can copy the card number, jot down the expiration date, and try to make unauthorized charges.

That's not to say that credit cards are risk free. Credit cards are surprisingly vulnerable both online and off. Thieves can break into merchant computers that store order information. Thieves might even pick up your credit card information from discarded order forms. Despite these risks, we continue to use credit cards.

Many people are concerned about their credit card data getting intercepted as it travels over the Internet. As you wrap up an online purchase and submit your credit card information, it is transmitted from your computer to the merchant's computer. Software called a packet sniffer, designed for legitimately monitoring network traffic, is occasionally used by unscrupulous hackers to intercept credit card numbers and other data traveling over the Internet.

**How can I keep my credit card number confidential?** When you submit credit card information, make sure the merchant provides a secure connection for transporting data. Typically, a secure connection is activated when you're in the final phases of checking out—as you enter your shipping and credit card information into a form and click a Submit button to send it. A secure connection encrypts your data. Even if your credit card number is intercepted, it cannot be deciphered and used. To make sure you have a secure connection, look for the lock icon. The Address box should also display a URL that begins with shttp:// or https:// (Secure HTTP), or contains ssl (Secure Sockets Layer).

### TRY IT!

**Identify a secure connection**

**1.** Start your browser and connect to the site: **www.walmart.com**.

**2.** Select any item and use the **Add to Cart** option to place it in your online shopping cart.

**3.** Click the **Proceed to Checkout** button.

**4.** At the checkout screen, do you see any evidence that you're using a secure connection?

**5.** Close your browser so that you don't complete the transaction.

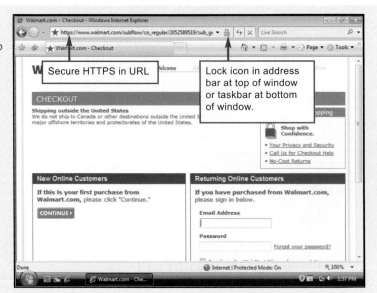

## AVOIDING E-MAIL SCAMS

**What are e-mail scams?** From time to time, you hear about con artists who have bilked innocent consumers out of their life savings. The Internet has its share of con artists, too, who run e-mail scams designed to collect money and confidential information from unsuspecting victims. E-mail scams are usually distributed in mass mailings called spam.

**What do I need to know about spam?** The Internet makes it easy and cheap to send out millions of e-mail solicitations. In the United States, the CAN-SPAM Act requires mass-mail messages to be labeled with a valid subject line. Recipients are supposed to be provided with a way to opt out of receiving future messages. Legitimate merchants and organizations comply with the law when sending product announcements, newsletters, and other messages. Unscrupulous spammers ignore the law and try to disguise their solicitations as messages from your friends, chat room participants, or co-workers (Figure 24).

| ! | 0 | ⚐ | From | Subject |
|---|---|---|---|---|
| | | | Winston | Welcome home |
| | | | Maria Robbert | Lunch on Wednesday? |
| | | | Jackie1405@aol.com | Party |
| | | | Datamation IT Update | [SPAM] Conference Focuses on IT |
| | | | FlyCharterAir.com | [SPAM] Charter Specials |
| | | | Sonja Crowder | Receive your V1agr&a |
| | | | Dwayne Thrman | It's new and successful |

**FIGURE 24**

Some e-mail systems use spam filters to flag suspected spam by adding [SPAM] to the subject line. Spam filters are not perfect, however. Some spam is not flagged and occasionally legitimate mail is mistaken for spam.

**Is spam dangerous?** Many spam messages contain legitimate information, including daily or weekly newsletters to which you've subscribed. Some spam messages, however, advertise illegal products. Others are outright scams to get you to download a virus, divulge your bank account numbers, or send in money for products you'll never receive.

Beware of spam containing offers that seem just too good to be true. For example, you might receive a message from an African businessman who is seeking your help to transfer a large sum of money from his country to yours (Figure 25). These messages are frauds.

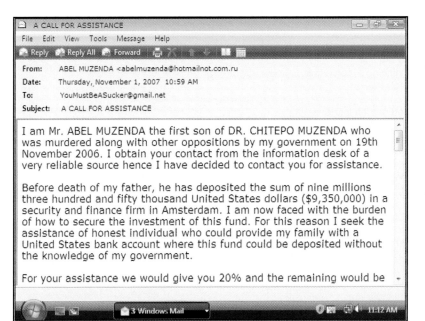

**FIGURE 25**

Many variations of this African money-transfer fraud—complete with deliberate grammatical errors—have circulated on the Internet for years. Victims who respond to these preposterous e-mails have found their bank accounts raided, their credit ratings destroyed, and their reputations ruined. According to the FBI, some victims have even been kidnapped!

**What's phishing?** Phishing (pronounced "fishing") is a scam that arrives in your e-mailbox looking like official correspondence from a major company, such as Microsoft, PayPal, eBay, MSN, Yahoo!, or America Online. The e-mail message is actually from an illegitimate source and is designed to trick you into divulging confidential information or downloading a virus. Links in the e-mail message often lead to a Web site that looks official, where you are asked to enter confidential information such as your credit card number, Social Security number, or bank account number.

The following are examples of phishing scams you should be aware of:

● A message from Microsoft with an attachment that supposedly contains a security update for Microsoft Windows. Downloading the attachment infects your computer with a virus.

● A message from America Online, complete with official-looking logos, that alerts you to a problem with your account. When you click the AOL Billing Center link and enter your account information, it is transmitted to a hacker's computer.

● A message that's obviously spam, but contains a convenient opt-out link. If you click the link believing that it will prevent future spam from this source, you'll actually be downloading a program that hackers can use to remotely control your computer for illegal activities.

**How do I avoid e-mail scams?** If your e-mail software provides spam filters, you can use them to block some unsolicited mail from your e-mailbox. Spam filters are far from perfect, however, so don't assume everything that gets through is legitimate. Use your judgment before opening any e-mail message or attachment.

Never reply to a message that you suspect to be fraudulent. If you have a question about its legitimacy, check whether it's on a list of known scams. Never click a link provided in an e-mail message to manage your account information. Instead, use your browser to go directly to the company's Web site and access your account as usual. Microsoft never sends updates as attachments. To obtain Microsoft updates, go to *www.microsoft.com* and click Windows Update or Office Update.

### ⌨ TRY IT!

**Arm yourself against e-mail scams**

**1.** Start your browser and connect to the site **www.antiphishing.org**. Click the Phishing Archive link and browse the list of recent phishing attacks.

**2.** Open your e-mail software and find out if it incudes spam filters. You can usually find this information by clicking Help on the menu bar and then typing "spam filter" in the search box.

**3.** Explore your options for configuring spam filters. If you use Microsoft Mail for e-mail (shown at right), you can find these settings by clicking **Tools** on the menu bar, and then clicking **Junk E-mail Options**.

Spam filters sometimes catch legitimate mail and group it with junk mail. You might want to keep tabs on your spam filters when they are first activated to make sure they are set to a level that eliminates most unwanted spam without catching too much legitimate mail.

**Orientation**

## PROTECTING YOUR PRIVACY

**How much information has been collected about me?** No matter what steps you take to protect your privacy, information about you is stored in many places and has the potential to be consolidated by government agencies, private businesses, and criminals.

Some databases are legitimate—those maintained by credit bureaus and medical insurance companies, for example. By law, you have the right to ask for a copy of these records and correct any errors you find. Many other databases, such as those maintained at e-commerce sites and those illegally acquired by hackers, are not accessible, and you have no way of checking the data they contain.

**Can I control who collects information about me?** To some extent, you can limit your exposure to future data collection by supplying personal data only when absolutely necessary. When filling out online forms, consider whether you want to or need to provide your real name and address.

You should also be careful about revealing personal information in chat rooms and other online forums. Many chat room participants are not who they appear to be. Some people are just having fun with fantasy identities, but others are trying to con people by telling hard luck stories and faking illnesses. In a chat room, never reveal personal information, such as your full name, address, or phone number. Resist the temptation to meet face to face with chat room participants. Taking simple steps to protect your privacy is an important part of your overall security plan (Figure 26).

### TRY IT!

**Check your privacy**

**1.** Start your browser and go Googling by connecting to **www.google.com**. Enter your name in the Search box. What turns up?

**2.** Connect to **www.peopledata.com** and click the **People Search** option. Enter your name and state of residence. Click the **Search** button. Notice all the information that's offered.

**3.** Connect to **www.ciadata.com** and scroll down the page to view the kind of information anyone can obtain about you for less than $100.

**4.** Connect to the Federal Trade Commission site:

**http://www.ftc.gov/bcp/conline/pubs/credit/crdright.htm**

At this site, you can read about your rights to view credit reports.

**FIGURE 26**

Computer Security Checklist

- Use a password to protect your data in case your computer is stolen.
- Don't leave your computer unattended in public places.
- Run antivirus software and keep it updated.
- Install software service packs and security patches as they become available, but make sure they are legitimate.
- Install and activate firewall software, especially if your computer is directly connected to the Internet by an ISDN, DSL, satellite, or cable connection.
- Do not publish or post personal information, such as your physical address, passwords, Social Security number, or account numbers, on your Web site, your online resume, or other online documents.
- Be wary of contacts you make in public chat rooms.
- Don't click pop-up ads.
- Install and activate antispyware and ad-blocking software.
- Do not reply to spam.
- Ignore e-mail offers that seem too good to be true.

# QuickCheck

**1.** The best defense against viruses is to use a phishing filter before opening e-mail attachments. True or false? _____

**2.** Intruders can access your computer by exploiting _____ flaws in a computer's operating system, browser, or e-mail software.

**3.** _____ is an online threat that compromises your privacy by piggybacking on pop-up ads and collecting personal information.

**4.** E-mail scams are usually distributed in mass mailings called _____.

 CHECK ANSWERS

# BookOnCD

**ELECTRONIC VERSIONS** of your textbook are designed to be portable, interactive learning environments. This section offers an interactive overview of the popular BookOnCD and other BookOn products have similar features.

## BOOKONCD BASICS

**What is the BookOnCD?** The BookOnCD is a multimedia version of your textbook with photos that come to life as videos, diagrams that become animations, screenshots that open to guided software tours, and computer-scored activities that will help improve your test scores.

**What's the most effective way to use the BookOnCD?** If you're used to reading documents and Web pages on your computer screen, you can use the BookOnCD for most of your reading and studying. As you work through a chapter, you'll be able to view the multimedia elements in context and take QuickChecks at the end of each section. If you prefer to read from your printed textbook, you can start the BookOnCD whenever you want to view a multimedia element or work with a computer-scored activity.

**How do I start the BookOnCD?** To start the BookOnCD and take advantage of its interactive features, follow the instructions in the TRY IT! box below.

> ### FLASH PLAYER
>
> The BookOnCD requires the Adobe Flash player for displaying labs. The Flash player is installed on most computers. If the BookOnCD cannot find your Flash player when it starts, you'll be directed to go online to download and install it.

### TRY IT!

**Start the BookOnCD**

**1.** Locate the button on your computer's CD or DVD drive and push it to open the tray.

**2.** Insert the BookOnCD into the tray, label side up.

**3.** Push the button on the drive to close it.

**4.** Wait a few seconds until the BookOnCD has loaded. The main Computer Concepts screen appears, along with the Tracking Options dialog box.

The BookOnCD allows you to save your scores for QuickChecks, practice tests, and other activities, but for this session you do not need to track this data.

**5.** To disable tracking, make sure the box *Save Tracking data* is empty. If the box contains a check mark, click the box to empty it.

**6.** Click the **OK** button. The Tracking Options dialog box closes and the BookOnCD is ready for use.

To disable tracking for a session, make sure this box is empty.

Orientation

**How do I navigate through the book?** The BookOnCD menu and toolbar, near the top of the screen, contain tools you can use for navigation. The Next and Back buttons turn one page at a time. To get to the first page of any chapter, you can select it from the Contents menu.

The BookOnCD pages mirror the pages in the printed book, so if you want to take the QuickCheck that's on page 21 of your printed textbook for example, you can use the Go to Page option on the toolbar to jump right to it.

**What are the other menu and navigation options?** The menu bar includes a Web Links menu with options that open your browser and connect to InfoWebLinks, the NP10 Web site, and the Course Technology Web site. The menu bar also includes a Help menu where you can access instructions and troubleshooting FAQs. The Glossary button provides access to definitions for key terms. An Annotation button appears when your instructor has posted comments or lecture notes. If your instructor has not posted annotations, the button will not appear.

**How do I exit the BookOnCD?** When you have completed a session and want to close the BookOnCD, you can click the [X] button in the upper-right corner of the title bar, or you can click the File menu and select Exit. Figure 27 helps you locate the Close button and BookOnCD navigation tools.

**FIGURE 27**

Key features of the BookOnCD menu bar and toolbar.

The Back button displays the previous page.

The Next button displays the next page.

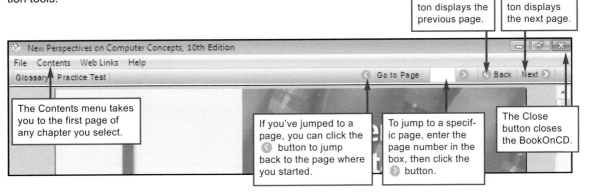

The Contents menu takes you to the first page of any chapter you select.

If you've jumped to a page, you can click the ◀ button to jump back to the page where you started.

To jump to a specific page, enter the page number in the box, then click the ▶ button.

The Close button closes the BookOnCD.

⌨ **TRY IT!**

**Open a chapter and navigate the BookOnCD**

1. Click **Contents** on the menu bar. The contents menu appears.

2. Click **Chapter 2**.

3. When Chapter 2 appears, click the **Next** button twice until you see page 56.

4. Click the **Back** button twice to go back to the first page of Chapter 2.

5. Click the white box on the right side of Go to Page. Type 89, then click the **Go to Page** ▶ button.

6. Click the ◀ **Go to Page** button. Now you should be back at the first page of Chapter 2.

7. Scroll down the page until you can see the Chapter Contents listing. As shown at right, you can use this list to quickly jump to Sections A, B, C, D, or E, Issues, Computers in Context, Labs, and End-of-Chapter activities.

8. Click ▶ **Section D** to jump to Section D.

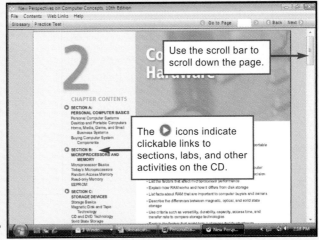

Use the scroll bar to scroll down the page.

The ▶ icons indicate clickable links to sections, labs, and other activities on the CD.

## MULTIMEDIA AND COMPUTER-SCORED ACTIVITIES

**What kinds of multimedia are included in the BookOnCD?**
Figures in your book marked with the ▶ icon morph into multimedia screentours, animations, and videos. A screentour takes you on a guided software tour—even if you don't have the software installed on your computer! Animations and videos visually expand on the concepts presented in the text.

**How do I access screentours and other multimedia?** To access multimedia elements, simply click the ▶ CLICK TO START icon while using the BookOnCD.

**Which activities are computer scored?** Figure 28 lists the BookOnCD activities that are computer scored. You can use these activities to gauge how well you remember and understand the material you read in the textbook.

Suppose you're reading Chapter 2. Work with the TRY IT! below to see how multimedia and computer-scored activities work.

**FIGURE 28**

BookOnCD Computer-Scored Activities

**Interactive Summary**

**Interactive Situation Questions**

**Practice Tests**

**Concept Map**

**QuickChecks**

**Lab QuickChecks**

### ⌨ TRY IT!

**Explore multimedia and computer-scored activities**

**1.** Use the **Go to Page** control to jump to page 79.

**2.** On page 79, Figure 2-23 contains a ▶ CLICK TO START icon. Click it to launch the video.

**3.** When you want to stop the video, click any blank area of the BookOnCD page. To restart the video, click the ▶ CLICK TO START icon again.

**4.** Now, try a computer-scored QuickCheck. Use the **Go to Page** control to get to page 75 and scroll down the page until you can see the entire set of QuickCheck questions.

**5.** Click the answer box for question 1, and then type your answer. Most answers are a single word. Upper and lower-case have no effect on the correctness of your answer.

**6.** Press the **Tab** key to jump to question 2, and then type your answer. Don't worry if you don't know the answer, you haven't actually read Chapter 2 yet. Just make a guess for now.

**7.** When you have answered all the questions, click the ▶ CHECK ANSWERS icon. The computer indicates whether your answer is correct or incorrect.

**8.** Continue to click **OK** to check the rest of your answers.

**9.** When you've reviewed all your answers, the computer presents a score summary. Click **OK** to close the dialog box

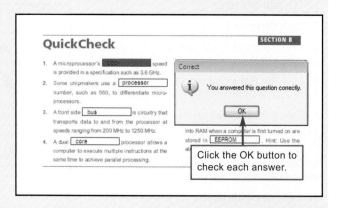

## NEW PERSPECTIVES LABS

**What about labs?** Your textbook gives you access to two kinds of labs. New Perspectives Labs are part of the BookOnCD. Student Edition Labs are located at the NP10 Web site. You'll learn how to access Student Edition Labs in Section E.

New Perspectives Labs give you hands-on experience applying concepts and using software discussed in each chapter. Labs on the BookOnCD are divided into topics, and each topic ends with a QuickCheck so that you can make sure you understand key concepts.

In addition to lab QuickChecks, each New Perspectives Lab also includes a set of assignments located in the Lab section of each chapter. Your instructor might require you to complete these assignments. You can submit them on paper, on disk, or as an e-mail message, according to your instructor's directions.

**How do I launch a lab?** First, navigate to the lab page using the New Perspectives Labs option from the Chapter Contents list or type in the corresponding page number from the printed book. Click the lab's ● icon to start it.

### TRY IT!

**Open a New Perspectives Lab**

**1.** Click **Contents** on the BookOnCD menu bar and select **Chapter 1**.

**2.** Scroll down to the Chapter Contents list and click ● **New Perspectives Labs**.

**3.** When the New Perspectives Labs page appears, click ● **Operating a Personal Computer**.

**4.** The lab window opens. Click the 🔁 button to view objectives for Topic 1.

**5.** Click the 🔁 button again to view page 1 of the lab. Read the information on the page, and then continue through the lab, making sure to follow any numbered instructions.

**6.** After page 8, you will encounter the first QuickCheck question. Click the correct answer, and then click the **Check Answer** button. After you find out if your answer was correct, click the 🔁 button to continue to the next question. Complete all the QuickCheck questions for Topic 1.

**7.** For this TRY IT! you don't have to complete the entire lab. When you are ready to quit, click the 🔁 button.

**8.** Click the 🔁 button again. Your Lab QuickCheck results are displayed.

**9.** Click the **OK** button to return to the BookOnCD.

# TRACKING YOUR SCORES

## Can I save scores from QuickChecks, labs, and other activities?

To save your scores, you have to create a Tracking file. The file can be located on a floppy disk, your computer's hard disk, a USB flash drive, or a network drive where you have permission to store files.

### ⌨ TRY IT!

#### Create a Tracking file

**1.** Make sure your BookOnCD is open.

**2.** Click **File** on the BookOnCD menu bar, then click **Change Tracking Options**.

**3.** When the Tracking Options dialog box appears, click the **Create** button.

**4.** When the Create Tracking File dialog box appears, enter the requested data (see illustration above right), then click **Continue**. The Save As dialog box appears.

**5.** Use the Save As dialog box to specify the location and name for your Tracking file. (See the illustration below right.)

**6.** After selecting a name and location for your Tracking file, click the **Save** button.

**7.** Back at the Tracking Options dialog box, make sure there is a check mark in the box labeled *Save Tracking data*, then click the **OK** button. Now your Tracking file is ready to receive your scores.

#### Complete a Practice Test

To start tracking your scores, you can complete a Practice Test.

**1.** Click the **Practice Test** button located on the BookOnCD toolbar.

**2.** The first question of a 10-question Practice Test appears. Answer the question, then click the **Next** button.

**3.** Answer the remaining questions, then click the **Check Answers** button.

**4.** When you see your score summary, click the **OK** button. You can then step through each of your answers or view a study guide.

**5.** Click the **Study Guide** button. A browser window opens to display each Practice Test question, your answers, and corresponding page numbers in your textbook.

**6.** Click the ❎ button on your browser window to close the Study Guide.

**7.** Click the **Close** button on the Practice Test window to close it and save your scores.

#### View the contents of your Tracking file

**1.** Click **File** on the BookOnCD menu bar.

**2.** Click **View Tracking Report**. Your computer opens your browser and displays a

summary score for the Practice Test you completed. The list of summary scores grows as you save additional Practice Tests, QuickChecks, Interactive Summaries, Interactive Situation Questions, and Lab QuickChecks.

**3.** To close the Tracking Report, close the browser window by clicking its ❎ button.

ORIENTATION

O-31

**How do I submit scores from my Tracking file?** You can use the Submit Tracking Data option on the File menu to send your scores to your instructor. The files are sent over an Internet service called WebTrack. Before you begin, make sure you have the following:

- An Internet connection
- Your instructor's WebTrack address
- Tracking file (If you've stored your data on a USB flash drive, make sure it is connected; if your data is on a floppy disk, make sure it is inserted in the drive.)

**Are the scores erased from my Tracking file when they are sent?** No. Your scores remain in your file—a copy is sent to your instructor. If your instructor's computer malfunctions and loses your data, you can resubmit your Tracking file. It is a good idea to back up your Tracking file using the Back Up Tracking File option on the File menu. If your file is damaged or lost, you'll have a copy.

**TRY IT!**

**Send your Tracking data**

1. Click **File** on the BookOnCD menu bar, then click **Submit Tracking Data**.

2. Make sure your instructor's Web Track address is correctly displayed in the Tracking Data Destination dialog box, then click **Continue**.

3. Your computer opens a browser window, makes an Internet connection, and contacts the WebTrack server.

4. When the WebTrack screen appears, make sure the information displayed is correct, then click the **Submit** button.

5. When you see a message that confirms your data has been submitted, you can close the browser window by clicking the [X] button.

6. Close your BookOnCD before you continue to the next section in the Orientation.

# QuickCheck

**SECTION D**

1. When you use the BookOnCD a(n) [_____] button appears if your instructor has posted comments or lecture notes.

2. Figures in the book marked with an @ sign morph into multimedia screentours, animations, and videos. True or false? [_____]

3. New Perspectives [_____] are divided into topics and each topic ends with a QuickCheck.

4. To save your scores on computer-scored activities you have to create a [_____] file.

▶ CHECK ANSWERS

## SECTION E

# NP10 Web Site

**THE INTERNET** offers access to information that's useful to just about everyone, and New Perspectives students are no exception. Your textbook includes the information you need to access the New Perspectives NP10 Web site, where you can continue the learning experience you began with your printed textbook and BookOnCD.

### WEB SITE RESOURCES

**What kinds of Web resources accompany my textbook?** The New Perspectives NP10 Web site—NP10 Web site, for short—includes activities and information to help you extend your knowledge and prepare for tests. Figure 29 highlights the features you'll find on the NP10 Web site.

**FIGURE 29**

NP10 Web Site Features

**Detailed Learning Objectives**
An expanded version of the Learning Objectives included at the beginning of each chapter.

**Chapter Overview CourseCasts**
Listen to a 5-minute audio presentation of chapter highlights on your computer or download to your MP3 player to study on the go.

**Chapter FlashCard CourseCasts**
Interact with downloadable audio flash cards to review key terms from the chapter.

**Test Yourself**
Each test contains 10 randomly selected questions from the chapter.

**Student Edition Labs**
Get hands-on practice with some of the concepts presented in a chapter.

**CNET Videos**
Watch a video clip from a recent CNET show and explore new tech trends.

**InfoWebLinks**
Follow Web links to find the most current information on equipment, concepts, and software you read about in a chapter.

**Online Games**
Have some fun while refreshing your memory about key concepts that might appear on the exam.

**TechBuzz**
Find out about cutting edge technology in the magazine-like TechBuzz section of the Web site.

## WEB SITE ACCESS

**How do I access the NP10 Web site?** You can get to the NP10 Web site in several ways:

- Open your browser and type *www.course.com/np/concepts10*. Your browser will display the main page of the NP10 Web site. From there, you can click links to each chapter's activities and information.

- Open your BookOnCD or other BookOn product and click any  link. These links take you directly to the information or activity specified along with the link.

**Do I need a password?** Yes. The first time you connect to the NP10 Web site, you must register for a CoursePort account. When you have completed the short registration process, you can access the NP10 Web site. Use the New User Registration link to create your CoursePort account.

### TRY IT!

**Access the NP10 Web site**

1. Start your browser.

2. Click the address box and type:

Make sure to use all lowercase letters, insert no spaces, and use the / slash, not the \ slash.

3. Press the **Enter** key. The CoursePort Login screen is displayed.

4. If you are accessing the NP10 Web site for the first time, click the **New User Registration** link and follow the instructions to create your account.

5. Once you've created a CoursePort account, you can log in by entering your Username and Password, then clicking the **Enter** button.

6. The Welcome screen contains links to activities for each chapter of the textbook. Click the button for Chapter 1 at the top of the screen. Your browser displays links to activities for the first chapter in your textbook.

7. You can always return to the Welcome screen by clicking the Home button on the Chapter toolbar. Click the **Home** button now.

8. Use your browser's [X] Close button to exit the NP10 Web site. If you are using a dial-up connection, you might have to manually disconnect from the Internet by double-clicking the icon in the lower-right corner of your screen, and then clicking Disconnect.

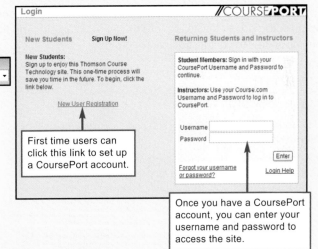

First time users can click this link to set up a CoursePort account.

Once you have a CoursePort account, you can enter your username and password to access the site.

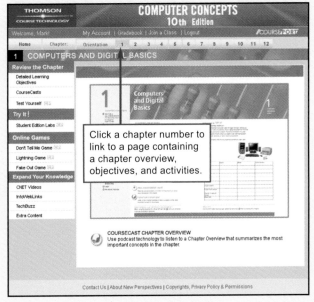

Click a chapter number to link to a page containing a chapter overview, objectives, and activities.

## WEB SITE TOUR

**How do I use the resources at the NP10 Web site?** The NP10 Web site is designed to help you review chapter material, prepare for tests, and extend your understanding of various topics.

When you have completed a chapter, you can work with the CNET videos, TechBuzz, and InfoWebLinks to explore chapter topics in more depth or gather material for class projects.

If you like a challenge, use the online games as a review activity; you'll get high scores if you understand the chapter material.

Test Yourself is a great way to prepare for tests because you'll be answering questions similar to those in your instructor's test bank.

For last minute review, load up your iPod with the Chapter Overview and Key Term FlashCard CourseCasts. You can listen to them for a quick refresher on your way to the test!

**Can I submit scores from Web site activities to my instructor?** You can track your results from the Test Yourself, Student Edition Labs, and Online Games through CoursePort's Universal Gradebook. Follow the steps in the box below to explore the NP10 Web site and find out how to submit scores to your instructor.

### TRY IT!

**Explore the NP10 Web site**

**1.** Connect to the NP10 Web site and then click the link for **Chapter 1**.

**2.** Click the **TechBuzz** link. This online magazine about technology trends changes every few months so you can keep current with new digital gadgets, computer equipment, and software.

**3.** Click the **InfoWeb** link. When you see a list of InfoWebLinks for Chapter 1, click the **Supercomputer** link. Read the short overview, and then click the first blue underlined link. Use the **Back** button on your browser window to get back to the Chapter 1 main page of the NP10 Web site.

**4.** Click the **CNET Videos** link. Take a few minutes to watch a video.

**5.** Click the **Chapter Overview CourseCast** link. Click the Listen Online button to start the chapter overview. You can use the download button if you want to store a CourseCast on your computer or portable music player. When you're ready to continue the tour, use the on-screen buttons to return to the Chapter 1 page.

**6.** Click the link to the **Lightning** game. Try your hand at a few questions, and then go back to the main Chapter 1 Web page.

**7.** Click the **Test Yourself** link. Complete a 10-question quiz. Your scores will be saved to the Universal Gradebook.

**8.** Click **Gradebook** on the CoursePort menu at the top of the Chapter main page to find instructions for printing your scores or e-mailing them to your instructor.

InfoWebLinks provide lots of information to supplement what you've read in the textbook.

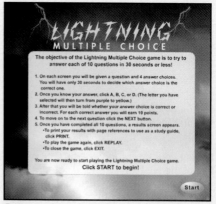

Online games, such as Lightning, Don't Tell Me, and Fake Out provide a fun way to review chapter material.

## STUDENT EDITION LABS

**How do I access the Student Edition Labs?** Student Edition Labs help you review the material presented in the textbook and extend your knowledge through dynamic observation and step-by-step practice.

 **TRY IT!**

### Work with Student Edition Labs

**1.** Make sure you're connected to the NP10 Web site and then click the link for **Chapter 1**.

**2.** Click the link for **Student Edition Labs**.

**3.** Click the link for **Chapter 1 Student Edition Labs**. The lab typically takes a few seconds to load, depending on the speed of your Internet connection.

**4.** Take a few minutes to walk through the section How to Use This Lab.

**5.** Click the **Understanding the Motherboard** link to start that lab.

**6.** Complete the first section of the lab, including the Intro, Observe, Practice, and Review activities.

**7.** When you've completed the review activity, a report containing your results is displayed. Use the Print button to print your report, or return to the NP10 Web site. If your instructor has activated your class, your score will be recorded to the Gradebook.

**8.** Exit the lab by clicking the [X] button.

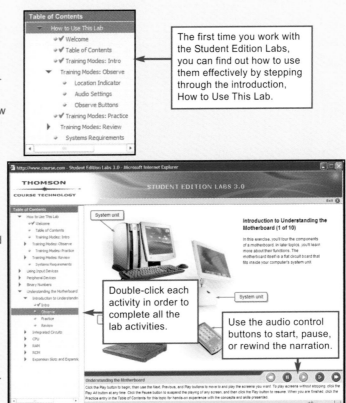

# QuickCheck

1. To access the NP10 Web site, you need a user-name and password. True or false? [_____]

2. When you're at the NP10 Web site, you can use the [_____] button to display the Welcome screen.

3. The Chapter [_____] is a 5-minute audio presentation of chapter highlights.

4. The Student Edition [_____] help you review through dynamic observation and step-by-step practice.

▶ CHECK ANSWERS

NEW PERSPECTIVES

# COMPUTER CONCEPTS

JUNE JAMRICH PARSONS • DAN OJA

EDITION
**10**

# 1

# Computers and Digital Basics

## LEARNING OBJECTIVES

• List the major technologies fueling the digital revolution

• Explain the concept of convergence and how it applies to digital devices

• Describe some ways in which digital technology affects society

• Define the term computer and explain input, output, processing, storage, and the stored program concept

• List the characteristics of personal computers, servers, mainframes, and supercomputers

• Describe similarities and differences in PDAs, portable players, and smart phones

• Describe the purpose of microcontrollers

• Differentiate between data and information, analog and digital

• Describe how digital devices represent numbers, text, images, and sound

• Explain the difference between bits and bytes, and the technical meaning of common prefixes, such as kilo, mega, and giga

• Demonstrate that you understand the general concept of how 0s and 1s are handled by integrated circuits

• Describe the relationship between compilers, interpreters, object code, and source code

• Briefly explain how a microprocessor's ALU and control unit work

• Provide examples of single-factor and two-factor authentication

• Describe how hackers can steal passwords

• List the principles of creating secure passwords and keeping them safe

## PRE-ASSESSMENT QUIZ

Take the pre-assessment quiz to find out how much you know about the topics in this chapter.

## MULTIMEDIA and INTERACTIVE ELEMENTS

When using the BookOnCD, BookOnFlashDrive, or other NP10 BookOn product, the ▶ icons are clickable to access multimedia resources.

BEFORE YOU READ ON, **TRY IT**

**WHAT'S MY DIGITAL PROFILE?**

The average American consumer owns 26 digital devices. Before you begin Chapter 1, take an inventory of your digital equipment to find their brands, models, and serial numbers. Tuck this information in a safe place. It can come in handy when you need to call technical support, arrange for repair services, or report missing equipment.

**1**. Fill in the following table for any digital equipment you own, rent, lease, or use.

|  | Brand | Model | Serial Number |
|---|---|---|---|
| Computer |  |  |  |
| Keyboard |  |  |  |
| Mouse |  |  |  |
| Monitor |  |  |  |
| Printer |  |  |  |
| Digital camera |  |  |  |
| Digital music player |  |  |  |
| Internet or network device |  |  |  |
| Other (list) |  |  |  |

**WEB SITE**

Visit the NP10 Web site to access additional resources ⓦ that accompany this chapter.

# All Things Digital

**IN A SIMPLER TIME** of poodle skirts, saddle shoes, and pony tails, consumers used a telephone to communicate, switched on a radio for music, watched the television for news, went to a movie theater for entertainment, trudged to the library for research, and headed to the nearest pizza joint for a game of pinball. Today, technology offers a dizzying number of choices for entertainment, information, and communication. It has changed the fabric of life in significant ways. We're using innovative new products, adjusting to industries in transformation, watching new markets emerge, and grappling with complex issues that have the potential to influence culture, politics, and economics on a global scale. Section A offers an overview of digital technology within the context of social and economic change.

## THE DIGITAL REVOLUTION

**What is the digital revolution?** The **digital revolution** is an ongoing process of social, political, and economic change brought about by digital technology, such as computers and the Internet. The digital revolution became a significant factor in the 1980s, as computers and other digital devices became popular and as the Internet opened global communications.

The term digital revolution was probably coined as a parallel to the term industrial revolution, and in that sense it promises to bring about a similar level of social and economic change. The digital revolution is creating an Information Society, in which generating, distributing, and manipulating information becomes a significant economic and cultural activity.

The digital revolution is ongoing. Every day new digital innovations challenge the status quo and require societies to make adjustments to traditions, lifestyles, and legislation.

**What technologies are fueling the digital revolution?** A constellation of technologies, including digital electronics, computers, communications networks, the Web, and digitization, are fueling the digital revolution. Before you learn about these technologies in greater detail later in the book, the following overview explains the big picture.

**What's the significance of digital electronics?** Digital electronics use electronic circuits to represent data. In the 1940s and 1950s engineers began to develop digital electronic devices and refine the electronic components used to build them. Transistors and then integrated circuits, which we call computer chips, were key factors in making electronic devices increasingly smaller and less expensive (Figure 1-1).

Consumers first became acquainted with digital electronics through digital watches that appeared in 1972 and then with handheld electronic calculators popularized by Texas Instruments in 1973. Today, digital electronic devices include computers, portable media players such as iPods, digital cameras and camcorders, cell phones, radios and televisions, GPSs (global positioning systems), DVD and CD players, e-book readers, and arcade games. Even cars and appliances, such as microwave ovens, refrigerators, and washing machines, include digital electronics for control, monitoring, and fault diagnosis.

---

**TERMINOLOGY NOTE**

The word *digital* comes from the root *digit*. In Latin, the word *digitus* means finger or toe. The modern use of the term *digital* is probably derived from the idea of counting on your fingers.

---

**FIGURE 1-1**

Digital devices, such as this wireless mouse, are built from solid state circuit boards and computer chips, making them small, light, fast, inexpensive, and durable.

Without digital electronics, you'd still be listening to bulky vacuum-tube radios instead of toting sleek iPods, computers would be huge machines, priced far beyond the reach of individuals, and your favorite form of entertainment would probably be foosball.

**When did computers step into the picture?** Engineers built the first digital computers during World War II for breaking codes and calculating ballistic missile trajectories. By the 1950s, a few computers were being used for business data processing applications, such as payroll and inventory management. Businesses adopted computers with increasing fervor as benefits for cutting costs and managing mountains of data became apparent.

During the antiestablishment era of the 1960s, the digital revolution was beginning to transform organizations, but had little effect on ordinary people. As with many technologies, computers were initially viewed with some measure of suspicion by consumers, who worried that impersonal data processing machines were reducing people to numbers.

When the first personal computers became available in 1976, sales got off to a slow start. Without compelling software applications, personal computers, such as the Apple II, seemed to offer little for their $2,400 price. As the variety of software increased, however, consumer interest grew. In 1982, *Time* magazine's annual Man of the Year award went to the computer, an indication that computers had finally gained a measure of acceptance by the person in the street (Figure 1-2).

As generations of computer users since that time have discovered, computers are handy devices. They displaced typewriters for creating documents, obsoleted mechanical calculators for number crunching, and took games to an entirely new dimension. Ambitious parents snapped up computers and educational software for their children and school systems set about equipping schools with computer labs.

In 1982, computers might have gained recognition in *Time* magazine, but fewer than 10% of U.S. households had a computer. Working on a standalone computer wasn't for everyone. People without interest in typing up corporate reports or school papers, crunching numbers for accounting, or playing computer games weren't tempted to become active soldiers in the digital revolution. Social scientists even worried that people would become increasingly isolated as they focused on computer activities rather than social ones. Computer ownership increased at a gradual pace until the mid-1990s, and then it suddenly accelerated as shown in the graph in Figure 1-3.

**FIGURE 1-2**

The computer was *Time* magazine's Machine of the Year in 1982.

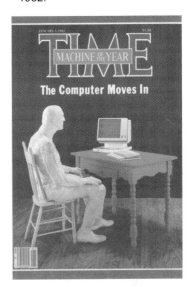

**FIGURE 1-3**

Household ownership of personal computers in the United States

*Source: U.S. Census Bureau*

## What caused the sudden upswing in computer ownership?

The second phase of the digital revolution materialized when the Internet was opened to public use. The **Internet** is a global computer network originally developed as a military project, then handed over to the National Science Foundation for research and academic use. When commercial Internet use was first allowed in 1995, companies such as AOL and Compuserve began to offer Internet access and e-mail to a quickly growing list of subscribers. **E-mail**, a form of electronic communication, was an application for the masses and finally a reason to buy a computer and join the digital revolution.

In addition to e-mail, the Internet offers many ways for people to communicate and interact. The Internet has turned the old idea of social isolation on its head; instead of computers reducing human interaction, computer networks encourage new types of interpersonal communications and relationships.

**Bulletin boards**, which allow members to post comments and questions that can be read and responded to by others, were one of the first online social scenes. Although postings and responses were sometimes days apart, hostile or inflammatory postings led to flame wars that subsided only when moderators stepped in.

**Chat groups** where people exchange typed messages in real time offered a more compelling environment than bulletin boards, and remain popular today. **Blogs**, short for Web logs, are personal journals posted online for general public access. A typical blog includes commentary by the author as well as links to additional information. Bloggers even enjoy the same protections under the law as journalists.

**Online social networks**, such as MySpace (Figure 1-4) and Friendster, have become wildly popular. To become a member of an online social network, you fill out a questionnaire to create your virtual identity and identify a list of friends. You can then choose to interact with your friends or with friends of those friends. This networking technique called *circle of friends* offers a level of comfort that members are interacting with friends of friends, rather than with strangers who might be encountered in chat rooms.

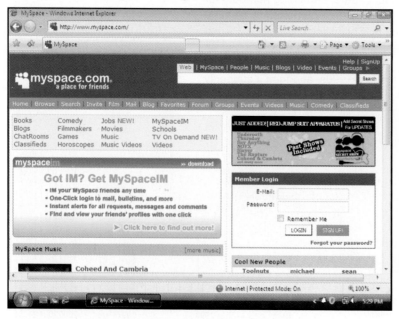

**FIGURE 1-4**

Online social networks offer netizens a place to look up old friends and meet friends of friends.

The Internet allows people to share resources as well as interact. Individuals' computers can be linked together in grid networks with powerful processing capabilities. One of the most ambitious grid computing efforts, SETI@home uses the Internet to connect the personal computers of more than 3 million volunteers from all over the world to analyze deep space radio signals in the search for extraterrestrial life.

A **computer network** is a group of computers linked by wired or wireless technology to share data and resources. Network technology existed before the Internet became popular, but the first computer networks were mainly deployed in schools and businesses. They were complicated to set up, unreliable, and offered only local connectivity. Network technology eventually became consumer-friendly, allowing homeowners to connect multiple computers to share printers, files, and an Internet connection.

Wireless networks offered even more advantages and Wi-Fi hotspots sprung up in airports, coffee shops, and hotels. Whereas the Internet enhanced communications, wireless network technology offered convenience and made digital information as accessible as radio stations.

**What about the Web?** When historians look back on the digital revolution, they are certain to identify the Web as a major transformative influence. The **Web** (short for World Wide Web) is a collection of linked documents, graphics, and sounds that can be accessed over the Internet. The Web has changed centuries-old business models, revolutionized the flow of information, and created a new virtual world.

Online stores pioneered by Amazon.com transformed the face of retailing. Rummage sales have gone global with Web sites such as eBay. Consumers now have more direct access to products and services, such as music downloads and airline reservations.

The publisher of telephone's ubiquitous Yellow Pages used to advertise "Let your fingers do the walking." That catch-phrase has never been more true as Web surfers' fingers jog miles over their keyboards each day to find answers, read the news, get sports scores, and check the weather report. In 2006 there were over 80 million Web sites, each with hundreds or thousands of pages containing information.

Fallout from the massive pool of Web-based information includes the proliferation of misinformation and disinformation. Anyone can post virtually anything on the Web, so researchers and ordinary netizens who use the Web have had to develop strategies to sift for the truth.

A key aspect of the Web is that it adds content and substance to the Internet. Without the Web, the Internet would be like a library without any books or a railroad without any trains. From storefronts to online magazines to multiplayer games, the Web has made Internet access a compelling digital technology for just about everyone.

**Cyberspace** is a term that refers to entities that exist largely within computer networks (Figure 1-5). The virtual world isn't reality in the sense of bricks and mortar, flesh and blood. You might envision online stores as similar to the shops in your local mall, but in reality they are simply a collection of data and images stored at a Web site. The Web defines much of the landscape of cyberspace, and its graphics and sounds make things seem real.

**How does digitization factor into the digital revolution?** **Digitization** is the process of converting text, numbers, sound, photos, and video into data that can be processed by digital devices. Some of the most obvious effects of the digital revolution can be attributed to digitization.

**FIGURE 1-5**

The term *cyberspace* was coined by science fiction writer William Gibson in his novelette *Burning Chrome*.

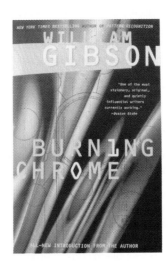

Digital images have changed the photographic industry. More than 80% of all cameras sold are digital, and the market for camera film is dwindling rapidly. One-hour photo processing labs, so popular in the 1990s, are disappearing from the strip-market landscape now that consumers can easily print their snapshots at home or from a Wal-Mart photo kiosk.

Digital imaging, such as computed tomography used in CAT scans, has had profound effects in medicine. The advantage of digital images is that they can be easily stored and transmitted. For example, rather than sending an x-ray to a consulting physician by overnight mail, a digital x-ray can be quickly transmitted over the Internet. Digital images can also be easily modified, encouraging all sorts of creative uses, but rendering photographic evidence somewhat less authoritative than it was in the pre-digital past.

Digital video is responsible for special effects in movies, new trends in 3-D animation, portable video, and surging consumer interest in home video. The film industry has become much more technology oriented and job openings reflect the need for specialists in graphics and motion video. Feature-length 3-D animated films are responsible for stunning technology breakthroughs, such as the ability to realistically depict the movement of clothing on a moving character and animate individual strands of hair or fur (Figure 1-6).

**FIGURE 1-6**

Animators at Pixar Studios created software called Fizt to individually simulate each of the 3 million hairs that flow and flutter as the furry main character moves.

At the consumer level, computer gaming is probably the most significant force driving research into faster computers and more sophisticated graphics processing.

Digital music first became popular when Internet-based file sharing networks like Napster offered free music downloads. The term **download** refers to the practice of copying a file from a remote computer to a local computer, such as when you copy a song from the Internet to your computer's hard disk. By disregarding copyrights and enabling users to pirate copyrighted music, file-sharing networks ran afoul of the law and many were forced to shut down. Apple and other astute companies saw a business opportunity in digital music, and online music stores, such as iTunes, quickly became popular.

Online music stores are transforming the industry, changing the way music is marketed, bought, and played. The ability to purchase a single song, rather than an entire album is making recording artists reconsider some of the shovelware they've been producing to bulk up albums.

Human speech can also be digitized. Weather reports on weatherband radio are read by computerized voice synthesizers. Automated telephone systems understand caller comments by using voice recognition. United Airlines' sophisticated telephone-based reservation system can handle an entire reservation without asking customers to use their phone keypads.

## CONVERGENCE

**What is convergence?** Your cell phone has a camera. Your clock has a radio. Your thermometer also reports the humidity. Your PDA plays digital music. All these are examples of technological **convergence**, a process by which several technologies with distinct functionalities evolve to form a single product.

In the pre-digital days, convergence often meant combining two technologically different devices in a single box. Old clock-radios, for example, combined a transistor radio and wind-up clock into a single case. Digital technology makes convergence much easier. Modern digital clock radios use a single microchip programmed for clock and radio functionality.

Convergence is currently doing its magic on cell phones, PDAs, computers, portable music players, digital cameras, GPSs, and e-book readers. These devices are gradually acquiring overlapping features and seem to be headed toward becoming a single device.

Another technology in convergence is voice communication. The current mix of land lines, cell phones, and Voice over IP burdens consumers with multiple handsets, numbers, and rate plans. Most people would like to have a single telephone number that can be used while at home, at work, or traveling. The phone must have a full set of features, such as emergency 911, caller ID, and voice mail. One vision for voice communication convergence is a Voice over IP phone that operates over home-, school-, or work-based broadband Internet connections, and switches automatically to a mobile network for use in other locations.

**How does convergence affect the typical consumer?**
Convergence tends to offer enhanced functionality and convenience. An average consumer owns more than 26 digital devices. Rather than juggle a cell phone, portable media player, camera, PDA, and computer, combining their features puts your data in a single device with a single charger.

The potential downside of convergence is quality. Especially in the initial stages of development, multipurpose devices rarely offer the same quality as the standalone devices they replace. For example, digital cameras tacked onto cell phones offer much lower resolution and fewer photo settings than a standalone digital camera. The marketplace is usually a good testing ground where consumer spending weeds out products that don't offer an acceptable mix of quality and convenience.

**Why does convergence seem to take so long?** Technology sometimes outstrips society's ability to deal with it. Many aspects of the digital revolution challenge the adaptability of societies and individuals. Laws and customs tend to change more slowly than technology, therefore technologies might be ready for deployment, but people and institutions just aren't ready for them.

Apple's foray into handheld computers illustrates the barriers that can hinder convergence. In 1993 Apple introduced a handheld device called the Newton that featured a small screen, personal organizer software, e-mail, and network connectivity. You'll recognize these features as being similar to today's PDAs. Unfortunately, the Newton was too large to fit in a shirt pocket and its handwriting recognition failed to recognize all but the most painstakingly printed characters. But the real problem was that people just didn't have much use for the product and it was discontinued after 6 years.

In 2004 Apple risked another foray into the handheld market, this time with a portable media player called the iPod. In contrast to the Newton, the iPod became an immediate hit because a huge population of young music lovers immediately recognized its value. By 2006 iPod fans had posted images depicting their ultimate iPod, and guess what? It merges a portable media player with a qwerty keyboard, camera, organizer software, and network connectivity (Figure 1-7).

Apple ran into a snag for deploying any type of cell phone with iTunes capability, however. Cell phone companies were reluctant to allow customers to pay iTunes for music, rather than paying their cell phone carrier. When ring tones are sold for up to $3 each, 99 cents for downloading an entire song from iTunes didn't leave much revenue to split between cell phone carriers and Apple.

**TERMINOLOGY NOTE**

Voice over IP (VoIP) refers to voice conversations that are routed over the Internet, rather than landlines or cellular phones. It is also called IP telephony or Internet telephony.

**FIGURE 1-7**

iPod fans created a mockup image of their dream machine—an iPod cell phone with PDA and digital media functionality.

## DIGITAL SOCIETY

### How does digital technology affect freedom and democracy?

Freedom of speech is the cornerstone of democracy. It can be defined as being able to speak freely without censorship or fear of reprisal. The concept is not limited to speaking, but includes all forms of expression, including writing, art, and symbolic actions. The more inclusive term freedom of expression is sometimes used instead of freedom of speech.

Freedom of speech is not an absolute. Most societies prohibit or repress some types of expression, such as hate speech, libel, pornography, and flag burning. Although freedom of expression is guaranteed under the U.S. Constitution, the European Convention on Human Rights, and the Universal Declaration of Human Rights, these documents recognize the necessity for some restrictions, which might vary from one society to the next. Incidents ranging from the controversy over teaching evolution in schools to the Arab world's fury over cartoons of Mohammed illustrate that societies draw the freedom of speech line in different places. The types of expression that are allowed or prohibited in a particular country are, in many respects, a reflection of its culture (Figure 1-8).

Digital technologies and communications networks make it easy to cross cultural and geographic boundaries. News, television shows, music, and art from all over the globe are accessible on the Internet. The Internet has the potential to expand freedom of speech by offering every person on the globe a forum for personal expression using personal Web sites, blogs, chat groups, and collaborative Wikis. Anonymous Internet sites such as Freenet, and **anonymizer tools** that cloak a person's identity even make it possible to exercise freedom of speech in situations where reprisals might repress it.

Internet information that seems innocuous in some cultures is not acceptable in others. Governments, parents, and organizations sometimes find it necessary to censor the Internet by limiting access and filtering content. China has some of the most draconian Internet censorship in the world. It blocks access to Web sites such as the BBC, The New York Times, Amnesty International, and Human Rights Watch. U.S. firms allegedly supplied the Chinese government with software necessary to erect its sophisticated filtering system. Search engines Google and Yahoo! have been accused of censoring search results for China-based Web surfers.

Chinese Internet censorship seems excessive, but it is by no means the only instance of free speech suppression. eBay has banned listings for any merchandise that could "promote or glorify hatred, violence or racial intolerance, or items that promote organizations with such views (e.g., KKK, Nazis, neo-Nazis, Skinhead Aryan Nation)." Parents frequently use filtering software such as Net Nanny and CYBER sitter. The U.S. Digital Millennium Copyright Act censored technical information by making it a crime to publish information about cracking DVD and CD copy protection.

Despite attempts to censor and filter speech on the Internet, it seems clear that digital technology opens the door to freedom of expression in unprecedented ways. Limitations on Internet speech are likely to change, too, as technology evolves and as societies come to grips with the balance between freedom and responsibility.

**FIGURE 1-8**

The 1960 movie *Inherit the Wind* was based on the trial of John Scopes who was accused of violating a state law that prohibited teaching evolution in state-funded schools.

**TERMINOLOGY NOTE**

A Wiki is one or more collaborative documents posted on the Web that can be viewed and changed by users. For example, Wikipedia is a collection of documents that form an encyclopedia. Visitors to the Wikipedia Web site can view definitions and information on a huge variety of topics and make changes to entries that are not correct or complete.

**Has digital technology changed the way we view privacy?**
Citizens of free societies have an expectation of privacy, which in the words of Supreme Court Justices Warren and Brandeis is "the right to be let alone." Digital technology use has exerted substantial pressure to diminish privacy by making it possible to easily collect and distribute data about individuals without their knowledge or consent.

In the United States, the expectation of privacy is derived from Fourth Amendment protections against unreasonable searches and seizures. The Fourth Amendment was formulated long before digital technologies such as e-mail and GPS devices. Legislation and court decisions pertaining to new technologies do not always strike the right balance between privacy and competing principles, such as free speech or free trade.

Privacy also encompasses confidentiality—the expectation that personal information will not be collected or divulged without permission. Internet marketers have a whole bag of tricks for getting personal information, and hackers are adept at breaking into sensitive databases to obtain confidential information.

Surveillance is viewed by many people as an invasion of privacy. Digital technology, such as GPS devices embedded in cell phones and cars, could allow everyone to be followed all of the time.

Some individuals dismiss the erosion of privacy saying "I have nothing to hide, so I don't care." But even they typically don't want stores, hackers, and curious onlookers to have access to data about what they buy, read, and watch, who they call, where they travel, and what they say.

Digital technology has not so much changed the way we view privacy—most citizens still have a reasonable expectation that their private lives will remain so. Instead, technology may help us develop a better appreciation for privacy and an understanding of the nuances that differentiate private and public spaces.

**How does digital technology affect intellectual property?**
**Intellectual property** refers to the ownership of certain types of information, ideas, or representations. It includes patents, trademarks, and copyrighted material, such as music, photos, software, books, and films. In the past, such works were difficult and expensive to copy.

Digital technology has made it easy to produce copies with no loss in quality from the original. Pirating—illegal copying and distribution of copyrighted material—is simple and inexpensive. It has caused significant revenue loss for software publishers, recording studios, and film producers. The fight against piracy takes many forms, from passing strict anti-piracy laws, to scrambling, encryption, and digital rights management schemes that physically prevent copying (Figure 1-9).

Digital technology adds complexity to intellectual property issues. Artists used to cut out various photos and paste them together to form a collage.

**FIGURE 1-9**

Most movie-goers have seen the rock-video style "Stealing" trailer. Consumer education is one front in the war against piracy.

 CLICK TO START

It is certainly easy to download images from the Web and paste them into reports, onto Web pages, and incorporate them into works of art, but without permission such digital cut and paste is not allowed.

Some films contain scenes that parents would rather their children not see. Even some scenes from family-oriented Harry Potter films might be too intense for young viewers. So, why not simply edit them out digitally to make a new DVD that the little tykes can watch? Such modifications are not allowed under current U.S. law, even for private viewing.

The law allows you to make a backup copy of software CDs or DVDs you legally own. However, if a CD, for example, is copy protected to prevent you from making a copy, it is against the law to break the copy protection. So, legally you have a right to a backup, but you don't have a way to legally create one!

Bucking protectionist trends are **open source** projects that promote copying, free distribution, peer review, and user modification. Linux is an open-source computer operating system that can be modified and freely distributed. Open source application software includes the popular OpenOffice.org suite, Avast! antivirus, Firefox Web browser, and Thunderbird e-mail.

Digital technology makes it possible to copy and modify films, music, software, and other data, but a tricky balancing act is required to allow consumers flexibility to use data while protecting the income stream to artists, performers, and publishers.

### What effect does digital technology have on the economy?
Digital technology is an important factor in global and national economies, in addition to affecting the economic status of individuals. **Globalization** can be defined as the worldwide economic interdependence of countries that occurs as cross-border commerce increases and as money flows more freely among countries. Consumers gain access to a wide variety of products, including technology products manufactured in locations scattered all over the globe. Countries that benefit from significant technology output include the United States, China, India, South Korea, and Finland (Figure 1-10).

Global communications technology offers opportunities for teleworkers in distant countries. Customer service lines for U.S. based companies, such as IBM, Dell, and Hewlett-Packard, are often staffed by offshore technicians who earn far more than they could if working for a locally-based company.

Globalization, fueled by digital technology, has controversial aspects, however. Worker advocates object to the use of cheap offshore labor that displaces onshore employees.

Individuals are affected by the **digital divide**, a term that refers to the gap between people who have access to technology and those who do not. Typically, digital have-nots face economic barriers.

**FIGURE 1-10**

Finland is a world leader in wireless technology. Its flagship technology company, Nokia, is responsible for about 25% of the country's exports.

They cannot afford computers, cell phones, and Internet access, or they are located in an economically depressed region where electricity is not available to run digital devices, power satellite dishes, and pick up Internet signals. But technology offers opportunity even to digital have-nots. For example, the Village Phone Project provides a small loan to entrepreneurs known as "village phone ladies" who sell minutes on their cell phones to neighbors who cannot afford their own land lines or cell phones (Figure 1-11).

Globalization is an ongoing process that will have far reaching effects on people in countries with developed technologies and those with emerging economies. Digital technology will be called upon to open additional economic opportunities without disrupting the lifestyles of currently prosperous nations.

**So what's the point?** Learning about digital technology is not just about circuits and electronics, nor is it only about digital gadgets, such as computers and portable music players. Digital technology permeates the very core of modern life. Understanding how this technology works and thinking about its potential can help you comprehend many issues related to privacy, security, freedom of speech, and intellectual property. It will help you become a better consumer and give you insights into local and world events.

You might even come to realize that some people who are responsible for making decisions about technology have only a vague idea of how it works. Without a solid grasp of technology problems, there can be little hope of finding effective solutions. As you continue to read this textbook, don't lose sight of the big picture. On one level, in this course you might be simply learning about how to use a computer and software. On a more profound level, however, you are accumulating knowledge about digital technology that applies to broader cultural and legal issues that are certain to affect your life far into the future.

**FIGURE 1-11**

In less technically developed countries such as Uganda and Bangladesh women make a living by selling cell phone time to their neighbors.

# QuickCheck

1. Computer ownership increased at a gradual pace from the late 1970s until the mid-1990s, and then it suddenly accelerated after the [blank] opened for commercial use.

2. Online social [blank], such as MySpace and Friendster, added a virtual dimension to the way people interact.

3. [blank] is a term that refers to objects and entities that exist largely within computer networks.

4. [blank] is the process of converting text, numbers, sound, animation, photos, and video into data that can be processed by digital devices.

5. [blank] is a process by which several technologies with distinct functionalities evolve to form a single product.

▶ CHECK ANSWERS

# Digital Devices

**WHETHER YOU REALIZE IT** or not, you already know a lot about the devices that fuel the digital revolution. You've picked up information from commercials and news articles, from books and movies, from conversations and correspondence—perhaps even from using a variety of digital devices and trying to figure out why they don't always work! The quintessential digital device is the computer. Section B provides an overview that's designed to help you start organizing what you know about digital devices, starting with computers.

## COMPUTER BASICS

**What is a computer?** The word *computer* has been part of the English language since 1646, but if you look in a dictionary printed before 1940, you might be surprised to find a computer defined as a person who performs calculations! Prior to 1940, machines designed to perform calculations were referred to as calculators and tabulators, not computers. The modern definition and use of the term computer emerged in the 1940s, when the first electronic computing devices were developed.

Most people can formulate a mental picture of a computer, but computers do so many things and come in such a variety of shapes and sizes that it might seem difficult to distill their common characteristics into an all-purpose definition. At its core, a **computer** is a multipurpose device that accepts input, processes data, stores data, and produces output, all according to a series of stored instructions (Figure 1-12).

**FIGURE 1-12**

A computer can be defined by its ability to accept input, process data, store data, and produce output, all according to a set of instructions from a computer program.

Computers produce output on devices such as screens and printers.

A computer accepts input from an input device, such as a keyboard, mouse, scanner, or digital camera.

Data is processed in the CPU according to instructions that have been loaded into the computer's memory.

A computer uses disks, CDs, and DVDs to permanently store data.

▶ CLICK TO START

**What is input?** Computer **input** is whatever is typed, submitted, or transmitted to a computer system. Input can be supplied by a person, by the environment, or by another computer. Examples of the kinds of input that computers can accept include words and symbols in a document, numbers for a calculation, pictures, temperatures from a thermostat, audio signals from a microphone, and instructions from a computer program. An input device, such as a keyboard or mouse, gathers data and transforms it into a series of electronic signals for the computer to store and manipulate.

**What is output?** **Output** is the result produced by a computer. Some examples of computer output include reports, documents, music, graphs, and pictures. Output devices display, print, or transmit the results of processing.

**What does *process data* mean?** Technically speaking, **data** refers to the symbols that represent facts, objects, and ideas. Computers manipulate data in many ways, and this manipulation is called **processing**. Some of the ways that a computer can process data include performing calculations, modifying documents and pictures, keeping track of your score in a fast-action game, drawing graphs, and sorting lists of words or numbers (Figure 1-13).

In a computer, most processing takes place in a component called the **central processing unit** or **CPU**. The CPU of most modern computers is a **microprocessor**, which is an electronic component that can be programmed to perform tasks based on data it receives. You'll learn more about microprocessors later in the chapter. For now, visualize a microprocessor as the little black box that's the brain of a digital device.

**How do computers store data?** A computer stores data so that it will be available for processing. Most computers have more than one place to put data, depending on how the data is being used. **Memory** is an area of a computer that temporarily holds data waiting to be processed, stored, or output. **Storage** is the area where data can be left on a permanent basis when it is not immediately needed for processing. Data is typically stored in files. A computer file, usually referred to simply as a **file**, is a named collection of data that exists on a storage medium, such as a hard disk, floppy disk, CD, DVD, or flash drive. A file can contain data for a term paper, Web page, e-mail message, or music video. Some files also contain instructions that tell the computer how to perform various tasks.

**What's so significant about a computer's ability to store instructions?** The series of instructions that tells a computer how to carry out processing tasks is referred to as a **computer program**, or simply a program. These programs form the **software** that sets up a computer to do a specific task. When a computer *runs* software, it performs the instructions to carry out a task.

Take a moment to think about the way you use a simple handheld calculator to balance your checkbook each month. You're forced to do the calculations in stages. Although you can store data from one stage and use it in the next stage, you cannot store the sequence of formulas—the program—required to balance your checkbook. Every month, therefore, you have to perform a similar set of calculations. The process would be much simpler if your calculator remembered the sequence of calculations and just asked you for this month's checkbook entries.

**FIGURE 1-13**

An unsorted list is input to the computer, which processes it and produces a sorted list as output.

The idea of a **stored program** means that a series of instructions for a computing task can be loaded into a computer's memory. These instructions can easily be replaced by a different set of instructions when it is time for the computer to perform another task. This ability makes computers multipurpose machines.

The stored program concept allows you to use your computer for one task, such as word processing, and then easily switch to a different type of computing task, such as editing a photo or sending an e-mail message. It is the single most important characteristic that distinguishes a computer from other simpler and less versatile digital devices, such as watches, calculators, and pocket-sized electronic dictionaries.

**What kinds of software do computers run?** Computers run two main types of software: application software and system software. A computer can be *applied* to many tasks, such as writing, number crunching, video editing, and online shopping. **Application software** is a set of computer programs that helps a person carry out a task. Word processing software, for example, helps people create, edit, and print documents. Personal finance software helps people keep track of their money and investments. Video editing software helps people create and edit home movies—and even some professional films.

Whereas application software is designed to help a person carry out a task, the primary purpose of **system software** is to help the computer system monitor itself in order to function efficiently. An example of system software is a computer **operating system** (OS), which is essentially the master controller for all the activities that take place within a computer. Although an operating system does not directly help people perform application-specific tasks, such as word processing, people do interact with the operating system for certain operational and storage tasks, such as starting programs and locating data files.

## PERSONAL COMPUTERS, SERVERS, MAINFRAMES, AND SUPERCOMPUTERS

**Are computers categorized in any way?** At one time it was possible to define three distinct categories of computers. Mainframes were housed in large, closet-sized metal frames. Minicomputers were smaller, less expensive, and less powerful computers that were able, nevertheless, to provide adequate computing power for small businesses. Microcomputers were clearly differentiated from computers in other categories because their CPUs consisted of a single microprocessor chip.

Today, microprocessors are no longer a distinction between computer categories because just about every computer uses one or more microprocessors as its CPU. The term *minicomputer* has fallen into disuse and the terms microcomputer and mainframe are used with less and less frequency.

Computers are versatile machines that can perform a truly amazing assortment of tasks, but some computers are better suited than others for certain tasks. Categorizing computers is a way of grouping them according to criteria such as usage, cost, size, and capability. Experts don't necessarily agree on the categories or the devices placed in each category, but commonly used computer categories include personal computers, servers, mainframes, and supercomputers.

**TERMINOLOGY NOTE**

The term *personal computer* is sometimes abbreviated as *PC*. However, PC can also refer to a specific type of personal computer that descended from the original IBM PC and runs Windows software.

In this book, PC refers to IBM PC descendants. It is not used as an abbreviation for personal computer.

**What is a personal computer?** A **personal computer** is a micro-processor-based computing device designed to meet the computing needs of an individual. It typically provides access to a wide variety of computing applications, such as word processing, photo editing, and e-mail.

Personal computers are available as desktop or portable models, and in a variety of *form factors*, a term that refers to the dimensions of the unit that holds the computer circuitry. You'll learn more about the wide variety of personal computer form factors in the Hardware chapter. For now, simply remember that computers like those pictured in Figure 1-14 are classified as personal computers.

**FIGURE 1-14**

Personal computer designs run the gamut from drab gray boxes to colorful curvy cases.

**What is a workstation?** The term **workstation** has two meanings. It can simply refer to an ordinary personal computer that is connected to a network. A second meaning refers to powerful desktop computers used for high-performance tasks, such as medical imaging and computer-aided design, that require a lot of processing speed. Some workstations contain more than one micro-processor, and most have circuitry specially designed for creating and displaying three-dimensional and animated graphics. Workstations, such as the one pictured in Figure 1-15, typically cost a bit more than an average personal computer.

**FIGURE 1-15**

A workstation resembles a desktop computer, but typically features more processing power and storage capacity.

**Is an Xbox a personal computer?** A **videogame console**, such as Nintendo's Wii, Sony's PlayStation, or Microsoft's Xbox, are not generally referred to as personal computers because of their history as dedicated game devices. They originated as simple digital devices that connected to a TV set and provided only a pair of joysticks for input.

Today's videogame consoles contain microprocessors that are equivalent to any found in a fast personal computer, and they are equipped to produce graphics that rival those on sophisticated workstations. Add-ons such as keyboards, DVD players, and Internet access make it possible to use a videogame console to watch DVD movies, send and receive e-mail, and participate in online activities such as multiplayer games. Despite these features, videogame consoles like the one in Figure 1-16 fill a specialized niche and are not considered a replacement for a personal computer.

**FIGURE 1-16**

A videogame console includes circuitry similar to a personal computer's, but its input and output devices are optimized for gaming.

**What makes a computer a server?** In the computer industry, the term *server* has several meanings. It can refer to computer hardware, to a specific type of software, or to a combination of hardware and software. In any case, the purpose of a **server** is to *serve* computers on a network (such as the Internet or a home network) by supplying them with data.

Any software or digital device, such as a computer, that requests data from a server is referred to as a **client**. For example, on a network, a server might respond to a client's request for a Web page. Another server might handle the steady stream of e-mail that travels among clients from all over the Internet. A server might also allow clients within a network to share files or access a centralized printer.

Remarkably, just about any personal computer, workstation, mainframe, or supercomputer can be configured to perform the work of a server. That fact should emphasize the concept that a server does not require a specific type of hardware. Nonetheless, computer manufacturers categorize some of their computers as servers because they are especially suited for storing and distributing data on a network. Server prices vary, depending on configuration, but tend to be more similar to workstation prices than personal computer prices. Despite impressive performance on server-related tasks, these machines often do not include features such as sound cards, DVD players, and other fun accessories that consumers expect on their desktop computers. Most consumers would not want to buy a server to replace a desktop computer.

**What's so special about a mainframe computer?** A **mainframe computer** (or simply a mainframe) is a large and expensive computer capable of simultaneously processing data for hundreds or thousands of users. Mainframes are generally used by businesses or governments to provide centralized storage, processing, and management for large amounts of data. Mainframes remain the computer of choice in situations where reliability, data security, and centralized control are necessary.

The price of a mainframe computer typically starts at several hundred thousand dollars and can easily exceed $1 million. Its main processing circuitry is housed in a closet-sized cabinet (Figure 1-17), but after large components are added for storage and output, a mainframe computer system can fill a good-sized room.

**How powerful is a supercomputer?** A computer falls into the **supercomputer** category if it is, at the time of construction, one of the fastest computers in the world (Figure 1-18).

**FIGURE 1-17**

This IBM z9 109 mainframe computer weighs 2,672 pounds and is about 6.5 feet tall.

**FIGURE 1-18**

The BlueGene/L supercomputer topped the list as the world's fastest computer when it was upgraded in 2006.

Because of their speed, supercomputers can tackle complex tasks and compute-intensive problems that just would not be practical for other computers. A **compute-intensive** problem is one that requires massive amounts of data to be processed using complex mathematical calculations. Molecular calculations, atmospheric models, and cosmological research are all examples of projects that require massive numbers of data points to be manipulated, processed, and analyzed.

Common uses for supercomputers include breaking codes, modeling worldwide weather systems, and simulating nuclear explosions. One impressive simulation designed to run on a supercomputer tracked the movement of thousands of dust particles as they were tossed about by a tornado.

At one time, supercomputer designers focused on building specialized, very fast, and very large CPUs. Today, most supercomputer CPUs are constructed from thousands of microprocessors. Of the 500 fastest supercomputers in the world, the majority use microprocessor technology.

## PDAS, PORTABLE PLAYERS, AND SMART PHONES

**Are handheld devices computers?** Handheld digital devices include familiar gadgets such as iPods, Blackberries, and Verizon's LG VX9800 smart phone. These devices incorporate many computer characteristics. They accept input, produce output, process data, and include storage capabilities. Handheld devices vary in their programmability and their versatility, however. Technically, these devices would be classified as computers, but only some of them are customarily referred to as computers.

**What is a handheld computer?** The gadgets currently touted as handheld computers are descended from PDAs. A **PDA** (personal digital assistant) is a pocket-sized digital appointment book with a small qwerty keyboard or a touch-sensitive screen, designed to run on batteries and be used while holding it. Originally, PDAs were not equipped for voice communications, which distinguished them from the emerging cell phone market. PDAs synchronized appointment data and contact lists with desktop computers by exchanging data over a dedicated wired or wireless connection.

A **handheld computer** is essentially a PDA enhanced with features such as removable storage, e-mail, Web access, voice communications, built-in camera, and GPS. Handheld computers also offer a variety of application software, but they do not typically run the same full-featured software versions as personal computers. Instead, they run special scaled-down versions of word processing, spreadsheet, and other application software. Examples of handheld computers with PDA ancestors include the Dell Axim and Hewlett-Packard iPAQ (Figure 1-19).

**INFOWEBLINKS**

What's the latest news about supercomputers? Visit the **Supercomputer InfoWeb** to learn more about these amazing machines.

 CLICK TO CONNECT
www.course.com/np/concepts10/ch01

**INFOWEBLINKS**

Learn more about the latest PDAs, players, and smart phones by visiting the **Handheld InfoWeb**.

 CLICK TO CONNECT
www.course.com/np/concepts10/ch01

**FIGURE 1-19**

Many handheld computers feature a small keyboard, while others accept handwriting input.

**How do smart phones fit into the picture?** Smart phones are descended from basic cell phones that were originally designed exclusively for voice communications. Their simple design offered a numeric keypad, a small screen, and just enough memory for a few names and phone numbers. Keypad data entry required the now-familiar thumbing such as pressing the 7 key four times to produce the letter *s*.

From the cell phone's humble origins emerged a digital device called a **smart phone**, which in addition to voice communication, includes features such as full qwerty keypad, text messaging, e-mail, Web access, removable storage, camera, FM radio, digital music player, and software options for games, financial management, personal organizer, GPS, and maps.

Smart phones, like the one in Figure 1-20, contain a microprocessor and have many characteristics of computers. They are not, however, usually referred to as computers because of their origins as a special-purpose device with keypad input and limited programmability.

**How are iPods classified?** iPods are an enhancement on MP3 players designed to play music stored in a type of file called MP3 (which stands for MPEG-1 Audio Layer-3). The basic idea behind these players was to convert music from CDs or download it from the Web to your computer, then transfer it to the player. Sharing MP3 files on the Web became hugely popular despite its questionable legality. After many music sharing sites were shut down, Apple created a legal music store called iTunes on the Web where music is stored in a proprietary, copy-protected file format and sold by the song or by the album. The iPod (Figure 1-21) was designed as the repository for consumers' iTunes music collections and enhanced versions of the device now store and play video and photos as well.

iPods and similar devices are classified as **portable media players** because their main strength is playing music, showing videos, and storing photos. Like other handheld digital devices, these players have many computer characteristics. An iPod, for example, contains a microprocessor, accepts input, has significant storage capacity on its built-in hard disk, and outputs stored music, video, and images. Most portable media players, however, have very limited programmability. They are not designed for users to add software and their lack of a keyboard or touch screen puts severe limits on data entry.

**Why is it hard to see much difference in handheld devices?** Whether they fall into the handheld computer, smart phone, or portable media player categories, today's handheld digital devices have many features in common. The lines that separate these devices are blurry because the market is in a state of convergence. Currently, size and battery life seem to be the factors preventing a single device from integrating all the features possible for a handheld device. Technology, however, is likely to solve those problems soon.

## MICROCONTROLLERS

**What is a microcontroller?** Have you ever wondered how a guided missile reaches its target or how your refrigerator knows when to initiate a defrost cycle? What controls your microwave oven, your television remote, TiVos, digital thermometers, watches, and clocks? Many common appliances and machines are controlled by embedded microcontrollers. A **microcontroller** is a special-purpose microprocessor that is built into the machine it controls. A microcontroller is sometimes called a computer-on-a-chip because it includes many of the elements common to computers.

**FIGURE 1-20**

Smart phones include qwerty keyboards, cameras, and digital music players.

**FIGURE 1-21**

The iPod and other portable media players work with music, videos, and photos.

**How does a microcontroller work?** Consider the microcontroller in a Subzero refrigerator. It accepts user input for desired temperatures in the refrigerator and freezer compartments. It stores these desired temperatures in memory. Temperature sensors collect additional input of the actual temperatures. The microcontroller processes the input data by comparing the actual temperature to the desired temperature. As output, the microcontroller sends signals to activate the cooling motor as necessary. It also generates a digital readout of the refrigerator and freezer temperatures.

**Is a microcontroller really a computer?** Recall that a computer is defined as a multipurpose device that accepts input, produces output, stores data, and processes it according to a stored program. A microcontroller seems to fit the input, processing, output, and storage criteria that define computers. Some microcontrollers can even be reprogrammed to perform different tasks.

Technically, a microcontroller could be classified as a computer, just as smart phones, and portable media players can be. Despite this technicality, however, microcontrollers tend to be referred to as processors rather than as computers because in practice they are used for dedicated applications, not as multipurpose devices.

**Why are microcontrollers significant?** Microcontrollers, such as the one in Figure 1-22, can be embedded in all sorts of everyday devices, enabling machines to perform sophisticated tasks that require awareness and feedback from the environment. When combined with wireless networks, devices with embedded processors can relay information to Web sites, cell phones, and a variety of data collection devices. Machines and appliances with embedded processors tend to be smarter about their use of resources, such as electricity and water, so they can be environmentally friendly.

Perhaps the most significant effect of microcontrollers is that they are an almost invisible technology, one that doesn't require much adaptation or learning on the part of the people who interact with microcontrolled devices. However, because microcontrollers remain mostly out-of-sight-and-out-of-mind, it is easy for their use to creep into areas that could be detrimental to quality of life, privacy, and freedom. That innocuous GPS chip in your cell phone, for example, can be useful if you're lost and need 911 assistance, but it could potentially become a tool for surreptitious surveillance.

**FIGURE 1-22**

A microcontroller is usually mounted on a circuit board and then installed in a machine or appliance using wires to carry input and output signals.

# QuickCheck

1. A computer accepts input, processes data, stores data, and produces [＿＿＿＿＿] according to a series of instructions.

2. The term *microprocessor* is a synonym for the term *microcomputer*. True or false? [＿＿＿＿＿]

3. The [＿＿＿＿＿] program concept enables computers to be multipurpose devices.

4. A(n) [＿＿＿＿＿] specializes in compute-intensive problems.

5. A(n) [＿＿＿＿＿] is a special-purpose microprocessor that is built into the machine it controls.

▶ CHECK ANSWERS

# Digital Data Representation

**COMPUTERS AND OTHER DIGITAL DEVICES** store all sorts of "stuff," including text, numbers, music, images, speech, and video. The amazing aspect of digital technology is that all these different elements are distilled down to simple pulses of electricity and stored as 0s and 1s. Understanding the data representation concepts presented in Section C will help you grasp the essence of the digital world and get a handle on all the jargon pertaining to bits, bytes, megahertz, and gigabytes.

## DATA REPRESENTATION BASICS

**What is data?** As you learned earlier in the chapter, data refers to the symbols that represent people, events, things, and ideas. Data can be a name, a number, the colors in a photograph, or the notes in a musical composition.

**Is there a difference between data and information?** In everyday conversation, people use the terms *data* and *information* interchangeably. Nevertheless, some technology professionals make a distinction between the two terms. They define data as the symbols that represent people, events, things, and ideas. Data becomes information when it is presented in a format that people can understand and use. As a general rule, remember that (technically speaking) data is used by machines, such as computers; information is used by humans.

**What is data representation?** **Data representation** refers to the form in which data is stored, processed, and transmitted. For example, devices such as PDAs, iPods, and computers store numbers, text, music, photos, and videos in formats that can be handled by electronic circuitry. Those formats are data representations. Data can be represented using digital or analog methods.

**What's the difference between analog and digital?** For a simple illustration of the difference between analog and digital, consider the way you can control the lights in a room using a traditional light switch or a dimmer switch (Figure 1-23). A traditional light switch has two discrete states—on and off. There are no in-between states, so this type of light switch is digital. A dimmer switch, on the other hand, has a rotating dial that controls a continuous range of brightness. It is, therefore, analog.

**Digital data** is text, numbers, graphics, sound, and video that has been converted into discrete digits such as 0s and 1s. In contrast, **analog data** is represented using an infinite scale of values.

**How does digital data work?** Imagine that you want to send a message by flashing a light. Your light switch offers two states: on and off. You could use sequences of ons and offs to represent various letters of the alphabet. To write down the representation for each letter, you can use 0s and 1s. The 0s represent the off state of your light switch; the 1s indicate the on state. For example, the sequence on on off off would be written 1100, and you might decide that sequence represents the letter A.

**FIGURE 1-23**

A computer is a digital device, more like a standard light switch than a dimmer switch.

Digital devices are electronic and so you can envision data flowing within these devices as pulses of light. In reality, digital signals are represented by two different voltages, such as +5 volts and 0 volts. They can also be represented by two different tones as they flow over a phone line. Digital data can also take the form of light and dark spots etched onto the surface of a CD or the positive and negative orientation of magnetic particles on the surface of a hard disk. Regardless of the technology, however, digital data is always represented by two states denoted as 0 and 1.

The 1s and 0s used to represent digital data are referred to as binary digits. It is from this term that we get the word *bit*—*bi*nary digi*t*. A **bit** is a 0 or 1 used in the digital representation of data.

## REPRESENTING NUMBERS, TEXT, AND PICTURES

**How do digital devices represent numbers?** Numeric data consists of numbers that might be used in arithmetic operations. For example, your annual income is numeric data, as is your age. The price of a bicycle is numeric data. So is the average gas mileage for a vehicle, such as a car or SUV. Digital devices can represent numeric data using the binary number system, also called base 2.

The **binary number system** has only two digits: 0 and 1. No numeral like 2 exists in this system, so the number two is represented in binary as 10 (pronounced *one zero*). You'll understand why if you think about what happens when you're counting from 1 to 10 in the familiar decimal system. After you reach 9, you run out of digits. For ten, you have to use the digits 10—zero is a placeholder and the 1 indicates one group of tens.

In binary, you just run out of digits sooner—right after you count to 1. To get to the next number, you have to use the zero as a placeholder and the 1 indicates one group of 2s. In binary then, you count 0 (zero), 1 (one), 10 (one zero), instead of counting 0, 1, 2 in decimal. If you need to brush up on binary numbers, refer to Figure 1-24 and to the lab at the end of the chapter.

The important point to understand is that the binary number system allows digital devices to represent virtually any number simply by using 0s and 1s.

| Decimal (Base 10) | Binary (Base 2) |
|:---:|:---:|
| 0 | 0 |
| 1 | 1 |
| 2 | 10 |
| 3 | 11 |
| 4 | 100 |
| 5 | 101 |
| 6 | 110 |
| 7 | 111 |
| 8 | 1000 |
| 9 | 1001 |
| 10 | 1010 |
| 11 | 1011 |
| 1000 | 1111101000 |

**FIGURE 1-24**

The decimal system uses ten symbols to represent numbers: 0, 1, 2, 3, 4, 5, 6, 7, 8, and 9. The binary number system uses only two symbols: 0 and 1.

## How do digital devices represent words and letters?

**Character data** is composed of letters, symbols, and numerals that are not used in arithmetic operations. Examples of character data include your name, address, and hair color. Just as Morse code uses dashes and dots to represent the letters of the alphabet, a digital computer uses a series of bits to represent letters, characters, and numerals. Figure 1-25 illustrates how a computer can use 0s and 1s to represent the letters and symbols in the text *HI!*

Digital devices employ several types of codes to represent character data, including ASCII, EBCDIC, and Unicode. **ASCII** (American Standard Code for Information Interchange, pronounced *ASK ee*) requires only seven bits for each character. For example, the ASCII code for an uppercase *A* is 1000001. ASCII provides codes for 128 characters, including uppercase letters, lowercase letters, punctuation symbols, and numerals.

A superset of ASCII, called **Extended ASCII**, uses eight bits to represent each character. For example, Extended ASCII represents the uppercase letter *A* as 01000001. Using eight bits instead of seven bits allows Extended ASCII to provide codes for 256 characters. The additional Extended ASCII characters include boxes, circles, and other graphical symbols. Figure 1-26 lists the Extended ASCII character set.

**FIGURE 1-25**

A computer treats the letters and symbols in the word *HI!* as character data, which can be represented by a string of 0s and 1s.

# HI!

01001000   01001001   00100001

**FIGURE 1-26**

The Extended ASCII code uses eight 1s and 0s to represent letters, symbols, and numerals. The first 32 ASCII characters are not shown in the table because they represent special control sequences that cannot be printed. The two blank entries are space characters.

| char | code | char | code | char | code | char | code | char | code | char | code | char | code | char | code |
|---|---|---|---|---|---|---|---|---|---|---|---|---|---|---|---|
| (space) | 00100000 | > | 00111110 | \ | 01011100 | z | 01111010 | ÿ | 10011000 | ‖ | 10110110 | ╘ | 11010100 | ≥ | 11110010 |
| ! | 00100001 | ? | 00111111 | ] | 01011101 | { | 01111011 | Ö | 10011001 | ╖ | 10110111 | ╒ | 11010101 | ≤ | 11110011 |
| " | 00100010 | @ | 01000000 | ^ | 01011110 | \| | 01111100 | Ü | 10011010 | ╕ | 10111000 | ╓ | 11010110 | ⌠ | 11110100 |
| # | 00100011 | A | 01000001 | _ | 01011111 | } | 01111101 | ¢ | 10011011 | ╣ | 10111001 | ╫ | 11010111 | ⌡ | 11110101 |
| $ | 00100100 | B | 01000010 | ` | 01100000 | ~ | 01111110 | £ | 10011100 | ║ | 10111010 | ╪ | 11011000 | ÷ | 11110110 |
| % | 00100101 | C | 01000011 | a | 01100001 |  | 01111111 | ¥ | 10011101 | ╗ | 10111011 | ┘ | 11011001 | ≈ | 11110111 |
| & | 00100110 | D | 01000100 | b | 01100010 | Ç | 10000000 | ₧ | 10011110 | ╝ | 10111100 | ┌ | 11011010 | ° | 11111000 |
| ' | 00100111 | E | 01000101 | c | 01100011 | ü | 10000001 | ƒ | 10011111 | ╜ | 10111101 | █ | 11011011 | ∙ | 11111001 |
| ( | 00101000 | F | 01000110 | d | 01100100 | é | 10000010 | á | 10100000 | ╛ | 10111110 | ▄ | 11011100 | · | 11111010 |
| ) | 00101001 | G | 01000111 | e | 01100101 | â | 10000011 | í | 10100001 | ┐ | 10111111 | ▌ | 11011101 | √ | 11111011 |
| * | 00101010 | H | 01001000 | f | 01100110 | ä | 10000100 | ó | 10100010 | └ | 11000000 | ▐ | 11011110 | ⁿ | 11111100 |
| + | 00101011 | I | 01001001 | g | 01100111 | à | 10000101 | ú | 10100011 | ┴ | 11000001 | ▀ | 11011111 | ² | 11111101 |
| , | 00101100 | J | 01001010 | h | 01101000 | å | 10000110 | ñ | 10100100 | ┬ | 11000010 | α | 11100000 | ■ | 11111110 |
| - | 00101101 | K | 01001011 | i | 01101001 | ç | 10000111 | Ñ | 10100101 | ├ | 11000011 | β | 11100001 |  | 11111111 |
| . | 00101110 | L | 01001100 | j | 01101010 | ê | 10001000 | ª | 10100110 | ─ | 11000100 | Γ | 11100010 | | |
| / | 00101111 | M | 01001101 | k | 01101011 | ë | 10001001 | º | 10100111 | ┼ | 11000101 | π | 11100011 | | |
| 0 | 00110000 | N | 01001110 | l | 01101100 | è | 10001010 | ¿ | 10101000 | ╞ | 11000110 | Σ | 11100100 | | |
| 1 | 00110001 | O | 01001111 | m | 01101101 | ï | 10001011 | ⌐ | 10101001 | ╟ | 11000111 | σ | 11100101 | | |
| 2 | 00110010 | P | 01010000 | n | 01101110 | î | 10001100 | ¬ | 10101010 | ╚ | 11001000 | µ | 11100110 | | |
| 3 | 00110011 | Q | 01010001 | o | 01101111 | ì | 10001101 | ½ | 10101011 | ╔ | 11001001 | τ | 11100111 | | |
| 4 | 00110100 | R | 01010010 | p | 01110000 | Ä | 10001110 | ¼ | 10101100 | ╩ | 11001010 | Φ | 11101000 | | |
| 5 | 00110101 | S | 01010011 | q | 01110001 | Å | 10001111 | ¡ | 10101101 | ╦ | 11001011 | Θ | 11101001 | | |
| 6 | 00110110 | T | 01010100 | r | 01110010 | É | 10010000 | « | 10101110 | ╠ | 11001100 | Ω | 11101010 | | |
| 7 | 00110111 | U | 01010101 | s | 01110011 | æ | 10010001 | » | 10101111 | ═ | 11001101 | δ | 11101011 | | |
| 8 | 00111000 | V | 01010110 | t | 01110100 | Æ | 10010010 | ░ | 10110000 | ╬ | 11001110 | ∞ | 11101100 | | |
| 9 | 00111001 | W | 01010111 | u | 01110101 | ô | 10010011 | ▒ | 10110001 | ╧ | 11001111 | φ | 11101101 | | |
| : | 00111010 | X | 01011000 | v | 01110110 | ö | 10010100 | ▓ | 10110010 | ╨ | 11010000 | ε | 11101110 | | |
| ; | 00111011 | Y | 01011001 | w | 01110111 | ò | 10010101 | │ | 10110011 | ╤ | 11010001 | ∩ | 11101111 | | |
| < | 00111100 | Z | 01011010 | x | 01111000 | û | 10010110 | ┤ | 10110100 | ╥ | 11010010 | ≡ | 11110000 | | |
| = | 00111101 | [ | 01011011 | y | 01111001 | ù | 10010111 | ╡ | 10110101 | ╙ | 11010011 | ± | 11110001 | | |

An alternative to the 8-bit Extended ASCII code, called **EBCDIC** (Extended Binary-Coded Decimal Interchange Code, pronounced *EB seh dick*), is usually used only by older, IBM mainframe computers.

**Unicode** (pronounced *YOU ni code*) uses sixteen bits and provides codes for 65,000 characters—a real bonus for representing the alphabets of multiple languages. For example, Unicode represents an uppercase *A* in the Russian Cyrillic alphabet as 0000010000010000.

**Why do ASCII and Extended ASCII provide codes for 0, 1, 2, 3, 4, 5, 6, 7, 8, and 9?** While glancing at the table of ASCII codes in Figure 1-26 you might have wondered why the table contains codes for 0, 1, 2, 3, and so on. Aren't these numbers represented by the binary number system? A computer uses Extended ASCII character codes for 0, 1, 2, 3 to represent numerals that are not used for calculations. For example, you don't typically use your Social Security number in calculations, so it is considered character data and represented using Extended ASCII. Likewise, the numbers in your street address can be represented by character codes rather than binary numbers.

**How can bits be used to store images?** Images, such as photos, pictures, line art, and graphs, are not small, discrete objects like numbers or the letters of the alphabet. To work with images, they must be digitized.

Images can be digitized by treating them as a series of colored dots. Each dot is assigned a binary number according to its color. For example, a green dot might be represented by 0010 and a red dot by 1100, as shown in Figure 1-27. A digital image is simply a list of color numbers for all the dots it contains.

**How can bits be used to store sound?** Sound, such as music and speech, is characterized by the properties of a sound wave. You can create a comparable wave by etching it onto a vinyl platter—essentially how records were made in the days of jukeboxes and record players. You can also represent that sound wave digitally by sampling it at various points, and then converting those points into digital numbers. The more samples you take, the closer your points come to approximating the full wave pattern. This process of sampling, illustrated in Figure 1-28, is how digital recordings are made.

**FIGURE 1-27**

An image can be digitized by assigning a binary number to each dot.

A red dot might be digitized as 1100.

**FIGURE 1-28**

A sound wave can be sampled at fraction-of-a-second time intervals. Each sample is recorded as a binary number and stored.

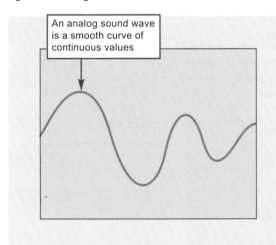

An analog sound wave is a smooth curve of continuous values

To digitize a wave, it is sliced into vertical segments, called samples. For purposes of illustration, this one-second sound wave was sliced into 30 samples.

## QUANTIFYING BITS AND BYTES

**How can I tell the difference between bits and bytes?** The ads for digital devices typically include lots of abbreviations relating to bits and bytes. A few key concepts can help you understand what these abbreviations mean. Even though the word *bit* is an abbreviation for binary digit, it can be further abbreviated, usually as a lowercase *b*.

On older digital devices, bits were handled in groups, and terminology from that era is still used. A group of 8 bits is called a **byte** and is usually abbreviated as an uppercase *B*.

Transmission speeds are typically expressed in bits, whereas storage space is typically expressed in bytes. For example, a cable Internet connection might transfer data from the Internet to your computer at 3 mega*bits* per second. In an iPod ad, you might notice that it can store up to 60 giga*bytes* of music and video.

**What do the prefixes kilo-, mega-, and giga- mean?** When reading about digital devices, you'll frequently encounter references such as 50 kilobits per second, 1.44 megabytes, and 2.8 gigahertz. Kilo, mega, giga, and similar terms are used to quantify digital data.

In common usage, *kilo*, abbreviated as K, means a thousand. For example, $50 K means $50,000. In the context of computers, however, 50K means 51,200. Why the difference? In the decimal number system we use on a daily basis, the number 1,000 is 10 to the 3rd power, or $10^3$. For digital devices where base 2 is the norm, a kilo is precisely 1,024, or $2^{10}$. A **kilobit** (abbreviated Kb or Kbit) is 1,024 bits. A **kilobyte** (abbreviated KB or Kbyte) is 1,024 bytes. Kilobytes are often used when referring to the size of small computer files.

The prefix *mega* means a million, or in the context of bits and bytes, precisely 1,048,576 (the equivalent of $2^{20}$). A **megabit** (Mb or Mbit) is 1,048,576 bits. A **megabyte** (MB or MByte) is 1,048,576 bytes. Megabytes are often used when referring to the size of medium to large computer files or to floppy disk capacity.

In technology lingo, the prefix *giga* refers to a billion, or precisely 1,073,741,824. As you might expect, a **gigabit** (Gb or Gbit) is approximately one billion bits. A **gigabyte** (GB or GByte) is one billion bytes. Gigabytes are typically used to refer to storage capacity.

Computers—especially mainframes and supercomputers—sometimes work with huge amounts of data, and so terms such as tera- (trillion), peta- (thousand trillion), and exa- (quintillion) are also handy. Figure 1-29 summarizes the terms commonly used to quantify computer data.

**TERMINOLOGY NOTE**

What's a kibibyte? Some computer scientists have proposed alternative terminology to dispel the ambiguity in terms such as *mega* that can mean 1,000 or 1,024. They suggest the following prefixes:

Kibi = 1,024
Mebi = 1,048,576
Gibi = 1,073,741,824

| | | | |
|---|---|---|---|
| Bit | One binary digit | Gigabit | $2^{30}$ bits |
| Byte | 8 bits | Gigabyte | $2^{30}$ bytes |
| Kilobit | 1,024 or $2^{10}$ bits | Terabyte | $2^{40}$ bytes |
| Kilobyte | 1,024 or $2^{10}$ bytes | Petabyte | $2^{50}$ bytes |
| Megabit | 1,048,576 or $2^{20}$ bits | Exabyte | $2^{60}$ bytes |
| Megabyte | 1,048,576 or $2^{20}$ bytes | | |

**FIGURE 1-29**

Quantifying Digital Data

## CIRCUITS AND CHIPS

**How do digital devices store and transport all those bits?**
Because most digital devices are electronic, bits take the form of electrical
pulses that can travel over circuits in much the same way that electricity
flows over a wire when you turn on a light switch. All the circuits, chips, and
mechanical components that form a digital device are designed to work
with bits.

At the simplest level, you can envision bits as two states of an electric circuit; the state used for a 1 bit would be *on* and the state for a 0 bit would be
*off*. In practice, the 1 bit might be represented by an elevated voltage, such
as +5 volts, whereas a 0 bit is represented by a low voltage, such as 0.

**What's inside?** If it weren't for the miniaturization made possible by digital electronic technology, computers, cell phones, and portable music
players would be huge, and contain a complex jumble of wires and other
electronic gizmos. Instead, today's digital devices contain relatively few
parts that include some chips and one or more circuit boards.

**What's a computer chip?** The terms *computer chip*, *microchip*, and
*chip* originated as technical jargon for *integrated circuit*. An **integrated circuit** (IC), such as the one pictured in Figure 1-30, is a super-thin slice of
semiconducting material packed with microscopic circuit elements, such as
wires, transistors, capacitors, logic gates, and resistors.

**Semiconducting materials** (or semiconductors), such as
silicon and germanium, are substances with properties
between those of a conductor (like copper) and an insulator
(like wood). To fabricate a chip, the conductive properties
of selective parts of the semiconducting material can be
enhanced to essentially create miniature electronic
pathways and components, such as transistors.

Integrated circuits are packaged in protective carriers that vary in shape
and size. Figure 1-31 illustrates some chip carriers, including small
rectangular DIPs (dual in-line packages) with caterpillar-like legs protruding from a black, rectangular body; and pincushion-like PGAs
(pin-grid arrays).

**FIGURE 1-30**

A computer chip is classified by
the number of miniaturized
components it contains—from
small-scale integration (SSI) of
fewer than 100 components per
chip to ultra large-scale integration (ULSI) of more than 1
million components per chip.

A DIP has two rows of pins
that connect the IC circuitry
to a circuit board.

A PGA is a square chip
package with pins arranged in
concentric squares, typically
used for microprocessors.

**FIGURE 1-31**

Integrated circuits can be used
for microprocessors, memory,
and support circuitry. They are
housed within a ceramic carrier.
These carriers exist in several
configurations, or chip packages, such as DIPs and PGAs.

**How do chips fit together?** The electronic components of most digital devices are mounted on a circuit board called a **system board**, motherboard, or main board. The system board houses all essential chips and provides connecting circuitry between them. In Figure 1-32, you can see what's inside a typical desktop computer, a Palm Pilot, and a cell phone.

**FIGURE 1-32**

The electronic components of computers, PDAs, and cell phones have many similar elements, including microchips and circuit boards.

# QuickCheck

1. Most computers are [                    ] devices that work with discrete numbers, such as 1s and 0s.

2. The [                ] number system represents numeric data as a series of 0s and 1s.

3. A computer uses [                ] codes to represent the numerals in your Social Security number and street address, whereas it uses [                ] numbers for numeric data such as your age.

4. A(n) [                ] is approximately one billion bytes.

5. A(n) [                ] circuit contains microscopic elements, such as wires, transistors, and capacitors, that are packed onto a very small square of semiconducting material.

▶ CHECK ANSWERS

# Digital Processing

**COMPUTERS AND OTHER DIGITAL DEVICES** process data, but how do they know what to do with it? The instructions you issue aren't 0s and 1s that a digital device can work with. So what goes on inside the box? Section D explains the programs that make digital devices tick. You'll discover that although digital devices appear to perform very complex tasks, under the hood they are really performing some very simple operations, but doing them at lightning speed.

## PROGRAMS AND INSTRUCTION SETS

**How do digital devices process data?** Computers, portable media players, handheld computers, and smart phones all work with digital data. That data is manipulated under the control of a computer program, or software. But how do digital circuits know what those program instructions mean? Let's take a closer look at programs to see how they are created and how digital devices work with them.

**Who creates programs?** Computer programmers create programs that control digital devices. These programs are usually written in a high-level **programming language**, such as C, Basic, COBOL, or Java.

Programming languages use a limited set of command words such as Print, If, Write, Display, and Get to form sentence-like statements designed as step-by-step directives for the processor chip. An important characteristic of most programming languages is that they can be written with simple tools, such as a word processor, and they can be understood by programmers. A simple program to select a song on your iPod might contain the statements shown in Figure 1-33.

```
Display Playlist

Get Song

Play Song
```

**FIGURE 1-33**

The program for an iPod displays a list of songs that the user can choose to play. A program works behind the scenes to display the list, get your selection, process it, and play the song.

The human-readable version of a program, like the one above, created in a high-level language by a programmer is called **source code**. Source code is an important first step in programming application software, batch files, and scripts that you'll learn about in later chapters. However, just as a digital device can't work directly with text, sounds, or images until they have been digitized, source code has to be converted into a digital format before the processor can use it.

**How does source code get converted?** The procedure for translating source code into 0s and 1s can be accomplished by a compiler or an interpreter. A **compiler** converts all the statements in a program in a single batch, and the resulting collection of instructions, called **object code**, is placed in a new file (Figure 1-34). Most of the program files distributed as software contain object code that is ready for the processor to execute.

FIGURE 1-34

A compiler converts statements written in a high-level programming language into object code that the processor can execute.

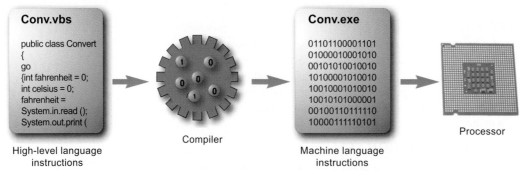

High-level language instructions     Compiler     Machine language instructions     Processor

▶ CLICK TO START

As an alternative to a compiler, an **interpreter** converts and executes one statement at a time while the program is running. After the statement is executed, the interpreter converts and executes the next statement, and so on (Figure 1-35).

FIGURE 1-35

An interpreter converts high-level statements one at a time as the program is running.

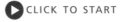

High-level language instructions     Interpreter     Processor

▶ CLICK TO START

Compilers and interpreters don't simply convert the characters from source code into 0s and 1s. For example, in the first line of the iPod program, Display Playlist, a compiler would not simply convert the *D* into its ASCII equivalent. No, computers are a little trickier than that.

**What does the conversion process produce?** A microprocessor is hard wired to perform a limited set of activities, such as addition, subtraction, counting, and comparisons. This collection of preprogrammed activities is called an **instruction set**. Instruction sets are not designed to carry out any specific task, such as word processing or playing music. Instead, an instruction set is designed to be general purpose so that programmers can use it in creative ways for the wide variety of tasks performed by all kinds of digital devices.

Each instruction has a corresponding sequence of 0s and 1s. For example, 00000100 might correspond to Add. The list of codes for a microprocessor's instruction set, called **machine language**, can be directly executed by the processor's circuitry. A set of machine language instructions for a program is called **machine code**.

A machine code instruction has two parts: the op code and the operands. An **op code**, which is short for operation code, is a command word for an operation such as add, compare, or jump. The **operand** for an instruction specifies the data, or the address of the data, for the operation. In the following instruction, the op code means add and the operand is 1, so the instruction means Add 1.

A single high-level instruction very often converts into multiple machine language instructions. Figure 1-36 illustrates the number of machine-language instructions that correspond to a simple high-level program.

```
#include <stdio.h>
int main (int argc, char *argv[])
{
    int I;
    int sum = 0;

    for (I=0; I<=100; I++) sum += I * I;
    printf ("The sum 0..100=%d\n",sum);
}
```

```
00100111101111011111111111100000
10101111101111110000000000010100
10101111101001000000000000100000
10101111101001010000000000100100
10101111101000000000000000011000
10101111101000000000000000011100
10001111101011100000000000011100
10001111101110000000000000011000
00000001110011100000000000011001
00100101110010000000000000000001
00101001000000010000000001100101
10101111101010000000000000011100
00000000000000000111100000010010
00000011000011111100100000100001
00010100001000001111111111110111
10101111101110010000000000011000
00111100000000100000010000000000
10001111101001010000000000011000
00001100000010000000000000111011 00
00100100100000010000000010000110000
```

FIGURE 1-36

Many machine language instructions might be needed to equal a simple high-level program that counts to 100.

To summarize what you should now know about programs and instruction sets, a programmer creates human-readable source code using a programming language. A compiler or interpreter converts source code into machine code. Machine code instructions are a series of 0s and 1s that correspond to a processor's instruction set.

## PROCESSOR LOGIC

**What happens inside a computer chip?** A microprocessor contains miles of microscopic circuitry and millions of miniature components divided into different kinds of operational units, such as the ALU and the control unit.

The **ALU** (arithmetic logic unit) is the part of the microprocessor that performs arithmetic operations, such as addition and subtraction. It also performs logical operations, such as comparing two numbers to see if they are the same. The ALU uses **registers** to hold data that is being processed, just as you use a mixing bowl to hold the ingredients for a batch of cookies.

The microprocessor's **control unit** fetches each instruction, just as you get each ingredient out of a cupboard or the refrigerator. Data is loaded into the ALU's registers, just as you add all the ingredients to the mixing bowl. Finally, the control unit gives the ALU the green light to begin processing, just as you flip the switch on your electric mixer to begin blending the cookie ingredients. Figure 1-37 illustrates a microprocessor control unit and ALU preparing to add 2 + 3.

FIGURE 1-37

The control unit fetches the ADD instruction, then loads data into the ALU's registers where it is processed.

**What happens when a computer executes an instruction?** The term **instruction cycle** refers to the process in which a computer executes a single instruction. Some parts of the instruction cycle are performed by the microprocessor's control unit; other parts of the cycle are performed by the ALU. The steps in this cycle are summarized in Figure 1-38.

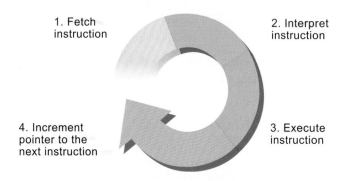

1. Fetch instruction

2. Interpret instruction

4. Increment pointer to the next instruction

3. Execute instruction

**FIGURE 1-38**

The instruction cycle includes four activities.

**What role does the control unit play?** The instructions that a computer is supposed to process for a particular program, are held in memory. When the program begins, the memory address of the first instruction is placed in a part of the microprocessor's control unit called an instruction pointer. The control unit can then fetch the instruction by copying data from that address into its instruction register. From there, the control unit can interpret the instruction, gather the specified data, or tell the ALU to begin processing. Figure 1-39 helps you visualize the control unit's role in processing an instruction.

RAM

Address M1
Add two numbers

Address M2
Put result in M3

Address M3

Control Unit

Instruction Pointer
M1

Add Two Numbers

ALU
4+5

**FIGURE 1-39**

The control unit fetches instructions, interprets them, fetches data, and tells the ALU which processing operations to perform.

**When does the ALU swing into action?** The ALU is responsible for performing arithmetic and logical operations. It uses registers to hold data ready to be processed. When it gets the go-ahead signal from the control unit, the ALU processes the data and places the result in an accumulator. From the accumulator, the data can be sent to memory or used for further processing. Figure 1-40 on the next page helps you visualize what happens in the ALU as the computer processes data. What happens after an instruction is executed? When the computer completes an instruction, the control unit increments the instruction pointer to the memory address of the next instruction, and the instruction cycle begins again.

**FIGURE 1-40**

The ALU uses data from its registers to perform arithmetic and logical operations. The results are placed in another register, called the accumulator.

**Do I need to know all this detailed stuff?** A computer that you use to play a 3-D action game has the same instruction set as the computer your great-grandmother uses to type (slowly) e-mail messages. All the complex game activities of tracking characters, generating sound, and displaying constantly changing graphics have to be performed using the standard instruction set. Your computer can only keep up with your action figure if it has a fast processor—much faster than the one needed by your great-grandmother.

What you should take away from the discussion about programming and instruction sets is the idea that computers and other digital devices perform a wide array of complex tasks by performing a very limited set of machine language instructions very fast. As you learn more about microprocessors, this concept will help you understand the significance of microprocessor performance, such as speed and word size, which you'll learn about in the next chapter.

**INFOWEBLINKS**

For more details on the inner workings of your computer's processor, visit the **CPU InfoWeb**.

 CLICK TO CONNECT

www.course.com/np/concepts10/ch01

# QuickCheck

SECTION D

1. The human-readable version of a program, created in a high-level language by a programmer is called [          ] code.

2. A compiler converts all the statements in a program in a single batch, and the resulting collection of instructions is called [          ] code.

3. In a machine code instruction such as 00000100 00000001 the left-most number is the op code and the remaining numbers are [          ].

4. The ALU in your computer's microprocessor performs [          ] and logical operations.

5. The microprocessor's [          ] unit fetches each instruction.

CHECK ANSWERS

# Password Security

USER IDS, passwords, and personal identification numbers (PINs) are a fact of everyday life in the information age. They are required for activities such as using ATMs and debit cards, logging into Windows, accessing wireless networks, making an iTunes purchase, instant messaging, reading e-mail, and file sharing. Many Web sites encourage memberships and offer perks if you sign up. Section E provides information about selecting secure passwords and managing the mountain of passwords you collect and tend to forget.

## AUTHENTICATION PROTOCOLS

**What is an authentication protocol?** Security experts use the term **authentication protocol** to refer to any method that confirms a person's identity using something the person knows, something the person possesses, or something the person is. For example, a person might know a password or PIN. A person might possess an ATM card or a credit card. A person can also be identified by **biometrics**, such as a fingerprint, facial features (photo), or retinal pattern (Figure 1-41).

Authentication protocols that use more than one means of identification are more secure than others. Two-factor authentication, which verifies identity using two independent elements of confirmation such as an ATM card and PIN, is more secure than single-factor authentication, such as a password. Computer-related security is primarily based on passwords associated with user IDs. The level of protection offered by single-factor authentication depends on good password selection and management on the part of users.

**What is a user ID?** A **user ID** is a series of characters—letters and possibly numbers or special symbols—that becomes a person's unique identifier, similar to a Social Security number. It is also referred to as a username, login, screenname, online nickname, or handle. User IDs are typically public. Because they are not secret, they do not offer any level of security.

User IDs are significant because they are the name on an account, such as e-mail or iTunes, that requires a password. When you first apply for or set up an account, you might be supplied with a user ID or you might be asked to create one. Often a user ID is a variation of your name. Brunhilde Jefferson's user ID might be bjeffe, bjefferson, brunhilde_jefferson, or bjeff0918445. It is also becoming common to use your e-mail address as a user ID.

The rules for creating a user ID are not consistent throughout all applications, so it is important to read instructions carefully before finalizing your user ID. For example, spaces might not be allowed in a user ID. Hence, the underline in brunhilde_jefferson is used instead of a space. There might be a length limitation, so Ms. Jefferson might have to choose a short user ID, such as bjeffe.

**FIGURE 1-41**

Two-factor authentication typically uses a password or PIN, combined with a biometric identification, such as this retinal scan.

Some computers that host password-protected resources don't differentiate between uppercase and lowercase letters, and would consider the user IDs B_Jefferson and b_jefferson to be the same. Other computers are **case sensitive** and differentiate between uppercase and lowercase. On such computers, if Ms. Jefferson selected Brun_Jeff as her user ID, she would not be able to gain access by typing brun_jeff. To avoid such problems, most people stick to lowercase letters for their user IDs.

**What is a password?** A **password** is a series of characters that verifies a user ID and guarantees that you are the person you claim to be. Although you might be assigned a password, typically you are asked to provide your own. In some situations you might be given a temporary password, and then asked to change it as soon as you successfully log in for the first time. Passwords and user IDs are typically created on a registration or enrollment screen similar to the one in Figure 1-42.

**User Name & Password**

*Enter a
Username:                          (Must be at least 8
                                   characters)

*Enter a
Password:                          (Must be at least 8
                                   characters and
*Confirm                           include one number)
Password:

View our privacy policy to learn how we protect your information.

**ENROLL NOW!»**

**FIGURE 1-42**

When you create an account, you are typically asked to enter a user ID and password.

**What if I forget my password?** Login screens for many applications provide a "forgot my password" link. Clicking this link checks your identity using your answer to a personal question. If your identity checks out, your password is e-mailed to you. A personal question provides an alternative authentication protocol to ensure that you are not a hacker pretending to have lost a password.

Personal questions and answers are usually set up at the same time you create an account. After selecting a password, you are required to choose a question that you must answer before your forgotten password is e-mailed to you. This question might be something like: What is your mother's maiden name? What is your favorite color? or Where were you born? You should be careful about the question you choose because public information like your mother's maiden name or the town of your birth can be researched by any hacker.

**What is the difference between a password and a PIN?** Both passwords and PINs are classified as *something the user knows* authentication methods. In practice, PINs tend to be a sort sequence of numbers that can be entered using a numeric keypad, whereas passwords tend to be longer sequences of letters, numbers, and special characters that require a full qwerty keyboard for entry. PINs are typically used with two-factor authentication protocols, whereas passwords are used in conjunction with single-factor authentication protocols.

For example, ATMs require a bank card (something you possess) and a PIN (something you know). In contrast, passwords are associated with single-factor authentication used for networks, Web sites, and other situations in which the hardware for dealing with ID cards is not available.

## PASSWORD HACKS

**How serious is password theft?** To a hacker, obtaining the password for a specific user ID can be even more rewarding than a burglar figuring out the combination to a house safe. Once hackers get into a user account, a wealth of personal information can be at their fingertips. This information could be anything from juicy e-mail gossip to Social Security numbers, credit card numbers, bank account numbers, health data, and other private details. When someone gains unauthorized access to your personal data and uses it illegally, it is called **identity theft**. Victims of this increasingly common crime often don't realize what is happening until it's too late.

Armed with your password and other personal data, a cybercriminal can rack up bills using your credit card, apply for a mortgage using your financial data, create fake accounts in your name, send embarrassing e-mail messages, or wreak havoc on your bank account. Once a thief breaks into an online account, he or she can also change your password and you will no longer be able to log in. Password theft is serious and pervasive, so it is important to understand how hackers get passwords and how you can protect yours.

**How can hackers get my password?** Hackers can employ a whole range of ways to steal passwords. Some primitive means include shoulder surfing, which is looking over your shoulder as you type in your password, and dumpster diving, which is going through your trash.

Password thieves can easily find your password if you write it down on a yellow sticky note hidden under your keyboard or in plain sight on top of your monitor. If a hacker doesn't have physical access to your work area but your computer is connected to a network, your password can be discovered by a hacker using a remote computer and software tools that systematically guess your password, intercept it, or trick you into revealing it.

A **dictionary attack** helps hackers guess your password by stepping through a dictionary containing thousands of the most commonly used passwords. Password dictionaries can be found on black hat sites and packaged with password cracking software, such as John the Ripper. Unfortunately, dictionary attacks are often enough to break a password because many users choose passwords that are easy to remember and likely to be in the most commonly used list (Figure 1-43).

**TERMINOLOGY NOTE**

*Hacker* can refer to a skilled programmer or to a person who manipulates computers with malicious intent. The terms *black hat* and *cracker* are also used to refer to a malicious or criminal hacker.

**FIGURE 1-43**

Some of the most commonly used passwords are included in the dictionaries packaged with password cracking software.

| | | | | | |
|---|---|---|---|---|---|
| 12345 | internet | jordan | alex | newyork | jonathan |
| abc123 | service | michael | apple | soccer | love |
| password | canada | michelle | avalon | thomas | marina |
| computer | hello | mindy | brandy | wizard | master |
| 123456 | ranger | patrick | chelsea | Monday | missy |
| tigger | shadow | 123abc | coffee | asdfgh | monday |
| 1234 | baseball | andrew | dave | bandit | monkey |
| a1b2c3 | donald | bear | falcon | batman | natasha |
| qwerty | harley | calvin | freedom | boris | ncc1701 |
| 123 | hockey | changeme | gandalf | dorothy | newpass |
| xxx | letmein | diamond | golf | eeyore | pamela |
| money | maggie | matthew | green | fishing | pepper |
| test | mike | miller | helpme | football | piglet |
| carmen | mustang | ou812 | linda | george | poohbear |
| mickey | snoopy | tiger | magic | happy | pookie |
| secret | buster | trustno1 | merlin | iloveyou | rabbit |
| summer | dragon | 12345678 | molson | jennifer | rachel |

The **brute force attack** also uses password-cracking software, but its range is much more extensive than the dictionary attack. Because it exhausts all possible keys to decrypt a password, a brute force attack can run for days or even as long as a week to crack some passwords.

If hackers can't guess a password, they can use another technique called **sniffing**, which intercepts information sent out over computer networks. Sniffing software is used legitimately by network administrators to record network traffic for monitoring and maintenance purposes. The same software can also be used for illicit activities. If your user ID and password travel over a network as unencrypted text they can easily fall into the hands of a password thief.

An even more sophisticated approach to password theft is **phishing**, in which a hacker poses as a legitimate representative of an official organization such as your ISP, your bank, or an online payment service in order to persuade you to disclose highly confidential information. Mostly through e-mail or instant messaging, a fake customer representative or administrator asks you to visit a Web page to confirm billing information or verify your account by providing your password, credit card number, or Social Security number. If you examine phishing messages more closely, you might realize that the Web sites referred to are fake. However, seasoned hackers try to make the URLs look as close as possible to the official Web sites they claim to represent (Figure 1-44).

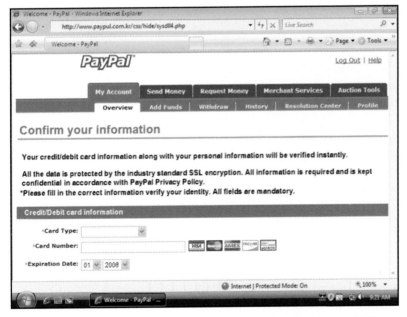

**FIGURE 1-44**

A fake Web site can look very similar to the real thing, but this fraudulent site originates in Korea.

As users became better at identifying phishing messages, password thieves resorted to the use of keyloggers. Short for *keystroke logging*, a keylogger is software that secretly records a user's keystrokes and sends the information to a hacker. A keylogger is a form of malicious code called a Trojan horse, or Trojan. Trojans are computer programs that seem to perform one function while actually doing something else. They can be embedded in e-mail attachments, software downloads, and even files. Trojans are discussed in more detail in the security section of the Software chapter.

## SECURE PASSWORDS

**How do I create a secure password?** With password theft becoming more and more widespread, security experts recommend using a strong, secure password for financial transactions such as those that involve your PayPal or bank accounts. A strong, secure password is one that is easy to remember but difficult to crack. Figure 1-45 offers guidelines for selecting secure passwords and avoiding ones that are easily crackable.

**FIGURE 1-45**

Tips for creating secure passwords

- Use passwords that are at least 8 characters in length. The longer the password, the tougher it is to crack.

- Use a combination of letters, numbers, and special characters such as $, #, if permitted.

- Use uppercase and lowercase letters if the hosting computer is case sensitive.

- Use a pass phrase, that is, one that is based on the first letters of a verse from a favorite poem or song. For example, the words from the nursery rhyme "Jack and Jill went up the hill" can be converted to jjwuth. You can then insert special characters and numbers, and add some uppercase letters to create a password that still makes sense to you personally, such as J&J w^th! This type of password appears random to anyone else but you.

- Do not use a password based on public information such as your phone number, Social Security number, driver's license number, or birthday. Hackers can easily find this information, and other personal facts such as names of your spouse, children, or pets.

- Avoid passwords that contain your entire user ID or part of it. A user ID of bjeffe coupled with a password of bjeffe123 is an easy target for password thieves.

- Steer clear of words that can be found in the dictionary, including foreign words. Dictionary attacks can utilize foreign language dictionaries. Even common words spelled backwards, such as *drowssap* instead of *password*, are not tricky enough to fool password-cracking software.

**FIGURE 1-45**

Tips for creating secure passwords

**How do I protect my password?** Once you have selected a strong password, you must take steps to keep it safe. Do not share your password with anyone. Avoid writing down a password. If possible, memorize it. If you must write down a password, do not leave it in an obvious place such as under your keyboard or mouse pad. Recording passwords in an unencrypted file stored on your computer is risky, too, especially if you have more than one password. A hacker who gains access to that file can use the password to access all your accounts.

If you think one of your passwords has been compromised, change it immediately. Even if you have no evidence of password tampering, security experts recommend that you change your password periodically, say every six months. When you change your passwords, do not just make a slight variation to your current one. For example, do not change just4Me1 to just4Me2. You should not reuse your old passwords either, so it's best to keep a password history list.

Aside from good password maintenance habits, computer maintenance is also essential. Make sure that your entire computer is protected by security software, which is explained in the Software chapter.

**How do I deal with all my passwords and user IDs?** You can accumulate many passwords and user IDs—from online banking, your ISP, online shopping sites, online music store, and maybe even from your favorite news and information Web sites. The more passwords and user IDs you have, the more difficult they become to remember.

How many times have you had to click on the "I forgot my password" link when you logged in to an online account? Your passwords provide the most protection if they are unique, but accessing even 25 different Web sites that require 25 different user IDs and 25 corresponding passwords requires quite a memory. To add to the confusion, you must also regularly change passwords to your critical accounts!

Instead of using 25 different user IDs and passwords, you need some way to reduce the number of things you have to memorize. First, strive to select a unique user ID that you can use for more than one site. Remember that people with your name who selected user IDs before you might have already taken the obvious user IDs. For example, when John Smith selects a user ID, you can bet that other people have already used johnsmith, jsmith, and john_smith. To keep his user ID unique, John might instead select jsl2wm (the first letters in John Smith loves 2 watch movies).

Next, you can maintain two or three tiers of passwords—the top level for high security, the second level for medium security, and the third level for low security. If you do not have too many accounts, you can opt for just two tiers—for high and low security. You can then select two passwords. Use the high-security password for accessing critical data, such as online banking, for managing an online stock portfolio, or for your account at an online bookstore that stores a copy of your billing and credit card information.

Use your low-security password in situations where you don't really care if your security is compromised. Some places on the Internet want you to establish an account with a user ID and password just so that they can put you on a mailing list. At other sites, your user ID and password provide access to information, but none of your own data (a credit card number, for example) is stored there. It is not necessary to change your low-security password very often. Figure 1-46 provides more information about tiered passwords.

**Tier 1:** High security
**Password:** BBx98$$NN26
**Uses:**
Online banking
PayPal
iTunes
Amazon.com

**Tier 2:** Low security
**Password:** Rover
**Uses:**
New York Times archive
Google
Wikipedia
PhotoSIG

**FIGURE 1-46**

Tiered passwords have the advantage of being easy to remember, however, the disadvantage is that a hacker who discovers one of your passwords will be able to use it to access many of your accounts.

**What is a password manager?** A **password manager** is utility software that generates secure passwords and stores them along with user IDs and their corresponding sites. When you want to log in to an online account, your password manager recognizes the sites and automatically retrieves and transmits the appropriate user ID and password. The data stored by a password manager is encrypted to protect it from hackers. You need only one master password to access all the password manager data.

The big advantage of a password manager is that you can use unique and secure passwords for every one of your online accounts. You don't have to worry if the passwords are difficult to remember because the software keeps track of them (Figure 1-47).

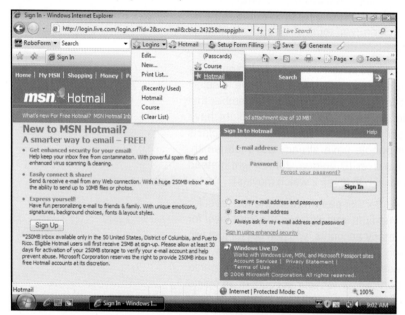

**FIGURE 1-47**

Password managers help you keep track of all your passwords.

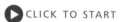 CLICK TO START

In addition to generating and tracking your passwords, most password managers provide other features, such as password strength meters and form fillers. A password strength meter indicates whether your passwords are secure enough—a feature that is useful if you've created your own passwords, rather than using your password manager to generate them. Form fillers automatically enter data into online Web forms such as those that request billing data when you order at an online shopping site. Many form fillers also match a Web form's URL against a set of valid URLs that you have provided in order to avoid sending data to a fake Web site that you have been lured to visit by a phishing message. When entering passwords, form fillers are not collecting your password from the keyboard; therefore, a hacker's keylogger cannot secretly record keystrokes.

There are several free, shareware, or open source password managers, such as KeyWallet, Whisper 32, PasswordMaker, and Password Safe. Some password managers offer portable versions. A portable password manager does not have to be installed on a computer before it is used. Instead, you can carry it around on a USB flash drive so that your passwords are available wherever you go, such as your school lab, the library, or your work. When you remove the flash drive, your portable password manager leaves no traces of passwords behind (Figure 1-48).

For extra protection against intruders who might search your computer for passwords, a flash drive that contains a password manager can be unplugged when you are not accessing password protected sites. You can also remove the flash drive from your computer when you're out so that your nosy roommate can't snoop through your computer files.

New password management techniques are being developed, but some offer their own set of potential security problems. For example, Web-based password managers could make attractive targets for password thieves. Breaking into a single site, a password thief could harvest thousands of passwords. As new password management technologies appear, make sure you evaluate them carefully before trusting them with your valuable data.

**FIGURE 1-48**

Some password managers are portable so that you can carry them with you on a USB flash drive.

# QuickCheck

1. A(n) _____ protocol is any method that confirms a person's identity using something the person knows, something the person possesses, or something the person is.

2. Two-factor authentication methods, which verify identity using two _____ elements of confirmation such as an ATM card and PIN, are typically more secure than single-factor authentication.

3. A(n) _____ is software that secretly records a user's keystrokes and sends the information to a hacker.

4. Tiered passwords have the advantage of reducing the number of passwords you have to remember, however, their disadvantage is that a hacker who discovers one of your passwords will be able to use it to access many of your accounts. True or false? _____

5. A(n) _____ manager is utility software that generates secure passwords and stores them along with user IDs and their corresponding sites.

 CHECK ANSWERS

# Are You Being Tracked?

**IN THE BOOK** *Harry Potter and the Prisoner of Azkaban*, Harry acquires a magical item called the Marauder's Map, which shows the location of every teacher and student at the Hogwarts School of Witchcraft and Wizardry. A group of students at the Massachusetts Institute of Technology became fascinated by the idea of a tracking map and constructed one of their own. It is rather amazing that a fictional magic device could so easily become reality.

In the context of Harry Potter, tracking technology seems fun, but in real life this apparently innocent tracking technology could be used by governments, corporations, and possibly criminals to monitor the daily activities of ordinary people. Location privacy can be defined as the ability to prevent other parties from learning one's current or past location. Tracking technology could have a significant effect on our ability to keep our daily lives private.

A location-enabled device (sometimes referred to as a location-aware device) is one that can determine its geographic location. Most are handheld mobile devices, but tracking chips can also be embedded in items as varied as cars, shipping cartons, product labels, clothing, and passports. Three technologies are used to equip devices with location awareness: GPS, cellular networks, and RFID.

A global positioning system, or GPS, uses a receiver inside a mobile device to triangulate a location based on signals from three or more earth-orbiting satellites. GPS technology is used for handheld GPS locator devices and automobile tracking services such as OnStar. GPS is a one-way technology; data travels to the GPS device, but the device does not transmit its position back to a satellite. However, coordinates from a GPS system can be transmitted over a different network, such as the cellular phone system or wireless network. For example, a tourist might rent a virtual tour guide device that narrates points of interest on a walking tour. The device collects information from a GPS satellite and when the tourist reaches an attraction, begins narrating.

Unbeknownst to the tourist, however, the device transmits its location to the tour operator's office. Not only does the tour operator know the tourist's location, but that information could be passed to a third party marketer or to immigration officials.

Wireless networks, such as a cellular phone system, can determine location based on the antenna to which it broadcasts. An antenna's coverage area ranges from a few miles up to 20 miles. The location of a mobile device and the person using it can be roughly determined to be within the range of the antenna it is currently transmitting to. A more precise location can be triangulated using multiple antennae. With current technology, triangulation from cellular phone antennae is less accurate than with GPS; current technology pinpoints a location to within 50-150 meters. Locations can be tracked only within range of cell towers. In contrast, GPS tracking is essentially worldwide.

Wireless transmissions are bi-directional; unlike one-way GPS, most mobile devices can transmit a location back to a base station. Cellular phone companies originally used this capability to determine when customers were roaming out of the home coverage area.

Currently, location data from cellular phones is also available for use by emergency responders to locate people in need of assistance. More controversially, bi-directional tracking devices have been embedded in rental cars to determine whether the car is exceeding the speed limit or is being used for unauthorized travel across state lines.

New child-tracking services offered by cellular phone carriers allow parents to track their cell-phone equipped children on a Web-based map. Parents can even set up boundaries and if their child crosses out of the approved area, an alarm sounds on the parent's computer or cell phone.

Law enforcement agencies have tried to gain access to location information to track suspected criminals and in some states, motor vehicle officials are considering plans to implant tracking devices in license plates.

RFID (radio frequency identification) technology is based on a special-purpose computer chip equipped with a microscopic antenna that receives and responds to radio-frequency queries from a transceiver. Whenever the chip is within range of a transceiver, its signal can be picked up. RFID chips are so small that they are almost unnoticeable. They can be implanted in animals or people, incorporated into a credit card or passport, and tucked away in clothing or other commercial products.

RFID product labels were originally designed to streamline warehouse and retail store operations, so that products could be scanned without removing them from shipping crates or shopping carts. They became controversial because consumers were not necessarily able to locate or remove the RFID device. Further, RFID-enabled items could be linked to a specific individual if an RFID labeled item was purchased with a credit card. It also seemed possible that unauthorized people could hijack RFID signals and track a person by, for example, picking up the signals emitted by her Benneton sweater.

Tracking technology has many uses. Employers can use location data to make sure employees are not spending too much time in the smoking area or break room. Cell phone carriers can collaborate with aggressive marketers to turn your cell phone into a handheld carnival barker who tries to coax you into nearby stores or restaurants. Data from a location-enabled device could be correlated with health clinics, bars, or adult bookstores allowing trackers to make inferences about a person's lifestyle.

The use of tracking technology is spreading and it seems clear that laws and regulations are necessary to prevent abusive practices. The Communications Act of 1934 requires that carriers only use a customer's confidential information for providing services specifically requested by that customer. The so called E911 Act that required wireless service providers to equip phones with GPS capability added location data to the list of information that is supposed to be kept confidential, and it prohibited certain marketing uses of customers' location data. Unfortunately, a bill that was proposed in 2001 requiring location-based services to obtain permission from customers before disclosing location information was not passed into law.

Privacy advocates are demanding strict protocols for collecting, using, storing, and distributing location information. They face opposition, however, from law enforcement officials who would like to explore ways location technology can be used to track criminals, and prevent terrorism. Commercial interest in this technology for marketing and advertising is also high and consumers might be willing to give up some measure of privacy for economic incentives, such as free OnStar service in exchange for listening to location-based advertising while driving.

The outcome of conflicting interests will determine if location-tracking technology can be implemented in such a way that the rights and privacy of individuals are protected.

**INFOWEBLINKS**

You'll find lots more information about tracking devices at the **Digital Surveillance InfoWeb**.

 CLICK TO CONNECT
www.course.com/np/concepts10/ch01

# What Do You Think?

1. Should users of location-enabled devices be informed when location tracking is in use?

○ Yes    ○ No    ○ Not sure

2. Do you think most people are aware of the privacy issues associated with location-enabled devices?

○ Yes    ○ No    ○ Not sure

3. Should users of location-aware devices be permitted to enable and disable tracking features on their devices?

○ Yes    ○ No    ○ Not sure

▶ SAVE RESPONSES

# Marketing

**WALKING OUT THE GATE** of ancient Pompeii, you might have come across an eye-catching sign extolling the virtues of a popular tavern in the next town. The sign was a clever bit of marketing designed to target thirsty travelers and drum up business. Throughout the centuries, handbills, newspaper ads, television commercials, radio spots, and mass mail campaigns were all important tools of the marketing industry. Now, computers have opened new vistas for communicating with consumers.

The American Marketing Association defines marketing as an organizational function and a set of processes for creating, communicating, and delivering value to customers and for managing customer relationships in ways that benefit the organization and its stakeholders. A person-in-the-street definition might simply be that marketing is an attempt to sell products.

Computers first played a role in marketing as a research tool for quickly crunching numbers from consumer surveys, sales figures, and projections. Statistics derived from that data helped companies focus development efforts on the most promising products and market them effectively. Marketing research data made one fact very clear: even the most effective advertising could not convince everyone to buy a particular product. A costly prime-time television ad, for example, might be seen by millions of viewers, but many of them had no interest at all in the advertised product. To better target potential buyers, marketers turned to direct marketing.

Direct marketing attempts to establish a one-to-one relationship with prospective customers rather than waiting for them to learn about a product from general, impersonal forms of advertising, such as billboards, radio spots, television commercials, and newspaper ads. The first direct marketing techniques included personalized letters, catalogs, and telemarketing. Customer names, addresses, and telephone numbers were mined from extensive computer databases maintained by mailing list brokers. Lists could be tailored in rudimentary ways to fit target markets. Selling snow tires? Get a list of consumers in northern states. Hawking a new brand of disposable razors? Get a list of men.

"Dear Carmen Smith, you might already have won…" Just about everyone in America has received a personalized sweepstakes mailing. Initially, personalized names were crudely inserted using dot matrix printers, but today high-speed laser printers dash off thousands of personalized letters per hour and use graphics capabilities to affix signatures that appear to have been hand-signed in ink.

Telemarketing is a technique for telephone solicitation. Computerized autodialers make it possible for telemarketers to work efficiently. An autodialer is a device that can dial telephone numbers stored in a list. It can also generate and dial telephone numbers using a random or sequential number generator.

A *smart* autodialer, called a predictive dialer, increases a telemarketer's efficiency even more by automatically calling several numbers at the same time and only passing a call to the marketer when a person answers. If you've picked up the telephone only to hear silence or a disconnect, it was likely an autodialer that connected to more than one person at the same time and dropped your call. Preemptive dialers eliminate telemarketing time that would be otherwise wasted with busy signals, answering machines, and so on.

The Internet opened up dramatic new horizons in direct marketing by providing an inexpensive conduit for collecting information about potential customers and distributing targeted direct marketing. According to author Jim Sterne, "The Internet and the World Wide Web have become the most important new communication media since television, and ones that are fundamentally reshaping contemporary understanding of sales and marketing." Today, a vast amount of information flows over the Internet and marketers are trying to harness that information to most efficiently communicate their message to prospective customers.

Market analysts are interested in consumer opinions about companies and products. Analysts for companies like Ford, Microsoft, and Sony track opinions on the Internet by monitoring message boards, discussion sites, and blogs. Software tools, such as Intelliseek and Cymfony, are similar to Google's Web search technology, but are refined to sift through blogs for conjunctions of words such as *Ford Ranger*, *love*, and *dependable* to guess that a blogger is happy with a particular vehicle.

E-commerce Web sites offer a global distribution channel for small entrepreneurs as well as multinational corporations. Consumers can locate e-commerce sites using a search engine. Some search engines allow paid advertising to appear on their sites. Clever marketers use search engine optimization techniques to get their Web sites to the top of search engine lists.

Another way to drive traffic to an e-commerce site is banner advertising that clutters up Web pages with inviting tag lines for free products. Clicking the ad connects consumers to the site. The cost of placing a banner ad depends on the click-through rate—the number of consumers who click an ad. Sophisticated banner ad software displays the banner ad across an entire network and monitors click-through rates. Not only does this software keep track of click throughs for billing purposes, it can automatically adjust the sites that carry each ad to maximize click-through rates.

The word *marketing* combined with *Internet* is often associated with the tidal wave of spam that's currently crashing into everyone's Inbox. These mass spam e-mails, however bothersome, are a very crude form of direct marketing. Typically, spammers use

unscrubbed mailing lists containing many expired, blocked, and invalid e-mail addresses. This hit-or-miss strategy is cheap. Ten million e-mail addresses can be rented for as low as $100 and server bandwidth provided by e-mail brokers costs about $300 per million messages sent.

Marketing professionals regard massive e-mail spamming with some degree of scorn because most lists don't narrow the focus to the most promising customers. Worse yet, consumers react by installing spam filters. Some spammers try to evade spam filters. More than one Web site offers marketers a free service that analyzes mass e-mail solicitations using a Spam filter simulator. If the solicitation can't get through the filter, the service offers suggestions on what to change so the message slips through.

In contrast to gratuitous spammers, marketing professionals have learned that opt-in mailing lists have much higher success rates. Consumers who have asked for information more often appreciate receiving it and act on it. Opt-in consumers are also more willing to divulge information that develops an accurate profile of their lifestyle so marketers can offer them the most appropriate products.

Most consumers would agree that the marketing industry needs professionals who are socially responsible. In describing the qualifications for marketing professionals, the Bureau of Labor and Statistics states the obvious when it says, "Computer skills are vital because marketing, product promotion, and advertising on the Internet are increasingly common." In preparing for a marketing career, a knowledge of computers, the Web, and the Internet are important. Equally important is preparation in statistical analysis, psychology, and ethics, along with coursework that covers legal and regulatory aspects of the technology-driven marketing industry.

**INFOWEBLINKS**

You'll find additional information about this Computers in Context topic by visiting the **Computers and Marketing InfoWeb**.

# New Perspectives Labs

## On the BookOnCD

To access the New Perspectives labs for Chapter 1, start the BookOnCD, BookOnFlashDrive, or other NP10 BookOn product and then click the icon next to the lab title below.

### ▶ OPERATING A PERSONAL COMPUTER

**IN THIS LAB YOU'LL LEARN:**

- How to start a Windows computer
- What to do when a computer is in sleep mode
- How to deactivate a screen saver
- How to select a different screen saver
- How to use the Alt, Ctrl, Esc, Num Lock, Caps Lock, Windows, Fn, Backspace, Delete, and arrow keys
- The difference between forward and backward slashes
- How to start and exit a program
- How to close a program that is not responding
- When to use the reset button
- How to shut down Windows

**LAB ASSIGNMENTS**

1. Start the interactive part of the lab. Make sure you've enabled Tracking if you want to save your QuickCheck results. Perform each lab step as directed, and answer all the lab QuickCheck questions. When you exit the lab, your answers are automatically graded and your results are displayed.

2. Make a note of the brand and location of the computer you're using to complete these lab assignments.

3. Use the Start button to access your computer's Control Panel folder. Describe the status of your computer's power saver settings.

4. Preview the available screen savers on the computer you use most frequently. Select the screen saver you like the best and describe it in a few sentences.

5. What is the purpose of an Fn key? Does your computer keyboard include an Fn key? Explain why or why not.

6. In your own words, describe what happens when you (a) click the Close button, (b) hold down the Ctrl, Alt, and Del keys, (c) press the reset button, and (d) select the Shut Down option.

### ▶ WORKING WITH BINARY NUMBERS

**IN THIS LAB YOU'LL LEARN:**

- The difference between the binary number system and the decimal number system
- How to count in binary
- How to convert decimal numbers into binary numbers
- How to convert binary numbers into decimal numbers
- How to use the Windows Calculator to convert numbers
- How to work with powers of two

**LAB ASSIGNMENTS**

1. Start the interactive part of the lab. Make sure you've enabled Tracking if you want to save your QuickCheck results. Perform each lab step as directed, and answer all the lab QuickCheck questions. When you exit the lab, your answers are automatically graded and your results are displayed.

2. Using paper and pencil, manually convert the following decimal numbers into binary numbers. Your instructor might ask you to show the process that you used for each conversion.

   a. 100     b. 1,000     c. 256
   d. 27      e. 48        f. 112
   g. 96      h. 1,024

3. Using paper and pencil, manually convert the following binary numbers into decimal numbers. Your instructor might ask you to show the process that you used for each conversion.

   a. 100      b. 101       c. 1100
   d. 10101    e. 1111      f. 10000
   g. 1111000  h. 110110

4. Describe what is wrong with the following sequence:

   10  100  110  1000  1001  1100  1110 10000

5. What is the decimal equivalent of $2^0$? $2^1$? $2^8$?

# Key Terms

Make sure you understand all the boldfaced key terms presented in this chapter. If you're using the NP10 BookOnCD, BookOnFlashDrive, or other NP10 BookOn product, you can use this list of terms as an interactive study activity. First, try to define a term in your own words, and then click the term to compare your definition with the definition presented in the chapter.

# Interactive Summary

To review important concepts from this chapter, fill in the blanks to best complete each sentence. When using the NP10 BookOnCD or other BookOn product, click the Check Answers buttons to automatically score your answers.

**SECTION A:** The [_____] revolution is an ongoing process of social, political, and economic change brought about by technologies such as computers and the Internet. The [_____] is a global computer network originally developed as a military project, adapted for research and academic use, and then for commercial use. [_____], a form of electronic communication, was an application for the masses and finally a reason to buy a computer and join the digital revolution. Another aspect of the digital revolution is [_____], a process by which several technologies with distinct functionalities evolve to form a single product. Technology has the potential to spread ideas, such as freedom and democracy, but it might have a chilling effect on [_____], or "the right to be left alone." It might also affect intellectual [_____] because digital technology has made it easy to produce copies with no loss in quality from the original. And although technology-driven [_____] has an effect on the economy, activists worry about the digital [_____] that separates people who have access to technology and those who do not.

▶ CHECK ANSWERS

**SECTION B:** A [_____] is a multipurpose device that accepts input, processes data, stores data, and produces output according to a series of stored instructions. Before a computer processes data, it is temporarily held in [_____]. This data is then processed in the central processing [_____]. The series of instructions that tells a computer how to carry out processing tasks is referred to as a computer [_____], which forms the [_____] that sets up a computer to do a specific task. Data is typically stored in a [_____], which is a named collection of data that exists on a storage medium, such as a hard disk, floppy disk, CD, DVD, or flash drive. The idea of a [_____] program means that a series of instructions for a computing task can be loaded into a computer's memory. [_____] software is a set of computer programs that helps a person carry out a task. [_____] software helps the computer system monitor itself in order to function efficiently. For example, a computer [_____] system (OS) is essentially the master controller for all the activities that take place within a computer. Computers are grouped into categories. A [_____] computer is a type of microcomputer designed to meet the needs of an individual. The term [_____] can refer to an ordinary personal computer that is connected to a network or to a powerful desktop computer used for high-performance tasks. A [_____] is, at the time of its construction, one of the fastest computers in the world. A [_____] computer is large, expensive, and capable of simultaneously processing data for hundreds or thousands of users. A [_____] computer is essentially a PDA enhanced with features such as removable storage, e-mail, and Web access. A [_____] is a special-purpose microprocessor that can control a device, such as a refrigerator or microwave oven.

▶ CHECK ANSWERS

## SECTION C:

[                    ] data is processed, stored, and transmitted as a series of 1s and 0s. Each 1 or 0 is called a [                    ] . Eight bits, called a [                    ] , represent one character—a letter, number, or punctuation mark. Data becomes [                    ] when it is presented in a format that people can understand and use. [                    ] data consists of numbers that might be used in arithmetic operations. It can be represented digitally using the [                    ] number system. [                    ] data is composed of letters, symbols, and numerals that are not used in arithmetic operations. This data is represented using [                    ] , EBCDIC, or Unicode. Data is quantified using terms such as [                    ] or kibibyte (1024 bytes), and prefixes, such as [                    ] or mebi (1,048,576), and giga or [                    ] (1,073,741,824). The bits that represent data travel as electronic pulses through [                    ] circuits, sometimes called computer chips. These chips are made from [                    ] materials and are housed in chip carriers that can be plugged into the [                    ] board of a digital device.

▶ CHECK ANSWERS

## SECTION D:

Software is usually written in high-level [                    ] languages, such as C, Basic, COBOL, and Java. The human-readable version of a program, created in a high-level language by a programmer is called [                    ] code. A [                    ] or interpreter converts this high-level code into [                    ] code. A microprocessor is hard wired to perform a limited set of activities, such as addition, subtraction, counting, and comparisons. This collection of preprogrammed activities is called an [                    ] set. Each instruction begins with an [                    ] code, which is a command word for an operation such as add, compare, or jump. Most instructions also include an [                    ] that specifies the data, or the address of the data, for the operation. The processor's ALU uses [                    ] to hold data that is being processed. The processor's [                    ] unit fetches each instruction, sends data to the registers, and signals the ALU to begin processing.

▶ CHECK ANSWERS

## SECTION E:

Passwords and user IDs are the most common authentication [                    ] . Password theft has become a serious security problem, that has lead to many cases of [                    ] theft, when unauthorized individuals gain access to personal data. Hackers discover and steal passwords using a variety of techniques. A [                    ] attack tries passwords from a list of commonly used passwords. A [                    ] force attack tries every possible combination of letters and numbers. [                    ] intercepts information sent out over computer networks. [                    ] uses fraudulent Web sites or e-mail messages to fool unsuspecting readers into entering passwords and other personal information. A [                    ] is software that secretly records a user's keystrokes and sends them to a hacker. To keep passwords safe, you should consider using tiered passwords or password [                    ] software that generates secure passwords and keeps track of which password corresponds to each site you access.

▶ CHECK ANSWERS

# Interactive Situation Questions

Apply what you've learned to some typical computing situations. When using the NP10 BookOnCD, BookOnFlashDrive, or any other NP10 BookOn product, you can type your answers, and then use the Check Answers button to automatically score your responses.

1. Suppose that you walk into an office and see the devices pictured to the right. You would probably assume that they are the screen and keyboard for a [          ] computer, workstation, or server.

2. You receive an e-mail message asking you to join a circle of friends. You assume that the message was generated in conjunction with an online [          ] network, such as MySpace, and if you become a member, you will be able to socialize online.

3. You go to the iTunes music store and purchase an album. When you see the [          ] message at the top of the screen, you know that the songs are being transferred from the remote iTunes server to your local computer.

4. You're visiting an antique shop and notice a collection of old fashioned radios. They actually feature a dial for tuning in different radio stations. You immediately recognize this as a(n) [          ] device because it deals with an infinite scale of values, rather than discrete values.

5. While attending a meeting at work you hear one of the executives wondering if "unit code" would be helpful. After a moment of puzzlement, you realize that the executive really meant [          ], and that it would allow your company software to be translated into the Cyrillic alphabet used by the Russian language.

6. You have a new storage device that offers 2 GB of storage space. It is currently empty. Your friend wants to give you a large digital photo that's 16 MB. Will it fit on your storage device. Yes or no? [     ]

7. Your bank is giving customers the choice of using a 4-digit PIN or a password that can contain up to 10 letters and numbers. The [          ] is more secure, so that's what you decide to use.

8. You need to select a password for your online PayPal account. Which of the following passwords would be the LEAST secure: jeff683, hddtmrutc, gargantuan, fanhotshot, bb#ii22jeffry, or high348? [          ]

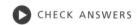 CHECK ANSWERS

# Interactive Practice Tests

Practice tests that consist of 10 multiple-choice, true/false, and fill-in-the-blank questions are available on both the NP10 BookOn products and the NP10 Web site. The questions are selected at random from a large test bank, so each time you take a test, you'll receive a different set of questions. Your tests are scored immediately, and you can print study guides that help you find the correct answers for any questions that you missed.

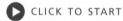 CLICK TO START

# Study Tips

Study Tips help you to organize and consolidate the information in a unit by making lists, outlines, charts, and sketches. You can use paper and pencil or word processing software to complete most of the Study Tip activities.

1. Make sure you can use your own words to correctly answer each of the red focus questions that appear throughout the chapter.

2. List the technologies that are fueling the digital revolution.

3. Give at least 5 examples of convergence.

4. Describe at least two social, political, and economic affects of the digital revolution.

5. Use a diagram to explain how a computer makes use of input, processing, storage, memory, output, and the stored program concept.

6. List, briefly describe, and rank (in terms of computing capacity) the characteristics of each computer category described in Section B of this chapter.

7. Describe the difference between system software, an operating system, application software, and a computer program.

8. Explain the difference between digital and analog.

9. List various ways to digitally represent character and numeric data.

10. Without looking back at the chapter, list as many terms as you can that relate to quantifying bits and bytes.

11. Use the terms integrated circuits, microprocessor, and system board in a meaningful sentence.

12. Describe how compilers and interpreters work with high level programming languages, source code, and object code.

13. Make a storyboard showing how a microprocessor's ALU would add the numbers 2 and 8.

14. Create five secure passwords and five passwords that might be easy to crack.

15. Fill in the blanks on the concept map shown below to show the relationships between programming and processing concepts described in this chapter.

# Concept Map

CHECK ANSWERS

# Projects

 CRITICAL THINKING

Whether you're taking this course to fulfill a graduation requirement, to improve your career options, or just for fun, take a few minutes to evaluate what you expect to gain from this course. Look through the table of contents of this textbook and select the five sections that you think will be most interesting, and the five sections that seem to be the least relevant to you. Incorporate your thoughts in two or three paragraphs that you e-mail to your instructor.

 GROUP PROJECT

Form a group with four or five other students. Each student in the group should ask at least five friends if they have 1) a computer, 2) a cell phone, 3) a portable music player, 4) dial-up Internet access, 5) high speed Internet access. Consolidate the data from all members of your group into an Excel spreadsheet, and then graph it. How do your statistics coincide with nationwide statistics for digital ownership? Graph or write a summary and make sure you site your sources for national statistics.

 CYBERCLASSROOM

Your instructor should provide each student with the e-mail addresses of four or five other students who will form a team, and designate a team leader. The team leader should find a news story about a technology issue from a source such as *www.news.google.com* and send it to one of the other students on the team. That student should add his or her opinion and comments, then send the message to another student in the group. Each student should use a different font color and initial their comments. When the message has circulated to all team members, it should be sent to your instructor. Make sure every member of the team is using antivirus software because, as you learned in the chapter, hackers can take advantage of unprotected computers.

 MULTIMEDIA PROJECT

Screenshots can be useful tools for learning, documentation, and troubleshooting. Any time you need to show someone what's displayed on your computer screen, you can press the Print Screen (PrtScr) key, which stores a copy of the screen into memory. From there, you can paste the screenshot into a document you're creating with a word processor. You can also paste it into a graphics program, such as Microsoft Paint and then edit it. For this project, take a screenshot, and paste it into a Word document. Under the screenshot, enter a description of the software and the purpose of the screen you captured.

 RESUME BUILDER

Several Web sites offer career aptitude assessments that claim to help you select a career that's suited to your personality and background. Use a search engine to locate three free Web-based career aptitude tests. Take the tests. If you are asked to sign up, make sure you exercise caution in the amount of personal information you divulge. After completing the tests, compare the results. Do they all point you in a similar career direction? What is your reaction to the results? Which test do you think was the most valid and why? Provide your instructor with your analysis, along with the URLs for the Web sites that provided the tests.

 GLOBALIZATION

Although the Internet provides a global communications network, communication between people still depends on finding a common language. For this project, explore the Web and experiment with ways in which technology is being used to close the language gap. You might start at Google or Wikipedia and look at the selection of languages they offer. Chronicle your exploration, making sure to document the Web sites you visited. What are your conclusions about Internet use by non-English speakers?

 ISSUE

The Issue section of this chapter focused on the increasing use of digital devices that can track a person's location. Tracking technology has advantages and disadvantages. It has been used to track down terrorists and to find missing children, but it can also be abused by government and private companies. For this project, begin by scanning some of the links at the Digital Surveillance InfoWeb. Add to your knowledge by using a search engine, such as Google, to scan recent information about location aware devices. Make a list of at least ten legitimate and useful applications of digital tracking. Make another list of ten abusive uses of tracking technology. Cite your sources for each item you list.

 COMPUTERS IN CONTEXT

The Computers in Context section highlighted new technologies used in the marketing industry. Think of a product that you recently bought. Now, suppose you work for the company that produces the product and you've been assigned to create a marketing campaign. Create a table in which the first column contains a short description of every way you can think of to market the product. In the second column of the table, indicate the main technology used to communicate the marketing message. In column 3, indicate which of the methods would be considered direct marketing. In column 4 rank the marketing methods from most expensive (10) to least expensive (1). (You can use the Web to get estimated costs for various types of advertising.) Finally, in column 5 rank the marketing methods from most effective (10) to least effective (1). Submit your table following your instructor's guidelines for format and style.

# On the Web

## STUDENT EDITION LABS

Ⓦ **CLICK TO ACCESS THE NP10 WEB SITE**
or open your browser and connect to www.course.com/np/concepts10/ch01.
Lab results can be stored in the Universal Gradebook.

Work hands-on in structured simulations practicing important skills and concepts

### BINARY NUMBERS

In the Binary Numbers Student Edition Lab, you will learn the following topics and skills:

- Comparing binary numbers to decimal numbers
- Adding binary numbers manually
- Converting binary numbers to decimal equivalents

### UNDERSTANDING THE MOTHERBOARD

In the Understanding the Motherboard Student Edition Lab, you will learn the following topics and skills:

- Identifying components of the motherboard, such as integrated circuits, the CPU, RAM, ROM, and expansion slots and cards
- Modifying the way Windows handles virtual memory on a system
- Installing expansion cards into a PC

### CHAPTER COURSECAST

Use your computer or iPod to hear a five-minute audio presentation of chapter highlights.

### FLASHCARD COURSECAST

Interact with audio flashcards to review key terms from the chapter.

### DETAILED OBJECTIVES

Make sure that you've achieved all the objectives for a chapter before it's time for your test!

### TEST YOURSELF

Review chapter material by taking these ten-question tests, then send your results to the Universal Gradebook.

### ONLINE GAMES

Have some fun while refreshing your memory about key concepts that might appear on the next test. You can even send your results to the Universal Gradebook!

### AND MORE!

At the NP10 Web site you'll also find TechBuzz, CNET videos, Extra Content, and InfoWebLinks.

# 2

# Computer Hardware

## CHAPTER CONTENTS

## LEARNING OBJECTIVES

- Label the main components of a personal computer system
- List the advantages and disadvantages of various desktop and portable computer form factors
- Describe the target markets for home, media, game, and small business computers
- List important factors to consider when shopping for a new computer
- Explain how upgrades and mods fit into a computer purchase decision
- List the factors that affect microprocessor performance
- Explain how RAM works and how it differs from disk storage
- List facts about RAM that are important to computer buyers and owners
- Describe the differences between magnetic, optical, and solid state storage
- Use criteria such as versatility, durability, capacity, access time, and transfer rate to compare storage technologies
- Explain the factors that might help a shopper decide whether to purchase a CRT, LCD, or plasma monitor
- Compare and contrast the technologies and applications for ink jet, laser, and dot matrix printers
- Describe the components of a computer's expansion bus, including various types of expansion slots and cables
- Explain the hardware compatibility considerations, device drivers, and procedures involved in installing a peripheral device
- List ways you can protect your computer system hardware from theft and damage

 **PRE-ASSESSMENT QUIZ**

Take the pre-assessment quiz to find out how much you know about the topics in this chapter.

**MULTIMEDIA and INTERACTIVE ELEMENTS**
When using the BookOnCD, BookOnFlashDrive, or other NP10 BookOn product, the ▶ icons are clickable to access multimedia resources.

BEFORE YOU READ ON, **TRY IT**

## HOW POWERFUL IS MY COMPUTER?

As you read Chapter 2, you'll learn that some computers are more powerful than others because they can store more data and process data faster. To find out how your home, work, or lab computer stacks up, you'll need to know a few of its specifications. Before you begin to read this chapter, check your computer's specifications by doing the following:

1. Start your computer.

2. Click the Start button, then click Control Panel.

3. Double-click the System icon or link to open the System Properties dialog box. (If you're in Category View, click System and Maintenance first.)

4. If you see a window with tabs, make sure the General tab is displayed.

5. Record information about your computer similar to the information provided for the sample computer in the table.

6. Then, just to get an idea of the other equipment you've got attached to your computer, click the link or icon for Device Manager. (You might have to click the Hardware tab first).

7. Browse through the list. When you're done, close all the dialog boxes by clicking the [X] buttons.

| | Sample Computer | Your Computer |
|---|---|---|
| Computer Manufacturer | Hewlett-Packard | |
| Computer Model | HP Pavilion | |
| Processor Manufacturer | AMD | |
| Processor Type | Athlon 64 X2 | |
| Processor speed | 2.4 GHz | |
| Number of processors | 1 (Dual core) | |
| RAM capacity | 1.93 GB | |

## WEB SITE

Visit the NP10 Web site to access additional resources Ⓦ that accompany this chapter.

# Personal Computer Basics

**WHETHER YOU ARE SHOPPING** for a new computer, using your trusty laptop, or troubleshooting a system glitch, it is useful to have some background about computer system components and how they work. Section A begins with a framework for understanding the vast number of options available for putting together a personal computer system, and then wraps up with some tips on interpreting the jargon in computer ads and negotiating the digital marketplace.

## PERSONAL COMPUTER SYSTEMS

**What's a personal computer system?** The term *personal computer system* has at least two meanings. It can broadly refer to any computer system that uses personal computers for core processing operations. Such systems would include school labs and small business networks. In a more limited context, the term personal computer system refers to a personal computer, software, and peripheral devices that can be connected together for use by a single individual. This chapter focuses on computers in the latter context to make sure you're familiar with the hardware tools that make a computer system tick.

**What are the components of a typical personal computer system?** The centerpiece of a personal computer system is, of course, a personal computer. In addition, most systems include peripheral devices. The term **peripheral device** designates input, output, and storage equipment that might be added to a computer system to enhance its functionality. Popular peripheral devices include printers, digital cameras, scanners, joysticks, and speakers.

A personal computer system usually includes the components shown in Figure 2-1. These components are described briefly on the next page. They are defined and discussed in more detail later in the chapter.

**FIGURE 2-1**

A typical personal computer system includes the system unit and a variety of storage, input, and output devices.

CLICK TO START

- **System unit.** The **system unit** is the case that holds the computer's main circuit boards, microprocessor, memory, power supply, and storage devices. Depending on the computer design, the system unit might also include other built-in devices, such as a keyboard and speakers.

- **Keyboard.** Most personal computer systems are equipped with a keyboard as the primary input device.

- **Mouse.** A mouse is an input device designed to manipulate on-screen graphical objects and controls.

- **Hard disk drive.** A hard disk drive is the main storage device on a personal computer system. It is usually mounted inside the computer's system unit and can store billions of characters of data. A small external light indicates when the drive is reading or writing data.

- **CD and DVD drives.** A CD drive is a storage device that uses laser technology to work with data on computer or audio CDs. A DVD drive can work with data on computer CDs, audio CDs, computer DVDs, or DVD movie disks. Some CD and DVD drives are classified as *read only* devices that cannot be used to write data onto disks. They are typically used to access data from commercial software, music, and movie CDs or DVDs. *Writable* CD and DVD drives, however, can be used to store and access data.

- **Other storage.** Personal computers sometimes include a floppy disk drive, which is a low-capacity storage device once found on virtually all computers. Floppy disks are disappearing as USB flash storage devices become more popular.

- **Sound system.** The sound system for a personal computer can output digital music, digitally recorded speech, and a variety of sound effects called system sounds designed to draw your attention to various messages and events. To produce sounds, a computer uses a circuit board called a sound card, which is typically housed in the system unit. A computer's sound card sends signals to speakers, which can be external devices or built into the system unit.

- **Display system.** A personal computer display system consists of two parts. Circuitry, called a graphics card, converts raw digital data into images that can be shown on a display device. Display devices, often called computer screens or monitors, present visual output, such as documents, photos, and videos. Personal computer systems can use several types of display technologies, including CRTs and LCDs. Display devices are usually built into the system unit of portable computers, but exist as standalone devices for computers that spend most of their time on a desk.

- **Network and Internet access.** Many personal computer systems include built-in circuitry for wired or wireless connections to a computer network. Networking features are useful for constructing a home network or connecting to public networks in coffee shops and airports. Internet connections require a modem. Modems that establish an Internet connection using a standard telephone line are often built into the system unit. Modems for cable, satellite, and other types of Internet access are usually separate components.

- **Printer.** A computer printer is an output device that produces computer-generated text or graphical images on paper.

---

**TERMINOLOGY NOTE**

The word *peripheral* is a relatively old part of computer jargon that dates back to the days of mainframes when the CPU was housed in a giant box and all input, output, and storage devices were housed separately. Technically, a peripheral is any device that is not part of the CPU.

In the world of personal computers, however, the use of the term *peripheral* varies and is often used to refer to any components that are not housed inside the system unit. Many personal computer owners do not think of a hard disk drive as a peripheral device, but technically it is one.

2

## DESKTOP AND PORTABLE COMPUTERS

**What is the significance of different computer designs?** The industrial design principle that "form follows function" applies to computers. If you need a computer that's functional for mobile applications, you would not consider hauling around a large, heavy unit designed to remain on a desk. Instead, you would look for a computer "form" that suits your mobile "function."

In the computer industry, the term **form factor** refers to the size and dimensions of a component, such as a system board or system unit. Personal computers are available in all sorts of form factors; some are small and some are large; some are designed to remain on a desk, whereas others are designed to be portable.

**What are the characteristics of desktop computers?** A **desktop computer** fits on a desk and runs on power from an electrical wall outlet. The main component of a typical desktop computer is a system unit that houses the processor, memory, storage devices, display circuitry, and sound circuitry. A desktop computer's keyboard, mouse, and display screen are typically separate components that are connected to the main unit by cables.

The first personal computers were desktop models, and this style remains popular for offices, schools, and homes. Because their components can be manufactured economically, desktop computers typically provide the most computing power for your dollar. The price of an entry-level desktop computer starts at $300 or a bit less, but most consumers select more powerful models that cost between $800 and $1,100.

A desktop computer's system unit can be housed in a vertical case or a horizontal case. Most horizontal units are placed under the monitor to save desk space. Horizontal system units were once the most common desktop computer configuration, however, they are much less popular now that manufacturers offer a wider variety of options.

One of those options is a vertical system unit, which can be placed on the desk, on the floor, or in a cubbyhole beneath the desk. The case for a vertical system unit is often referred to as a *tower*. Tower cases provide plenty of space for gamers and "modders" who want to soup up their machines by adding storage devices, lighted power cables, or accelerated graphics cards. Tower units are also the form factor of choice for computer owners who might want to upgrade components in the future because it is easy to get inside the case and swap out parts.

Another desktop computer option is a cube-shaped mini case, which is smaller than a tower unit and sometimes sports a handle. Mini cases are popular with gamers because they can be easily carried to LAN parties where they are networked together for multiplayer games.

Some manufacturers eliminate the separate system unit by incorporating computer circuitry in the back of a flat-panel screen or into a keyboard. Figure 2-2 illustrates some popular desktop form factors.

A tower unit can be placed on the desk or on the floor.

A small form factor desktop is easy to carry, but is not classified as a portable computer because it requires power from a wall outlet and does not run on batteries.

The circuitry for this desktop model is integrated into the case that holds the screen.

**How do portable computers differ from desktops?** A **portable computer** (also referred to as a mobile computer) is a small, lightweight personal computer with screen, keyboard, storage, and processing components integrated into a single unit that runs on power supplied by an electrical outlet or a battery. Portable computers are ideal for mobile uses because they are easy to carry and can be used outdoors, in airports, and in classrooms without the need for a nearby electrical outlet. Portable computers are classified as notebooks, tablets, and ultra-mobiles (Figure 2-3).

**What is a notebook computer?** A **notebook computer** (also referred to as a laptop), is a small, lightweight portable computer that opens like a clamshell to reveal a screen and keyboard. Notebook computers cost a bit more than desktop computers with similar computing power and storage capacity.

Notebook computers are coveted by students because they don't take up too much space in crowded dorm rooms and they are fairly easy to carry around campus. On average, a notebook computer weighs about 5 pounds, but some ultra-light notebooks weigh in at about 2 pounds. The price of an entry-level notebook computer starts around $500. Consumers often spend between $800 and $1,200, however, to get the features and performance they want. A fully-loaded notebook computer with widescreen display can cost more than $4,000.

**What is a tablet computer?** A **tablet computer** is a portable computing device featuring a touch-sensitive screen that can be used as a writing or drawing pad. A *slate* tablet configuration resembles a high-tech clipboard and lacks a built-in keyboard (although one can be attached). A *convertible* tablet computer is constructed like a notebook computer, but the screen folds face up over the keyboard to provide a horizontal writing surface.

Tablet computers shine for applications that involve handwritten input. Most tablet computers are also configured to accept voice input. These capabilities are particularly useful for insurance adjusters who do most of their work at the scene of accidents and natural disasters, real estate agents who need access to data while out with clients, and healthcare workers who are moving quickly from one patient to the next.

Since tablet computers were first introduced in 2002, their price has remained high, starting at about $1,000, but more typically costing $1,400 to $2,300.

**What is an ultra-mobile computer?** An **ultra-mobile PC** (UMPC) is a small form factor tablet computer designed to run most of the software available for larger portable computers. About the size of a paperback book and weighing in at 2 pounds, a typical UMPC does not have a physical keyboard, but one can be displayed on its small, touch-sensitive screen. UMPCs are equipped for wireless Internet access to the Web and e-mail. Many UMPCs are equipped with GPS and can be used to listen to music, watch videos, and play games. A typical UMPC costs from $500-$900.

**FIGURE 2-3**

Portable computers include a screen and keyboard in one unit and can run on batteries.

A notebook computer is small and lightweight, giving it the advantage of portability. It can be plugged into an electrical outlet, or it can run on battery power.

A slate is a type of tablet computer that's similar in size to a notebook computer, but features a touch-sensitive screen that can be used for input instead of a keyboard.

An ultra-mobile PC is a smaller, lighter version of the slate-style tablet computer.

## HOME, MEDIA, GAME, AND SMALL BUSINESS SYSTEMS

**What's the significance of designations, such as home, media, small business, or game systems?** When studying computer ads and browsing vendor Web sites, you're likely to see some computer systems designated as home systems, whereas others are designated as game systems, small business systems, or media systems. These designations are created by computer vendors to help consumers sort through the sometimes mind-boggling variety of configuration options.

**What differentiates a home computer from other types?** The idea of a home computer system probably developed because Microsoft offered Home and Professional versions of the Windows operating system. Windows Home version targeted less sophisticated users and originally was not meant to be used extensively for networking.

Today, a **home computer system** offers a hardware platform with adequate, but not super-charged support for most computer applications, including Web browsing, e-mail, working with photos, downloading music, and working with general productivity applications, such as word processing. Software applications run normally, but graphics and games might be a bit slow.

The target market for home computer systems is families with young children and adults who are occasional users. A home system is often synonymous with a budget system, with prices starting at $300 including a monitor.

**What is a Media Center PC?** Apple Computers, Inc. discovered a hidden market when it began to promote music and video applications for its iMac computers. When Microsoft introduced a version of Windows called Media Center Edition (MCE), PC hardware manufacturers quickly produced computers optimized for consumers who want to integrate their computers, televisions, home theaters, and audio systems.

A **Media Center PC** officially uses Windows Media Center Edition operating system, but computers with other operating systems can be equipped with media features using third-party software. These computers are sometimes called media PCs or entertainment PCs.

Key components of a media PC include a remote control device and wireless keyboard that allow you to control your computer from your couch, a graphics system that includes TV tuner circuitry to display television programs on a computer monitor, and software for displaying digital photos as a slide show on a computer display, television, projection TV, computer projection device, or home theater (Figure 2-4). Media PCs also include a variety of connectors for speakers, VCRs, and cassette players.

**FIGURE 2-4**

Intel's Viiv technology complements Microsoft's Multimedia Center Edition with a fast microprocessor and chips dedicated to producing vivid graphics, smooth video, and vibrant surround sound.

**What's so great about a gaming PC?** Some of the most cutting-edge computers are designed for gaming. Not only do these machines feature the fastest processors, they are also stuffed with memory, include state-of-the-art sound capabilities, and feature dual graphics processors (Figure 2-5).

Although some manufacturers produce gaming notebook computers, most serious gamers tend to select desktop models because they are easier to customize and offer a little more power per dollar. Some overlap exists between media PCs and gaming PCs. Both may use the Windows Media Center Edition operating system for flexibility in handling video and music. Gamers like to have it all, so when they're taking a break from intense online multiplayer competition, they can relax and unwind watching their favorite Sci-Fi shows on their widescreen LCD screens.

The technophile features of a gaming computer come with a steep price premium. Computers start at $2000 and quickly climb past the $4000 price point.

**What are the characteristics of a small business computer?** Computers marketed for small business applications tend to be middle-of-the-line models pared down to essentials. A medium-speed processor, moderate amount of RAM, and sensible disk capacity are adequate for basic business applications, such as word processing, spreadsheet analysis, accounting, and e-mail. Easy networking options allow small business computers to connect with other computers in an office environment.

With price tags in the $500-600 range, small business computers like the one advertised in Figure 2-6 remain cost-effective because they are not loaded with memory, fancy graphics cards, or audio systems typical on home or media computers. Small business computers might not include a CD or DVD drive and often do not include speakers. The computers used in small businesses tend to be desktop models, rather than notebooks, because they are less expensive, easier to repair, and are less likely to be lost or stolen.

**FIGURE 2-5**

Game computers feature state-of-the-art components for processing, graphics, and audio.

# 20/20 VISION

The innovative NVIDIA® nForce 590 SLI MCP chipset for Intel lets you control just how much graphics power your XPS 700 has. You will sit in awe of the massive resolution and incredible frame rates driving the XPS 700 graphics experience, supported by one to four cards from NVIDIA® or ATI®.

**An All Out Graphics Assault**
The ultimate gaming solution includes the optional NVIDIA® Quad SLI™ Technology equipped with the power of NVIDIA's next Generation 7 series graphics card delivering a relentless 48 gigapixels per second of graphics performance and 6 teraflops of graphics-computing power. 96 pixel pipes and 2GB of on-board memory will let you max-out all your in-game graphics settings, bringing you inside the action with stunning clarity and mind-blowing effects.

**FIGURE 2-6**

Small business owners want a cost effective solution without bells and whistles.

**» HP Compaq 2000 series**

Our lowest price PC designed for small office environments and basic application usage such as word processors, spreadsheets, internet browsing and email.

NEW

- **Starting at: $349.00***
- Essential features at affordable prices.
- Microsoft Windows XP Professional SP2, Microsoft Windows XP Home SP2 or Mandrake Linux
- Choice of Intel Celeron D or Intel Pentium 4 processors or Pentium 4 with Hyper-Threading Technology
- Windows Vista Capable

## BUYING COMPUTER SYSTEM COMPONENTS

**How do I get started?** The process of buying your own computer system is not cut and dried. Some experts advocate assessing your computing needs first, whereas other experts suggest researching features and prices. The trick is to do your homework for the entire system before jumping into a purchase of any one component. Remember that you will be purchasing peripherals, software, and accessories in addition to a computer. To prepare for a computer purchase you should complete the following activities:

- Browse through computer magazines and online computer stores to get a general idea of features and prices.

- Decide on a budget and stick to it.

- Make a list of the ways you plan to use your computer.

- Select a platform.

- Decide on a form factor.

- Select peripherals, software, and accessories.

**Where can I find product information?** You can start by looking at ads in current computer magazines, such as *PC Computing*, *PC Magazine*, *CPU*, and *MacWorld*. You might visit computer stores online or in a nearby mall to get a general idea of prices and features.

**How can I make sense of all the jargon in computer ads?** Computer ads are loaded with jargon and acronyms, such as RAM, ROM MHz, GB, USB, and PCI. You're sure to spot lots of this computer lingo in ads like the one in Figure 2-7.

When you complete this chapter, you should be able to sort out the terminology used in a typical computer ad. For terms you encounter that are not covered in this textbook, you can google the term or refer to online dictionaries and encyclopedias, such as Webopedia, Whatis.com, or Wikipedia.

**What can I expect to pay for a new computer?** Computers are sold at price points ranging from a few hundred dollars to several thousand dollars. Computer price points can be roughly grouped into three categories.

A computer priced higher than US$2,000 is the computer equivalent of a luxury automobile. Computers in this price range contain one or more fast processors, a generous amount of RAM, and a copious amount of disk space. These computers contain state-of-the-art components and should not have to be replaced as quickly as less expensive computers. Computer game enthusiasts and anyone planning to work extensively with video editing are likely to require a high-end computer that costs over US$2,000.

Computers that retail for between US$800 and $2,000 might be considered the four-door sedans of the computer marketplace because a majority of buyers select computers in this price range. These popular computers lack the flashy specifications of their state-of-the-art cousins, but provide ample computing power to meet the needs of an average user.

**FIGURE 2-7**

A typical computer ad provides specifications couched in lots of computer jargon.

- Intel Pentium EE 965 64-bit dual core processor 3.73 GHz with Hyper-Threading 1066 MHz FSB
- 2 MB L2 cache
- 2 GB 533 MHz SDRAM (max. 4 GB)
- 160 GB SATA HD (7200 rpm)
- 48X CD-RW + 16X DVD+RW/+R with double layer write capable
- 3.5" 1.44 MB floppy disk drive
- 19" LCD TV/monitor
- 512 MB NVidia PCI graphics card
- Sound Blaster PCI sound card
- Altec Lansing speakers
- U.S. Robotics 56 Kbps modem
- Mouse and keyboard
- External drive bays: 2 5.25" bays for disk, tape, or CD drives; 1 3.5" bay for a floppy drive
- Internal drive bays: 1 HDD bay
- 8 USB ports: 2 front, 6 back
- 2 serial, 1 parallel, and 1 video port
- 1 network port (RJ45 connector)
- 4 PCI slots and 1 AGP slot
- Windows Vista operating system
- Home/small business software bundle
- 3-year limited warranty

In the computer industry, the equivalent of a compact car is a sub-$800 computer. The technology in these computers is usually a year or two old and you can expect reduced processor speed, memory capacity, and drive capacity. Nevertheless, budget computers feature many of the same components that owners coveted in their state-of-the-art computers a few years back. You might have to replace a budget computer sooner than a more expensive computer, but it should be serviceable for typical applications.

**Why is it important to figure out how I'm going to use my new computer?** Computers can help you perform such a wide variety of tasks that it can be impossible to predict all the ways you might use your new machine in the future. You can, however, make a list of the ways you plan to immediately use your computer and that list can help you think about the features you'll need. Some computer-based activities require more processing or storage capacity than others. Therefore, if you have some ideas about your computer usage, you're more likely to buy the right computer and not have to purchase expensive upgrades for it later. Figure 2-8 offers some guidelines to help you evaluate how your plan for using a computer might affect your purchase decision.

**FIGURE 2-8**

Situations such as those listed in the left column help to narrow down the mind-boggling number of choices offered to computer shoppers.

| Usage Plan | Purchase Recommendation |
|---|---|
| You plan to use your computer for popular tasks such as e-mail, browsing the Web, playing a few games, managing your checkbook, downloading digital music, and writing school papers. | A mid-priced computer with standard features might meet your needs. |
| You're on a budget. | A budget-priced computer will handle the same applications as a mid-priced computer, but some tasks might run more slowly. |
| You plan to work on accounting and budgeting for a small business. | Consider one of the business systems offered by your computer vendor. |
| You spend lots of time playing computer games. | Buy a computer with the fastest processor and graphics card you can afford. |
| You plan to work extensively with video editing or desktop publishing. | Select a computer system with a fast processor, lots of hard disk capacity, and a graphics card loaded with memory. |
| Someone who will use the computer has special needs. | Consider purchasing appropriate adaptive equipment, such as a voice synthesizer or one-handed keyboard. |
| You plan to use specialized peripheral devices. | Make sure the computer you purchase can accommodate the devices you plan to use. |
| Your work at home overlaps your work at school or on the job. | Shop for a computer that's compatible with the ones you use at school or work. |
| You want to work with specific software, such as a game or graphics tool. | Make sure you select a computer that meets the specifications listed on the software box or Web site. |
| You're buying a new computer to replace an old one. | If you have a big investment in software, you should select a new computer that's compatible with the old one. |

**How important is compatibility?** Suppose that you want to do some assignments at home using the same software provided by your school lab. Maybe you want to transport data back and forth between your job and home. Or, perhaps your child wants to use a computer at home like the one at school. Computers that operate in essentially the same way are said to be *compatible*. To assess whether two computers are compatible, you have to consider if they run the same software and use the same peripheral devices.

Today, there are three personal computer platforms: PC, Mac, and Linux. The **PC platform** is based on the design for one of the first personal computer superstars—the IBM PC. The great grandchildren of the IBM PC are on computer store shelves today—a huge selection of personal computer brands and models manufactured by companies such as Lenovo, Hewlett-Packard, Dell, and Gateway. The Windows operating system was designed specifically for these personal computers and, therefore, the PC platform is sometimes called the Windows platform. Most of the examples in this book pertain to PCs because they are so popular.

The **Mac platform** is based on a proprietary design for a personal computer called the Macintosh, manufactured almost exclusively by Apple Computer, Inc. The Mac lineup includes the iMac, MacBook, Mac mini, and Mac Pro computers, all running the Mac OS operating system.

At one time, the PC and Mac platforms were not compatible because of hardware and operating system differences. Application software designed for Macs did not typically work with PCs and vice versa.

The compatibility situation has changed because many Mac computers now use the same microprocessors as PCs. If you have a Mac computer with an Intel processor (sometimes called an Intel Mac), you can install Windows on it and run Windows software.

The ability to run Windows offers Mac owners access to software from the PC and Mac platforms, and makes it possible to use the Mac OS to run one application, then switch to Windows to run another application. This capability can come in handy, for example, if a parent who uses Windows software is sharing a computer with an elementary-school student who is working with Macs at school.

The **Linux platform** is essentially a standard PC with the Linux operating system installed. As with Intel Macs, Linux computers can be configured to boot into either Linux or Windows operating systems. Linux is typically the platform selected for technical applications.

**What about software?** Most computers are sold with a pre-installed operating system, which typically includes a Web browser and e-mail software. Some computers are bundled with application software that you can use to create documents, crunch numbers, and produce presentations. Check the software situation carefully. The trend today is for manufacturers to install trial software that you can use free for a few months. To continue using the software beyond the trial period, however, you have to pay for it. Such software is "included" but not "free." Buyer beware.

If you're purchasing a computer to do a task that requires specialized software, you should factor its cost into the cost of your computer system. Check the specifications listed on the software box to make sure your new computer has enough memory and processing speed to run it.

**TERMINOLOGY NOTE**

Computers that are compatible with the PC platform are usually referred to simply as PCs. Computers in the Mac platform are referred to as Macs.

**Can I upgrade a computer to make it more powerful?** When shopping for a computer system, your budget might not stretch to cover the cost of all the equipment you want. Or, you might wonder if you can extend the life of your current computer by upgrading key components. Some components are easy to add or change, whereas others are not. Figure 2-9 summarizes the most popular computer equipment upgrades, indicates their average time for completion, cost, difficulty level, and accessibility.

**FIGURE 2-9**

Popular upgrades at a glance; in the Accessibility column, internal upgrades require you to open the system unit.

2

| Upgrade | Time | Cost (US$) | Difficulty | Accessibility |
|---|---|---|---|---|
| Replace processor | 1-5 hours | $200-600 | Difficult and not recommended | Internal |
| Add memory | 30-60 minutes | $50-300 | Moderate | Internal |
| Add external hard drive | 10-15 minutes | $100-300 | Easy | External |
| Replace internal hard disk drive | 1-2 hours | $50-500 | Somewhat difficult | Internal |
| Replace graphics card | 1 hour | $150-500 | Moderate | Internal |
| Switch to wireless keyboard and mouse | 15 minutes | $50-100 | Easy | External |
| Add USB port or digital camera memory card reader | 15 minutes | $20-200 | Easy | External |
| Add second display screen | 5-10 minutes | $250-500 | Easy | External |
| Add or replace speakers | 5-10 minutes | $50-500 | Easy | External |
| Replace CD or DVD drive | 1-2 hours | $50-150 | Moderate | Internal |

**What is a mod?** Upgrades and add-ons, such as those listed in Figure 2-9, are usually sanctioned and approved by computer manufacturers and vendors. However, some creative computer owners, called modders, work with unsanctioned modifications. In the context of computing a **mod** is a custom, hand-built modification to a computer system component.

Mods are analogous to hotrods in many ways. Just as hot rod construction begins with a standard car chassis, a computer mod begins with standard, off-the-shelf components. Hot rods can be chopped and jacked, fenders removed, windows added, engines chromed, and chassis painted in day-glo colors. Computer mods often include custom paint jobs, glowing lights, and clear plexiglass side panels that offer a view of the system board.

**Where do modders find components?** Modders have built computers using discarded microwave ovens, vintage televisions, gumball machines, Legos, suitcases, and toys—all items that can be picked up in thrift stores or rummage sales.

Electronic components, such as cold cathode lights and neon string lights, can be scavenged from a variety of sources. Radio Shack offers a collection of products for modders, but a much more extensive selection of modding components can be found at Web sites that specialize in modding. Figure 2-10 illustrates a creative mod that uses see-through and lighting effects.

**FIGURE 2-10**

Mods are customized computers that sport radical modifications, such as see-through cases and lighted cables.

**Where is the best place to buy a computer?** Consumers have many choices for computer vendors. Manufacturers such as Dell and Apple sell computers online at company Web sites, where you can easily configure a computer system with various features and get a price quote.

Computers and peripherals are also sold at office stores, such as OfficeMax, and electronics stores, such as Best Buy or Circuit City. You might have the option of working with a locally-owned computer boutique. Most consumer advocates suggest shopping around, comparing prices, service, and warranties.

Before you make a final decision on computer equipment or software, ask the following questions: Does your new equipment or software come with technical support? How long does the support last? How can you contact technical support? Is it free? Is the support staff knowledgeable? What is the duration of the equipment warranty? Does it cover the cost of parts and labor? Where do repairs take place? Who pays shipping costs for equipment that is sent to the manufacturer for repair? How long do repairs typically take? With the answers to these questions in hand along with your decisions about budget, form factor, and platform, you can be confident that you're making a savvy computer purchase.

# QuickCheck

**SECTION A**

1. Popular _____ devices include printers, digital cameras, scanners, joysticks, and speakers.

2. The first popular personal computers were _____ models, and this style remains popular for offices, schools, and homes.

3. Portable computers are classified as notebooks, _____, and ultra-mobiles.

4. Key components of a(n) _____ PC include a remote control device, TV tuner, and Viiv technology.

5. To assess whether two computers are _____, you have to consider if they run the same software and use the same peripheral devices.

▶ CHECK ANSWERS

# Microprocessors and Memory

**2**

**A TYPICAL COMPUTER AD** contains a long list of specifications that describe a computer's components and capabilities. Savvy shoppers understand how these specifications affect computer performance and price. Most computer specifications begin with the microprocessor type and speed. Computer manufacturers want consumers to think that faster is better, but is there a point at which you can pay for speed you won't need? Computer ads also contain information about a computer's memory capacity. Lots of memory can add hundreds of dollars to the cost of a computer. Consumers are right to ask "How much RAM is enough?" Section B explains how microprocessors and memory affect computer performance and price.

## MICROPROCESSOR BASICS

**What exactly is a microprocessor?** As you learned in Chapter 1, a microprocessor (sometimes simply referred to as a processor) is an integrated circuit designed to process instructions. It is the most important, and usually the most expensive, component of a computer. Although a microprocessor is sometimes mistakenly referred to as a computer on a chip, it can be more accurately described as a CPU on a chip because it contains—on a single chip—circuitry that performs essentially the same tasks as the central processing unit (CPU) of a classic mainframe computer.

**What does it look like?** Looking inside a computer, you can usually identify the microprocessor because it is the largest chip on the system board, although it might be hidden under a cooling fan. Most of today's microprocessors are housed in a PGA (pin grid array) chip package, as shown in Figure 2-11.

**What makes one microprocessor perform better than another?** Computer ads typically include microprocessor specifications related to performance. For example, an ad might describe a microprocessor as "Intel® Pentium® Extreme Edition Dual-Core with HT Technology 3.20 GHz, 800M Hz FSB, 2 MB Cache." A microprocessor's performance is affected by several factors, including clock speed, bus speed, word size, cache size, instruction set, and processing techniques.

**What do MHz and GHz have to do with computer performance?** A specification, such as 3.20 GHz, that you see in a computer ad indicates the speed of the **microprocessor clock**—a timing device that sets the pace for executing instructions. Most computer ads specify the speed of a microprocessor in megahertz or gigahertz. **Megahertz** (MHz) means a million cycles per second. **Gigahertz** (GHz) means a billion cycles per second.

A cycle is the smallest unit of time in a microprocessor's universe. Every action a processor performs is measured by these cycles. It is important, however, to understand that the clock speed is not equal to the number

**FIGURE 2-11**

Today's microprocessors are typically housed in a PGA chip package.

of instructions a processor can execute in one second. In many computers, some instructions occur within one cycle, but other instructions might require multiple cycles. Some processors can even execute several instructions in a single clock cycle.

A specification such as 3.2 GHz means that the microprocessor's clock operates at a speed of 3.2 billion cycles per second. All other things being equal, a computer with a 3.2 GHz processor is faster than a computer with a 1.5 GHz processor or a 933 MHz processor (Figure 2-12).

Some chipmakers differentiate chips by clock speed whereas other chipmakers use model numbers, called processor numbers (PN). Processor numbers do not correspond to a particular clock speed but they can indicate speed relative to other processors within the same family. For example, the Pentium 570 processor has a higher processor number and is faster than the Pentium 550. Processor numbers cannot be compared across product families, however. An Intel M 755 processor is not faster than the Pentium 4 560. Even though 755 is a larger number than 560, the M processor and Pentium 4 are in different processor families. Their processor numbers cannot be compared to each other.

**What is FSB?** FSB stands for **front side bus**, a term that refers to the circuitry that transports data to and from the microprocessor. A fast front side bus moves data quickly and allows the processor to work at full capacity. In today's computers, FSB speed (technically its frequency) is measured in megahertz (MHz) and ranges from 200 MHz to 1250 MHz. Higher numbers indicate faster FSB speeds. Some processor manufacturers use a technology called **HyperTransport** to increase the speed of data moving to the processor.

**What impact does word size have on performance?** **Word size** refers to the number of bits that a microprocessor can manipulate at one time. Word size is based on the size of registers in the ALU and the capacity of circuits that lead to those registers. A processor with a 32-bit word size, for example, has 32-bit registers, processes 32 bits at a time, and is referred to as a 32-bit processor. Processors with a larger word size can process more data during each processor cycle—a factor that leads to increased computer performance. Today's personal computers typically contain 32-bit or 64-bit processors.

**How does the cache size affect performance?** **Cache** (pronounced "cash") is special high-speed memory that allows a microprocessor to access data more rapidly than from memory located elsewhere on the system board. A large cache can increase computer performance. Some computer ads specify cache type and capacity. A **Level 1 cache** (L1) is built into the processor chip, whereas a **Level 2 cache** (L2) is located on a separate chip and takes a little more time to get data to the processor. Cache capacity is usually measured in kilobytes.

**FIGURE 2-12**

Computer ads provide processor specifications, but how about the processor in your current computer? You can discover your processor's specs using the Windows Control Panel or third-party software, such as CPU-Z.

**TERMINOLOGY NOTE**

Other terms for front side bus include system bus and memory bus.

Cache is sometimes called RAM cache, cache memory, CPU cache, or internal cache.

**How does an instruction set affect performance?** As chip designers developed various instruction sets for microprocessors, they added increasingly complex instructions, each requiring several clock cycles for execution. A microprocessor with such an instruction set uses **CISC** (complex instruction set computer) technology. A microprocessor with a limited set of simple instructions uses **RISC** (reduced instruction set computer) technology. A RISC processor performs most instructions faster than a CISC processor. It might, however, require more of these simple instructions to complete a task than a CISC processor requires for the same task. Most processors in today's personal computers use CISC technology.

A processor's ability to handle graphics can be enhanced by adding specialized graphics and multimedia instructions to a processor's instruction set. 3DNow!, MMX, and SSE-3 are examples of instruction set enhancements sometimes mentioned in computer ads. Although instruction set enhancements have the potential to speed up games, graphics software, and video editing, they offer speed enhancements only with software designed to utilize these specialized instructions.

**Can a microprocessor execute more than one instruction at a time?** Some processors execute instructions "serially"—that is, one instruction at a time. With **serial processing**, the processor must complete all steps in the instruction cycle before it begins to execute the next instruction. However, using a technology called **pipelining**, a processor can begin executing an instruction before it completes the previous instruction. Many of today's microprocessors also perform **parallel processing**, in which multiple instructions are executed at the same time. Pipelining and parallel processing, illustrated in Figure 2-13, enhance processor performance.

To get a clearer picture of serial, pipelining, and parallel processing technology, consider an analogy in which computer instructions are pizzas. Serial processing executes only one instruction at a time, just like a pizzeria with one oven that holds only one pizza. Pipelining is similar to a pizza conveyor belt. A pizza (instruction) starts moving along the conveyor belt into the oven, but before it reaches the end, another pizza starts moving along the belt. Parallel processing is similar to a pizzeria with many ovens. Just as these ovens can bake more than one pizza at a time, a parallel processor can execute more than one instruction at a time.

**What's a dual core processor?** As an alternative to using more than one processor, some computers have a single chip containing the circuitry for two microprocessors. A **dual core processor** is faster than one with a single core. To gain maximum speed, however, your computer's operating system and software should be optimized for dual core processing. Windows supports it, as do some games and graphics software.

**What is HT?** The abbreviation HT (or HTT), which appears in many computer ads, stands for **Hyper-Threading Technology** and refers to circuitry that enables a single processor to simulate two processors. Hyper-Threading speeds up some applications, but does not offer the performance boost of dual core technology.

**With so many factors to consider, how can I compare microprocessor performance?** Various testing laboratories run a series of tests to gauge the overall speed of a microprocessor. The results of these tests—called **benchmarks**—can then be compared to the results for other microprocessors. The results of benchmark tests are usually available on the Web and published in computer magazine articles.

**FIGURE 2-13**

Microprocessor designers have developed techniques for serial processing, pipelining, and parallel processing.

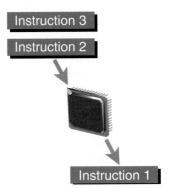

In serial processing, one instruction is processed at a time.

In pipelining, an instruction can begin to be processed before the previous instruction's processing is complete.

In parallel processing, multiple instructions can be processed at the same time.

## TODAY'S MICROPROCESSORS

**Which companies produce most of today's popular micro-processors?** Intel is the world's largest chipmaker and supplies a sizeable percentage of the microprocessors that power PCs. In 1971, Intel introduced the world's first microprocessor—the 4004. Intel's 8088 processor powered the original IBM PC. Since the debut of the IBM PC in 1985, Intel has introduced numerous microprocessors that have been used by most major computer manufacturers.

AMD (Advanced Micro Devices) is Intel's chief rival in the PC chip market. AMD's Athlon and Opteron processors are direct competitors to Intel's Pentium and Itanium lines. AMD processors are less expensive than comparable Intel models and have a slight performance advantage according to some benchmarks.

Historically, Motorola and IBM were the main chip suppliers for Apple computers, but Apple began a transition to Intel chips in 2005. IBM produces RISC-based POWER processors for servers and other high-performance computers. Transmeta Corporation specializes in chips for mobile computing devices, such as tablet computers.

**Which microprocessor is best for my PC?** The microprocessor that's best for you depends on your budget and the type of work and play you plan to do. The microprocessors marketed with the current crop of computers can handle most business, educational, and entertainment applications (Figure 2-14). You'll want to consider the fastest processor offerings if you typically engage in processing-hungry activities, such as 3-D animated computer games, desktop publishing, multitrack sound recording, or video editing.

**Can I replace my computer's microprocessor with a faster one?** It is technically possible to upgrade your computer's microprocessor, but computer owners rarely do so. The price of the latest, greatest microprocessor can often get you more than halfway to buying an entirely new computer system. Technical factors also discourage microprocessor upgrades. A microprocessor operates at full efficiency only if all components in the computer can also handle the faster speeds. In many cases, installing a new processor in an old computer can be like attaching a huge outboard engine to a canoe. In both cases, too much power can lead to disaster.

**What is overclocking?** **Overclocking** is a technique for increasing the speed of a computer component, such as a processor, graphics card, motherboard, or memory. When successful, overclocking can increase the processing power of a slow component to match that of a faster, more expensive component. Overclocking is popular with gamers who want to squeeze every bit of processing speed out of their computers.

**Why doesn't everyone overclock?** Overclocking is very risky. Additional electrical power pumped into a component also increases heat output. Overclocked components can overheat and even catch fire. To maintain safe operating temperatures, modders install supplemental cooling systems, sometimes using heavy-duty heatsinks, big fans, liquid oxygen, dry ice, or other refrigerants.

**FIGURE 2-14**

Today's popular server, desktop, and mobile microprocessors.

| Processor | Application |
|-----------|-------------|

| | |
|-----------|-------------|
| Core | Desktops, portables |
| Xeon | Servers |
| Itanium | Servers |
| Pentium D | Servers, desktops |
| Pentium 4 | Servers, desktops |
| Pentium Extreme Edition | Desktops |
| Celeron Celeron M | Desktops Portables |
| Pentium M | Notebooks, PDAs |
| Mobile Pentium 4 | Notebooks, PDAs |

## AMD

| | |
|-----------|-------------|
| Opteron | Servers |
| Athlon 64 | Desktops, portables |
| Turion 64 | Notebooks, PDAs |
| Sempron | Desktops |
| Mobile Sempron | Notebooks, PDAs |

**INFOWEBLINKS**

For updates on popular microprocessors, you can connect to the **Microprocessor Update InfoWeb**.

CLICK TO CONNECT
www.course.com/np/concepts10/ch02

## RANDOM ACCESS MEMORY

**What is RAM? RAM** (random access memory) is a temporary holding area for data, application program instructions, and the operating system. In a personal computer, RAM is usually several chips or small circuit boards that plug into the system board within the computer's system unit.

A computer's RAM capacity is invariably included in the list of specifications in a computer ad (Figure 2-15). The amount of RAM in a computer can affect the overall price of a computer system. To understand how much RAM your computer needs and to understand computer ad terminology, it is handy to have a little background on how RAM works and what it does.

**Why is RAM so important?** RAM is the "waiting room" for the computer's processor. It holds raw data waiting to be processed as well as the program instructions for processing that data. In addition, RAM holds the results of processing until they can be stored more permanently on disk or tape (Figure 2-16).

### FIGURE 2-15

A computer ad typically specifies the amount and type of RAM.

- Intel Pentium EE 965 64-bit dual core processor 3.73 GHz with Hyper-Threading 1066 MHz FSB
- 2 MB L2 cache
- 2 GB 533 MHz SDRAM (max. 4 GB)
- 160 GB SATA HD (7200 rpm)
- 48X CD-RW + 16X DVD+RW/+R with double layer write capable
- 3.5" 1.44 MB floppy disk drive

### FIGURE 2-16

RAM is the computer equivalent of the waiting room at an airport or a train station. It holds data waiting to be processed, stored, displayed, or printed.

RAM

Let's look at an example. When you use personal finance software to balance your checkbook, you enter raw data for check amounts, which is held in RAM. The personal finance software sends to RAM the instructions for processing this data. The processor uses these instructions to calculate your checkbook balance and sends the results back to RAM. From RAM, your checkbook balance can be stored on disk, displayed, or printed.

In addition to data and application software instructions, RAM also holds operating system instructions that control the basic functions of a computer system. These instructions are loaded into RAM every time you start your computer, and they remain there until you turn off your computer.

**How does RAM differ from hard-disk storage?** People who are new to computers sometimes tend to confuse RAM and hard-disk storage, maybe because both components hold data, because they typically are "hidden" inside the system unit, or because they can both be measured in gigabytes. To differentiate between RAM and hard-disk storage, remember that RAM holds data in circuitry that's directly connected to the system board, whereas hard-disk storage places data on magnetic media. RAM is temporary storage; hard-disk storage is more permanent. In addition, RAM usually has less storage capacity than hard-disk storage.

**How does RAM work?** In RAM, microscopic electronic parts called **capacitors** hold the bits that represent data. You can visualize the capacitors as microscopic lights that can be turned on or off. A charged capacitor is "turned on" and represents a "1" bit. A discharged capacitor is "turned off" and represents a "0" bit. Each bank of capacitors holds eight bits—one byte of data. A RAM address on each bank helps the computer locate data, as needed, for processing (Figure 2-17).

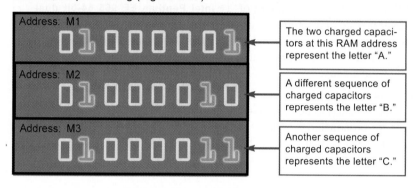

Address: M1 — The two charged capacitors at this RAM address represent the letter "A."

Address: M2 — A different sequence of charged capacitors represents the letter "B."

Address: M3 — Another sequence of charged capacitors represents the letter "C."

**FIGURE 2-17**

Each RAM location has an address and uses eight capacitors to hold the eight bits that represent a byte.

 CLICK TO START

In some respects, RAM is similar to a chalkboard. You can use a chalkboard to write mathematical formulas, erase them, and then write an outline for a report. In a similar way, RAM can hold numbers and formulas when you balance your checkbook, and then can hold the outline of your English essay when you use word processing software. RAM contents can be changed just by changing the charge of the capacitors.

Unlike disk storage, most RAM is **volatile**, which means it requires electrical power to hold data. If the computer is turned off or the power goes out, all data stored in RAM instantly and permanently disappears. When someone exclaims, "Rats! I just lost my document," it often means the person was entering the text of a document (which was being held in RAM), and the power went out before the data was saved on disk.

**How much RAM does my computer need?** RAM capacity is expressed in megabytes or gigabytes. Today's personal computers typically feature between 256 MB and 2 GB of RAM. The amount of RAM your computer needs depends on the software you use. RAM requirements are routinely specified on the outside of a software package (Figure 2-18). If you need more RAM, you can purchase and install additional memory up to the limit the computer manufacturer sets. For good basic performance, a computer running Windows software should have at least 256 MB of RAM. Games, desktop publishing, graphics, and video applications tend to run more smoothly with at least 512 MB of RAM.

**Can my computer run out of memory?** Suppose that you want to work with several programs and large graphics at the same time. Will your computer eventually run out of memory? The answer is "probably not." Today's personal computer operating systems are quite adept at allocating RAM space to multiple programs. If a program exceeds its allocated space, the operating system uses an area of the hard disk, called **virtual memory**, to store parts of programs or data files until they are needed. By selectively exchanging the data in RAM with the data in virtual memory, your computer effectively gains almost unlimited memory capacity.

Too much dependence on virtual memory can slow down your computer's performance, however, because getting data from a mechanical device, such as a hard disk drive, is much slower than getting data from an elec-

**FIGURE 2-18**

Minimum RAM requirements are typically displayed on the package of a software product.

**Minimum System Requirements:**

- Windows Vista/XP/2000/NT4 Pentium III with 64 MB of RAM
- Windows ME/98(SE)/98, Pentium III with 32 MB of RAM
- 40 MB hard drive space
- CD-ROM drive
- Mouse
- Internet connection (optional)
- Printer (optional)
- Scanner or digital camera with 32-bit twain interface (optional)

tronic device, such as RAM. To minimize virtual memory use, load up your computer with as much RAM as possible.

**Do all computers use the same type of RAM?** No. RAM components vary in speed, technology, and configuration. Many computer ads provide information on all three aspects of RAM, but consumers who want lots of fast RAM for 3-D gaming and desktop publishing have to wade through a thicket of acronyms and technical jargon. To unlock the meaning of RAM specifications, such as "1 GB 533 MHz SDRAM," you need an understanding of a few more acronyms and abbreviations.

RAM speed is often expressed in nanoseconds or megahertz. One **nanosecond** (ns) is 1 billionth of a second. In the context of RAM speed, lower nanosecond ratings are better because it means the RAM circuitry can react faster to update the data it holds. For example, 8 ns RAM is faster than 10 ns RAM.

RAM speed can also be expressed in MHz (millions of cycles per second). Just the opposite of nanoseconds, higher MHz ratings mean faster speeds. For example, 533 MHz RAM is faster than 400 MHz RAM.

Most of today's personal computers use SDRAM or RDRAM. SDRAM (synchronous dynamic RAM) is fast and relatively inexpensive. Recent innovations, such as dual channel technology and double data rate (DDR) have increased SDRAM speed. RDRAM (rambus dynamic RAM) was first developed for the popular Nintendo 64 game system and then adapted for use in personal computers. RDRAM is more expensive than SDRAM and is usually found in high-performance workstations. RAM is configured as a series of DIP chips soldered onto a small circuit board, as shown in Figure 2-19.

**FIGURE 2-19**

SDRAM is the most popular type of RAM in today's computers. It is typically available on a small circuit board called a DIMM (dual inline memory module). When adding memory to a computer, check with the computer manufacturer to make sure you purchase the correct RAM type and speed.

## READ-ONLY MEMORY

**How is ROM different from RAM?** **ROM** (read-only memory) is a type of memory circuitry that holds the computer's startup routine. ROM is housed in a single integrated circuit—usually a fairly large, caterpillar-like DIP package—which is plugged into the system board.

Whereas RAM is temporary and volatile, ROM is permanent and non-volatile. ROM holds "hard-wired" instructions that are a permanent part of the circuitry and remain in place even when the computer power is turned off. This is a familiar concept to anyone who has used a hand calculator that includes various "hard-wired" routines for calculating square roots, cosines, and other functions. The instructions in ROM are permanent, and the only way to change them is to replace the ROM chip.

**If a computer has RAM, why does it need ROM too?** When you turn on your computer, the microprocessor receives electrical power and is ready to begin executing instructions. As a result of the power being off, however, RAM is empty and doesn't contain any instructions for the microprocessor to execute. Now ROM plays its part. ROM contains a small set of instructions called the **ROM BIOS** (basic input/output system). These instructions tell the computer how to access the hard disk, find the operating system, and load it into RAM. After the operating system is loaded, the computer can understand your input, display output, run software, and access your data.

## EEPROM

**Where does a computer store its basic hardware settings?** To operate correctly, a computer must have some basic information about storage, memory, and display configurations. For example, your computer needs to know how much memory is available so that it can allocate space for all the programs you want to run. RAM goes blank when the computer power is turned off, so configuration information cannot be stored there. ROM would not be a good place for this information, either, because it holds data on a permanent basis. If, for example, your computer stored the memory size in ROM, you could never add more memory—well, you might be able to add it, but you couldn't change the size specification in ROM. To store some basic system information, your computer needs a type of memory that's more permanent than RAM, but less permanent than ROM. EEPROM is just the ticket.

**EEPROM** (electrically erasable programmable read-only memory) is a non-volatile chip that requires no power to hold data. EEPROMs replace CMOS technology that required power from a small battery integrated into the system board.

When you change the configuration of your computer system—by adding RAM, for example—the data in EEPROM must be updated. Some operating systems recognize such changes and automatically perform the update. You can manually change EEPROM settings by running your computer's setup program, as described in Figure 2-20.

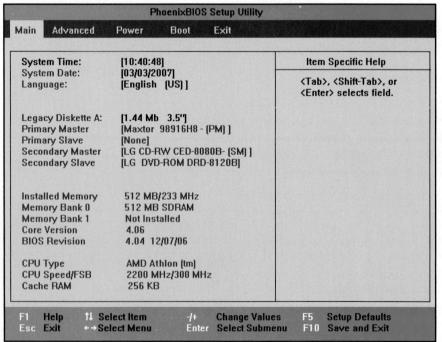

**FIGURE 2-20**

EEPROM holds computer configuration settings, such as the date and time, hard disk capacity, number of floppy disk drives, and RAM capacity. To access the EEPROM setup program, hold down the F1 key as your computer boots. But be careful! If you make a mistake with these settings, your computer might not be able to start.

If you mistakenly enter the Setup program, follow the on-screen instructions to exit and proceed with the boot process. In Figure 2-20, the Esc (Escape) key allows you to exit the Setup program without making any changes to the EEPROM settings.

**What information about memory performance is most important?** Even though ROM and EEPROM have important roles in the operation of a computer, RAM capacity really makes a difference you can notice. The more data and programs that can fit into RAM, the less time your computer will spend moving data to and from virtual memory. With lots of RAM, you'll find that documents scroll faster, games respond more quickly, and many graphics operations take less time than with a computer that has a skimpy RAM capacity.

Most ads specify RAM capacity, speed, and type. Now when you see the specification "512 MB 400 MHz SDRAM (max. 2 GB)" in a computer ad, you'll know that the computer's RAM capacity is 512 megabytes (enough to run most of today's software), that it operates at 400 megahertz (fairly fast), and that it uses SDRAM (a little slower and less expensive than RDRAM). You'll also have important information about the maximum amount of RAM that can be installed in the computer—2 GB, which is more than enough for the typical computer owner who does a bit of word processing, surfs the Web, and plays computer games.

# QuickCheck

1. A microprocessor's [_____] speed is provided in a specification such as 3.6 GHz.

2. Some chipmakers use a [_____] number, such as 560, to differentiate microprocessors.

3. A front side [_____] is circuitry that transports data to and from the processor at speeds ranging from 200 MHz to 1250 MHz.

4. A dual [_____] processor allows a computer to execute multiple instructions at the same time to achieve parallel processing.

5. RAM is [_____], which means that it cannot hold data when the computer power is off.

6. A computer does not usually run out of RAM because it can use an area of the hard disk called [_____] memory.

7. The instructions for loading the operating system into RAM when a computer is first turned on are stored in [_____]. Hint: Use the abbreviation.

CHECK ANSWERS

# Storage Devices

**COMPUTER MANUFACTURERS** typically try to entice consumers by configuring computers with a variety of storage devices, such as a floppy disk drive, hard disk drive, and some sort of CD or DVD drive. What's the point of having so many storage devices? As it turns out, none of today's storage technologies is perfect. One technology might provide fast access to data, but it might also be susceptible to problems that could potentially wipe out all your data. A different technology might be more dependable, but it might have the disadvantage of relatively slow access to data.

Smart shoppers make sure their new computers are equipped with a variety of storage devices. Informed computer owners understand the strengths and weaknesses of each storage technology so that they can use these devices with maximum effectiveness. In this section, you'll learn many secrets that can make you a smart storage technology buyer and owner. The storage technologies you'll learn about are now used in a variety of devices—from digital cameras to player pianos—so an understanding of storage technology can be useful outside the boundaries of personal computing.

## STORAGE BASICS

**What are the basic components of a data storage system?** A data storage system has two main components: a storage medium and a storage device. A **storage medium** (storage media is the plural) is the disk, tape, CD, DVD, paper, or other substance that contains data. A **storage device** is the mechanical apparatus that records and retrieves data from a storage medium. Storage devices include floppy disk drives, hard disk drives, tape drives, CD drives, DVD drives, and flash drives. The term *storage technology* refers to a storage device and the media it uses.

**How does a storage system interact with other computer components?** You can think of your computer's storage devices as having a direct pipeline to RAM. Data gets copied from a storage device into RAM, where it waits to be processed. After data is processed, it is held temporarily in RAM, but it is usually copied to a storage medium for more permanent safekeeping.

As you know, a computer's processor works with data that has been coded into bits that can be represented by 1s and 0s. When data is stored, these 1s and 0s must be converted into some kind of signal or mark that's fairly permanent, but can be changed when necessary.

Obviously, the data is not literally written as "1" or "0." Instead, the 1s and 0s must be transformed into changes in the surface of a storage medium. Exactly how this transformation happens depends on the storage technology. For example, hard disks store data in a different way than CD-ROMs. Three types of storage technologies are commonly used for personal computers: magnetic, optical, and solid state.

**TERMINOLOGY NOTE**

The process of storing data is often referred to as writing data or saving a file because the storage device writes the data on the storage medium to save it for later use.

The process of retrieving data is often referred to as reading data, loading data, or opening a file.

**Which storage technology is best?** Each storage technology has its advantages and disadvantages. If one storage system was perfect, we wouldn't need so many disk and tape drives connected to our computers! To compare storage devices, it is useful to apply the criteria of versatility, durability, speed, and capacity.

**How can one storage technology be more versatile than another?** Some storage devices can access data from only one type of medium. More versatile devices can access data from several different media. A floppy disk drive, for example, can access only floppy disks, whereas a DVD drive can access computer DVDs, DVD movies, audio CDs, computer CDs, and CD-Rs.

**What makes a storage technology durable?** Most storage technologies are susceptible to damage from mishandling or other environmental factors, such as heat and moisture. Some technologies are more susceptible than others to damage that could cause data loss. CDs and DVDs tend to be more durable than hard disks, for example.

**What factors affect storage speed?** Quick access to data is important, so fast storage devices are preferred over slower devices. **Access time** is the average time it takes a computer to locate data on the storage medium and read it. Access time for a personal computer storage device, such as a disk drive, is measured in milliseconds (thousandths of a second). One millisecond (ms) is one-thousandth of a second. Lower numbers indicate faster access times. For example, a drive with a 6 ms access time is faster than a drive with an access time of 11 ms.

Access time is best for random-access devices. **Random access** (also called direct access) is the ability of a device to "jump" directly to the requested data. Floppy disk, hard disk, CD, DVD, and solid state drives are random-access devices, as are the memory cards used in digital cameras. A tape drive, on the other hand, must use slower **sequential access** by reading through the data from the beginning of the tape. The advantage of random access becomes clear when you consider how much faster and easier it is to locate a song on a CD (random access) than on a cassette tape (sequential access).

**Data transfer rate** is the amount of data a storage device can move per second from the storage medium to the computer. Higher numbers indicate faster transfer rates. For example, a CD-ROM drive with a 600 KBps (kilobytes per second) data transfer rate is faster than one with a 300 KBps transfer rate.

**What's important about storage capacity?** In today's computing environment, higher capacity is almost always preferred. Storage capacity is the maximum amount of data that can be stored on a storage medium, and it is measured in kilobytes, megabytes, gigabytes, or terabytes.

Storage capacity is directly related to **storage density**, the amount of data that can be stored in a given area of a storage medium, such as the surface of a disk. The higher the storage density, the more data is stored. Storage density can be increased by making the particles representing bits smaller, by layering them, packing them closer together, or standing them vertically (Figure 2-21).

**FIGURE 2-21**

Vertical storage produces higher storage capacities than horizontal storage.

With horizontal storage, particles are arranged end to end, and use of the disk surface is not optimized.

With vertical storage, particles stand on end so that many more can be packed on the disk surface.

## MAGNETIC DISK AND TAPE TECHNOLOGY

**What is magnetic disk and tape technology?** Hard disk, floppy disk, and tape storage technologies can be classified as **magnetic storage**, which stores data by magnetizing microscopic particles on a disk or tape surface. The particles retain their magnetic orientation until that orientation is changed, thereby making disks and tapes fairly permanent but modifiable storage media. A **read-write head** mechanism in the disk drive can magnetize particles to write data, and sense the particles' polarities to read data. Figure 2-22 shows how a computer stores data on magnetic media.

**FIGURE 2-22**

Before data is stored, particles on the surface of the disk are scattered in random patterns. The disk drive's read-write head magnetizes the particles, and orients them in a positive (north) or negative (south) direction to represent 0 and 1 bits.

Data stored magnetically can be easily changed or deleted simply by changing the magnetic orientation of the appropriate particles on the disk surface. This feature of magnetic storage provides lots of flexibility for editing data and reusing areas of a storage medium containing unneeded data.

Data stored on magnetic media such as floppy disks can be unintentionally altered by magnetic fields, dust, mold, smoke particles, heat, and mechanical problems with a storage device. Placing a magnet on a floppy disk, for example, is a sure way of losing data.

Magnetic media gradually lose their magnetic charge, resulting in lost data. Some experts estimate that the reliable life span of data stored on magnetic media is about three years. They recommend that you refresh your data every two years by recopying it.

**Why are hard disk drives so popular?** Hard disk technology is the preferred type of main storage for most computer systems for three reasons. First, it provides lots of storage capacity. Second, it provides fast access to files. Third, a hard disk is economical. The cost of storing a megabyte of data is about 1/17th of a penny. You'll find hard disk drives in all kinds of digital devices, including personal computers, iPods, and TiVos.

**How does hard disk technology work?** As the main storage device on most computers, a **hard disk drive** contains one or more platters and their associated read-write heads. A **hard disk platter** is a flat, rigid disk made of aluminum or glass and coated with magnetic iron oxide particles. More platters mean more data storage capacity. The platters rotate as a unit on a spindle, making thousands of rotations per minute.

Each platter has a read-write head that hovers over the surface to read data. The head hovers only a few microinches above the disk surface, as shown in Figure 2-23 on the next page.

**TERMINOLOGY NOTE**

You often see the terms *hard disk* and *hard disk drive* used interchangeably. You might also hear the term *fixed disk* used to refer to hard disks.

**FIGURE 2-23**

Hard disk platters and read-write heads are sealed inside the drive case or cartridge to screen out dust and other contaminants.

▶ CLICK TO START

Personal computer hard disk platters are typically 3.5" in diameter, with storage capacities ranging from 40 to 500 GB. Miniature hard drives (sometimes called microdrives), such as the 1.8" drive featured on Apple's iPod digital music player, store 30 to 80 GB.

Hard disk access times of 6 to 11 ms are not uncommon, whereas a floppy or CD takes about half a second to spin up to speed and find data. Hard disk drive speed is sometimes measured in revolutions per minute (rpm). The faster a drive spins, the more rapidly it can position the read-write head over specific data. For example, a 7,200 rpm drive is able to access data faster than a 5,400 rpm drive.

Computer ads typically specify the capacity, access time, and speed of a hard disk drive. So "160 GB 8 ms 7200 RPM HD" means a hard disk drive with 160 gigabyte capacity, access time of 8 milliseconds, and speed of 7,200 revolutions per minute. Ads rarely specify the amount of data that a hard drive can transfer, but the average data transfer rate is about 50 megabytes per second.

**What's all this business about Ultra ATA, EIDE, SCSI, and DMA?** Computer ads use these acronyms to describe hard disk drive technology. A hard drive mechanism includes a circuit board called a **hard disk controller** that positions the disk and read-write heads to locate data. Disk drives are classified according to their controllers. Popular types of drive controllers include SATA, Ultra ATA, EIDE, and SCSI. Although computer ads often specify the hard drive controller type, consumers don't really have much choice. If you want a 160 GB drive, for example, your hardware vendor is likely to offer only one brand of drive with one type of controller. Figure 2-24 shows a typical controller mounted on a hard disk drive.

The storage technology used on many PCs transfers data from a disk, through the controller, to the processor, and finally to RAM before it is actually processed. Computer ads sometimes specify this technology. For example, DMA (direct memory access) technology allows a computer to transfer data directly from a drive into RAM, without intervention from the processor. This architecture relieves the processor of data-transfer duties and frees up processing cycles for other tasks. UDMA (ultra DMA) is a faster version of DMA technology.

**FIGURE 2-24**

A hard disk controller circuit board is typically mounted in the hard disk drive case.

**What's the downside of hard disk storage?** Hard disks are not as durable as many other storage technologies. The read-write heads in a hard disk hover a microscopic distance above the disk surface. If a read-write head runs into a dust particle or some other contaminant on the disk, it might cause a **head crash**, which damages some of the data on the disk. To help prevent contaminants from contacting the platters and causing head crashes, a hard disk is sealed in its case. A head crash can also be triggered by jarring the hard disk while it is in use. Although hard disks have become considerably more rugged in recent years, you should still handle and transport them with care. You should also make sure that you make a backup copy of the data stored on your hard disk in case of a head crash.

**Can I use a second hard disk drive to increase storage space?** You can increase the storage capacity of your computer by adding a second hard disk drive, which can also provide backup for your primary drive. Hard disk drives are available as internal or external units. Internal drives are inexpensive and can be easily installed in a desktop computer's system unit. External drives are slightly more expensive and connect to a desktop or notebook computer using a cable.

**What is floppy disk technology?** One of the oldest storage technologies, floppy disks are classified as magnetic storage because data is stored by magnetizing microscopic particles on the disk surface. A **floppy disk** is a round piece of flexible mylar plastic covered with a thin layer of magnetic oxide and sealed inside a protective casing (Figure 2-25). If you break open the disk casing (something you should never do unless you want to ruin the disk), you would see that the mylar disk inside is thin and literally floppy.

At one time, just about every personal computer included a floppy disk drive designed for high-density (HD) double-sided (DS) disks. Floppy disks are also referred to as floppies or diskettes. It is not correct to call them hard disks even though they seem to have a "hard" or rigid plastic case. The term hard disk refers to an entirely different storage technology.

A floppy disk's 1.44 MB capacity is not really sufficient for today's media-intensive applications. Many MP3 music files and photos are too large to fit on a floppy. In the past, floppy disks were extensively used to distribute software. CDs and DVDs offer more capacity for distributing the huge files for today's software applications. Web downloads offer more convenience for smaller files.

**What's the purpose of a tape drive?** As you have learned, a head crash can easily destroy hard disk data. Protecting the vast amount of data on the hard disk is of particular concern because it would be difficult and time-consuming to reconstruct. A backup copy of the data on a hard disk can be made with a variety of storage devices, including tape drives. A **tape drive** is a device that reads data from and writes data to a long stream of recordable media similar to the tapes used in audio cassettes.

Tape drives are primarily used on business computers. Unlike CDs and DVDs, a tape backup device is not suitable for everyday storage tasks. To find out why, you need to understand how a tape drive works.

**How does a tape drive work?** A tape is a sequential, rather than a random-access, storage medium. Essentially, data is arranged as a long sequence of bits that begins at one end of the tape and stretches to the other end. The beginning and end of each file are marked with special header labels. To locate a file, the tape drive must start at one end of the

**FIGURE 2-25**

A standard floppy disk drive reads and writes data on a 3.5" HD DS floppy disk.

tape and read through all the data until it finds the right header label. A tape can contain hundreds or—in the case of a mainframe—thousands of feet of tape. Access time is measured in seconds, not in milliseconds as for a hard disk drive. Tape is simply too slow to be practical as a computer's main storage device. Chapter 4 provides more information about the backup process, tape backups, and alternative ways to back up personal computer data.

## CD AND DVD TECHNOLOGY

**Is there a difference between CD and DVD technology?** Today, most computers come equipped with some type of **CD drive** or **DVD drive**, designed to work with a variety of CDs and DVDs. CD and DVD technologies are similar, but storage capacities differ.

**CD** (compact disc) technology was originally designed to hold 74 minutes of recorded music. The original CD standard was adapted for computer storage with capacity for 650 MB of data. Later improvements in CD standards increased the capacity to 80 minutes of music or 700 MB of data.

**DVD** (digital video disc or digital versatile disk) is a variation of CD technology that was originally designed as an alternative to VCRs, but was quickly adopted by the computer industry to store data. The initial DVD standard offered 4.7 GB (4,700 MB) of data storage; that's about seven times as much capacity as a CD. Subsequent improvements in DVD technology offer even more storage capacity. A **double layer DVD** has two recordable layers on the same side and can store 8.5 GB of data. An **HD-DVD** can store 15 GB per layer on a single side; a **Blu-ray DVD** (BD) has 25 GB capacity per layer.

**How do CD and DVD drives work?** CD and DVD storage technologies are classified as **optical storage**, which stores data as microscopic light and dark spots on the disk surface. The dark spots, shown in Figure 2-26, are called **pits**. The lighter, non-pitted surface areas of the disk are called **lands**.

CD and DVD drives contain a spindle that rotates the disk over a laser lens. The laser directs a beam of light toward the underside of the disk. The dark pits and light lands on the disk surface reflect the light differently. As the lens reads the disk, these differences are translated into the 0s and 1s that represent data (Figure 2-27).

**FIGURE 2-26**

As seen through an electron microscope, the pits on an optical storage disk look like small craters. Each pit is less than 1 micron (one millionth of a meter) in diameter—1,500 pits lined up side by side are about as wide as the head of a pin.

**FIGURE 2-27**

CD and DVD drives use a laser to read data from the underside of a disk.

Drive spindle spins disk

Laser lens directs a beam of light to the underside of the CD-ROM disk

Laser pickup assembly senses the reflectivity of pits and lands

Tracking mechanism positions a disk track over the laser lens

The surface of an optical disk is coated with clear plastic, making the disk quite durable and less susceptible to environmental damage than data recorded on magnetic media. An optical disk, such as a CD, is not susceptible to humidity, fingerprints, dust, magnets, or spilled soft drinks. Scratches on the disk surface can interfere with data transfer, but a good buffing with toothpaste can erase the scratch without damaging the underlying data. An optical disk's useful life is estimated to be more than 30 years. Figure 2-28 illustrates the layers of an optical disk.

FIGURE 2-28

CDs and DVDs are constructed with one or more layers of recording surface sandwiched between protective plastic.

**How fast are CDs and DVDs?** The original CD drives could access 150 KB of data per second. The next generation of drives doubled the data transfer rate and were consequently dubbed "2X" drives. Transfer rates seem to be continually increasing. A 52X CD drive, for example, transfers data at 80 Mbps, which is still relatively slow compared to a hard disk drive's transfer rate of 5,000 Mbps.

The speed of a DVD drive is measured on a different scale than a CD drive. A 1X DVD drive is about the same speed as a 9X CD drive. Today's DVD drives typically have 16X speeds for a data transfer rate of 177.28 Mbps.

**What's the significance of ROM, R, and RW?** Optical technologies are grouped into three categories: read-only, recordable, and rewritable.

**Read-only technology** (ROM), stores data permanently on a disk, which cannot be subsequently added to or changed. Read-only disks, such as CD-ROMs, CD-DAs, DVD-Video, and DVD-ROMs are typically pre-pressed during mass production and used to distribute software, music, and movies.

**Recordable technology** (R) uses a laser to change the color in a dye layer sandwiched beneath the clear plastic disk surface. The laser creates dark spots in the dye that are read as pits. The change in the dye is permanent, so data cannot be changed once it has been recorded.

**Rewritable technology** (RW) uses phase change technology to alter a crystal structure on the disk surface. Altering the crystal structure creates patterns of light and dark spots similar to the pits and lands on a CD. The crystal structure can be changed from light to dark and back again many times, making it possible to record and modify data much like on a hard disk.

**What are my choices for CD and DVD media?** Several CD and DVD formats are currently popular for use in personal computers:

- **CD-DA** (compact disc digital audio), more commonly known as audio CD, is the format for commercial music CDs. Music is typically recorded on audio CDs by the manufacturer, but can't be changed by the consumer.

- **DVD-Video** (digital versatile disc video) is the format for commercial DVDs that contain feature-length films.

- **CD-ROM** (compact disc read-only memory, pronounced "cee dee rom") was the original format for storing computer data. Data is stamped on the disk at the time it is manufactured. Data cannot be added, changed, or deleted from these disks.

- **DVD-ROM** (digital versatile disk read-only memory) contains data stamped onto the disk surface at the time of manufacture. Like CD-ROMs, the data on these disks is permanent, so you cannot add or change data.

- **CD-R** (compact disc recordable) disks store data using recordable technology. The data on a CD-R cannot be erased or modified once you record it. However, most CD-R drives allow you to record your data in multiple sessions. For example, you can store two files on a CD-R disk today, and add data for a few more files to the disk at a later time.

- **DVD+R** or **DVD-R** (digital versatile disk recordable) disks store data using recordable technology similar to a CD-R, but with DVD storage capacity.

- **CD-RW** (compact disc rewritable) disks store data using rewritable technology. Stored data can be recorded and erased multiple times, making it a very flexible storage option.

- **DVD+RW** or **DVD-RW** (digital versatile disk rewritable) disks store data using rewritable technology similar to CD-RW, but with DVD storage capacity.

**Are rewritable CD or DVD drives an acceptable replacement for a hard disk?** A rewritable CD or DVD drive is a fine addition to a computer system, but is not a good replacement for a hard disk drive. Unfortunately, the process of accessing, saving, and modifying data on a rewritable disk is relatively slow compared to the speed of hard disk access.

**Can I use a single drive to work with any CD or DVD media?** Most CD drives can read CD-ROM, CD-R, and CD-RW disks, but cannot read DVDs. Most DVD drives can read CD and DVD formats. Storing computer data and creating music CDs requires a recordable or rewritable device. As you can see from the table in Figure 2-29, the most versatile optical storage device is a DVD R/RW/CD-RW combo.

**TERMINOLOGY NOTE**

Even though CD-ROM and ROM-BIOS both contain the word *ROM*, they refer to quite different technologies. ROM BIOS refers to a chip on the system board that contains permanent instructions for the computer's boot sequence. A CD-ROM drive is an optical storage device that's usually installed in one of the system unit's drive bays.

**FIGURE 2-29**

CD and DVD Capabilities

| | Play Audio CDs | Play DVD Movies | Read CD Data | Read DVD Data | Create Music CDs | Store Data on CDs | Store Data on DVDs |
|---|---|---|---|---|---|---|---|
| **CD-ROM Drive** | ✔ | | ✔ | | | | |
| **CD-R Drive** | ✔ | | ✔ | | ✔ | ✔ | |
| **CD-RW Drive** | ✔ | | ✔ | | ✔ | ✔ | |
| **DVD/CD-RW Drive** | ✔ | ✔ | ✔ | ✔ | ✔ | ✔ | |
| **DVD R/RW/CD-RW Drive** | ✔ | ✔ | ✔ | ✔ | ✔ | ✔ | ✔ |

## SOLID STATE STORAGE

**What is solid state storage? Solid state storage** (sometimes called flash memory) is a technology that stores data in erasable, rewritable circuitry, rather than on spinning disks or streaming tape. It is widely used in portable consumer devices, such as digital cameras, MP3 music players, notebook computers, PDAs, and cell phones.

Solid state storage is portable and provides fairly fast access to data. It is an ideal solution for storing data on mobile devices and transporting data from one device to another.

**How does solid state storage work?** Solid state storage contains a gridwork or circuitry. Each cell in the grid contains two transistors that act as gates. When the gates are open, current can flow and the cell has a value that represents a "1" bit. When the gates are closed by a process called Fowler-Nordheim tunneling, the cell has a value that represents a "0" bit.

Very little power is required to open or close the gates, which makes solid state storage ideal for battery-operated devices, such as digital cameras and PDAs. Once the data is stored, it is **non-volatile**—the chip retains the data without the need for an external power source.

**FIGURE 2-30**

Media Center PCs typically include card readers for solid state memory cards.

Solid state storage provides fast access to data because it includes no moving parts. Solid state storage is very durable—it is virtually impervious to vibration, magnetic fields, or extreme temperature fluctuations. On the downside, the capacity of solid state storage does not currently match that of hard disks, or DVDs. The cost per megabyte of storage—about 3¢—is significantly higher than for magnetic or optical storage.

**What are my options for solid state storage?** Several types of solid state storage are available to today's consumers. The formats for these small, flat cards include CompactFlash, MultiMedia, SecureDigital (SD), and SmartMedia. Because digital photography is so popular, some Media Center PCs have a built-in **card reader** to make it simple to transfer photos from your camera to your computer (Figure 2-30).

Moving data in the other direction, a computer can download MP3 music files and store them on a solid state memory card. That card can be removed from the computer and inserted into a portable MP3 player, so you can listen to your favorite tunes while you're on the go.

For even more versatility, solid state USB flash drives and U3 drives can be used to store computer data files and programs.

**What is a USB flash drive?** A **USB flash drive**, such as Sony's MicroVault, the SanDisk Cruzer, or the Kingston Traveler, is a portable storage device that plugs directly into a computer's USB port using a built-in connector (Figure 2-31).

Also called thumb drives, pen drives, jumpdrives, and keychain drives, USB flash drives are about the size of a highlighter pen and so durable that you can literally carry them on your key ring. Files stored on a USB flash drive can be opened, edited, deleted, and run just as though those files were stored on magnetic or optical media. You might say that USB flash drives are the new floppy disks because not only can you access files as if they were stored on disks, but you can run software from them, too (Figure 2-32).

**FIGURE 2-31**

A USB flash drive plugs directly into a computer's USB port.

2

**FIGURE 2-32**

To run software from a USB Flash drive, you can double-click the program name in Windows Explorer.

USB flash drives have capacities ranging from 16 MB to 8 GB. They have maximum data transfer speeds of about 100 Mbps, but most commonly operate in the range of 18-28 megabytes per second. When you want to remove a USB flash drive from a computer, you should use the appropriate onscreen eject control. For example, on PCs, you would use the Safely Remove Hardware icon, located on the right side of the Windows task bar.

**What is a U3 drive?** A **U3 drive** (sometimes called a U3 smart drive) is a special type of USB flash drive that is preconfigured to autoplay when it is inserted into a computer. It runs an application called Launchpad, which is similar to the Windows Start menu, and lists programs that can be accessed from the U3 drive. Software applications for U3 drives are available at the U3 Web site.

## STORAGE WRAPUP

**Can I add storage to my computer?** You can increase storage capacity by adding hard drives and you can add storage flexibility by installing additional types of storage devices.

External storage devices, such as external hard disk drives, CD drives, DVD drives, and USB flash drives, simply plug into connectors built into your computer's system unit. They can be easily detached when you want to move your computer or if your external drive contains a backup that you want to store away from your computer. Before you disconnect any storage device, make sure you understand the manufacturer's instructions for doing so. On PCs, you usually have to use the Safely Remove Hardware icon on the Windows taskbar. Macs usually provide an eject icon next to the drive listing.

As an alternative to an external drive, you can install storage devices inside your computer's system unit case in "parking spaces" called **drive bays**. An external drive bay provides access from outside the system unit—a necessity for a storage device with removable media, such as floppy disks, CDs, tapes, and DVDs. Internal drive bays are located deep inside the system unit and are designed for hard disk drives, which don't use removable storage media. Most desktop and notebook computers include at least one internal drive bay and one or more external bays (Figure 2-33).

**FIGURE 2-33**

Most notebook computers provide bays for one floppy disk drive, one hard disk drive, and one CD or DVD drive.

An empty drive bay located on the side of a notebook computer

Most desktop computers have several drive bays, some accessible from outside the case, and others—designed for hard disk drives—without any external access. Empty drive bays are typically hidden from view with a face plate.

CLICK TO START

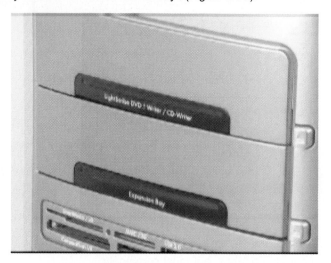

**INFOWEBLINKS**

To get an update on the latest computer storage technologies, connect to the **Storage Frontiers InfoWeb**.

W   CLICK TO CONNECT

www.course.com/np/concepts10/ch02

**What are the relative advantages and disadvantages of each type of computer storage device?** Earlier in the chapter you read that no storage technology is perfect. While hard disk drives offer fast and inexpensive access, they are not the most durable technology. CD and DVD technology is durable, but slow, and flash drives are expensive when compared to other storage media. The table in Figure 2-34 summarizes the relative advantages and disadvantages of each storage technology covered in this section.

**FIGURE 2-34**

Storage Technology Comparison

| Storage device | Cost of device (Average) | Capacity | Cost of media (disk/tape) | Cost per MB (Average) | Data Transfer rate | Technology | Portable |
|---|---|---|---|---|---|---|---|
| Floppy disk | $30 | 1.44 MB | $0.24 in bulk | $0.17 | 62.5 KBps | Magnetic | Yes |
| CD-RW | $65 | 700 MB | $0.58 in bulk | $0.0008 | 150 KBps-7.8 MBps (for 1-52x) | Optical | Yes |
| DVD+RW | $110 | 4.7 GB | $0.80 in bulk | $0.0002 | 1.35-32.4 MBps (for 1- 24x) | Optical | Yes |
| Flash drive | $14-$200 | 16 MB–8 GB | | $0.05 | 10-30 MBps | Solid State | Yes |
| Hard drive (Internal) | $30-$400 | 20 GB–750 GB | | $0.0005 | 150-300 MBps | Magnetic | No |
| Hard drive (External) | $70-$750 | 5 GB-1000 GB | | $0.0008 | 12-480 MBps | Magnetic | Yes |
| Tape | $500-$1000 | 2 GB–800 GB compressed | $2–$90 in bulk | $0.0001 | 2-160 MBps | Magnetic (sequential) | No |

# QuickCheck

1. _____ time is the average time it takes a computer to locate data on a storage medium and read it.

2. A disk drive is a(n) _____ access device, whereas a tape drive is a(n) _____ access device.

3. Higher disk _____ provides increased storage capacity.

4. A magnetic storage device uses a read-write _____ to magnetize particles that represent data.

5. Hard disks are susceptible to head _____ , so it is important to make backup copies.

6. Data on an optical storage medium, such as a DVD, is stored as pits and _____ .

7. CD-RW technology allows you to write data on a disk, and then change that data. True or false? _____

8. A USB flash drive uses solid _____ technology to store data and programs.

▶ CHECK ANSWERS

# Input and Output Devices

**THIS SECTION** provides an overview of the most popular input and output devices for personal computers. It begins with input devices, including keyboards, mice, trackpads, joysticks, and touch screens. Next, a survey of computer display devices helps you sort out the differences among CRT, LCD, and plasma displays. A guide to printers describes today's most popular printer technologies and provides a handy comparison chart. You'll learn about other peripheral devices in later chapters. You'll also take a look at the computer's expansion bus—the components that carry data to peripheral devices. With an understanding of how the expansion bus works, you'll be able to select, install, and use all kinds of peripherals.

## BASIC INPUT DEVICES

**What devices can I use to get data into a computer?** Most computer systems include a keyboard and pointing device, such as a mouse, for basic data input. Touch-sensitive screens offer an additional input option. Other input devices, such as scanners, digital cameras, and graphics tablets, are handy for working with graphical input. Microphones and electronic instruments provide input capabilities for sound and music.

**What's special about a computer keyboard's design?** The design of most computer keyboards is based on the typewriter's QWERTY layout, which was engineered to keep the typewriter's mechanical keys from jamming. In addition to the basic typing keypad, desktop and notebook computer keyboards include a collection of function keys designed for computer-specific tasks. Most desktop computer keyboards also include a calculator-style numeric keypad, plus an editing keypad with keys such as End, Home, and Page Up, to efficiently move the screen-based insertion point. You can even find tiny keyboards on handheld devices—entering text and numbers is an important part of most computing tasks.

**What does a pointing device do?** A **pointing device** allows you to manipulate an on-screen pointer and other screen-based graphical controls. The most popular pointing devices for personal computers include mice, trackballs, pointing sticks, trackpads, and joysticks.

**How does a mouse work?** A standard desktop computer includes a **mouse** as its primary pointing device. Many computer owners also add a mouse to their notebook computers. A mouse includes one or more buttons that can be clicked to input command selections, such as "Start" and "Shut down." To track its position, a computer mouse uses either mechanical or optical technology (Figure 2-35).

Most computer owners prefer the performance of an optical mouse because it provides more precise tracking, greater durability, less maintenance, and more flexibility to use the mouse on a wide variety of surfaces without a mouse pad.

**FIGURE 2-35**

A mechanical mouse (top) reads its position based on the movement of a ball that rolls over a mouse pad placed on a desk.

An optical mouse (bottom) uses an onboard chip to track a light beam as it bounces off a surface, such as a desk, clipboard, or mouse pad.

## When would I use other pointing devices?

When would I use other pointing devices? Alternative pointing devices, such as those pictured in Figure 2-36 can be used when a mouse is not available or does not provide adequate control.

FIGURE 2-36

Alternative Pointing Devices

2

Pointing stick

Trackpad

Trackball

Joystick

A **pointing stick**, or TrackPoint, looks like the tip of an eraser embedded in the keyboard of a notebook computer. It is a space-saving device that you can push up, down, or sideways to move the on-screen pointer. A **trackpad** is a touch-sensitive surface on which you can slide your fingers to move the on-screen pointer. Pointing sticks and trackpads are typically supplied with notebook computers so that it is not necessary to carry a mouse as an extra component.

A **trackball** looks like a mechanical mouse turned upside down. You use your fingers or palm to roll the ball and move the pointer. Controlling a trackball uses a different set of muscles than controlling a mouse, so some computer owners periodically switch to a trackball to prevent stress injuries.

A **joystick** looks like a small version of a car's stick shift. Moving the stick provides input to on-screen objects, such as a pointer or an action figure in a computer game. Joysticks can include several sticks and buttons for arcade-like control when playing computer games. Some joysticks are designed for people who have physical disabilities that prevent them from using a standard mouse.

## How does a touch screen work?

How does a touch screen work? Tablet computers, many PDAs, UMPCs, retail store self checkouts, and information kiosks collect input from a **touch screen**, which overlays a display screen. The most commonly used touch screen technology is a transparent panel coated with a thin layer of electrically conductive material that senses a change in the electrical current when touched. This "resistive" technology is fairly durable. It is not susceptible to dust or water, but it can be damaged by sharp objects.

**FIGURE 2-37**

Most touch screens use resistive technology that registers a change in electrical current when touched.

The coordinates for a touch event are processed in essentially the same way as a mouse click. For example, if you touch your PDA screen at the location of a button labeled "Calendar" the area you touch generates coordinates and sends them to the processor. The processor compares the coordinates to the image displayed on the screen to find out what is at the coordinates, and then responds, in this case by opening your appointment calendar.

The resistive technology used in today's touch screens can be operated with bare fingers or a stylus (Figure 2-37). Processing technology can interpret a single touch or more complex input such as handwriting.

## DISPLAY DEVICES

**What are my options for display devices?** A computer display screen is usually classified as an output device because it typically shows the results of a processing task. Some screens, however, can be classified as both input and output devices because they include touch-sensitive technology that accepts input. Three technologies are used for computer display devices: CRT, LCD, and plasma (Figure 2-38).

A **CRT** (cathode ray tube) display device uses the same sort of glass tube as a standard television. Gun-like mechanisms in the tube spray beams of electrons toward the screen and activate individual dots of color that form an image. CRT display devices, often simply called monitors, offer an inexpensive and dependable computer display. They are bulky, however, and consume a fair amount of power.

An **LCD** (liquid crystal display) produces an image by manipulating light within a layer of liquid crystal cells. Modern LCD technology is compact in size, lightweight, and provides an easy-to-read display. LCDs are standard equipment on notebook computers. Standalone LCDs, referred to as LCD monitors or flat panel displays, are popular for desktop computers. The advantages of LCD monitors include display clarity, low radiation emission, portability, and compactness. LCD technology has become price competitive with CRTs and most new computers now ship with LCD displays.

**Plasma screen** technology creates an on-screen image by illuminating miniature colored fluorescent lights arrayed in a panel-like screen. Plasma screens are compact, lightweight, and more expensive than LCD and CRT monitors.

CRT, LCD, and plasma screens can be equipped with NTSC (standard American television) or HDTV (high-definition television) circuitry so they accept television signals from an antenna or cable. This technology lets you simultaneously view computer data and television on the same display device using split-screen or picture-in-picture format.

**Which display technology produces the best image?** Image quality is a factor of screen size, dot pitch, width of viewing angle, refresh rate, resolution, and color depth. Screen size is the measurement in inches from one corner of the screen diagonally across to the opposite corner. Typical monitor screen sizes range from 13" to 21". On some displays, the viewable image does not stretch to the edge of the screen. Instead, a black border makes the image smaller than the size specified. Many computer ads now include a measurement of the **viewable image size** (vis).

**Dot pitch** (dp) is a measure of image clarity. A smaller dot pitch means a crisper image. Technically, dot pitch is the distance in millimeters between like-colored **pixels**—the small dots of light that form an image. A dot pitch between .26 and .23 is typical for today's display devices.

A display device's **viewing angle width** indicates how far to the side you can still clearly see the screen image. A wide viewing angle indicates that you can view the screen from various positions without compromising image quality. CRT and plasma screens offer the widest viewing angles. Graphics artists tend to prefer CRT screens, which display uniform color from any angle.

A CRT's **refresh rate** (also referred to as vertical scan rate) is the speed at which the screen is repainted. The faster the refresh rate, the less the screen flickers. Refresh rate is measured in cycles per second, or Hertz (Hz), and is

**FIGURE 2-38**

Display Device Technology

CRT

LCD

Plasma

### INFOWEBLINKS

For up-to-the-minute information on the latest and greatest graphics cards, monitors, and LCD displays, check out the **Display Devices InfoWeb.**

CLICK TO CONNECT
www.course.com/np/concepts10/ch02

adjustable using Control Panel settings in Windows. A refresh rate of at least 75 Hz produces a fairly flicker-free display.

The number of colors a monitor can display is referred to as **color depth** or bit depth. Most PC display devices have the capability to display millions of colors. When set at 24-bit color depth (sometimes called True Color), your PC can display more than 16 million colors—and produce what are considered photographic-quality images. Windows allows you to select resolution and color depth. The most popular setting is 24-bit color at 1024 x 768 resolution.

The number of horizontal and vertical pixels that a device displays on a screen is referred to as its **resolution**. The resolution for many early PC displays was referred to as **VGA** (Video Graphics Array). Higher resolutions were later provided by **SVGA** (Super VGA), **XGA** (eXtended Graphics Array), **SXGA** (Super XGA), and **UXGA** (Ultra XGA). Widescreen resolutions, such as **WUXGA**, offer the same aspect ratio as high definition television. Figure 2-39 summarizes the most common PC resolutions.

At higher resolutions, text and other objects appear smaller, but the computer can display a larger work area, such as an entire page of a document. The two screens in Figure 2-40 help you compare a display set at 640 x 480 resolution with a display set at 1024 x 768 resolution.

**FIGURE 2-39**

Common PC Resolutions

| | |
|---|---|
| VGA | 640 x 480 |
| SVGA | 800 x 600 |
| XGA | 1024 x 768 |
| SXGA | 1280 x 1024 |
| UXGA | 1600 x 1200 |
| WUXGA | 1920 x 1200 |

**FIGURE 2-40**

The screen on the left shows 1024 x 768 resolution. Notice the size of text and other screen-based objects. The screen on the right shows 640 x 480 resolution. Text and other objects appear larger on the low-resolution screen, but you see a smaller portion of the screen desktop.

### What are the components of a typical computer display system?

In addition to a display device, such as a monitor, a computer display system also requires graphics circuitry that generates the signals for displaying an image on the screen. One type of graphics circuitry, referred to as integrated graphics, is built into a computer's system board. Graphics circuitry can also be supplied by a small circuit board called a **graphics card** (graphics board or video card), like the one in Figure 2-41.

A graphics card typically contains a **graphics processing unit** (GPU) and special video memory, which stores screen images as they are processed but before they are displayed. Lots of video memory is the key to lightning-fast screen updating for fast action games, 3-D modeling, and graphics-intensive desktop publishing. In addition to video memory, most graphics cards contain special graphics accelerator technology to further boost performance.

**FIGURE 2-41**

A graphics card is a small circuit board that plugs into the system board.

92

## PRINTERS

**What printer technologies are available for personal computers?**
Printers are one of the most popular output devices available for personal
computers. Today's best-selling printers typically use ink jet or laser technology. An old printer technology called dot matrix is also used in some
applications.

**How does an ink jet printer work?** An **ink jet printer** has a nozzle-
like print head that sprays ink onto paper to form characters and graphics.
The print head in a color ink jet printer consists of a series of nozzles, each
with its own ink cartridge. Most ink jet printers use CMYK color, which
requires only cyan (blue), magenta (pink), yellow, and black inks to create a
printout that appears to have thousands of colors. Alternatively, some printers use six or eight ink colors to print midtone shades that create slightly
more realistic photographic images.

Ink jet printers, such as the one in Figure 2-42, outsell all other types of
printers because they are inexpensive and produce both color and black-
and-white printouts. They work well for most home and small business
applications. Small, portable ink jet printers meet the needs of many mobile
computer owners. Ink jet technology also powers many photo printers,
which are optimized to print high-quality images produced by digital cameras and scanners.

**How do laser printers compare to ink jet printers?** A **laser printer**,
such as the one in Figure 2-43, uses the same technology as a photocopier
to paint dots of light on a light-sensitive drum. Electrostatically charged ink
is applied to the drum and then transferred to paper. Laser technology is
more complex than ink jet technology, which accounts for the higher price of
laser printers.

A basic laser printer produces only black-and-white printouts. Color laser
printers are available, but are somewhat more costly than basic black-and-
white models. Laser printers are often the choice for business printers,
particularly for applications that produce a high volume of printed material.

**FIGURE 2-42**

Most ink jet printers are small,
lightweight, and inexpensive,
yet produce very good-quality
color output.

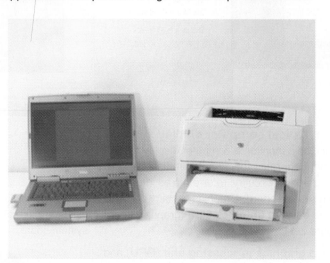

**FIGURE 2-43**

Laser printers are a popular
technology when high-volume
output or good-quality printouts
are required.

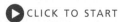

▶ CLICK TO START

**What is a dot matrix printer?** When PCs first appeared in the late
1970s, dot matrix printers were the technology of choice, and they are still
available today. A **dot matrix printer** produces characters and graphics by
using a grid of fine wires. As the print head noisily clatters across the paper,
the wires strike a ribbon and paper in a pattern prescribed by your PC. Dot

matrix printers can print text and graphics—some even print in color using a multicolored ribbon.

Today, dot matrix printers, like the one in Figure 2-44, are used primarily for "back-office" applications that demand low operating cost and dependability, but not high print quality.

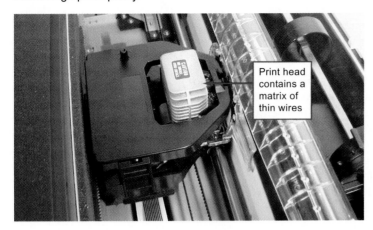

Print head contains a matrix of thin wires

**FIGURE 2-44**

Unlike laser and ink jet technologies, a dot matrix printer actually strikes the paper and, therefore, can print multipart carbon forms.

Characters are formed from a pattern of dots created as the wires strike an inked ribbon.

**What features should I look for in a printer?** Printers differ in resolution, speed, duty cycle, operating costs, duplex capability, and memory.

- **Resolution.** The quality or sharpness of printed images and text depends on the printer's resolution—the density of the gridwork of dots that create an image. Printer resolution is measured by the number of dots printed per linear inch, abbreviated as dpi. At normal reading distance, a resolution of about 900 dpi appears solid to the human eye, but a close examination reveals a dot pattern. If you want magazine-quality printouts, 900 dpi is sufficient resolution. If you are aiming for resolution similar to expensive coffee-table books, look for printer resolution of 2,400 dpi or higher.

- **Print speed.** Printer speeds are measured either by pages per minute (ppm) or characters per second (cps). Color printouts typically take longer than black-and-white printouts. Pages that contain mostly text tend to print more rapidly than pages that contain graphics. Typical speeds for personal computer printers range between 6 and 30 pages per minute.

- **Duty cycle.** In addition to printer speed, a printer's **duty cycle** determines how many pages a printer is able to churn out. Printer duty cycle is usually measured in pages per month. For example, a personal laser printer has a duty cycle of about 3,000 pages per month (ppm)—that means roughly 100 pages per day. You wouldn't want to use it to produce 5,000 campaign brochures for next Monday, but you would find it quite suitable for printing 10 copies of a five-page outline for a meeting tomorrow.

- **Operating costs.** The initial cost of a printer is only one of the expenses associated with printed output. Ink jet printers require frequent replacements of relatively expensive ink cartridges. Laser printers require toner cartridge refills or replacements. Dot matrix printers require replacement ribbons. When shopping for a printer, you can check online resources to determine how often you'll need to replace printer supplies and how much they are likely to cost.

- **Duplex capability.** A **duplex printer** can print on both sides of the paper. This environment-friendly option saves paper but can slow down the print process, especially on ink-jet printers that pause to let the ink dry before printing the second side.

• **Memory.** A computer sends data for a printout to the printer along with a set of instructions on how to print that data. **Printer Control Language** (PCL) is the most widely used language for communication between computers and printers, but **PostScript** is an alternative printer language that many publishing professionals prefer. The data that arrives at a printer along with its printer language instructions require memory. A large memory capacity is required to print color images and graphics-intensive documents. Some printers let you add memory to improve printing of such pages.

• **Networkability.** If your personal computer system is not networked to other computers in your house, apartment, or dorm, you can attach a print-er directly to your computer. If your computer is part of a network, you can share your printer with other network users, who essentially send their print jobs to your computer's printer for output. Another way to configure net-work printing for multiple users is to purchase a network-enabled printer that connects directly to the network, rather than to one of the computers on a network. The network connection can be wired or wireless. The advantage of a network-ready printer is that it can be placed in a location convenient for all the network users.

Figure 2-45 provides comparative information for ink jet, laser, and dot matrix printers. For specific information on a particular brand and model of printer, check the manufacturer's Web site.

**INFOWEBLINKS**

Before you shop for a printer, take a look at the buying tips in the **Printer Buyer's Guide InfoWeb**.

 CLICK TO CONNECT
www.course.com/np/concepts10/ch02

**FIGURE 2-45**

Printer Comparison

| Printer Type | Max. Resolution | Speed | Duty Cycle | Operating Cost | Memory |
|---|---|---|---|---|---|
| Ink Jet (B&W) (color graphics) | 4800 x 1200 | 2–7 ppm 1–2 ppm | 3,000 ppm | 1–7¢/page 6–18¢/page | 256 KB–2 MB |
| Laser (B&W) (color graphics) | 2400 dpi | 10–20 ppm 2–4 ppm | 150,000 ppm | 2–4¢/page 2–4¢/page | 8–120 MB |
| Dot Matrix (B&W) | 72–360 dpi | 5–6 ppm | 6,000–60,000 ppm | 1.5–2¢/page | 2–128 KB |

## INSTALLING PERIPHERAL DEVICES

**Is it difficult to install a new peripheral device?** At one time, installing computer peripherals required a screwdriver and extensive knowl-edge of ports, slots, boards, and device drivers. Today, many peripheral devices connect to an external **USB** (universal serial bus) port and Windows automatically loads their device drivers, making installation as simple as plugging in a table lamp. USB is currently the most popular tech-nology for connecting peripherals (Figure 2-46).

On most new computer models, USB ports are conveniently located on the front or sides of the system unit for easy access. Many kinds of peripheral devices—including mice, scanners, and joysticks—are available with USB connections. Several types of storage devices, such as USB flash drives, also use USB connections.

There are still occasions, however, when a simple USB connection is not available. Installing high-end graphics and sound cards for a multimedia or serious gaming computer typically requires you to open the system unit.

Whether you are working with a simple USB connection or more complex equipment, a little information about the computer's data bus will arm you with the information you need to negotiate the steps for installing most peripheral devices.

**FIGURE 2-46**

Plugging a cable into a USB port is the simplest way to con-nect peripheral devices to a computer.

**How does a computer move data to and from peripheral devices?** When you install a peripheral device, you are basically creating a connection for data to flow between the device and the computer. Within a computer, data travels from one component to another over circuits called a **data bus**. One part of the data bus runs between RAM and the microprocessor. The segment of the data bus to which peripheral devices connect is called the **expansion bus** (or the I/O bus). As data moves along the expansion bus, it can travel through expansion slots, expansion cards, ports, and cables (Figure 2-47).

**FIGURE 2-47**

The expansion bus connects the computer system board to peripheral devices.

Microprocessor  System bus  RAM  Expansion bus  Expansion slots and expansion cards  Cable  Printer or other peripherals

Hard disk drive

**What's an expansion slot?** An **expansion slot** is a long, narrow socket on the system board into which you can plug an expansion card. An **expansion card** is a small circuit board that gives a computer the capability to control a storage device, an input device, or an output device. Expansion cards are also called expansion boards, controller cards, or adapters.

Expansion cards are built for only one type of slot. If you plan to add or upgrade a card in your computer, you must make sure the right type of slot is available on the system board. Most desktop computers provide four to eight expansion slots, some containing factory-installed expansion cards, such as modems, graphics cards, sound cards, and network cards. Figure 2-48 shows how to plug an expansion card into an expansion slot.

**FIGURE 2-48**

An expansion card simply slides into an expansion slot and is secured with a small screw. Before you open the case, make sure you unplug the computer and ground yourself—that's technical jargon for releasing static electricity by using a special grounding wristband or by touching both hands to a metal object.

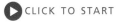 CLICK TO START

Expansion slots are classified as ISA, PCI, or AGP:

- **ISA** (Industry Standard Architecture) slots are an old technology, used today only for some modems and other relatively slow devices. Many new computers have few or no ISA slots.

- **PCI** (Peripheral Component Interconnect) slots offer fast transfer speeds and a 32-bit or 64-bit data bus. These slots typically house a graphics card, sound card, video capture card, modem, or network interface card. PCI Express is a high speed version used by today's fastest graphics cards.

- **AGP** (Accelerated Graphics Port) slots provide a high-speed data pathway primarily used for graphics cards.

**FIGURE 2-49**

Expansion Ports

**Do notebook computers contain expansion slots?** Most notebook computers are equipped with several USB ports and a special type of external slot called a **PC slot** or PCMCIA slot (Personal Computer Memory Card International Association). Typically, a notebook computer has only one of these slots, but the slot can hold more than one **PC card** (also called PCMCIA expansion cards or Card Bus cards). Notebook owners are advised to use the USB ports and PC slot, rather than opening the notebook's system unit.

**What is an expansion port?** An **expansion port** is any connector that passes data in and out of a computer or peripheral device. It is similar to an electrical outlet because you can plug things in to make a connection.

An expansion port is often housed on an expansion card so that it is accessible through an opening in the back of the computer's system unit. A port might also be built into the system unit case of a desktop or notebook computer. The built-in ports supplied with a computer usually include a mouse port, keyboard port, serial port, and USB ports. Figure 2-49 illustrates the major types of expansion ports on a typical desktop computer.

**How do I know which cable to use?** With so many types of ports, you can expect a corresponding variety of cables. If a cable is supplied with a peripheral device, you can usually figure out where to plug it in by matching the shape of the cable connector to the port. Some manufacturers also color code ports and plugs to make them easy to match. Figure 2-50 on the next page provides information about the computer cables you're most likely to encounter.

**Why do some peripheral devices include a disk or CD?** Some devices require software to establish communication with your computer. The directions supplied with your peripheral device include instructions on how to install the software. Typically, you use the software disk or CD one time to get everything set up, and then you can put the disk away in a safe place. You'll learn more about this software, called a device driver, in the next chapter.

Long-time computer techies probably remember the days when installing a peripheral device meant messing around with little electronic components called dip switches and a host of complex software settings called IRQs. Fortunately, today's PCs include a feature called **Plug and Play** (PnP) that automatically takes care of these technical details. Although it took several years to refine Plug and Play technology, it works quite well for just about every popular peripheral device. If PnP doesn't work, your computer simply won't recognize the device and won't be able to exchange data with it. If you've got a stubborn peripheral device, check the manufacturer's Web site for a device driver update, or call the manufacturer's technical support department.

**What's the most important thing to remember about installing peripherals?** Installing a peripheral device is not difficult when you remember that it's all about using the expansion bus to make a connection between the system board and a peripheral device. The cable you use must match the peripheral device and a port on the computer. If the right type of port is not available, you might have to add an expansion card. Once the connection is made, PnP should recognize the new device. If not, you'll probably have to install driver software and perhaps seek technical assistance.

**FIGURE 2-50**

Common Personal Computer Cables and Connectors

| | CONNECTOR | DESCRIPTION | DEVICES |
|---|---|---|---|
| | USB | Connects to USB port, which sends data over a single data line and can support up to 127 devices. USB-1 carries data at speeds up to 12,000 Kbps; USB-2, at 480,000 Kbps. | Modem, keyboard, joystick, scanner, mouse, external hard disk drive, MP3 player, digital camera |
| | IEEE 1394 | Connects to the FireWire port, which sends data at 400,000 Kbps. | Video camera, DVD player |
| | VGA HDB-15 | Connects to the video port. | Monitor |

# QuickCheck

**SECTION D**

1. Computer [_____] devices include mice, trackpads, trackballs, and joysticks.

2. In the context of computer displays, [_____] rate refers to the speed at which the screen image is repainted.

3. The number of dots that form an image on a monitor or printer is referred to as [_____].

4. A printer with [_____] printing capability can print on both sides of the paper.

5. AGP, PCI, and ISA are types of expansion [_____].

6. A(n) [_____] port provides one of the fastest, simplest ways to connect peripherals.

▶ CHECK ANSWERS

# Hardware Security

**THE INFORMATION** that computers contain and process has become practically priceless to every PC owner. Just about everyone depends on a computer for information and communication. A stolen computer, even if it's low-priced, can be a huge loss if it holds valuable financial data or months of research. A broken PC can easily cost hundreds of dollars to repair, especially if the data is damaged and needs to be recovered. For trouble-free computer use, is important to secure and regularly maintain your computer equipment, just as you would with your home and car.

## ANTI-THEFT DEVICES

**What can I do to prevent my computer from being stolen?** Computers have rapidly become prime targets for thieves. Many security breaches have been traced to stolen computers. The portability of notebook computers makes them particularly easy for a thief to grab, just as a wallet or a handbag would be. Figure 2-51 contains important tips for protecting your notebook computer from theft.

**FIGURE 2-51**

Tips for Preventing Computer Theft

- Never leave your notebook computer unattended, especially when you are in a coffee shop, the library, or at the airport.

- If you have to leave your notebook computer in your car, never leave it in plain view. Lock it up in the trunk or cover it up.

- Carry your notebook computer in an inconspicuous carrying case.

- Record your notebook computer's make, model, and serial number and store them away from the computer. Most notebook computers cannot be recovered because the police do not have this tracking information.

- Consider securing your notebook computer with an anti-theft device.

**How do computer anti-theft devices work?** Several computer anti-theft devices are available. Most can be used for both desktops and notebook computers.

The Kensington Security Slot is a security mechanism that's factory-installed on many personal computers. It docks with a special lock that can be attached to a cable. The cable can be fastened to a desk to prevent theft as shown in Figure 2-52.

**FIGURE 2-52**

The Kensington Security Slot is an industry standard way to secure a computer to a desk.

Notebook computers can also be fastened with tie-down brackets or stored in a specially designed locker that can be installed under a desk or in a closet. Another option for securing notebook computers is a security plate that's affixed to the underside of the computer or to a desk (Figure 2-53).

Computer motion sensor alarms, similar to those for automobiles, can be installed on desktop or notebook computers and armed so that any movement triggers audible alarm sounds or recorded verbal warnings.

In addition to locks designed to secure a computer's system unit, there are also several types of storage device locks designed to prevent unauthorized access to your computer's floppy, CD, and DVD drives.

**If my computer is stolen can authorities recover it?** Your chances of recovering a stolen computer improve if you have taken some steps in advance, such as recording the computer's serial number, affixing a tracking label, or installing tracking software.

STOP (Security Tracking of Office Property) plates leave an indelible tattoo on your computer equipment. It takes 800 pounds of force to remove a plate, which contains a unique ID number, a warning message, and an 800 number to report a stolen computer. Each plate ID number is registered in the international STOP database, thereby making it virtually impossible for a thief to resell a computer that has a STOP label.

Tracking and recovery software, such as Computrace, StealthSignal, and CyberAngel secretly sends a message as soon as a thief uses a stolen computer to log onto the Internet. This message contains the computer's exact location and is directed to a tracking or monitoring center. Some tracking software products can be configured to delete the data on the stolen computer.

## SURGE PROTECTION AND BATTERY BACKUP

**What is a power surge?** To ensure that your computer stays in good running condition, it is essential that you protect it from the unavoidable power surges or spikes that endanger many electrical appliances and equipment. A **power surge** is a sudden increase or spike in electrical energy, affecting the current that flows to electrical outlets. Computers and peripheral devices require a stable current and are particularly sensitive to these sudden bursts of electrical energy. The overload can slowly damage your computer's circuit boards and other electrical components. Over time, even small, repeated power surges can shorten your PC's life.

Power surges can originate from a number of sources: downed power lines, power grid switching by the electric company, faulty wiring, and large appliances like refrigerators and air conditioners powering on and off. However, one of the most powerful sources is lightning. Lightning or electrical storms cause extremely large power surges and consequently pose a real threat to your computer equipment.

**How can I protect my computer from power surges?** You can protect your computer equipment from power surges by plugging it into a surge strip instead of directly into a wall outlet. For added protection during thunderstorms, shut down your computer, turn off all your peripheral devices, and unplug the surge strip and all computer-related cables from wall outlets, including the telephone line for your modem.

**What is a surge strip and how does one work?** A **surge strip** (also called a surge suppressor or surge protector) is a device that contains electrical outlets protected by circuitry that blocks surges and spikes. Some surge strips also have sockets for modem connections that prevent surges from traveling down telephone or cable lines and into your computer (Figure 2-54).

A surge strip monitors the electrical current that passes from the outlet to all the devices plugged into the strip. When it detects a surge or spike, it redirects the extra current to a grounded circuit. A big power surge can burn out a surge strip while it tries to protect your equipment. Some surge strips have an indicator light that warns you if the surge strip is no longer functioning properly. Check the manufacturer's documentation to determine if you should discard the depleted strip, reset it, or install a new fuse.

**What is a UPS?** A **UPS** (uninterruptible power supply) is a device that not only provides surge protection, but also furnishes your computer with battery backup power during a power outage. If your computer is connected to a UPS when a power outage occurs, you can save what you're doing and shut down your PC properly. Depending on your system's configuration, a UPS with a high-performance battery might give you enough backup power to keep your computer up and running for several hours, allowing you to continue to work during the entire blackout or brownout.

Most UPSs have two types of sockets: one type offers battery backup plus surge protection, and the other offers only surge protection. The surge-only sockets are for printers, which use so much power that they can quickly drain the battery. Manufacturers advise against the use of battery backup for printers because it's not economical. Some UPS units also provide fax and cable modem protection. American Power Conversion, the largest manufacturer of small UPSs, helps you choose a UPS based on your system's configuration and the amount of run time you want during a power failure. Figure 2-55 illustrates the major components of a UPS.

**FIGURE 2-54**

A surge strip offers outlets for power plugs and might also provide protection for modem cables.

**FIGURE 2-55**

An uninterruptible power supply (UPS) not only protects electronic equipment from power surges, it also provides battery power during power outages.

Surge-only outlets

Surge and battery backup outlets

2

## BASIC MAINTENANCE

**Can I prevent hardware problems?** Computer component failures can be caused by manufacturing defects and other circumstances beyond your control. You can, however, undertake some preventive maintenance that can add years to the life of your computer equipment, just as regular tune-ups lengthen the life of your car. Preventive maintenance can save you more than the cost of repairs; you also save the time you would've lost while tracking down problems and arranging for repairs. Regular cleaning of your PC's components and peripheral devices helps to keep your system in good condition.

**How do I clean the keyboard?** Always shut down your PC before you clean your keyboard so that you don't inadvertently type in commands that you don't want your system to do. Also, disconnect your keyboard and remember where the connection is. Flip the keyboard over and shake it gently to get rid of any small pieces of dirt between the keys. A can of compressed air is effective for blowing off the dust and dislodging larger debris. A vacuum cleaner can pop off and suck away the keys on your keyboard, so be very careful if you use one to clean your keyboard.

You can use cotton swabs just slightly moistened with a mild cleaning fluid to clean the sides of keys. Wipe the tops of the keys with a soft cloth, again slightly dampened with a mild cleaning solution. Allow your keyboard to dry before you reconnect it to your PC. Avoid spills into your keyboard by not setting your drinks too close to it. A flexible clear plastic keyboard cover can also prevent damage from spills and sticky fingers. Figure 2-56 provides more information on cleaning your computer keyboard.

**FIGURE 2-56**

Carefully use a Q-tip and a can of compressed air or a vacuum cleaner to remove dust and debris from your keyboard.

▶ CLICK TO START

**How do I get dust and fingerprints off my computer screen?** Dust and fingerprint smudges can easily accumulate on your computer screen and make it quite difficult to read. You should clean your screen on a regular basis, at least weekly. It's always best to turn off your monitor before you clean because a blank screen will reveal all the smudges, dust, and dirt.

You can safely clean CRT screens with a household glass cleaner because they are made of glass. Spray the cleaner on a lint-free, soft cloth, but never directly on the screen. The dripping liquid can seep through your monitor and damage the inside circuits.

Because LCD screens are not made of glass, they are even more delicate than CRTs. It is safest to use commercial LCD cleaners. Again, do not spray directly on the panel. Dampen your lint-free, soft cloth with the cleaner. If you choose to purchase lint-free wipes, make sure they are non-abrasive. Some computer equipment manufacturers recommend the microfiber cloths used for wiping eyeglasses.

**Should I be concerned about my computer's operating temperature?** High-performance processors, hard drives, graphics cards, and several other computer components generate a lot of heat. Overheating can lead to computer breakdown because it can wear out internal components and chips.

Most desktop computers have a fan mounted on the power supply that runs continuously to maintain the proper temperature inside of the system unit. Additional cooling fans might also be used to cool the microprocessor or graphics card. Notebook computers also have cooling fans, but the fans come on only after the processor reaches a certain temperature (Figure 2-57).

**FIGURE 2-57**

Fans that cool your computer vent outside the case. Keep the area around your computer clear for good air circulation.

It is important to be aware of the ventilation around your computer system and ensure that the fans are able to draw air from the room and blow it across the inside components. If your computer is in an enclosed space, such as a cabinet, you might need to cut out a hole at the back to give your PC some room to "breathe." You should also be aware of the temperature in the room in which your computer resides. Several vendors sell temperature monitors and extra cooling fans if you think your equipment is overheating.

Dust particles, dirt, and even your pet's hair can collect on and around the cooling fans and impede their performance. You should regularly use a can of compressed air or a vacuum cleaner hose to clean out debris from the vents and fans. You should, however, exercise extreme caution when you clean out your computer's system case. First, make sure that you've turned off your PC, monitor, and all other related devices. Stay a couple of inches away from all components as you dust, especially if you're using a vacuum cleaner hose. Do not touch the system board, and make sure not to knock any cables loose.

Computer monitors also heat up quickly. They have top and rear vents for releasing heat, and you should keep them clear of dust, dirt, and other obstacles. Do not put papers, books, or other items on top of a monitor.

**Are there any other components that need TLC?** To avoid read or write errors, you also want your CD, DVD, and floppy drives to function properly. Retailers provide cleaning kits for many types of storage devices and media. Also examine your CDs and DVDs for scratches and fingerprints. Clean them with a soft cloth slightly dampened with water. If the smudges don't come off, a little isopropyl alcohol might help.

If you work with a mechanical mouse, you should clean it periodically. Unplug the mouse, remove the bottom cover and the ball inside it, and then use a cotton swab to clean out the dirt that has accumulated around the rollers. If you own a wireless mouse, you'll have to change the battery at least every six months.

**What is a good computer maintenance routine?** Aside from cleaning your computer equipment on a regular basis, you should do the preventive maintenance tasks listed in Figure 2-58. You'll learn how to do these tasks in later chapters.

**FIGURE 2-58**

Tips for Regular Computer Maintenance

- Back up your files regularly, particularly those that are most important to you. You might want to perform daily incremental backups of critical data and monthly backups of all your files. You should also test your backup procedures periodically.
- Run utilities that ensure peak performance for your hard disk drive. In Windows, these utilities include Disk Cleanup and Disk Defragmenter. It's best to do this maintenance on a weekly basis.
- Delete your browser's history and cache files on a monthly basis in order to free up space for your temporary files. The free space results in faster downloads from the Internet.
- Apply the latest operating system, driver, and security updates.
- Scan your computer for viruses and spyware once a week.
- Keep antivirus and spyware definitions updated.

## TROUBLESHOOTING AND REPAIR

**How can I tell if something is wrong with my computer?** There are several telltale signs that your computer is in trouble. The most obvious one is your PC's failure to power up. A loud beep at start-up time can also indicate a problem. If your computer's screen remains blank or error messages appear, you might have a hardware problem.

Hardware problems can also show up as unexpected restarts at random intervals, or as a peripheral device that stops working. Some problems are intermittent and might seem to be resolved only to come back when they are least convenient to deal with.

Many seasoned users have encountered the **blue screen of death** (also called BSoD), that suddenly replaces the usual graphical screen display with an enigmatic error message written in white text against a bright blue background. The blue screen of death indicates that the operating system has encountered an error from which it cannot recover, and the computer no longer accepts any commands.

Hardware problems can quickly escalate and some can eventually make your computer non-functional or make your data impossible to access. Any computer problem that prevents you from working as usual should be taken seriously. A little time spent troubleshooting can save you lots of annoyance down the road.

**How do I troubleshoot a hardware problem?** You might be able to solve many hardware problems by simply following the basic guidelines for troubleshooting listed in Figure 2-59.

FIGURE 2-59

Troubleshooting Tips

- Stay calm and don't jump to any conclusions until you've thought everything through.

- Write down all error messages and any other information that goes with them.

- Make sure all components are plugged in and that there are no loose cables. For example, if your monitor's cable is loose, the indicator light will be off and your screen will be blank.

- If you can, try to duplicate the problem by going through the same steps that led you to it.

- Look for troubleshooting and repair tips in your user's manual, your vendor's Web site, or even through a search engine. If you search the Internet by typing in the error message number or keywords in the error message, you might discover that at least one person has already found a solution to your problem.

- Run your spyware and antivirus software. Lurking viruses, worms, Trojan Horses, and spyware (discussed in the next chapter), can cause strange and unexplainable occurrences in your computer system. For example, spyware can cause your computer to keep displaying a pop-up ad no matter how you try to close it.

- A simple reboot of your computer might clear up the problem. Windows always requires a reboot when it displays the blue screen of death on your screen. However, a more serious problem underlying a BSoD will not be resolved with a reboot. To reboot a PC, hold down the Ctrl, Alt, and Del keys at the same time. When the Task Manager window appears, hold down the Ctrl, Alt, and Del keys once again.

Troubleshooting and diagnostic tools can help you find the source of a problem and fix it. For example, Windows offers interactive troubleshooting tools formatted as a series of simple questions, answers, and recommendations. You might have to borrow a computer to run these tools if your computer is totally out of commission. Figure 2-60 illustrates a simple troubleshooting session.

FIGURE 2-60

To access a Windows troubleshooter, use the Start menu to select Help and Support, then look for the link to Troubleshooting or Fixing a Problem.

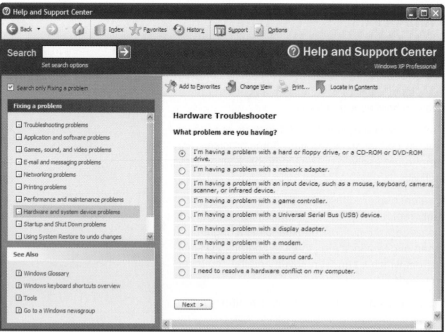

**What is Safe Mode?** If Windows encounters a critical problem that is keeping it from operating normally, it starts up in Safe Mode the next time you reboot your computer. **Safe Mode** is a limited version of Windows that allows you to use your mouse, monitor, and keyboard, but no other peripheral devices (Figure 2-61). While in Safe Mode you can use Control Panel's Add/Remove Programs to uninstall recently added programs or hardware that might be interfering with the operation of other components.

**What if I can't solve the problem myself?** If you are unable to fix a hardware problem after following the basic guidelines for troubleshooting, get ready to call the technical support center for the device or component that is malfunctioning. You can also consider asking for help from a knowledgeable person or from computer repair professionals like the Geek Squad. Make sure you have all the data they might need, such as warranty information, purchase date, serial number, brand, model, and operating system. You will also have to provide the error message and all information that came with it. You might also have to describe the steps that led you to the problem.

**FIGURE 2-61**

To enter Safe Mode, you can press the F8 function key as your PC boots.

However you resolve the problem, write down the solution. You never know when you might need it again!

# QuickCheck

1. The Kensington Security [_____] is an industry standard security mechanism that's factory-installed on many personal computers.

2. A power [_____] is a sudden increase or spike in electrical energy, affecting the current that flows to electrical outlets.

3. Most UPSs have two types of sockets: one type offers [_____] backup plus surge protection, and the other offers only surge protection.

4. Many seasoned users have encountered the blue screen of [_____] that suddenly replaces the usual graphical screen display with an enigmatic error message written in white text against a bright blue background.

5. [_____] Mode is a stripped down version of Windows, designed for troubleshooting.

CHECK ANSWERS

# Where Does All the e-Garbage Go?

**MANUFACTURING** an average desktop computer with a CRT monitor requires 48 pounds of chemicals and 529 pounds of fossil fuels, according to a United Nations study. That makes producing a computer more materials-intensive than manufacturing an automobile. Extending the lifespan of your computer might be environmentally friendly, but keeping up with technology probably means replacing your computer every few years.

When it is time to replace your computer, is there a way to do it in an environmentally safe way? The National Recycling Coalition estimates that 500 million computers will become obsolete by 2007. In the United States alone, almost eight printer cartridges are discarded every second. A recycling company called GreenDisk estimates that about 1 billion floppy disks, CDs, and DVDs end up in landfills every year.

U.S. landfills already hold more than 2 million tons of computer and electronic parts, which contain toxic substances such as lead, cadmium, and mercury. A computer monitor, for example, can contain up to eight pounds of lead. An Environmental Protection Agency (EPA) report sums up the situation: "In this world of rapidly changing technology, disposal of computers and other electronic equipment has created a new and growing waste stream."

Many computers end up in landfills because their owners are unaware of potential environmental hazards and simply toss them in the garbage. In addition, PC owners typically are not given information on options for disposing of their old machines. Instead of throwing away your old computer, you might be able to sell it; donate it to a local school, church, or community program; have it hauled away by a professional recycling firm; or send it back to the manufacturer. Some artists even accept old computers and use parts in jewelry and craft projects.

With the growing popularity of Internet auctions and dedicated computer reclamation sites, you might be able to get some cash for your old computer. At Web sites such as the Computer Recycle Center at *www.recycles.com*, you can post an ad for your old stuff. Off the Web, you can find several businesses, such as Computer Renaissance, that refurbish old computers and sell them in retail stores.

*Recycled Computer Creations by Gregory Steele, Marquette, MI*

Donating your old computer to a local organization doesn't actually eliminate the disposal problem, but it does delay it. Unfortunately, finding a new home for an old computer is not always easy. Most schools and community organizations have few resources for repairing broken equipment, so if your old computer is not in good working order, it could be more of a burden than a gift. In addition, your computer might be too old to be compatible with the other computers in an organization. It helps if you can donate software along with your old computer. To ensure a legal transfer, include the software distribution disks, manuals, and license agreement. And remember, once you donate the software, you cannot legally use it on your new computer unless it is freeware or shareware.

If you cannot find an organization to accept your computer donation, look in your local Yellow Pages or on the Internet for an electronics recycling firm, which will haul away your computer and recycle any usable materials.

Despite private sector options for selling, donating, or recycling old computers, many governments are worried that these voluntary efforts will not be enough to prevent massive dumping of an ever-growing population of obsolete computers.

Many states have taken legislative action to curtail the rampant disposal of obsolete computer equipment. For example, Massachusetts has banned televisions and computer monitors from its landfills.

In Maine it is illegal to dispose of computers or monitors—they have to be recycled in an environmentally sound way. But recycling can be costly—equipment needs to be collected, sorted, disassembled, and shipped to processing or disposal plants.

Basic to the issue of reducing electronic waste is the question of "Who pays?" Should it be the taxpayer, the individual consumer, the retailer, or the computer manufacturer?

A few years ago, Californians were faced with the prospect of tax hikes to deal with alarming increases in electronic waste, but activists questioned if tax increases were fair to individual taxpayers who generate very little electronic waste. Now, consumers buying computers in California have to pay a recycling fee at the time of purchase.

Other lawmakers propose to make manufacturers responsible for recycling costs and logistics. "Extended producer responsibility" refers to the idea of holding manufacturers responsible for the environmental effects of their products through the entire product life cycle, which includes taking them back, recycling them, or disposing of them. Maryland requires computer manufacturers to ante up an annual fee for electronic waste disposal.

Proposed legislation in Europe would require manufacturers to accept returns of their old equipment free of charge and take appropriate steps to recycle it. The economics of a mandatory take-back program are likely to increase product costs because manufacturers would typically pass on recycling costs to consumers.

Some manufacturers currently participate in voluntary producer responsibility programs. Consumers who buy Hewlett-Packard toner cartridges are provided with a postage-paid shipping box so they can return the cartridges for recycling. Using IBM's PC Recycling Service, consumers can ship any make of computer, including system units, monitors, printers, and optional attachments, to a recycling center for $29.99.

The EPA (Environmental Protection Agency) advocates a national plan in which consumers, retailers, and manufacturers can cooperate to reduce electronic waste. Its Plug-in to eCycling Web site makes the point that "No national infrastructure exists for collecting, reusing, and recycling electronics." With laws that differ from state to state, consumers are often confused about how to dispose of their unwanted computers, monitors, CDs, and ink cartridges.

U.S. Legislators are trying to hammer out the details of an e-waste bill that provides tax incentives for companies that recycle and requires consumers to recycle computers, monitors, and other electronic devices. The United States is not alone in its efforts. Lawmakers in the European Union, Great Britain, Australia, China, and Japan are also addressing ways to manage the electronic waste stream and keep our planet green.

**INFOWEBLINKS**

You'll find much more information about how you can recycle an old computer by connecting to the **Computer Recycling InfoWeb.**

**W** CLICK TO CONNECT
www.course.com/np/concepts10/ch02

## What Do You Think?

ISSUE

1. Have you ever thrown away an old computer or other electronic device? ○ Yes  ○ No  ○ Not sure

2. Are you aware of any options for recycling electronic equipment in your local area? ○ Yes  ○ No  ○ Not sure

3. Would it be fair for consumers to pay a recycling tax on any electronic equipment that they purchase? ○ Yes  ○ No  ○ Not sure

 SAVE RESPONSES

## COMPUTERS IN CONTEXT

# Military

**IN ENGINES OF THE MIND,** Joel Shurkin writes, "If necessity is the mother of invention, then war can be said to be its grandmother." The military, an early pioneer in computer and communication technologies, continues to be the driving force behind technologies that have revolutionized everyday life. During World War II, the U.S. military initiated a classified research program, called Project PX, to develop an electronic device to calculate artillery firing tables; by hand, each table required weeks of grueling calculations. Project PX produced ENIAC (Electrical Numerical Integrator And Calculator), one of the first general-purpose electronic computers. When ENIAC was completed in 1946, the war was over, but ENIAC's versatile architecture could be used for other calculations, such as designing hydrogen bombs, predicting weather, and engineering wind tunnels. ENIAC's technology evolved into the computers used today.

After Project PX, the military continued to support computer research. Like most large corporations, the military used mainframe computers to maintain personnel, inventory, supply, and facilities records. This data was distributed to terminals at other locations through rudimentary networks. Because all data communication flowed through the mainframe, a single point of failure for the entire system was a possible risk. A malfunction or an enemy "hit" could disrupt command and control, sending the military into chaos. Therefore, the armed forces created the Advanced Research Projects Agency (ARPA) to design a distributed communications system that could continue operating without a centralized computer. The result was ARPANET, which paved the way for the data communications system we know today as the Internet. ARPANET was activated in 1967, but the .mil domain that designates U.S. military Web sites was not implemented until 1984.

The U.S. Department of Defense (DoD) currently maintains two data communications networks: SIPRNet, a classified (secret-level) network, and NIPRNet, which provides unclassified services. The DoD's public Web site, called DefenseLINK, provides official information about defense policies, organizations, budgets, and operations.

Computers and communications technology have also become an integral part of high-tech military operations. U.S. Apache helicopters, for example, are equipped with computer-based Target Acquisition Designation Sights, laser range finder/designators, and Pilot Night Vision Sensors. These arcade-style controls are also used by tank drivers in the U.S. Army's 4th Infantry Division. Each vehicle in this "Digitized Division" is equipped with a Force 21 Battle Command Brigade and Below system, which works like a battlefield Internet to transmit data on the location of friendly and enemy forces from one vehicle to another using wireless communication.

Much like a video game, the Force 21 touch screen shows friendly troops in blue, and a global positioning satellite (GPS) system updates their positions automatically. Enemy troops spotted by helicopters are shown as red icons. To get information on any friendly or enemy vehicle, a soldier can simply touch one of these blue or red icons. To send text messages—much like cell phone and computer instant messaging—a soldier touches the Message button. The built-in GPS system provides location and route information, much like sophisticated mapping programs in luxury cars.

Force 21 computers are installed in shock-resistant cases and equipped with a cooling system that eliminates the need for a fan, which might pull in dust, dirt, or water. The computers run Sun Microsystem's Solaris operating system because it is less vulnerable to viruses and intrusion attacks than Microsoft Windows. To prevent enemy capture and use, Force 21 computers have a self-destruct mechanism that can be triggered remotely.

In addition to pilots and tank drivers, battlefield soldiers will soon be equipped with "wearable" computer and communications equipment. The $2 billion Land Warrior program will provide high-tech "wearable" weaponry, such as the Army's Integrated Helmet Assembly Subsystem. IHAS is a helmet-mounted display screen that a soldier wears over the dominant eye to view graphical data, digital maps, thermal images, intelligence information, and troop locations. The display is updated by a wireless network connection every 30 seconds. Land warrior gear also includes a weapon-mounted video camera, so that soldiers can view and fire around corners and acquire targets in darkness.

The military has also conducted research in computer simulations that are similar to civilian computer games. "Live" military training is dangerous—weapons are deadly and equipment costs millions of dollars. With computer simulations, however, troops can train in a true-to-life environment without physical harm or equipment damage. Flying an F-16 fighter, for example, costs about $5,000 an hour, but flying an F-16 simulator costs only $500 per hour. The military uses simulators to teach Air Force pilots to fly fighter jets, Navy submarine officers to navigate in harbors, and Marine infantry squads to handle urban combat. Military trainers agree that widespread use of computer games helps prepare troops to adapt quickly to simulations.

A 24-year-old preflight student at Pensacola Naval Air Station modified the Microsoft Flight Simulator game to re-create a T-34C Turbo Mentor plane's con-

trols. After logging 50 hours on the simulator, the student performed so well on a real plane that the Navy used his simulation to train other pilots. Today, a growing cadre of computer and communications specialists are needed to create and maintain increasingly complex military systems.

An army once depended on its infantry, but today's high-tech army depends equally on its database designers, computer programmers, and network specialists. Even previously low-tech military jobs, such as mechanics and dietitians, require some computer expertise. Happily, new recruits are finding military computer systems easy to learn, based on their knowledge of civilian technologies, such as the Internet and computer games.

Although most citizens agree that an adequate national defense is necessary, the cost of defense-related equipment, personnel, and research remains controversial. In 1961, President Dwight Eisenhower warned "We must guard against the acquisition of unwarranted influence, whether sought or unsought, by the military-industrial complex." Many socially motivated citizens and pacifists protested diverting tax dollars from social and economic programs to the military-industrial complex Eisenhower cautioned against. In retrospect, however, military funding contributed to many technologies we depend on today. For example, detractors tried to convince the government that Project PX was doomed to failure, but without ENIAC research, computers might not exist today. Skeptics saw no future for the fruits of ARPANET research, but it led to the Internet, which has changed our lives significantly.

**INFOWEBLINKS**

You'll find lots more information related to this Computers in Context topic at the **Computers and the Military InfoWeb**.

www.course.com/np/concepts10/ch02

# New Perspectives Labs

## On the BookOnCD

To access the New Perspectives labs for Chapter 2, start the BookOnCD, BookOnFlashDrive, or other NP10 BookOn product and then click the icon next to the lab title below.

### ▶ BENCHMARKING

#### IN THIS LAB YOU'LL LEARN:

- Which computer performance factors can be measured by benchmark tests

- How to run a test that identifies a computer's processor type, RAM capacity, and graphics card type

- How to run benchmarking software that analyzes a computer's processor speed and graphics processing speed

- How to interpret the results of a benchmark test

- How to compare the results from benchmark tests that were performed on different system configurations

- When benchmark tests might not provide accurate information on computer performance

#### LAB ASSIGNMENTS

1. Start the interactive part of the lab. Make sure you've enabled Tracking if you want to save your QuickCheck results. Perform each lab step as directed, and answer all the lab QuickCheck questions. When you exit the lab, your answers are automatically graded and your results are displayed.

2. If Microsoft Word is available, use the System Info button to analyze the computer you typically use. Provide the results of the analysis along with a brief description of the computer you tested and its location (at home, at work, in a computer lab, and so on).

### PROCESSOR BENCHMARKS

| Processor | Quake III Arena | PCMark04 |
|-----------|-----------------|----------|
| "Supernova EE" | 548 | 5198 |
| "Pulsar FX" | 551 | 5020 |

3. From the Processor Benchmarks table above, which fictional processor appears to be faster at graphics processing? Which processor appears to be better at overall processing tasks?

4. Explain why you might perform a benchmark test on your own computer, but get different results from those stated in a computer magazine, which tested the same computer with the same benchmark test.

5. Use a search engine on the Web to find benchmark ratings for one of Intel's Core Duo processors and one of AMD's Athlon 64 Dual-Core processors. Are the benchmarks different? What would account for the benchmark results?

# Key Terms

Make sure you understand all the boldfaced key terms presented in this chapter. If you're using the NP10 BookOnCD, BookOnFlashDrive, or other NP10 BookOn product, you can use this list of terms as an interactive study activity. First, try to define a term in your own words, and then click the term to compare your definition with the definition presented in the chapter.

Access time, 77

AGP, 96

Benchmarks, 69

Blue screen of death, 103

Blu-ray DVD, 81

Cache, 68

Capacitors, 72

Card reader, 84

CD drive, 81

CD, 81

CD-DA, 82

CD-R, 83

CD-ROM, 83

CD-RW, 83

CISC, 69

Color depth, 91

CRT, 90

Data bus, 95

Data transfer rate, 77

Desktop computer, 58

Dot matrix printer, 92

Dot pitch, 90

Double layer DVD, 81

Drive bays, 86

Dual core processor, 69

Duplex printer, 93

Duty cycle, 93

DVD drive, 81

DVD, 81

DVD+R, 83

DVD+RW, 83

DVD-R, 83

DVD-ROM, 83

DVD-RW, 83

DVD-Video, 82

EEPROM, 74

Expansion bus, 95

Expansion card, 95

Expansion port, 96

Expansion slot, 95

Floppy disk, 80

Form factor, 58

Front side bus, 68

Gigahertz, 67

Graphics card, 91

Graphics processing unit, 91

Hard disk controller, 79

Hard disk drive, 78

Hard disk platter, 78

HD-DVD, 81

Head crash, 80

Home computer system, 60

Hyper-Threading Technology, 69

HyperTransport, 68

Ink jet printer, 92

ISA, 96

Joystick, 89

Lands, 81

Laser printer, 92

LCD, 90

Level 1 cache, 68

Level 2 cache, 68

Linux platform, 64

Mac platform, 64

Magnetic storage, 78

Media Center PC, 60

Megahertz, 67

Microprocessor clock, 67

Mod, 65

Mouse, 88

Nanosecond, 73

Non-volatile, 84

Notebook computer, 59

Optical storage, 81

Overclocking, 70

Parallel processing, 69

PC card, 96

PC platform, 64

PCI, 96

PC slot, 96

peripheral device, 56

Pipelining, 69

Pits, 81

Pixels, 90

Plasma screen, 90

Plug and Play, 96

Pointing device, 88

Pointing stick, 89

Portable computer, 59

PostScript, 94

Power surge, 99

Printer Control Language, 94

RAM, 71

Random access, 77

Read-only technology, 82

Read-write head, 78

Recordable technology, 82

Refresh rate, 90

Resolution, 91

Rewritable technology, 82

RISC, 69

ROM BIOS, 74

ROM, 73

Safe Mode, 105

Sequential access, 77

Serial processing, 69

Solid state storage, 84

Storage density, 77

Storage device, 76

Storage medium, 76

Surge strip, 100

SVGA, 91

SXGA, 91

System unit, 57

Tablet computer, 59

Tape drive, 80

Touch screen, 89

Trackball, 89

Trackpad, 89

U3 drive, 85

Ultra-mobile PC, 59

UPS, 100

USB flash drive, 85

USB, 94

UXGA, 91

VGA, 91

Viewable image size, 90

Viewing angle width, 90

Virtual memory, 72

Volatile, 72

Word size, 68

WUXGA, 91

XGA, 91

# Interactive Summary

To review important concepts from this chapter, fill in the blanks to best complete each sentence. When using the NP10 BookOnCD or other BookOn product, click the Check Answers buttons to automatically score your answers.

**SECTION A:** The core of a personal computer system include the computer system [_____], display device, keyboard, and mouse. Personal computers come in a variety of [_____] factors. A [_____] computer fits on a desk, runs on power from an electrical wall outlet, and can be housed in a horizontal case or vertical [_____] case. A [_____] computer (also referred to as a mobile computer) is a small, lightweight personal computer with screen, keyboard, storage, and processing components integrated into a single unit that runs on power supplied by an electrical outlet or a battery. Three categories of these computers include notebook computers, [_____] computers, and ultra-mobile PCs. Personal computers are sometimes designated as home, media, small business, or game systems to help consumers select the computer that's right for their needs. Although the Mac platform was not previously [_____] with the PC platform, the situation is changing now that Intel Macs use the same [_____] as PCs. Consumers can sometimes save money by installing upgrades after purchase, however replacing a [_____] is difficult and not recommended. Some computer owners make unauthorized modifications to their computer systems called [_____]. For information on the latest computers, mods, and prices, consumers can check computer magazines and Web sites.

CHECK ANSWERS

**SECTION B:** The microprocessor and memory are two of the most important components in a computer. The microprocessor is an [_____] circuit, which is designed to process data based on a set of instructions. In most of today's personal computers, microprocessor performance is measured by the speed of the microprocessor [_____]. A specification such as 3.2 GHz means that the microprocessor's clock operates at a speed of 3.2 [_____] cycles per second. Other factors affecting overall processing speed include word size, cache size, instruction set complexity, parallel processing, and pipelining. Most personal computers only contain one main microprocessor, but many of today's dual [_____] processors contain the circuitry for two microprocessors. Computers contain various kinds of memory. Random [_____] memory is a special holding area for data, program instructions, and the [_____] system. It stores data on a temporary basis until the processor makes a data request. The speed of RAM circuitry is measured in [_____] or in megahertz (MHz). RAM is different from disk storage because it is [_____], which means that it can hold data only when the computer power is turned on. Computers also contain Read [_____] memory, which is a type of memory that provides a set of "hard-wired" instructions that a computer uses to boot up. A third type of memory, called by its acronym [_____], is a non-volatile chip that contains configuration settings, such as hard disk size and RAM capacity.

CHECK ANSWERS

## SECTION C:

Today's personal computers use a variety of storage technologies. [＿＿＿＿] storage technologies, such as hard disks, floppy disks, and tapes, store data as magnetized particles. A hard disk provides multiple [＿＿＿＿] for data storage that are sealed inside the drive case or cartridge to prevent airborne contaminants from interfering with the read-write heads. Hard disks are less durable than floppy disks, so it is important to make a copy of the data they contain. [＿＿＿＿] storage technologies store data as a series of [＿＿＿＿] and lands on the surface of a CD or DVD. Storage technologies, such as CD-[＿＿＿＿], provide good data storage capacity, but do not allow you to alter the disk's contents. [＿＿＿＿] technology allows you to write data on a CD or DVD, but you cannot delete or change that data. [＿＿＿＿] technology allows you to write and rewrite data on a CD or DVD. [＿＿＿＿] state storage technologies, such as USB flash drives, store data by activating electrons in a microscopic grid of circuitry.

▶ CHECK ANSWERS

## SECTION D:

Most computer systems include a keyboard and some type of [＿＿＿＿] device for basic data [＿＿＿＿]. For output, most computers include a display device. A [＿＿＿＿] produces an image by spraying electrons toward the screen. [＿＿＿＿] technology produces an image by manipulating light within a layer of liquid crystal cells. [＿＿＿＿] screen technology creates an on-screen image by illuminating miniature fluorescent lights arrayed in a panel-like screen. Image quality for a display device is a factor of screen size, dot [＿＿＿＿], viewing angle width, resolution, refresh [＿＿＿＿], and color [＿＿＿＿]. A typical computer display system consists of the display device and a [＿＿＿＿] card. For printed output, most PC owners turn to [＿＿＿＿] jet printers, although [＿＿＿＿] printers are a popular option when low operating costs and high duty cycle are important. A [＿＿＿＿] matrix printer is sometimes used for back-office applications and printing multipart forms. Installing a peripheral device is not difficult when you remember that it uses the [＿＿＿＿] bus to make a connection between the computer and peripheral device. Many of today's peripherals connect to a [＿＿＿＿] port. If the right type of port is not available, you might have to add an [＿＿＿＿] card.

▶ CHECK ANSWERS

## SECTION E:

For trouble-free computer use, is important to secure and regularly [＿＿＿＿] your computer equipment. Anti-theft devices include computer locks and tie-down brackets. Computers can be protected from power surges and [＿＿＿＿] by connecting to a surge strip. An [＿＿＿＿] power supply can also protect against surges, plus it can supply backup power in case of a power outage. Keeping your computer's [＿＿＿＿] vents free of dust can help to keep its operating temperature within operational levels. You can also clean off the screen and shake dirt out of the keyboard. Problems such as the blue screen of [＿＿＿＿] require troubleshooting. Windows offers interactive troubleshooting tools formatted as a series of simple questions, answers, and recommendations. Booting into [＿＿＿＿] Mode can also be a helpful step in the troubleshooting process.

▶ CHECK ANSWERS

# Interactive Situation Questions

Apply what you've learned to some typical computing situations. When using the NP10 BookOnCD, BookOnFlashDrive, or any other NP10 BookOn product, you can type your answers, and then use the Check Answers button to automatically score your responses.

1. Suppose you're reading a computer magazine and you come across the ad pictured to the right. By looking at the specs, you can tell that the microprocessor was manufactured by which company? [_____]

2. The capacity of the hard disk drive in the ad is [_____] GB and the memory capacity is [_____] GB.

3. The computer in the ad appears to have a(n) [_____] controller card for the hard disk drive.

4. You are thinking about upgrading the microprocessor in your three-year-old computer, which has a 2.6 MHz Pentium microprocessor and 512 MB of RAM. Would it be worthwhile to spend $500 to install a 3.8 GHz Pentium processor? Yes or no? [_____]

5. You're in the process of booting up your computer and suddenly the screen contains an assortment of settings for date and time, hard disk drive, and memory capacity. From what you've learned in this chapter, you surmise that these settings are stored in [_____] , and that they are best left unmodified.

6. You're looking for a portable storage device that you can use to transport a few files between your home computer and your school computer lab. The school lab computers have no floppy disk drives, but do have USB ports. You should be able to transport your files using a USB [_____] drive.

7. You want to add a storage device to your computer that reads CD-ROMs, DVD-ROMs, DVD-Videos, and CD-Rs. A DVD/CD-RW will do the job. True or false? [_____]

**SUP-R GAME DESKTOP MODEL EE2007**

- Athlon™ 64 FX-57
- 1 GB 400 MHz SDRAM
- 160 GB UltraATA HD (7200 rpm)
- 16x DVD / 52x36x52x CD-RW Drive
- 3.5" 1.44 MB FDD
- 21" 24 dp monitor
- Dual NVIDIA® GeForce™ 6800 Ultra PCI Express 512MB
- Creative Sound Blaster® Audigy®
- Altec Lansing speakers
- Gigbit Ethernet port
- 3-year limited warranty*
- Windows Vista

**$ 1799**

8. You are a professional graphics designer. A(n) [_____] is likely to give you the best colors from all viewing angles, whereas a(n) [_____] may not show true colors when viewed from some angles.

9. Suppose that you volunteer to produce a large quantity of black-and-white leaflets for a charity organization. It is fortunate that you have access to a(n) [_____] printer with a high duty cycle and low operating costs.

▶ CHECK ANSWERS

# Interactive Practice Tests

Practice tests that consist of 10 multiple-choice, true/false, and fill-in-the-blank questions are available on both the NP10 BookOn products and the NP10 Web site. The questions are selected at random from a large test bank, so each time you take a test, you'll receive a different set of questions. Your tests are scored immediately, and you can print study guides that help you find the correct answers for any questions that you missed.

▶ CLICK TO START

# Study Tips

Study Tips help you to organize and consolidate the information in a unit by making lists, outlines, charts, and sketches. You can use paper and pencil or word processing software to complete most of the Study Tip activities.

2

1. Make sure you can use your own words to correctly answer each of the red focus questions that appear throughout the chapter.

2. Draw a set of quick sketches that show each of the following form factors: desktop tower, desktop horizontal, small form factor desktop, notebook, slate tablet, convertible tablet, UMPC.

3. Create a short consumer brochure that lists 5 characteristics that would help consumers choose among a home, media, game, or small business computer system.

4. Describe the three price-points for personal computers and indicate which price point best fits your computing needs.

5. Explain how Intel Macs are changing the old idea that PCs and Macs are not compatible.

6. Make sure you can list at least three computer upgrades that are easy and explain the upgrade that is most difficult to make.

7. List and describe the factors that affect microprocessor performance.

8. Name two companies that produce microprocessors, and list some of the models that each company produces.

9. List four types of memory and briefly describe how each one works.

10. Describe the advantages and disadvantages of magnetic storage, optical storage, and solid state storage.

11. Create your own diagram to illustrate how the data bus connects RAM, the microprocessor, and peripheral devices.

12. Summarize what you know about how a graphics card can affect a monitor's resolution.

13. Make a table with three columns, labeled Input, Output, and Storage. Page through the chapter and for each device you encounter, place it in one or more of the columns as appropriate.

14. List three ways you can protect your computer from theft.

15. Make a list of ways to keep your computer clean, prevent it from overheating, and protect it from power anomalies.

16. Think about the last time you had a problem with computer hardware or software. Would any of the steps in Figure 2-59 have helped you solve the problem faster? If not, what guidelines would you add to the list in the figure?

17. Fill in the blanks on the concept map below to show the hierarchy of system unit components.

# Concept Map

 CHECK ANSWERS

# Projects

 ## CRITICAL THINKING

Steve Jobs, co-founder of Apple Computers, coined the idea that computers should be consumer appliances like toasters that could be setup easily, used by anyone, and "democratically priced" so they were affordable to everyone. An opposing philosophy, championed by many PC owners, is that computers should be flexible modular systems that can be easily customized, upgraded, and modified by anyone with a moderate degree of technical savvy. Which philosophy do you personally prefer? What do you think is the preference of the majority of computer shoppers? If you were a computer designer, how would you provide your customers with flexibility while making it approachable for non-techies? Incorporate your ideas in a one-page e-mail message or attachment and submit it to your instructor.

 ## GROUP PROJECT

For this project, work in groups of three or four. The group should select a digital device, such as a printer, scanner, digital camera, Web camera, digital video camera, digital music player, video capture card, digitizing tablet, or accelerated 3-D graphics card. If a member of your group owns the device, that's a plus. Create promotional materials for a tradeshow booth featuring your "product." You might include a product photo, list of specifications, and a short instruction manual. If time permits, your instructor might ask your group to present your sales pitch or a demonstration to the rest of the class.

 ## CYBERCLASSROOM

E-mail the other members of your team a technical support question based on a theoretical problem you're having with your computer. They should try to solve the problem using their current expertise and relevant Web sites. At the end of the project, evaluate your team's success rate based on the difficulty of the problems and the efficiency of their troubleshooting.

 ## MULTIMEDIA PROJECT

Search the Web for "modding" and collect ideas for souping up your computer system unit, keyboard, and mouse. Make sure you check out options for clear lexan and metallic cases, along with lighting options. Download photos from the Web and print them out, keeping track of sources. Using ideas from your collection of photos, sketch out plans for your ultimate modded computer. Submit your plan along with a list of the sources you used to get ideas and images.

 ## RESUME BUILDER

Use the Web and other resources to learn about the computers and other technologies used in your career field or profession of interest to you. Develop the information you find into a format similar to the Computers in Context section of each chapter in this textbook. Make sure you select two photos to accompany your narrative and include a list of relevant InfoWebLinks.

 ## GLOBALIZATION

Computer ownership is growing worldwide and providing access to productivity tools and a global communications infrastructure. For this project, look for statistics and graphs showing the increase in computer ownership over time. How does it compare to telephone, television, and radio ownership? Are any aspects of this data unexpected or surprising? Gather your graphs and analysis into a two- to three-page executive summary.

 ## ISSUE

The Issue section of this chapter focused on the potential for discarded computers and other electronic devices to become a significant environmental problem. For this project, write a two- to five-page paper about recycling computers, based on information you gather from the Internet. To begin this project, consult the Computer Recycling InfoWeb (see page 107) and link to the recommended Web pages to get an in-depth overview of the issue. Next, determine the specific aspect of the issue you will present in your paper. You might, for example, decide to focus on toxic materials that end up in landfills or barriers that discourage shipping old computers across national borders. Whatever aspect of the issue you present, make sure you can back up your discussion with facts and references to authoritative articles and Web pages. Follow your professor's instructions for formatting citations and for submitting your paper by e-mail or as a printed document.

 ## COMPUTERS IN CONTEXT

The Computers in Context section of this chapter focused on computer and communication technologies pioneered by the military and then adopted into civilian use. For this project, research one of two topics:

- The use of notebook computers in combat environments and how design innovations for military use might affect the design of your next computer
- Developments in wearable computers and how soldiers and civilians might use them

To begin the project, survey the material in the Computers and the Military InfoWeb (page 109). Use a Web search engine to locate additional material relevant to the topic you've selected. Then write a two- to four-page paper about your findings and include graphics to illustrate your points. Make sure you cite sources for your material. Follow your professor's instructions for formatting and submitting your paper.

# On the Web

## STUDENT EDITION LABS

Work hands-on in structured simulations practicing important skills and concepts

### PERIPHERAL DEVICES

In the Peripheral Devices Student Edition Lab, you will learn the following topics and skills:

- Identifying commonly used peripheral devices, such as display devices, printers, scanners, digital cameras and storage devices

- Adjusting display properties on a monitor and printer settings on a printer

- Identifying storage devices and their appropriate uses

### USING INPUT DEVICES

In the Using Input Devices Student Edition Lab, you will learn the following topics and skills:

- Using a keyboard, including using the function keys and the numeric keypad

- Using a mouse, including double-clicking, right-clicking and dragging objects

- Identifying other input devices, such as touchpads, stylus, microphones, and digital video cameras.

### CHAPTER COURSECAST

Use your computer or iPod to hear a five-minute audio presentation of chapter highlights.

### TEST YOURSELF

Review chapter material by taking these ten-question tests, then send your results to the Universal Gradebook.

### FLASHCARD COURSECAST

Interact with audio flashcards to review key terms from the chapter.

### ONLINE GAMES

Have some fun while refreshing your memory about key concepts that might appear on the next test. You can even send your results to the Universal Gradebook!

### DETAILED OBJECTIVES

Make sure that you've achieved all the objectives for a chapter before it's time for your test!

### AND MORE!

At the NP10 Web site you'll also find TechBuzz, CNET videos, Extra Content, and InfoWebLinks.

# 3

# Computer Software

## CHAPTER CONTENTS

## LEARNING OBJECTIVES

- Describe the way software is categorized and identify the purpose for each major software category
- Explain the key features and uses for word processing, desktop publishing, and Web authoring software
- Describe the major features of spreadsheet software
- Describe the key features of database software
- List the types of software available for graphics, video, music, education and reference, entertainment, and business
- List guidelines that are important for software shoppers
- Describe the rights granted by copyright law, commercial software licenses, shareware licenses, freeware licenses, open source licenses, and public domain software
- Explain how to install and uninstall software, whether it is supplied on CDs or as a Web download
- Differentiate between local, portable, and Web applications
- Describe the purpose of software updates, patches, and service packs
- List and describe the various types of malware mentioned in this chapter
- Explain how antivirus software works

 **PRE-ASSESSMENT QUIZ**

Take the pre-assessment quiz to find out how much you know about the topics in this chapter.

---

**MULTIMEDIA and INTERACTIVE ELEMENTS**
When using the BookOnCD, BookOnFlashDrive, or other NP10 BookOn product, the ▶ icons are clickable to access multimedia resources.

BEFORE YOU READ ON, **TRY IT**

## IS MY SOFTWARE UP TO DATE?

Chapter 3 introduces you to basic concepts about computer software. Before you begin reading, take a glance at the software installed on your home, work, or school computer. Want to know if your software is up to date? You can use the "About" feature of any software package to find its version number and discover if a service pack (SP) has been installed.

1. Start your computer.

2. Click the Start button.

3. Click the All Programs option to display a list of installed software.

4. Point to items in the list that have a ▶ symbol to see a sublist of software programs.

5. As you read through the list of installed software, jot down the names of any that you're not familiar with. When you read the chapter, you might find out what they do.

6. Look for Internet Explorer in the list of programs.

7. Click Internet Explorer to open the program.

8. Click the Help menu, then click About Internet Explorer. A dialog box appears. It contains a version number like 6.0 or 7.0, and it might also contain a service pack number like SP2. You'll learn the significance of version numbers and service packs when you read the chapter.

9. Click the OK button to close the About Internet Explorer window, then click the ⊠ button to close the Internet Explorer program.

10. Explore the About dialog box for other software on your computer. Does it provide more or less information than the Internet Explorer Dialog box?

---

## WEB SITE
Visit the NP10 Web site to access additional resources Ⓦ that accompany this chapter.

# Software Basics

**COMPUTER SOFTWARE** determines the types of tasks a computer can help you accomplish. Some software helps you create documents, while other software helps you block viruses or fine tune your computer's performance. Section A delves into the characteristics of application software, utilities, and device drivers.

## SOFTWARE CATEGORIES

**What is software?** As you learned in Chapter 1, the instructions that tell a computer how to carry out a task are referred to as a computer program. These programs form the software that prepares a computer to do a specific task, such as document production, photo editing, virus protection, file management, or Web browsing.

**How is software categorized?** The two main categories are system software and application software. System software is designed for computer-centric tasks, whereas application software is designed to help people accomplish real-world tasks. For example, you would use system software to diagnose a problem with your hard disk drive or Internet connection, but you would use application software to edit a photo or write a term paper. System software and application software categories can be further divided into subcategories, as shown in Figure 3-1.

> **TERMINOLOGY NOTE**
>
> The term *software* was once used for all non-hardware components of a computer. In this context, software referred to computer programs and to the data the programs used. It could also refer to any data that existed in digital format, such as documents or photos. Using today's terminology, however, the documents and photos you create are usually classified as *data* rather than as software.

**FIGURE 3-1**

Software can be classified into categories.

## APPLICATION SOFTWARE

**Why is it called application software?** When you hear the word *application*, your first reaction might be to envision a financial aid application or a form you fill out to apply for a job, a club membership, or a driver's license. The word application has other meanings, however. One of them is a synonym for the word *use*. A computer certainly has many uses, such as creating documents, crunching numbers, drawing designs, and editing photographs. Each use is considered an application, and the software that provides the computer with instructions for each use is called application software, an application, or simply an *app*.

There are thousands of useful software applications designed for personal use or business use. You'll get a detailed look at some of the most popular application software later in the chapter.

**What is productivity software?** Some types of application software are referred to as productivity software. Many different definitions exist for this popular term. In general, however, **productivity software** can be defined as any type of application software that has the potential to help people do their work more efficiently.

The term might have originated in reference to software tools used by businesses to increase secretarial efficiency at routine office tasks, such as typing, filing, and basic bookkeeping. The applications that are most commonly associated with productivity software include word processing, spreadsheets, schedulers, and database management systems. Graphics software, presentation software, and desktop publishing software are also sometimes classified as productivity applications.

**What is groupware?** Another type of application software, called **groupware**, is designed to help several people collaborate on a single project using local networks or Internet connections. Groupware usually provides the capability to maintain schedules for group members, automatically select meeting times for the group, facilitate communication by e-mail or other channels, distribute documents according to a prearranged schedule or sequence, and allow multiple people to contribute to a single document.

**How do I run application software?** Techniques for running applications depend on your computer's operating system, but on most personal computers, you can double-click a desktop icon or select the application from a menu, as shown in Figure 3-2.

**FIGURE 3-2**

When using a PC, you can usually start application software using the Start menu or a desktop icon.

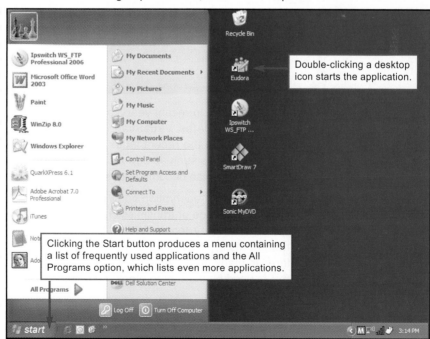

Double-clicking a desktop icon starts the application.

Clicking the Start button produces a menu containing a list of frequently used applications and the All Programs option, which lists even more applications.

► CLICK TO START

## UTILITY SOFTWARE

**What is utility software?** A type of system software called **utility software** is designed to help you monitor and configure settings for your computer system equipment, the operating system, or application software. Examples of utility software include diagnostic and maintenance tools, setup wizards, communications programs, and security software.

Typically, utility software targets a specific task, and includes a much more limited set of features than application software. LIke all system software, utilities focus on computer-centric tasks such as blocking viruses or diagnosing hard disk errors, rather than real-world tasks such as document production or accounting. On a PC, you can access some utility software from desktop icons or the Start menu, just like application software. Other utilities can be accessed from Windows Control Panel (Figure 3-3).

**FIGURE 3-3**

Windows Control Panel provides access to many utilities. You can open the Control Panel using the Windows Start menu.

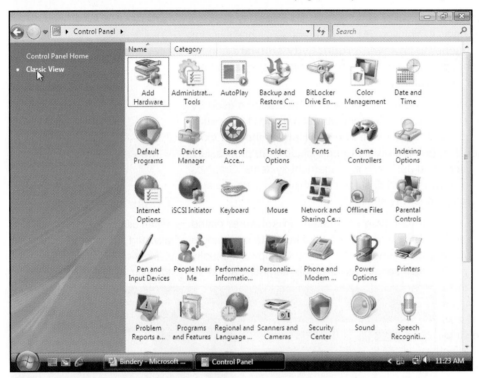

**What are the most popular utilities?** In recent years, antivirus software, such as Norton AntiVirus and McAfee VirusScan, has been a popular category of utility software. With the recent influx of nuisance ads, intrusion attempts, and spam, utilities such as pop-up ad blockers, personal firewalls, and spam filters have also become best-sellers.

Other security-related utilities include file-encryption software, such as PGP, that scrambles file contents for storage or transmission. For people nervous about the trail of Web sites they leave behind, utilities like 12Ghosts Wash remove Internet history lists, files, and graphics from locations that can be scattered in many parts of the hard disk. Filtering software, such as Net Nanny, is used by parents to block their children from viewing objectionable Web sites.

Acrobat Reader is a long-time favorite utility that transforms all kinds of files into a portable format that can be created and read by any computer on which it is installed. Acrobat is especially handy for distributing documents created using expensive desktop publishing software that's not likely to be installed on many people's computers.

Computer owners like to customize their screen-based desktops with screensavers that display clever graphics when the machine is idle. *Skins* that customize the look and feel of media players and DVD burners are also popular (Figure 3-4).

Another popular category of utility software is system utilities, such as Norton SystemWorks, and System Mechanic. These utilities can track down and fix disk errors, repair corrupted files, and give your PC a performance-enhancing tune-up.

A final group of utilities worth mentioning is designed for backing up files, cleaning up hard disks, and shredding files so they can't be recovered. Utilities such as Recover My Files, VirtualLab, and R-Undelete can help you recover files deleted by mistake.

**What are desktop widgets?** A **desktop widget** (sometimes called a dashboard widget or control) is a specialized utility program that appears on a computer's screen-based desktop, looks like a control, and might display a snippet of information. Some examples of desktop widgets include clocks, calendars, calculators, news aggregators, sticky notes, and weather stations. Widgets are usually configured to autostart when a computer boots up, and remain on the desktop until the computer is shut down. Widgets can also be corralled in a sidebar or dashboard.

Widgets are sometimes designed to be transparent so that they don't obscure other objects. Figure 3-5 illustrates some popular desktop widgets.

**FIGURE 3-4**

Skins that change the appearance of Windows Media Player are an example of popular utilities.

**FIGURE 3-5**

Desktop widgets are available for all kinds of tasks.

CLICK TO START

## DEVICE DRIVERS

**What is a device driver?** A **device driver** is software that helps a peripheral device establish communication with a computer. This type of system software is used by printers, monitors, graphics cards, sound cards, network cards, modems, storage devices, mice, and scanners. Once installed, a device driver automatically starts when it is needed. Device drivers usually run in the background, without opening a window on the screen.

Suppose you connect a new printer to your computer. When you install it, you also install a printer driver. Whenever you initiate a print job, the device driver runs in the background to send data to the printer. The printer driver signals you only if it runs into a problem, such as if the printer is not connected or it runs out of paper.

On a PC, if you need to change the settings for a device driver or update it, you can usually access the driver by using the Start menu's Programs or All Programs option. Otherwise, open the Control Panel and then open the System icon. On the Hardware tab, click the Device Manager button to view a list of all your computer system hardware and corresponding device drivers, as shown in Figure 3-6.

**FIGURE 3-6**

The Windows Device Manager offers access to device drivers. You can typically check if they are working and change settings. You can also check the device driver's version number to compare it with the most recent version posted online.

# QuickCheck

1. The two main software categories are _____ software and application software.

2. _____ software can be defined as any type of application software that has the potential to help people do their work more efficiently.

3. A type of application software that is called _____ is designed to help several people collaborate on a single project using local networks or Internet connections.

4. A type of system software referred to as _____ software is designed to help you monitor and configure settings for your computer system equipment, the operating system, or application software.

5. A device _____ is software usually run in the background without opening a window and is designed to help a peripheral device establish communication with a computer.

⊙ CHECK ANSWERS

# Popular Applications

**MOST COMPUTERS INCLUDE** some basic word processing, e-mail, and Internet access software, but computer owners invariably want additional software to increase their computers' productivity, business, learning, or entertainment capabilities. Section B provides an overview of the vast array of application software that's available for personal computers.

## DOCUMENT PRODUCTION SOFTWARE

**How can my computer help me with my writing?** Whether you are writing a 10-page paper, generating software documentation, designing a brochure for your new startup company, or laying out the school newspaper, you will probably use some form of **document production software**. This software assists you with composing, editing, designing, printing, and electronically publishing documents. The three most popular types of document production software are word processing, desktop publishing, and Web authoring (Figure 3-7).

**Word processing software**, such as Microsoft Word, has replaced typewriters for producing many types of documents, including reports, letters, memos, papers, and manuscripts. Word processing software gives you the ability to create, spell-check, edit, and format a document on the screen before you commit it to paper.

**Desktop publishing software** (abbreviated DTP) takes word processing software one step further by helping you use graphic design techniques to enhance the format and appearance of a document. Although today's word processing software offers many page layout and design features, DTP software products, such as QuarkXPress and Adobe InDesign, have sophisticated features to help you produce professional-quality output for newspapers, newsletters, brochures, magazines, and books.

**Web authoring software** helps you design and develop customized Web pages that you can publish electronically on the Internet. Only a few years ago, creating Web pages was a fairly technical task that required authors to insert HTML tags, such as <a href="contents.htm">. Now Web authoring software products, such as Microsoft FrontPage and Macromedia Dreamweaver, help nontechnical Web authors by providing easy-to-use tools for composing the text for a Web page, assembling graphical elements, and automatically generating HTML tags.

**How does document production software help me turn my ideas into sentences and paragraphs?** Document production software makes it easy to let your ideas flow because it automatically handles many tasks that might otherwise distract you. For example, you don't need to worry about fitting words within the margins. A feature called *word wrap* determines how your text will flow from line to line by automatically moving words down to the next line as you reach the right margin. Imagine that the sentences in your document are ribbons of text; word wrap bends the ribbons. Changing the margin size just means bending the ribbon in different

3

**FIGURE 3-7**

Popular document production software includes Microsoft Word, QuarkXPress, and Macromedia Dreamweaver.

**INFOWEBLINKS**

This InfoWeb is your guide to today's best-selling **Document Production Software**.

 CLICK TO CONNECT
www.course.com/np/concepts10/ch03

places. Even after you type an entire document, adjusting the size of your right, left, top, and bottom margins is simple (Figure 3-8).

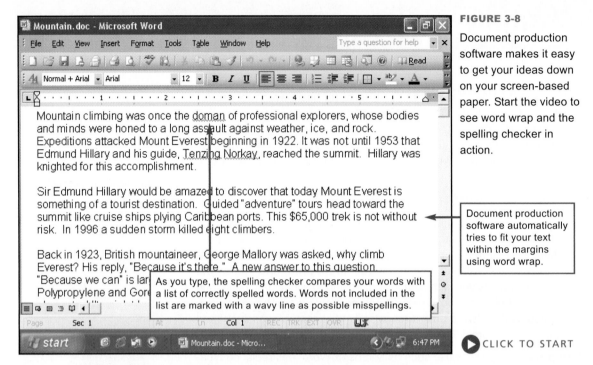

**FIGURE 3-8**

Document production software makes it easy to get your ideas down on your screen-based paper. Start the video to see word wrap and the spelling checker in action.

Document production software automatically tries to fit your text within the margins using word wrap.

▶ CLICK TO START

**What if I'm a bad speller?** Most document production software includes a **spelling checker** that marks misspelled words in a document. You can easily correct a misspelled word as you type, or you can run the spelling checker when you finish entering all the text. Some software even has an autocorrecting capability that automatically changes a typo, such as *teh*, to the correct spelling (*the*).

Although your software's spelling checker helps you correct misspellings, it cannot guarantee an error-free document. A spelling checker works by comparing each word from your document to a list of correctly spelled words that is stored in a data file called a **spelling dictionary**. If the word from your document is in the dictionary, the spelling checker considers the word correctly spelled. If the word is not in the dictionary, the word is counted as misspelled. Sounds okay, right? But suppose your document contains a reference to the city of Negaunee. This word is not in the dictionary, so the spelling checker considers it misspelled, even though it is spelled correctly. Proper nouns and scientific, medical, and technical words are likely to be flagged as misspelled, even if you spell them correctly, because they do not appear in the spelling checker's dictionary.

Now suppose that your document contains the phrase *a pear of shoes*. Although you meant to use *pair* rather than *pear*, the spelling checker will not catch your mistake because *pear* is a valid word in the dictionary. Your spelling checker won't help if you have trouble deciding whether to use *there* or *their*, *its* or *it's*, or *too* or *to*. Remember, then, that a spelling checker cannot substitute for a thorough proofread.

**Can document production software improve my writing?** Because word processing software tends to focus on the writing process, it offers several features that can improve the quality of your writing. These features may not be available in desktop publishing software or Web authoring software, which focus on the format of a document.

Your word processing software is likely to include a **thesaurus**, which can help you find a synonym for a word so that you can make your writing more varied and interesting. A **grammar checker** reads through your document and points out potential grammatical trouble spots, such as incomplete sentences, run-on sentences, and verbs that don't agree with nouns.

Your word processing software might also be able to analyze the reading level of your document using a standard **readability formula**, such as the Flesch-Kincaid reading level. You can use this analysis to find out if your writing matches your target audience, based on sentence length and vocabulary.

**Can document production software help me break bad writing habits?** Most word processing, DTP, and Web authoring software includes a **Search and Replace** feature. You can use this feature to hunt down mistakes that you typically make in your writing. For example, you might know from experience that you tend to overuse the word *typically*. You can use Search and Replace to find each occurrence of *typically*, and then you can decide whether you should substitute a different word, such as *usually* or *ordinarily*.

**How do I get my documents to look good?** The **format** for a document refers to the way that all the elements of a document—text, pictures, titles, and page numbers—are arranged on the page. The final format of your document depends on how and where you intend to use it. A school paper, for example, simply needs to be printed in standard paragraph format—perhaps double spaced and with numbered pages. Your word processing software has all the features you need for this formatting task. A brochure, newsletter, or corporate report, on the other hand, might require more ambitious formatting, such as columns that continue on noncontiguous pages and text labels that overlay graphics. You might consider transferring your document from your word processing software to your desktop publishing software for access to more sophisticated formatting tools. For documents that you plan to publish on the Web, Web authoring software usually provides the most useful set of formatting tools.

The look of your final document depends on several formatting factors, such as font style, paragraph style, and page layout. A **font** is a set of letters that share a unified design. Font size is measured as **point size**, abbreviated pt. (One point is about 1/72 of an inch.) Figure 3-9 illustrates several popular fonts included with document production software.

**INFOWEBLINKS**

You can add to your font collection by downloading font files from the **Font InfoWeb**.

 CLICK TO CONNECT
www.course.com/np/concepts10/ch03

| Font | Size |
|---|---|
| Times New Roman Font | 8 pt. |
| Times New Roman Font | 10 pt. |
| Times New Roman Font | 12 pt. |
| Times New Roman Font | 16 pt. |
| **Times New Roman Font** | **16 pt. Bold** |
| Times New Roman Font | 16 pt. Green |
| Arial Font | 16 pt. |
| Comic Sans MS | 16 pt. |
| Georgia Font | 16 pt. Bold Gold |
| Dotto | 24 pt. Orange |

**FIGURE 3-9**

You can vary the font style by selecting character formatting attributes, such as bold, italics, underline, superscript, and subscript. You can also select a color and size for a font. The font size for the text in a typical paragraph is set at 8, 10, or 12 pt. Titles can be as large as 72 pt.

**Paragraph style** includes the alignment of text within the margins and the space between each line of text. **Paragraph alignment** refers to the horizontal position of text—whether it is aligned at the left margin, aligned at the right margin, or **fully justified** so that the text is aligned evenly on both the right and left margins. Your document will look more formal if it is fully justified, like the text in this paragraph, than if it has an uneven or ragged right margin. **Line spacing** (also called **leading**, pronounced "LED ing") refers to the vertical spacing between lines. Documents are typically single spaced or double spaced, but word processing and DTP software allow you to adjust line spacing in 1 pt. increments.

Instead of individually selecting font and paragraph style elements, document production software typically allows you to define a **style** that lets you apply several font and paragraph characteristics with a single click. For example, instead of applying bold to a title, changing its font to Times New Roman, centering the text, and then adjusting the font size to 18 pt., you can define a Document Title style as 18 pt., Times New Roman, centered, bold. You can then apply all four style characteristics at once simply by selecting the Document Title style (Figure 3-10).

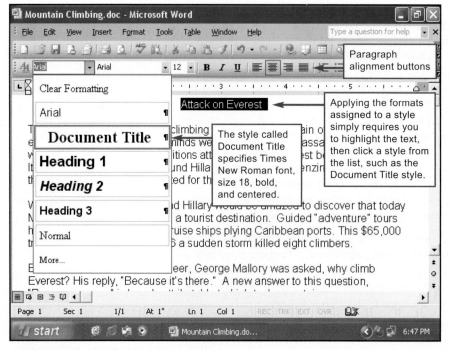

**FIGURE 3-10**

By defining a style, you can apply multiple font attributes with a single click.

▶ CLICK TO START

**Page layout** refers to the physical position of each element on a page. In addition to paragraphs of text, these elements might include:

● **Headers and footers.** A **header** is text that you specify to automatically appear in the top margin of every page. A **footer** is text that you specify to automatically appear in the bottom margin of every page. You might put your name and the document title in the header or footer of a document so that its printed pages won't get mixed up with those of another printed document.

● **Page numbers.** Word processing and DTP software automatically number the pages of a document according to your specifications, usually placing the page number within a header or footer. A Web page, no matter what its length, is all a single page, so Web authoring software typically doesn't provide page numbering.

- **Graphical elements.** Photos, diagrams, graphs, and charts can be incorporated in your documents. **Clip art**—a collection of drawings and photos designed to be inserted in documents—is a popular source of graphical elements.

- **Tables.** A **table** is a grid-like structure that can hold text or pictures. For printed documents, tables are a popular way to produce easy-to-read columns and rows of data and to position graphics. It may sound surprising, but for Web pages, tables provide one of the few ways to precisely position text and pictures. As a result, Web page designers make extensive and very creative use of tables.

Most word processing software is page-oriented, meaning that it treats each page as a rectangle that can be filled with text and graphics. Text automatically flows from one page to the next. In contrast, most DTP software is frame-oriented, allowing you to divide each page into several rectangular-shaped **frames** that you can fill with text or graphics. Text flows from one frame to the next, rather than from page to page (Figure 3-11).

### Attack on Everest
#### by Janell Chalmers

Mountain climbing was once the domain of professional explorers, whose bodies and minds were honed to a long assault against weather, ice, and rock. Expeditions attacked Mount Everest

Wrapping text around a frame adds interest to the layout.

til 1953 guide. Tenzing Norkay, reached the summit. Hillary was knighted for this accomplishment.

Sir Edmund Hillary would be amazed to discover that today Mount Everest has become something of a tourist destination. Guided "adventure" tours head toward the summit like cruise ships plying

Caribbean ports. This $65,000 trek is not without risk. In 1996 a sudden storm killed eight climbers.

Back in 1923, British mountaineer, George Mallory was asked, why climb Everest? His reply, "Because it's there." A new answer to this question, "Because we can" may be largely attributable to new high-tech mountain gear. Nylon, polypropylene and Gore-Tex clothing provide light, yet warm protection from the elements. New, high-tech ultraviolet lenses protect eyes from dangerous snowblindness.

An other gear makes the mountain seem less

*"Because it's there."*
George Mallory

**FIGURE 3-11**

DTP frames give you exact control over the position of elements on a page, such as a figure and a caption on top of it.

One frame holds the centered title and author's byline. This text is linked to the text in subsequent frames.

Guide lines that do not appear on printouts help align text and graphical elements.

Text can link to frames on the next page or on any page of the document.

▶ CLICK TO START

### Does document production software increase productivity?
Word processing software, in particular, provides several features that automate tasks and allow you to work more productively. For example, suppose that you want to send prospective employers a letter and your resume. Instead of composing and addressing each letter individually, your software can perform a **mail merge** that automatically creates personalized letters by combining the information in a mailing list with a form letter. Some additional capabilities of word processing software include:

- Automatically generating a table of contents and an index for a document

- Automatically numbering footnotes and positioning each footnote on the page where it is referenced

- Providing document templates and document wizards that show you the correct content and format for a variety of documents, such as business letters, fax cover sheets, and memos

- Exporting a document into HTML format for use on the Web

## SPREADSHEET SOFTWARE

**What is a spreadsheet?** A **spreadsheet** uses rows and columns of numbers to create a model or representation of a real situation. For example, your checkbook register is a type of spreadsheet because it is a numerical representation of the cash flowing in and out of your bank account. Today, **spreadsheet software**, such as Microsoft Excel, provides tools to create electronic spreadsheets. It is similar to a smart piece of paper that automatically adds up the columns of numbers you write on it. You can use it to make other calculations, too, based on simple equations that you write or more complex, built-in formulas. As an added bonus, spreadsheet software helps you turn your data into a variety of colorful graphs. It also includes special data-handling features that allow you to sort data, search for data that meets specific criteria, and print reports.

Spreadsheet software was initially popular with accountants and financial managers who dealt with paper-based spreadsheets, but found the electronic version far easier to use and less prone to errors than manual calculations. Other people soon discovered the benefits of spreadsheets for projects that require repetitive calculations—budgeting, maintaining a grade book, balancing a checkbook, tracking investments, calculating loan payments, and estimating project costs.

Because it is so easy to experiment with different numbers, spreadsheet software is particularly useful for **what-if analysis**. You can use what-if analyses to answer questions such as "What if I get an A on my next two economics exams? But what if I get only Bs?" "What if I invest $100 a month in my retirement plan? But what if I invest $200 a month?"

**What does a computerized spreadsheet look like?** You use spreadsheet software to create an on-screen **worksheet**. A worksheet is based on a grid of columns and rows. Each **cell** in the grid can contain a value, label, or formula. A **value** is a number that you want to use in a calculation. A **label** is any text used to describe data. For example, suppose that your worksheet contains the value $486,000. You could use a label to identify this number as Income (Figure 3-12).

**INFOWEBLINKS**

For links to today's best-selling spreadsheet software, connect to the **Spreadsheet InfoWeb**.

 CLICK TO CONNECT
www.course.com/np/concepts10/ch03

**FIGURE 3-12**

In a worksheet, each column is lettered and each row is numbered. The intersection of a column and row is called a cell. Each cell has a unique cell reference, or *address*, derived from its column and row location. For example, A1 is the cell reference for the upper-left cell in a worksheet because it is in column A and row 1. You can select any cell and make it the active cell by clicking it. Once a cell is active, you can enter data into it.

You can format the labels and values on a worksheet in much the same way as you would format text in a word processing document. You can change fonts and font size, select a font color, and select font styles, such as bold, italic, and underline.

**How does spreadsheet software work?** The values contained in a cell can be manipulated by formulas placed in other cells. A **formula** works behind the scenes to tell the computer how to use the contents of cells in calculations. You can enter a simple formula in a cell to add, subtract, multiply, or divide numbers. More complex formulas can be designed to perform just about any calculation you can imagine. Figure 3-13 illustrates how a formula might be used in a simple spreadsheet to calculate savings.

**FIGURE 3-13**

When a cell contains a formula, it displays the result of the formula rather than the formula itself. To view and edit the formula, you use the Formula bar.

You can think of the formula as working behind the scenes to perform calculations and then display the result.

▶ CLICK TO START

**FIGURE 3-14**

Functions are special formulas provided by spreadsheet software.

A formula, such as =D4-D5+((D8/B2)*110), can contain **cell references** (like D4 and D5), numbers (like 110), and **mathematical operators**, such as the multiplication symbol (*), the division symbol (/), the addition symbol, and the subtraction symbol. Parts of a formula can be enclosed in parentheses to indicate the order in which the mathematical operations should be performed. The operation in the innermost set of parentheses—in this case, (D8/B2)— should be performed first.

You can enter a formula from scratch by typing it into a cell, or you can use a built-in preset formula called a **function**, provided by the spreadsheet software. To use a function, you simply select one from a list, as shown in Figure 3-14, and then indicate the cell references of any values you want to include in the calculation.

**What happens when I modify a worksheet?** When you change the contents of any cell in a worksheet, all the formulas are recalculated. This **automatic recalculation** feature ensures that the results in every cell are accurate for the information currently entered in the worksheet.

Your worksheet is also automatically updated to reflect any rows or columns that you add, delete, or copy within the worksheet. Unless you specify otherwise, a cell reference is a **relative reference**—that is, a reference that can change from B4 to B3, for example, if row 3 is deleted and all the data moves up one row.

If you don't want a cell reference to change, you can use an absolute reference. An **absolute reference** never changes when you insert rows or copy or move formulas. Understanding when to use absolute references is one of the key aspects of developing spreadsheet design expertise. Figure 3-15 and its associated tour provide additional information about relative and absolute references.

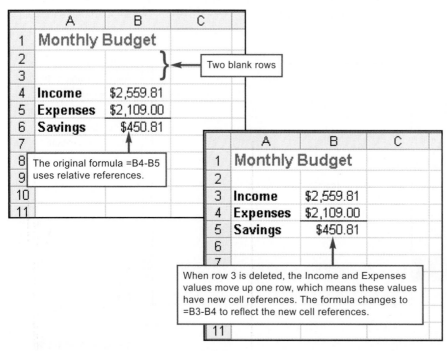

**FIGURE 3-15**

As shown in the examples, relative references within a formula can change when you change the sequence of a worksheet's rows and columns. An absolute reference is anchored so that it always refers to a specific cell.

▶ CLICK TO START

**How will I know which formulas and functions to use when I create a worksheet?** To create an effective and accurate worksheet, you typically must understand the calculations and formulas that are involved. If, for example, you want to create a worksheet that helps you calculate your final grade in a course, you need to know the grading scale and understand how your instructor plans to weight each assignment and test.

Most spreadsheet software includes a few templates or wizards for pre-designed worksheets, such as invoices, income-expense reports, balance sheets, and loan payment schedules. Additional templates are available on the Web. These templates are typically designed by professionals and contain all the necessary labels and formulas. To use a template, you simply plug in the values for your calculation.

## "NUMBER CRUNCHING" SOFTWARE

**Aside from spreadsheets, what other "number crunching" software is available?** Spreadsheet software provides a sort of blank canvas on which you can create numeric models by simply painting values, labels, and formulas. The advantage of spreadsheet software is the flexibility it provides—flexibility to create customized calculations according to your exact specifications. The disadvantage of spreadsheet software is that—aside from a few predesigned templates—you are responsible for entering formulas and selecting functions for calculations. If you don't know the formulas or don't understand the functions, you're out of luck.

In contrast to the blank canvas approach provided by spreadsheet software, other number crunching software works more like paint by numbers. It provides a structured environment dedicated to a particular number crunching task, such as statistical analysis, mathematical modeling, or money management.

**Statistical software** helps you analyze large sets of data to discover relationships and patterns. Products such as SPSS and Statsoft STATISTICA are helpful tools for summarizing survey results, test scores, experiment results, or population data. Most statistical software includes graphing capability so that you can display and explore your data visually.

**Mathematical modeling software** provides tools for solving a wide range of math, science, and engineering problems. Students, teachers, mathematicians, and engineers, in particular, appreciate how products such as Mathcad and Mathematica help them recognize patterns that can be difficult to identify in columns of numbers (Figure 3-16).

### INFOWEBLINKS

For more information about popular "number crunching" software, take a look at the **Numeric Software InfoWeb**.

 CLICK TO CONNECT
www.course.com/np/concepts10/ch03

**FIGURE 3-16**

Mathematical modeling software helps you visualize the product of complex formulas. Here the points from a sphere are graphed onto a plane, to demonstrate the principles behind the Astronomical Clock of Prague.

**Money management software** offers a variety of tools for tracking monetary transactions and investments. In this software category, **personal finance software**, such as Microsoft Money and Intuit Quicken, is designed to keep records of income, expenses, assets, and liabilities using a simple checkbook-like user interface. This software also automates routine financial tasks, such as budgeting, investing, check writing, and bill paying. Many personal financial software products provide direct links to online banking services, so you can use them to check account balances, transfer funds, and pay bills.

Personal financial software produces reports and graphs that show you where your money goes. For example, you can analyze various aspects of your cash flow, such as how much you spent on entertainment last month and how that compares to the previous month.

**Tax preparation software** is a specialized type of personal finance software designed to help you gather your annual income and expense data, identify deductions, and calculate tax payments. Popular products, such as Intuit TurboTax, even accept data directly from personal finance software to eliminate hours of tedious data entry.

## DATABASE SOFTWARE

**What is a database?** The term *database* has evolved from a specialized technical term into a part of our everyday vocabulary. In the context of modern usage, a **database** is simply a collection of data that is stored on one or more computers. A database can contain any sort of data, such as a university's student records, a library's card catalog, a store's inventory, an individual's address book, or a utility company's customers. Databases can be stored on personal computers, LAN servers, Web servers, mainframes, and even handheld computers.

**What is database software?** **Database software** helps you enter, find, organize, update, and report information stored in a database. Microsoft Access, FileMaker Pro, and askSam are three of the most popular examples of database software for personal computers. Oracle and MySQL are popular server database software packages. For PDAs, popular choices include HanDBase, Mobile DB, dbNow, and JFile.

**How does a database store data?** Database software stores data as a series of records, which are composed of fields that hold data. A **record** holds data for a single entity—a person, place, thing, or event. A **field** holds one item of data relevant to a record. You can envision a record as a Rolodex or index card and a series of records as a table (Figure 3-17).

**TERMINOLOGY NOTE**

Database software is also referred to as database management software (DBMS).

**FIGURE 3-17**

A single database record is similar to a Rolodex card or an index card. A series of records is usually depicted in table format.

| Song Title | Performer | Composer | CD | Date | Record Label | Length |
|---|---|---|---|---|---|---|
| Seven Years | Norah Jones | Lee Alexander | Come Away with Me | 02/01/2002 | Blue Note | 2:24 |
| Shoot the Moon | Norah Jones | Jesse Harris | Come Away with Me | 02/02/2002 | Blue Note | 3:57 |
| Summertime | Janis Joplin | George Gershwin | Greatest Hits | 08/31/1999 | Sony | 3:28 |
| Summertime | Sarah Vaughan | George Gershwin | Compact Jazz | 06/22/1987 | Polygram | 4:34 |

Some database software provides tools to work with more than one collection of records, as long as the records are somehow related to each other. For example, MTV might maintain a database pertaining to jazz music. One series of database records might contain data about jazz songs. It could contain fields such as those shown in Figure 3-17. Another series of records might contain biographical data about jazz performers, including name, birth date, and home town. It might even include a field for the performer's photo.

These two sets of records can be related by the name of the performing artist, as shown in Figure 3-18.

**FIGURE 3-18**

The two sets of records are related by the Performer field. The relationship allows you to select Norah Jones from the Jazz Performers records and jump to any records in the Jazz Songs records that Norah Jones performed.

**How do I create records?** Database software provides the tools you need to define fields for a series of records. Figure 3-19 shows a simple form you might use to specify the fields for a database.

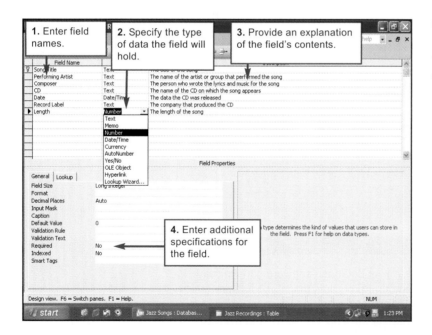

**FIGURE 3-19**

Database software provides tools for specifying fields for a series of records.

 CLICK TO START

**When can I enter data?** After you've defined fields for a series of records, you can enter the data for each record. Your database software provides a simple-to-use data entry form that allows you to easily fill in the data for each field. Instead of typing data into a database, you can also import data from a commercial database, such as a customer mailing list. You can even download databases from the Web, and then import the data into fields you have defined with your database software.

**How do I locate specific data?** Many databases contain hundreds or thousands of records. If you want to find a particular record or a group of records, scrolling through every record is much too cumbersome. Instead, you can enter a **query** to perform a search, and the computer will quickly locate the records you seek.

Most database software provides one or more methods for making queries. A **query language**, such as SQL (Structured Query Language), provides a set of commands for locating and manipulating data. To locate all performances of *Summertime* before 1990 from a Jazz Songs database, you might enter a query such as:

Select * from JazzSongs where SongTitle = 'Summertime' and Date < '1990'

In addition to a formal query language, some database software provides **natural language query** capabilities. To make such queries, you don't have to learn an esoteric query language. Instead, you can simply enter questions, such as:

Who performed Summertime before 1990?

As an alternative to a query language or a natural language query, your database software might allow you to **query by example** (QBE), simply by filling out a form with the type of data you want to locate. Figure 3-20 illustrates a query by example for *Summertime* performances before 1990.

> **TERMINOLOGY NOTE**
>
> A query is a set of keywords and operators that describe information you want to find.

**FIGURE 3-20**

When you query by example, your database software displays a blank form on the screen, and you enter examples of the data that you want to find.

**How can I use search results?** Your database software can typically help you print reports, export data to other programs (such as to a spreadsheet where you can graph the data), convert the data to other formats (such as HTML so that you can post the data on the Web), and transmit data to other computers.

Whether you print, import, copy, save, or transmit the data you find in databases, it is your responsibility to use it appropriately. Never introduce inaccurate information into a database. Respect copyrights, giving credit to the person or organization that compiled the data. You should also respect the privacy of the people who are the subject of the data. Unless you have permission to do so, do not divulge names, Social Security numbers, or other identifying information that might compromise someone's privacy.

## GRAPHICS SOFTWARE

**What kind of software do I need to work with drawings, photos, and other pictures?** In computer lingo, the term **graphics** refers to any picture, drawing, sketch, photograph, image, or icon that appears on your computer screen. **Graphics software** is designed to help you create, manipulate, and print graphics. Some graphics software products specialize in a particular type of graphic, while others allow you to work with multiple graphics formats. If you are really interested in working with graphics, you will undoubtedly end up using more than one graphics software product.

**Paint software** (sometimes called image editing software) provides a set of electronic pens, brushes, and paints for painting images on the screen. A simple program called Microsoft Paint is included with Windows. More sophisticated paint software products include Corel Paint Shop Pro and Procreate Painter. Many graphic artists, Web page designers, and illustrators use paint software as their primary computer-based graphics tool.

**Photo editing software**, such as Adobe Photoshop, includes features specially designed to fix poor-quality photos by modifying contrast and brightness, cropping out unwanted objects, and removing red eye. Photos can also be edited using paint software, but photo editing software typically offers tools and wizards that simplify common photo editing tasks.

**Drawing software** provides a set of lines, shapes, and colors that can be assembled into diagrams, corporate logos, and schematics. The drawings created with tools such as Adobe Illustrator and Macromedia Freehand tend to have a flat cartoon-like quality, but they are very easy to modify, and look good at just about any size. Figure 3-21 illustrates a typical set of tools provided by drawing software.

**FIGURE 3-21**

Drawing software provides tools for creating and manipulating graphics.

**3-D graphics software** provides a set of tools for creating wireframes that represent three-dimensional objects. A wireframe acts much like the framework for a pop-up tent. Just as you would construct the framework for the tent and then cover it with a nylon tent cover, 3-D graphics software can cover a wireframe object with surface texture and color to create a graphic of a 3-D object (Figure 3-22 on the next page).

**FIGURE 3-22**

3-D graphics software provides tools for creating a wireframe that represents a 3-D object. Some 3-D software specializes in engineering-style graphics, while other 3-D software specializes in figures.

**CAD software** (computer-aided design software) is a special type of 3-D graphics software designed for architects and engineers who use computers to create blueprints and product specifications. AutoCAD is one of the best-selling professional CAD products. TurboCAD is a low-cost favorite. Scaled-down versions of professional CAD software provide simplified tools for homeowners who want to redesign their kitchens, examine new landscaping options, or experiment with floor plans.

**Presentation software** supplies the tools you need for combining text, photos, clip art, graphs, animations, and sound into a series of electronic slides, like those in Figure 3-23. You can display electronic slides on a color monitor for a one-on-one presentation or use a computer projection device for group presentations. You can also output the presentation as overhead transparencies, paper copies, or 35 mm slides. Popular presentation software products include Microsoft PowerPoint and Harvard Graphics.

**FIGURE 3-23**

A computer-based presentation consists of a series of slides, created with presentation software.

3

## MUSIC SOFTWARE

**Why would I need music software?** You don't have to be a musician or composer to have a use for music software. Many types of music software are available. You might be surprised to find how many of them come in handy.

It is possible—and easy—to make your own digital voice and music recordings, which you store on your computer's hard disk. Your operating system might supply **audio editing software**, such as Sound Recorder or you can download open source software, such as Audacity (Figure 3-24).

**FIGURE 3-24**

Audio editing software provides controls much like those on a tape recorder. Menus offer additional digital editing features, such as speed control, volume adjustments, clipping, and mixing.

Audio editing software typically includes playback as well as recording capabilities. A specialized version of this software called karaoke software integrates music files and on-screen lyrics—everything you need to sing along with your favorite tunes.

Music can be stored in a variety of digital formats on a computer or on a portable audio player, such as Apple's iPod. Digital music formats, such as MP3 and AAC, are not the same formats used to store music on commercial audio CDs. These file formats take up much less storage space than on the original CD.

A variety of software allows you to convert music from commercial CDs for use on computers and portable audio players. **CD ripper software** pulls a track off an audio CD and stores it in raw digital format on your computer's hard disk. **Audio encoding software** (sometimes called an *audio format converter*) converts the raw audio file into a format such as MP3 or AAC. After the file is converted, you can listen to it on your computer, or you can transfer it to a portable MP3 player.

**Ear training software** targets musicians and music students who want to learn to play by ear, develop tuning skills, recognize notes and keys, and develop other musical skills. **Notation software** is the musician's equivalent of a word processor. It helps musicians compose, edit, and print the notes for their compositions. For non-musicians, **computer-aided music software** is designed to generate unique musical compositions simply by selecting the musical style, instruments, key, and tempo. **MIDI sequencing software** and software synthesizers are an important part of the studio musician's toolbox. They're great for sound effects and for controlling keyboards and other digital instruments.

**TERMINOLOGY NOTE**

Some CD ripper software also includes audio encoding software so that ripping and encoding seem to happen within a single operation.

**INFOWEBLINKS**

At the **Music Software InfoWeb**, you'll find detailed information on popular software in this category.

W  CLICK TO CONNECT
www.course.com/np/concepts10/ch03

## VIDEO EDITING AND DVD AUTHORING SOFTWARE

**What can video editing software do?** The popularity of computer-based video editing can be attributed to video editing software, such as Windows Movie Maker and Apple iMovie, now included with Windows computers and Macs. **Video editing software** provides a set of tools for transferring video footage from a camcorder to a computer, clipping out unwanted footage, assembling video segments in any sequence, adding special visual effects, and adding a sound track. Despite an impressive array of features, video editing software is relatively easy to use, as explained in Figure 3-25.

**FIGURE 3-25**

Video editing software, such as Adobe Premiere, helps you import a series of video clips from a camera or VCR, arrange the clips in the order of your choice, add transitions between clips, and add an audio track.

With the growing popularity of writable DVD drives, desktop video authors now want to transfer their productions to DVDs and watch them on standard DVD players connected to television sets or projectors. **DVD authoring software** offers tools for creating DVDs with Hollywood-style menus. Just like commercial movies, desktop videos can now include menu selections such as Play Movie, Scene Selection, and Special Features. You can use the remote control for your DVD player to scroll through and select menu options. Examples of DVD authoring software include Sonic DVDit, ULead DVD MovieFactory, Apple iDVD, and Adobe Encore DVD.

## EDUCATIONAL AND REFERENCE SOFTWARE

**How can I use my computer for learning new things?** **Educational software** helps you learn and practice new skills. For the youngest students, educational software, such as MindTwister Math and 3D Froggy Phonics, teaches basic arithmetic and reading skills. Instruction is presented in game format, and the levels of play are adapted to the player's age and ability.

For older students and adults, software is available for such diverse educational endeavors as learning languages, training yourself to use new software, learning how to play the piano or guitar, improving keyboarding skills, and even learning managerial skills for a diverse workplace. Exam preparation software is available for standardized tests such as the SAT, GMAT, and LSAT. Web-based distance education software tools, such as WebCT and Blackboard, help instructors keep track of student progress and provide students with interactive study and testing activities.

**What's reference software?** **Reference software** provides a collection of information and a way to access that information. This type of software includes massive amounts of data—unlike database software, which is shipped without any data. The reference software category spans a wide range of applications—from encyclopedias to medical references, from map software to trip planners, and from cookbooks to telephone books. The options are as broad as the full range of human interests.

Because of the quantity of data it includes, reference software is generally shipped on a CD or DVD, or can be accessed on the Web. Encyclopedias are the most popular software packages in this category. Bestsellers include Microsoft Encarta and Britannica's CD. An encyclopedia on CD-ROM or the Web has several advantages over its printed counterpart. Finding information is easier, for example. Also, electronic formats take up less space on your bookshelf and include interesting video and audio clips. A single CD is cheaper to produce than a shelf full of hard-bound printed books. These lower production costs translate to more affordable products and allow an average person to own a comprehensive encyclopedia.

## ENTERTAINMENT SOFTWARE

**What's the best-selling entertainment software?** Computer games are the most popular type of entertainment software. Over $7 billion of computer and video games are sold each year in the United States alone. Computer games are generally classified into subcategories, such as role-playing, action, adventure, puzzles, simulations, sports, and strategy/war games, as described in Figure 3-26.

**FIGURE 3-26**

Game Categories

| Type of Game | Description | Examples |
|---|---|---|
| Role-playing | Based on a detailed story line—often one that takes place in a medieval world populated with dastardly villains and evil monsters—the goal is to build a character into a powerful entity that can conquer the bad guys and accumulate treasure. | Diablo, EverQuest, Icewind Dale, Planescape |
| Action | Like arcade games, action games require fast reflexes as you maneuver a character through a maze or dungeon. | Quake, Doom, Unreal Tournament, Enter the Matrix, Tomb Raider |
| Adventure | Similar to role-playing games except that the focus is on solving problems rather than building a character into a powerful wizard or fighter. | Myst, The Longest Journey, Return to Monkey Island |
| Puzzle | Include computerized versions of traditional board games, card games, and Rubik's cube-like challenges. | Tetris, Lemmings |
| Simulation | Provide a realistic setting, such as the cockpit of an airplane. Players must learn to manipulate controls using the keyboard, joystick, or special-purpose input device. A great way to get your adrenaline pumping without expenses or risks. | Flight Simulator, NASCAR Racing, Mech Warrior |
| Sports | Place participants in the midst of action-packed sports events, such as a football game, baseball game, hockey final, soccer match, or golf tournament. Most sports games offer arcade-like action and require quick reflexes. | NBA Live, MVP Baseball, SimGolf |
| Strategy | Players (one player might be the computer) take turns moving characters, armies, and other resources in a quest to capture territory. | Age of Empires, Sim City, Warcraft |

**How do multiplayer games work?** Multiplayer games provide an environment in which two or more players can participate in the same game. Even some of the earliest computer games, like Pong, supplied joysticks for two players. Today's multiplayer games are a far cry from those simplistic games. Now numerous players can use Internet technology to band together or battle one another in sophisticated virtual environments.

Large-scale multiplayer games, such as Battlefield 1942 and EverQuest, operate on multiple Internet servers, each one with the capacity to handle thousands of players at peak times. A new twist in online multiplayer games is persistent metaworlds, in which objects remain even when play ends. If one player drops an object, for example, it will be there when other players pass by.

## BUSINESS SOFTWARE

**Do businesses use specialized software?** *Business software* is a broad term that describes vertical and horizontal market software, which helps businesses and organizations accomplish routine or specialized tasks.

**What is vertical market software?** **Vertical market software** is designed to automate specialized tasks in a specific market or business. Examples include patient management and billing software that is specially designed for hospitals, job estimating software for construction businesses, and student record management software for schools. Today, almost every business has access to some type of specialized vertical market software designed to automate, streamline, or computerize key business activities.

**What is horizontal market software?** **Horizontal market software** is generic software that just about any kind of business can use. **Payroll software** is a good example of horizontal market software. Almost every business has employees and must maintain payroll records. No matter what type of business uses it, payroll software must collect similar data and make similar calculations to produce payroll checks and W-2 forms. Accounting software and project management software are additional examples of horizontal market software. **Accounting software** helps a business keep track of the money flowing in and out of various accounts. **Project management software** is an important tool for planning large projects, scheduling project tasks, and tracking project costs.

# QuickCheck

**SECTION B**

1. Various kinds of [_____] production software provide tools for creating and formatting printed and Web-based materials.

2. A spelling checker will find an error in "The sailor tied a complex not." True or false? [_____]

3. [_____] software provides a sort of blank canvas on which you can create numeric models by simply painting values, labels, and formulas.

4. [_____] software stores data as a series of records and allows you to establish relationships between different types of records.

5. CD [_____] software transfers files from an audio CD to your computer's hard disk.

6. [_____] authoring software allows you to add Hollywood-style menus to digital videos.

▶ CHECK ANSWERS

# Buying Software

**SAVVY SOFTWARE SHOPPERS** have a good sense of what to buy and where to find it. Section C offers some shopping tips for expanding your computer's software repertoire. The section ends with a discussion of software copyrights—important information that will help you understand the difference between legal and illegal software copying.

## CONSUMER BASICS

**What are the most essential applications and utilities to have?** In addition to an operating system, your computer should have browser software, an e-mail client, word processing software, a security suite, graphics viewer, and software that lets you burn files onto CDs and DVDs. You will probably also want compression software that lets you shrink big graphics files before e-mailing them, graphics software for editing photos, and some type of diagnostic software for troubleshooting hardware and software problems. For entertainment, you might want sound recording and playback software, as well as a few computer games.

**Should I use the apps and utilities that come with the operating system?** Most operating systems include a handful of small applications and a good variety of useful utility software. You'll want to thoroughly explore what your operating system has to offer before you spend money on third-party software. Figure 3-27 contains a list of the most frequently used apps and utilities offered by the Microsoft Windows operating system.

| Software | Function |
| --- | --- |
| Internet Explorer | Browse the Web |
| Windows Explorer | Keep track of files and folders |
| WordPad | Perform basic word processing |
| Notepad | Edit text |
| Calculator | Add, subtract, and calculate basic functions |
| Paint | Edit bitmap images, such as photos |
| Sound Recorder | Digitize music and voice input from a microphone |
| Windows Media Player | Play music and videos |
| Backup | Make backups of hard disk files |
| Disk defragmenter | Arrange data on hard disk for optimal efficiency |
| Security Center | Set security levels for Internet and network access |
| Windows Firewall | Block intrusion attempts |

**FIGURE 3-27**

The Windows operating system includes many useful applications and utilities. You can evaluate these offerings before considering whether to supplement them with third-party versions.

If you want utilities other than those included with your computer's operating system, you can explore software offered by third-party vendors. As it turns out, third-party vendors also offer utilities designed for the same tasks as those packaged with operating systems and you might want to consider those as well.

There are two reasons why some computer owners prefer utilities produced by third-party vendors over those packaged with an operating system. Operating system utilities are sometimes not as dependable as third-party utilities designed by companies that specialize in system maintenance or security.

For example, Symantec's Norton SystemWorks has a long track record of producing dependable diagnostic utilities, and McAfee's Security Suite was successfully protecting computers from viruses and intrusions long before Microsoft developed its own set of Security Center utilities.

Additionally, some operating system utilities are not as full featured as third-party versions. For example, although Windows supplies a file compression utility that reduces file size for quick transmission or efficient storage, many computer owners prefer to use third-party utilities, such as WinZip, WinAce, IZArc, QuickZip, or PKZIP, that offer a variety of compression options.

**What is the advantage of a software suite?** A **software suite** is a collection of application software sold as a single package. Office suites, such as Microsoft Office, StarOffice, OpenOffice.org, and WordPerfect Office, include applications to boost basic productivity: word processing, spreadsheet, and e-mail software. Graphics suites, such as Adobe Creative Suite, Macromedia Studio MX, and CorelDRAW Graphics Suite, typically include paint, draw, and Web graphics tools. Media suites such as InterVideo MediaOne provide tools for creating music CDs and video DVDs. Security suites include tools to scan your computer for viruses and prevent online intrusions.

Purchasing a software suite is usually much less expensive than purchasing the applications separately. Another advantage is usability. Because all the applications in a suite are produced by the same software publisher, they tend to use similar user interfaces and provide an easy way to transport data from one application to another. The disadvantage of a software suite is that you might pay for applications you don't need. Figure 3-28 lists the components of several popular software suites.

**FIGURE 3-28**

Software suites are available in many application categories, such as productivity, antivirus, graphics, and media.

**Microsoft Office XP Professional**

Word
Excel
Outlook
PowerPoint
Publisher
Access

**Norton SystemWorks**

Norton AntiVirus
Norton Utilities
Norton Goback
Norton Cleanup
Norton Checkit
    Diagnostics
Norton System
    Optimizer

**Adobe Creative Suite**

Adobe Illustrator
Adobe Photoshop
Adobe InDesign
Adobe Acrobat
    Professional
Adobe
    GoLive

**InterVideo MediaOne**

WinDVD
Disc Master
Smart Backup
InterVideo Photo Album
DVD Copy

**How do I know if a software program will work on my computer?**
Tucked away at the software publisher's Web site or printed on the software
package (Figure 3-29) you'll find **system requirements**, which specify the
operating system and minimum hardware capacities necessary for a software product to work correctly.

**FIGURE 3-29**

System requirements typically
can be found on the software
box or posted on the download
site.

**System Requirements**

Operating Systems: Windows 95/98/2000/Me/XP/Vista
Processor: Pentium class computer
Memory: 16 MB or more
Hard Disk Space: 10 MB free
Network Protocol: TCP/IP
Network Connection: 10/100 Ethernet LAN/WAN,
cable modem, DSL router, ISDN router, or dial-up modem

**eCourse Internet Works**
2007 eCourseWare Corp. All
rights reserved. eCourse is
a registered trademark of
eCourseWare Corp.

**Where can I find out about the latest, greatest software?** New
software appears so quickly that it can seem impossible to keep up with it.
However, a collection of publications and Web sites can help you keep
abreast of software developments that might improve your computing experience.

Computer and technology magazines, such as *Wired*, *Macworld*, and *PC
Computing*, usually include software reviews in every issue. Some magazines focus on games, while others specialize in business or power apps,
but if you find a computer magazine that you enjoy reading, it is likely to
include information about software that interests you.

Most computer magazines have companion Web sites and some of those
significantly extend the material offered in the magazine's printed pages.
ZDnet and Cnet (*reviews.cnet.com*), for example, offer in-depth comparison
reviews written by experts and tested under laboratory conditions.

Consumer-oriented Web sites also offer reviews. For example, a site at
*www.toptenreviews.com* contains easy-to-understand, in-depth checklists
that make it easy to compare the features of popular software packages.

User reviews and ratings can be found at download sites, such as
*www.download.com* and comparison shopping sites, such as
*www.bizrate.com*, *Amazon.com*, and *newegg.com*. You might also find a
blog or news feed that focuses on the type of software you typically use.

**Where can I get software?** Software is sold in some surprising places.
You might find graphics software at your local art supply store. Your favorite
beauty salon might carry *Cosmopolitan*'s makeup and hairstyle makeover
software. You might even find homeopathic medicine software on sale at a
health food store. Of course, software is also available from traditional
sources, including office stores, computer superstores, electronics superstores, and discount stores as well as local computer stores. You can buy
software from mail-order catalogs, the software publisher's Web site, and
software download sites.

**What's included in a typical software package?** The key ingredients necessary to install new software are the files that contain the programs and data. These files might be supplied on **distribution media**—one or more CDs or DVDs that are packaged in a box, along with an instruction manual. The files might also be supplied as an Internet download that contains program modules and the text of the instruction manual.

**Is it better to buy software in a box or download it?** Boxed software can be purchased in a store or shipped to you by mail. The box usually includes distribution CDs and an installation manual. It might also include a more extensive user manual, but many software publishers have cut costs by supplying user manuals online or as an extra cost item. The advantage of distribution CDs is their availability in case your hard disk fails and you have to reinstall your software. Boxed software can give you a physical record of your registration code, serial number, and certificate of authenticity, which might be necessary for reinstallation.

You can download software from a Web site instead of buying it in a box. Downloading can be convenient. It saves you a trip to the store and you don't have to wait for a mail order package to arrive. Depending on the speed of your Internet connection, however, downloads can tie up your computer for a few hours. Even with a fast connection a download can be interrupted and you might have to call customer service to restart it without paying for the product again.

Downloading can be risky. Some download sites display an irritating number of ads and are sometimes exploited by hackers. Software downloaded from less reputable sites might contain viruses. When possible you should download directly from the software publisher's Web site or from a download site operated by a reputable business, such as a computer magazine or retailer. In any case, it is good practice to scan downloaded files for viruses before installing them.

Prices for boxed software and Web downloads can vary, so if you have the time to shop around, you are likely to save some money.

## SOFTWARE COPYRIGHTS AND LICENSES

**What is a software copyright?** After you purchase a software package, you might assume that you can install it and use it in any way you like. In fact, your purchase entitles you to use the software only in certain prescribed ways. In most countries, computer software, like a book or movie, is protected by a copyright.

A **copyright** is a form of legal protection that grants the author of an original work an exclusive right to copy, distribute, sell, and modify that work, except under special circumstances described by copyright laws. These exceptions include:

- The purchaser has the right to copy software from distribution media or a Web site to a computer's hard disk in order to install it.

- The purchaser can make an extra, or backup, copy of the software in case the original copy becomes erased or damaged, unless the process of making the backup requires the purchaser to defeat a copy protection mechanism designed to prohibit copying.

- The purchaser is allowed to copy and distribute sections of a software program for use in critical reviews and teaching.

**INFOWEBLINKS**

To read the actual text of software copyright laws, connect to the **Software Copyright InfoWeb**.

 CLICK TO CONNECT
www.course.com/np/concepts10/ch03

Most software displays a **copyright notice**, such as © *2007 eCourse*, on one of its screens. This notice is not required by law, however, so programs without a copyright notice are still protected by copyright law. People who circumvent copyright law and illegally copy, distribute, or modify software are sometimes called software pirates, and their illegal copies are referred to as pirated software.

**Can I tell if software is pirated?** Software pirates are getting more and more aggressive and pirated software is not always easy to identify. Some unsuspecting consumers have inadvertently obtained pirated software, even when paying full price from a reputable source. According to the Software & Information Industry Association (SIIA), the attributes in Figure 3-30 could indicate that a software product is pirated.

Widespread pirating of Microsoft products has led to preventive measures such as Certificates of Authenticity and expensive-to-duplicate holographic images on CD labels.

If you suspect that software is pirated, it is best not to buy it or install it. If you have questions about a product's authenticity, you can contact the SIIA or the legitimate software publisher.

**What is a software license?** In addition to copyright protection, computer software is often protected by the terms of a software license. A **software license**, or *license agreement*, is a legal contract that defines the ways in which you may use a computer program. Software licenses can impose additional restrictions on software use, or they can offer additional rights to consumers. For example, most software is distributed under a **single-user license** that limits use to one person at a time. However, some software publishers offer licenses for multiple users to schools, organizations, and businesses.

A **site license** is generally priced at a flat rate and allows software to be used on all computers at a specific location. A **multiple-user license** is priced per user and allows the allocated number of people to use the software at any time. A **concurrent-use license** is priced per copy and allows a specific number of copies to be used at the same time.

**Where is the license?** For personal computer software, you can find the license on the outside of the package, on a separate card inside the package, on the CD packaging, or in one of the program files. Most legal contracts require signatures before the terms of the contract take effect. This requirement becomes unwieldy with software—imagine having to sign a license agreement and return it before you can use a new software package. To circumvent the signature requirement, software publishers typically use two techniques to validate a software license: shrink-wrap licenses and EULAs.

**What is a shrink wrap license?** When you purchase computer software, the distribution media are usually sealed in an envelope, plastic box, or shrink wrapping. A **shrink-wrap license** goes into effect as soon as you open the packaging. Figure 3-31 explains more about the mechanics of a shrink-wrap license.

**FIGURE 3-30**

According to the Software & Information Industry Association, pirated software can sometimes be identified by these characteristics:

- Software sold in a clear CD-ROM jewel case with no accompanying documentation, license, registration card or Certificate of Authenticity
- Software that is marked as "Academic" product
- Software marked as "OEM" or "For Distribution Only With New PC Hardware"
- Software CD-ROMs with handwritten labels
- Backup disks that you receive from a computer retailer containing handwritten labels
- Poor graphics and coloring of accompanying materials (label on the inside of the jewel case)
- Multiple programs from many different publishers on a single CD-ROM (commonly referred to as Compilation CDs)
- If a computer retailer loads software on your PC, and you request the original manual and the dealer responds by saying purchase a third-party book (eg., "WordPerfect 2000 for Dummies"), this often indicates that the software installed by the retailer is illegal
- Photocopied manuals

**FIGURE 3-31**

When software has a shrink-wrap license, you agree to the terms of the software license by opening the package. If you do not agree with the terms, you should return the software in its unopened package.

**What is a EULA?** A **EULA** (end-user license agreement) is displayed on-screen when you first install software. After reading the software license on the screen, you can indicate that you accept the terms of the license by clicking a designated button—usually labeled OK, I agree, or I accept. If you do not accept the terms, the software does not load and you will not be able to use it.

**When I accept a software license, what am I agreeing to do?** Software licenses are often lengthy and written in legalese, but your legal right to use the software continues only as long as you abide by the terms of the software license. Therefore, you should understand the software license for any software you use. To become familiar with a typical license agreement, you can read through the one in Figure 3-32.

**Software License Agreement**

**Important - READ CAREFULLY:** This License Agreement ("Agreement") is a legal agreement between you and eCourse Corporation for the software product, eCourse GraphWare ("The SOFT-WARE"). By installing, copying, or otherwise using the SOFTWARE, you agree to be bound by the terms of this Agreement. The SOFTWARE is protected by copyright laws and international copyright treaties. The SOFTWARE is licensed, not sold.

**GRANT OF LICENSE.** This Agreement gives you the right to install and use one copy of the SOFTWARE on a single computer. The primary user of the computer on which the SOFTWARE is installed may make a second copy for his or her exclusive use on a portable computer.

**OTHER RIGHTS AND LIMITATIONS.** You may not reverse engineer, decompile, or disassemble the SOFTWARE except and only to the extent that such activity is expressly permitted by applicable law.

The SOFTWARE is licensed as a single product; its components may not be separated for use on more than one computer. You may not rent, lease, or lend the SOFTWARE.

You may permanently transfer all of your rights under this Agreement, provided you retain no copies, you transfer all of the SOFTWARE, and the recipient agrees to the terms of this Agreement. If the software product is an upgrade, any transfer must include all prior versions of the SOFTWARE.

You may receive the SOFTWARE in more than one medium. Regardless of the type of medium you receive, you may use only one medium that is appropriate for your single computer. You may not use or install the other medium on another computer.

**WARRANTY.** eCourse warrants that the SOFTWARE will perform substantially in accordance with the accompanying written documentation for a period of ninety (90) days from the date of receipt. TO THE MAXIMUM EXTENT PERMITTED BY APPLICABLE LAW, eCourse AND ITS SUPPLIERS DISCLAIM ALL OTHER WARRANTIES AND CONDITIONS EITHER EXPRESS OR IMPLIED, INCLUDING, BUT NOT LIMITED TO, IMPLIED WARRANTIES OF MERCHANTABILITY, FITNESS FOR A PARTICULAR PURPOSE, TITLE, AND NON-INFRINGEMENT, WITH REGARD TO THE SOFTWARE PRODUCT.

**FIGURE 3-32**

When you read a software license agreement, look for answers to the following questions:

Am I buying the software or licensing it?

When does the license go into effect?

Under what circumstances can I make copies?

Can I rent the software?

Can I sell the software?

What if the software includes a distribution CD and a set of distribution floppy disks?

Does the software publisher provide a warranty?

Can I loan the software to a friend?

**Are all software licenses similar?** From a legal perspective, there are two categories of software: public domain and proprietary. **Public domain software** is not protected by copyright because the copyright has expired, or the author has placed the program in the public domain, making it available without restriction. Public domain software may be freely copied, distributed, and even resold. The primary restriction on public domain software is that you are not allowed to apply for a copyright on it.

**Proprietary software** has restrictions on its use that are delineated by copyright, patents, or license agreements. Some proprietary software is distributed commercially, whereas some of it is free. Based on licensing rights, proprietary software is distributed as commercial software, demoware, shareware, freeware, and open source software.

**What is commercial software?** **Commercial software** is typically sold in computer stores or at Web sites. Although you buy this software, you actually purchase only the right to use it under the terms of the software license. A license for commercial software typically adheres closely to the limitations provided by copyright law, although it might give you permission to install the software on a computer at work and on a computer at home, provided that you use only one of them at a time.

**What is demoware?** Some commercial software is available as a trial version, sometimes called demoware. **Demoware** is distributed for free and often comes pre-installed on new computers, but it is limited in some way until you pay for it. Demoware publishers can use a variety of techniques to limit the software. It might remain functional for a set number of days before expiring and requiring payment. It might run for a limited amount of time—for example 60 minutes—each time you launch it. Demoware could be configured so that you can run it for only a limited number of times. Or, key features, such as printing, might be disabled. Disabled features account for demoware's less-than-flattering nickname of crippleware.

Demoware publishers usually take steps to prevent users from uninstalling and reinstalling the demo to circumvent time limitations. Users who want to unlock the full version of a demo can typically do so by following links to the software publisher's Web site and using a credit card to purchase a registration code. The software can then be restarted and used without further interruption after the registration code is entered.

**Is shareware the same as demoware?** The characteristics of shareware sound very similar to those of demoware. **Shareware** is copyrighted software marketed under a try-before-you-buy policy. It typically includes a license that permits you to use the software for a trial period. To use it beyond the trial period, you must pay a registration fee. The original idea behind shareware was that payment would be on the honor system. Unlike crippled or time-limited demoware, shareware was supposed to be fully-functioning software.

Shareware was conceived as a low-cost marketing and distribution channel for independent programmers. Thousands of shareware programs are available, encompassing just about as many applications as commercial software. A shareware license usually encourages you to make copies of the software and distribute them to others. Copying, considered a bad thing by commercial software publishers, can work to the advantage of shareware authors, but only if users pay for the product. Unfortunately many shareware authors collect only a fraction of the money they deserve for their programming efforts.

Today, many shareware authors use demoware techniques to limit their programs until payment is received. The term shareware is used today to refer to programs distributed by independent programmers, whereas demoware tends to be used when referring to trial versions of software from big software firms, such as Microsoft, Adobe Systems, and Oracle.

**What about freeware?** **Freeware** is copyrighted software that—as you might expect—is available for free. It is fully functional and requires no payment for its use. Because the software is protected by copyright, you cannot do anything with it that is not expressly allowed by copyright law or by the author. Typically, the license for freeware permits you to use the software, copy it, and give it away, but does not permit you to alter it or sell it. Many utility programs, device drivers, and some games are available as freeware.

**What is open source software?** **Open source software** makes uncompiled program instructions—the source code—available to programmers who want to modify and improve the software. Open source software may be sold or distributed free of charge in compiled form, but it must, in every case, also include the source code. Linux is an example of open source software, as is FreeBSD—a version of UNIX designed for personal computers. OpenOffice.org—a full-featured productivity suite—is another popular example open source software. Despite the lack of restrictions on distribution and use, open source software is copyrighted and is not public domain.

Many open source characteristics also apply to free software (not to be confused with freeware, which you are not supposed to modify or resell). Both open source and free software can be copied an unlimited number of times, distributed for free, sold, and modified. The philosophies behind open source and free software are slightly different, but their licenses are really quite similar.

Two of the most common open source and free software licenses are BSD and GPL. The **BSD license** originated as the Berkeley Software Distribution license for a UNIX-like operating system. The license is simple and short (Figure 3-33).

**FIGURE 3-33**

Open source and free software licenses include BSD and GPL. The wording of the BSD license is very simple.

Copyright (c) 2007, [Publisher]

All rights reserved.

Redistribution and use in source and binary forms, with or without modification, are permitted provided that the following conditions are met:

* Redistributions of source code must retain the above copyright notice, this list of conditions, and the following disclaimer.

* Redistributions in binary form must reproduce the above copyright notice, this list of conditions and the following disclaimer in the documentation and/or other materials provided with the distribution.

* Neither the name of the Publisher nor the names of its contributors may be used to endorse or promote products derived from this software without specific prior written permission.

THIS SOFTWARE IS PROVIDED BY THE PUBLISHER AND CONTRIBUTORS "AS IS" AND ANY EXPRESS OR IMPLIED WARRANTIES, INCLUDING, BUT NOT LIMITED TO, THE IMPLIED WARRANTIES OF MERCHANTABILITY AND FITNESS FOR A PARTICULAR PURPOSE ARE DISCLAIMED. IN NO EVENT SHALL THE PUBLISHER AND CONTRIBUTORS BE LIABLE FOR ANY DIRECT, INDIRECT, INCIDENTAL, SPECIAL, EXEMPLARY, OR CONSEQUENTIAL DAMAGES (INCLUDING, BUT NOT LIMITED TO, PROCUREMENT OF SUBSTITUTE GOODS OR SERVICES; LOSS OF USE, DATA, OR PROFITS; OR BUSINESS INTERRUPTION) HOWEVER CAUSED AND ON ANY THEORY OF LIABILITY, WHETHER IN CONTRACT, STRICT LIABILITY, OR TORT (INCLUDING NEGLIGENCE OR OTHERWISE) ARISING IN ANY WAY OUT OF THE USE OF THIS SOFTWARE, EVEN IF ADVISED OF THE POSSIBILITY OF SUCH DAMAGE.

The **GPL** (General Public License) was developed for a free operating system called GNU. GPL is slightly more restrictive than BSD because it requires derivative works to be licensed under a GPL. That means if you get a really cool computer game that's licensed under GPL and you modify the game to create a new level, you have to distribute your modification under the GPL license. You cannot legally market your modification under a commercial software license. There are currently three versions of the GPL license. Their differences are of interest primarily to software developers.

**Should a software license affect my purchase decision?** Savvy software buyers typically consider software licenses before they make a purchase. Understanding a software license helps you stay on the right side of the law and can save you money.

Before purchasing software, make sure the license allows you to use the software the way you want to. If you plan to install the software on more than one computer or introduce modifications, make sure the license allows you to do so.

Some commercial software, such as security software, requires annual renewal. If you don't want to pay the fee every year, you might consider open source security software instead. Informed consumers tend to make better buying decisions. Just remember that many software programs exist and you can usually find alternatives with similar features offered under various licensing terms.

**3**

# QuickCheck

1. One advantage of a software [_____] is that each application tends to have a similar user interface and it is usually easy to transport data from one application to another.

2. System [_____] specify the operating system and minimum hardware capacities required for software to work correctly.

3. If the opening screen of a software application contains no copyright notice, it is not protected by copyright law. True or false? [_____]

4. [_____] domain software is not copyrighted, making it available for use without restriction, except that you cannot apply for a copyright on it.

5. A [_____]-use license is priced per copy and allows a specific number of copies to be used at the same time.

6. [_____] source software is distributed with its source code so that it can be legally modified and redistributed.

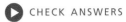 CHECK ANSWERS

# Installing Software and Upgrades

**IT'S SURPRISING HOW QUICKLY** your collection of software can grow as you discover new ways to use your computer for school, work, and play. Before you can use software, you have to install it on your computer. As you read Section D, you'll find out how to install software from CDs or from downloads, how to upgrade your software, and how to eliminate some of the software you no longer need.

## INSTALLATION BASICS

**What's included in a typical software package?** Whether it's on a CD or downloaded from the Web, today's software is typically composed of many files. For example, the eVideo-In Pro software includes numerous files with extensions such as .exe, .dll, and .hlp, as shown in Figure 3-34.

**FIGURE 3-34**

The files required by the eVideo-In Pro software contain user-executable programs, support programs, and data.

At least one of the files included in a software package is an **executable file** designed to be started by users or automatically launched by the operating system. On PCs, these programs are stored in files that typically have .exe file extensions and are sometimes referred to as user-executable files or exe files (pronounced E-X-E).

Other files supplied with a software package contain support programs for the computer to use in conjunction with the main executable file. A support program can be called, or activated, by the main program as needed. In the context of Windows software, support programs often have file extensions such as .dll and .ocx.

In addition to program files, many software packages also include data files. As you might expect, these files contain any data that is necessary for a task, but not supplied by the user, such as Help documentation, a word list for an online spell checker, synonyms for a thesaurus, or graphics for the software's toolbar icons. The data files supplied with a software package sport file extensions such as .txt, .bmp, and .hlp. Figure 3-35 can help you visualize how multiple files work together as one software application.

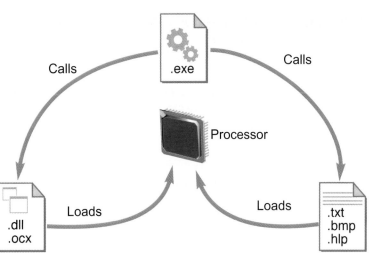

**FIGURE 3-35**

The main executable file provides the primary set of instructions for the computer to execute and calls various support programs and data files as needed.

With some operating systems, including Windows, one software program might share some common files with other software. These shared files are often supplied by the operating system and perform routine tasks, such as displaying the Print dialog box, which allows you to select a printer and specify how many copies you want to print. Shared files are not typically distributed with software because they should already exist on your computer. The installation routine attempts to locate these files. It then notifies you if any files are missing, and provides instructions for installing them.

**Why does software require so many files?** The use of a main executable file plus several support programs and data files offers a great deal of flexibility and efficiency for software developers. Support programs and data files from existing programs can usually be modified by developers for other programs without changing the main executable file. This modular approach can significantly reduce the time required to create and test the main executable file, which usually contains a long and fairly complex program. The modular approach also allows software developers to reuse their support programs in multiple software products and adapt preprogrammed support modules for use in their own software.

Modular programming techniques are of interest mainly to people who create computer programs; however, these techniques affect the process of installing and uninstalling software. It is important, therefore, to remember that computer software typically consists of many files that contain user-executable programs, support programs, and data.

**Is it necessary to install software?** **Software installation** (sometimes referred to as setup) is a process that places a program into a computer so that it can be run or executed. Installation can simply be a matter of copying files to a computer or plugging in a USB flash drive, or it can be a more formal process that requires a series of steps and configurations. Installation procedures depend on your computer's operating system and whether the software is a local, Web, or portable application.

For purposes of this discussion, we'll look at software installation under the Windows operating system. The procedure features some quirks and complexities that don't exist with the Mac and Linux platforms, and because Windows use is so pervasive, understanding how to install software on a PC is useful and practical.

## INSTALLING LOCAL APPLICATIONS

**What is a local application?** A **local application** is software that is designed to reside on a computer's hard disk. When you install a local application, its files are placed in the appropriate folders on your computer's hard disk, and then your computer performs any software or hardware configurations necessary to make sure the program is ready to run.

Most local applications contain a **setup program** that guides you through the installation process. During the installation process, the setup program usually performs the following activities:

- Copies files from distribution media or downloads files to specified folders on the hard disk

- Uncompresses files that have been distributed in compressed format

- Analyzes the computer's resources, such as processor speed, RAM capacity, and hard disk capacity, to verify that they meet or exceed the minimum system requirements

- Analyzes hardware components and peripheral devices to select appropriate device drivers

- Looks for any system files and players, such as Internet Explorer or Windows Media Player, that are required to run the program but are not supplied on the distribution media or download

- Updates necessary system files, such as the Windows Registry and the Windows Start menu, with information about the new software

**What is the Windows Registry?** The **Windows Registry** is a database that keeps track of your computer's peripheral devices, software, preferences, and settings. You'll learn more about the Registry in the operating system chapter, but the important concept to understand is that when you install software on the hard disk, information about the software is recorded in the Registry.

**Are all the software files installed in the same folder?** Most executable files and data files for new software are placed in the folder you specify. Some support programs for the software, however, might be stored in other folders, such as Windows\System. The location for these files is determined by the software installation routine. Figure 3-36 maps out the location of files for a typical Windows software installation.

### TERMINOLOGY NOTE

Although the term *local application* seems to imply application software as opposed to system software, it is also used in a broader sense to refer to any system or application software that is installed locally on the hard disk.

**FIGURE 3-36**

When you install software, its files might end up in different folders. Files for the eVideo-In Pro software are installed in two folders.

| Windows\System | | |
|---|---|---|
| File name | Size | Type |
| eVidmdbg.dll | 20 KB | Support Program |
| eVidodec32.dll | 92 KB | Support Program |
| eVidwave.dll | 37 KB | Support Program |
| Version.dll | 24 KB | Support Program |
| eVidpodbc.dll | 955 KB | Support Program |
| eVidgain.dll | 116 KB | Support Program |
| eVgateway.ocx | 42 KB | Support Program |

Distribution CDs

| Program Files\eVideo-In Pro | | |
|---|---|---|
| File name | Size | Type |
| eVidpro.exe | 5,500 KB | Main Executable Program |
| eVidpro.hlp | 275 KB | Help File |
| eVidcore.hlp | 99 KB | Help File |
| eVidcore.dll | 1,425 KB | Support Program |
| eVidpro.dll | 1,517 KB | Support Program |
| Readme.doc | 65 KB | Data File |
| eVdplugin.dll | 813 KB | Support Program |
| eVdtrans.dll | 921 KB | Support Program |

**How do I install local applications from CDs and DVDs?** The process of installing a local application from distribution CDs or DVDs is quite straightforward. You insert the CD or DVD and close the tray. A setup program should autostart and then guide you through the process of selecting the hard disk location for the program files and acknowledging the EULA. Figure 3-37 shows what to expect when you use a setup program to install local apps from CDs or DVDs.

**FIGURE 3-37**

Installing from Distribution Media

1 Insert the first distribution CD or DVD. The setup program should start automatically. If it does not, look for a file called Setup.exe and then run it.

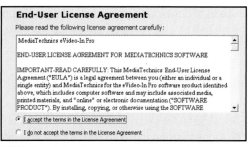

2 Read the license agreement, if one is presented on the screen. By agreeing to the terms of the license, you can proceed with the installation.

3 Select the installation option that best meets your needs. If you select a full installation, the setup program copies all files and data from the distribution medium to the hard disk of your computer system. A full installation gives you access to all features of the software.

If you select a custom installation, the setup program displays a list of software features for your selection. After you select the features you want, the setup program copies only the selected program and data files to your hard disk. A custom installation can save space on your hard disk.

4 Follow the prompts provided by the setup program to specify a folder to hold the new software program. You can use the default folder specified by the setup program or a folder of your own choosing, You can also create a new folder during the setup process.

5 If the software includes multiple distribution CDs, insert each one in the specified drive when the setup program prompts you.

6 When the setup is complete, start the program you just installed to make sure it works.

**How do I install downloaded software?** The installation process is slightly different for Windows software that you download. Usually all the files needed for the new software are **zipped** to consolidate them into one large file, which is compressed to decrease its size and reduce the download time. As part of the installation process, this downloaded file must be reconstituted, or **unzipped**, into the original collection of files.

It is a good idea to store original unzipped files for downloaded software on a CD or in a hard disk folder that you back up periodically. If your computer's hard drive malfunctions, you can use these files to reconstitute your software without having to download all of it again. Figure 3-38 maps out the process of downloading and installing local apps.

**FIGURE 3-38**

Installing Downloaded Software

**1** At the distribution Web site, locate any information pertaining to installing the software. Read it. You might also want to print it.

**2** Click the download link.

**3** If you are downloading from a trusted site and have antivirus software running, click the Open button in the File Download dialog box.

**4** Wait for the download to finish. Typically, the setup program included in the download starts automatically.

**5** Use the setup program to specify a folder to hold the new software program. You can use the default folder specified by the setup program or a folder of your own choosing. You can also create a new folder during the setup process.

**6** Wait for the setup program to uncompress the downloaded file and install the software in the selected directory. During this process, respond to license agreement and other prompts. When the installation is complete, test the software to make sure it works.

Downloadable software can be provided in several different formats. Some automatically install themselves, but others require manual procedures. A downloadable file typically is set up as a **self-installing executable file**, **self-executing zip file**, or **non-executing zip file** (Figure 3-39).

FIGURE 3-39

Downloadable File Formats

### Self-installing Executable Files

Under the most automated installation system, the process of downloading new software automatically initiates the entire installation process.

The software download is packaged as one large file with an .exe extension. This file automatically unzips itself and starts the setup program. You simply follow the setup program prompts to acknowledge the license agreement, indicate the folder for the software files, and complete the installation.

### Self-executing Zip Files

Downloaded files with .exe extensions do not always install themselves. Some are simply self-executing zip files, which automatically unzip the software's files, but do not automatically start the setup program.

To install software from a self-executing zip file, you start the executable file to unzip the files for the new software. One of these files will be the Setup.exe program. Next, you manually start the setup program and follow its prompts to complete the installation.

### Non-executing Zip Files

If you download software and it arrives as one huge file with a .zip extension, you must locate this file on your hard disk and then use Windows XP or a program such as WinZip to unzip it.

After unzipping the file, you must run the setup program to acknowledge the license agreement, indicate the folder for the software files, and complete the installation.

**What if my software requires activation?** **Product activation** is a means of protecting software from illegal copying by requiring users to enter a product key or activation code before the software can be used. Activation is usually part of the software installation process, but it can also occur when demoware times out. Failure to enter a valid code prohibits the program from launching.

Product activation is not the same as registration, which is designed to collect demographic information from consumers, although a few software publishers tie activation and registration together.

Software can be activated over the phone or more commonly on the Internet. Usually a message appears onscreen instructing you to enter a serial number or validation code supplied on the distribution medium, packaging material, or download site. The information you enter is either checked against a database or used to create a hash value.

Checking an activation code against a database, makes sure that the code you've entered has not been used before. If the code is a duplicate, the license for that copy of the software is being used by someone else and you will have to call customer service to straighten out the problem.

A **hash value** is a unique number derived from encoding one or more data sets, such as names, serial numbers, and validation codes. Product validation can create a hash value based on your validation code and your computer's internal serial number, effectively tying the software to use on one specific computer.

Validation codes are very important. You should keep a list of them in a safe place, along with other configuration information for your computer system.

## INSTALLING PORTABLE SOFTWARE AND WEB APPS

**What is portable software?** **Portable software** is designed to run from removable storage, such as a CD or USB flash drive. Program files do not exist on the hard disk, no configuration data is stored on the hard disk, and no entries need to be made in the Windows Registry. When the media containing the portable software is removed from the computer, no trace of it is left there.

Your BookOnCD is an example of portable software. To use it, you simply insert the CD containing the program files. Other examples of portable applications include OpenOffice.org, Thunderbird (e-mail), Firefox (browser), and FileZilla (upload and download), designed to run from USB flash drives.

**How do I install portable software?** Portable software is so simple to install that it is sometimes referred to as install-free software. Installation is simply a matter of getting program files to the media on which they are supposed to run. For example, suppose that you want to run Portable OpenOffice.org from a USB flash drive. You can download the Portable OpenOffice.org zip file and then simply unzip it so that the files end up on the USB flash drive (Figure 3-40).

**What are Web apps?** A **Web application** (or Web app*)* is software that is accessed with a Web browser. Instead of running locally, much of the program code for the software runs on a remote computer connected to the Internet or other computer network. Web apps are available for many of the same applications that run locally, such as e-mail, calendars, databases, photo sharing, project management, maps, games, and even word processing.

**FIGURE 3-40**

Portable OpenOffice.org offers word processing, spreadsheet, database, graphics, and presentation modules that can be run from a USB flash drive and transported from one computer to another.

CLICK TO START

**How do I install Web apps?** Some Web apps, such as Gmail and Yahoo! Mail, require no installation at all on your local computer. These applications use browser software as the e-mail client software, making it possible to access your e-mail from any computer that has a browser and an Internet connection.

Some Web applications, such as Google Earth, require a client-side program to be installed on your local computer. The Internet sites that host Web apps typically include instructions if installation is necessary. You can print the instructions if they look somewhat tricky.

## SOFTWARE UPDATES

**What are updates, patches, and service packs?** Software publishers regularly update their software to add new features, fix bugs, and update its security. Types of software updates (also called upgrades), include new versions, patches, and service packs.

Periodically software publishers produce new versions of their software designed to replace older versions. To keep these updates straight, each version carries a version or revision number. For example, version 1.0 might be replaced by a newer version 1.1 or version 2.0. Updating to a new version usually involves a fee, but it is typically less costly than purchasing the new version off the shelf.

A **software patch** is a small section of program code that replaces part of the software you currently have installed. The term **service pack**, which usually applies to operating system updates, is a set of patches that correct problems and address security vulnerabilities. Software patches and service packs are usually free.

**How do I get updates?** Software publishers have various ways of notifying customers about updates. Many allow you to set your preferences for how you would like to receive notifications and updates. If you have registered your software—usually by connecting to the publisher's Web site during or after an installation—you might receive an e-mail notice when an update is available. Alternatively, you can check the publisher's Web site from time to time.

Some software provides an Automatic Update option that periodically checks the software publisher's Web site for updates, downloads updates automatically, and installs them without user intervention. The advantage of Automatic Update is convenience. The disadvantage is that changes can be made to your computer without your knowledge.

Some software checks the Web to see if an update is available and gives you the option of downloading and installing it, as shown in Figure 3-41.

**FIGURE 3-41**

Adobe Acrobat periodically checks the publisher's Web site. When updates are available, it displays a notification screen that can be used to download and install the update if the user wants to do so.

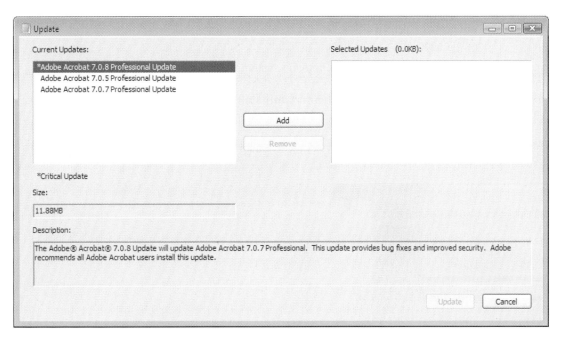

3

**When should I update my software?** It is always a good idea to install patches and service packs when they become available. The revised code they contain often addresses security vulnerabilities and the sooner you patch up those holes, the better.

Version updates are a slightly different story. Many savvy computer owners wait to update for a few weeks or months after new software versions become available. The reason they wait is to find out how other users like the new version. If Internet chatter indicates some major flaws, it can be prudent to wait until the publisher is able to address them with patches.

**How do I install an update?** A new version update usually installs in a similar way as you installed the original version, by activating a setup program, displaying a license agreement, and adding updated entries to your computer's Start menu. To combat piracy, many software publishers require users to enter a validation code to complete an update.

Patches and service packs are usually distributed over the Internet and automatically install themselves when you download them.

**When I install an update, what happens to the old version?** The result of an update depends on several factors. Most patches and service pack installations cannot be reversed. A new version installation typically overwrites the old version, but you might have the option to keep the old version just in case you have trouble with the new one and need to revert back to the previous version. The documentation for the update should explain your options for retaining or overwriting old versions.

## UNINSTALLING SOFTWARE

**How do I know what software is installed on my computer?** When working with a PC, there are several places you can look to see what software is installed. The All Programs menu lists most, if not all, of your installed applications. A few applications might not appear on this list if they were installed in a non-standard way.

You can find information about drivers by using Control Panel's System option. Click the Device Manager option on the Hardware tab to view a list of your computer's hardware. Clicking a device from the list links to information about the device driver, including its publisher, date, and version.

**How do I get rid of software?** With some operating systems, such as DOS, you can remove software simply by deleting its files. Other operating systems, such as Windows and Mac OS, include an **uninstall routine**, (Figure 3-42) which deletes the software's files from various folders on your computer's hard disk. The uninstall routine also removes references to the program from the desktop and from operating system files, such as the file system and, in the case of Windows, the Windows Registry.

**FIGURE 3-42**

The menu option that you use to launch a program might also include an uninstall option.

If an uninstall routine is not provided by the software, you can use the uninstall procedure supplied by your computer's operating system (Figure 3-43).

**FIGURE 3-43**

Uninstall options in Windows XP (right) and Windows Vista (left) list installed software and give you the option to select a program for deletion.

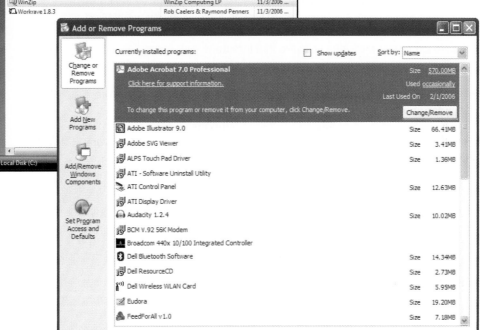

▶ CLICK TO START

# QuickCheck

SECTION D

1. At least one of the files included in a software package is an [_____] file designed to be started by users.

2. A [_____] application is software that is designed to reside on a computer's hard disk.

3. Usually all the files for downloaded software are zipped to consolidate them into one large file. True or false? [_____]

4. [_____] software is designed to run from removable storage, such as a CD or USB flash drive.

5. A software [_____] is a small section of program code that replaces part of the software you currently have installed.

▶ CHECK ANSWERS

# Security Software

THE DAYS WHEN VIRUSES were the greatest threat to computers are long gone. Today a virus is just one of many categories of malicious software, or malware, that can wreak havoc on computer systems and networks. Deluged with such a huge assortment of threats to their systems and often unable to distinguish one type of threat from another, individual computer users and businesses have had to defend themselves by purchasing all kinds of security software. Section E explains how you can use security software to combat malicious software that threatens your computer.

## SECURITY SOFTWARE BASICS

**What is security software?** **Security software** is designed to protect computers from various forms of destructive software and unauthorized intrusions. One of the first security software offerings was created by Dr. Peter Tippett, an emergency room physician who took a page from conventional medicine and applied it to computer viruses. The security software developed by Dr. Tippett was sold to Symantec Corporation in 1992 and incorporated into the popular Norton AntiVirus software.

Security software can be classified into various types: antivirus, anti-spyware, anti-spam, and firewalls. Each type focuses on a specific security threat.

**What are malware threats?** The terms **malicious software** and **malware** refer to any computer program designed to surreptitiously enter a computer, gain unauthorized access to data, or disrupt normal processing operations. Malware includes viruses, worms, Trojans, bots, and spyware.

Malware is created and unleashed by individuals referred to as hackers, crackers, black hats, or cybercriminals. The motivation behind malware is varied. Some malware was intended to be a relatively harmless prank or mildly annoying vandalism. Other malware was created to distribute political messages or to disrupt operations at specific companies. In an increasing number of cases, the motivation is monetary gain. Malware designed for identity theft or extortion has become a very real threat to individuals and corporations. Organized crime bosses, drug traffickers, and terrorists are joining forces with cybercriminals to increase the sophistication of their activities (Figure 3-44).

Emerging security threats often combine and refine old exploits, blurring the lines between viruses, worms, and other kinds of malware. For example, a Trojan horse might carry a bot that turns a victim's computer into a distribution point for a mass-mailing worm. Security experts use the term **blended threat** to describe malware that combines more than one type of malicious program. Although the nuances of blended threats are beyond the scope of this chapter, it is important to understand the threats posed by viruses, worms, Trojans, bots, and spyware if you hope to avoid identity theft and other inconvenient computing incidents.

**FIGURE 3-44**

Security breaches were once little more than pranks, but today's threats from organized crime and terrorists are serious concerns, not only for individuals, but for corporations and governments.

**What is a virus?** A **computer virus** is a set of program instructions that attaches itself to a file, reproduces itself, and spreads to other files. A common misconception is that viruses spread themselves from one computer to another. They don't. Viruses can replicate themselves only on the host computer. A key characteristic of viruses is their ability to lurk in a computer for days or months, quietly replicating themselves. While this replication takes place, you might not even know that your computer has contracted a virus; therefore, it is easy to inadvertently spread infected files to other people's computers.

In addition to replicating itself, a virus might deliver a payload, which could be as harmless as displaying an annoying message or as devastating as corrupting the data on your computer's hard disk. It can corrupt files, destroy data, display an irritating message, or otherwise disrupt computer operations. A trigger event, such as a specific date, can unleash some viruses. For example, the Michelangelo virus triggers on March 6, the birthday of artist Michelangelo. Viruses that deliver their payloads on a specific date are sometimes referred to as time bombs. Viruses that deliver their payloads in response to some other system event are referred to as logic bombs.

Viruses spread when people distribute infected files by exchanging disks and CDs, sending e-mail attachments, exchanging music on file-sharing networks, and downloading software from the Web.

**What is a worm?** A **computer worm** is a self-replicating program designed to carry out some unauthorized activity on a victim's computer. Worms can spread themselves from one computer to another without any assistance from victims. They can enter a computer through security holes in browsers and operating systems, as e-mail attachments, and by victims clicking on infected pop-up ads or links contained in e-mails.

Mass-mailing worms such as Klez, Netsky, MyDoom, Sasser, and Bagle (also called Beagle) have made headlines and caused havoc on personal computers, LANs, and Internet servers. A **mass-mailing worm** spreads by sending itself to every address in the address book of an infected computer. To make these worms difficult to track, the *From* line of the infected message sometimes contains a spoofed address of a randomly selected person from the e-mail address book.

Although e-mail is currently the primary vehicle used to spread worms, hackers have also devised ways to spread worms over file-sharing networks, such as Kazaa. Some worms are designed to spread over instant messaging links. Worms such as Cabir and Symbos_skulls can even infect mobile phones.

**What is a Trojan Horse?** A **Trojan horse** (sometimes simply called a *Trojan*) is a computer program that seems to perform one function while actually doing something else. Unlike a worm, a Trojan is not designed to spread itself to other computers. Also differing from viruses and worms, Trojans are not typically designed to replicate themselves. Trojans are standalone programs that masquerade as useful utilities or applications, which victims download and install unaware of their destructive nature.

Trojan horses are notorious for stealing passwords using a **keylogger**—a type of program that records keystrokes. Another type of Trojan called a **Remote Access Trojan** (RAT) has backdoor capabilities that allow remote hackers to transmit files to victims' computers, search for data, run programs, and use a victim's computer as a relay station for breaking into other computers.

**INFOWEBLINKS**

The old saying "know thy enemy" applies to malicious software. To learn more details about current threats, visit the **Virus Descriptions InfoWeb**.

 CLICK TO CONNECT
www.course.com/np/concepts10/ch03

3

**TERMINOLOGY NOTE**

A *spoofed address* is one that is misleading or incorrect. In the case of e-mail, it is not the actual address of the person or computer that sent the e-mail message. Spoofed addresses make it difficult or impossible to trace mail back to the sender.

**What is a bot?** Any software that can automate a task or autonomously execute a task when commanded to do so is called an intelligent agent. Because an intelligent agent behaves somewhat like a robot, it is often called a **bot**.

Good bots perform a variety of helpful tasks such as scanning the Web to assemble data for search engines like Google. Some bots offer online help, while others monitor chat groups for prohibited behavior and language. Bad bots, on the other hand, are controlled by hackers and designed for unauthorized or destructive tasks. They can be spread by worms or Trojans. Most bad bots are able to initiate communications with a central server on the Internet to receive instructions. A computer under the control of a bad bot is sometimes referred to as a **zombie** because it carries out instructions from a malicious leader.

Like a spider in its web, the person who controls many bot-infested computers can link them together into a network called a **botnet**. Experts have discovered botnets encompassing more than one million computers. Botmasters who control botnets use the combined computing power of their zombie legions for many types of nefarious tasks such as breaking into encrypted data, carrying out Denial of Service attacks against other computers, and sending out massive amounts of spam.

**What is spyware?** **Spyware** is a type of program that secretly gathers personal information without the victim's knowledge, usually for advertising and other commercial purposes. Once it is installed, spyware starts monitoring Web-surfing and purchasing behavior, and sends a summary back to one or more third parties. Just like Trojans, spyware can monitor keystrokes and relay passwords and credit card information to cybercriminals.

Spyware can get into a computer using exploits similar to those of Trojans. It can piggyback on seemingly legitimate freeware or shareware downloads. You can also inadvertently allow spyware into your computer by clicking innocuous but infected pop-up ads or surfing through seemingly valid and secure but compromised Web sites.

**What does malware do?** Once viruses, worms, bots, Trojans, and spyware enter your computer, they can carry out a variety of unauthorized activities, such as those listed in Figure 3-45.

> **TERMINOLOGY NOTE**
>
> A *Denial of Service attack* is designed to generate a lot of activity on a network by flooding its servers with useless traffic—enough traffic to overwhelm the server's processing capability and essentially bring all communications and services to a halt.

**FIGURE 3-45**

Malware Activities

- Display irritating messages and pop-up ads.
- Delete or modify your data.
- Encrypt your data and demand ransom for the encryption key.
- Upload or download unwanted files.
- Log your keystrokes to steal your passwords and credit card numbers.
- Propagate malware and spam to everyone on your e-mail address book or your instant messaging buddy list.
- Disable your antivirus and firewall software.
- Block access to specific Web sites and redirect your browser to infected Web sites.
- Cause response time on your system to deteriorate.
- Allow hackers to remotely access data on your computer.
- Allow hackers to take remote control of your machine and turn it into a zombie.
- Link your computer to others in a botnet that can send millions of spam e-mails or wage Denial of Service attacks against Web sites.
- Cause network traffic jams.

**How do I know if my computer is infected?** Watch out for the symptoms of an infected computer listed in Figure 3-46.

FIGURE 3-46

Symptoms of Infection

3

- Irritating messages or sounds
- Frequent pop-up ads, at times with pornographic content
- The sudden appearance of a new Internet toolbar on your browser's home page
- An addition to your Internet favorites list that you didn't put there
- Prolonged system start-up
- Slower than usual response to mouse clicks and keyboard strokes
- Browser or application crashes
- Missing files
- Your computer's security software becomes disabled and it cannot be restarted
- Periodic network activity when you are not actively browsing or sending e-mail
- Your computer reboots itself frequently

Some malware does a good job of cloaking itself, so victims are unaware of its presence. Cloaking techniques are great defense mechanisms because when victims aren't aware of malware, they won't take steps to eradicate it. Many victims whose computers were part of massive botnets never knew their computers were compromised.

Some hackers cloak their work using rootkits. The term **rootkit** refers to software tools used to conceal malware and backdoors that have been installed on a victim's computer. Rootkits can hide bots, keyloggers, spyware, worms, and viruses. With a rootkit in place, hackers can continue to exploit a victim's computer with little risk of discovery. Rootkits are usually distributed by Trojans.

**How do I avoid security threats?** The Orientation section at the beginning of this book listed some techniques for safe computing. That list is worth repeating (Figure 3-47).

FIGURE 3-47

Avoiding Security Threats

- Install and activate security software on every computing device you own.
- Keep software patches and operating system service packs up to date.
- Do not open suspicious e-mail attachments.
- Obtain software only from reliable sources, and before running it use security software to scan for malware.
- Do not click pop-up ads—to make the ad go away, right-click the ad's taskbar button and select the Close option.
- Avoid unsavory Web sites.
- Disable the option *Hide extensions for known file types in Windows* so you can avoid opening files with more than one extension, such as a file called game.exe.zip.

**What's a virus hoax?** Some virus threats are very real, but you're also likely to get e-mail messages about so-called viruses that don't really exist. A **virus hoax** usually arrives as an e-mail message containing dire warnings about a supposedly new virus on the loose. When you receive an e-mail message about a virus or any other type of malware, don't panic. It could be a hoax.

You can check one of the many antivirus software Web sites to determine whether you've received a hoax or a real threat. The Web sites also provide security or virus alerts, which list all the most recent legitimate malware threats. If the virus is a real threat, the Web site can provide information to determine whether your computer has been infected. You can also find instructions for eradicating the virus. If the virus threat is a hoax, by no means should you forward the e-mail message to others.

**INFOWEBLINKS**

Some Web sites specialize in tracking hoaxes. For links to these sites, visit the **Hoax InfoWeb**.

 CLICK TO CONNECT

www.course.com/np/concepts10/ch03

## SECURITY SUITES

**What is a security suite?** A **security suite** integrates several security modules to protect against the most common types of malware, unauthorized access, and spam. Security suites might include additional features such as WiFi detection that warns of possible intrusions into your wireless network and parental controls for monitoring and controlling children's Internet usage. A security suite, like the one in Figure 3-48, typically includes antivirus, firewall, and privacy modules.

**FIGURE 3-48**

McAfee Security Suite includes modules for Virusscan, Personal Firewall, Privacy Service, and Spamkilller.

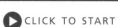 CLICK TO START

**What are the advantages and disadvantages of a security suite?** A security suite costs less than purchasing standalone security modules. In addition, a single interface for accessing all of the security suite's features is much less complex than having to learn how to configure and run several different products.

When installing a security suite you are typically required to uninstall or disable all other antivirus, anti-spyware, and firewall software on your computer. Most security suites cannot run concurrently with standalone security products, and overlapping security coverage from two similar products can cause glitches. Therefore, one disadvantage of security suites is that you become dependent on your security package's vendor, who becomes the sole protector of your computer from malicious code. In addition, suites may not have the best individual security components, but you cannot pick and choose. However, competition between security suite vendors tends to increase the quality of security offerings.

**INFOWEBLINKS**

If you don't have security software for your computer you should get it. Use the **Antivirus Software InfoWeb** to link to Web sites where you can purchase and download various types of security software.

 CLICK TO CONNECT

www.course.com/np/concepts10/ch03

**Where can I purchase a security suite?** The most popular security suites include Symantec Norton Internet Security, McAfee Internet Security Suite, Alwil Avast!, Trend Micro PC-cillin Internet Security, and Panda Platinum Internet Security. They can be purchased in most office, electronics, and computer stores, or downloaded from the Web.

It is also worth looking into your ISP's free security offerings. For example, Comcast provides its customers with McAfee security products, all accessible through Comcast's special toolbar. AOL gives its customers a security package that combines McAfee's main security products with its own home-grown security features, such as parental control and spam filters.

A security suite is often pre-installed on a new computer. However, usually it is demoware, so you have the option of purchasing it after the trial period, normally 60 days. Typically, there is also an annual subscription fee for continued use and regular updates. When you renew your subscription, you might have an option to upgrade to a newer version for an extra $10-20. There are also open source versions of antivirus software, which do not require annual subscription fees.

**Is open source security software as dependable as commercial security suites?** Open source security software, like all open source software, is distributed with its source code. Because the source code is open for examination, black hats can view the code and look for security holes. They can potentially plot strategies to disable security protection or sneak past its defenses. Proponents of open source software, however, claim that because the code is open, security holes are likely to be discovered and fixed by white hats before they can be exploited by hackers. Vulnerabilities have been discovered in both open source and commercial security products.

Whether open source products, such as ClamWin (Figure 3-49) or commercial security software, each security suite has unique strengths and weaknesses, which can change as the suites are updated. Before you purchase a security suite, read current reviews and check user ratings at consumer Web sites.

## ANTIVIRUS MODULES

**What is antivirus software?** **Antivirus software** is a type of utility software that looks for and eradicates viruses, Trojan horses, worms, and bots. Most antivirus software also scans for spyware, although some security software publishers offer spyware detection as a separate module. Antivirus software is included in security suites or can be purchased as a standalone module. Antivirus software is available for all types of computer and data storage, including handhelds, personal computers, USB flash drives, and servers.

**How does antivirus software work?** Modern antivirus software attempts to identify malware by searching your computer's files and memory for virus signatures. A **virus signature** is a section of program code, such as a unique series of instructions, that can be used to identify a known malicious program, much as a fingerprint is used to identify an individual.

Antivirus software scans for virus signatures in programs, data files, incoming and outgoing e-mail and attachments, and inbound instant message attachments. Antivirus software can also watch for unusual activity such as a considerably large number of e-mail messages being sent out from your computer.

**FIGURE 3-49**

Open source antivirus software ClamWin comes in a portable version to protect USB flash drives.

Most antivirus programs can also scan for virus signatures in zip files, which is important when downloading zipped software and receiving zipped e-mail attachments.

### How do I activate and deactivate my antivirus software?

Installation and activation procedures vary for each virus protection product. However, once you have installed your antivirus software, the best and safest practice is to keep it running full time in the background so that it checks every e-mail message as it arrives and scans all files the moment you access them. The scanning process requires only a short amount of time, which creates a slight delay in downloading e-mail and opening files.

When installing some application or utility software you might be instructed to deactivate your antivirus software. You can usually right-click the icon on your computer's taskbar that corresponds to your antivirus software and then select the exit or disable option. Do not forget to reactivate your antivirus software as soon as the installation is completed.

### How should I configure my antivirus software?
For the most extensive protection from malware, you should look for and enable the features of your antivirus software listed in Figure 3-50.

**FIGURE 3-50**

Configuration Settings for Antivirus Software

- Start scanning when the computer boots.
- Scan all programs when they are launched and document files when they are opened.
- Scan other types of files, such as graphics, if you engage in some risky computing behaviors and are not concerned with the extra time required to open files as they are scanned.
- Scan incoming mail and attachments.
- Scan incoming instant message attachments.
- Scan outgoing e-mail for worm activity such as mass-mailing worms.
- Scan zip (compressed) files.
- Scan for spyware, sometimes called pups (potentially unwanted programs).
- Scan all files on the computer's hard disk at least once a week.

### How do I keep my antivirus software up-to-date?
Two aspects of your antivirus software periodically need to be updated. First, the antivirus program itself might need a patch or update to fix bugs or improve features. Second, the list of virus signatures has to be updated to keep up with the latest malware developments. Virus signatures and other information that antivirus software uses to identify and eradicate malware is stored in one or more files usually referred to as **virus definitions**. Antivirus program updates and revised virus definitions are packaged into a file that can be manually or automatically downloaded. If your antivirus software is part of a security suite, the update might also include patches for other security software modules, such as the anti-spam module or firewall.

Most antivirus products are preconfigured to regularly check for updates, download them, and install them without user intervention. If you would rather control the download and installation process yourself, you can configure your antivirus software to alert you when updates are ready. In any case, you should manually check for updates periodically just in case the auto-update function has become disabled.

**How often should I do a system scan?** Most experts recommend that you configure your antivirus software to periodically scan all the files on your computer. With the proliferation of malware attacks, it's best to schedule a weekly system scan. Because a full system scan can significantly slow down your computer, schedule the scan for a time when you are not usually using your computer, but it is turned on.

You can also run a manual scan of your entire computer or of specific files. For example, suppose you download a program and you want to make sure it is virus free before you install and run it. You can use Windows Explorer to locate and right-click the downloaded file, then select the *Scan* option from the pop-up menu (Figure 3-51).

**What does quarantine mean?** If, during the scanning process, your virus protection software identifies a virus, worm, Trojan horse, or bot in a file or attachment, it can try to remove the infection, put the file into quarantine, or simply delete the file. A **quarantined file** typically contains suspicious code, such as a virus signature. For your protection, most antivirus software encrypts the file contents and isolates it in a quarantine folder, so it can't be inadvertently opened or accessed by a hacker. If the infected file ends up on a quarantine list, your antivirus software might give you the option of trying to disinfect the file or deleting it.

**How dependable is antivirus software?** Today's antivirus software is quite dependable, but not infallible. A fast-spreading worm can reach your computer before a virus definition update arrives, some spyware can slip through the net, and cloaking software can hide some viral exploits. Despite occasional misses, however, antivirus software and other security software modules are constantly weeding out malware that would otherwise infect your computer. It is essential to use security software, but also important to take additional precautions, such as making regular backups of your data.

**FIGURE 3-51**

Before installing and running a downloaded file, you can scan it by right-clicking the file name and selecting the Scan option.

# QuickCheck

1.  The term [_____] threat describes malware that combines more than one type of malicious program.

2.  A key characteristic of [_____] is their ability to lurk in a computer for days or months, quietly replicating themselves.

3.  Unlike a [_____] , a Trojan is not designed to spread itself to other computers.

4.  The term [_____] refers to software tools used to conceal malware and backdoors that have been installed on a victim's computer.

5.  When antivirus software finds a virus signature, it typically [_____] the file by encrypting it and moving it to an isolated folder.

▶ CHECK ANSWERS

# How Serious is Software Piracy?

**SOFTWARE IS EASY TO STEAL.** You don't have to walk out of a Best Buy store with a $495 DVD Workshop software box under your shirt. You can simply borrow your friend's DVD Workshop distribution CDs and install a copy of the program on your computer's hard disk. It seems so simple that it couldn't be illegal. But it is.

Piracy takes many forms. End-user piracy includes friends loaning distribution disks to each other and installing software on more computers than the license allows. Although it is perfectly legal to lend a physical object, such as a sweater, to a friend, it is not legal to lend digital copies of software and music because, unlike a sweater that can be worn by only one person at a time, copies of digital things can be simultaneously used by many people.

Counterfeiting is the large-scale illegal duplication of software distribution media, and sometimes, even its packaging. According to Microsoft, many software counterfeiting groups are linked to organized crime and money-laundering schemes that fund a diverse collection of illegal activities, such as smuggling, gambling, extortion, and prostitution. Counterfeit software is sold in retail stores and through online auctions—often the packaging looks so authentic that buyers have no idea they have purchased illegal goods.

Internet piracy uses the Web as a way to illegally distribute unauthorized software. In Net jargon, the terms *appz* and *warez* (pronounced as "wares" or "war EZ") refer to pirated software. Some warez has even been modified to eliminate serial numbers, registration requirements, expiration dates, or other forms of copy protection. The Business Software Alliance (BSA) estimates that more than 800,000 Web sites illegally sell or distribute software.

In many countries, including the United States, software pirates are subject to civil lawsuits for monetary damages and criminal prosecution, which can result in jail time and stiff fines. Nonetheless, software piracy continues to have enormous impact. According to a BSA and IDC 2006 Piracy Study, $60 billion of software was legitimately purchased worldwide, but software worth a whopping $34 billion was pirated.

A small, but vocal, minority of software users, such as members of GNU (which stands for "Gnu's Not UNIX"), believes that data and software should be freely distributed. Richard Stallman writes in the GNU Manifesto, "I consider that the golden rule requires that if I like a program I must share it with other people who like it. Software sellers want to divide users and conquer them, making each user agree not to share with others. I refuse to break solidarity with other users in this way. I cannot in good conscience sign a nondisclosure agreement or a software license agreement."

Is software piracy really damaging? Who cares if you use a program without paying for it? Software piracy is damaging because it has a negative effect on the economy. Software production makes a major contribution to the United States economy, employing more than 2 million people and accounting for billions of dollars in corporate revenue. It fuels economic development in countries such as India, China, and Malaysia. A BSA economic impact study concluded that lowering global piracy from an average of 36% to only 26% would add more that 1 million jobs and $400 billion in worldwide economic growth.

Decreases in software revenues can have a direct effect on consumers, too. When software publishers are forced to cut corners, they tend to reduce customer service and technical support. As a result, you, the consumer, get put on hold when you call for technical support, find fewer free technical support sites, and encounter customer support personnel who are only moderately knowledgeable about their products. The bottom line—software piracy negatively affects customer service.

As an alternative to cutting support costs, some software publishers might build the cost of software piracy into the price of the software. The unfortunate result is that those who legitimately license and purchase software pay an inflated price. The BSA and

IDC reported about 35% of the software currently in use is pirated. Vietnam, Zimbabwe, and Indonesia have the world's highest piracy rates—90% of the software used in Vietnam and Zimbabwe is believed to be pirated. The figure is 87% in Indonesia. In China the piracy rate is 86%. In the United States, an estimated 21% of software is pirated. In Japan, the rate is 28%.

**Piracy Rates by Region** (as percent of total in use)

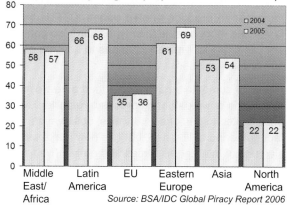

Source: BSA/IDC Global Piracy Report 2006

Although the rate of business software piracy might be declining, total piracy appears to be growing by one or two percentage points each year. Analysts fear that the Internet is a major factor in piracy growth. As Internet access becomes available to subscribers in countries such as China, piracy could skyrocket. To make matters worse, increased access to high-speed Internet connections makes it much easier to quickly download large software files.

As a justification of high piracy rates, some observers point out that people in many countries simply might not be able to afford software priced for the U.S. market. This argument could apply to China, where the average annual income is equivalent to about US$3,500, and in North Korea, where the average income is only US$900. A Korean who legitimately purchases Microsoft Office for US$250 would be spending more than one-quarter of his or her annual income.

Many countries with a high incidence of software piracy, however, have strong economies and respectable per capita incomes. To further discredit the theory that piracy stems from poverty, India—which has a fairly large computer-user community, but a per capita income of only US$1,600—is not among the top 20 countries with high rates of software piracy.

If economic factors do not account for the pervasiveness of software piracy, what does? The incidence of piracy seems to be higher among small business and individual users than corporations and government agencies. Two-thirds of college and university students see nothing unethical about swapping or downloading digital copyrighted software, music, and movie files without paying for them and more than half of the respondents believe it is acceptable to do so in the workplace.

Some analysts suggest that people need more education about software copyrights and the economic implications of piracy. Other analysts believe that copyright enforcement must be increased by implementing more vigorous efforts to identify and prosecute pirates.

**INFOWEBLINKS**

You can read the GNU Manifesto and other thought-provoking articles about software piracy by going to the **Copyright and Piracy InfoWeb**.

 CLICK TO CONNECT
www.course.com/np/concepts10/ch03

# What Do You Think?

ISSUE

1. Do you believe that software piracy is a serious issue?    ○ Yes   ○ No   ○ Not sure

2. Do you know of any instances of software piracy?    ○ Yes   ○ No   ○ Not sure

3. Do you think that most software pirates understand that they are doing something illegal?    ○ Yes   ○ No   ○ Not sure

4. Should software publishers try to adjust software pricing for local markets?    ○ Yes   ○ No   ○ Not sure

 SAVE RESPONSES

## COMPUTERS IN CONTEXT

# Journalism

**IN THE ANCIENT WORLD,** news spread by word of mouth, relayed by bards and merchants who traveled from town to town—in essence, the first reporters to broadcast the news. The news business is all about gathering and disseminating information as quickly as possible. Technology has played a major role in news reporting's evolution from its bardic roots to modern 24-hour live news networks.

Johann Gutenberg's printing press (ca. 1450), the first technological breakthrough in the news business, made it feasible to publish news as printed notices tacked to walls in the town square. As paper became more economical, resourceful entrepreneurs sold broadsheets to people eager for news, and the concept of a newspaper was born. The first regularly published newspapers appeared in Germany and Holland in 1609, and the first English newspaper, the Weekly News, was published in 1622.

But the news spread slowly. In the early 1800s, it took four weeks for newspapers in New York to receive reports from London. With the advent of the telegraph in 1844, however, reporters from far-flung regions could wire stories to their newspapers for publication the next day. The first radio reporters in the 1920s offered live broadcasts of sports events, church services, and variety shows. Before the 1950s, black-and-white newsreels shown in movie theaters provided the only visual imagery of news events, but television gave viewers news images on a nightly basis.

Technology has benefited print journalism, too. For decades, typesetters transferred reporters' handwritten stories into neatly set columns of type. Today, reporters use computers and word processing software to tap out their stories and run a preliminary check of spelling and grammar.

Stories are submitted by computer network to editors, who also use word processing software to edit stories to fit time and space constraints. The typesetting process has been replaced by desktop publishing software and computer to plate (CTP) technology. Digital pages produced with desktop publishing software are sent to a raster image processor (RIP), which converts the pages into dots that form words and images. After a page has been RIPed, a platesetter uses lasers to etch the dots onto a physical plate, which is then mounted on the printing press to produce printed pages. CTP is much faster and more flexible than typesetting, so publishers can make last-minute changes to accommodate late-breaking stories.

Personal computers have also added a new dimension to the news-gathering process. Reporters were once limited to personal interviews, observation, and fact gathering at libraries, but can now make extensive use of Internet resources and e-mail. Web sites and online databases provide background information on all sorts of topics. Other resources include newsgroups and chat rooms, where reporters can monitor public opinion on current events and identify potential sources.

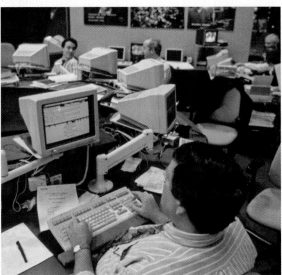

Most major networks maintain interactive Web sites that offer online polls and bulletin boards designed to collect viewers' opinions. Although online poll respondents are not a representative sample of the population, they can help news organizations gauge viewer opinions and determine whether news coverage is comprehensive and effective.

E-mail has changed the way reporters communicate with colleagues and sources. It's often the only practical method for contacting people in remote locations or distant time zones, and it's useful with reluctant sources, who feel more comfortable providing information under the cloak of anonymous Hotmail or Yahoo! accounts. Vetting e-mail sources—verifying credentials such as name, location, and occupation—can be difficult, however, so reporters tend not to rely on these sources without substantial corroboration.

For broadcast journalism, digital communications play a major role in today's live-on-the-scene television reporting. Most news organizations maintain remote production vans, sometimes called satellite news gathering (SNG) trucks, that travel to the site of breaking news, raise their antennas, and begin to broadcast. These complete mobile production facilities include camera control units, audio and video recording equipment, and satellite or microwave transmitters.

On-the-scene reporting no longer requires a truck full of equipment, however. Audiovisual editing units and video cameras have gone digital, making them easier to use and sized to fit in a suitcase. A new breed of backpack journalists carry mini-DV cameras, notebook computers, and satellite phones. Jane Ellen Stevens, a pioneer backpack journalist specializing in science and technology, has reported since 1997 from remote locations, such as a space camp in Russia.

Backpack journalists can connect their minicams to notebook computers with a FireWire cable, transfer their video footage to the hard disk, and then edit the footage using consumer-level video editing software. The resulting video files, compressed for transmission over a satellite phone, are sent to newsroom technicians, who decompress and then broadcast them—all in a matter of seconds.

One drawback of backpack journalists' use of minicams and compression is that the video quality usually isn't as crisp as images filmed with studio cameras. News organizations with high standards were once hesitant to use this lower quality video, but have found that viewers would rather see a low-quality image now than a high-quality image later. To many viewers, a few rough edges just make the footage seem more compelling, more "you are there."

A memorable tour de force in SNG was the brainchild of David Bloom, an NBC reporter embedded with the U.S. Army 3rd Infantry Division during Operation Iraqi Freedom. He helped modify an M-88 tank recovery vehicle into a high-tech, armored SNG vehicle. The $500,000 Bloommobile featured a gyrostabilized camera that could produce jiggle-free video as the tank blasted over sand dunes at 50 mph. Tragically, Bloom died while covering the conflict, but many viewers vividly remember his exhilarating reports as the Bloommobile raced down desert roads, trundled along with army supply convoys, and narrowly escaped enemy fire.

Computers, the Internet, and communications technology make it possible to instantly broadcast live reports across the globe, but live reporting is not without controversy. A reporter who arrives at the scene of a disaster with microphone in hand has little time for reflection, vetting, and cross-checking, so grievous errors, libelous images, or distasteful video footage sometimes find their way into news reports.

Jeff Gralnick, former executive producer for ABC News, remarks, "In the old days, we had time to think before we spoke. We had time to write, time to research and time to say, 'Hey, wait a minute.' Now we don't even have the time to say, 'Hey, wait a nanosecond.' Just because we can say it or do it, should we?" Technology has given journalists a powerful arsenal of tools for gathering and reporting the news, but has also increased their accountability for accurate, socially responsible reporting.

**INFOWEBLINKS**

You'll find lots more information related to this topic at the **Computers and Journalism InfoWeb**.

www.course.com/np/concepts10/ch03

# New Perspectives Labs

## On the BookOnCD

To access the New Perspectives labs for Chapter 3, start the BookOnCD, BookOnFlashDrive, or other NP10 BookOn product and then click the icon next to the lab title below.

▶ **INSTALLING AND UNINSTALLING SOFTWARE**

### IN THIS LAB YOU'LL LEARN:

- How to use a setup program to install Windows application software from a distribution CD
- The difference between typical, compact, and custom installation options
- How to specify a folder for a new software installation
- How to install downloaded software
- How to install an upgrade
- How to uninstall a Windows application
- What happens, in addition to deleting files, when you uninstall a software application
- How to locate the program that will uninstall a software application
- Why you might not want to delete all of the files associated with an application

### LAB ASSIGNMENTS

1. Start the interactive part of the lab. Make sure you've enabled Tracking if you want to save your QuickCheck results. Perform each lab step as directed, and answer all the lab QuickCheck questions. When you exit the lab, your answers are automatically graded and your results are displayed.

2. Browse the Web and locate a software application that you might like to download. Use information supplied by the Web site to answer the following questions:
   a. What is the name of the program and the URL of the download site?
   b. What is the size of the download file?
   c. According to the instructions, does the download file appear to require manual installation, is it a self-executing zip file, or is it a self-installing executable file?

3. On the computer you typically use, look through the list of programs (click Start, then select All Programs to see a list of them). List the names of any programs that include their own uninstall routines.

4. On the computer you typically use, open the Control Panel and then open the Add/Remove Programs dialog box. List the first 10 programs that are currently installed on the computer.

# Key Terms

Make sure you understand all the boldfaced key terms presented in this chapter. If you're using the NP10 BookOnCD, BookOnFlashDrive, or other NP10 BookOn product, you can use this list of terms as an interactive study activity. First, try to define a term in your own words, and then click the term to compare your definition with the definition presented in the chapter.

3

# Interactive Summary

To review important concepts from this chapter, fill in the blanks to best complete each sentence. When using the NP10 BookOnCD or other BookOn product, click the Check Answers buttons to automatically score your answers.

**SECTION A:** Computer software can be grouped into two main categories. [_____] software is designed for computer-centric tasks, whereas [_____] software is designed to help people accomplish real-world tasks. These two main categories can be further divided into subcategories. [_____] software is designed to help you monitor and configure settings for your computer system equipment, the operating system, or application software. Many software packages in this category appear as desktop [_____] that display controls and snippets of information for clocks, calendars, calculators, news aggregators, sticky notes, and weather stations. Device [_____] are a type of system software that helps a computer establish communication with peripheral devices. [_____] software can be defined as any type of application software that has the potential to help people do their work more efficiently. [_____] is designed to help several people collaborate on a single project using local networks or Internet connections.

CHECK ANSWERS

**SECTION B:** Document [_____] software assists you with composing, editing, designing, printing, and electronically publishing documents. The three most popular types of document production software include word processing, desktop publishing, and Web authoring. [_____] software is similar to a smart piece of paper that automatically adds up the columns of numbers you write on it. You can use it to make other calculations, too, based on simple equations that you write or more complex, built-in formulas. Because it is so easy to experiment with different numbers, this type of software is particularly useful for [_____] analyses. [_____] software helps you store, find, organize, update, and report information stored in one or more tables. When two sets of records are [_____], database software allows you to access data from both tables at the same time. [_____] software, including paint, photo editing, drawing, 3-D, and presentation software, is designed to help you create, manipulate, and print images. Music and video editing software, educational and reference software, and entertainment software round out the most popular categories of personal computer software.

For businesses, [_____] market software is designed to automate specialized tasks in a specific market or business. [_____] market software is generic software that can be used by just about any kind of business.

CHECK ANSWERS

## SECTION C:

Most new computers include an operating system, essential utilities, and some basic application software. If you want utilities other than those included with your computer's operating system, you can explore software offered by [              ] party vendors. When shopping for application software, consider software [              ], which are a collection of application software sold as a single package. All the bundled applications usually have similar controls and data can be easily transferred from one application to another. Software can be purchased in a box containing [              ] media, such as CDs or DVDs, or as a download. [              ] software, such as commercial software, is protected by copyright that grants an exclusive right to copy, distribute, sell, and modify that work to its author. Public [              ] software is not protected by copyright. A software [              ] can extend or limit the rights granted by copyright. Demoware and [              ] are distributed free of charge, but require payment for continued use. Freeware is copyrighted software that can be used for free, but cannot be altered or resold. [              ] source software is distributed with its source code, and can be modified, sold, and redistributed.

▶ CHECK ANSWERS

## SECTION D:

The process of [              ] software places a program into a computer so that it can be executed or run. The main program is stored in an [              ] file that might call additional programs as necessary. Most programs are [              ] applications, designed to be installed on a hard disk. A [              ] program, included with the software, guides you through the installation process. For downloaded software, the first step in the installation process is usually to [              ] the distribution file that was compressed to conserve space and reduce download time. In contrast to local applications, [              ] software is designed to run from removable storage, such as a CD or USB flash drive. On PCs these apps require no entries in the Windows Registry. [              ] applications are designed to be accessed with a browser. Some require no installation on your local computer, whereas others require a small client-side program. Software publishers regularly update their software to add new features, fix bugs, and update its security. A software [              ] is a small section of program code that replaces part of the software you currently have installed. The term service [              ], which usually applies to operating system updates, is a set of patches that correct problems and address security vulnerabilities. To remove software from a PC, it is important to use an [              ] routine, rather than simply deleting program files.

▶ CHECK ANSWERS

## SECTION E:

Security software can be classified into various types: antivirus, anti-spyware, anti-spam, and firewalls. Each type focuses on a specific security threat. A computer [              ] is a set of program instructions that attaches itself to a file, reproduces itself, and spreads to other files. A computer [              ] is a self-replicating program designed to carry out some unauthorized activity on a victim's computer. In the context of computing, a Trojan [              ] is a computer program that seems to perform one function while actually doing something else. For example, it might steal passwords using a type of program called a [              ] that records keystrokes. A Remote Access Trojan sets up [              ] capabilities that allow remote hackers to access files on victims' computers. [              ] programs can turn computers into zombies and link them together into [              ]. [              ] is a type of program that secretly gathers personal information without the victim's knowledge, usually for advertising and other commercial purposes. To combat malware, it is important to use [              ] software that looks for virus signatures. Most computer owners obtain this software as one module in a security [              ].

▶ CHECK ANSWERS

# Software Key Terms

# Interactive Situation Questions

Apply what you've learned to some typical computing situations. When using the NP10 BookOnCD, BookOnFlashDrive, or any other NP10 BookOn product, you can type your answers, and then use the Check Answers button to automatically score your responses.

**1.** You've volunteered to create some graphics for a nonprofit organization, but you'll need a variety of graphics software tools for the organization's computer. Your first choice is to consider a graphics [            ] that bundles together paint, draw, and Web graphics software.

**2.** Suppose that you've been hired to organize a professional skateboard competition. When you consider how you'll need to use computers, you realize that you must collect information on each competitor and keep track of every competitive event. With at least two types of related records, you'll probably need to use [            ] software.

**3.** Imagine that you just purchased a new software package. You insert the distribution CD, but nothing happens. No problem—you can manually run the [            ] program, which will start the install routine.

**4.** You are preparing to download a new software program from the Web. The download consists of one huge file with an .exe extension. You recognize this as a self-[            ] executable file that will automatically unzip itself and start the installation routine.

**5.** You download an open source software program from the Web. You assume that the download includes the uncompiled [            ] code for the program as well as the [            ] version.

**6.** You're in the process of receiving some e-mail messages when your antivirus software pops up an alert. You assume that it has discovered a virus [            ] in an attachment for one of the e-mail messages and has [            ] the file.

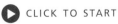 CHECK ANSWERS

# Interactive Practice Tests

Practice tests that consist of 10 multiple-choice, true/false, and fill-in-the-blank questions are available on both the NP10 BookOn products and the NP10 Web site. The questions are selected at random from a large test bank, so each time you take a test, you'll receive a different set of questions. Your tests are scored immediately, and you can print study guides that help you find the correct answers for any questions that you missed.

CLICK TO START

# Study Tips

Study Tips help you to organize and consolidate the information in a unit by making lists, outlines, charts, and sketches. You can use paper and pencil or word processing software to complete most of the Study Tip activities.

1. Make sure you can use your own words to correctly answer each of the red focus questions that appear throughout the chapter.

2. List at least three examples of system software and five examples of utility software.

3. List three types of productivity software, and at least five categories of application software.

4. Describe the strengths of word processing, DTP, and Web authoring software.

5. Explain how a spelling checker works and why it is not a substitute for proofreading.

6. Draw a sketch of a simple worksheet and label the following: columns, rows, cell, active cell, values, labels, formulas, and Formula bar.

7. Explain the difference between an absolute reference and a relative reference, giving an example of each.

8. List five types of "number crunching" software that you can use instead of spreadsheet software.

9. Describe how you would use each of the six types of graphics software described in this chapter.

10. Read the license agreement in Figure 3-32 and answer each of the questions in the corresponding figure caption.

11. Explain the differences in installing local software, portable software, and Web apps.

12. Describe the process of installing software from a distribution CD, and contrast it with the process of installing downloaded software.

13. Explain the differences between proprietary software, commercial software, shareware, open source software, freeware, and public domain software.

14. Explain the differences between self-installing executable files, self-executing zip files, and non-executing zip files.

15. Explain the purpose of a software patch and describe how it differs from a service pack.

16. Create a table that summarizes the differences between various types of malware based on their method of distribution and exploits.

17. Draw a story board to illustrate how antivirus software works.

18. Fill in the blanks on the concept map below to show the hierarchy of software described in this chapter.

**3**

# Concept Map

CHECK ANSWERS

# Projects

 CRITICAL THINKING

Have you heard about the "24-hour rule" for software that says you can legally use any software for free for 24 hours without paying for it? How about your right to use so-called abandoned software that's no longer supported or that was created by a company now out of business? Both the 24-hour rule and the concept of abandoned software are urban legends and have no basis in copyright law. Does it seem to you that most people don't have the facts about copyrights? How strong a factor is that in the proliferation of software piracy? What are your thoughts about the connection between knowing the copyright rules and following them? Put your thoughts in order, write them up, and send them to your instructor.

 GROUP PROJECT

Form a group with at least two of your classmates. Now imagine that your college (or business) has decided to negotiate with software publishers to offer students (or employees) a bundled software package at a greatly discounted price. Your group's job is to select the 15 software products for the bundle. Your group must make sure the software effectively meets the major needs of the students at your school (or employees in your workplace). Use Internet resources to look at the range of software available and make your selections. Make sure you take advantage of group members' expertise and experience with software products. Arrange your final list into categories like those in Figure 3-1.

 CYBERCLASSROOM

Some productivity packages, such as Microsoft Word, include features designed for group collaboration. Learn how to use revision marks. Create a document at least three paragraphs long about your favorite computer software and circulate it to all team members as an e-mail attachment for comment using revision marks.

 MULTIMEDIA PROJECT

Find a photo from one of your old albums or at an antique store. Scan the photo into digital format. Use graphics software to improve the photo quality. Your instructor might run a contest to see which students can most dramatically improve their original photos.

 RESUME BUILDER

Use the Web and other resources to compile a list of the software used in your current or future career field. Are there standard packages that job applicants need to know how to use? If so, what can you find out about those packages on the Web? If your career field does not use any standard software packages, explain why you think that is the case. Also, make a list of the software packages you're familiar with. As you consider your school and career goals for the next year, list at least five additional software packages you would like to learn. Explain why they would be helpful. Submit your lists to your instructor by e-mail.

 GLOBALIZATION

Computer games are big business. They are exported worldwide and accessed by communities of online players around the globe. For this project gather information about the most internationally popular computer games. Try some of them yourself to see what they're all about. What effect, if any, would you expect these games to have on individual players living in the cultures of 1) industrialized countries, 2) Middle-eastern countries, and 3) developing countries? Summarize your ideas in one or two pages.

 ISSUE

The Issue section of this chapter focused on copyrights and software piracy. For this project, you will write a two- to five-page paper about this issue based on information you gather from the Internet. To begin this project, consult the Copyright and Piracy InfoWeb, and link to the recommended Web pages to get an in-depth overview of the issue. Armed with this background, select one of the following viewpoints and statements and argue for or against it:

• Free software advocates: As an enabling technology, software should be freely distributed, along with its modifiable source code.

• Librarians: Copyright laws, especially the Digital Millennium Copyright Act, minimize the needs of the public and go too far in their efforts to protect the rights of software authors.

• Software Publishers Association: Strong copyright laws and enforcement are essential for companies to publish and support high-quality software.

 COMPUTERS IN CONTEXT

The Computers in Context section of this chapter focused on computer and communications technology used by reporters and journalists. Technology has had a major effect on backpack journalists who use small-scale digital devices to gather and report the news. For this project, use a Web search engine to collect information on the advantages and disadvantages of backpack journalism. In your research, you should explore technical issues, such as the cost of equipment, video quality, and transmission capabilities. Also explore ethical issues pertaining to on-the-spot news reporting.
Summarize your research in a two- to four-page paper.

# On the Web

## STUDENT EDITION LABS

**W** **CLICK TO ACCESS THE NP10 WEB SITE**
or open your browser and connect to www.course.com/np/concepts10/ch03.
Lab results can be stored in the Universal Gradebook.

### WORD PROCESSING

In the Word Processing Student Edition Lab, you will learn the following topics and skills:

- Opening, saving, and printing a document
- Moving the insertion point and entering and editing text
- Moving and deleting blocks of text
- Inserting graphics and formatting your document
- Checking your document for spelling errors

### SPREADSHEETS

In the Spreadsheets Student Edition Lab, you will learn the following topics and skills:

- Entering labels, values, and formulas
- Selecting and naming ranges
- Inserting functions
- Formatting a worksheet
- Creating a chart

### INSTALLING AND UNINSTALLING SOFTWARE

In the Installing and Uninstalling Software Student Edition Lab, you will learn the following topics and skills:

- Installing software from a distribution CD
- Installing downloaded software
- Understanding the differences between upgrades, updates, and patches
- Uninstalling software applications

### DATABASES

In the Databases Student Edition Lab, you will learn the following topics and skills:

- Entering and editing data
- Understanding the relationships between tables
- Sorting data
- Creating an index
- Creating queries
- Applying filters
- Creating and modifying reports

### PRESENTATION SOFTWARE

In the Presentation Software Student Edition Lab, you will learn the following topics and skills:

- Adding text, graphics, animations, and sound to slides
- Using slide layouts and design templates
- Understanding the slide master
- Previewing, viewing, and printing a presentation

### KEEPING YOUR COMPUTER VIRUS FREE

In the Keeping Your Computer Virus Free Student Edition Lab, you will learn the following topics and skills:

- Using antivirus software
- Virus detection and prevention

3

### CHAPTER COURSECAST

Use your computer or iPod to hear a five-minute audio presentation of chapter highlights.

### FLASHCARD COURSECAST

Interact with audio flashcards to review key terms from the chapter.

### DETAILED OBJECTIVES

Make sure that you've achieved all the objectives for a chapter before it's time for your test!

### TEST YOURSELF

Review chapter material by taking these ten-question tests, then send your results to the Universal Gradebook.

### ONLINE GAMES

Have some fun while refreshing your memory about key concepts that might appear on the next test. You can even send your results to the Universal Gradebook!

### AND MORE!

At the NP10 Web site you'll also find TechBuzz, CNET videos, Extra Content, and InfoWebLinks.

# 4

## CHAPTER CONTENTS

# Operating Systems and File Management

## LEARNING OBJECTIVES

- Describe the way operating systems handle each computer resource
- Identify operating systems used on today's personal computers, PDAs, and servers; describe their strengths and weaknesses
- Explain the significance of multitasking, multithreading, and multi-processing
- List six steps that occur during the PC boot process
- Explain the relationship between an operating system and a user interface
- Give examples of tasks that might benefit from dual booting or virtu-al machine capability
- Describe the significance of file formats; list at least 10 commonly used formats and their extensions
- Create valid names for files and folders, plus demonstrate that you can construct and trace file paths
- Demonstrate how to use file management features of application software and operating system utilities
- Describe how a computer physically stores data on disks, but repre-sents this storage system with a logical model
- Demonstrate that you can implement a viable backup and restore plan
- Compare the advantages and disadvantages of using tapes, floppy disks, a second hard disk, CDs, networks, and Web sites for backups
- Explain the importance of a recovery disk

 **PRE-ASSESSMENT QUIZ**

Take the pre-assessment quiz to find out how much you know about the topics in this chapter.

**MULTIMEDIA and INTERACTIVE ELEMENTS**
When using the BookOnCD, BookOnFlashDrive, or other NP10 BookOn product, the ▶ icons are clickable to access multimedia resources.

BEFORE YOU READ ON, **TRY IT**

## IS MY COMPUTER'S HARD DISK GETTING FULL?

Parts of Chapter 4 focus on files—how to create them, where to store them, and how to keep them safe. Your computer's hard disk stores a high percentage of the programs you use and the data files you create. You might wonder if your hard disk is getting full. To find out, you can use the My Computer icon.

**1.** Start your computer and make sure you can see the Windows desktop.

**2.** If you are using Windows Vista, Click the Search, type **C:**, and then press the Enter key

If you are using an earlier version of Windows, double-click the My Computer icon. If that icon is not on your desktop, click the Start button and click My Computer from the menu that appears.

**3.** Right-click Local disk (C:) to display the pop-up menu.

**4.** Click Properties.

**5.** A Local Disk Properties dialog box should appear containing statistics about your computer's hard disk.

**6.** Using the blanks on the figure to the right, jot down the statistics for used space, free space, and capacity, and then sketch in the slices of the pie chart for your computer.

**7.** Also jot down the file system used by your computer in the blank provided. You'll learn the significance of the file system when you read the chapter.

## WEB SITE

Visit the NP10 Web site to access additional resources Ⓦ that accompany this chapter.

SECTION **A**

# Operating System Basics

**AN OPERATING SYSTEM** is an integral part of virtually every computer system. It fundamentally affects how you can use your computer. Can you run two programs at the same time? Can you connect your computer to a network? Does your computer run dependably? Does all your software have a similar look and feel, or do you have to learn a different set of controls and commands for each new program you acquire? To answer questions like these, it is helpful to have a clear idea about what an operating system is and what it does. Section A provides an overview of operating system basics to help you understand this essential part of computer systems.

## OPERATING SYSTEM ACTIVITIES

**What is an operating system?** An **operating system** (abbreviated OS) is a type of system software that acts as the master controller for all activities that take place within a computer system. It is one of the factors that determines your computer's compatibility and platform. Most personal computers are sold with a preinstalled operating system, such as Microsoft Windows or Mac OS (Figure 4-1). A third operating system called Linux is typically used for high-end workstations and servers. A variety of other operating systems, such as DOS, UNIX, Solaris, and BeOS, are also available.

**FIGURE 4-1**

Windows (left) is typically pre-installed on IBM-compatible computers manufactured by companies such as Dell and Hewlett-Packard. Mac OS (right) is preinstalled on Apple Macintosh computers.

**Is the Windows operating system the same as Windows software?** No. Although it is true that an operating system is software, terms such as Windows software, Mac software, or Linux software are used to refer to application software. Windows software, for example refers to applications designed to run on computers that have Microsoft Windows installed as the operating system. A program called Microsoft Word for Windows is an example of Windows software; it is a word processing program designed to run under the Windows operating system. Mac software is designed to run under Mac OS and Linux software is designed to run under the Linux operating system.

**What does an operating system do?** The most obvious responsibility of your computer's operating system is to provide an environment for running software. Your computer's operating system, application software, and device drivers are organized similar to the chain of command in an army. You issue a command using application software. Application software tells the operating system what to do. The operating system tells the device drivers, device drivers tell the hardware, and the hardware actually does the work. Figure 4-2 illustrates this chain of command for printing a document or photo.

**FIGURE 4-2**

A command to print a document is relayed through various levels of software, including the operating system, until it reaches the printer.

4

**2.** The word processing application signals the operating system that a document must be sent to the printer.

Printer Driver

**4.** The device driver controls the printer as it prints the document.

**1.** You issue the Print command while using application software, such as a word processor.

**3.** The operating system communicates the document data to the device driver for the printer.

The operating system interacts with application software, device drivers, and hardware to manage a computer's resources. In the context of a computer system, the term **resource** refers to any component that is required to perform work. For example, the processor is a resource. RAM, storage space, and peripherals are also resources. While you interact with application software, your computer's operating system is busy behind the scenes with resource management tasks such as those listed in Figure 4-3.

**FIGURE 4-3**

Operating System Tasks

Manage memory

Manage processor resources

Keep track of storage resources

Ensure that input and output proceed in an orderly manner

Establish basic elements of the user interface

**How do operating systems manage processor resources?** In an earlier chapter, you learned how the control unit directs activities within the microprocessor. Operating systems also control the microprocessor—just at a slightly higher level. Every cycle of a computer's microprocessor is a resource for accomplishing tasks.

Many activities—called *processes*—compete for the attention of your computer's microprocessor. Commands are arriving from programs you're using, while input is arriving from the keyboard and mouse. At the same time, data must be sent to the display device or printer, and Web pages are arriving from your Internet connection. To manage all these competing processes, your computer's operating system must ensure that each process receives its share of microprocessor cycles.

When using Windows, you can open Task Manager to see a list of processes that are being executed by the microprocessor (Figure 4-4).

**FIGURE 4-4**

The Windows operating system displays a list of processes when you hold down the Ctrl, Alt, and Del keys. Most processes are legitimate programs that run in the background to carry out tasks for the operating system, device drivers, and applications. Occasionally a bot or worm will launch rogue processes. If you want to know if a process is legitimate, you can google its name using any search engine.

**How do operating systems handle so many processes?** During a typical computing session, your computer might run an average of 50 processes. Ideally, the operating system should be able to help the microprocessor switch seamlessly from one process to another. Depending on the capabilities of the operating system and computer hardware, processes can be managed by multitasking, multithreading, and multiprocessing.

**Multitasking** provides process and memory management services that allow two or more tasks, jobs, or programs to run simultaneously. Most of today's operating systems, including the OS on your personal computer, offer multitasking services.

Within a single program, **multithreading** allows multiple parts, or threads, to run simultaneously. For example, one thread for a spreadsheet program might be waiting for input from the user while other threads perform a long calculation in the background. Multithreading can speed up performance on single or multiple processor computers.

Many new computers include dual core processors or multiple processors. An operating system's **multiprocessing** capability supports a division of labor among all the processing units.

**How does an operating system manage memory?** A microprocessor works with data and executes instructions stored in RAM—one of your computer's most important resources. When you want to run more than one program at a time, the operating system has to allocate specific areas of memory for each program, as shown in Figure 4-5.

When multiple programs are running, the OS should prevent a **memory leak**—a situation in which instructions and data from one area of memory overflow into memory allocated to another program. If an OS falls down on the job and fails to protect each program's memory area, data can get corrupted, programs can crash, and your computer displays error messages, such as "General Protection Fault" or "Program Not Responding." Your PC can sometimes recover from a memory leak if you use the Ctrl+Alt+Del key sequence to close the corrupted program.

**How does the OS keep track of storage resources?** Behind the scenes, an operating system acts as a filing clerk that stores and retrieves files from your disks and CDs. It remembers the names and locations of all your files and keeps track of empty spaces where new files can be stored. Later in the chapter, you'll explore file storage in more depth and learn how the operating system affects the way you create, name, save, and retrieve files.

**Why does the operating system get involved with peripheral devices?** Every device connected to a computer is regarded as an input or output resource. Your computer's operating system communicates with device driver software so that data can travel smoothly between the computer and peripheral resources. If a peripheral device or driver is not performing correctly, the operating system makes a decision about what to do—usually it displays an on-screen message to warn you of the problem.

Your computer's operating system ensures that input and output proceed in an orderly manner, using buffers to collect and hold data while the computer is busy with other tasks. By using a keyboard buffer, for example, your computer never misses one of your keystrokes, regardless of how fast you type or what else is happening in your computer at the same time.

**Are different operating systems needed for different computing tasks?** One operating system might be better suited to some computing tasks than others. To provide clues to their strengths and weaknesses, operating systems are informally categorized and characterized using one or more of the following terms:

A **single-user operating system** expects to deal with one set of input devices—those that can be controlled by one user at a time. Operating systems for handheld computers and many personal computers fit into the single-user category. DOS is an example of a single-user operating system.

A **multiuser operating system** allows a single computer—often a mainframe—to deal with simultaneous input, output, and processing requests from many users. One of its most difficult responsibilities is to schedule all the processing requests that a centralized computer must perform. IBM's OS/390 is one of the most popular mainframe multiuser operating systems.

A **network operating system** (also referred to as a server operating system) provides communications and routing services that allow computers to share data, programs, and peripheral devices. Novell NetWare, for example, is almost always referred to as a network operating system. The difference between network services and multiuser services can seem a little hazy—especially because operating systems such as UNIX, Linux,

**FIGURE 4-5**

The operating system allocates a specific area of RAM for each program that is open and running. The operating system is itself a program, so it requires RAM space, too.

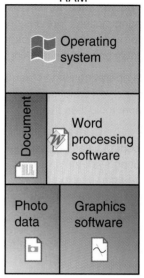

RAM

The term *buffer* is technical jargon for a region of memory that holds data waiting to be transferred from one device to another.

4

and Sun Microsystem's Solaris offer both. The main difference, however, is that multiuser operating systems schedule requests for processing on a centralized computer, whereas a network operating system simply routes data and programs to each user's local computer, where the actual processing takes place.

A **desktop operating system** is one that's designed for a personal computer—a desktop, notebook, or tablet computer. The computer you use at home, at school, or at work is most likely configured with a desktop operating system, such as Microsoft Windows or Mac OS. Typically, these operating systems are designed to accommodate a single user, but might also provide networking capability. Today's desktop operating systems invariably provide multitasking capabilities.

Some operating system vendors characterize their products as home or professional versions. The home version usually has fewer network management tools than the professional version.

**Do I ever interact directly with the OS?** Although its main purpose is to control what happens behind the scenes of a computer system, many operating systems provide helpful tools, called operating system utilities, that you can use to control and customize your computer equipment and work environment. For example, Microsoft Windows offers its users controls to do the following activities.

- **Launch programs.** When you start your computer, Windows displays graphical objects, such as icons, the Start button, and the Programs menu, which you can use to start programs.

- **Manage files.** A useful utility, called Windows Explorer, allows you to view a list of files, move them to different storage devices, copy them, rename them, and delete them.

- **Get help.** Windows offers a Help system you can use to find out how various commands work.

- **Customize the user interface.** The Windows Control Panel, accessible from the Start menu, provides utilities that help you customize your screen display and work environment.

- **Configure equipment.** The Control Panel also provides access to utilities that help you set up and configure your computer's hardware and peripheral devices (Figure 4-6).

**FIGURE 4-6**

Many Windows utilities can be accessed from the Control Panel. You'll find it by clicking the Start button. The Classic View shown here displays all Control Panel options; Category View organizes the options into groups.

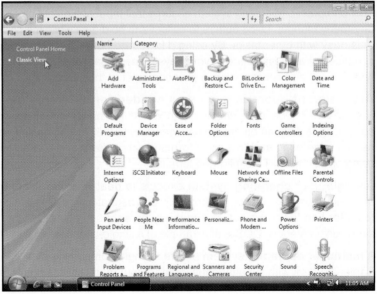

## USER INTERFACES

**What is a user interface?** A **user interface** can be defined as the combination of hardware and software that helps people and computers communicate with each other. Your computer's user interface includes a display device, mouse, and keyboard that allow you to view and manipulate your computing environment. It also includes software elements, such as icons, menus, and toolbar buttons.

**How does the operating system affect the user interface?** The operating system's user interface defines the so-called look and feel of compatible software. For example, application software that runs under Windows uses a standard set of menus, buttons, and toolbars based on the operating system's user interface. Originally, computers had a **command-line interface** that required users to type memorized commands to run programs and accomplish tasks (Figure 4-7).

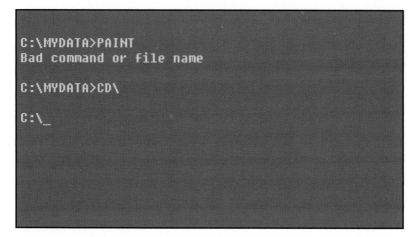

C:\MYDATA>PAINT
Bad command or file name

C:\MYDATA>CD\

C:\_

**FIGURE 4-7**

A command-line user interface requires users to type commands. Here the prompt C:\MYDATA> means the computer is looking at the MYDATA folder of drive C. The user has tried to start a program called Paint, but that program does not exist in the current folder, so the computer has produced an error message "Bad command or file name."

Most computers today feature a graphical user interface, abbreviated as GUI and pronounced as "gooey" or "gee you eye". A **graphical user interface** provides a way to point and click a mouse to select menu options and manipulate graphical objects displayed on the screen.

GUIs were originally conceived at the prestigious Xerox PARC research facility. In 1984, developers at Apple Computer, Inc. turned the idea into a commercial success with the launch of its popular Macintosh computer, which featured a GUI operating system and applications. Graphical user interfaces didn't really catch on in the PC market until 1992 when Windows 3.1 became standard issue on most PCs.

**What are the basic elements of a GUI?** GUIs are based on graphical objects that can be manipulated using a mouse or other input device. Each graphical object represents a computer task, command, or real-world object. Icons and windows can be displayed on a screen-based **desktop** as explained in Figure 4-8 on the next page. An **icon** is a small picture that represents a program, file, or hardware device. A **window** is a rectangular work area that can hold a program, data, or controls.

The Start menu offers options for running programs, searching for files, accessing configuration settings, and getting help.

The taskbar contains the Start button, Quick Start bar, and Notification area.

**FIGURE 4-8**

Microsoft Windows displays a desktop that can contain icons, menus, windows, and taskbars.

A **button** is a graphic—usually rectangular in shape—that can be clicked to make a selection. Buttons can be arranged in a **menu bar**, **toolbar**, or **taskbar** (Figure 4-9).

**FIGURE 4-9**

Buttons and command options can be arranged on menu bars (top), toolbars (center), or taskbars (bottom).

**What's the point of menus and dialog boxes?** Menus were developed as a response to the difficulties many people experienced trying to remember command words and syntax for command-line user interfaces. A **menu** displays a list of commands or options. Each line of the menu is referred to as a menu option or a menu item. Menus are popular because you simply choose the command you want from a list. Also, because all the commands on the list are valid, it is not possible to invoke invalid commands that generate errors.

You might wonder how a menu can present all the commands you might want to use. Obviously, there are many possibilities for combining command words so there could be hundreds of menu options. Two methods are generally used to present a reasonably sized list of options: submenus and dialog boxes.

A **submenu** is an additional set of commands that the computer displays after you make a selection from the main menu. Sometimes a submenu displays another submenu providing even more command choices (Figure 4-10).

FIGURE 4-10

Menu options with a ▶ symbol lead to submenus.

Instead of leading to a submenu, some menu options lead to a dialog box. A **dialog box** displays the options associated with a command. You fill in the dialog box to indicate specifically how you want the command carried out, as shown in Figure 4-11.

FIGURE 4-11

Dialog boxes can contain a variety of controls.

Dialog boxes display controls that you manipulate with a mouse to specify settings and other command parameters. Figure 4-12 explains how to use some of the dialog box controls that you are likely to encounter in Windows, Mac, or Linux environments.

FIGURE 4-12

Dialog box controls offer a variety of ways to enter specifications for tasks you'd like the software to carry out.

Registered To:

Text box

Keyboard Sensitivity: Less · Neutral · More

Slider bar

Optimize for: ○ Maximum
Large buffer size.
● Minimum
Small buffer size.

Radio buttons

4

**How similar are the user interfaces for Windows, Mac OS, and Linux?** All of the popular desktop operating systems use graphical user interfaces that are more similar than they are different. Regardless of whether you use Windows, Mac OS, or Linux, you'll encounter a fairly standard set of on-screen controls. They might differ in their visual design, but it is easy to determine how to use them. In the next section of the chapter, you'll learn more about the similarities and differences in today's popular operating systems.

## THE BOOT PROCESS

**Where is the operating system stored?** In some digital devices—typically handhelds and videogame consoles—the entire operating system is small enough to be stored in ROM. For most other computers, the operating system program is quite large, so most of it is stored on a hard disk. During the boot process, the operating system kernel is loaded into RAM. The **kernel** provides essential operating system services, such as memory management and file access. The kernel stays in RAM all the time your computer is on. Other parts of the operating system, such as customization utilities, are loaded into RAM as they are needed.

**What is the boot process?** The sequence of events that occurs between the time that you turn on a computer and the time that it is ready for you to issue commands is referred to as the **boot process**, or booting your computer.

Your computer's small **bootstrap program** is built into special ROM (read-only memory) circuitry housed in the computer's system unit. When you turn on a computer, the ROM circuitry receives power and begins the boot process by executing the bootstrap program. Six major events happen during the boot process:

● **Power up.** When you turn on the power switch, the power light is illuminated, and power is distributed to the computer circuitry.

● **Start boot program.** The microprocessor begins to execute the bootstrap program that is stored in ROM.

● **Power-on self-test.** The computer performs diagnostic tests of several crucial system components.

● **Identify peripheral devices.** The operating system identifies the peripheral devices that are connected to the computer and checks their settings.

● **Load operating system.** The operating system is copied from the hard disk to RAM.

● **Check configuration and customization.** The microprocessor reads configuration data and executes any customized startup routines specified by the user.

**Why doesn't a computer simply leave the operating system in memory?** Most of a computer's memory is volatile random access memory (RAM), which cannot hold any data when the power is off. Although a copy of the operating system is housed in RAM while the computer is in operation, this copy is erased as soon as the power is turned off. In addition to RAM, computers have non-volatile memory circuitry, such as ROM and EEPROM, which can store data even when the power is off. Typically, ROM and EEPROM are not nearly large enough to store an entire operating system.

**TERMINOLOGY NOTE**

The term *boot* comes from the word *bootstrap*, which is a small loop on the back of a boot. Just as you can pull on a big boot using a small bootstrap, your computer boots up by first loading a small program into memory, and then it uses that small program to load a large operating system.

Given the volatility of RAM and the insufficient size of ROM and EEPROM, computer designers decided to store the operating system on a computer's hard disk. During the boot process, a copy of the operating system is transferred into RAM where it can be accessed quickly whenever the computer needs to carry out an input, output, or storage operation (Figure 4-13).

**Do computers ever have trouble loading the operating system?** Problems loading the operating system are rare, except when a disk has been inadvertently left in the floppy disk drive. Before computers were equipped with hard disk drives, floppy disks were used to store the operating system and application software. As a legacy from these early machines, today's computers first check the floppy disk drive for a disk containing the operating system. If it doesn't find a disk in the drive, it proceeds to look for the operating system on the hard disk. However, if a floppy disk happens to be hanging around in drive A, the computer assumes that you want to boot from it and looks for the operating system on that disk. The error message "Non-system disk or disk error" is the clue to this problem. Remove the floppy disk and press any key to resume the boot process.

**How do I know when the operating system is loaded?** The operating system is loaded and the boot process is complete when the computer is ready to accept your commands. Usually, the computer displays an operating system prompt or a main screen. The Windows operating system, for example, displays the Windows desktop when the boot process is complete.

**FIGURE 4-13**

The bootstrap program copies the operating system into RAM, where it can be directly accessed by the processor to carry out input, output, or storage operations.

Boot program
tells hard disk
to load the OS

Hard disk   Operating
system        ROM
kernel loaded
into RAM

RAM

Operating
system is
available
as needed

Processor

4

# QuickCheck

1. An operating system manages a computer's [_____] , such as RAM, storage, and peripherals.

2. To run more than one program at a time, the operating system must allocate a specific area of [_____] for each program.

3. The core part of an operating system is called its [_____] .

4. A(n) [_____] program stored in ROM tells the hard disk to load the operating system into RAM.

5. A user [_____] encompasses the hardware and software that helps people and computers communicate with each other.

CHECK ANSWERS

# Today's Operating Systems

**CONSUMERS CAN SELECT** from several operating systems for their personal computers and handheld devices. What makes these operating systems different? What are their strengths and weaknesses? Section B offers an operating system overview designed to give you a basic familiarity with their features.

## MICROSOFT WINDOWS

**What's the best-selling operating system?** **Microsoft Windows** is installed on more than 80% of the world's personal computers. The Windows operating system gets its name from the rectangular work areas that appear on the screen-based desktop. Each work area window can display a different document or program, providing a visual model of the operating system's multitasking capabilities (Figure 4-14).

**FIGURE 4-14**

Microsoft Windows XP (top) and Windows Vista (bottom) use similar GUI controls, although the appearance of icons and other graphical elements is slightly different. See if you can match the elements on the Windows XP screen to those pointed out on the Windows Vista screen.

▶ CLICK TO START

**What do I need to know about the evolution of Windows?** The first versions of Windows, including Windows 3.1, were sometimes referred to as *operating environments* rather than operating systems because they required DOS to supply the operating system kernel. Windows operating environments primarily supplied a point-and-click user interface, complete with graphical screen displays and mouse input. Windows operating environments evolved into today's comprehensive operating systems, which do not require the DOS kernel.

From its inception, the Windows operating system was designed to run on Intel or Intel-compatible microprocessors. As those chips evolved from 16-bit to 32-bit, and then to 64-bit architectures, Windows evolved to keep pace. In addition, Windows developers added and upgraded features, such as networking and the file system. They also refined the user interface by attempting to make it more visually attractive and easier to use. Since its introduction in 1985, Windows has evolved through several versions, listed in Figure 4-15.

**What are the strengths of Windows?** The number and variety of programs that run on Windows are unmatched by any other operating system, a fact that contributes to Windows being the most widely used desktop operating system. For the best selection of software, especially for games and vertical market business software, Windows is the operating system of choice.

The variety of hardware platforms that run Windows is also a significant strength. You can use a desktop computer, notebook, PDA, ultra-mobile, PC, or tablet computer and see a familiar set of Windows icons and menus. Features such as handwriting recognition contribute to the versatility of Windows, allowing it to control PDAs and tablet computers with touch screens.

The Windows user community is also a strength. A vast amount of documentation, including tutorials and troubleshooting guides, can be found online and on the shelves of most bookstores. Microsoft's official site, *www.microsoft.com*, includes thousands of pages of easily searchable information. Third-party sites, such as Paul Thurrott's Super Site for Windows, also offer tips, tools, and troubleshooting guides.

When it comes to hardware and peripheral devices, Windows offers excellent support in the form of built-in drivers and Plug and Play functionality. With the largest user base of any platform, Windows computer owners are the target market for the majority of hardware manufacturers. Many of the fastest graphics cards and the coolest joysticks are offered exclusively for the Windows platform.

**What are Window's weaknesses?** Windows has been criticized for two major weaknesses: reliability and security. The reliability of an operating system is usually gauged by the length of time it operates without glitches. Unfortunately, Windows tends to become unstable with more frequency than other operating systems. Slow system response, programs that stop working, and error messages can be symptoms of a Windows malfunction. Rebooting usually clears the error condition and

**FIGURE 4-15**

Windows Timeline

**2007 Windows Vista**
Featured 64-bit support, enhanced security, and more flexible file management. Also more powerful search capabilities and live icons that show document thumbnails.

**2001 Windows XP**
Featured an updated user interface, used the Windows 2000 32-bit kernel, and supported FAT32 and NTFS file systems.

**2000 Windows Me**
The last Windows version to use the original Windows kernel that accesses DOS.

**2000 Windows 2000**
Billed as a "multipurpose network OS for businesses of all sizes" and featured enhanced Web services.

**1998 Windows 98**
Increased stability was a big feature of this Windows version, which also included the Internet Explorer browser.

**1995 Windows 95**
Featured a revised user interface. Supported 32-bit processors, TCP/IP, dial-up networking, and long file names.

**1993 Windows NT**
Provided management and security tools for network servers and the NTFS file system.

**1992 Windows for Workgroups**
Provided peer-to-peer networking, e-mail, group scheduling, and file and printer sharing.

**1992 Windows 3.1**
Introduced program icons and the file folder metaphor.

**1990 Windows 3.0**
Introduced graphical controls.

**1987 Windows 2.0**
Introduced overlapping windows and expanded memory access.

**1985 Windows 1.0**
Divided the screen into rectangular windows that allowed users to work with several programs at the same time.

returns a computer to normal functionality, but the time wasted shutting down and waiting for a reboot adds unnecessary frustration to the computing experience.

Of the major desktop operating systems, Windows has the reputation for being the most vulnerable to viruses, worms, and other attacks. Some portion of Windows' vulnerability is because its huge user base makes it the biggest target. In addition, anti-establishment sentiments make Microsoft a hip adversary for rebellious hackers. Even so, Windows has many security holes which are found and exploited. Although Microsoft is diligent in its efforts to patch security holes, its programmers are always one step behind the hackers, and while users wait for patches their computers are vulnerable.

**What's the difference between the home and professional versions of Microsoft Windows?** Microsoft typically offers several versions, called "editions," of the Windows operating system for various markets. Home, Professional, Media Center, and Workstation editions are designed for personal computers. Server editions are designed for LAN, Internet, and Web servers. Embedded editions are designed for handheld devices, such as PDAs and mobile phones. Figure 4-16 categorizes some of the most popular past and present Windows offerings.

**FIGURE 4-16**

Microsoft offers several versions of Windows, designed for different computing tasks and equipment.

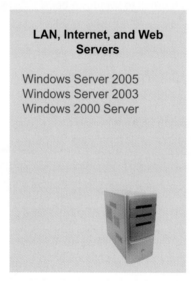

**Personal Computers**

Windows Vista
Windows XP Home Edition
Windows XP Professional
Windows XP Media Center
    Edition
Windows XP Tablet PC
    Edition
Windows 2000 Professional
Windows Me
Windows 98

**LAN, Internet, and Web Servers**

Windows Server 2005
Windows Server 2003
Windows 2000 Server

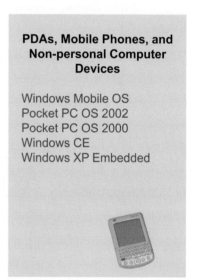

**PDAs, Mobile Phones, and Non-personal Computer Devices**

Windows Mobile OS
Pocket PC OS 2002
Pocket PC OS 2000
Windows CE
Windows XP Embedded

## MAC OS

**Is Mac OS similar to Windows?** **Mac OS** stands for Macintosh Operating System and it is the OS designed for Apple Computer's Macintosh line of computer systems. Although Mac OS was developed several years before Windows, both operating systems base their user interfaces on the graphical model pioneered at Xerox PARC. Both interfaces feature multiple rectangular work areas to reflect multitasking capabilities. Both operating systems provide basic networking services. A quick comparison of Figures 4-14 and 4-17 shows that both Mac and Windows interfaces use a mouse for pointing to and clicking various icons and menus.

**FIGURE 4-17**

You can tell when you're using Mac OS by the Apple logo that appears on the menu bar. The Mac OS X interface includes all the standard elements of a GUI, including icons, menus, windows, and taskbars.

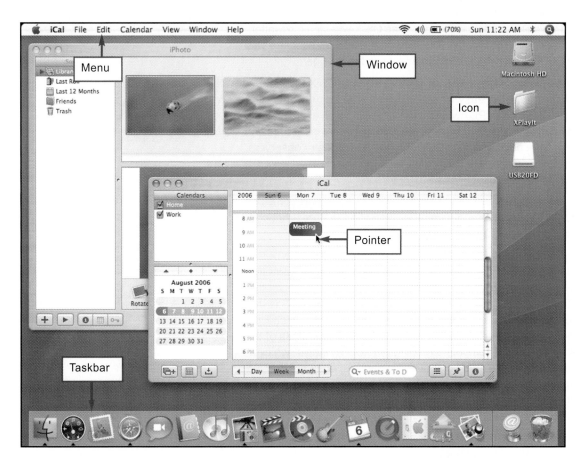

4

CLICK TO START

**What do I need to know about the evolution of Mac OS?** Like Windows, Mac OS has been through a number of revisions (Figure 4-18). The original Classic Mac OS was designed for a line of Macintosh computers based on the Motorola 68000 microprocessor.

In 2001, Classic Mac OS was rewritten to run on Macintosh computers containing PowerPC microprocessors produced by IBM. The new Mac OS was called Mac OS X (the X can either be pronounced as "ten" or the letter X). Mac OS X was much more sophisticated than its predecessor, with better memory management and multitasking capabilities.

In 2006, Macintosh hardware changed significantly with the switch from PowerPC to Intel processors. Mac OS X was again rewritten. The first version of Mac OS X to support the Intel architecture was Mac OS X version 10.4, sometimes referred to as Tiger.

**What are the strengths of Mac OS?** Mac OS X has a reputation for being an easy to use, reliable, and secure operating system. Back when PC owners were struggling with an inscrutable command-line operating system, Macintosh owners were breezing along with a point and click GUI. According to industry observers, Macintosh developers have always been in the lead when it comes to intuitive user interface design.

The operating system kernel of Mac OS X is based on UNIX and includes industrial strength memory protection features that contribute to a low incidence of errors and glitches.

Mac OS X inherited a strong security foundation from UNIX that tends to limit the number of security holes and the damage that can be done by hackers who manage to slip in. Another factor that contributes to the security of computers running Mac OS is that fewer viruses are designed to target the Mac user base because it is much smaller than the Windows user base. Regardless of the relative security of computers running Mac OS X, Macintosh owners should practice safe computing by applying software and OS patches as they become available, activating wireless network encryption, not opening suspicious e-mail attachments, and not clicking links embedded in e-mail messages.

In addition to reliability and security, Mac OS X offers strong backward compatibility, dual boot options, and a good virtual machine platform.

**What is backward compatibility?** **Backward compatibility** refers to the ability to work with products designed for prior-generation hardware or software. For example, suppose you have a computer and lots of great software, but you purchase a faster machine with an upgraded operating system. If that operating system is backward compatible with the operating system on your old computer, you can use all of your old applications.

Macintosh computer developers, like their counterparts at Microsoft, have been careful to provide capabilities to run prior-generation software on new OS versions. For PowerPC Mac owners who wanted to run application software designed for the earlier generation of Mac hardware, OS X provided an emulation

**FIGURE 4-18**

Mac OS Timeline

**2006** **Mac OS X (Desktop edition for Intel processor)**
Kernel ported to Intel codebase, support for old PowerPC software offered using Rosetta emulation, version Leopard.

**2001** **Mac OS X (Desktop edition for PowerPC)**
New kernel based on Unix-like, open source code called XNU, proprietary GUI called Aqua featuring softer edges and translucent colors, multi-user, multitasking, versions Cheetah, Puma, Jaguar, Panther, and Tiger.

**1999** **Mac OS 9**
Visually controversial metallic-look user interface, support for multiple users, Sherlock search utility searches the Internet as well as local storage devices, CD burning software, designed to run on IBM Power PC chips, Classic emulation for running software designed for Motorola chips.

**1997** **Mac OS 8**
Full-color GUI, designed to run on Motorola 68000 and IBM Power PC processors, supported large file sizes and file names up to 255 characters.

**1991** **System 7/ Mac OS**
User interface icons colorized, virtual memory and personal file sharing introduced, shipped with the popular QuickTime video software, balloon help identified the function of icons, 32-bit compatible.

**1988** **System 6**
Introduced multitasking, no built-in support for virtual memory.

**1984** **Classic Mac OS**
Grayscale graphical user interface featuring icons and menus that could be manipulated by a mouse. Singletasking, limited memory management, file system creates data forks and resource forks.

mode. An emulation program called Rosetta allows software applications designed for PowerPC Macs to run on Intel Macs. Software developers also have the option of shipping software in Universal Binary format, which includes a PowerPC and Intel version of the application. The correct version is automatically run when the application runs.

The ability to run prior-generation applications is important because software developers typically require several months to produce applications for new hardware or operating systems. While waiting for new applications, consumers can use emulators to run software they might have purchased for an older computer and have access to a much larger library of programs than would initially be available for a new hardware platform.

**What is dual boot?** Mac OS X on an Intel Mac offers the ability to run Windows and Windows application software in addition to software designed for the Macintosh. Software called Boot Camp is a **dual boot** utility that can switch between Mac OS X and Windows XP. When booting, you can select either Mac OS X or Windows (Figure 4-19). To change operating systems, you have to reboot.

**FIGURE 4-19**

On a Macintosh computer with Boot Camp, you can boot into Mac OS X or into Windows XP.

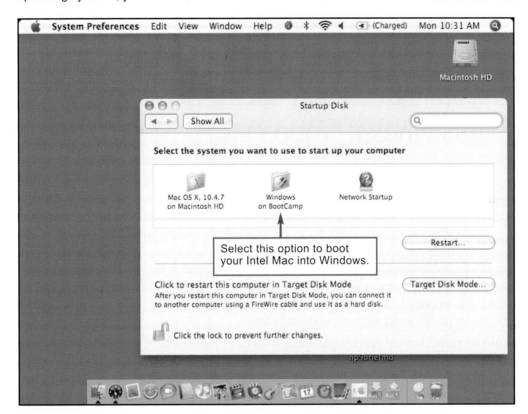

**What is a virtual machine?** The Intel version of Mac OS X is also a good platform for **virtual machine** technologies that allow you to use one computer to simulate the hardware and software of another. Each virtual machine has its own simulated processor, RAM, video card, input and output ports, and operating system. Each machine can also run most software that's compatible with the virtual hardware and operating system.

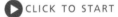 CLICK TO START

Popular virtual machine software called Parallels Desktop can run on most computers with Intel microprocessors, including the Intel Mac. The computer boots into native Mac OS X, but users can create a virtual machine running guest operating systems, such as Windows XP. The virtual machine's desktop appears in a window on the Macintosh screen.

Theoretically, your Mac desktop could display a virtual Windows XP computer, a virtual Linux computer, and a native Mac OS X computer (Figure 4-20).

**FIGURE 4-20**

On a Mac with virtual Windows and Linux, switching from one operating system to another is as simple as selecting a window. When switched to the Windows work area, you can run games, business software, and other applications designed for the Windows OS. Clicking the Linux work area, you could run Linux applications from its vast collection of open source software. Returning to the Mac OS X desktop, you could run your collection of high-end graphics and multimedia iLife software designed exclusively for the Macintosh.

**What are the weaknesses of Mac OS?** The weaknesses of Mac OS include a somewhat limited selection of software and its use of resource forks. A decent collection of software is available for computers that run Mac OS, although the selection is not as vast as the Windows collection. Many of the most prolific software publishers produce one version of their software for Windows and another, similar version for Mac OS.

Macintosh computer owners might find that many popular software titles are not available for Mac OS X. The selection of games, for example, is much sparser than for Windows, although it should be noted that the selection of graphics software for Mac OS X is as good or better than the selection available for Windows. Open source software, including OpenOffice.org, is usable on Macs only with emulation software.

**What is a resource fork?** In most operating systems a file is a single unit that contains data or program code. Files maintained by the Macintosh operating system, however, can have two parts, called forks. The **data fork** is similar to files in other operating systems. It contains data, such as the text for a document, the graphics for a photo, or the commands for a program. The **resource fork** is a companion file that stores information about the data in the data fork, such as the file type and the application that created it.

Although resource forks have advantages on their native Macintosh platform, they pose difficulties for transferring files to other platforms. In today's networked world in which everyone wants to share data, the resource fork presents a potential bottleneck to the free flow of data. To transfer Mac files to a PC, for example, requires a conversion process that bundles the resource fork information with the data fork.

## UNIX AND LINUX

**Are UNIX and Linux the same?** The **UNIX** operating system was developed in 1969 at AT&T's Bell Labs. It gained a good reputation for its dependability in multiuser environments, and many versions of it became available for mainframes and microcomputers.

In 1991, a young Finnish student named Linus Torvalds developed the **Linux** (pronounced LIH nucks) operating system. Linux was inspired by and loosely based on a UNIX derivative called MINIX, created by Andrew Tanenbaum. Linux continues to gain popularity as an operating system for personal computers, though it is not as popular for desktop applications as Windows or Mac OS.

**What are the strengths of Linux?** Linux is rather unique because it is distributed along with its source code under the terms of a General Public License (GPL), which allows everyone to make copies for their own use, to give to others, or to sell. This licensing policy has encouraged programmers to develop Linux utilities, software, and enhancements. Linux is primarily distributed over the Web.

Although Linux is designed for microcomputers, rather than mainframes, it shares several technical features with UNIX, such as multitasking, virtual memory, TCP/IP drivers, and multiuser capabilities. These features make Linux a popular operating system for e-mail and Web servers as well as for local area network servers.

**What are the weaknesses of Linux?** Linux typically requires a bit more tinkering than the Windows and Mac desktop operating systems. The comparatively limited number of programs that run under Linux also discourages many nontechnical users from selecting it as the OS for their desktop and notebook computers. A constantly growing collection of high-quality open source software is becoming available for the Linux platform, but many of these applications are targeted toward business and technical users.

Several Web sites offer a **Linux distribution**, which is a package that contains the Linux kernel, system utilities, applications, and an installation routine. Beginner-friendly Linux distributions include Fedora, Ubuntu, and SUSE. Most of these distributions include a GUI module that provides a user interface similar to the one pictured in Figure 4-21.

**FIGURE 4-21**

Linux users can choose from several graphical interfaces. Pictured here is the popular KDE graphical desktop.

 CLICK TO START

## DOS

**Why do I keep hearing about DOS?** Old-timers in the computer industry sometimes reminisce about DOS. It was the first operating system that many of them used, and its cryptic command-line user interface left an indelible impression. **DOS** (which rhymes with toss) stands for Disk Operating System. It was developed by Microsoft—the same company that later produced Windows—and introduced on the original IBM PC in 1982. Although IBM called this operating system PC-DOS, Microsoft marketed it to other companies under the name MS-DOS.

DOS software, such as Visicalc, used command-line interfaces and rustic menus that users controlled with the keyboard's arrow keys (Figure 4-22).

**FIGURE 4-22**

When using Visicalc, you could press the slash key (/) to call up the main menu, which simply listed the first letter of each command. For example, F was the Format command, so if you wanted to format a cell, you pressed F to see a list of letters, such as C, L, and R—the commands for centering, left alignment, and right alignment.

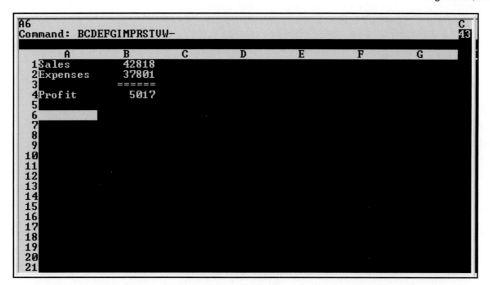

After more than 20 years, remnants of DOS still linger in the world of personal computers because it provided part of the operating system kernel for Windows versions 3.1, 95, 98, and Me.

During the peak of its popularity, thousands of software programs were produced for computers running DOS. You can occasionally find some of these programs on the Internet, and run them using the MS-DOS Prompt option (Windows 98, Me, NT, and 2000) or the Command Prompt option (Windows XP) on the Windows Start menu. DOS also offers handy troubleshooting utilities, such as Ping, Tracert, Copy *, msconfig, and netstat used by tech-savvy computer users. DOS programs look rather unsophisticated by today's standards, so for many of today's computer owners, DOS and DOS software are nothing more than footnotes in the history of the computer industry.

## HANDHELD OPERATING SYSTEMS

**What are the options for handheld operating systems?** Three operating systems dominate the realm of handheld computers: Palm OS, Windows Mobile OS, and Symbian OS shown in Figure 4-23.

**Palm OS** is produced by PalmSource, a spinoff of the company that produced some of the first commercially successful PDAs. Palm OS is currently used for popular PDAs such as palmOne Zire and Sony CLIE. It also powers Fossil's wristwatch PDA and smartphones from manufacturers such as palmOne, Samsung, and Kyocera.

**FIGURE 4-23**

Mobile devices use operating systems such as Windows Mobile OS (below), Palm OS (top of next page), and Symbian OS (next page).

Windows Mobile OS

**Windows Mobile OS** is an operating system built on the Microsoft Windows CE technology. As a cousin to Windows XP, Windows Mobile OS sports some features similar to those found on the Windows desktop. Windows Mobile OS is the operating system for a variety of PDAs, phone-enabled PDAs, and smartphones.

**Symbian OS** is a multitasking, multithreaded operating system popular on Ericsson and Nokia smartphones. Symbian can be easily programmed with languages such as C++, Visual Basic, or Personal Java, and so some interesting third-party freeware and shareware is available.

**Are operating systems for handheld devices similar to desktop operating systems?** Operating systems for handheld and desktop devices provide many similar services, such as scheduling processor resources, managing memory, loading programs, managing input and output, and establishing the user interface. But because handheld devices tend to be used for less sophisticated tasks, their operating systems are somewhat simpler and significantly smaller.

By keeping the operating system small, it can be stored in ROM. Without the need to load the OS from disk into RAM, a handheld device's operating system is ready almost instantly when the unit is turned on. Operating systems for handheld devices provide built-in support for touch screens, handwriting input, wireless networking, and cellular communications.

Palm OS

Symbian OS

# QuickCheck SECTION B

1. The Windows operating system was designed to run on Motorola and IBM processors. True or false? [ ]

2. A(n) [ ]-compatible operating system should run application software designed for the operating system's prior generations.

3. A(n) [ ] boot computer could boot into Windows, and then reboot into Mac OS.

4. A computer configured with the correct set of [ ] machines could run Windows in a window on the Mac desktop.

5. A resource [ ] is a companion file created by Mac OS to store information about the file and its data.

6. [ ] is an open source operating system that can run on the desktop, but tends to be used for server applications instead.

7. Windows Mobile, Palm, and Symbian are examples of operating systems used for handheld devices. True or false? [ ]

▶ CHECK ANSWERS

# File Basics

**THE TERM FILE WAS USED** for filing cabinets and collections of papers long before it became part of the personal computer lexicon. Today, computer files in digital format offer a compact and convenient way to store documents, photos, videos, and music. Computer files have several characteristics, such as a name, format, location, size, and date. To make effective use of computer files, you'll need a good understanding of these file basics, and that is the focus of Section C.

## FILE NAMES AND EXTENSIONS

**What is a computer file?** As you learned in Chapter 1, a computer file—or simply a file— is defined as a named collection of data that exists on a storage medium, such as a disk, CD, DVD, or tape. A file can contain a group of records, a document, a photo, music, a video, an e-mail message, or a computer program.

When you use word processing software, the text you enter for a document is stored as a file. You can give the file a name, such as *A History of Film Noir*. A music file, such as *Bach Brandenberg Concertos* that you download over the Internet is stored as a file, too.

**What are the rules for naming files?** Every file has a name and might also have a file extension. When you save a file, you must provide a valid file name that adheres to specific rules, referred to as **file-naming conventions**. Each operating system has a unique set of file-naming conventions. Figure 4-24 lists file naming conventions for the current versions of Windows.

**Is there a maximum length for file names?** DOS and Windows 3.1 limited file names to eight characters. With that limitation, it was often difficult to create descriptive file names. A file name such as HseBud06 might be used for a file containing a household budget for 2006. With such cryptic file names, it was not always easy to figure out what a file contained. As a result, files were sometimes difficult to locate and identify. Today, most operating systems allow you to use longer file names.

Current versions of Windows support file names up to 255 characters long. That limitation includes the entire file path—drive letter, folders, file name, and extension. A file name limitation of 255 characters gives you the flexibility to use descriptive file names, such as Household Budget 2007, so that you can easily identify what a file contains.

**What is a file extension?** A **file extension** (sometimes referred to as a file name extension) is an optional file identifier that is separated from the main file name by a period, as in Paint.exe. As you become familiar with file extensions, they will provide a clue to the file's contents. Files with .exe extensions are executable files that your computer can run. Paint.exe, for example, is a graphics utility packaged with the Windows operating system. Files with .dat extensions are typically data files. Files with .doc extensions contain word processing documents.

**FIGURE 4-24**

Windows File-naming Conventions

| | |
|---|---|
| Case sensitive | No |
| Maximum length of file name | File name and extension cannot exceed 255 characters |
| Spaces allowed | Yes |
| Numbers allowed | Yes |
| Characters not allowed | * \ : < > \| " / ? |
| File names not allowed | Aux, Com1, Com2, Com3, Com4, Con, Lpt1, Lpt2, Lpt3, Prn, Nul |

**Why are certain characters not allowed in a file name?** If an operating system attaches special significance to a symbol, you might not be able to use it in a file name. For example, Windows uses the colon (:) character to separate the device letter from a file name or folder, as in *C:Music.* A file name that contains a colon, such as *Report:2007,* is not valid because the operating system would become confused about how to interpret the colon. When you use Windows applications, avoid using the symbols : * \ < > | " / and ? in file names.

**What are reserved words?** Some operating systems also contain a list of **reserved words** that are used as commands or special identifiers. You cannot use these words alone as a file name. You can, however, use these words as part of a longer file name. For example, under Windows, the file name *Nul* would not be valid, but you could name a file something like *Nul Committee Notes.doc* or *Null Set.exe.*

In addition to *Nul,* Windows users should avoid using the following reserved words as file names: *Aux, Com1, Com2, Com3, Com4, Con, Lpt1, Lpt2, Lpt3,* and *Prn.*

**What else should I know about creating file names?** Some operating systems are case sensitive, but not those you typically work with on personal computers. Feel free to use uppercase and lowercase letters in file names that you create on PCs and Macs.

You can also use spaces in file names. That's a different rule than for e-mail addresses where spaces are not allowed. You've probably noticed that people often use underscores or periods instead of spaces in e-mail addresses such as Madi_Jones@msu.edu. That convention is not necessary in file names, so a file name such as Letter to Madi Jones is valid.

## FILE DIRECTORIES AND FOLDERS

**How do I designate a file's location?** To designate a file's location, you must first specify the device where the file is stored. As shown in Figure 4-25, each of a PC's storage devices is identified by a device letter—a convention that is specific to DOS and Windows. The main hard disk drive is usually referred to as drive C. A device letter is usually followed by a colon, so the hard disk drive could be designated as C:.

Although the floppy disk drive is traditionally designated as drive A and the hard disk drive is designated as drive C, device letters for CD, DVD, and USB flash drives are not standardized. For example, the CD-writer on your computer might be assigned device letter E, whereas the CD-writer on another computer might be assigned device letter R.

**What is a disk partition?** A **disk partition** is a section of a hard disk drive that is treated as a separate storage unit. Most PCs are configured with a single hard disk partition that contains the operating system, programs, and data. However, it is possible to create more than one hard disk partition. For example, a PC owner might set up one partition for operating system files and another partition for programs and data. This arrangement sometimes can speed up the process of disinfecting a computer that has been attacked by malicious software.

Partitions can be assigned drive letters. In the example above, the operation system files would be stored in partition C. The program and data file partition would probably be designated as drive D. Partitions are not the same thing as folders. Partitions are more permanent, and a special utility is required to create, modify, or delete them.

4

**FIGURE 4-25**

The Windows operating system labels storage devices with letters, such as A: and C:.

| Name | Type |
|---|---|
| **Hard Disk Drives** | |
| Local Disk (C:) | Local Disk |
| **Devices with Removable Storage** | |
| 3½ Floppy (A:) | 3½-Inch Floppy Disk |
| DVD/CD-RW Drive (D:) | CD Drive |
| **Network Drives** | |
| files on 'Mtcnas' (H:) | Network Drive |

**TERMINOLOGY NOTE**

Drive letter assignments are based on conventions that date back to the first PCs. The original IBM PCs shipped with a single floppy disk drive and it was designated drive A. An enhanced PC later shipped with two floppy disk drives, designated A and B. When hard disks were eventually added to PC systems, they were designated drive C.

**Do I have to remember where I put each file?** Your computer's operating system maintains a list of files called a **directory** for each storage disk, tape, CD, DVD, or USB flash drive. The main directory is referred to as the **root directory**. On a PC, the root directory is identified by the device letter followed by a backslash. For example, the root directory of the hard disk would be C:\. A root directory can be subdivided into smaller lists. Each list is called a **subdirectory**.

**What is a folder?** When you use Windows, Mac OS, or a Linux graphical file manager, each subdirectory is depicted as a **folder**. Folders help you envision your files as if they were stored in a filing cabinet. Each folder can hold related items, for example, a set of documents, sound clips, and photos for a school project. You can create and name folders to meet your needs. You might create a folder called *Documents* to hold reports, letters, and so on. You can create another folder called *My Music* to hold your MP3 files and a folder called *Music of the Congo* to hold music and document files for a music class project.

Folders can be created within other folders. You might, for example, create a *Jazz* folder within the *My Music* folder to hold your jazz collection and another folder named *Reggae to* hold your reggae collection.

A folder name is separated from a drive letter and other folder names by a special symbol. In Microsoft Windows, this symbol is the backslash ( \ ). For example, the folder for your reggae music (within the *My Music* folder on drive C) would be written as *C:\ My Music\Reggae*.

A computer file's location is defined by a **file specification** (sometimes called a **path**), which includes the drive letter, folder(s), file name, and extension. Suppose that you have stored an MP3 file called *Marley One Love* in the *Reggae* folder on your hard disk. Its file specification is shown in Figure 4-26.

**FIGURE 4-26**

A file specification provides the name and location of a file.

# C:\My Music\Reggae\Marley One Love.mp3

| Drive letter | Primary folder | Secondary folder | File name | File extension |

**What's the significance of a file's size?** A file contains data, stored as a group of bits. The more bits, the larger the file. **File size** is usually measured in bytes, kilobytes, or megabytes. Knowing the size of a file can be important. Compared to small files, large files fill up storage space more quickly, require longer transmission times, and are more likely to be stripped off e-mail attachments by a mail server. Your computer's operating system keeps track of file sizes and supplies that information when you request a listing of files.

**Is the file date important?** Your computer keeps track of the date that a file was created or last modified. The **file date** is useful if you have created several versions of a file and want to make sure you know which version is the most recent. It can also come in handy if you have downloaded several updates of a software package, such as an MP3 player, and you want to make sure you install the latest version.

## FILE FORMATS

**Why should I know about file formats?** Some operating systems do a fairly good job of shielding users from the intricacies of file formats. For example, Windows uses a file association list to link a file extension to its corresponding application software. This handy feature allows you to open a data file without first opening an application, simply by double-clicking the file from a desktop icon or selecting it from the Documents list that's accessible from the Start menu.

Of course, your application software also shields you from the messy task of searching through directories to find the files it will open. When you use the Open dialog box, most applications automatically comb through the files on a specified device and in a specified folder to display only those that have the correct file extensions.

With all this help from the operating system and your application software, it might seem that knowing about file formats is unimportant. You might, however, find it useful to understand file formats so that you can easily accomplish tasks such as those listed in Figure 4-27.

**What determines a file's format?** Although a file extension is a good indicator of a file's format, it does not really define the format. You could use the Rename command to change a QuickTime movie called Balloons.mov to Balloons.doc. Despite the .doc extension, the file is still in QuickTime format because the data elements in the file are arranged in a specific configuration unique to QuickTime.

The format of a file might include a header, data, and possibly an end-of-file marker. A **file header** is a section of data at the beginning of a file that contains information about a file—typically the date it was created, the date it was last updated, its size, and its file type.

A file header should not be confused with the headers appearing at the top of each page in a document created with a word processor. Instead, envision a file header as a hidden Post-It note that's attached to the beginning of a file. Although it is hidden to users, computers can read the information in a file header to determine the file's format.

The remaining contents of a file depend on whether it contains text, graphics, audio, or multimedia data. A text file, for example, might contain sentences and paragraphs interspersed with codes for centering, boldfacing, and margin settings. A graphics file might contain color data for each pixel, followed by a description of the color palette. The **file format** dictates the arrangement of this data. Figure 4-28 illustrates the layout for a Windows bitmap file and contrasts it with the layout of a GIF file.

**FIGURE 4-27**

Understanding file formats helps you perform the following tasks:

- Figure out the correct format for e-mail attachments that you send to friends or colleagues.
- Find the right player software for music and media files that you download from the Web.
- Discover how to work with a file that doesn't seem to open.
- Convert files from one format to another.

**INFOWEBLINKS**

The **File Formats InfoWeb** provides a list of file extensions and their corresponding software.

 CLICK TO CONNECT
www.course.com/np/concepts10/ch04

| Bitmap File Format | GIF File Format |
|---|---|
| File header | File header |
| Bitmap header | Logical screen descriptor |
| Color palette | Global color table |
| Bitmap data | Local image descriptor |
| | Local color table |
| | Image data |
| | End-of-file character |

**FIGURE 4-28**

Although bitmap and GIF file formats contain graphics, the file layouts differ.

**Which file formats am I most likely to encounter?** A software program typically consists of at least one executable file with an .exe file extension. It might also include a number of support programs with extensions such as .dll, .vbx, and .ocx. Configuration and startup files usually have .bat, .sys, .ini, and .bin extensions. In addition, you'll find files with .hlp and .tmp extensions. Files with .hlp extensions hold the information for a program's Help utility. Files with .tmp extensions are temporary files. When you open a data file with software applications, such as word processors, spreadsheets, and graphics tools, your operating system makes a copy of the original file and stores this copy on disk as a temporary file. It is this temporary file that you work with as you view and revise a file.

To the uninitiated, the file extensions associated with programs and the operating system might seem odd. Nevertheless, executable and support files—even so-called temporary files—are crucial for the correct operation of your computer system. You should not manually delete them. The table in Figure 4-29 lists the file extensions typically associated with the Windows operating system and executable files.

**FIGURE 4-29**

OS and Executable Extensions

| Type of File | Description | Extension |
| --- | --- | --- |
| Batch file | A sequence of operating system commands executed automatically when the computer boots | .bat |
| Configuration file | Information about programs the computer uses to allocate the resources necessary to run them | .cfg  .sys  .mif<br>.bin  .ini |
| Help | The information displayed by on-screen Help | .hlp |
| Temporary file | A sort of scratch pad that contains data while a file is open, but is discarded when you close the file | .tmp |
| Support program | Program instructions executed along with the main .exe file for a program | .ocx  .vbx<br>.vbs  .dll |
| Program | The main executable files for a computer program | .exe  .com |

The list of data file formats is long, but becoming familiar with the most popular formats and the type of data they contain is useful. Figure 4-30 provides this information in a convenient table. Where noted, a file format is associated with a particular software program.

**FIGURE 4-30**

Data File Extensions

| Type of File | Extension |
| --- | --- |
| Text | .txt  .dat  .rtf  .doc (Microsoft Word and WordPad)  .wpd (WordPerfect) |
| Sound | .wav  .mid  .mp3  .au  .ra (RealAudio) |
| Graphics | .bmp  .pcx  .tif  .wmf  .gif  .jpg  .png  .eps  .ai (Adobe Illustrator) |
| Animation/video | .flc  .fli  .avi  .mpg  .mov (QuickTime)  .rm (RealMedia)  .wmv (Windows Media Player) |
| Web pages | .htm  .html  .asp .vrml |
| Spreadsheets | .xls (Microsoft Excel)  .wks (Lotus 1-2-3)  .dif |
| Database | .mdb (Microsoft Access) |
| Miscellaneous | .pdf (Adobe Acrobat)  .ppt (Microsoft PowerPoint)  .zip (WinZip)<br>.pub (Microsoft Publisher)  .qxp (QuarkExpress) |

**How do I know which files a program will open?** A software application can open files that exist in its **native file format**, plus several additional file formats. For example, Microsoft Word opens files in its native DOC (.doc) format, plus files in formats such as HTML (.htm or .html), Text (.txt), and Rich Text Format (.rtf). Within the Windows environment, you can discover which formats a particular software program can open by looking at the *Files of type* list in the Open dialog box, as shown in Figure 4-31.

**FIGURE 4-31**

An application's *Files of type* list usually displays the file formats a program can open. You can also look for an Import option on the File menu.

**Why can't I open some files?** Suppose you receive an e-mail attachment called Cool.tif. "Aha!" you say to yourself, "My Photoshop software ought to open that file." You try—several times—but all you get is an error message. When a file doesn't open, one of three things probably went wrong:

- The file might have been damaged—a techie would call it corrupted—by a transmission or disk error. Although you might be able to use file recovery software to repair the damage, it is usually easier to obtain an undamaged copy of the file from its original source.

- Someone might have inadvertently changed the file extension. While renaming the Cool file, perhaps the original .bmp extension was changed to .tif. If you have a little time, you can change the file extension and try to open the file. If a file contains a graphic, chances are that it should have the extension for one of the popular graphics formats, such as .bmp, .gif, .jpg, .tif, or .png. Otherwise, you should contact the source of the file to get accurate information about its real format.

- Some file formats exist in several variations, and your software might not have the capability to open a particular variation of the format. You might be able to open the file if you use different application software. For example, Photoshop might not be able to open a particular file with a .tif file extension, but Corel Paint Shop Pro might open it.

**What if all my software fails to open a particular file format?** Although a computer might be able to discover a file's format, it might not necessarily know how to work with it. Just as you might be able to identify a helicopter, you can't necessarily fly it without some instructions. Your computer also requires a set of instructions to use most file formats. These instructions are provided by software. To use a particular file format, you must make sure your computer has the corresponding software.

Suppose you download a file with an .rm extension and none of your current software works with this file format. Several Web sites provide lists of file extensions and their corresponding software. By looking up a file extension in one of these lists, you can find out what application software you'll need to find, buy, download, and install.

Many files downloaded from the Web require special player or reader software. For example, PDF text files require software called Acrobat Reader, MP3 music files require software called an MP3 player, and RM video files require the RealMedia Player software. Typically, you can follow a link from the Web page that supplied your file download to find a site from which you can download the necessary player or reader software.

**How do I know what kinds of file formats I can send to my friends, colleagues, and instructor?** Unless you know what application software is installed on your friends' computers, you won't know for certain whether they can open a particular file you've sent. There's a good chance, however, that your friends can open files saved in common document formats such as Microsoft Word's DOC or Adobe Acrobat's PDF format; graphics formats such as PNG, TIFF, or JPEG; and music formats such as MP3 and AIF. You should check with the recipient before sending files in less common, proprietary formats, such as Adobe Illustrator's AI format and QuarkExpress's QXP format.

**Is it possible to convert a file from one format to another?** Perhaps you created a Word document on your PC, but you need to convert it into a format that's usable by your colleague who owns a Mac. Or suppose you want to convert a Word document into HTML format so that you can post it on the Web. You might also want to convert a Windows bitmap (.bmp) graphic into GIF format so that you can include it on a Web page. The easiest way to convert a file from one format to another is to find an application program that works with both file formats. Open the file using that software, and then use the Export option, or the Save As dialog box, to select a new file format, assign the file a new name, and save it (Figure 4-32).

**FIGURE 4-32**

An easy way to convert a file from one format to another is to open it with an application that supports both file formats, and then use the Save As dialog box to select an alternative file format.

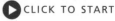
CLICK TO START

**Will a converted document be identical to the original?** Many file formats convert easily to another format, and the resulting file is virtually indistinguishable from the original. Some conversions, however, do not retain all the characteristics of the original file. When you convert a DOC file into HTML format, for example, the HTML page does not contain any of the headers, footers, superscripts, page numbers, special characters, or page breaks that existed in the original DOC file.

When you need a conversion routine for an obscure file format, or if you need to convert between many different file formats, consider specialized conversion software, available through commercial or shareware outlets.

**INFOWEBLINKS**

Conversion software runs the gamut from simple shareware to industrial-strength commercial packages. The **Conversion Software InfoWeb** will help you compare what's available.

 CLICK TO CONNECT

www.course.com/np/concepts10/ch04

4

# QuickCheck

SECTION C

1. Windows file-naming [＿＿＿＿＿＿] are different than for Linux.

2. When using Windows, you cannot use a reserved word, such as Aux, as a file name. True or false? [＿＿＿＿]

3. On a computer running Windows, the hard disk letter is usually designated as [＿＿＿＿＿].

4. The root directory of a disk can be divided into smaller lists called [＿＿＿＿＿＿], that are depicted as folders.

5. A file's location is defined by a file path, which includes the drive letter, one or more [＿＿＿＿＿＿], file name, and extension.

6. A file's [＿＿＿＿＿＿] can be important information when you are planning to transmit it to another computer over a network.

7. A file [＿＿＿＿＿＿] is a section of data at the beginning of a file that contains information about the file type.

8. The [＿＿＿＿＿＿] file format for Microsoft Word is DOC.

▶ CHECK ANSWERS

# File Management

**FILE MANAGEMENT ENCOMPASSES** any procedure that helps you organize your computer-based files so that you can find and use them more efficiently. Depending on your computer's operating system, you can organize and manipulate your files from within an application program or by using a special file management utility the operating system provides. Section D offers an overview of application-based and operating system-based file management.

## APPLICATION-BASED FILE MANAGEMENT

### How does a software application help me manage files?

Applications, such as word processing software or graphics software, typically provide a way to open files and save them in a specific folder on a designated storage device. An application might also have additional file management capabilities, such as deleting, copying, and renaming files. Take a look at an example of the file management capabilities in a typical Windows application—Microsoft Word.

Suppose you want to write a letter to the editor of your local newspaper about the rising tide of graffiti in your neighborhood. You would open your word processing software and type the document. As you type, the document is held in RAM. At some point, you'll want to save the document. To do so, you click File on the menu bar, and then select the Save As option. The Save As dialog box, shown in Figure 4-33, opens and allows you to specify a name for the file and its location on one of your computer's storage devices.

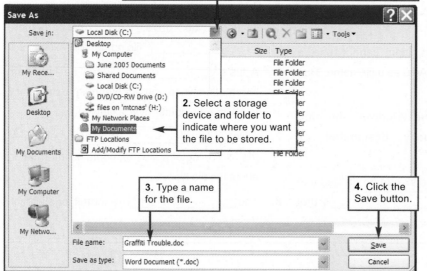

**FIGURE 4-33**

The Save As dialog box is used to name a file and specify its storage location.

**What's the difference between the Save option and the Save As option?** Most Windows applications provide a curious set of options on the File menu. In addition to the Save As option, the menu contains a Save option. The difference between the two options is subtle, but useful. The Save As option allows you to select a name and storage device for a file, whereas the Save option simply saves the latest version of a file under its current name and at its current location.

A potentially confusing aspect of these options occurs when you try to use the Save option for a file that doesn't yet have a name. Because you can't save a file without a name, your application displays the Save As dialog box, even though you selected the Save option. The flowchart in Figure 4-34 will help you decide whether to use the Save or Save As command.

**What other options are available in the Save As dialog box?** The Save As dialog box displayed by Windows applications allows you to do more than just save a file. You can use it to rename a file, delete a file, or create a folder, as shown in Figure 4-35.

**FIGURE 4-34**

Should I use the Save or Save As command?

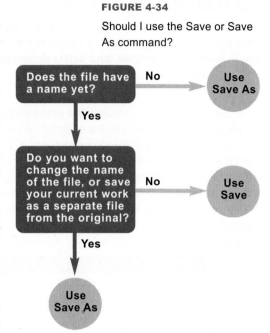

**FIGURE 4-35**

The Save As dialog box not only helps you name a file and designate its destination drive, but also allows you to rename files, delete files, create folders, and rename folders.

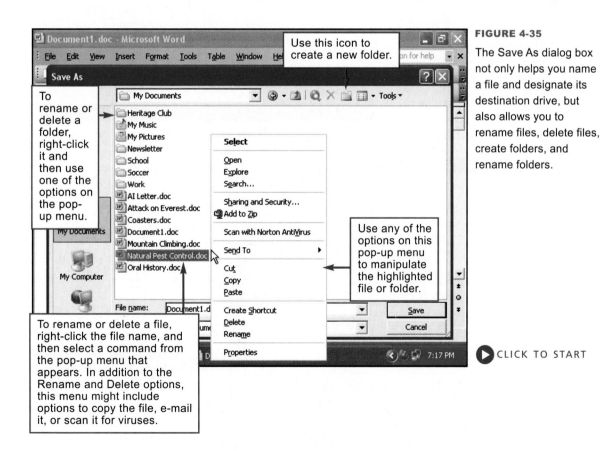

CLICK TO START

## FILE MANAGEMENT UTILITIES

### How does the operating system help me manage files?

Although most application software gives you access to commands you can use to save, open, rename, and delete individual files, you might want to work with groups of files or perform other file operations that are inconvenient within the Open or Save dialog boxes.

Most operating systems provide **file management utilities** that give you the big picture of the files you have stored on your disks and help you work with them. For example, Windows provides a file management utility that can be accessed from the My Computer icon or from the Windows Explorer option on the Start menu. On computers with Mac OS, the file management utilities are called the Finder and Spotlight. These utilities, shown in Figure 4-36, help you view a list of files, find files, move files from one place to another, make copies of files, delete files, discover file properties, and rename files.

**TERMINOLOGY NOTE**

Utilities called desktop search tools help you also find and access information stored in e-mails, Web pages, and contact lists in addition to data and program files. Desktop search tools are offered by third-party vendors such as Google and Yahoo! They are also being added to operating system utilities.

**FIGURE 4-36**

The Windows file management utility can be tailored to show files as icons (top) or as a list (middle).
Mac OS provides a file management utility called the Finder (bottom).

## FILE MANAGEMENT METAPHORS

**How can a file management utility help me visualize my computer's file storage?** File management utilities often use some sort of storage metaphor to help you visualize and mentally organize the files on your disks and other storage devices. These metaphors are also called **logical storage models** because they are supposed to help you form a mental (logical) picture of the way in which your files are stored.

**What storage metaphors are typically used for personal computers?** After hearing so much about files and folders, you might have guessed that the filing cabinet is a popular metaphor for computer storage. In this metaphor, each storage device of a computer corresponds to one of the drawers in a filing cabinet. The drawers hold folders and the folders hold files.

Another storage metaphor is based on a hierarchical diagram that is sometimes referred to as a tree structure. In this metaphor, a tree represents a storage device. The trunk of the tree corresponds to the root directory. The branches of the tree represent folders. These branches can split into small branches representing folders within folders. The leaves at the end of a branch represent the files in a particular folder. Figure 4-37 illustrates the tree lying on its side so that you can see the relationship to the metaphor shown in the next figure, Figure 4-38.

The tree structure metaphor offers a useful mental image of the way in which files and folders are organized. It is not, however, particularly practical as a user interface. Imagine the complexity of the tree diagram from Figure 4-37 if it were expanded to depict branches for hundreds of folders and leaves for thousands of files.

For practicality, storage metaphors are translated into more mundane screen displays. Figure 4-38 shows how Microsoft programmers combined the filing cabinet metaphor with the tree structure metaphor in the Windows Explorer file management utility.

**FIGURE 4-37**

You can visualize the directory of a disk as a tree on its side. The trunk corresponds to the root directory, the branches to folders, and the leaves to files.

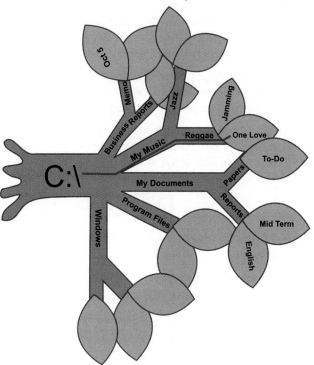

**FIGURE 4-38**

Windows Explorer borrows folders from the filing cabinet metaphor and places them in a hierarchical structure similar to a tree on its side.

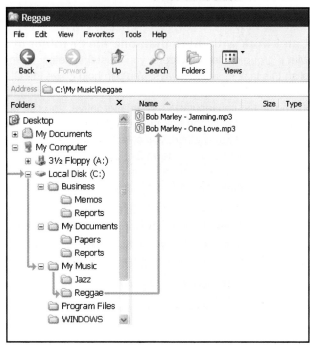

## WINDOWS EXPLORER

**How do I use a file management utility?** As an example of a file management utility, take a closer look at **Windows Explorer**, a utility program bundled with the Windows operating system and designed to help you organize and manipulate the files stored on your computer.

The Windows Explorer window is divided into two window panes. The pane on the left side of the window lists each of the storage devices connected to your computer, plus several important system objects, such as My Computer, My Network Places, and the Desktop.

An icon for a storage device or other system object can be expanded by clicking its corresponding plus-sign icon. Expanding an icon displays the next level of the storage hierarchy—usually a collection of folders.

A device icon or folder can be opened by clicking directly on the icon rather than on the plus sign. Once an icon is opened, its contents appear in the pane on the right side of the Windows Explorer window. Figure 4-39 illustrates how to manipulate the directory display.

**FIGURE 4-39**

Windows Explorer makes it easy to drill down through the levels of the directory hierarchy to locate a folder or file.

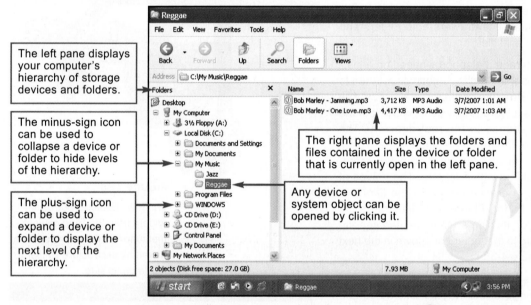

The left pane displays your computer's hierarchy of storage devices and folders.

The minus-sign icon can be used to collapse a device or folder to hide levels of the hierarchy.

The plus-sign icon can be used to expand a device or folder to display the next level of the hierarchy.

The right pane displays the folders and files contained in the device or folder that is currently open in the left pane.

Any device or system object can be opened by clicking it.

 CLICK TO START

**Can I work with more than one file or folder at a time?** To work with a group of files or folders, you must first select them. You can accomplish this task in several ways. You can hold down the Ctrl key as you click each item. This method works well if you are selecting files or folders that are not listed consecutively. As an alternative, you can hold down the Shift key while you click the first item and the last item you want to select. By using the Shift key method, you select the two items that you clicked and all the items in between. Windows Explorer displays all the items you selected by highlighting them. After a group of items is highlighted, you can use the same copy, move, or delete procedure that you would use for a single item.

**What can I do with the folders and files that are listed in Windows Explorer?** In addition to locating files and folders, Windows Explorer provides a set of procedures (shown in Figure 4-40 on the next page) that help you manipulate files and folders in the following ways:

● **Rename.** You might want to change the name of a file or folder to better describe its contents.

- **Copy.** You can copy a file from one device to another—for example, from a floppy disk in drive A to the hard disk in drive C. You can also make a copy of a document so that you can revise the copy and leave the original intact.

- **Move.** You can move a file from one folder to another or from one storage device to another. When you move a file, it is erased from its original location, so make sure you remember the new location of the file. You can also move entire folders and their contents from one storage device to another storage device, or move them to a different folder.

- **Delete.** You can delete a file when you no longer need it. You can also delete a folder. Be careful when you delete a folder because most file management utilities also delete all the files within a folder.

**FIGURE 4-40**

Windows Explorer helps you delete, copy, move, and rename files.

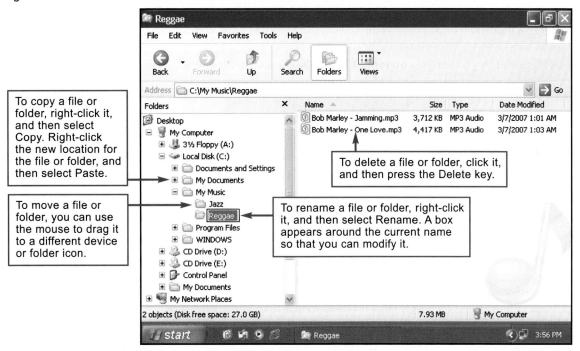

To copy a file or folder, right-click it, and then select Copy. Right-click the new location for the file or folder, and then select Paste.

To move a file or folder, you can use the mouse to drag it to a different device or folder icon.

To delete a file or folder, click it, and then press the Delete key.

To rename a file or folder, right-click it, and then select Rename. A box appears around the current name so that you can modify it.

## FILE MANAGEMENT TIPS

A file management utility provides tools and procedures to help you keep track of your program and data files, but these tools are most useful when you have a logical plan for organizing your files and when you follow some basic file management guidelines. The following tips pertain to managing files on your own computer. When working with files on lab computers, follow the guidelines from your instructor or lab manager.

- **Use descriptive names.** Give your files and folders descriptive names, and avoid using cryptic abbreviations.

- **Maintain file extensions.** When renaming a file, keep the original file extension so that you can easily open it with the correct application software.

- **Group similar files.** Separate files into folders based on subject matter. For example, store your creative writing assignments in one folder and your MP3 music files in another folder.

- **Organize your folders from the top down.** When devising a hierarchy of folders, consider how you want to access files and back them up. For example, it is easy to specify one folder and its subfolders for a backup. If your important data is scattered in a variety of folders, however, making backups is more time consuming.

- **Consider using the My Documents default directory.** Windows software typically defaults to the *My Documents* folder for storing data files. You might want to use *My Documents* (Figure 4-41) as your main data folder, and add subfolders as necessary to organize your files.

- **Do not mix data files and program files.** Do not store data files in the folders that hold your software—on Windows systems, most software is stored in subfolders of the *Program Files* folder.

- **Don't store files in the root directory.** Although it is acceptable to create folders in the root directory, it is not a good practice to store programs or data files in the root directory of your computer's hard disk.

- **Access files from the hard disk.** For best performance, copy files from floppy disks or CDs to your computer's hard disk before accessing them.

- **Follow copyright rules.** When copying files, make sure you adhere to copyright and license restrictions.

- **Delete or archive files you no longer need.** Deleting unneeded files and folders helps keep your list of files from growing to an unmanageable size.

- **Be aware of storage locations.** When you save files, make sure the drive letter and folder name specify the correct storage location.

- **Back up!** Back up your folders regularly.

## PHYSICAL FILE STORAGE

**Is data stored in specific places on a disk?** So far, you've seen how an operating system such as Windows can help you visualize computer storage as files and folders. This logical storage model, however, has little to do with what actually happens on your disk. The structure of files and folders you see in Windows Explorer is called a logical model because it is supposed to help you create a mental picture. The **physical storage model** describes what actually happens on the disks and in the circuits. As you will see, the physical model is quite different from the logical model.

Before a computer can store a file on a disk, CD, or DVD, the storage medium must be formatted. The **formatting** process creates the equivalent of electronic storage bins by dividing a disk into **tracks** and then further dividing each track into **sectors**. Tracks and sectors are numbered to provide addresses for each data storage bin. The numbering scheme depends on the storage device and the operating system. On floppy, Zip, and hard disks, tracks are arranged as concentric circles; on CDs and DVDs, one or more tracks spiral out from the center of the disk (Figure 4-42).

**FIGURE 4-41**

Windows XP supplies a series of default folders, including *My Documents*, that many users find convenient for storing their data.

**FIGURE 4-42**

A process called formatting prepares the surface of a disk to hold data.

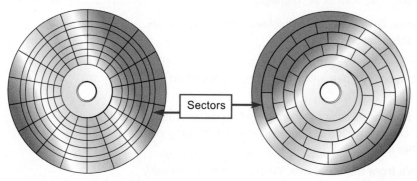

Disks are divided into tracks and wedge-shaped sectors—each side of a floppy disk typically has 80 tracks divided into 18 sectors. Each sector holds 512 bytes of data.

On a typical CD, a single track is about three miles long and is divided into 336,000 sectors. Each sector holds 2,048 bytes of data.

**How does a disk get formatted?** Today, most floppy, Zip, and hard disks are preformatted at the factory; however, computer operating systems provide **formatting utilities** you can use to reformat some storage devices—typically floppy and hard disks. Formatting utilities are also supplied by the companies that manufacture hard disk drives, writable CD and DVD drives, and CD/DVD recording software.

When you use a formatting utility, it erases any data that happens to be on the disk, and then prepares the tracks and sectors necessary to hold data. You might consider reformatting some of your old floppy disks (instead of just deleting the files they contain) if you really want to make them blank before you reuse them. The screen tour associated with Figure 4-43 demonstrates how to use Windows to format a floppy disk.

**FIGURE 4-43**

Windows includes a floppy disk formatting utility, which can be accessed from the A: (Floppy disk) icon in the My Computer window or Windows Explorer.

**4**

▶ CLICK TO START

**How does the operating system keep track of a file's location?** The operating system uses a **file system** to keep track of the names and locations of files that reside on a storage medium, such as a hard disk. Different operating systems use different file systems. Most versions of Mac OS use the Macintosh Hierarchical File System (HFS). Ext2fs (extended 2 file system) is the native file system for Linux. Windows NT, 2000, XP, and Vista use a file system called **NTFS** (New Technology File System). The file system for Windows 3.1 was called FAT16. Windows 95, 98, and Me use a file system called **FAT32**.

To speed up the process of storing and retrieving data, a disk drive usually works with a group of sectors called a **cluster** or a "block." The number of sectors that form a cluster varies, depending on the capacity of the disk and the way the operating system works with files. A file system's primary task is to maintain a list of clusters and keep track of which are empty and which hold data. This information is stored in a special index file. If your computer uses the FAT32 file system, for example, this index file is called the **File Allocation Table** (FAT). If your computer uses NTFS, it is called the **Master File Table** (MFT).

Each of your disks contains its own index file so that information about its contents is always available when the disk is in use. Unfortunately, storing this crucial file on disk also presents a risk because if the index file is

damaged by a hard disk head crash or corrupted by a virus, you'll generally lose access to all the data stored on the disk. Index files become
damaged all too frequently, so it is important to back up your data.

When you save a file, your PC's operating system looks at the index file to
see which clusters are empty. It selects one of these empty clusters,
records the file data there, and then revises the index file to include the new
file name and its location.

A file that does not fit into a single cluster spills over into the next contiguous
(meaning adjacent) cluster, unless that cluster already contains data. When
contiguous clusters are not available, the operating system stores parts of a
file in noncontiguous (nonadjacent) clusters. Figure 4-44 helps you visualize how an index file, such as the MFT, keeps track of file names and
locations.

**Master File Table**

| File | Cluster | Comment |
| --- | --- | --- |
| MFT | 1 | Reserved for MFT files |
| DISK USE | 2 | Part of MFT that contains list of empty sectors |
| Bio.txt | 3, 4 | Bio.txt file stored in clusters 3 and 4 |
| Jordan.wks | 7, 8, 10 | Jordan.wks file stored noncon-tiguously in clusters 7, 8, and 10 |
| Pick.wps | 9 | Pick.wps file stored in cluster 9 |

**FIGURE 4-44**

Each colored cluster on the disk contains part of a file. Bio.txt is stored in contiguous clusters. Jordan.wks is stored in noncontiguous clusters. A computer locates and displays the Jordan.wks file by looking for its name in the Master File Table.

When you want to retrieve a file, the OS looks through the index for the file
name and its location. It moves the disk drive's read-write head to the first
cluster that contains the file data. Using additional data from the index file,
the operating system can move the read-write heads to each of the clusters
containing the remaining parts of the file.

**What happens when a file is deleted?** When you click a file's icon
and then select the Delete option, you might have visions of the read-write
head somehow scrubbing out the clusters that contain data. That doesn't
happen. Instead, the operating system simply changes the status of the
file's clusters to "empty" and removes the file name from the index file. The
file name no longer appears in a directory listing, but the file's data remains
in the clusters until a new file is stored there. You might think that this data is
as good as erased, but it is possible to purchase utilities that recover a lot of
this supposedly deleted data—law enforcement agents, for example, use
these utilities to gather evidence from deleted files on the computer disks of
suspected criminals.

To delete data from a disk in such a way that no one can ever read it, you
can use special **file shredder software** that overwrites supposedly empty
sectors with random 1s and 0s. You might find this software handy if you
plan to donate your computer to a charitable organization, and you want to
make sure your personal data no longer remains on the hard disk.

**Can deleted files be undeleted?** The Windows Recycle Bin and similar utilities in other operating systems are designed to protect you from accidentally deleting hard disk files you actually need. Instead of marking a file's clusters as available, the operating system moves the file to the Recycle Bin folder. The deleted file still takes up space on the disk, but does not appear in the usual directory listing.

Files in the Recycle Bin folder can be undeleted so that they again appear in the regular directory. The Recycle Bin can be emptied to permanently delete any files it contains.

**How does a disk become fragmented?** As a computer writes files on a disk, parts of files tend to become scattered all over the disk. These **fragmented files** are stored in noncontiguous clusters. Drive performance generally declines as the read-write heads move back and forth to locate the clusters containing the parts of a file. To regain peak performance, you can use a **defragmentation utility**, such as Windows Disk Defragmenter, to rearrange the files on a disk so that they are stored in contiguous clusters (Figure 4-45).

**FIGURE 4-45**

Defragmenting a disk helps your computer operate more efficiently. Consider using a defragmentation utility at least once a month to keep your computer running in top form.

4

**Fragmented disk**

On the fragmented disk (left), the purple, orange, and blue files are stored in noncontiguous clusters.

When the disk is defragmented (right), the sectors of data for each file are moved to contiguous clusters.

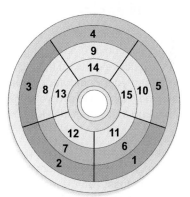

**Defragmented disk**

# QuickCheck

1. The _____ option on an application's File menu allows you to save the latest version of a file under its current name and at its current location.

2. A storage _____ , such as a filing cabinet or tree, helps you visualize and mentally organize your computer files.

3. Windows _____ is utility software provided by the operating system and designed to help you organize and manipulate files.

4. A hard disk stores data in concentric _____ , which are divided into wedge-shaped _____ .

5. File _____ software overwrites deleted files with random 1s and 0s.

▶ CHECK ANSWERS

# Backup Security

**COMPUTER EXPERTS UNIVERSALLY RECOMMEND** that you make backups of your data. It sounds pretty basic, right? Unfortunately, this advice tells you what to do, not how to do it. It fails to address some key questions, such as: Do I need special backup equipment and software? How often should I make a backup? How many of my files should I back up? What should I do with the backups? In this section you'll find the answers to your questions about backing up data that's stored on a personal computer. You'll begin by looking at backup basics, and then review your equipment and software options. Along the way, you should pick up lots of practical tips to keep your data safe.

## BACKUP BASICS

**Why do I need to make backups?** Have you ever mistakenly copied an old version of a document over a new version? Has your computer's hard disk drive gone on the fritz? Did a virus wipe out your files? Has lightning fried your computer system? These kinds of data disasters are not rare; they happen to everyone. You can't always prevent them, so you need a **backup** that stores the files needed to recover data that's been wiped out by operator error, viruses, or hardware failures.

**What's the best backup plan?** A good backup plan allows you to restore your computing environment to its pre-disaster state with a minimum of fuss. Unfortunately, no single backup plan fits everyone's computing style or budget. You must devise your own backup plan that's tailored to your particular computing needs.

The list in Figure 4-46 outlines factors you should consider as you formulate your own backup plan.

**FIGURE 4-46**

Guidelines for Formulating a Backup Plan

- Decide how much of your data you want, need, and can afford to back up.
- Create a realistic schedule for making backups.
- Make sure you have a way to avoid backing up files that contain viruses.
- Find out what kind of boot disks you might need to get your computer up and running after a hard disk failure or boot sector virus attack.
- Make sure you can test your restore procedure so that you can successfully retrieve the data you've backed up.
- Find a safe place to keep your backups.
- Decide what kind of storage device you'll use to make backups.
- Select software to handle backup needs.

**How often should I back up my data?** Your backup schedule depends on how much data you can afford to lose. If you're working on an important project, you might want to back up the project files several times a day. Under normal use, however, most people schedule a once-a-week backup. If you work with a To Do list, use it to remind yourself when it is time to make a backup.

**How do I avoid backing up files that contain viruses?** Viruses can damage files to the point that your computer can't access any data on its hard disk. It is really frustrating when you restore data from a backup only to discover that the restored files contain the same virus that wiped out your data. If your antivirus software is not set to constantly scan for viruses on your computer system, you should run an up-to-date virus check as the first step in your backup routine.

**How do I choose a backup device?** The backup device you select depends on the value of your data, your current equipment, and your budget. Most computer owners use what they have—a writable CD, DVD, or floppy disk drive. For added convenience and security, some consumers purchase an external hard disk drive (Figure 4-47). Businesses sometimes use tape drives for backups. If you have several backup options available, use the table in Figure 4-48 to evaluate the strengths and weaknesses of each one.

**FIGURE 4-47**

An external hard disk drive typically connects to your computer's USB port. The drive can easily be disconnected when not in use and stored in a safe place.

**FIGURE 4-48**

Storage Capacities and Costs of Backup Media

| | Device Cost | Media Cost | Capacity | Comments |
|---|---|---|---|---|
| **Floppy disk** | $30 (average) | 25¢ | 1.44 MB | Low capacity means that you have to wait around to feed in disks |
| **Removable hard disk** | $130 (average) | $50 | 35 GB (average) | Fast, limited capacity, but disks can be removed and locked in a secure location |
| **External hard disk** | $200 (average) | N/A | 250 GB (average) | Fast and convenient, but might hold only one backup |
| **Network server** | Assume a business or school supplies free access | N/A | Depends on space allocated to user | Fast and convenient, but make sure that the server is regularly backed up |
| **CD-R** | $40 (average) | 15¢ | 680 MB | Limited capacity, can't be reused, long shelf life |
| **CD-RW** | $50 (average) | 25¢ | 680 MB | Limited capacity, reusable, very slow |
| **Writable DVD** | $100 (average) | 25¢ | 4.7 GB | Good capacity, reasonable media cost, higher capacity coming soon |
| **Tape** | $2,000 (average) | $80 | 200 GB (average) | Most convenient but expensive for capacity equal to today's hard drives |
| **USB Flash drive** | $15–$500 | N/A | 32 MB–4 GB | Convenient and durable, but high-capacity models are expensive |
| **Web site** | N/A | $15.00 per month | 1 GB | Transfer rate depends on your Internet connection; security and privacy of your data might be a concern |

**Where should I keep my backups?** If your backups are on an external hard disk or removable media, keep your backups in a safe place. Don't keep them at your computer desk because a fire or flood that damages your computer could also wipe out your backups. In addition, a thief who steals your computer might also scoop up nearby equipment and media. Storing your backups at a different location is the best idea. If offsite storage isn't practical, at least move them to a room apart from your computer.

**How can I be sure that my backup works?** If your computer's hard disk crashes, you do not want to discover that your backups are blank! To prevent such a disastrous situation, it is important to enable the read after write or compare option backup software provides. These options force the software to check the data in each sector as it is written to make sure it is copied without error. You should also test your backup by trying to restore one file. Try it with one of your least important data files, just in case your backup is faulty.

## DATA FILE BACKUP

**What's the easiest way to back up my important data?** Today, most computers are equipped with a writable CD or DVD drive with adequate storage capacity for a typical computer owner's data files. An easy way to back up your important data is simply by copying selected files to a writable CD or DVD. No special software is necessary for this task. The software supplied with your CD or DVD writer includes a formatting routine that prepares a disk to hold data and allows you to select the files you want to copy, or "burn," as a backup (Figure 4-49).

**FIGURE 4-49**

Use the software supplied with your CD or DVD drive to format disks and copy files.

**How do I find the files I need to backup?** If your strategy is to back up your important data files, the procedure can be simplified if you've stored all these files in one folder or its subfolders. For example, Windows users might store their data files in folders contained in the *My Documents* folder. A folder called *My Documents\Music* might hold MP3 files, a *My Documents\Reports* folder can hold reports, a *My Documents\Art* folder can hold various graphics files, and so on. With your data files organized under the umbrella of a single folder, you are less likely to omit an important file when you make backups.

Some applications, such as financial software, create files and update them without your direct intervention. If you have the option during setup, make sure these files are stored under the My Documents umbrella. Otherwise, you must discover the location of the files and make sure they are backed up with the rest of your data.

In addition to data files you create, a few other types of data files might be important to you. Consider making backups of the files listed in Figure 4-50.

- **Internet connection information.** Your ISP's phone number and IP address, your user ID, and your password are often stored in an encrypted file somewhere in the *Windows\System* folder. Your ISP can usually help you find this file.

- **E-mail folders.** If you're using POP e-mail software, your e-mail folder contains all the e-mail messages you've sent and received, but not deleted. Check the Help menu on your e-mail program to discover the location of these files.

- **E-mail address book.** Your e-mail address book might be stored separately from your e-mail messages. To find the file on a Windows computer, use the Search or Find option on the Start menu to search for "Address Book."

- **Favorite URLs.** If you're attached to the URLs you've collected in your Favorites or Bookmarks list, you might want to back up the file that contains this list. To find the file, search your hard disk for "Favorites" or "Bookmarks."

- **Downloads.** If you paid to download any files, you might want to back them up so that you don't have to pay for them again. These files include software, which usually arrives in the form of a compressed .exe file that expands into several separate files as you install it. For backup purposes, the compressed .exe file should be all you need.

- **Validation codes and other configuration information.** If you keep a running list of validation or activation codes that correspond to your software, then it is important to copy this information in case your hard disk crashes and you have to reinstall your software. Additional configuration or procedural notes can also come in handy when it comes time to reload a hard disk after a crash.

**How do I restore files from my data file backups?** Restoring from a data file backup is easy. You simply copy files from your backup to your hard disk. If, for example, you inadvertently delete an important file and discover that you have done so only after you've cleaned out your computer's Recycle Bin, then you can retrieve the file from your backup.

If your hard drive crashes and you have to install a new one, the process of retrieving your files is a bit more complex. First, you have to reload the operating system on your hard disk. That task is explained a little later in this section. Then you have to reinstall all of your software and device drivers. As the final step, you can copy your data files back to the hard disk. To avoid a lengthy manual rebuild of your hard disk, you might consider system backups and recovery disks.

**What is system restore?** System Restore (Windows Me and XP) and System Protection (Windows Vista) are operating systems utilities that periodically set a **restore point** that is a snapshot of your computer settings. If a hard disk problem causes system instability, you might be able to roll back to a restore point when your computer was operational. Restore points are set automatically when you install new software. You can manually set restore points, too. For example, you might want to set a restore point before setting up a network or installing new hardware. System restore can be accessed from the Start menu by choosing Accessories and then selecting System Tools.

## SYSTEM BACKUP

**What does backup software do?** To make a backup, you can use **backup software**—a set of utility programs designed to back up and restore files. Backup software usually includes options that make it easy to schedule periodic backups, define a set of files that you want to regularly back up, and automate the restoration process.

Backup software differs from most copy routines because it typically compresses all the files for a backup and places them in one large file. Under the direction of backup software, this file can spread across multiple tapes if necessary. The file is indexed so that individual files can be located, uncompressed, and restored.

**Where can I get backup software?** Backup software is supplied with most tape drives and other backup devices. Some versions of Windows include Microsoft Backup software (Figure 4-51), which you can usually find by clicking the Start button, and then selecting Accessories and System Tools. You can also purchase and download backup software from companies that specialize in data protection software.

### INFOWEBLINKS

For current links to backup software information, reviews, and manufacturers, visit the **Backup Software InfoWeb**.

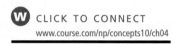 CLICK TO CONNECT
www.course.com/np/concepts10/ch04

**FIGURE 4-51**

Microsoft Widows includes backup software with Windows XP (left) and Windows Vista (right).

CLICK TO START

Whatever backup software you use, remember that it needs to be accessible when it comes time to restore your data. If the only copy of your backup software exists on your backup media, you will be in a Catch-22 situation. You won't be able to access your backup software until you restore the files from your backup, but you won't be able to restore your files until your backup software is running! Make sure you keep the original distribution CD for your backup software or a disk-based copy of any backup software you downloaded from the Web.

**How do I use backup software?** Backup software provides tools for scheduling backup dates and selecting the files you want to back up. The scheduling feature allows you to automate the backup process and reduces the chance that you'll forget to make regular backups. Backup software can also save time and storage space by offering options for full, differential, or incremental backups.

**What is a full backup?** A **full backup** makes a fresh copy of every file in the folders you've specified for the backup. In contrast to a full-system backup, a full backup does not necessarily contain every file on your computer. A full backup might contain only your data files, for example, if those are the files you want to regularly back up.

**What is a differential backup?** A **differential backup** makes a backup of only those files that were added or changed since your last full backup session. After making a full backup of your important files, you can make differential backups at regular intervals. If you need to restore all your files after a hard disk crash, first restore the files from your full backup, and then restore the files from your latest differential backup.

**What is an incremental backup?** An **incremental backup** makes a backup of the files that were added or changed since the last backup—not necessarily the files that changed from the last full backup, but the files that changed since any full or incremental backup. After making a full backup of your important files, you can make your first incremental backup containing the files that changed since the full backup. When you make your second incremental backup, it will contain only the files that changed since the first incremental backup. To restore files from an incremental backup, files from a full backup are restored first, followed by files from each incremental backup, starting with the oldest and ending with the most recent. The video associated with Figure 4-52 describes the difference between full, differential, and incremental backups.

**FIGURE 4-52**

Full, incremental, and differential backups each take a slightly different approach to backing up files.

 CLICK TO START

**What about backing up the Windows Registry?** Windows users often hear a variety of rumors about backing up the Windows Registry. The Registry, as it is usually called, is an important group of files the Windows operating system uses to store configuration information about all the devices and software installed on a computer system. If the Registry becomes damaged, your computer might not be able to boot up, launch programs, or communicate with peripheral devices. It is a good idea to have an extra copy of the Registry in case the original file is damaged.

As simple as it sounds, backing up the Registry can present a bit of a problem because the Registry is always open while your computer is on. Some software that you might use for backups cannot copy open files. If you use such software, it might never back up the Registry. Windows users whose backup plans encompass all files on the hard disk must make sure their backup software provides an option for including the Windows Registry. Even if a full-system backup is not planned, many experts recommend that you at least copy the Registry to a separate folder on the hard disk or to a floppy disk. If you do so, you should update this copy whenever you install new software or hardware.

**How many backups do I need?** Most experts recommend that you keep more than one set of backups. If you use recordable CDs or DVDs for your backups, then you simply burn a new disk each time you back up. If you are using rewritable media, such as removable hard disks, tapes, or CD-RWs, then you can reuse your backups—typically by rotating three backup disks or tapes.

To maintain a rotating backup, use one disk or tape for the first backup, and then use a different disk or tape for the next backup. Use another disk or tape for the third backup. For the fourth backup, you can overwrite the data on the first backup; for the fifth backup, overwrite the data on the second backup, and so on. So that you know which backup is the most recent, write the date of the backup on the disk or tape label.

## BOOT AND RECOVERY DISKS

**What is a boot disk?** If your computer's hard disk is out of commission, you might wonder how it can access the operating system files needed to carry out the boot process. If your hard disk fails or a virus wipes out the boot sector files on your hard disk, you won't be able to use your normal boot procedure.

For such emergencies, it is essential to have on hand a removable storage medium that you can use to boot your PC.

A **boot disk** is a removable storage medium containing the operating system files needed to boot your computer without accessing the hard disk. CDs, DVDs, and even USB flash drives are currently the typical media used for boot disks, although in the past the standard medium was the floppy disk.

**What is a DOS boot disk?** A **DOS boot disk** enables your computer to boot into DOS instead of Windows. If your computer runs Windows and contains a floppy disk drive, you can make your own DOS boot disk using My Computer or Windows Explorer, as shown in Figure 4-53.

**FIGURE 4-53**

To create a DOS boot disk, insert a blank floppy disk in drive A. Open My Computer or Windows Explorer, and then right-click the Drive A icon. Select Format and check the box labeled Create an MS-DOS startup disk.

After you've created your floppy boot disk, you should write-protect it to prevent possible virus infection and to keep anyone from accidentally writing over it. Slide the tab at the top of the floppy to activate write protection. Manufacturer and PC-related Web sites, such as *freepctech.com*, also provide free downloads for creating various types of boot disks, including DOS boot disks.

**How do I start my computer with a DOS boot disk?**   Simply insert your DOS boot disk in the appropriate drive (or plug in the USB flash drive containing the boot disk files) to boot your computer. Because a DOS boot disk is designed to boot into DOS, not Windows, your computer is booted and ready for commands when you see a prompt, such as A:> on the screen.

**What if my computer doesn't boot from the boot disk?** Your computer should detect the boot disk and be able to start up from it. If the boot disk doesn't seem to work, you can check the following:

● **The computer's boot configuration.** Your computer might not be configured to boot from the drive where you've inserted your boot disk. Most PCs are configured to boot from drive C, but you can change that setting by using the Bios Setup menu, which is accessible by pressing the Setup menu function key (usually F2) just after you flip on the power switch.

● **The boot disk.** Your floppy, CD, or DVD might not be a valid boot disk or it might have errors on it. If possible, use a functioning computer to verify that your boot disk is bootable and readable. Make sure that your boot disk has no scratches or smudges on it.

● **The cable connections.** Check for any loose cables, which can prevent any system components from functioning.

**How do I use a DOS boot disk?** In the DOS environment, you or any technician you're working with can run some diagnostic tools. For example, to check for hard drive errors type in chkdsk. You can also fix certain problems, such as corrupted Registry entries, with the use of DOS commands.

Even after you've diagnosed and fixed your computer's problems, however, you still have to restore your entire working environment to its original state before your computer crashed. This requires reinstalling Windows, service packs, device drivers, utilities, and application software. You also must reestablish all your user settings and recover all your data. Going through these steps to restore a hard disk can take several hours or even days (Figure 4-54).

**FIGURE 4-54**

When restoring a hard disk from scratch, you'll need access to all the original system and application software disks shipped with your computer or installed after it was purchased.

**What is a recovery disk?** A **recovery disk** (sometimes referred to as a recovery CD) is a bootable CD, DVD, or other media that contains a complete copy of your computer's hard disk as it existed when shipped from the manufacturer. It contains the operating system, device drivers, utilities, and even software that was bundled in with your computer. You can use a recovery disk to return your computer to its factory default state. However, a recovery disk will not restore your data files, any software that you installed, or any configuration setting you've made since you unwrapped your computer from its shipping box.

**Where can I get a recovery disk?** Recovery disks are sometimes included with new computers as a CD or DVD. If you don't receive one, you should check the manufacturer's Web site for a downloadable version. The operating system might also supply a method for creating recovery disks. For example, the Windows XP Backup Utility creates a set of Automated System Recovery disks (Figure 4-55).

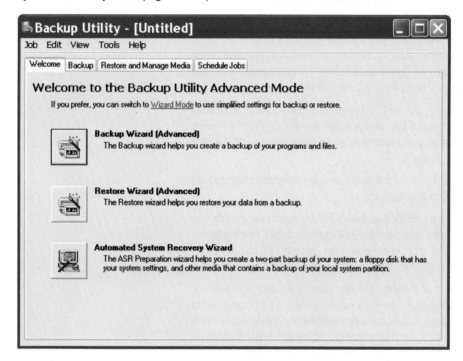

**FIGURE 4-55**

Windows XP includes an Automated System Recovery Wizard that helps you create a boot disk containing your system settings.

Several manufacturers no longer include recovery disks. Instead, they store an exact image of the hard disk with all factory-installed device drivers and software in a hidden partition (sometimes called a recovery partition) on the hard drive. Consumers are provided with a special utility to copy the image from the recovery partition to the main partition to restore the hard disk to its original state. Recovery partitions are convenient for restoring a corrupted device driver or software module because you can simply copy or reinstall the file from the recovery partition to the main partition. The files in the recovery partition are not accessible, however, if your computer's hard disk fails. Therefore, don't be misled into thinking that a recovery partition can help you restore your computer after a hard disk failure.

**Is there any way to make a recovery disk that contains my computer's settings?** You can create a **custom recovery CD** that contains your computer's current settings and device drivers. To do so, you must create a bootable image of the essential files using disk imaging software, such as Norton Ghost. Your custom recovery disk can only restore your system to its state on the date you made the image. It's important to create a new recovery disk every time you make significant changes to your hardware, software, or user settings.

Norton Ghost is a product of Symantec, which also provides a more specialized recovery disk called the Symantec Recovery Disk. In case of an emergency, you can use this disk to boot Windows, reinstall your device drivers, and establish a recovery environment where you can run tasks such as scanning your computer for viruses, restoring files and folders from a backup image, and checking disks for errors. The Symantec Recovery Disk is included with Norton Ghost and Norton Save and Restore.

Certain PC manufacturers have pre-installed Norton Ghost and the recovery environment on some of their computers. These machines might not require the Symantec Recovery Disk. Keyboard keys are set up to start the recovery environment. Check your manufacturer's specific instructions for recovery from system failure.

The contents and capabilities of recovery disks vary. Some are designed to restore your computer to its like-new state and wipe out all your data. Others attempt to restore user settings, programs, and data. Before you depend on a recovery disk, make sure you know what it contains and how to use it in case of a system failure.

4

# QuickCheck

1. When backing up selected files, rather than making a full backup, you should make a copy of the Windows [          ] and keep it updated every time you install new hardware or software.

2. The backup process is simplified if you store all your important data files in a single [          ] .

3. One of the best devices for home backup is a(n) [          ] hard disk drive.

4. A(n) [          ] backup copies only those files that have changed since your last backup session.

5. A(n) [          ] CD helps restore a computer system by loading hardware drivers and user settings as well as the operating system.

 CHECK ANSWERS

# Cyberterrorists or Pranksters?

**IT DOESN'T TAKE** any special digital expertise to mastermind some computer crimes. Setting fire to a computer doesn't require the same finesse as writing a stealthy virus, but both can have the same disastrous effect on data. Old-fashioned crimes, such as arson, that take a high-tech twist because they involve a computer can be prosecuted under traditional laws.

Traditional laws do not, however, cover the range of possibilities for computer crimes. Suppose a person unlawfully enters a computer facility and steals backup tapes. That person might be prosecuted for breaking and entering. But would common breaking and entering laws apply to a person who uses an off-site terminal to enter a computer system without authorization? And what if a person copies a data file without authorization? Has that file really been stolen if the original remains on the computer?

Many countries have computer crime laws that specifically define computer data and software as personal property. These laws also define as crimes the unauthorized access, use, modification, or disabling of a computer system or data. But laws don't necessarily stop criminals. If they did, we wouldn't have to deal with malicious code and intrusions.

## Computer Crime Gambits

**Data diddling:** Unauthorized alterations to data stored on a computer system, such as a student changing grades stored in a school's computer.

**Identity theft:** Unauthorized copying of personal information, such as credit card numbers, passwords, Social Security numbers, and bank account PINs.

**Salami shaving:** Redirecting small, unnoticeable amounts of money from large amounts.

**Denial of Service:** An attempt to disrupt the operations of a network or computer system, usually by flooding it with data traffic.

**Information theft:** Unauthorized access to a computer system, such as military or government computers, to gain restricted information.

**Virus distribution:** Launching viruses, worms, and Trojan horses.

**Vandalism:** Intentional defacement of Web sites.

Computer crimes—costly to organizations and individuals—include a variety of gambits, such as virus distribution, data diddling, identity theft, and salami shaving.

One of the first computer crime cases involved a worm unleashed on the ARPANET in 1988 that quickly spread through government and university computer systems. The worm's author, Robert Morris, was convicted and sentenced to three years' probation, 400 hours of community service, and a $10,000 fine. This relatively lenient sentence was imposed because Morris claimed he had not intended to cripple the entire network.

A 1995 high-profile case involved a computer hacker named Kevin Mitnick, who was accused of breaking into dozens of corporate, university, government, and personal computers. Although vilified in the media, Mitnick had the support of many hackers and other people who believed that the prosecution grossly exaggerated the extent of his crimes. Nonetheless, Mitnick was sentenced to 46 months in prison and ordered to pay restitution in the amount of $4,125 during his three-year period of supervised release. The prosecution was horrified by such a paltry sum—an amount that was much less than its request for $1.5 million in restitution.

*Forbes* reporter Adam L. Penenberg took issue with the 46-month sentence imposed by Judge Marianne Pfaelzer and wrote, "This in a country where the average prison term for manslaughter is three years. Mitnick's crimes were curiously innocuous. He broke into corporate computers, but no evidence indicates that he destroyed data. Or sold anything he copied. Yes, he pilfered software—but in doing so left it behind. This world of bits is a strange one, in which you can take something and still leave it for its rightful owner. The theft laws designed for payroll sacks and motor vehicles just don't apply to a hacker."

In 2005 a German teenager confessed to creating the Sasser computer worm that was blamed for shutting down British Airways and Delta Airlines flight check-ins, hospitals and government offices in Hong Kong, part of Australia's rail network, Finnish banks, British Coast Guard stations, and millions of other computers worldwide. The teen was given a suspended sentence of 21 months and was required to perform 30 hours of community service. Microsoft paid a $250,000 reward to the two people who tipped off German police to the virus author's identity. The teen now holds a job at a computer company that creates antivirus software.

Officials also made two arrests in connection with the Blaster worm. A 24-year-old Romanian citizen and an American teenager apparently downloaded copies of the worm source code, altered it slightly, and sent their versions back out again. The Romanian was allegedly angered by his treatment by one of his professors. The American teenager was just trying to see what he could get away with.

Under Romanian law, distributing a virus can mean a 15-year prison sentence. The U.S. Patriot Act and the Cyber-Security Enhancement Act carry even stiffer penalties—anywhere from 10 years to life in prison.

A CNET reporter questions the harshness of such penalties: "What bothers me most is that here in the United States, rapists serve, on average, 10 years in prison. Yet if, instead of assaulting another human being, that same person had released a virus on the Net, the criminal would get the same or an even harsher sentence."

Law makers hope that stiff penalties will deter cyber criminals. U.S. Attorney John McKay is quoted as saying, "Let there be no mistake about it, cyber-hacking is a crime. It harms persons, it harms individuals, it harms businesses. We will investigate, track down, and prosecute cyber-hackers."

These cases illustrate our culture's ambivalent attitude toward computer hackers. On the one hand, they are viewed as evil cyberterrorists who are set on destroying the glue that binds together the Information Age. From this perspective, hackers are criminals who must be hunted down, forced to make restitution for damages, and prevented from creating further havoc.

From another perspective, hackers are viewed more as Casper the Friendly Ghost in our complex cyber-machines—as moderately bothersome entities whose pranks are tolerated by the computer community, along with software bugs and hardware glitches. Seen from this perspective, a hacker's pranks are part of the normal course of study that leads to the highest echelons of computer expertise. "Everyone has done it," claims one hacking devotee, "even Bill Gates (founder of Microsoft) and Steve Jobs (founder of Apple Computer)."

Which perspective is right? Are hackers dangerous cyberterrorists or harmless pranksters? Before you make up your mind about computer hacking and cracking, you might want to further investigate several landmark cases by following links at the Computer Crime InfoWeb.

**INFOWEBLINKS**

Who's in the cybercrime news? How are cybercriminals caught? The **Computer Crime InfoWeb** provides answers to these questions and more.

CLICK TO CONNECT

www.course.com/np/concepts10/ch04

# What Do You Think?

ISSUE

1. Should a computer virus distribution sentence carry the same penalty as manslaughter?

○ Yes  ○ No  ○ Not sure

2. Should it be a crime to steal a copy of computer data while leaving the original data in place and unaltered?

○ Yes  ○ No  ○ Not sure

3. Should hackers be sent to jail if they cannot pay restitution to companies and individuals who lost money as the result of a prank?

○ Yes  ○ No  ○ Not sure

4. Do you think that a hacker would make a good consultant on computer security?

○ Yes  ○ No  ○ Not sure

▶ SAVE RESPONSES

# COMPUTERS IN CONTEXT

# Law Enforcement

**SIRENS WAIL.** Blue lights strobe the night. A speeding car slows and pulls off to the side of the road. It looks like a routine traffic stop, but the patrol car is outfitted with a mobile data computer. The police officers on this high-tech force have already checked the speeding car's license plate number and description against a database of stolen cars and cars allegedly used in kidnapping and other crimes.

Mounted in the dashboard of marked and unmarked police cars, a mobile data computer resembles a notebook computer with its flat-panel screen and compact keyboard. Unlike a consumer-grade notebook, however, the computers in police cruisers use hardened technology designed to withstand extreme conditions, such as high temperatures in parked vehicles. The dashboard-mounted computer communicates with an office-based server using a wireless link, such as short-range radio, CDPD (cellular digital packet data) technology, or Wi-Fi. With this wireless link, police officers can access data from local, state, and national databases.

One national database, the National Crime Information Center (NCIC), is maintained by the FBI and can be accessed by authorized personnel in local, state, and federal law enforcement agencies. The system can process more than 2.4 million queries per day related to stolen vehicles, wanted criminals, missing persons, violent gang members, stolen guns, and members of terrorist organizations. The officers who pulled over the speeding car received information from the NCIC that the car was stolen, so they arrested the car's occupant and took him to the police station for booking.

At the police station, digital cameras flash and the suspect's mug shot is automatically entered into an automated warrants and booking system. The system stores the suspect's complete biographical and arrest information, such as name, aliases, addresses, Social Security number, charges, and arrest date. The system also checks for outstanding warrants against the suspect, such as warrants for other thefts. Booking agents can enter those charges into the system, assign the new inmate to a cell, log his personal items, and print a photo ID or wrist band.

Automated warrants and booking systems have been proved to increase police productivity. New York City's system handles more than 300,000 bookings per year, with gains in productivity that have put nearly 300 officers back into action investigating crimes and patrolling neighborhoods.

As part of the booking process, the suspect is fingerprinted. A standard fingerprint card, sometimes called a ten-print card, contains inked prints of the fingers on each hand, plus name, date of birth, and other arrest information. Now, however, instead of using ink, a biometric scanning device can electronically capture fingerprints. Text information is entered using a keyboard and stored with digital fingerprint images.

The fingerprint information can be transmitted in digital format from local law enforcement agencies to the FBI's Automated Fingerprint Identification System (AFIS). This biometric identification methodology uses digital imaging technology to analyze fingerprint data. Using sophisticated algorithms, AFIS can classify arriving prints for storage or search the collection of 600 million fingerprint cards for matching prints.

Conventional crimes, such as car theft, are often solved by using standard investigative techniques with information from computer databases. To solve cybercrimes, however, often the special skills of computer forensic investigators are required.

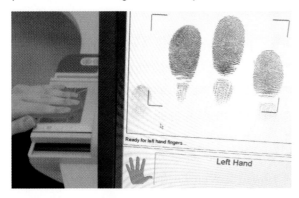

Ready for left hand fingers...

Left Hand

Computer forensics is the scientific examination and analysis of data located on computer storage media, conducted to offer evidence of computer crimes in court. Computer crimes can be separated into two categories. The first includes crimes that use computers, such as transmitting trade secrets to competitors, reproducing copyrighted material, and distributing child pornography. The second includes crimes targeted at computers, such as Denial of Service attacks on servers, Web site vandalism, data theft, and destructive viruses. Computer forensics can be applied to both categories.

Whether investigators suspect that a computer is the origin of a cyber attack or contains evidence, the first step in the forensic process is to use disk imaging software to make an exact replica of the information stored on the hard disk. The disk image is collected on a write-once medium that cannot be altered with planted evidence, and the forensic scientist begins analyzing the disk image data with simple search software that looks through files for keywords related to the crime. In the case of the Gap-Toothed Bandit who was convicted for robbing nine banks, analysis of the disk image revealed word processing files containing notes he handed to tellers demanding money.

Criminals typically attempt to delete files with incriminating evidence, but a good forensic scientist can retrieve data from deleted files with undelete software or data recovery software. Temporary Internet or cache files can also yield evidence, pointing law enforcement officers to Web sites the suspect visited that might be fronts for illegal activity.

When a computer is a target of a cyber attack, forensic investigators use three techniques to track the source. The first option is to make an immediate image of the server's hard disk and look through its log files for evidence of activity coming from unauthorized IP addresses. A second technique is to monitor the intruder by watching login attempts, changes to log files, and file access requests. Sophisticated intruders might be able to detect such monitoring, however, and cover their tracks. A third technique is to create a honeypot—an irresistible computer system or Web site containing fake information that allows investigators to monitor hackers until identification is possible.

Despite the many techniques and tools available to forensic investigators, they have three main constraints. First, they must adhere to privacy regulations and obtain warrants to set up wiretaps or gather information from ISPs about their customers. Second, they must scrupulously document their procedures so that the evidence they produce cannot be discredited in court as planted or fabricated. Third, forensic investigators must examine a wide range of alternatives pertaining to the crime, such as the chance that an IP or e-mail address used to commit a cybercrime doesn't belong to an innocent bystander being spoofed by the real hacker.

Privacy, documentation, and evidentiary constraints cost forensic investigators time, and failure to adhere to strict standards can sometimes allow criminals to avoid conviction and penalties. But even within these constraints, careful forensic investigation is an important aspect of catching and convicting high-tech criminals.

**INFOWEBLINKS**

For more information about police and FBI technology, connect to the **Computers in Law Enforcement InfoWeb**.

 CLICK TO CONNECT
www.course.com/np/concepts10/ch04

# New Perspectives Labs

## On the BookOnCD

To access the New Perspectives labs for Chapter 4, start the BookOnCD, BookOnFlashDrive, or other NP10 BookOn product and then click the icon next to the lab title below.

### WORKING WITH WINDOWS EXPLORER

**IN THIS LAB YOU'LL LEARN:**

- How to access Windows Explorer
- How to expand and collapse the directory structure
- How to rename or delete a file or folder
- The basic principles for creating an efficient directory structure for your files
- How to create a folder
- How to select a single file or a group of files
- How to move files from one folder to another

#### LAB ASSIGNMENTS

1. Start the interactive part of the lab. Make sure you've enabled Tracking if you want to save your QuickCheck results. Perform each lab step, and answer all the lab QuickCheck questions.

2. Use Windows Explorer to look at the directory of the hard disk or floppy disk that currently contains most of your files. Draw a diagram showing the hierarchy of folders. Write a paragraph explaining how you could improve this hierarchy, and draw a diagram to illustrate your plan.

3. On a blank floppy disk or USB Flash drive, create three folders: Music, Web Graphics, and Articles. Within the Music folder, create four additional folders: Jazz, Reggae, Rock, and Classical. Within the Classical folder, create two more folders: Classical MIDI and Classical MP3. If you have Internet access, go on to #4.

4. Use your browser software to connect to the Internet, and then go to a Web site, such as *www.zdnet.com* or *www.cnet.com*. Look for a small graphic (remember, the capacity of a floppy disk is only 1.44 MB!) and download it to your Web Graphics folder. Next, use a search engine to search for "classical MIDI music." Download one of the compositions to the Music\Classical\Classical MIDI folder. Open Windows Explorer and expand all the directories for drive A. Open the Music\Classical\Classical MIDI folder and make sure your music download appears. Capture a screenshot. Follow your instructor's directions to submit this screenshot as a printout or an e-mail attachment.

### BACKING UP YOUR COMPUTER

**IN THIS LAB YOU'LL LEARN:**

- How to start the Windows Backup utility
- How to use the Backup Wizard
- How to create a backup job
- Which files to select for a backup job
- How to back up the Windows Registry
- The advantages and disadvantages of using a password to protect your backup data
- The implications of compressing your backup data
- How to restore data from an entire backup job
- How to restore a single file from a backup

#### LAB ASSIGNMENTS

1. Start the interactive part of the lab. Make sure you've enabled Tracking if you want to save your QuickCheck results. Perform each lab step as directed, and answer all the lab QuickCheck questions. When you exit the lab, your answers are automatically graded and your results are displayed.

2. Describe where most of your data files are stored, and estimate how many megabytes of data (not programs) you have in all these files. Next, take a close look at these files and estimate how much data (in megabytes) you cannot afford to lose. Finally, explain what you think would be the best hardware device for backing up this amount of data.

3. Draw a sketch or capture a screenshot of the Microsoft Backup window's toolbar. Use ToolTips, ScreenTips, or the window's status bar to find the name of each toolbar button. Use this information to label the buttons on your sketch or screenshot.

4. Assume that you will use Microsoft Backup to make a backup of your data files. Describe the backup job you would create—specify the folders you must include. It is not necessary to list individual files unless they are not within one of the folders you would back up. Make sure you indicate whether you would use password protection, the type of compression you would select, and how you would handle the Windows Registry.

# Key Terms

Make sure you understand all the boldfaced key terms presented in this chapter. If you're using the NP10 BookOnCD, BookOnFlashDrive, or other NP10 BookOn product, you can use this list of terms as an interactive study activity. First, try to define a term in your own words, and then click the term to compare your definition with the definition presented in the chapter.

Backup, 222
Backup software, 226
Backward compatibility, 198
Boot disk, 228
Boot process, 192
Bootstrap program, 192
Button, 190
Cluster, 219
Command-line interface, 189
Custom recovery CD, 231
Data fork, 200
Defragmentation utility, 221
Desktop, 189
Desktop operating system, 188
Dialog box, 191
Differential backup, 227
Directory, 206
Disk partition, 205
DOS, 202
DOS boot disk, 228
Dual boot, 199
FAT32, 219
File Allocation Table, 219
File date, 206
File extension, 204
File format, 207
File header, 207
File management utilities, 214

File shredder software, 220
File size, 206
File specification, 206
File system, 219
File-naming conventions, 204
Folder, 206
Formatting, 218
Formatting utilities, 219
Fragmented files, 221
Full backup, 227
Graphical user interface, 189
Icon, 189
Incremental backup, 227
Kernel, 192
Linux, 201
Linux distribution, 201
Logical storage model, 215
Mac OS, 197
Master File Table, 219
Memory leak, 187
Menu, 190
Menu bar, 190
Microsoft Windows, 194
Multiprocessing, 186
Multitasking, 186
Multithreading, 186
Multiuser operating system, 187
Native file format, 209

Network operating system, 187
NTFS, 219
Operating system, 184
Palm OS, 202
Path, 206
Physical storage model, 218
Recovery disk, 230
Reserved words, 205
Resource, 185
Resource fork, 200
Restore point, 225
Root directory, 206
Sectors, 218
Single-user operating system, 187
Subdirectory, 206
Submenu, 191
Symbian OS, 203
Taskbar, 190
Toolbar, 190
Tracks, 218
UNIX, 201
User interface, 189
Virtual machine, 199
Window, 189
Windows Explorer, 216
Windows Mobile OS, 203

4

# Interactive Summary

To review important concepts from this chapter, fill in the blanks to best complete each sentence. When using the NP10 BookOnCD or other BookOn product, click the Check Answers buttons to automatically score your answers.

**SECTION A:** An operating system interacts with application software, device drivers, and hardware to manage a computer's [_____], such as the processor, memory, and input/output devices. To allow two or more programs to run simultaneously, an OS can offer [_____] services. Within a single program, [_____] allows multiple parts, or threads, to run simultaneously. An operating system's [_____] capability supports a division of labor among all the processing units. When multiple programs are running, the OS should prevent a memory [_____], that is a situation in which instructions and data from one area of memory overflow into memory allocated to another program. Operating systems are informally categorized and characterized using one or more of the following terms: A [_____] -user operating system expects to deal with one set of input devices—those that can be controlled by one person at a time. A

[_____] -user operating system is designed to deal with input, output, and processing requests from many users. A [_____], or server, operating system provides process and memory management services that allow two or more programs to run simultaneously. A [_____] operating system is one that's designed for a personal computer—either a desktop or notebook computer.

In addition to behind-the-scenes activities, operating systems also provide helpful tools, called operating system [_____] that you can use to control and customize your computer equipment and work environment. In addition, many operating systems also influence the "look and feel" of your software, or what's known as the user [_____]. The core part of an operating system is called the [_____], which is loaded into RAM during the [_____] process. ▶ CHECK ANSWERS

**SECTION B:** Popular [_____] operating systems include Microsoft Windows, Mac OS, and Linux. The first versions of Windows were sometimes referred to as operating [_____] rather than operating systems because they required DOS to supply the operating system kernel. Windows has evolved to keep pace with 16-bit to 32-bit, and [_____] -bit architectures. Its strengths include a huge library of Windows [_____], support for a variety of peripheral devices, and plenty of documentation. Two of the weakest features of Microsoft Windows are reliability and [_____].

Mac OS evolved from the original Classic Mac OS designed for [_____] computers based on the Motorola 68000 microprocessor. In 2001, Mac OS X was released for Apple's new line of computers using IBM's PowerPC processor. OS X was again revised for a line of computers using [_____]

processors. Mac OS X offers [_____] compatibility for prior-generation applications. Intel Macs can be set up to dual [_____] Mac OS and Windows. Intel Macs also offer a good platform for [_____] machine technologies that allow you to use one computer to simulate the hardware and software of another. One of the potential problems with Mac OS is its use of [_____] forks, which make cross-platform file sharing clumsy. Linux is an [_____] source operating system that is used extensively for servers. One of the reasons it has not become a popular desktop OS is that it requires a bit more technical savvy than Windows or Mac OS. Developed by Microsoft and supplied on the original IBM PCs, [_____] was one of the first operating systems for personal computers. Operating systems for PDAs are typically smaller than PC operating systems and can fit in [_____]. ▶ CHECK ANSWERS

**SECTION C:** A computer [_____] is a named collection of data that exists on a storage medium, such as a hard disk, floppy disk, CD, DVD, or tape. Every file has a name and might also have a file extension. The rules that specify valid file names are called file-naming [_____] . These rules typically do not allow you to use certain characters or [_____] words in a file name. A file [_____] is usually related to a file format—the arrangement of data in a file and the coding scheme used to represent the data. A software program's [_____] file format is the default format for storing files created with that program. A file's location is defined by a file [_____] (sometimes called a path), which includes the storage device, folder(s), file name, and extension. In Windows, storage devices are identified by a drive letter, followed by a [_____] . An operating system maintains a list of files called a directory for each storage disk, tape, CD, or DVD. The main directory of a disk is sometimes referred to as the [_____] directory, which can be subdivided into several smaller lists called subdirectories that are depicted as [_____] .

▶ CHECK ANSWERS

**4**

**SECTION D:** File [_____] encompasses any procedure that helps you organize your computer-based files so that you can find and use them more effectively. [_____] -based file management uses tools provided with a software program to open and save files. Additional tools might also allow you to create new folders, rename files, and delete files. The Save and Save As dialog boxes are examples of these file management tools. Most operating systems provide file management [_____] that give you the "big picture" of the files you have stored on your disks. The structure of folders that you envision on your disk is a [_____] model, which is often represented by a storage [_____] , such as a tree structure or filing cabinet. Windows [_____] is an example of a file management utility provided by an operating system. Windows Explorer allows you to find, rename, copy, move, and delete files and folders. In addition, it allows you to perform these file management activities with more than one file at a time. The way that data is actually stored is referred to as the [_____] storage model. Before a computer stores data on a disk, CD, or DVD, it creates the equivalent of electronic storage bins by dividing the disk into [_____] , and then further dividing the disk into [_____] . This dividing process is referred to as [_____] . Each sector of a disk is numbered, providing a storage address that the operating system can track. Many computers work with a group of sectors, called a [_____] , to increase the efficiency of file storage operations. An operating system uses a file [_____] to track the physical location of files.

▶ CHECK ANSWERS

**SECTION E:** A backup is a copy of one or more files that has been made in case the original files become damaged. A good backup plan allows you to [_____] your computing environment to its pre-disaster state with a minimum of fuss. Your personal backup plan depends on the files you need to back up, the hardware you have available to make backups, and your backup software. In any case, it is a good idea to back up the Windows [_____] and make sure your files are free of [_____] . Backups should be stored in a safe place, away from the computer. Backups can be recorded on floppy disks, writable CDs and DVDs, networks, Web sites, a second hard disk, or tapes. Many computer owners depend on writable CDs for backups, and use My Computer or Windows [_____] to simply select files and copy files to the backup. [_____] drives and backup software are typically used in business situations when a full-system backup is desirable. Backup software differs from most copy routines because it [_____] all the files for a backup into one large file. In addition to file backups, you should have a [_____] disk containing the operating system files and settings needed to start your computer without accessing the hard disk.

▶ CHECK ANSWERS

# Interactive Situation Questions

Apply what you've learned to some typical computing situations. When using the NP10 BookOnCD, BookOnFlashDrive, or any other NP10 BookOn product, you can type your answers, and then use the Check Answers button to automatically score your responses.

1. While using several programs at the same time, your computer displays an error message that refers to a program that is not responding. You recognize this message as one that might result from a [＿＿＿＿] leak and decide to close the non-responding program using Ctrl+Alt+Del.

2. Your friend wants to open a window on his Mac computer in which he can run Microsoft Windows and play some games designed for the Windows platform. You tell your friend to create a [＿＿＿＿] machine using software such as Parallels Desktop.

3. Suppose you are using Microsoft Word and you want to open a file. When your software lists the documents you can open, you can expect them to be in Word's [＿＿＿＿] file format, which is DOC.

4. Can you use a Windows application, create a document, and store it using the file name I L*ve NY ? Yes or no? [＿＿＿＿]

5. When you want to work with several files—to move them to different folders, for example—it would be most efficient to use a file management utility, such as Windows [＿＿＿＿].

6. When specifying a location for a data file on your hard disk, you should avoid saving it in the [＿＿＿＿] directory.

7. Your computer seems to be taking longer to store and retrieve files. You use a(n) [＿＿＿＿] utility to rearrange the files in contiguous clusters.

8. You have an old computer that you will donate to a school, but you want to make sure its hard disk contains no trace of your data. To do so, you should use file [＿＿＿＿] software that overwrites empty sectors with random 1s and 0s.

9. You just finished making a full backup on a set of DVDs. Before you depend on this backup, you should test it to make sure you can successfully [＿＿＿＿] the data in the event of a hard disk crash.

10. Your hard disk crashed for some unknown reason. Now when you switch on the computer power, all you get is an "Error reading drive C:" message. You use a(n) [＿＿＿＿] CD that contains the operating system files and device drivers needed to start your computer without accessing the hard disk.

▶ CHECK ANSWERS

# Interactive Practice Tests

Practice tests that consist of 10 multiple-choice, true/false, and fill-in-the-blank questions are available on both the NP10 BookOn products and the NP10 Web site. The questions are selected at random from a large test bank, so each time you take a test, you'll receive a different set of questions. Your tests are scored immediately, and you can print study guides that help you find the correct answers for any questions that you missed.

▶ CLICK TO START

# Study Tips

Study Tips help you to organize and consolidate the information in a unit by making lists, outlines, charts, and sketches. You can use paper and pencil or word processing software to complete most of the Study Tip activities.

1. Make sure you can use your own words to correctly answer each of the red focus questions that appear throughout the chapter.

2. Make sure you can list and describe the four main resources that an operating system manages.

3. Explain the term *memory leak*, and describe what you can do if one occurs on your PC.

4. Describe the difference between a graphical user interface and a command-line user interface.

5. Watch your computer while it boots and revise the list on page 192 so that it reflects what happens when your computer boots.

6. Describe five tasks for which you must interact directly with the operating system.

7. Study the figures of Windows, Mac OS, and Linux in Section B. If you were to start an unfamiliar computer, describe how you would identify its operating system.

8. Discuss the pros and cons of using Linux as a desktop operating system.

9. Make a list of five file names that are valid under the file-naming conventions for your operating system. Also create a list of five file names that are not valid, and explain the problem with each one.

10. Pick any five files on the computer that you typically use, and write out the full path for each one.

11. Make a list of at least 20 file extensions you find on the computer you use most often. Group these extensions into the following categories: system files, graphics files, sound files, text files, other.

12. Describe the difference between the Save and the Save As options provided by an application.

13. Explain the kinds of file management tasks that might best be accomplished using a file management utility such as Windows Explorer, instead of the Save As or Open dialog box provided by a software application.

14. Make sure that you can describe what happens in the MFT or FAT when a file is stored or deleted.

15. Describe the various types of boot disks that might help you recover from a hard disk crash.

16. Discuss the pros and cons of each type of backup hardware.

17. Make a list of backup tips that you think would help people devise a solid backup plan.

18. Fill in the blanks in the concept map below that illustrates the hierarchy of OS resource management activities.

**4**

# Concept Map

CHECK ANSWERS

# Projects

 CRITICAL THINKING

Think about the ways you typically interact with a computer and how the operating system factors into that interaction. What aspects of the operating system do you like? Which aspects could be improved? Organize your thoughts into an annotated list and e-mail it to your instructor.

 GROUP PROJECT

Keeping files and folders organized is a skill worth developing. Work with one or two other people to streamline the organization of folders and files on a computer storage device, such as a hard disk or flash drive. The storage device should contain at least 100 files. You can have the computer generate a listing of the files by connecting to *www.support.microsoft.com*, searching for article 196158, and following the instructions you find there for "How to Create a Text File List of the Contents of a Folder." Once you have a document containing the list, you can edit it to indicate how you would rearrange the files into a better structure of folders. Use a series of indents or Microsoft Word's outlining function to show the hierarchy of files and folders. Annotate your list by indicating the kinds of files you expect to be stored in each folder.

 CYBERCLASSROOM

Create an e-mail message that describes your backup equipment and plan along with the date of your last backup. In the subject line, include your name and the title "Original Backup Plan." Send the message to other members of your team and solicit comments and questions.

Based on the feedback you receive, use a word processor to revise your backup plan so it gives you improved protection against losing files. Using copy and paste, add the text of your Original Backup Plan and all the comments you received from your team. Your final document should contain your Revised Backup Plan, your Original Backup Plan, and your team's comments. Send this document to your instructor as an e-mail attachment.

 MULTIMEDIA PROJECT

Suppose you work for a software company and you are tasked with designing the user interface for a new handheld electronic toy for children ages 8-12. Write a paragraph describing how children will use the toy, then sketch out the main screen. Use callouts to describe how each of the screen elements is supposed to work.

 RESUME BUILDER

In today's job market, versatility is valuable. For this project, find a computer that runs an operating system different from the one you normally use. Spend at least 30 minutes working with this alternative operating system. Write a one-page description of your initial reaction, including aspects you liked and did not like.

 GLOBALIZATION

Computers are used worldwide, but all of the major operating systems originated in English-speaking countries. Take a look at the operating system that you use in the context of global users who might not speak English and who might not have grown up with Western customs. Describe at least five aspects of your operating system that would have to be modified to be acceptable to global users.

 ISSUE

The Issue section of this chapter focused on cybercrime. For this project, write a two- to five-page opinion paper about the "right to hack," based on information that you gather from the Internet. To begin this project, consult the Computer Crime InfoWeb (see page 233), and link to the recommended Web pages to get an in-depth overview of the issue. Armed with this background, select one of the following statements and argue for or against it:

• People have the "right" to hone their computing skills by breaking into computers.

• A person who creates a virus is perfectly justified in releasing it if the purpose is to make everyone aware of these security breaches.

• Computer crimes are no different from other crimes, and computer criminals should be held responsible for the damage they cause.

Whatever viewpoint you decide to present, make sure you back it up with facts and references to authoritative articles and Web pages. Follow your professor's instructions for submitting your paper by e-mail or as a printed document.

 COMPUTERS IN CONTEXT

The Computers in Context section focused on computer use in law enforcement. For this project, use Web-based resources to search for cases in which computer forensic evidence was used in a criminal or civil investigation. Write a paragraph about the case's particulars, including a description of the alleged criminal activity. Next, create a list of elements, such as e-mail messages, attachments, files, and server logs, that were the focus of the forensic investigation. Follow up with a summary of the outcome. Was the suspect found guilty? Was a penalty imposed? Finally, state your opinion of how forensic evidence affected the case. Was it key evidence required to make the case, or did it simply support other physical evidence? Was the computer forensic evidence solid or open to interpretation and challenges from the defense? Make sure you include the URLs used for your research, and check with your professor for instructions on submitting this project on disk, by e-mail, or in print.

# On the Web

## STUDENT EDITION LABS

**W CLICK TO ACCESS THE NP10 WEB SITE**
or open your browser and connect to www.course.com/np/concepts10/ch04.
Lab results can be stored in the Universal Gradebook.

### MAINTAINING A HARD DRIVE

In the Maintaining a Hard Drive Student Edition Lab, you will learn the following topics and skills:

- Defragmenting a hard disk
- Running ScanDisk
- Detecting system and program failure
- Freeing up disk space

### MANAGING FILES AND FOLDERS

In the Managing Files and Folders Student Edition Lab, you will learn the following topics and skills:

- Using Windows Explorer to manage files and folders
- Deleting and restoring files
- Creating, naming, copying, and moving folders
- Changing folder options and properties

### BACKING UP YOUR COMPUTER

In the Backing Up Your Computer Student Edition Lab, you will learn the following topics and skills:

- Creating a backup
- Creating an incremental backup
- Backing up the Windows Registry
- Scheduling backup jobs
- Restoring an entire backup

### USING WINDOWS

In the Using Windows Student Edition Lab, you will learn the following topics and skills:

- Identifying common elements of Windows software
- Working with the taskbar and Start menu
- Using menus, toolbars, and dialog boxes

 **CHAPTER COURSECAST**

Use your computer or iPod to hear a five-minute audio presentation of chapter highlights.

 **FLASHCARD COURSECAST**

Interact with audio flashcards to review key terms from the chapter.

 **DETAILED OBJECTIVES**

Make sure that you've achieved all the objectives for a chapter before it's time for your test!

 **TEST YOURSELF**

Review chapter material by taking these ten-question tests, then send your results to the Universal Gradebook.

 **ONLINE GAMES**

Have some fun while refreshing your memory about key concepts that might appear on the next test. You can even send your results to the Universal Gradebook!

 **AND MORE!**

At the NP10 Web site you'll also find TechBuzz, CNET videos, Extra Content, and InfoWebLinks.

# 5

# LANs and WLANs

## LEARNING OBJECTIVES

- Describe the characteristics of PANs, NANs, LANS, MANs, and WANs
- Diagram the five most common network topologies
- Diagram Shannon's model of a communications network
- List the types of cables and other links typically used for data communications networks
- Make a list of network devices and explain the role of each one
- Describe the role of communications protocols
- Explain the difference between packet switching and circuit switching technology
- Describe how to set up wired and wireless networks
- List various ways to share files over a LAN
- List security measures for wired and wireless networks
- List and define types of encryption that help secure computer networks and data

 **PRE-ASSESSMENT QUIZ**

Take the pre-assessment quiz to find out how much you know about the topics in this chapter.

---

**MULTIMEDIA and INTERACTIVE ELEMENTS**
When using the BookOnCD, BookOnFlashDrive, or other NP10 BookOn product, the ▶ icons are clickable to access multimedia resources.

BEFORE YOU READ ON, **TRY IT**

## IS MY COMPUTER CONNECTED TO ANY NETWORKS?

Chapter 5 introduces computer networks and explains how handy they are for sharing files and accessing the Internet at home, at school, or in a business. Your computer might be connected to a home network or it might have access to a campus network or a local wireless hotspot. To discover the networks that your computer can access, do the following steps:

**1.** Click the Start button on the Windows taskbar, select Connect To. If you are using Windows XP, select Show all connections. If you're using Windows Vista, select Open Network and Sharing Center.

**2.** When the network dialog box appears, click the Maximize button so that the window fills the screen.

**3.** Study the information displayed in the window. How many networks are listed? _____

**4.** To view the status of a network in Windows XP, right-click it, then select Status from the pop-up menu. For Windows Vista, click the View status link.

**5.** Write down the status window information in any of the applicable red lines in the screen shot at right.

**6.** When you have recorded the information, close the Dialog boxes. You'll learn more about network status as you read this chapter.

# Network Building Blocks

**TODAY, NETWORKS ARE EVERYWHERE** and network technology is evolving rapidly. Just when you think you have got a handle on your home wireless network, along come technologies like 802.11n, MIMO, and WPA2. Although network technology continues to evolve, it is based on a set of fairly stable concepts. If you understand the network building blocks introduced in Section A, working with new network technologies will be a piece of cake.

## NETWORK CLASSIFICATIONS

**What's the purpose of a network?** In the early years of personal computers, networks were scarce. Most personal computers functioned as standalone units, and computing was essentially a solitary activity in which one person interacted with a limited set of software tools, such as a word processor, spreadsheet, database, and games.

Some computer engineers, however, had the foresight to anticipate that personal computers could be networked to provide advantages not available with standalone computers. One of the most significant network ideas was conceived by Bob Metcalfe in 1976. His plan for transporting data between computers, shown in Figure 5-1, has become a key element in just about every computer network.

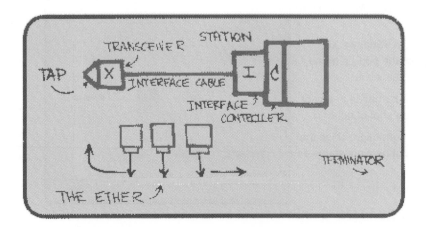

**FIGURE 5-1**

In 1976, Bob Metcalfe drew this diagram of a network technology, which he called Ethernet.

**How are computer networks classified?** Networks can be classified according to their size and geographic scope.

**PAN** (personal area network) is a term sometimes used to refer to the interconnection of personal digital devices within a range of about 30 feet (10 meters) and without the use of wires or cables. For example, a PAN could be used to wirelessly transmit data from a notebook computer to a PDA or portable printer.

A **NAN** (neighborhood area network) provides connectivity within a limited geographical area, usually spread over several buildings. These networks are becoming popular as local coffee shops and computer hobbyists offer wireless Internet connections to the public.

A **LAN** (local area network) is a data communications network that connects personal computers within a very limited geographical area—usually a single building. LANs use a variety of wired and wireless technologies. School computer labs and home networks are examples of LANs.

A **MAN** (metropolitan area network) is a public high-speed network capable of voice and data transmission within a range of about 50 miles (80 km). Examples of MANs include local Internet service providers, cable television companies, and local telephone companies.

A **WAN** (wide area network) covers a large geographical area and usually consists of several smaller networks, which might use different computer platforms and network technologies. The Internet is the world's largest WAN. Networks for nationwide banks and multi-location superstores can also be classified as WANs.

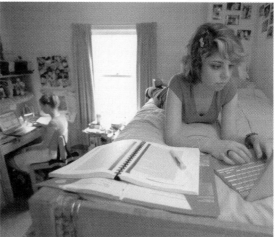

**Why is geographic scope important?** Localized networks typically include a small number of computers, which can be connected using basic equipment. As the area of network coverage expands, the number of workstations grows, specialized devices are sometimes required to boost signals, and the diversity of devices requires sophisticated management tools and strategies.

The focus of this chapter is on LANs because you are most likely to encounter this type of network in a school lab or small business. Also, if you intend to set up or upgrade a network in your home or dorm room, you will be working with LAN technologies (Figure 5-2).

**FIGURE 5-2**

The computer network in your dorm room is a LAN.

## LAN STANDARDS

**Are there different kinds of LANs?** In the past, a great diversity of LAN technologies existed as engineers pioneered various ideas to make data transport faster, more efficient, and more secure. Today, LANs are becoming more standardized, but several LAN standards remain necessary to accommodate networking environments that range from simple households to large businesses.

**What are LAN standards?** LAN technologies are standardized by the Institute of Electrical and Electronics Engineers (IEEE) *Project 802 - Local Network Standards*. IEEE standards are available for most types of commercial networks. An IEEE designation number, such as IEEE 802.3, is sometimes used to refer to a network standard in articles and advertisements. When you're shopping for equipment to connect your computer to a network, these designation numbers help you identify compatible network technologies.

**What are the most popular LAN standards?** Several LAN standards, including ARCnet, Token Ring, and FDDI, were popular in the past but are rarely used today. Today, most LANs are configured with Ethernet technology and use compatible Wi-Fi standards in applications that require wireless access. These standards are popular across the board for home and business installations. You'll learn more specifics about these popular networking technologies in sections B and C.

## NETWORK DEVICES

**What devices can be attached to a network?** You can think of a network as a spider web with many interconnecting points. Each connection point on a network is referred to as a **node**. A network node typically contains computers, networked peripherals, or network devices.

**How do computers connect to LANs?** A personal computer connected to a network is sometimes called a workstation. Other classes of computers, such as mainframes, supercomputers, servers, and handhelds, can also connect to LANs.

To connect to a LAN, a computer requires network circuitry, sometimes referred to as a **network interface card** (NIC). Network circuitry is often built into personal computers. If not, a NIC can be added to a slot in the system board, a USB port, or a notebook's PCMCIA slot.

**What is a networked peripheral?** A **networked peripheral**, or network-enabled peripheral, is any device that contains network circuitry to directly connect to a network. Printers, scanners, and storage devices are examples of devices that can be equipped to directly connect to a network instead of connecting to a workstation. Network-enabled printers and scanners are sometimes described as having "built-in networking." Some devices offer networking as an optional add-on. A storage device that directly connects to a network is called **network attached storage** (NAS).

**What are network devices?** A **network device**, or network appliance, is any electronic device that broadcasts network data, boosts signals, or routes data to its destination. Network devices include hubs, switches, routers, gateways, bridges, and repeaters. You will learn more about these devices later in the chapter. In the meantime, study Figure 5-3 for an example of a LAN that connects a variety of computers, peripherals, and network devices.

> **TERMINOLOGY NOTE**
>
> Throughout this chapter, the term *workstation* means a personal computer connected to a network.

> **TERMINOLOGY NOTE**
>
> Network interface cards are sometimes called network adapters or network cards.

**FIGURE 5-3**

A small LAN uses network devices to connect computers and peripherals.

Every device on a network requires network circuitry, such as a network interface card.

## CLIENTS, SERVERS, AND PEERS

### What is the difference between a network client and a server?

Network devices can function as clients or as servers. A server is a computer that provides services to other computers called clients. For example, an **application server** runs application software for network workstations. A **file server** stores files and supplies them to workstations on request. A **print server** handles jobs sent to network printers.

Servers are often dedicated to the task they perform, which means they are not assigned to users as workstations. Computers can be configured to perform both functions at the same time, but will not perform optimally in either role.

Networks that include one or more servers can operate in **client/server mode**, which you can envision as a hierarchical structure with servers at the top of the hierarchy (Figure 5-4).

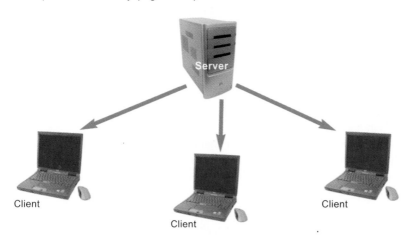

Client

Client

Client

**FIGURE 5-4**

In client/server mode, a server is the most important resource. Client computers are usually personal computers that use locally installed client software, such as a browser or e-mail package, to access the server.

5

### Can a network function without a server?

Networks do not require servers. Files and applications can be shared among workstations operating in **peer-to-peer mode**. In this mode, workstations can share responsibility for processing, storage, printing, and communications tasks (Figure 5-5). Popular file sharing networks such as Napster and BitTorrent operate in peer-to-peer mode.

Workstation

Workstation

Workstation

**FIGURE 5-5**

In peer-to-peer mode, workstations serve as both clients and servers.

### Should I choose client/server or peer-to-peer?

You don't have to choose one or the other. A network can function in client/server mode when necessary and also exchange data in peer-to-peer fashion. You can, for example, share files in peer-to-peer mode with several other computers on the network during the day, then in the evening when your friends come over to play computer games, you can configure one of your computers as a server that oversees game play on the other computers in your network that operate as clients for the duration of the game.

## PHYSICAL TOPOLOGY

**How are the devices on a LAN physically arranged?** The arrangement of devices in a network is referred to as its **physical topology**. Figure 5-6 illustrates star, ring, bus, mesh, and tree topologies; the pathways shown between nodes can be linked by physical cables or wireless signals.

**What are the advantages of each topology?** A network arranged as a **star topology** features a central connection point that links cables or handles wireless broadcasts to all workstations and peripherals. Many home networks are arranged in a star topology. The advantage of this topology is that any link can fail without affecting the rest of the network. Its primary disadvantage is that it requires quite a bit of cable to link all the devices—a disadvantage that disappears with wireless networks. Although the failure of a link does not affect the rest of the network, a device with a failed link would be cut off from the network and unable to receive data.

A **ring topology** connects all devices in a circle, with each device having exactly two neighbors. Data is transmitted from one device to another around the ring. This topology minimizes cabling, but failure of any one device can take down the entire network. Ring topologies, once championed by IBM, are infrequently used in today's networks.

A **bus topology** uses a common backbone to connect all network devices. The backbone functions as a shared communication link, which carries network data. The backbone stops at each end of the network with a special device called a terminator. Bus networks work best with a limited number of devices. Bus networks with more than a few dozen computers are likely to perform poorly, and if the backbone cable fails, the entire network becomes unusable.

A **mesh topology** connects each network device to many other network devices. Data traveling on a mesh network can take any of several possible paths from its source to its destination. These redundant data pathways make a mesh network very robust. Even if several links fail, data can follow alternative functioning links to reach its destination—an advantage over networks arranged in a star topology. The original plan for the Internet was based on mesh topology. Today, mesh topologies are used for some wireless networks. In a wireless mesh, data can be transported to nodes located far from a central access point, simply by hopping from one node to another.

A **tree topology** is essentially a blend of star and bus networks. Multiple star networks are connected into a bus configuration by a backbone. Tree topologies offer excellent flexibility for expansion—a single link to the backbone can add an entire group of star-configured devices. This link can be accomplished using the same type of hub that is used as the central connection point in a star network. Many of today's school and business networks are based on tree topologies.

**Can various networks be interconnected?** Yes. You can connect your home network to the Internet, for example. A LAN in your sorority or fraternity could be connected to your college campus network. A retail store might connect its cash register network to is financial network.

Two similar networks can be connected by a device called a **bridge**, which simply transfers data without regard to its format. Networks that use different topologies and technologies can be interconnected by using gateways.

**FIGURE 5-6**

Network Topologies

Star topology

Ring topology

Bus topology

Mesh topology

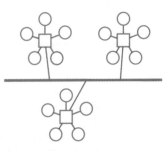

Tree topology

**Gateway** is a generic term for any device or software code used to join two networks, even if those networks use different protocols or address ranges. A gateway can be implemented completely in software, completely in hardware, or as a combination of the two. The device used to connect your home LAN to the Internet, for example, is a type of gateway.

## NETWORK LINKS

**What connects the nodes of a network?** Data can travel from one network device to another over a cable or through the air. A **communications channel**, or link, is a physical path or a frequency for signal transmissions. For example, Channel 12 on your TV tuner is a specific frequency used to broadcast audiovisual data for a television station. This data might also be carried over another channel, such as coaxial cable, as part of a cable TV system.

Data in a network with wired links travels from one device to another over cables (Figure 5-7). You'll learn more about wired LANs, such as Ethernet, HomePNA, and HomePlug, in Section B. Networks without wires transport data through the air, eliminating the need for cables. Section C contains more information on popular wireless network technologies, such as Wi-Fi and Bluetooth.

**FIGURE 5-7**

Cables and wireless technologies transport data from one network device to another.

**What's bandwidth?** Network links must move data and move it quickly. **Bandwidth** is the transmission capacity of a communications channel. Just as a four-lane freeway can carry more traffic than a two-lane street, a high-bandwidth communications channel can carry more data than a low-bandwidth channel. For example, the coaxial cable that brings you more than 100 channels of cable TV has a higher bandwidth than your home telephone line. The bandwidth of a channel carrying digital data is usually measured in bits per second (bps). The bandwidth of a channel carrying analog data is typically measured in hertz (Hz).

To better grasp the significance of bandwidth in a communications network, imagine a dial-up connection's 56 Kbps bandwidth as a narrow bike path that allows a limited amount of slow traffic. A 1.5 Mbps connection through your cable TV company is equivalent to a two-lane highway. A typical LAN, such as a college computer lab, might provide 100 Mbps bandwidth—equivalent to a 260-lane expressway.

High-bandwidth communications systems, such as cable TV and DSL, are sometimes referred to as **broadband**, whereas systems with less capacity, such as dial-up Internet access, are referred to as **narrowband**.

**TERMINOLOGY NOTE**

Hz is an abbreviation for hertz, which refers to the number of times a wave oscillates, or peaks, per second. Telephone signals are transmitted in the 1,200 Hz range. Many wireless networks transmit a 2.4 GHz signal that peaks 2.4 billion times per second.

## COMMUNICATIONS PROTOCOLS

**What is a protocol?** A protocol is a set of rules for interacting and nego-tiating. In some respects, it is like signals between the pitcher and catcher in a baseball game. Before the ball is thrown, the catcher and pitcher use hand signals to negotiate the speed and style of the pitch.

In the context of networks, a **communications protocol** refers to a set of rules for efficiently transmitting data from one network node to another. Just as a pitcher signals the catcher in baseball, two computers on a network might negotiate their communications protocols through a process called **handshaking**. The transmitting device sends a signal that means "I want to communicate." It then waits for an acknowledgement signal from the receiv-ing device. The two devices negotiate a protocol that both can handle. The sounds you hear as two modems or fax machines connect are examples of handshaking.

The best-known communications protocol is probably TCP/IP. It is the pro-tocol that regulates Internet data transport and has become a standard for LANs as well.

**What can communications protocols do?** Protocols set standards for encoding and decoding data, guiding data to its destination, and mitigat-ing the effects of interference. Specifically, protocols are responsible for the following aspects of network communications:

● Dividing messages into packets

● Affixing addresses to packets

● Initiating transmission

● Regulating the flow of data

● Checking for transmission errors

● Acknowledging receipt of transmitted data

**How does data travel over a network?** In 1948, Claude Shannon, an engineer at the prestigious Bell Labs, published an article describing a communications system model applicable to networks of all types, including today's computer networks.

In Shannon's model, data from a source, such as a network workstation, is encoded and sent as signals over a communications channel to a destina-tion, such as a network printer, storage device, server, or workstation. When data arrives at its destination, it is decoded. Transmission signals can be disrupted by interference called *noise*, which has the potential to corrupt data, making it erroneous or unintelligible (Figure 5-8).

**FIGURE 5-8**

A communications system basi-cally sends information from a source to a destination. Although the path between the source and destination might appear to be straight in the dia-gram, the data can pass through several devices, which convert it to electrical, sound, light, or radio signals; beam it up to satellites; route it along the least congested links; or clean up parts of the signal that have been distorted by noise.

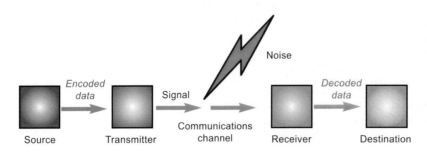

**What kind of signals travel over computer networks?** When data is transmitted over a network link it usually takes the form of an electromagnetic signal. You can think of these signals as waves that ripple through cables or through the air. Digital signals are transmitted as bits using a limited set of frequencies. Analog signals can assume any value within a specified range of frequencies. Figure 5-9 helps you visualize the difference between digital and analog waves.

**How can a network detect if a signal has been corrupted?** Digital networks—those that transmit digital signals—can be easily monitored to determine if interference has corrupted any signals. At its most primitive level, digital equipment is sensitive to only two frequencies—one that represents 1s and one that represents 0s. Suppose that a 0 is sent as -5 volts and a 1 is sent as +5 volts. What if, during transmission, some interference changes the voltage of a "perfect" 1 to +3 volts? When the signal is received, the receiving device realizes that +3 volts is not one of the two valid voltages. It guesses that a 1 bit (+5 volts) was actually transmitted, and cleans the signal by reestablishing its voltage to +5. Correcting errors is one of the responsibilities of protocols.

**What's a packet?** When you send a file or an e-mail message, you might suppose that it is transmitted as an entire unit to its destination. This is not the case. Your file is actually chopped up into small pieces called packets. A **packet** is a parcel of data that is sent across a computer network. Each packet contains the address of its sender, the destination address, a sequence number, and some data. When packets reach their destination, they are reassembled into the original message according to the sequence numbers (Figure 5-10).

**Why not just send an entire message?** Some communications networks, such as the telephone system, use a technology called **circuit switching**, which essentially establishes a dedicated, private link between one telephone and another for the duration of a call. This type of switching provides callers with a direct pipeline over which streams of voice data can flow. Unfortunately, circuit switching is rather inefficient. For example, when someone is on hold, no communication is taking place—yet the circuit is reserved and cannot be used for other communications.

A more efficient alternative to circuit switching is **packet switching** technology, which divides a message into several packets that can be routed independently to their destination. Messages divided into equal-size packets are easier to handle than an assortment of small, medium, large, and huge files.

Packets from many different messages can share a single communications channel, or circuit. Packets are shipped over the circuit on a first-come, first-served basis. If some packets from a message are not available, the system does not need to wait for them. Instead, the system moves on to send packets from other messages. The end result is a steady stream of data (Figure 5-11).

FIGURE 5-11

Packet switching networks (top) provide a more efficient communications system than circuit switching networks (bottom).

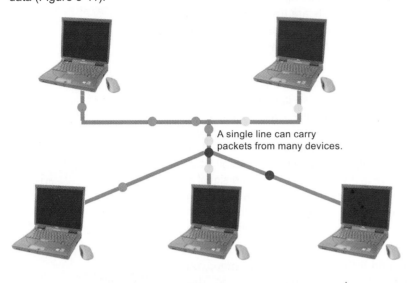

A single line can carry packets from many devices.

Each circuit dedicates an entire channel to one sender and one receiver.

**How are packets routed to their destinations?** Every packet that travels over a network includes the address of its destination device, similar to the way a letter contains the address of a house or mailbox. Communications protocols specify the proper format for addresses within a particular type of network. When a packet reaches a network node, a routing device examines the address and sends the packet along to its destination.

**How do devices get an address?** Network addresses are a potential source of confusion. Network devices can have a variety of addresses used for different purposes. Two commonly used addresses are MAC addresses and IP addresses.

**What is a MAC address?** In the context of networking, MAC stands for Media Access Control. A **MAC address** is a unique number assigned to a network interface card when it is manufactured. MAC addresses are used for some low-level network functions and can also be employed to establish network security.

**What is an IP address?** An **IP address** is a series of numbers used to identify a network device. IP addresses were originally used on the Internet, but now are the standard used for assigning addresses to devices in virtually every type of computer network. IP addresses are assigned to network computers, servers, peripherals, and devices. When written, an IP address such as 204.127.129.1 is separated into four sections by periods for the convenience of human readers. Each section is called an **octet** because in binary it is represented by eight bits.

**Where do IP addresses come from?** IP addresses can be assigned by ISPs or system managers. Assigned IP addresses are semi-permanent and stay the same every time you boot your computer. If you use an assigned IP address, you have to enter it when you configure your network access.

IP addresses can also be obtained through **DHCP** (Dynamic Host Configuration Protocol), a protocol designed to automatically distribute IP addresses. Most computers are preconfigured to get an IP address by sending a query to the network device acting as the DHCP server. The IP address assigned by DHCP is good for that session. The next time you boot up, you might be assigned a different address. The fact that your IP address changes each time you boot up isn't a problem. Your network keeps track of your IP address behind the scenes and unlike an e-mail address your IP address is not publicized as a permanent address that people use to send files and messages to you.

**What happens when data reaches its destination?** Even on a small home network, packets might not travel from the source directly to their destination. Like travelers routed from one airline hub to another, network traffic often travels through intermediary routing devices. Some networks include protocols to keep track of each node that a packet traverses on its journey.

When data reaches its destination, it is checked for errors one last time and then the packets are reassembled into their original configuration. Tracking data is appended or stripped off, depending on the application, and then the newly delivered file is ready to be stored or viewed on the destination device.

---

# QuickCheck

1. To connect to a LAN, a computer requires network circuitry, sometimes referred to as a network [_____] card.

2. A peer-to-peer network is simply a small version of a client/server network. True or false? [_____]

3. Communications [_____], such as TCP/IP, set standards for encoding and decoding data, guiding data to its destination, and mitigating the effects of noise.

4. A(n) [_____] switching network divides messages into small parcels and handles them on a first-come, first-served basis, whereas a(n) [_____] switching network establishes a dedicated connection between two devices.

5. A(n) [_____] address can be assigned to a network workstation by a DHCP server.

▶ CHECK ANSWERS

# Wired Networks

**WIRED NETWORKS** offer clear advantages over their wireless counterparts for applications that require security and fast access. If you're planning to host a LAN party, for example; if you frequently transfer large video files from one computer to another; if you're nervous about the security of wireless networks, or if you're sending big PostScript print jobs to a network printer, then a wired network should be your first choice. In Section B the focus is on wired technologies used for local area networks.

## WIRED NETWORK BASICS

**What is a wired network?** A **wired network** is one that uses cables to connect network devices. Familiar technologies such as telephone and cable television make extensive use of wired networks. Much of the Internet infrastructure is also wired. Before wireless technologies became available, local area networks were exclusively wired. Today, wired networks are used less frequently for home, school, and business networks. They remain the network technology of choice, however, for LANs that require fast and secure connectivity.

**What are the advantages of wired networks?** Wired networks are fast, secure, and simple to configure. A wired network transfers data over cables, which typically have high bandwidth and are shielded against interference. Wired connections are characteristically fast and reliable. The speed of a wired network is useful when accessing large files from a local server; file transfers on wired networks are significantly faster than on wireless networks.

Wired networks also offer a faster infrastructure for playing multiplayer computer games within the LAN (Figure 5-12). For Internet based multiplayer games however, the speed of the Internet connection rather than the LAN is usually the limiting factor.

Wired networks are more secure than their wireless counterparts because a computer can only join a network if it is physically connected by a cable. When you set up a wired network you don't have to worry about LANjackers accessing your network from the sidewalk outside your house, or your neighbor stumbling across your files because your wireless signal reaches past your property line.

Today's wired LANs are easy to set up and configure. Most computers are preconfigured with the hardware and software needed to join a wired network. Whether you want to link up a desktop or notebook, PC or Mac, you can pretty much just plug in to connect.

**What are the disadvantages of wired networks?** The cables that offer speed and security for a wired network are also its main weakness. Devices tethered to cables have limited mobility. Desktop computers tend to be better candidates for wired networks, whereas notebook computers can retain their mobility when they are not tethered to a cable.

**FIGURE 5-12**

Discerning multiplayer game players prefer a fast wired connection when playing head to head on a LAN.

Cables are unsightly, tend to get tangled, and collect dust. Running cables through ceilings, walls, and floors can be tricky or banned by your landlord. Some building codes prohibit network cables from running through air conditioning and heating ducts. When drilling holes for network cables, installers should take care to avoid electrical wires and other hazards.

**Are there various types of wired networks?** In the past, many wired network technologies vied for popularity. Today, the most popular LAN technology is Ethernet. Alternatives such as HomePNA and HomePlug technologies are available but much less frequently used.

## HOMEPNA AND POWERLINE NETWORKS

**What's HomePNA?** **HomePNA** (sometimes called HPNA) is a network technology that utilizes existing telephone wiring to connect network devices. Data transport follows the Ethernet model, but HPNA NICs and other network devices are specially designed to connect to standard telephone wall jacks and exchange data over premises telephone wiring (Figure 5-13).

**TERMINOLOGY NOTE**

In telecommunications and networking, premises wiring refers to cables and wires run within the structure of an office building, home, or other structure.

**FIGURE 5-13**

To form an HPNA network, workstations are equipped with HPNA NICs, which are connected to telephone wall jacks.

5

Existing home telephone wiring

Telephone jack — Workstation with HomePNA NIC

Telephone jack — Workstation with HomePNA NIC

Telephone jack — Workstation with HomePNA NIC

**Who should use HomePNA network technology?** If the structure of your building makes wiring difficult but you want the security of wired technology, then HomePNA might offer a solution. HomePNA works even when phone lines are not active, so as long as you have phone wires running throughout your building and telephone jacks are located where you want to put computers, you have a ready-made infrastructure for a HomePNA LAN. HomePNA also works in commercial settings. Several major hotels have found HomePNA to be a good solution to retrofit network access into guest rooms.

**What is the speed and range of HomePNA?** HomePNA operates at 10 Mbps, which is slower than Ethernet, but similar to wireless technology. With a HomePNA network, data transport speeds are sufficient for average local file and printer sharing activities, as well as Web browsing. For exchanging lots of large files locally, Fast Ethernet or Gigabit Ethernet would be preferable technologies. HomePNA works with up to 32 devices and supports up to 1000 feet (304 meters) of wiring between devices.

**INFOWEBLINKS**

For the latest information on HomePNA and HomePlug networks, connect to the **Home Network InfoWeb**.

 CLICK TO CONNECT
www.course.com/np/concepts10/ch05

**Can I talk on the phone while using the network?** When your computer is connected to a HomePNA network, you can typically use the phone to make a call and send information over the network at the same time because the network frequency is different from the voice frequency. You cannot, however, make a voice call while a dial-up Internet connection is active.

**What's a powerline network?** A **powerline network** uses premises electrical wiring to form the infrastructure for a LAN. Data, transmitted as low-frequency radio waves, travels along the electrical wiring from one network device to another at speeds of about 10 Mbps. Powerline network equipment is sold under HomePLC, HPLC, or HomePlug network labels.

**Why use powerline network technology?** If you want a wired network, cannot run wires, and don't have telephone jacks where you want to locate computers, a powerline network might suit your needs. Network adapters can be attached to computers with Ethernet ports, then plugged into any electrical wall outlet (Figure 5-14).

**What are the limitations of powerline networks?** The ease with which you can link computers on a powerline network depends on the path of the wiring through your building's circuit box. The length of wiring between devices is limited to about 1000 feet (304 meters). Networks in apartment buildings are only secure if each apartment has its own circuit breaker box. Otherwise signals from your network could be picked up by neighbors using powerline network equipment.

Another potential problem with powerline networks is that standard surge strips and UPSs suppress powerline network data signals as well as spikes and surges. Plugging your computer directly into a wall outlet risks damage by power fluctuations. To protect equipment on powerline networks, look for special power-line network rated surge strips from manufacturers such as Belkin or SurgeMaster.

## ETHERNET

**How does Ethernet work?** **Ethernet**, defined by IEEE 802.3, simultaneously broadcasts data packets to all network devices. A packet is accepted only by the device to which it is addressed (Figure 5-15).

**FIGURE 5-14**

A powerline NIC is cabled to a computer's Ethernet port and plugs into a wall outlet.

**FIGURE 5-15**

On an Ethernet, a packet is broadcast to every device, but is accepted only by the device to which it is addressed.

This workstation sends a packet addressed to workstation #23.

The packet is broadcast to every device.

Only workstation #23 accepts the packet.

An integral part of Ethernet technology relies on **CSMA/CD** protocol (Carrier Sense Multiple Access with Collision Detection). CSMA/CD takes care of situations in which two network devices attempt to transmit packets at the same time. A collision occurs and the signals do not reach their destination. CSMA/CD protocol detects the collision, deletes the colliding signals, resets the network, and prepares to retransmit the data. The two devices wait for random time periods before retransmitting to prevent a collision from reoccurring (Figure 5-16).

**FIGURE 5-16**

On an Ethernet, data travels on a first-come, first-served basis. If two workstations attempt to send data at the same time, a collision occurs. That data must be resent.

Data is sent from this workstation.

At the same time, data is sent from this workstation.

A collision occurs!

● CLICK TO START

**5**

**How fast is an Ethernet network?** The original Ethernet standard carried data over a coaxial cable bus topology at 10 Mbps. Today, Ethernet encompasses a family of LAN technologies that offer various data transmission rates over cables arranged in a bus or star topology. Of the Ethernet variations shown in Figure 5-17, **Fast Ethernet**, which operates at 100 Mbps, is currently the most popular for small to medium LANs, like those you might find in homes and small businesses. **Gigabit Ethernet**, with speeds of 1000 Mbps, is gaining popularity as equipment prices decrease.

| Ethernet Standard | IEEE Designation | Speed |
|---|---|---|
| 10BaseT Ethernet | IEEE 802.3 | 10 Mbps |
| Fast Ethernet | IEEE 802.3u | 100 Mbps |
| Gigabit Ethernet | IEEE 802.3z | 1000 Mbps |
| 10 Gig Ethernet | IEEE 802.3ae | 10 Gbps |

**FIGURE 5-17**

Ethernet Standards

**Why is Ethernet so popular?** Despite challenges from other technologies, Ethernet has emerged as the leading LAN technology. It is currently used in a high percentage of LANs worldwide. Ethernet's success is attributable to several factors:

● Ethernet networks are easy to understand, implement, manage, and maintain.

● As a nonproprietary technology, Ethernet equipment is available from a variety of vendors, and market competition keeps prices low.

● Current Ethernet standards allow extensive flexibility in network topology to meet the needs of small and large installations.

● Ethernet is compatible with popular Wi-Fi wireless networks, so it is easy to mix wired and wireless devices on a single network.

**INFOWEBLINKS**

Ethernet is definitely cool. See what the "Ether" is all about at the **Ethernet InfoWeb**.

Ⓦ CLICK TO CONNECT
www.course.com/np/concepts10/ch05

## ETHERNET EQUIPMENT

**What equipment do I need for an Ethernet network?** Ethernet is the quintessential wired network technology. If you have a basic understanding of how it is installed, you can apply that knowledge to putting together just about any network.

Ethernet equipment is widely available and fairly inexpensive. For a typical home network that accesses the Internet, you need the following equipment:

- Two or more Ethernet-ready computers
- An Ethernet router
- Surge strip or UPS
- Cables for each computer
- Internet access device, such as cable modem or DSL modem and corresponding cables

**How can I tell if a computer is Ethernet ready?** Many computers have a built-in Ethernet port located on the system case. The port looks very similar to an oversized telephone jack. If you have such a port, the next step is to determine its speed, as explained in Figure 5-18.

**INFOWEBLINKS**

Your basic shopping list for a simple Ethernet LAN is at the **Building a LAN InfoWeb**.

 CLICK TO CONNECT

www.course.com/np/concepts10/ch05

**FIGURE 5-18**

Checking a workstation for an Ethernet port

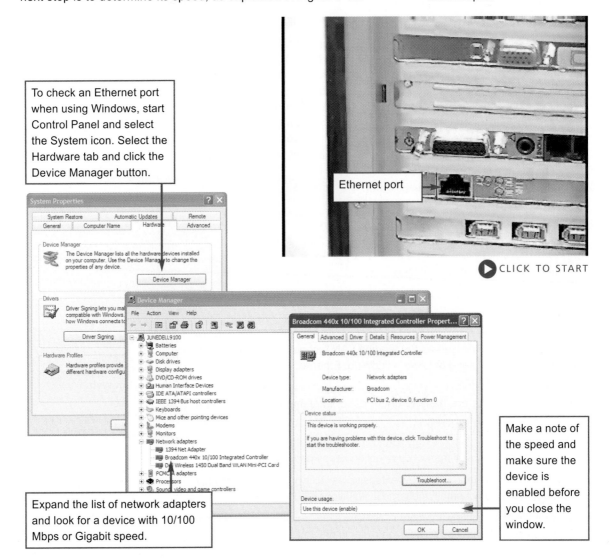

To check an Ethernet port when using Windows, start Control Panel and select the System icon. Select the Hardware tab and click the Device Manager button.

Ethernet port

CLICK TO START

Expand the list of network adapters and look for a device with 10/100 Mbps or Gigabit speed.

Make a note of the speed and make sure the device is enabled before you close the window.

**What if a computer doesn't have an Ethernet port?** If your computer has no Ethernet port, you can purchase and install an **Ethernet adapter** (also called an Ethernet card or NIC). Adapters like the one in Figure 5-19 simply plug into a USB port on the outside of your computer's system unit. Follow the manufacturer's installation instructions to install any necessary device drivers. Connecting an Ethernet adapter through the USB port is a good solution for notebook or desktop computers. If you're working with a desktop computer, you can install an Ethernet card in a PCI slot inside the computer case. For notebook computers, you can purchase and install an Ethernet adapter that slides into a PC card slot.

**FIGURE 5-19**

Ethernet adapters

Ethernet adapter for USB port     Ethernet adapter for PCMCIA slot     Ethernet adapter for PCI slot

**5**

**Should I buy an Ethernet hub, switch, or router?** A **network hub** is a device that links two or more nodes of a wired network. On a typical network, the hub accepts data from one of the computers and then broadcasts it to all of the other network nodes. Some devices receive data that is not meant for them, but their NICs filter out any data that is not intended for that destination.

A **network switch** is a more sophisticated connection device that sends data only to the devices specified as the destination. Using a switch instead of a hub can increase a network's performance and security because data isn't flowing indiscriminately to every device on the network.

A **network router** is a network device that can ship data from one network to another. Most routers are also switches that contain ports for connecting workstations. You might see a router/switch device advertised as "router with 4-port switch." A router/switch is particularly useful for connecting a home network to the Internet, so if you are planning to connect your network to the Internet, you should consider using one as the central point of your LAN (Figure 5-20).

**FIGURE 5-20**

An Ethernet router features a collection of ports for connecting servers, workstations, and peripheral devices.

**How many ports do I need?** Your hub, switch or router needs one port for each device you intend to wire to the network. A typical router, for example, has four or five ports for network devices. It also has a WAN port that is only used to connect the router to the Internet. If you want to attach more devices to a network, you can purchase an inexpensive hub that provides additional ports and connects to the router.

**What do I need to know about speed?** Ethernet routers are available at 10/100 Mbps or Gigabit speeds. If you have a Gigabit router and all the network computers have Gigabit Ethernet adapters, data will flow over all network connections at Gigabit speeds. If some computers have Gigabit adapters, whereas others have 10/100 Mbps adapters, a Gigabit router will ship data at a speed that corresponds to each adapter.

The only time you waste bandwidth is when you have a 10/100 Mbps router, but several of the network computers have Gigabit Ethernet adapters. In this case, the router cannot send data at Gigabit speeds, so the Gigabit adapters will receive data at the 100 Mbps rate.

Serious computer gamers who compete against each other over a LAN prefer Gigabit Ethernet equipment for adapters and routers. Some video-conferencing and streaming video applications might also benefit from high bandwidth equipment.

**What kind of cable do I need?** The devices in an Ethernet are connected with network cables terminated at each end with a plastic **RJ45 connector** (Figure 5-21). Network cables contain four pairs of copper wires. Each pair of wires is independently insulated and then twisted together, which is why network cable is sometimes referred to as twisted-pair cable. Shielded twisted-pair cable (STP) contains shielding, which reduces signal noise that might interfere with data transmitted over unshielded cable (UTP). The shielded cable is not significantly more expensive.

Network cables can be purchased in a variety of lengths. You'll need one for each workstation. When you calculate the length of each cable, make sure you consider the path that the cable will follow as it snakes along walls from the router to the workstation.

## ETHERNET SETUP

**What's the general procedure for setting up Ethernet?** Nowadays, it is easy to set up a wired network like the one in Figure 5-22.

To set up an Ethernet LAN:

- Run cables from the router to each workstation or server
- Run a cable between the router and the device used for your Internet connection
- Configure each workstation
- Configure the router

**How do I run the wiring?** Before you begin running wires, make sure the router, computers, and other devices are powered off. Connect cables between the router and the Ethernet ports on each workstation or server. Run a cable between your Internet device and the router's WAN port. Tuck the cables out of the way. You might want to use cable tacks to carefully secure each cable to the baseboards along your walls. Use the same precautions with your network cables as you would with power cords; do not run them across walkways or under carpets.

**FIGURE 5-21**

Network cables are terminated with plastic RJ45 connectors that are similar to, but larger than the connectors used for telephones.

**FIGURE 5-22**

A typical wired network uses a router as a central device for connecting workstations, a file server, and an Internet access device.

When the cables are in place, plug in the router, preferably through a surge strip or UPS, and then turn it on. One by one, power up each network device. Figure 5-23 walks you through the basic setup.

FIGURE 5-23

Installing a LAN

**1.** Place the router in a central location and plug it into a surge-protected outlet.

**2.** Run cables from the router to the Ethernet adapter in each workstation.

**3.** Run a cable from your Internet device and your router's WAN port.

**4.** Turn on network devices one at a time. Your operating system should automatically detect the NICs and establish a connection to the network.

► CLICK TO START

**5.** Use your computer's operating system network utilities to verify each connection. When using Windows, open the Start menu to access Control Panel. From there, access Network Connections.

**How do I configure each workstation?** Turn on one of the workstations and wait for it to boot. Your computer's operating system should automatically sense the network connection. If you are using Windows you can check your connection in the Network Connections window, as shown in Figure 5-24.

**FIGURE 5-24**

Windows displays details for a wired network connection in the Network Connections window.

**How do I configure the router?** The router's configuration data is stored in its EEPROM chip. To access the configuration data, open your browser and enter the router's address in the Address line. Most routers use http://192.168.1.1 or http://192.168.1.100 as their configuration address. You can check your router's documentation to verify. It is essential that you change the router's password to prevent unauthorized changes to your network. If you are connecting to the Internet, additional configuration might be necessary, as explained in the Internet chapter.

**How do I know when the network is ready?** Your operating system usually displays a message or icon to let you know when you are connected to a network. For example, Windows displays the Local Area Connection icon on the taskbar to indicate the status of a wired network. If that icon indicates the network is connected, it is ready for use.

# QuickCheck

**SECTION B**

1. A(n) _____ LAN simultaneously broadcasts data packets over all network links and uses CSMA/CD protocol to handle collisions.

2. A HomePNA network uses existing telephone wiring. True or false? _____

3. Fast Ethernet operates at _____ Mbps.

4. A network _____ is a device that links two or more nodes of a wired network and broadcasts it to all the network nodes.

5. A(n) _____ can connect the nodes of a LAN and also handle data transfer between a LAN and the Internet.

▶ CHECK ANSWERS

## SECTION C

# Wireless Networks

**WHO WANTS LOTS OF** unsightly wires and cables snaking through their living room or office space? Today's trend is to wireless LAN technology. Wireless LANS, dubbed WLANS, are easy to install, but it is important to secure them from intrusions. Section C supplies information on wireless LAN equipment and installation. You'll learn more about wireless security in Section E.

### WIRELESS BASICS

**What is a wireless network?** A **wireless network** transports data from one device to another without the use of cables or wires. Networks of all sizes, from PANs to LANs and WANs, can use wireless technologies, such as radio signals, microwaves, and infrared light.

**How do radio signals transport data?** Wireless devices can transport data as radio, microwave, or infrared signals. Most wireless networks transport data as **RF signals** (radio frequency signals). RF signals—commonly called radio waves—are sent and received by a **transceiver** (a combination of a transmitter and a receiver) that is equipped with an antenna. Workstations, peripheral devices, and network devices can be equipped with transceivers to send and receive data on wireless networks (Figure 5-25).

**How do microwaves transport data? Microwaves** (the waves themselves, not your oven!) provide another option for transporting data over wireless networks. Like radio waves, microwaves are electromagnetic signals, but they behave differently. Microwaves can be aimed in a single direction and have more carrying capacity than radio waves. However, microwaves cannot penetrate metal objects and work best for line-of-sight transmission when a clear path exists between the transmitter and receiver. Microwave installations typically provide data transport for large corporate networks.

**How does infrared transport data?** Today most people are familiar with remote controls that use **infrared light** beams to change television channels. Infrared can also carry data signals, but only for short distances and with a clear line of sight. Its most practical use seems to be for transmitting data between devices connected to a PAN.

**What are the advantages of wireless networks?** The main advantage of wireless networks is mobility. Wireless devices are not tethered to network cables, so battery operated workstations can be easily moved from room to room, or even outdoors. With wireless networks, there are no unsightly cables, and power spikes are much less likely to run through cables to damage workstations.

**Do wireless networks have disadvantages?** In the past, wireless network equipment was quite a bit more expensive than equivalent wired equipment. With the current popularity of wireless technologies, however, prices have equalized. When compared to wired networks, the main disadvantages of wireless networks are speed, range, licensing, and security.

**5**

**FIGURE 5-25**

Wireless equipment often sports an antenna for transmitting and receiving data signals.

**Why is wireless slower than wired?** Wireless signals are susceptible to interference from devices such as microwave ovens, cordless telephones, and baby monitors. When interference affects a wireless signal, data must be re-transmitted.

Despite interference, wireless networks are fast enough for most applications. Even the slowest wireless LAN technologies are faster than most Internet services, so online access from a wireless LAN is no slower than from a wired LAN. Wireless LANs are slower for intra-LAN operations, such as exchanging files and sharing printers. When lots of computer game players compete against each other over a LAN, a fast, wired network is desirable.

**What limits the range of a wireless network?** The range of a wireless signal can be limited by the type of signal, the transmitter strength, and the physical environment. Just as radio stations fade as you move away from their broadcasting towers, data signals fade as the distance between network devices increases. Signal range can also be limited by thick walls, floors, or ceilings (Figure 5-26).

**What's wrong with wireless security?** Wireless signals float through the air and penetrate walls. The signals that carry your wireless data can be accessed from outside your premises. Someone outside of your house, for example, could surreptitiously join your network, access files, and piggyback on your Internet connection. To make wireless network data useless to intruders, it should be encrypted. Later in the chapter you'll learn how to use encryption to secure a wireless LAN.

**How does licensing affect wireless networks?** Signals that are sent through the air are regulated by government agencies such as the Federal Communications Commission (FCC). To broadcast at most frequencies, such as those used by radio or television, a license is required. Only certain frequencies are unlicensed and available for public use. Unlicensed frequencies include 2.4 GHz and 5.8 GHz used by cordless telephones and baby monitors, and the 460 MHz frequency used for two-way citizens band radios. Wireless networks use unlicensed frequencies so that they can be set up without applying to the FCC for permission. The few unlicensed frequencies are crowded, however, and neighboring home networks that are forced to use the same frequencies pose security risks.

**What are the most popular technologies for wireless networks?** By far the most popular wireless LAN technology is Wi-Fi. A second wireless technology called Bluetooth is useful for some applications. Other wireless technologies, such as WiMAX and Zigbee are MAN or WAN technologies, typically used for fixed Internet access. Let's take a brief look at Bluetooth technology and then examine Wi-Fi networks in more detail.

**FIGURE 5-26**

On a wireless network, signal strength varies depending on distance from a transmitter and obstacles that might interfere with the signal.

## BLUETOOTH

**What is Bluetooth?** **Bluetooth** is a short-range wireless network technology that's designed to make its own connections between electronic devices, without wires, cables or any direct action from a user. Bluetooth networks form automatically when two or more Bluetooth devices come within range of each other. A Bluetooth network is sometimes called a **piconet**.

To form a network, a Bluetooth device can search for other Bluetooth devices within range. When another Bluetooth device is detected, it typically broadcasts what it is, for example a printer, a PC, or a cell phone. Before data is exchanged, the owners of the two Bluetooth devices have to exchange passkeys, or PINs (Figure 5-27). Once passkeys have been exchanged, the two Bluetooth devices form a trusted pair. Future communication between these two devices does not require the passkey to be re-entered.

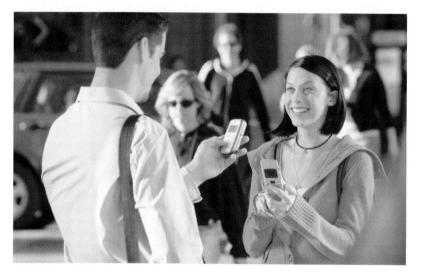

**FIGURE 5-27**

Owners of Bluetooth devices can beam data to other Bluetooth device owners.

**5**

**Where is Bluetooth used?** Bluetooth operates at the unlicensed 2.4 GHz frequency, so anyone can set up a Bluetooth network. Bluetooth is not typically used to connect a collection of workstations. Instead, Bluetooth connectivity replaces the short cables that would otherwise tether a mouse, keyboard, or printer to a computer.

Bluetooth can also be used to link devices in a PAN, connect home entertainment system components, provide hands-free cell phone operation in an automobile, link a cell phone to a wireless headset (Figure 5-28), and synchronize PDAs with desktop base stations.

Bluetooth is built into some peripheral devices. If you want these devices to communicate with your computer you can use a variety of add-on cards.

**What is the speed and range of Bluetooth?** Bluetooth offers peak transmission rates of only 1 Mbps (version 1.2) or 3 Mbps (version 2.0 +EDR) over a range of 3–300 feet (about 1–91 meters).

**FIGURE 5-28**

Bluetooth technology is used for wireless keyboards and mice, but it is also the technology used for wireless headsets and devices like Motorola's Bluetooth headset that clips to a motorcycle helmet so you don't miss important cell calls.

## WI-FI

**What is Wi-Fi?** **Wi-Fi** refers to a set of wireless networking technologies defined by IEEE 802.11 standards that are compatible with Ethernet. A Wi-Fi network transmits data as radio waves over 2.4 GHz or 5.8 GHz frequencies. When people refer to wireless networks they are usually talking about Wi-Fi.

Wi-Fi encompasses several standards, designated by letters b, a, g, and n. Some of these standards are cross compatible, which means that you can use them on the same wireless network. Figure 5-29 summarizes the specifications for each Wi-Fi standard.

**FIGURE 5-29**

Wi-Fi Standards

| IEEE Designation | Frequency | Speed | Range | Pros/Cons |
|---|---|---|---|---|
| IEEE 802.11b | 2.4 GHz | 11 Mbps | 100–300 feet | Original standard |
| IEEE 802.11a | 5 GHz | 54 Mbps | 25–75 feet | Not compatible with 802.11b, g, or n |
| IEEE 802.11g | 2.4 GHz | 54 Mbps | 100–150 feet | Faster than, but compatible with, 802.11b |
| IEEE 802.11n | 2.4/5 GHz | 200 Mbps | 100–150 feet | Faster but compatible with b and g |

**How do the speed and range of Wi-Fi compare to other network technologies?** On a wired network, the rated speed and range are usually quite close to actual performance. Wireless network speed and range, however, are often theoretical maximums, because signals can easily deteriorate. Although Wi-Fi 802.11n is capable of 200 Mbps speeds, in actual performance it is unlikely to match Fast Ethernet and is far slower than Gigabit Ethernet.

In a typical office environment, Wi-Fi's range varies from 25 to 150 feet (8–45 meters). Thick cement walls, steel beams, and other environmental obstacles can drastically reduce this range to the point that signals cannot be reliably transmitted. Wi-Fi signals can also be disrupted by interference from electronic devices operating at the same frequency, such as 2.4 GHz cordless telephones.

Wi-Fi speed and range can be improved with various technologies. For example, **MIMO** (multiple-input multiple-output) technology uses two or more antennae to essentially send multiple sets of signals between network devices (Figure 5-30).

**FIGURE 5-30**

MIMO-equipped devices usually have more than one antenna.

## WI-FI EQUIPMENT

**What equipment is required for a Wi-Fi network?** Wi-Fi equipment is widely available and fairly inexpensive. For a typical home network, you need the equipment listed in Figure 5-31.

**FIGURE 5-31**

Wireless Networking Equipment

Wireless-ready devices, such as computers and printers

Short piece of network cable to run between the router and one computer

Surge strip or UPS

Wireless router

**How can I tell if a device is wireless-ready?** Although cell phones and PDAs sometimes sport a small antenna that emphasizes their wireless communications capabilities, the antenna and transceiver for most notebook computers are hidden inside the case. You usually have to check your computer's documentation or on-screen utilities to discover if it has wireless capabilities (Figure 5-32).

**FIGURE 5-32**

Check the hardware listings to see if your computer has wireless capability. Use the System or Device Manager icon in the Windows Control Panel to look for a wireless or WLAN adapter.

5

**Can I add Wi-Fi?** If your computer is not pre-equipped with wireless circuitry, you can purchase and install a Wi-Fi card. A **Wi-Fi card** (also called a Wi-Fi adapter) is a wireless NIC that includes a transmitter, receiver, and antenna to transmit signals. Wi-Fi cards for notebook or tablet computers can plug into a PC slot or USB port. Wi-Fi capability can be added to a desktop computer as a Wi-Fi card that fits into a system unit slot with the antenna protruding out of the back or as a small box that connects to a USB port. Yet another option is to use a wireless adapter to convert a standard Ethernet port into a wireless port. Figure 5-33 illustrates various Wi-Fi cards.

**INFOWEBLINKS**

For the latest information on Wi-Fi equipment and pricing, check out the **Wireless LAN InfoWeb**.

**W** CLICK TO CONNECT
www.course.com/np/concepts10/ch05

**FIGURE 5-33**

Wi-Fi Cards

**Do I need a wireless router?** You can set up a wireless network in two ways (Figure 5-34). First, you can set up a **wireless ad-hoc network** in which devices broadcast directly to each other. The advantage of this configuration is cost. If your devices include factory-installed wireless networking circuitry, you don't need additional equipment. The disadvantage of an ad-hoc network is Internet access. Although you can access the Internet from an ad-hoc network, you'll have to designate one of the network computers as the gateway device. It will require a cable connection to your Internet modem, and it will have to be left on during the time anyone on your network might want to access the Internet.

A second option called a **wireless infrastructure network** uses a centralized broadcasting device, such as a wireless access point or router. A **wireless access point** is a device that transmits and receives wireless signals. A **wireless router** is a wireless access point that also includes routing circuitry that can connect a Wi-Fi network to the Internet. Wireless routers offer the most flexibility for Internet access and the best security options, so most experts recommend using one as the central point in your wireless network. The remaining information in this section pertains to wireless infrastructure networks that use wireless routers.

## WI-FI SETUP

**What's the general procedure for setting up a Wi-Fi network?** Setting up a Wi-Fi network involves a few simple steps.

- Set up the router
- Connect to the router with a computer
- Configure the router
- Access the router setup utility
- Create a new router password
- Enter an SSID for the network
- Activate WEP, WPA, or WPA2 and create an encryption key
- Set up the wireless workstations
- Connect an Internet access device

Let's see how you can apply these steps to set up a basic wireless network similar to the one in Figure 5-35.

........ Wireless connections

———— Wired connections

To an ISP and Internet

Cable, DSL, or satellite modem for Internet access

Router

File server

Printer          Workstation          Workstation          Workstation

**FIGURE 5-34**

Wireless ad-hoc networks transmit from one workstation to another, whereas an infrastructure network uses a centralized access point or router to relay signals to workstations.

Wireless ad-hoc network

Wireless infrastructure network

**FIGURE 5-35**

A wireless network typically includes several workstations connected wirelessly to a router; an Internet device connected by a cable to the router's WAN port; and possibly a file server linked with a wired or wireless connection.

**How do I set up a wireless router?** Place the wireless router in a central location relative to the network devices. Thick concrete walls and floors can significantly lower signal strength, so if you encounter such obstacles, you might have to consider a signal booster.

Connect the wireless router to a power outlet through a surge strip or UPS. A UPS will keep your network operational during a power outage. Your ability to access the Internet during a power outage depends on the power situation at your ISP. However, a network that consists of battery operated notebook computers and a wireless router connected to a UPS should be able to run for several hours during a blackout.

If you want your wireless network to access the Internet, connect the router to an Internet access device, such as a cable or DSL modem. Internet modems are typically connected to the router's WAN port using an Ethernet cable.

**How do I access the router's configuration utility?** Before using your wireless network, you should adjust router configuration settings for the default password, SSID, and encryption, as described later in this section. The configuration settings are stored in the router's EEPROM memory. You'll need to log into the configuration software to adjust settings. A router has no screen or keyboard of its own, so to access the router's configuration software, you have to connect a computer to the router. The easiest way to make this connection is with a short Ethernet cable. Although it might seem nonintuitive to use a wire to create a wireless network, the use of a cabled connection is detected automatically by Windows and that provides a direct link to the router without any preliminary setup.

Documentation for the router supplies a LAN address for the router and might also supply a default password. A LAN address is typically something like 192.168.1.1 or 192.168.1.100. Open your browser and type http:// and the router's LAN address in the Address line. Enter the default password, if one is necessary (Figure 5-36).

**FIGURE 5-36**

To access the router configuration utilities, use your browser.

**How do I change the default password?** Your wireless router configuration utility might look like the one in Figure 5-37. Your first step after logging on is to change the default password so that hackers can't gain access to your network and reconfigure it for their own malevolent schemes. Locate the setting for the administrator password and create a new one. Follow the recommendations in earlier chapters for creating a strong password. This password is only used to configure the router. It does not need to be conveyed to network users who simply want to set up their computers to send and receive data over the network.

**FIGURE 5-37**

Change the default password for your router when you install a wireless network.

 CLICK TO START

**What is an SSID?** An **SSID** (service set identifier) is the name of a wireless network. In areas where there are overlapping wireless networks, such as in a city or on a college campus, SSIDs help you log into the right network, rather than a network run by a hacker who will try to suck important information off your computer as soon as you connect.

**How do I set the SSID?** Most routers ship with a pre-defined SSID set by the manufacturer. Predefined SSIDs are typically very simple and publicly known. Use the router configuration software to change the default SSID. When you create an SSID, think of it as a user ID, rather than a password. Appropriate SSIDs would be similar to Acme Company, Java Joe Coffee Shop, Planters Inn of Miami, or Alpha Kappa Delta Phi.

**Should I broadcast my SSID?** When SSID broadcasting is turned on, any wireless device passing by can see that a network exists. Legitimate users can easily find the network and connect to it. With SSID broadcasting turned off, the public can't see it. Unfortunately, hackers armed with the right tools can see the network even if the SSID is not broadcast. Turning off SSID is a very weak form of security. Experts disagree about broadcasting your network's SSID. If you believe the potential for drive-by hacking is high, then you might not want to broadcast the SSID. In any case, SSID should be left on until you configure the rest of the devices that you plan to use on your network.

**Do I need to take any special steps to secure my wireless network?** Wireless networks are much more susceptible to unauthorized access and use than wired networks. Some measure of security can be gained by enabling encryption as explained in Section E.

**When is the router configuration complete?** Basic router configuration requires you to change the router password, enter an SSID, and activate encryption. Your wireless networking utility offers additional configuration options, but they are not needed for typical home and school networks. With your router configuration complete, you can close the router utility and set up the rest of the network.

**How do I set up workstations and other network devices?** To add computers and other devices to your wireless network, start by turning on another computer with wireless capability. Its wireless device driver should automatically find the network SSID and ask you to enter the wireless network key or passphrase.

**Can I mix wireless and wired devices?** Most wireless routers include ports for 4 Ethernet cables and a WAN port for a cable to an Internet device, such as a cable or DSL modem (Figure 5-38).

You can also wire some of your network workstations to the router. As a sample scenario, you might use a cable to connect the router and an old desktop computer that you plan to use as a game server or as a server for lots of video footage. You could also use a wired connection for the computer that you use to edit the video footage.

**FIGURE 5-38**

Most wireless routers (note the antenna) also include ports for wired Ethernet connections.

5

---

# QuickCheck

1. Today's most popular wireless LAN technology is compatible with Ethernet and called [          ].

2. [          ] is a short-range wireless network technology used for PANs.

3. In a wireless [          ] network, devices broadcast directly to each other rather than through a central broadcasting device.

4. A wireless [          ] network uses a centralized broadcasting device, such as a wireless access point or router.

5. When setting up a wireless network it is important to change the username and password, create a unique [          ] and enable encryption. (Hint: Use the acronym.)

▶ CHECK ANSWERS

SECTION D

# Using LANs

**LANS HAVE BECOME** an integral part of computing environments at home, at school, and at work. Many LANs are installed solely for distributing access to an Internet connection. That facet of LANs will be discussed in the next chapter. What else can you do with a LAN? Section D helps you explore the advantages and disadvantages of LANs, as well as providing practical tips on how to share files and printers.

## LAN ADVANTAGES AND CHALLENGES

**Why are LANs advantageous?** Today, the pervasiveness of LANs and other types of networks has dramatically changed the face of computing by offering **shared resources**—hardware, software, and data made available for authorized network users to access. LANs offer the following advantages:

● **LANs enable people to work together.** Using groupware and other specialized network application software, several people can work together on a single document, communicate by e-mail and instant messaging, take part in multiplayer computer games, and participate in online conferences and Webcasts (Figure 5-39).

**FIGURE 5-39**

LANs can be used for intra-LAN collaboration, or they can be connected to other networks for broader participation.

● **Sharing networked software can reduce costs.** Although purchasing and installing a single software copy for an entire LAN might be technically possible, it is typically not allowed under the terms of a single-user license agreement. However, software site licenses for network use are usually less expensive than purchasing single-user versions of a product for each network user.

● **Sharing data on a LAN can increase productivity.** To transfer data between standalone computers, a file is usually copied to some type of removable storage media, and then carried or mailed to the other computer where it is copied onto the hard disk. LANs can provide authorized users with access to data stored on network servers or workstations.

- **Sharing networked hardware can reduce costs.** In an office environment, for example, a single expensive color printer can be purchased and attached to a LAN, instead of the costly alternative of purchasing color printers for each employee who wants to generate color printouts.

- **Sharing networked hardware can provide access to a wide range of services and specialized peripheral devices.** A LAN can allow multiple users to access Internet services, including voice over IP, through a single Internet connection. Networked peripheral devices, such as scanners, photo printers, plotters, and high-capacity storage devices can be accessed by any authorized LAN users. In a home environment, a LAN can offer access to surveillance and monitoring devices from inside or outside the home. LANs can control entertainment devices, and supply them with downloaded music and videos (Figure 5-40).

**FIGURE 5-40**

Music and video can stream over wireless LANs to projectors, speakers, and televisions when devices are equipped for 802.11 networking.

A wireless projector streams video signals from a remote PC.

A wireless receiver connects to an audio system, so you can listen to music from your PC in any room.

A wireless media player can stream video to your television, and play digital music on your stereo system.

**Do LANs have disadvantages?** One disadvantage of LANs is that when a network malfunctions, all the resources you're accustomed to accessing are unavailable until the network is repaired.

Another disadvantage of LANs is their vulnerability to unauthorized access. Whereas a standalone computer is vulnerable to on-premises theft or access, network computers are vulnerable to unauthorized access from many sources and locations.

Through unauthorized use of a LAN workstation, intruders can access data stored on the network server or other workstations. LANs connected to the Internet are vulnerable to intrusions from remote computers in distant states, provinces, or countries. Wireless LANs can be tapped from a specially equipped "snooping" computer in a car that's being driven by a hacker.

LANs are also more vulnerable than standalone computers to malicious code. Whereas the most prevalent threat to standalone computers is disk-borne viruses, networks are susceptible to an ever-increasing number of worms, Trojan horses, and blended threats. If a virus gets through LAN security, every computer on the network is at risk.

Most computer owners are enthusiastic about the benefits provided by LANs and believe that those benefits outweigh the risks of intrusions and viruses—especially if their computers can be protected by security tools, such as antivirus software and firewalls. You'll learn more about LAN security threats and countermeasures later in this chapter.

## SHARING FILES

**How do I access network resources?** If you use Windows, it automatically detects available LANs any time you turn on a workstation. Depending on your network setup, you might be asked to log in by entering a user ID and password. Once access is established, you can use any shared resources for which you have been given authorization.

You can access shared data on other workstations in a variety of ways. For example, you can use My Computer to access shared resources listed under the My Network Places folder in Windows Explorer. Resources on other computers are listed as folders or drives; their names might indicate the computer on which they reside. Figure 5-41 shows a listing of available network resources.

**FIGURE 5-41**

Windows Explorer lists drives and folders that network users designate as shared. This example shows Workgroup1 offers access to two computers and one printer.

On some networks, My Network Places cannot find all the shared drives and folders, so some might not be listed. If you want to access a shared resource that is not listed, you can use the Map Network Drive tool. **Drive mapping** assigns a drive letter to a storage device located on a network workstation (Figure 5-42).

**FIGURE 5-42**

In this drive mapping example, a server's drive C is mapped as drive F by a workstation.
After the mapping is complete, the server's hard disk appears in the workstation's directory as drive F and can be used just as though it were a drive connected directly to the workstation.

► CLICK TO START

**How do I specify which resources can be shared by other workstations?** If your computer is part of a network, you can typically specify which of your drives and folders can be accessed from other network workstations. For security reasons, however, it is not advisable to allow shared access to the root directory of drive C on your computer.

You can allow other network users to view and edit files in the folders you've designated as shared, or you can limit access only to viewing. Figure 5-43 explains how to use Windows to designate a folder as shared.

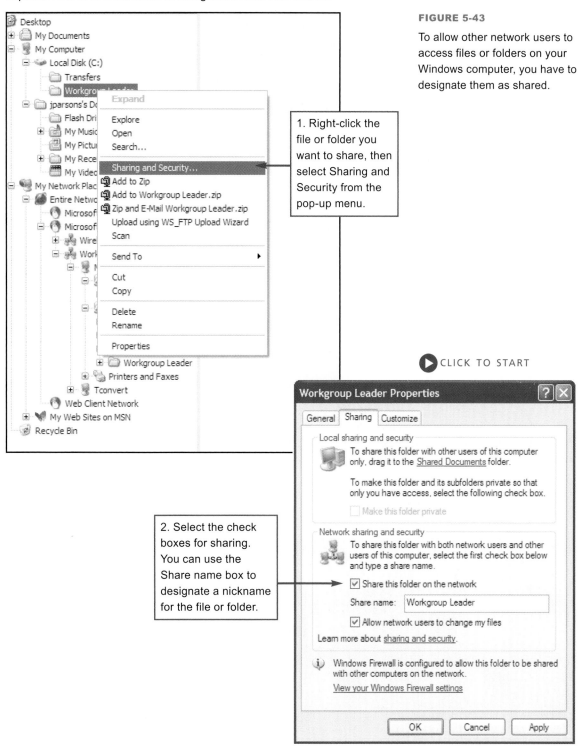

**FIGURE 5-43**

To allow other network users to access files or folders on your Windows computer, you have to designate them as shared.

1. Right-click the file or folder you want to share, then select Sharing and Security from the pop-up menu.

2. Select the check boxes for sharing. You can use the Share name box to designate a nickname for the file or folder.

CLICK TO START

**What is a file server?** A file server is a computer whose primary purpose is to be a repository for files that can be accessed by network workstations. A file server can reside on any personal computer. For example, you might designate one of your old desktop computers as a file server and use it to store lots of big video files that you don't want clogging up your local hard disk.

A file server connects to a LAN's router just like any other network device. You can also purchase a computing device advertised as a server. A server typically has no monitor or keyboard; its system unit contains a microprocessor, memory, high-capacity hard disk, and built-in network adapter. File servers are available as tower units or rack-mounted blade servers (Figure 5-44).

**Are file servers a good idea for home networks?** Whereas file servers are an essential component of most business networks, in many home networks, files are stored on workstations in shared folders rather than on a file server. A potential problem with this arrangement is that workstations must be turned on in order to access their files over a network. If you find yourself running all over the house turning on computers in order to find files, your network could be more effective with a file server. File servers are designed to run continuously day and night, so they are always on and their files are always accessible.

Another reason to consider a file server for a home network is backup. Rather than purchase external hard disk drives for each workstation's backup, one low-cost file server can supply enough space to back up files for several workstations.

**Do file servers require any special setup?** If you're using a file server without its own keyboard or monitor, its configuration software is accessible using a browser. To configure a file server, open a browser from any workstation, enter the file server's IP address, and provide the administrator ID and password.

## SHARING PRINTERS

**How can I set up a printer for network access?** There are three ways to set up a printer so it can be accessed from any workstation. You can set up printer sharing using a workstation printer, set up printer sharing using a print server, or install a printer with built-in networking (Figure 5-45).

**FIGURE 5-44**

Servers are sold as tower units (top) or as rack-mountable units (bottom), typically used for business applications.

**FIGURE 5-45**

Printers can be attached to LANS in various ways.

Printer attaches to one workstation

Printer attaches to print server, which connects to router

Printer attaches directly to router

**How does printer sharing work?** One way to share a printer over a network is to connect the printer to one of the workstations and then enable printer sharing. With printer sharing enabled, as long as the printer and workstation are turned on, any workstation on the network can send print jobs to the printer.

**How do I enable printer sharing?** If you're using Windows and you want to allow other users to share the printer that's attached to your workstation, use the Printers and Faxes dialog box as shown in Figure 5-46.

**FIGURE 5-46**

You can designate the printer attached to your computer as sharable over the network.

1. Open the Printer and Faxes dialog box, right-click the printer you want to designate as shared, and then select Sharing from the pop-up menu.

2. Select *Share this printer* and give the printer a nickname.

● CLICK TO START

**How do I send a print job to a shared printer?** Before you can send a print job to a shared printer attached to someone else's workstation, you have to make sure that the printer driver is installed on your computer (Figure 5-47). Once you've added the printer to your list of printers and faxes, you can select the printer from your software's Print dialog box.

**FIGURE 5-47**

To use a network printer, its printer driver must be installed on your computer.

Select *Add a printer* and follow the printer wizard to complete the shared printer setup.

**Can I set up a shared printer without tying up a workstation?**
You can use a network print server device to take the place of a workstation-controlled printer. By attaching a print server to a standard printer, you can access the printer from the network without going through a workstation. Print servers are available for wireless or wired networks. To set up a print server, connect it to the printer's USB port and access the configuration settings using your browser. Once the print server is configured, you can send print jobs to it using the same steps as for a shared printer.

**What about attaching a printer directly to the network?** A printer with built-in networking does not have to be attached to a workstation or a print server because it has its own NIC. This type of printer typically connects to the network hub or router using a cable. Once configured, print jobs are sent to it just as with shared printers.

## LAN PARTIES

**What is a LAN party?** A **LAN party** is a gathering of people who connect their own computers to a LAN, usually to play multiplayer computer games. LAN parties can take place in private homes, community centers, or other venues. Most private LAN parties max out at 12 or so attendees. Commercialized LAN parties are sponsored by computer hardware or software companies and can sometimes involve hundreds of players (Figure 5-48). LANs can also be used for Xbox System Links, in which players link their Xboxes to a LAN for gaming.

**Do LAN parties require special hardware?** Small LAN parties can use just about any wired or wireless LAN. Attendees usually bring their own computer, keyboard, monitor, mouse, headphones, surge strip, and network cables. The host of a LAN party usually supplies the basic network infrastructure including hubs and routers. The host should also make a few calculations ahead of time to ensure that the party venue has adequate power to prevent circuits from popping. The LAN party host might also provide a computer that is used as a dedicated application server that coordinates game play. However, the game server can run on one of the player's computers—usually the fastest computer gets this honor.

**What about software?** Multiplayer computer games, such as Quake, Doom, Counter-Strike, Unreal Tournament, and Battlefield 1942 are popular at LAN parties. Players can compete against each other, team up to play against other teams, or play against the game's artificial intelligence. Each player should have the game software installed and a unique validation key to a legal copy of the software. LAN parties are not a valid reason to pirate software.

## TROUBLESHOOTING

**What if my network stops working?** Network problems can stem from a variety of sources. Symptoms of network malfunctions are slow response time, intermittent outages, failure to access files from one workstation, and non-availability of network services to all workstations. To troubleshoot network problems, you have to consider the possibility of a problem with a workstation's hardware or settings; network links including cables and wireless signal strength; or network devices such as routers, servers, or NICs.

**FIGURE 5-48**

LAN's aren't just for business use!

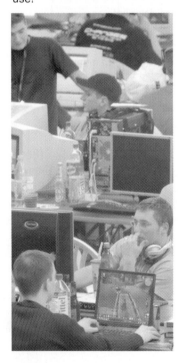

**Cables.** Make sure all network cables are firmly connected. If only one workstation is not accessing the network, you might try swapping cables with another workstation.

**Signal strength.** In a wireless network, check the signal strength. If the signal is weak, move the workstation closer to the access point, if possible.

**Interference.** If you have intermittent network outages, look for sources of interference, such as cordless phones, baby monitors, or construction equipment.

**Network devices.** Make sure your network hub, switch, router, or wireless access point is plugged in and functioning properly. Check the activity lights.

**Security.** If your network requires passwords, make sure you are using the correct password and that your password has not expired.

**Settings.** Make sure the network is enabled (Figure 5-49) and then use Control Panel to check the drivers for your network equipment.

**FIGURE 5-49**

The Network Connections tool, accessed from Control Panel, helps troubleshoot connection problems.

Dell Wireless WLAN 1450 Dual Band WLAN Mini-PCI Card

# QuickCheck

SECTION D

1. Networks offer shared _____ , such as printers, software applications, and storage space.

2. For security reasons it is not advisable to allow shared access to the _____ directory of your C: drive.

3. Before you can send a print job to a shared printer attached to someone else's workstation, you have to make sure that the printer _____ is installed on your computer.

4. A(n) _____ server is a computer whose primary purpose is to be a repository for files that can be accessed by network workstations.

5. A(n) _____ server can be connected to a LAN to run software for workstations or coordinate game play for a LAN party.

CHECK ANSWERS

# Security Through Encryption

**LOCAL AREA NETWORKS** are susceptible to a variety of threats. Many threats can be handled using techniques for standalone computers. Network equipment should be connected to power strips to prevent damage from power spikes. Data should be backed up in case of a hard drive failure. Workstations should be protected by antivirus software, and passwords should be required for network access. Wireless networks also should be protected by the use of encryption. In Section E you'll learn how to enable encryption on a wireless network, you'll find out how encryption works, and become familiar with other ways that encryption can be useful.

## WI-FI SECURITY

**What are the threats to my wireless network?** Compared to wired networks, wireless networks are much more susceptible to unauthorized access and use. To join a wired network, you have to gain physical access to the router and plug in a cable. To access many wireless networks, you simply boot up a wireless-enabled device such as a notebook computer within range of the wireless router. One threat to wireless network users is called an "evil twin." Users think they are logging onto a legitimate network, but its signals are being jammed by hackers who can extract passwords and credit card information from unsuspecting users.

With wireless network data floating freely through the air, hackers have an easy time intercepting signals by cruising through a business district or neighborhood with a Wi-Fi enabled notebook computer, a practice called **LAN jacking** or war driving ("war" stands for wireless access revolution).

LAN jackers can pinpoint the exact location of a wireless access point with the use of GPS (Global Positioning System) receivers or legitimate network-detecting and monitoring software such as NetStumbler (Figure 5-50).

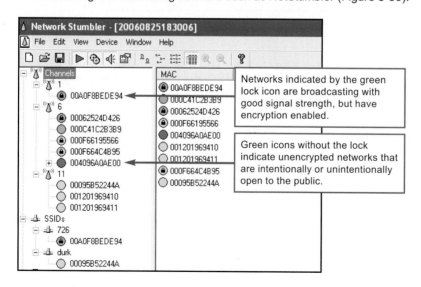

**FIGURE 5-50**

Software tools such as NetStumbler help locate and identify secured and unsecured networks. Once logged on to an unsecured wireless network, LAN jackers are free to do anything from stealing the network owner's credit card or bank information to attacking computers in other networks.

An offshoot of war driving is a gambit called **war chalking**. When wireless snoops find an unsecured network, they write specific symbols on walls, sidewalks, or lampposts to signal other wireless network seekers that they can tap into a wireless network in the area (Figure 5-51). War chalking is based on a convention established by hobos during the 1930's Great Depression. To help other vagabonds, hobos marked streets and homes with chalk symbols to indicate the best places for getting free handouts.

**FIGURE 5-51**

Warchalking identifies wireless networks. Open nodes are unsecured, closed nodes are well secured, WEP nodes are protected, but by easy-to-bypass security.

Open node          Closed node          WEP node

**5**

**How can I secure my wireless network?** Preventing Wi-Fi signal interception is difficult, but encrypting transmitted data makes it useless to intruders. **Wireless encryption** scrambles the data transmitted between wireless devices and then unscrambles the data only on devices that have a valid encryption key. Several types of encryption are available; some are more effective than others. You'll learn how encryption works later in the chapter.

**What are the types of wireless encryption?** The original wireless encryption was called **WEP** (Wired Equivalent Privacy) because it was designed to provide a level of confidentiality similar to that of a wired network. The original version of WEP is very easy to bypass. A second version of WEP uses stronger encryption but has several flaws that can easily be exploited by hackers.

**WPA** (Wi-Fi Protected Access) addresses some of WEP's weaknesses. It utilizes TKIP (Temporal Key Integrity Protocol) to encrypt data based on the user's password. TKIP also implements message integrity checking, making sure that packets have not been intercepted or tampered with in any way.

In contrast to WEP and WPA, much better security is offered by **WPA2**, which uses the same kind of strong encryption required by government agencies and businesses. It also replaces TKIP with CCMP (Counter-node CBC MAC Protocol), which rotates encryption keys and implements more rigorous message integrity checks.

**Which type of encryption should I use?** All devices on a network must use the same type of encryption. If you have even one device on your network that only supports WEP, for example, you will have to use WEP for the entire network. Although WEP is fairly easy for hackers to neutralize, it is better than leaving a network totally unprotected. WEP can discourage casual hackers and keep your neighbors out of your files if the range of your networks overlap.

The best type of encryption is WPA2, so use it if all the devices on your network support it. Certified Wi-Fi devices manufactured after March 2006 must support WPA2. Devices manufactured before that date might support only WEP or WPA, although several newer devices support both WEP and WPA. The Wi-Fi Alliance Web site provides a list of WPA and WPA2 certified products. If you have older equipment in your network, you might want to phase out each older device gradually so that you can upgrade your encryption from WEP, to WPA, to the more secure WPA2.

**How do I activate WEP, WPA, or WPA2?** To activate encryption for your wireless network open the router's configuration software. Earlier in the chapter you learned that most wireless routers can be configured by opening a browser and entering the router's IP number. Use the router configuration utilities to select WEP, WPA, or WPA2. In addition, you must create a wireless network key.

A **wireless network key** is the basis for scrambling and unscrambling the data transmitted between wireless devices. The key is similar to a password, only longer. Instructions for creating a valid key are usually given in the router's documentation or on-screen Help file. Typically, your key can use numbers 0-9 and letters A-F. Some router software requests that you enter a passphrase, such as notrespassingthismeansu! A hashing algorithm uses the passphrase to generate a wireless network key.

Don't use a key or passphrase that's easy for an intruder to decipher. Remember the key or passphrase you use to configure the router. Later, when you set up computers and other network devices, you will enter the same key so that every device on your network can encrypt and decrypt the data flowing on the network. Figure 5-52 illustrates how to activate wireless encryption.

**FIGURE 5-52**

The configuration utility used to set up wireless security is supplied by the router manufacturer. In this example security is being configured for a Linksys router.

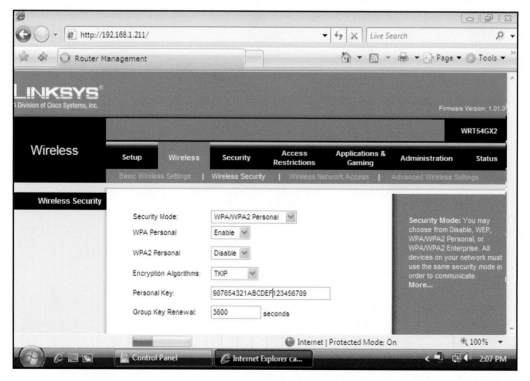

## ENCRYPTION

**Exactly what is encryption?** **Encryption** transforms a message in such a way that its contents are hidden from unauthorized readers. Encryption is designed to keep messages secret. In the context of computing, encryption can be used in many ways, including the following.

- Scrambling data sent over wired or wireless networks to prevent intrusions

- Securing credit card numbers and other personal information transferred from shoppers' computers to e-commerce sites

- Encrypting computer archives so that data they contain is unusable if the the archive is lost or compromised

- Scrambling the contents of e-mail messages to maintain privacy

**How does encryption work?** An original message—one that has not yet been encrypted—is referred to as **plaintext** or cleartext. An encrypted message is referred to as **ciphertext**. The process of converting plaintext into ciphertext is called encryption. The reverse process—converting ciphertext into plaintext—is called **decryption**.

Messages are encrypted by using a cryptographic algorithm and key. A **cryptographic algorithm** is a procedure for encrypting or decrypting a message. A **cryptographic key** (usually just called a key) is a word, number, or phrase that must be known to encrypt or decrypt a message.

For example, Julius Caesar made extensive use of an encryption method called simple substitution, which could have been used to turn the plaintext message "Do not trust Brutus" into GRQRWWUXVWEUXWXV. The cryptographic algorithm was to offset the letters of the alphabet. The key was 3 (Figure 5-53).

**FIGURE 5-53**

The algorithm for Caesar's encryption technique was to offset the letters of the alphabet—in this case by three letters. A simple transformation table was used to encrypt or decrypt a message. For example, if a "G" appears in the encrypted message, it would be a "D" in the original unencrypted message.

Ciphertext letters:

D E F G H I J K L M N O P Q R S T U V W X Y Z A B C

Equivalent plaintext letters:

A B C D E F G H I J K L M N O P Q R S T U V W X Y Z

**What's the difference between strong and weak encryption?** Caesar's simple substitution key is an example of **weak encryption** because it is easy to decrypt even without the algorithm and key. Unauthorized decryption is sometimes referred to as breaking or cracking a code. You could crack Caesar's code in several ways. For example, you could discover the key by making 25 different transformation tables, each with a different offset (assuming that the encryption method uses the letters of the alphabet in sequence and not at random). You could also analyze the frequency with which letters appear—in English documents, E, T, A, O, and N appear most frequently—and you can piece together the message by guessing the remaining letters.

**Strong encryption** is loosely defined as "very difficult to break." **AES** (Advanced Encryption Standard), the technology used for WPA2, is one of the strongest cryptographic algorithms. With continuous advances in technology, however, strong encryption is a moving target. Several encryption methods that were considered impossible to break 10 years ago have recently been cracked.

**How long does it take to break strong encryption?** Encryption methods can be broken by the use of expensive, specialized, code-breaking computers. The cost of these machines is substantial, but not beyond the reach of government agencies, major corporations, and organized crime. Encryption methods can also be broken by standard computer hardware—supercomputers, mainframes, workstations, and even personal computers. These computers typically break codes using a brute force attack, which consists of trying all possible keys (Figure 5-54).

The length of a computer-readable encryption key is measured in bits. A 32-bit key, for example, could be one of 4.2 billion ($2^{32}$) numbers. Surprisingly, it would be possible to try all these numbers and discover the key in less than a day by using an average personal computer.

To discover a 40-bit key, you would have to try about 1 trillion possible combinations—a week's worth of processing time on a personal computer. 56-bit and 64-bit encryption—once thought to be unbreakable by any computer in the private sector—require a lot of computing power, but have been broken by combining the power of many personal computers connected over the Internet. 128-bit encryption and 256-bit encryption are probably secure for several years. Most encryption today uses a 128-bit key.

Another way to understand how the length of a key affects the strength of encryption is to consider this guideline: Beginning with a 40-bit key, each additional bit doubles the time it would take to discover the key. If a personal computer takes one week to crack a 40-bit key, it takes two weeks to crack a 41-bit key, four weeks to crack a 42-bit key, and eight weeks to crack a 43-bit key. A 128-bit key takes $2^{(128-40)}$ times longer to crack than a 40-bit key—that's 309,485,009,821,345,068,724,781,056 times longer!

**What's public key encryption?** Caesar's encryption method is an example of **symmetric key encryption** in which the key used to encrypt a message is also used to decrypt the message. Symmetric key encryption is used to encrypt stationary data, such as corporate financial records. It is also used to encrypt the data that travels over wireless LANs.

Symmetric keys are not practical for e-mail and other situations in which the person receiving encrypted data does not have the key beforehand. E-mailing the key would be a major security problem because of the potential for a hacker to intercept it.

**Public key encryption** (PKE) eliminates the key-distribution problem, by using one key to encrypt a message, but another key is used to decrypt the message. Figure 5-55 illustrates how public key encryption works.

**FIGURE 5-54**

To discover a 4-digit PIN by brute force, a criminal must try, at most, 10,000 possibilities. Finding the key to computer data encrypted using a 32-bit key would involve about 4.2 billion possibilities.

**FIGURE 5-55**

Public key encryption uses two keys. A public key is used to encrypt a message. A private key is used to decrypt the message.

**1.** James sends the *public* key to JoBeth, but he keeps a *private* key.

**2.** JoBeth uses the public key to encrypt a message, which she sends back to James.

**4.** James can decrypt the message using his private key.

**3.** If the message and public key are intercepted by Draco, he cannot decrypt the message because he does not have the private key.

Public key encryption is a crucial technology for e-commerce and e-mail. When you use a secure connection to transmit a credit card number, the server sends a public key to your browser. Your browser uses this public key to encrypt the credit card number. After it is encrypted, no one—not even you—can use the public key to decrypt the message. The encrypted message is sent to a Web server, where the private key is used to decrypt it.

When personal computer users want to encrypt e-mail or other documents, they turn to public key encryption software called **PGP** (Pretty Good Privacy) software. When you first use PGP, the software generates a private key and a public key. You must keep your private key hidden. You e-mail the public key to the people you have authorized to send encrypted messages to you.

The people who receive your public key can store it in their PGP programs, which they then use to encrypt messages. When they send these messages to you, you can decrypt them using your private key. PGP software is available as a free download from several Web sites. Figure 5-56 contains an example of a public key generated by PGP.

-----BEGIN PGP PUBLIC KEY BLOCK-----

Version: 5.0

```
mQCNAi44C30AAAEEAL1r6BylvuSAvOKIk9ze9yCK+ZPPbRZrpXIRFBbe
+U8dGPMb9XdJS4L/cy1fXr9R9j4EfFsK/rgHV6i2rE83LjWrmsDPRPSaizz+
EQTIZi4AN99jiBomfLLZyUzmHMoUoE4shrYgOnkc0u101ikhieAFje77j/F3
596pT6nCx/9/AAURtCRBbmRyZSBCYBNhcmQgPGFiYWNhcmRAd2Vsb
C5zZi5jYS51cz6JAFUCBRAuOA6O7zYZz1mqos8BAXr9AgCxCu8CwGZR
dpfSs65r6mb4MccXvvfxO4TmPi1DKQj2FYHYjwYONk8vzA7XnE5aJmk5J
/dChdvfIU7NvVifV6of=GQv9
```

-----END PGP PUBLIC KEY BLOCK-----

**INFOWEBLINKS**

For additional resources on using ciphertext to protect data, including PGP software that you can use on your PC, connect to the **Encryption InfoWeb**.

 CLICK TO CONNECT
www.course.com/np/concepts10/ch05

FIGURE 5-56

PGP software generates a huge public key. Each person's public key is unique. You can e-mail this key to anyone who might want to send you an encrypted message.

5

# QuickCheck

1.  The original encryption method used for wireless networks was called [          ] , but the most secure wireless encryption is [          ] .

2.  [          ] key encryption uses the same key to encrypt a message as it does to decrypt the message.

3.  [          ] key encryption uses one key to encrypt a message, but another key to decrypt the message.

4.  [          ] is public key encryption software that is popular with personal computer owners who want to encrypt e-mail and data files. (Hint: Use the acronym.)

 CHECK ANSWERS

# Who's Stealing My Signals?

**A MAN WAS ARRESTED** in Florida recently and charged with unauthorized access to a computer network, a crime that's a third-degree felony and carries punishment ranging from probation to five years in prison. The accused man was allegedly piggybacking on his neighbor's wireless network to access the Internet. It appears to be one of the first cases of its kind in the United States.

Reporters and bloggers monitoring the case reported that the fault might actually rest with the network's owner who failed to implement wireless security. An especially aggressive posting on one blog also suggested that the network equipment manufacturer could be at fault for not enabling encryption as the default security setting.

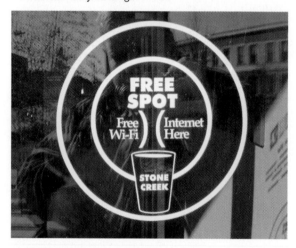

With the proliferation of home, school, and corporate wireless networks, hackers are expected to increasingly capitalize on unprotected household wireless systems to download child pornography, send threatening e-mails, and steal financial information. But what about casual interlopers who just want to borrow a little bandwidth from time to time?

One tech-savvy reporter relates that "on a trip to Colorado a fellow skier told me that although the hotel we were both staying at did not have a wireless network, an apartment complex down the street did. So I sat on their doorstep in the freezing cold to check e-mail with my laptop." He then wonders wryly if he should have rung the bell and asked if he could "please use their Wi-Fi."

Free wireless access is not unusual. Free community wireless access is offered in cities as diverse as San Francisco, Miami, New York, Prague, and Amsterdam. You can find it in airports, hotels, and coffee shops. Free wireless access is also offered by rogue WLANS operated by public spirited individuals who are more than willing to share their bandwidth with passersby. Rogue WLAN operators typically subscribe to a high-speed Internet access service. They pay their monthly fees, but instead of limiting access to their own personal use, they distribute their connections over wireless LANs to friends, neighbors, and just about anyone who passes by with the right computer equipment.

Setting up a Wi-Fi antenna is simple and inexpensive. A basic Wi-Fi antenna can be created with a few wires and an empty Pringles container. Fancier antennas require a ravioli can—really!

The 802.11 standard uses an unlicensed telecommunications spectrum, so it is perfectly legal to set up an antenna to transmit and receive Wi-Fi signals without obtaining a broadcast license. FCC regulations even prohibit landlords from limiting tenant use of or access to wireless networks. For example, network administrators at the University of Texas at Dallas attempted to prohibit students from installing private wireless access points in their dorm rooms because the signals interfered with access to the campus-wide wireless network. The university reversed its policy after reviewing FCC regulations.

Some free WLAN advocates envision a nationwide web of interconnected Wi-Fi networks that will form "a seamless broadband network built by the people, for the people." In this vision of a world connected by free WLANs, libraries can offer Internet access to people in low-income neighborhoods. Local schools could get wired without exorbitant cabling expenses. Parents, kids, and grandparents, as well as corporate executives, could exchange e-mail and instant messages from locations that include the kitchen table, the corner coffee shop, and the Little League field.

But some broadband providers, such as AT&T and Time Warner Cable, fear that every user of a free wireless network is one less paying customer. According to one industry analyst, "The telecom industries are addicted to the one-wire, one-customer philosophy." Sharing an Internet connection that is intended for single-user access does not coexist with this philosophy. Most subscriber agreements contain wording that limits use of a broadband connection to one user and perhaps immediate family members. Although wording varies from one provider to another, most agreements expressly prohibit subscribers from using their connections for commercial purposes. Some free WLAN operators don't believe that sharing is commercial use. "I'm sharing it with people," says one free WLAN provider, "I'm not selling it. I'm not making a profit off it."

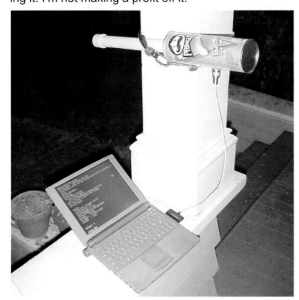

Whether or not free WLANs are legal, their benefits are tempered by several potentially negative repercussions. For example, tightening up subscriber agreements to eliminate the sharing loophole could affect many broadband subscribers who currently operate private wired or wireless networks that link several computers to a single Internet connection. Broadband providers could force private network operators to purchase more expensive multiuser licenses—an option that might be too expensive for many home networks.

The wisdom of unregulated network availability is called into question by the proliferation of free WLANs. A publicly accessible LAN that requires no passwords or accounts can be used anonymously for a variety of illegal and dangerous activities. Like drug dealers who use public telephones to avoid taps and traces, terrorists and other criminals can simply walk into a free WLAN zone, tap into the Internet, and walk away without leaving a trace.

Widespread distribution of free WLANs can reduce the bandwidth available to paying customers. If your neighbor sets up a free WLAN that becomes popular with customers in a nearby coffee house, your previously sedate network neighborhood might suddenly become an overcrowded metropolis with major Internet access traffic jams.

Despite possible repercussions, the free WLAN movement appears to be growing and becoming more controversial. Some industry analysts expect a battle similar to the one that ensued when Napster's peer-to-peer music-sharing network was attacked by the music industry. The free WLAN controversy could pit a group of telecommunications giants against a rag-tag alliance of free WLAN advocates. The outcome has the potential to affect broadband subscribers everywhere.

5

**INFOWEBLINKS**

The **Free WLAN InfoWeb** provides more details about Wi-Fi technology and renegade LANs.

 CLICK TO CONNECT
www.course.com/np/concepts10/ch05

# What Do You Think?

ISSUE

1. Have you ever accessed a free WLAN?                              ○ Yes  ○ No  ○ Not sure

2. Do you believe that rogue WLANs can survive alongside for-profit broadband ISPs?              ○ Yes  ○ No  ○ Not sure

3. Are broadband providers justified in limiting the terms of their service agreements to "one subscription, one customer"?       ○ Yes  ○ No  ○ Not sure

 SAVE RESPONSES

## COMPUTERS IN CONTEXT

# Education

**THE FIRST EDUCATIONAL** application of computers emerged in the 1960s, when huge mainframes with clunky interfaces introduced students to computer-aided instruction (CAI). Based on operant conditioning research by B. F. Skinner and Ivan Pavlov—remember dogs salivating when a bell rings?—CAI uses basic drill and practice: The computer presents a problem, the student responds, and the computer evaluates the response. Studies in the 1970s indicated that CAI systems, such as PLATO (Programmed Logic for Automated Teaching Operations), improved student test scores, but students found the mainframe's monochrome display and the CAI's regimented drill format boring. Recent incarnations of CAI, such as an alien-invader style elementary math program, use snazzy graphics and arcade formats to grab learners' attention.

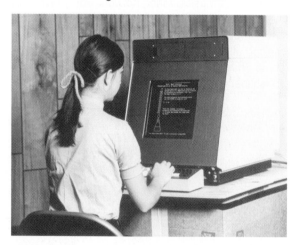

Educators looking for ways to harness computers' interactive and programmable nature arrived at the idea of computer-based training (CBT). CBT is formatted as a series of tutorials, beginning with a pretest to see whether students have the prerequisite skills and ending with a CAI-style drill and practice test to determine whether students can move on to the next tutorial segment. Today, CBT is a popular approach to learning how to use computer software.

Another educational approach, called computer-aided learning (CAL), uses the computer more as a source of information than an assessment mechanism. Students using CAL make decisions about their level of expertise, what material is relevant, and how to pace their own learning. Exploratory CAL environments include Seymour Papert's Logo programming language; students can investigate geometry concepts by using Logo to program a graphical turtle on-screen.

In addition to CAI, CBT, and CAL, simulations have become a popular educational tool. The computer mimics a real-world situation through a narrative description or with graphics. Students are given options and respond with a decision or an action. The computer evaluates each response and determines its consequences. Oregon Trail, a simulation popular with elementary school students, describes events that beset a group of pioneers traveling in a wagon train. Students respond to each event, while learning bits of history, money-handling skills, conservation, and decision making.

Most educators believe that computers can help create an individualized and interactive learning environment, which can make learning more effective and efficient. Although 99% of American public schools have computers and 93% of students use them in some way, these statistics can be deceiving. The reality falls far short of the ideal situation—every student having access to a computer throughout the school day.

The challenge is to figure out how to achieve the computers' potential in an educational setting when supplying computers for every student is often cost prohibitive. Compromise solutions have been tried with varying degrees of success. Some schools have installed learning labs where students go for scheduled lab time. In elementary schools, often a few computers are placed in special work areas of classrooms and used for small group projects or individual drill and practice. Some schools have relegated most computers to the library, where they are connected to the Internet and used for research. In some classrooms, a single computer can be used as an effective presentation device.

A few schools without the budget for enough desktop computers have opted for inexpensive PDAs instead. "Students need to use technology just as you and I do, not just one hour a day," says one teacher in support of PDAs. Students use standard PDA software for educational tasks: tracking nutritional intake for health class, collecting data from experiments in biology class, graphing functions in math class, translating phrases for French class, and maintaining to-do lists. The biggest drawback to more widespread educational use of PDAs, however, is a lack of software specifically designed for education.

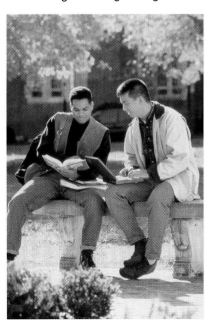

As another option, some schools—primarily colleges—have confronted the problem of computer access by requiring all incoming first-year students to purchase notebook computers. Many colleges, for example, provide Internet connections in dorm rooms and library study carrels or offer campuswide Wi-Fi service. Students can tote their notebook computers to class and take notes. They can contact instructors via e-mail, use the Internet as a research resource, and run educational software.

Another educational use of computers can be seen in distance education (DE) courses (also called distance learning). Historically, distance education meant correspondence study or courses delivered by radio or television, but the meaning has been broadened to encompass any educational situation in which students and instructors aren't in the same place. Therefore, most DE courses today require students to have access to a computer and an Internet connection. DE courses are offered to K-12 students, college students, military personnel, business people, and the general public. Most students who choose DE courses do so because they want to learn at their own pace, at a convenient time, and in a location close to home. Single parents who must deal with the realities of child care, working professionals who cannot relocate to a college town, and physically disabled students find distance education handy. Distance education has the potential of increasing the pool of students for a course by making it financially feasible; for example, an advanced Kanji course could be offered at a midwestern university with only 10 on-campus Japanese majors if enough distance education students can boost enrollment.

The Internet hosts a wide variety of DE courses, both credit-earning and noncredit courses. Several course management systems (CMSs), such as Blackboard and WebCT, help teachers prepare and manage DE courses. These systems are popular with degree-granting institutions that offer credit-earning DE courses in their course catalogs (subject to the usual course fees and requirements).

Course management software typically runs from a server maintained by a school system, college, or university. Using Web browsers, teachers access the CMS to post an online syllabus, develop Web pages with course content, create a database of questions for online assessment, manage e-mail, set up online discussion groups, and maintain a gradebook. Students using Internet-connected computers and standard Web browsers can access course materials, submit assignments, interact with other students, and take tests.

Computers and the Internet have opened opportunities for lifelong learning. Prospective students can use a search engine to easily find non-credit courses and tutorials for a wide range of topics, including pottery, dog grooming, radio astronomy, desktop publishing, and drumming. Some tutorials are free, and others charge a small fee. Several Web sites, such as Barnes & Noble University and Online-Learning.com, offer a good choice of fee-based or free courses. In a society that promotes learning as a lifelong endeavor, the Internet has certainly made it possible for students of all ages to pursue knowledge and skills simply by using a computer and an Internet connection.

**INFOWEBLINKS**

You'll find lots more information related to this Computers in Context topic at the **Computers and Education InfoWeb**.

W   CLICK TO CONNECT

www.course.com/np/concepts10/ch05

# New Perspectives Labs

## On the BookOnCD

To access the New Perspectives labs for Chapter 5, start the BookOnCD, BookOnFlashDrive, or other NP10 BookOn product and then click the icon next to the lab title below.

### ▶ LOCAL AREA NETWORKS

#### IN THIS LAB YOU'LL LEARN:

- The basic technology specifications for Ethernet and Wi-Fi networks
- To identify the parts of a router
- How to open the router configuration utility
- How to change a router's default password
- How to create an SSID
- The advantages and disadvantages of WEP, WPA, and WPA2 encryption
- How to enable wireless encryption
- How to determine a computer's wired or wireless networking capability
- How to connect a LAN to the Internet
- How to make sure a router is configured for DHCP

#### LAB ASSIGNMENTS

1. Start the interactive part of the lab. Perform each lab step as directed, and answer all the lab QuickCheck questions.

2. Use your computer's networking utilities to find out if your computer is LAN and/or WLAN ready. Make a note of the type and specifications of any network adapters installed in your computer.

3. Using the information you gathered from assignment 2, draw a sketch showing how your computer could be linked into a LAN.

4. Examine the networking utilities installed on your computer. If you are using Windows, you might find utilities such as Network Connections, Wireless Network Setup Wizard, and others. Look at each utility and write a one-paragraph description for each utility.

# Key Terms

Make sure you understand all the boldfaced key terms presented in this chapter. If you're using the NP10 BookOnCD, BookOnFlashDrive, or other NP10 BookOn product, you can use this list of terms as an interactive study activity. First, try to define a term in your own words, and then click the term to compare your definition with the definition presented in the chapter.

AES, 285
Application server, 249
Bandwidth, 251
Bluetooth, 267
Bridge, 250
Broadband, 251
Bus topology, 250
Ciphertext, 285
Circuit switching, 253
Client/server mode, 249
Communications channel, 251
Communications protocol, 252
Cryptographic algorithm, 285
Cryptographic key, 285
CSMA/CD, 259
Decryption, 285
DHCP, 255
Drive mapping, 276
Encryption, 285
Ethernet, 258
Ethernet adapter, 261
Fast Ethernet, 259
File server, 249
Gateway, 251
Gigabit Ethernet, 259
Handshaking, 252
HomePNA, 257
Infrared light, 265
IP address, 255
LAN, 247
LAN jacking, 282
LAN party, 280

MAC address, 254
MAN, 247
Mesh topology, 250
Microwaves, 265
MIMO, 268
NAN, 246
Narrowband, 251
Network attached storage, 248
Network device, 248
Network hub, 261
Network interface card, 248
Network router, 261
Network switch, 261
Networked peripheral, 248
Node, 248
Octet, 255
Packet, 253
Packet switching, 253
PAN, 246
Peer-to-peer mode, 249
PGP, 287
Physical topology, 250
Piconet, 267
Plaintext, 285
Powerline network, 258
Print server, 249
Public key encryption, 286
RF signals, 265
Ring topology, 250
RJ45 connector, 262
Shared resources, 274
SSID, 272

Star topology, 250
Strong encryption, 285
Symmetric key encryption, 286
Transceiver, 265
Tree topology, 250
WAN, 247
War chalking, 283
Weak encryption, 285
WEP, 283
Wi-Fi, 268
Wi-Fi card, 269
Wired network, 256
Wireless access point, 270
Wireless ad-hoc network, 270
Wireless encryption, 283
Wireless infrastructure network, 270
Wireless network, 265
Wireless network key, 284
Wireless router, 270
WPA, 283
WPA2, 283

5

# Interactive Summary

To review important concepts from this chapter, fill in the blanks to best complete each sentence. When using the NP10 BookOnCD or other BookOn product, click the Check Answers buttons to automatically score your answers.

**SECTION A:** Networks can be classified by geographical scope as PANs, [_____], MANs, NANs, and WANs. LAN technologies are standardized by the [_____] organization. Each connection point on a network is referred to as a [_____]. Nodes can contain computers, networked [_____], or network devices. Computers connected to a network require network circuitry, often housed on a network [_____] card (NIC). Networks that include one or more servers can operate in [_____]/server mode or peer-to-peer mode. Networks without a server typically operate in peer-to-peer mode. Physical network topologies include star, bus, [_____], mesh, and tree. Network nodes are linked by communications channels. High bandwidth channels are referred to as [_____], whereas low bandwidth channels are referred to as [_____]. Communications [_____], such as TCP/IP, divide messages into [_____], handle addressing, and manage routing.

▶ CHECK ANSWERS

**SECTION B:** Wired LANs are fast, secure, and simple to configure. HomePNA networks transport data over [_____] wiring and HomePlug networks transport data over [_____] wiring. Ethernet networks use CAT 5e/CAT 6 wiring with plastic [_____] connectors. Ethernet uses CSMA/CD to detect [_____]. [_____] Ethernet operates at 100 Mbps, whereas Gigabit Ethernet operates at [_____] Mbps. Ethernet is usually wired in a [_____] topology to a central device. A network [_____] is a device that accepts data from one workstation and broadcasts it to all of the other network nodes. A network [_____] is a more sophisticated connection device that sends data only to the devices specified as the destination. A network [_____] is a network device that can ship data from one network to another. You typically use your [_____] software to access the router's configuration utilities.

▶ CHECK ANSWERS

**SECTION C:** Most wireless LANs transport data using [          ] frequency signals. The most popular WLAN technology is Wi-Fi, but [          ] is used for PANs and other short-range connections. Wi-Fi is defined by the IEEE [          ] standards, and there are versions denoted by the letters a, b, g, and n. Computers on a Wi-Fi network must have wireless circuitry, such as a Wi-Fi adapter. Wireless networks can be set up as a wireless [          ] network in which devices broadcast directly to each other, or as a wireless [          ] network that uses a centralized broadcasting device, such as a wireless [          ] point or a wireless router. When setting up a wireless network it is important to change the default router password, create an [          ] to uniquely identify the network, and enable wireless encryption for security.

▶ CHECK ANSWERS

**SECTION D:** LANs allow people to share network resources, such as files, printers, and Internet connections. Unfortunately, LANs are vulnerable to unauthorized access and malware. To view the files stored on other network workstations, you can use a technique called drive [          ] that assigns a drive letter and displays a remote drive's contents. Under Windows, you can designate folders and printers as [          ] if you want to allow other workstations to access them. If you have many files that need to be accessed from various workstations, you might want to add a [          ] server to the network. If you would like everyone on a network to have access to a printer, but you prefer not to send print jobs through any of the workstations, you can add a [          ] server or attach a network-ready printer directly to the router. When using a network for a LAN party, usually one of the computers will be used as an [          ] server to coordinate game play. Network problems can stem from a variety of sources. Symptoms of network malfunctions are slow response time, intermittent outages, failure to access files from one workstation, and non-availability of network services to all workstations. To troubleshoot network problems, you have to consider the possibility of a problem with a workstation's hardware or settings; network links including cables and wireless signal strength; or network devices such as routers, servers, or NICs.

▶ CHECK ANSWERS

5

**SECTION E:** Compared to wired networks, wireless networks are much more susceptible to unauthorized access and use. Hackers have an easy time intercepting signals by cruising through a business district or neighborhood with a Wi-Fi enabled notebook computer, a practice called LAN [          ]. Preventing Wi-Fi signal interception is difficult, but wireless [          ] scrambles transmitted data and makes it useless to intruders. Originally, wireless networks were secured with [          ], but it proved too easy to crack. Much better security is offered by WPA and WPA2. An original message—one that has not yet been encrypted—is referred to as [          ] or cleartext. An encrypted message is referred to as [          ]. Messages are encrypted by a crypto-graphic [          ], which is a specific procedure for encrypting or decrypting a message. A cryptographic [          ] is a word, number, or phrase that must be known to encrypt or decrypt a message. [          ] key encryption uses the same key to encrypt and decrypt a message. [          ] key encryption eliminates the key-distribution problem, by using one key to encrypt a message, but another key is used to decrypt the message. The software for a popular implementation of public key encryption called Pretty [          ] Privacy can be downloaded from several Web sites and used to encrypt e-mail or other documents.

▶ CHECK ANSWERS

# Interactive Situation Questions

Apply what you've learned to some typical computing situations. When using the NP10 BookOnCD, BookOnFlashDrive, or any other NP10 BookOn product, you can type your answers, and then use the Check Answers button to automatically score your responses.

1. You're installing a LAN and you decide to go with Ethernet. You'll typically use Category [____] cables to connect each workstation to a(n) [_____].

2. You're setting up an Ethernet wired network using a router. To access the router and its configuration software, you open your [_____] and type the router's IP address.

3. You're trying to figure out if your computer has a built-in Ethernet port cable. You see the port pictured to the right. Is that the port you should use for your RJ45 connector? [_____]

4. You install an 802.11b network, but it seems to stop working at various times. To begin troubleshooting, you look for any devices, such as cordless phones, that use the [_____] GHz frequency.

5. Your PC is connected to a LAN, and you want to regularly access a file that's stored on one of the LAN workstations. You'd like to access that computer's hard disk as though it were connected to your own computer, so you decide to [_____] the workstation's hard disk drive as drive F.

6. You arrive at work and one of your co-workers tells you that the router is down. Is it correct to surmise that your workstation will not be able to access other workstations, but will be able to access the Internet? Yes or no? [_____]

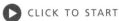

7. You're walking down the street in a large city and you spy a chalk circle on the sidewalk with "WEP" inside it. You realize that you're looking at an example of [_____] chalking and there is probably a wireless LAN nearby.

8. You've set up a wireless network using some new equipment and a few old Wi-Fi cards given to you by your roommates. One of the cards is equipped only for WEP, whereas all the other cards support WPA2. Your roommate tells you that in order to use all the cards, you'll have to disable wireless encryption. Is your roommate right? [_____]

▶ CHECK ANSWERS

# Interactive Practice Tests

Practice tests that consist of 10 multiple-choice, true/false, and fill-in-the-blank questions are available on both the NP10 BookOn products and the NP10 Web site. The questions are selected at random from a large test bank, so each time you take a test, you'll receive a different set of questions. Your tests are scored immediately, and you can print study guides that help you find the correct answers for any questions that you missed.

▶ CLICK TO START

# Study Tips

Study Tips help you to organize and consolidate the information in a unit by making lists, outlines, charts, and sketches. You can use paper and pencil or word processing software to complete most of the Study Tip activities.

1. Make sure you can use your own words to correctly answer each of the red focus questions that appear throughout the chapter.

2. Make a list of the advantages and another list of the disadvantages of creating and using a computer network.

3. Describe the characteristics of PANs, NANs, LANS, MANs, and WANs, plus provide an example of each.

4. Create a list of network devices mentioned in this chapter. Write a brief description of each one, and indicate whether it would typically be part of the Internet, a LAN, or both.

5. Draw diagrams of star, ring, bus, mesh, and tree network topologies. Make sure that you can trace the route of data over an Ethernet. Discuss how collisions are detected and/or avoided.

6. Make a list of network cabling options and wireless options. Explain the advantages/disadvantages of each.

7. Explain the difference between an analog signal and a digital signal. Why do most modern communications systems use digital signals?

8. Draw a diagram of Shannon's communications model. Apply this model to a Wi-Fi LAN by indicating which real-world devices would exist at various points in the model to originate data, encode it, transmit signals, and so on.

9. Make a list of the LAN standards described in this chapter. For each one, indicate the type of technology it uses, its maximum speed, range, and the devices available to set up network communications.

10. Describe the differences between SSIDs, IP addresses, MAC addresses, and wireless network keys.

11. Make a list of security concerns that are related to local area networks.

12. Describe the steps that you would take to (a) secure a wired LAN and (b) secure a wireless LAN.

13. Describe the difference between symmetric encryption and public key encryption. List five uses for each one.

14. Fill in the blanks on the concept map shown below to show the hierarchy of LAN technology.

5

# Concept Map

CHECK ANSWERS

# Projects

 CRITICAL THINKING

Wireless technology has become quite pervasive. Not only are computing devices wireless, but most people have other devices, such as security systems, baby monitors, and entertainment systems, that could be wirelessly networked. Play the role of a futurist and think about the ultimate wired home. Sketch out floor plans and show how you would set up wireless devices, including wireless access points.

 GROUP PROJECT

Form a group with three or four other students. Suppose you are all living in adjacent dorm rooms and decide to create a LAN to connect your computers. For this project, first describe the number, type, and location of the computers that will form your network. Next, decide what type of network technology you want to use: Ethernet, HomePNA, Wi-Fi, HomePlug, or a mixture. Create a diagram showing the location of each computer, the wiring path (for Ethernet), the location of electrical outlets (for HomePlug), the location of telephone outlets (for HomePNA), or potential signal interference (for wireless). Create a shopping list of the network components you need to purchase, and then use the Web to locate prices for each item on your list. Make sure you supply your instructor with the URLs for sites where you found pricing information.

 CYBERCLASSROOM

With a partner, research public key encryption (PKE) you could use to send encrypted e-mail back and forth. Do any utilities offered with your operating system offer PKE or would you have to use third-party software? If possible, set up encryption and send your partner an encrypted e-mail message or file. Describe the tools and procedure you used to your instructor.

 MULTIMEDIA PROJECT

Wireless technology is increasingly being used for home entertainment systems, including stereos, television, and home theaters. For this project choose either television, stereo, or projection systems. Research the wireless options for the equipment of your choice. Write a two-page how-to article describing how to set up a cool wireless system. Be sure to describe the system's benefits as well as how to assemble the equipment.

 RESUME BUILDER

Bluetooth advocates champion the idea of using Bluetooth devices to exchange electronic business cards. Suppose you're working in the technology department of a corporation and your boss asks you to research the value of this concept for the company's sales representatives. After you complete your research, write a one-page memo describing your findings about cost and usefulness.

 GLOBALIZATION

The model for telecommunications in most technologically advanced countries depends on large telecommunications corporations for telephone and Internet access. Can you envision ways in which people in technologically underdeveloped countries could benefit from inexpensive LAN and WLAN technologies? Jot down your initial thoughts, then search the Web for additional ideas. Write a one-page executive summary that describes your ideas.

 ISSUE

The Issue section of this chapter focuses on the use of Wi-Fi technology to build wireless LANs that provide free Internet access. For this project, write a two- to five-page paper that examines one aspect of the free WLAN controversy. You might explore Wi-Fi technology to learn more about how it works. You might look for examples of free WLANs and try to find what motivates their operators. Or you might research how broadband providers are reacting to free WLANs. To begin this project, consult the Free WLAN InfoWeb (see page 289) to get an overview of the controversy. Using that information as background, choose the focus for your paper and continue your research. As you write your paper, make sure you can back up your statements with facts and references to authoritative articles and Web pages.

 COMPUTERS IN CONTEXT

The Computers in Context section focuses on the many ways computers and Internet technology are used in education. For this project, identify a topic you'd like to learn more about, such as a hobby or your academic major. Under the heading "Topic Description," write a brief description of your topic, why it interests you, and what you would like to learn about it. Next, use a search engine, such as Google, to locate online tutorials about your topic. Under the heading "Available Tutorials," write a brief description of your search results. Indicate the number of tutorials you found on the topic, provide the URLs for at least three tutorials, and write a short description of each one. Take one of the free tutorials. Under the heading "Evaluation," describe the format for the tutorial, its ease of use, and what you learned.

# On the Web

## STUDENT EDITION LABS

**W CLICK TO ACCESS THE NP10 WEB SITE**
or open your browser and connect to www.course.com/np/concepts10/ch05.
Lab results can be stored in the Universal Gradebook.

Work hands-on in structured simulations practicing important skills and concepts

### NETWORKING BASICS

In the Networking Basics Student Edition Lab, you will learn the following topics and skills:

- Network architecture, hardware, and software
- Network protocols and utilities
- Networked resources
- Network security

### WIRELESS NETWORKING

In the Wireless Networking Student Edition Lab, you will learn the following topics and skills:

- Implementing wireless networks
- Wireless security

 **CHAPTER COURSECAST**

Use your computer or iPod to hear a five-minute audio presentation of chapter highlights.

 **FLASHCARD COURSECAST**

Interact with audio flashcards to review key terms from the chapter.

 **DETAILED OBJECTIVES**

Make sure that you've achieved all the objectives for a chapter before it's time for your test!

 **TEST YOURSELF**

Review chapter material by taking these ten-question tests, then send your results to the Universal Gradebook.

 **ONLINE GAMES**

Have some fun while refreshing your memory about key concepts that might appear on the next test. You can even send your results to the Universal Gradebook!

 **AND MORE!**

At the NP10 Web site you'll also find TechBuzz, CNET videos, Extra Content, and InfoWebLinks.

# 6

# The Internet

## CHAPTER CONTENTS

## LEARNING OBJECTIVES

- Briefly summarize the origins and development of the Internet
- Draw a conceptual diagram illustrating the Internet backbone, NAPs, NSPs, routers, and ISPs
- Draw a diagram to illustrate how computers on a LAN would access the Internet through a single DSL modem
- List at least five protocols used on the Internet and describe what they are used for
- Explain the differences between static IP addresses, dynamic IP addresses, private IP addresses, and domain names
- Explain when and why you might use Ping and Traceroute utilities
- Describe the advantages and disadvantages of dial-up, cable, DSL, ISDN, satellite, and fixed wireless Internet services
- Differentiate between portable Internet access and mobile Internet access
- Identify and describe the most prevalent types of portable Internet access
- Differentiate between WAP and wireless data services
- Describe the basic technology underlying chat and instant messaging services
- Explain how Voice over IP works
- Relate at least five examples of grid computing
- Describe how FTP differs from file sharing technologies such as BitTorrent
- Explain how hackers use the Internet to infiltrate computers
- List at least three steps you can take to secure your computer against Internet-based intrusions

 **PRE-ASSESSMENT QUIZ**

Take the pre-assessment quiz to find out how much you know about the topics in this chapter.

**MULTIMEDIA and INTERACTIVE ELEMENTS**
When using the BookOnCD, BookOnFlashDrive, or other NP10 BookOn product, the ▶ icons are clickable to access multimedia resources.

BEFORE YOU READ ON, **TRY IT**

### HOW FAST AND DEPENDABLE IS MY INTERNET CONNECTION?

You can access the Internet in various ways—using your phone line, your cable TV connection, or a personal satellite dish. Is your Internet connection fast enough for activities such as downloading DVDs and playing online multiplayer games? You can discover the speed of your Internet connection by doing the following steps.

**1.** Using Windows Vista, enter **command prompt** in the Search box. Using Windows XP, click the Start button, point to accessories, and then select Command Prompt from the list. This action opens what's called a "DOS Box."

**2.** Type **Ping www.google.com** and then press the Enter key.

**3.** Your computer makes four attempts to access the Google Web site and measures the time required for each attempt. Fill in the blanks below with the Ping statistics for your computer. When you read the chapter, you'll learn how those statistics stack up for videoconferencing, Voice over IP, and online multiplayer gaming.

**4.** Click the **✕** button to close the DOS box.

```
Command Prompt                                                    _  □  ✕
Microsoft Windows [Version 6.0.5600]
Copyright (c) 2006 Microsoft Corporation.  All rights reserved.

C:\Users\Sara>ping www.google.com

Pinging www.l.google.com [216.239.37.104] with 32 bytes of data:

Reply from 216.239.37.104: bytes=32 time=339ms TTL=241
Reply from 216.239.37.104: bytes=32 time=331ms TTL=241
Reply from 216.239.37.104: bytes=32 time=4088ms TTL=241
Reply from 216.239.37.104: bytes=32 time=196ms TTL=241

Ping statistics for 216.239.37.104:
    Packets: Sent = 4, Received = 4, Lost = 0 (0% loss),
Approximate round trip times in milli-seconds:
    Minimum = 196ms, Maximum = 4088ms, Average = 1238ms

C:\Users\Sara>_
```

PING STATISTICS FOR MY COMPUTER

Packets sent: _____

Packets received: _____

Packets lost: _____

Round trip minimum: _____ms

Round trip maximum: _____ms

Round trip average: _____ms

**WEB SITE**
Visit the NP10 Web site to access additional resources ⓦ that accompany this chapter.

# Internet Technology

**TO MOST PEOPLE,** the Internet seems like old hat. Even people who haven't used the Internet know a lot about it from watching the news, reading magazines, and watching movies. Using the Internet is actually pretty easy. Browsing Web sites, shopping at the Net mall, sending e-mail, and chatting online? No problem. But what makes the Internet "tick"? How can one network offer so much information to so many people? Section A pulls back the curtain and gives you a glimpse of what happens behind the scenes on the Net.

## BACKGROUND

**How did the Internet get started?** The history of the Internet begins in 1957 when the Soviet Union launched Sputnik, the first man-made satellite. In response to this display of Soviet superiority, the U.S. government resolved to improve its scientific and technical infrastructure. One of the resulting initiatives was the Advanced Research Projects Agency (ARPA).

ARPA swung into action with a project designed to help scientists communicate and share valuable computer resources. The ARPANET, created in 1969, connected computers at UCLA, Stanford Research Institute, University of Utah, and University of California at Santa Barbara (Figure 6-1). In 1985, the National Science Foundation (NSF) used ARPANET technology to create a similar, but larger, network, linking not just a few mainframe computers, but entire LANs at each site. Connecting two or more networks creates an internetwork, or internet. The NSF network was an internet (with a lowercase "i"). As this network grew throughout the world, it became known as the Internet (with an uppercase "I").

Early Internet pioneers—mostly educators and scientists—used primitive command-line user interfaces to send e-mail, transfer files, and run scientific calculations on Internet supercomputers. Finding information was not easy. Without search engines, Internet users relied on word of mouth and e-mail to keep informed about new data and its location. "The data you need is on the Stanford computer in a file called Chrome.txt" was typical of messages between colleagues.

**How did the Internet become so popular?** In the early 1990s, software developers created new user-friendly Internet access tools, and Internet accounts became available to anyone willing to pay a monthly subscription fee. Today, the Internet connects computers all over the globe and supplies information to people of all ages and interests.

**How big is the Internet today?** With an estimated 200 million nodes and 1 billion users, the Internet is huge. Although exact figures cannot be determined, it is estimated that Internet traffic exceeds 100 terabytes each week—about 100 trillion bytes. That's approximately 10 times the amount of data stored in the entire printed collection of the U.S. Library of Congress.

**FIGURE 6-1**

An original diagram of the ARPANET included four nodes, depicted as circles.

**TERMINOLOGY NOTE**

A few years ago, Wired News announced it would no longer capitalize the word *Internet*, a move supported by National Public Radio and several prominent linguists. Most style guides, however, still recommend that you capitalize references to the global communications network called the Internet.

## INTERNET INFRASTRUCTURE

**How is the Internet structured?** Surprisingly, the Internet is not owned or operated by any single corporation or government. It is a data communications network that grew over time in a somewhat haphazard configuration as networks connected to other networks and to the Internet backbone.

**What is the Internet backbone?** The **Internet backbone** is a network of high-capacity communications links that provides the main routes for data traffic across the Internet. At one time, the topology of the Internet backbone and interconnected networks might have resembled a spine with ribs connected along its length. Today, however, it more resembles a map of interstate highways with many junctures and redundant routes.

**How does the backbone tie the Internet together?** The Internet backbone consists of high-speed fiber-optic links connecting high-capacity routers that direct network traffic. Backbone links and routers are maintained by **network service providers** (NSPs), such as SBC/AT&T, Qwest, Sprint, and Verizon's MCI and UUNET divisions. NSP equipment and links are tied together by **network access points** (NAPs), so that, for example, data can begin its journey on a Verizon link and then cross over to a Sprint link, if necessary, to reach its destination.

NSPs supply Internet connections to large Internet service providers, such as AT&T WorldNet, AOL, and Comcast. An **Internet service provider** (ISP) is a company that offers Internet access to individuals, businesses, and smaller ISPs. Figure 6-2 shows a simplified conceptual diagram of the Internet backbone and its components.

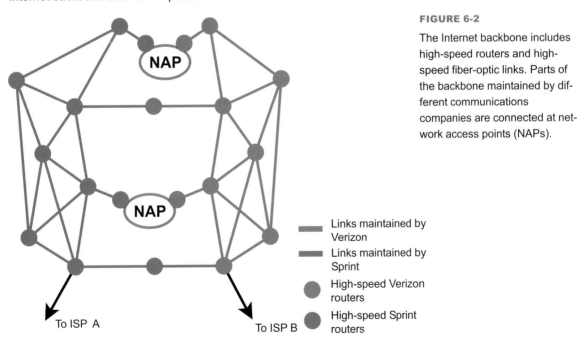

**FIGURE 6-2**

The Internet backbone includes high-speed routers and high-speed fiber-optic links. Parts of the backbone maintained by different communications companies are connected at network access points (NAPs).

Links maintained by Verizon

Links maintained by Sprint

High-speed Verizon routers

High-speed Sprint routers

**What kinds of network devices are part of an ISP?** An ISP operates routers, communication equipment, and other network devices that handle the physical aspects of transmitting and receiving data between their subscribers and the Internet. Many ISPs also operate e-mail servers to handle incoming and outgoing mail for their subscribers. Some ISPs have Web servers for subscriber Web sites. An ISP might operate a server that translates an address, such as *www.google.com*, into a valid IP address such as 208.50.141.12. ISPs can also maintain servers for chat groups, instant messaging, music file sharing, FTP, and other file transfer services (Figure 6-3).

**FIGURE 6-3**

ISP Equipment

**How does my computer fit into the structure of the Internet?**
To communicate with an ISP, your computer uses some type of communications device, such as a modem. A **modem** contains circuitry that converts the data-carrying signals from your computer to signals that can travel over various communications channels. The kind of modem you use depends on whether your ISP supplies dial-up, cable, satellite, or DSL Internet service.

A standalone computer can communicate with an ISP directly through a modem, or through a combination of a router and modem. If your computer is part of a network, the network's router typically handles the Internet connection. Figure 6-4 illustrates the difference between standalone and LAN Internet access. You'll learn more about connecting to the Internet using telephone, cable, satellite, and cellular links in Sections B and C.

**TERMINOLOGY NOTE**

The word *modem* is derived from the words *modulate* and *demodulate*. In communications lingo, modulation means changing the characteristics of a signal, as when a dial-up modem changes a digital pulse into an analog audio signal that travels over telephone lines. Demodulation means changing a signal back to its original state.

**FIGURE 6-4**

Your computer can connect to the Internet as a standalone device or part of a LAN. Your data first travels to your ISP, then to an NSP and out over the Internet backbone.

# INTERNET PROTOCOLS, ADDRESSES, AND DOMAINS

**What protocols are used by the Internet?** The Internet uses a variety of communications protocols to support basic data transport and services, such as e-mail, Web access, and downloading. Figure 6-5 briefly describes some of the main protocols used on the Internet.

FIGURE 6-5

Protocols Used on the Internet

| Protocol | Name | Function |
|---|---|---|
| TCP | Transmission Control Protocol | Creates connections and exchanges packets of data |
| IP | Internet Protocol | Provides devices with unique addresses |
| UDP | User Datagram Protocol | An alternative data transport to TCP used for DNS, Voice over IP, and file sharing |
| HTTP | Hypertext Transfer Protocol | Exchanges information over the Web |
| FTP | File Transfer Protocol | Transfers files between local and remote host computers |
| POP | Post Office Protocol | Transfers mail from an e-mail server to a client Inbox |
| SMTP | Simple Mail Transfer Protocol | Transfers e-mail messages from client computers to an e-mail server |
| VoIP | Voice over Internet Protocol | Transmits voice conversations over the Internet |
| IRC | Internet Relay Chat | Transmits text messages in real time between online users |
| BitTorrent | BitTorrent | Distributes files using scattered clients rather than a server |

**How significant is TCP/IP?** **TCP/IP** is the primary protocol suite responsible for message transmission on the Internet. A **protocol suite** is a combination of protocols that work together. **TCP** (Transmission Control Protocol) breaks a message or file into packets. **IP** (Internet Protocol) is responsible for addressing packets so that they can be routed to their destination. From a practical perspective, TCP/IP provides a protocol standard for the Internet that is easy to implement, public, free, and extensible.

**Does the Internet use a special addressing scheme?** In the previous chapter, you learned that IP addresses can be assigned to LAN workstations. IP addresses originated on the Internet as part of the TCP/IP protocol. IP addresses are used to uniquely identify computers on the Internet as well as on LANs. In the context of the Internet, these addresses are sometimes referred to as TCP/IP addresses or Internet addresses.

**How do IP addresses work on the Internet?** Every device on the Internet has an assigned IP address, such as 204.127.129.1, divided into four octets by periods. The numbers in each octet correspond to network classes. For example, an IP address that begins with a number between 128 and 191 corresponds to a Class B network, such as a large college campus. When delivering a packet of data, Internet routers use the first octet to get a general idea of where to send the packet. The rest of the IP address is used to drill down to the exact destination.

**Do octets correspond to the parts of e-mail or Web site addresses?** E-mail addresses, such as *imastudent@uga.edu* and Web site addresses such as *http://www.uga.edu* seem to be separated into parts with periods, similar to the octets in an IP address. The octets do not, however, map to the parts of a Web site address or e-mail address. So, even though *http://www.uga.edu* has an IP address of 128.192.1.9, the first octet, 128, does not correspond to *http://*. Nor does the second octet, 192, map to *www*.

**Do I need a permanent IP address?** A computer can have a permanently assigned **static IP address** or a temporarily assigned **dynamic IP address**. As a general rule, computers on the Internet that act as servers use static IP addresses. Typically, ISPs, Web sites, Web hosting services, and e-mail servers that always need to be found at the same address require static IP addresses. Most other Internet users have dynamic IP addresses. Figure 6-6 illustrates a tool you can use to find your IP address.

**FIGURE 6-6**

You can find your current IP address using Web-based tools. If your computer is part of a LAN, the address will be the one for your LAN's router.

**Why doesn't everyone have a static IP address?** The use of 12-digit addresses such as 128.192.100.100 provides approximately 4.3 billion unique addresses, but many of these are reserved for special purposes and devices, leaving a meager number for the estimated 1.2 billion Internet users. To avoid running out of static IP addresses, dynamic addresses are used whenever possible. Dynamic IP addresses can be handed out as necessary and reused as needed.

**How do I get a dynamic IP address?** Every ISP controls a unique pool of IP addresses, which can be assigned to subscribers. If you have the type of Internet connection that requires a modem to make a telephone connection, for example, your ISP's DHCP server assigns a temporary IP address to your computer for use as long as it remains connected. When you end a session, that IP address goes back into a pool of addresses that can be distributed to other subscribers when they log in.

Your computer is rarely assigned the same dynamic IP address it had during a previous session. As an IP nomad with no permanent address, you can't feasibly run a Web site or perform other server-related activities on your computer. For example, if you try to run an online store, its address would change every time you connect to the Internet and customers would not be able to find it.

If you want to operate a server, your ISP should be able to supply you with a service plan that includes a static IP address and that will supply adequate bandwidth for server activity.

**How does a dynamic IP address relate to an always-on connection?** Most high-speed Internet connections use always-on technology. An **always-on connection** is linked to your ISP and is online whenever your computer and modem are on, even if you are not actively accessing the Internet. An always-on connection can have a static or dynamic IP address. With an always-on connection your dynamic IP address might seem like a static one because the address can remain the same unless you turn off your modem or your service provider has an outage.

Always-on connections are convenient. You don't have to wait for a connection to be established before using your browser or sending e-mail. If you have an always-on connection, however, you should be aware that it poses a security risk. With an always-on connection, your computer is connected to the Internet for long periods of time with the same IP address, making it particularly vulnerable to hackers. In Section E you'll learn how routers and firewalls can protect computers that have always-on Internet connections.

**What's a domain name?** Although IP addresses work for communication between computers, people find it difficult to remember long strings of numbers. Therefore, many Internet servers also have an easy-to-remember name, such as *nike.com*. The official term for this name is *fully qualified domain name (FQDN)*, but most people just refer to it as a **domain name**. By convention, you should type domain names using all lowercase letters.

A domain name is a key component of Web addresses, e-mail addresses, and addresses on the Web called URLs. It is the Web server name in a Web address and the e-mail server name in an e-mail address. For example, in the Web address *www.msu.edu/infotech*, the domain name is *msu.edu*. In the e-mail address *jbillings@msu.edu*, the domain name is also *msu.edu*.

A domain name ends with an extension that indicates its **top-level domain**. For example, in the domain name *msu.edu*, *edu* indicates that the computer is maintained by an educational institution. Some of the most commonly used top-level domains are listed in Figure 6-7.

**FIGURE 6-7**

Top-level Domains

| Domain | Description |
|--------|-------------|
| biz | Unrestricted use; usually for commercial businesses |
| com | Unrestricted use; usually for commercial businesses |
| edu | Restricted to North American educational institutions |
| gov | Restricted to U.S. government agencies |
| info | Unrestricted use |
| int | Restricted to organizations established by international treaties |
| mil | Restricted to U.S. military agencies |
| net | Unrestricted use; traditionally for Internet administrative organizations |
| org | Unrestricted use; traditionally for professional and nonprofit organizations |

Country codes also serve as top-level domains. Canada's top-level domain is ca; the United Kingdom's is uk; Australia's is au. A domain with growing popularity is tv. Originally assigned to the small Polynesian island of Tuvalu, the tv domain is marketed by a professional management team and is available for a fee to media-related Web sites.

How are domain names related to IP addresses? Every domain name corresponds to a unique IP address that has been entered into a huge database called the **Domain Name System** (DNS). Any computer that hosts this database is referred to as a **domain name server**. A domain name, such as *travelocity.com*, must be converted into an IP address before packets can be routed to it. For example, when you type *www.travelocity.com* into your browser, the browser's first step is to contact a domain name server to get the IP address for the Travelocity Web server, as shown in Figure 6-8.

**FIGURE 6-8**

A domain name request is routed through your ISP to your designated domain name server, which searches through its database to find a corresponding IP address. The IP address can then be attached to packets, such as requests for Web pages.

**Is www part of domain names?** No. Suppose that a corporation operates a server with an IP address of 192.150.18.61. The DNS links that address to the domain name *adobe.com*, not *www.adobe.com*. Prefixes such as *http://*, *www*, and *ftp* correspond to protocols, ports, and services offered by Internet computers.

A server can handle multiple tasks such as operating a corporate Web site, managing e-mail, and fulfilling FTP download requests. Each service uses a designated port. A **port** can be described as a virtual device because it is not a physical circuit or mechanism, but rather a conceptual or abstract concept that allows a computer to perform more than one type of service. Port 80, for example, typically corresponds to Web services, such as the corporate Web site. E-mail uses port 110. Ports 20 and 21 customarily host FTP downloads. A computer can have hundreds of ports.

When you enter *http://www.adobe.com* in a browser, the DNS gets your request as far as the *adobe.com* server. The server at *adobe.com* is listening to all the data packets that arrive. Packets sent to Web sites with URLs that begin *http://www* are handled by port 80, usually to display a Web page.

**Do I need my own domain name?** For client-style Internet activities, such as Web browsing, e-mail, and chat, you do not need your own domain name. You might, however, want a domain name if you plan to operate your own Web server or if you establish a Web site using servers provided by a Web site hosting service.

Suppose you decide to set up a Web site called Rocky Mountain Photos. For customers to access your site by typing *www.rockymtnphotos.com*, you must obtain the *rockymtnphotos.com* domain name. In contrast, if your Web site is set up on a Web server supplied by your ISP, your own domain name might not be necessary because you use the domain of the ISP's Web server. For example, if you set up your Rocky Mountain Photos site on AOL's Hometown Web server, its address might be *hometown.aol.com/rockymtnphotos*.

**INFOWEBLINKS**

Where can you register a domain name? What are the current fees? These questions are answered at the **Domain Name InfoWeb.**

CLICK TO CONNECT
www.course.com/np/concepts10/ch06

**How do I get a domain name?** An organization called **ICANN** (Internet Corporation for Assigned Names and Numbers) is recognized by the United States and other governments as the global organization that coordinates technical management of the Internet's Domain Name System. It supervises several for-profit Accredited Domain Registrars, which handle domain name requests.

The first step in registering a domain name is to find out whether the name is available. By connecting to an Accredited Domain Registrar Web site, you can enter a domain name, as shown in Figure 6-9.

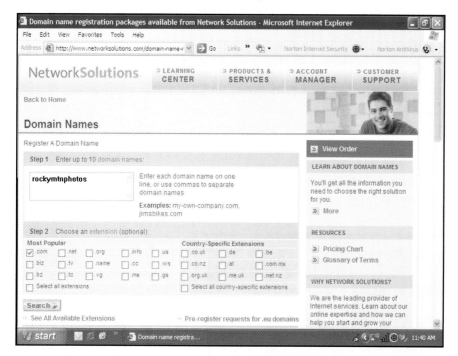

**FIGURE 6-9**

The first step in registering a domain name is to find out whether the name is currently in use or reserved for future use. If a domain name is not available, consider using a different top-level domain, such as biz instead of com. After you've found an available domain name, you can continue the registration process by filling out a simple online form.

CLICK TO START

**Is a fee required to obtain a domain name?** You can register a domain name for a minimal annual fee—currently between US$10 and $50, depending on the registration service.

Some domain names are not currently in use, yet they are not available because they are reserved. Internet entrepreneurs have made a business of registering high-profile domain names with the intention of reselling them. Some domain names carry price tags of over $500,000. Most domain name shoppers, however, can come up with a perfectly suitable domain name that's not reserved or in use.

## CONNECTION SPEED

**How fast is the Internet?** Data travels over the Internet at an incredible speed. On average, data within North America usually arrives at its destination in less than 1/10th of a second (100 ms) after it is sent. Data packets usually clip along the Internet backbone at blinding speeds. Data transport can slow down, however, when usage peaks during breaking news events, or when denial of service attacks break through security. Such slow-downs are temporary, however, and usually last only a few hours.

The elapsed time for data to make a round trip from point A to point B and back to point A is referred to as **latency**. Typically, latency averages 200 ms (milliseconds) or less in North America. Latency increases slightly for overseas transmissions. If you want to play online multiplayer games, it is best to have less than 100 ms latency. Good quality Voice over IP and videoconferencing require latency rates of 200 ms or less.

**Can I measure speed and latency?** You can run speed tests by linking to Internet-based utilities such as the Speakeasy Speed Test. You can also use a local Internet utility called **Ping** (Packet Internet Groper), which sends a signal to a specific Internet address and waits for a reply. If a reply arrives, Ping reports that the computer is online and displays the elapsed time for the round-trip message. You can use Ping before playing online games, using Voice over IP, or joining an online videoconference to make sure you have adequate speed for everything to run smoothly.

Ping also shows whether packets were lost in transmission. Packets can become lost when signal interference or network congestion overwhelms Internet servers and routers. Lost packets can cause jitter in Voice over IP communications and videoconferencing. Too many lost packets during an online gaming session can cause the game to stutter or stall. And if packets don't arrive in the correct order, your game character might seem to act randomly for a few seconds.

Another utility called **Traceroute** records a packet's path in addition to its round-trip speed. You can use Traceroute to analyze the latency of your data as it hops from one Internet router to the next. Figure 6-10 contains a Traceroute report.

**FIGURE 6-10**

In this example, Traceroute is used to monitor an Internet connection between a small lakeside cabin in northern Michigan and the HotWired Web site. The satellite connection has extremely high latency and timed out before the Web site could be accessed.

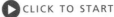

CLICK TO START

**How fast is a typical Internet connection?** The connection speeds you see advertised by ISPs refer to the amount of data that travels between a subscriber's computer and an ISP within a given time period. Connection speed is measured in Kbps (kilobits per second) or Mbps (megabits per second). The Internet connection speeds offered by various ISPs vary. Slow dial-up connections top out at 56 Kbps. High-speed (also called broadband) connections at 6000 Kbps (6 Mbps) are common. High-speed connections can display graphics quickly, show smoothly streaming video, handle net-based videoconferences, and deliver high-quality Voice over IP.

**What factors affect connection speed?** Your connection speed depends on whether you connect to your ISP using a telephone, cable television, satellite, or wireless link. Maximum speed can differ from actual speed because links are susceptible to interference that can hinder signals. Upstream speed can also differ from downstream speed.

**What are upstream and downstream speeds?** **Upstream speed** is the rate of data that is transmitted from your computer to the Internet. **Downstream speed** is the rate of data arriving at your computer. Many ISPs limit the speed of data flowing to and from their subscribers to make sure everyone gets an equal share of the bandwidth. In many cases, upstream speed is much slower than downstream speed.

When upstream speeds differ from downstream speeds, you have an **asymmetric Internet connection**. When upstream and downstream speeds are the same, you have a **symmetric Internet connection**. Asymmetric connections discourage subscribers from setting up Web and e-mail servers that would transmit lots of upstream data. For most users, however, an asymmetric connection is sufficient.

**What are my connection options?** Consumers have several options for connecting to the Internet. **Fixed Internet access** links your computer to an ISP from a stationary point, such as a wall socket or roof-mounted antenna. **Portable Internet access** allows you to easily move your access device, as in the case of vehicle-mounted satellite dishes that can be deployed when the vehicle is parked. **Mobile Internet access** allows you to use the Internet as you are on the go, such as using a cell phone to collect your e-mail while you are traveling by train.

You're not necessarily limited to a single Internet access option. Many consumers find it convenient to maintain fixed Internet access for home use, but use a portable or mobile method of Internet access while out and about. In Sections B and C you'll learn more about Internet access options.

> **TERMINOLOGY NOTE**
>
> In telecommunications, the term *asymmetric communications* refers to any system or device in which speed or quality differs between one direction and the other.

6

# QuickCheck

SECTION A

1. The Internet [_____] is a network of high-capacity communications links that provides the main routes for data traffic across the Internet.

2. An [_____] is a company that offers Internet access to individuals, businesses, and smaller ISPs. (Hint: Use the acronym.)

3. On the Internet, [_____] breaks a message into packets, and [_____] is responsible for addressing packets so that they can be routed to their destination.

4. Computers on the Internet that act as servers use [_____] IP addresses, whereas most other computers use [_____] IP addresses.

5. An Internet address, such as *msu.edu*, is called a fully qualified [_____] name.

6. The top-level domain for most schools and universities is [_____] .

7. When upstream speeds differ from downstream speeds, you have an asymmetrical Internet connection. True or false? [_____]

 CHECK ANSWERS

# Fixed Internet Access

ONE OF THE MOST challenging aspects of the Internet is selecting a service provider. In this section of the chapter, you'll learn about fixed Internet access, which is typically your main link to the Internet. You'll learn to evaluate the pros and cons of various fixed Internet options and discover why online interactive game players shun satellite Internet connections, but love cable Internet service. Plus, you'll find out which types of Internet access work best for Voice over IP.

## DIAL-UP CONNECTIONS

**What is a dial-up connection?** A **dial-up connection** is a fixed Internet connection that uses a voiceband modem and telephone lines to transport data between your computer and your ISP. Many ISPs, including AT&T Worldnet, AOL, and EarthLink offer dial-up Internet access. The service is typically less than $10 per month, but access speed is slow.

**How does a dial-up connection work?** When you use a dial-up connection, your computer's modem places a regular telephone call to your ISP. When the ISP's computer answers your call, a dedicated circuit is established between you and your ISP—just as though you had made a voice call and someone at the ISP had picked up the phone. The circuit remains connected for the duration of your call and provides a communications link that carries data between your computer and the ISP. As your data arrives at the ISP, a router sends it out over the Internet. Figure 6-11 illustrates the path of your data when you use a dial-up connection.

**FIGURE 6-11**

When you use an ISP to access the Internet, your data travels over local telephone lines to your ISP, which sends it onto the Internet.

Your computer and modem — Telephone wall jack — ISP's modem — ISP's router — ISP — To the Internet

**How does a voiceband modem work?** The signals that represent data bits exist in your computer as digital signals. The telephone system, however, expects to work with human voices, so it carries analog audio signals. A **voiceband modem**—usually referred to simply as a modem—converts the signals from your computer into signals that can travel over telephone lines. A modem transmits a 1,070 Hz tone for a 0 data bit and a 1,270 Hz tone for a 1 data bit.

When your computer's modem initiates a connection, it sends a signal that is equivalent to picking up the receiver of a telephone to get a dial tone. It then dials the ISP by emitting a series of tones—the same tones you'd produce if you punched in the ISP's number using a phone keypad. The modem then waits for the ISP's modem to answer the call. After the ISP's modem answers, the two modems begin to negotiate communications protocols, such as transmission rate. The series of beeps, tones, and whooshing sounds you hear when you connect to your ISP is the sound of your modem "talking" to the ISP's modem. This process of negotiation is sometimes called handshaking. When the negotiation is complete, data transmission can begin (Figure 6-12).

**FIGURE 6-12**

When you transmit data, your voiceband modem modulates the signal that carries your data. A modem at the other end of the transmission demodulates the signal.

Your computer generates a digital signal.

Your modem changes the digital signal into an analog audio signal.

The receiving modem converts the analog signal back into a digital signal.

### How fast is a voiceband modem?

Modem speeds are measured in bits per second. (If you're a stickler for details, you'll realize that bps is actually a measure of capacity, but everyone calls it speed.) Since 1998, most modems use a standard called V.90 to provide a theoretical maximum speed of 56 Kbps. Actual data transfer speeds are affected by factors such as the quality of your phone line and connection. Even with an excellent connection, however, a 56 Kbps modem tops out at about 44 Kbps.

Dial-up connections are asymmetrical; 44 Kbps is a typical downstream speed for a 56 Kbps modem. Upstream, the data rate drops to about 33 Kbps or less.

### Where can I get a voiceband modem?

Most computers have built-in voiceband modem circuitry. You can check the ports of your computer for one that accepts a standard telephone RJ-11 connector (Figure 6-13). Voiceband modems are also available for internal slots or external USB ports. To get connected, plug one end of a telephone cable into your computer's RJ-11 port and the other end into a telephone wall jack. Your computer's operating system typically includes configuration software. Your ISP will supply information, such as the dial-in number, for completing the configuration.

**FIGURE 6-13**

An RJ-11 port on your computer can be connected by cable to a telephone wall jack.

RJ-11 port

### Can I talk and send data at the same time?

When your computer is connected to your ISP over a dial-up connection, data is transmitted over the same frequencies normally used for voice conversations. If you have only one telephone line, you cannot pick up your telephone receiver, dial your friend, and carry on a voice conversation while you are sending data. Some modems use technology similar to call waiting that allows you to remain connected to your ISP and temporarily suspend data transfers while answering a voice call.

### Can I use an analog modem if my phone service is digital?

In many areas of the world, the telephone system uses digital rather than analog signals to send voice conversations. You can still use an analog modem because the sounds it emits are transported just as if they were voices. Digital telephone systems open up the possibilities for digital data transport options such as ISDN, DSL, and dedicated lines.

6

## DSL, ISDN, AND DEDICATED LINES

**What are the options for transporting digital data over telephone lines?** Although the standard equipment provided by telephone companies limits the amount of data you can transmit and receive over a voiceband modem, the telephone system's copper wire has a fair amount of capacity. Several services, such as ISDN, DSL, and dedicated lines take advantage of this capacity to offer high-speed digital communications links for voice and data.

**What is a dedicated line?** T1, T3, and T4 services are high-capacity dedicated lines that can be leased from the telephone company and are not shared by other customers. Speed ranges from 1.544 Mbps to 274 Mbps. These high-speed services are usually too expensive for individuals, but are leased by corporations and provide many of the links on the Internet backbone.

**What is ISDN? ISDN** (Integrated Services Digital Network) is a type of fixed Internet connection that moves data at speeds of 64 Kbps or 128 Kbps over ordinary telephone lines. Speed is symmetric, so you'll get the same data rates upstream as downstream. The service is usually obtained from a local telephone company or a dedicated ISDN service provider. ISDN availability and pricing vary from place to place.

**Do I need a modem for ISDN?** As with a dial-up connection, you use a telephone wall jack as your fixed point of connection, but instead of connecting your computer to a voiceband modem, you use a device called an **ISDN terminal adapter**, which sends digital signals. Although it is sometimes called an ISDN modem, a terminal adapter is not technically a modem because it doesn't modulate and demodulate the data signal. When installing ISDN, you typically receive an ISDN terminal adapter from your ISP (Figure 6-14).

**FIGURE 6-14**

ISDN requires a terminal adapter that can be added to an internal slot or USB port.

**Is an ISDN connection always on?** Basic ISDN service is like dial-up in that it makes a connection when you open a browser, e-mail, or other Internet applications, and disconnects when you've closed those applications. Connections are almost instantaneous, however, so ISDN users don't have to wait for lengthy dialing and handshaking as with dial-up connections. Some ISDN providers offer a service called always-on dynamic ISDN (AO/DI), which remains connected to an ISP as long as the computer and terminal adapter are on. Although AO/DI offers a slight performance enhancement, an always-on connection increases your computer's vulnerability to hackers.

**Why would I want ISDN?** ISDN allows you to use your telephone line for voice calls and transmit data at the same time. ISDN service is faster than dial-up. It is sometimes classified as high-speed Internet service, but it is not in the league of truly high-speed Internet connections, such as DSL and cable. If you have no other high-speed options, if ISDN is available, and if the price isn't too exorbitant, you might consider replacing your dial-up connection with ISDN.

**What is DSL? DSL** (digital subscriber line) is a high-speed, digital, always-on, Internet access technology that runs over standard phone lines. It is one of the fastest Internet connections that's affordable to individual consumers. Several variations of this technology exist, including ADSL (asymmetric DSL, with downstream speed faster than upstream speed), SDSL (symmetric DSL, with the same upstream and downstream speed), HDSL (high-rate DSL), VDSL (very high speed DSL), and DSL lite.

**TERMINOLOGY NOTE**

The acronym xDSL refers to the entire group of DSL technologies (including symmetric DSL, HDSL, and so on). xDSL is not a separate variation of DSL.

**How does DSL work?** Data is transmitted to and from your local telephone switching station in pure digital form, bypassing the bottleneck of analog-to-digital-to-analog conversion and escaping the requirement to use the narrow bandwidth allocated to voice transmissions. The result is fast data transmission over standard copper telephone cable.

DSL uses some fairly sophisticated technology to superimpose digital signals over the unused frequency spectrum of an ordinary telephone line. A DSL connection can simultaneously carry voice and data, if permitted by your DSL provider. Voice and data signals travel over telephone lines to your telephone company's local switching station. There, the voice signals are separated from the data signals. Voice signals are routed to the regular telephone system; data signals are routed to your ISP and then to the Internet (Figure 6-15).

**INFOWEBLINKS**

Nationwide, DSL vendors are grouping and regrouping. How might this affect your Internet access? You'll find up-to-date consumer information at the **DSL InfoWeb**.

 CLICK TO CONNECT
www.course.com/np/concepts10/ch06

**FIGURE 6-15**

Voice and data signals travel over DSL to a special device at the local telephone switching station, where they are divided and routed to an ISP or to the regular telephone network.

**6**

**How fast is DSL?** The speed of a DSL connection varies according to the characteristics of your telephone line and your distance from the telephone company's switching station. Current DSL technology can transport data at speeds up to 6 Mbps downstream for a distance of about 1.25 miles (2 km). DSL signals deteriorate over distance, however. For DSL to work, your connection has to be within about 3 miles (5 km) of your telephone company's switching station. The distance requirement only pertains to the distance between you and the switching station. Once the signal arrives at the switch and is handed off to the ISP, it can travel the Internet backbone anywhere in the world.

**How do I get DSL service?** In many areas, DSL is a joint venture between the telephone company and an ISP. The telephone company is responsible for physical cabling and voice transmission. An ISP is responsible for data traffic. Some DSL installations require trained service technicians, whereas others can be handled by consumers. Prior to installation, you can contact your telephone company to find out if DSL is available in your area. Your DSL service provider will supply you with instructions for the installation.

**Do I need special equipment for DSL?** DSL installations typically require a modem and filters (Figure 6-16). DSL is digital, so data doesn't need to be changed into analog signals and then back to digital as it does when you use a dial-up connection. DSL signals have to be modulated, however, so they can travel on non-voice frequencies. A **DSL modem** is a device that connects a computer to a telephone line and converts computer data signs into signals compatible with DSL.

**DSL filters** prevent voiceband signals from interfering with DSL signals. Professionally installed business DSL systems typically use a single external filter. Self-installed DSL kits provide filters that you connect to every device in your home that uses the telephone line.

**FIGURE 6-16**

DSL Equipment

A DSL filter is essentially a line extension. For example to filter a telephone, unplug the phone, plug the filter into the wall jack, and plug the phone cable into the filter.

A DSL modem plugs into your computer's USB or Ethernet port.

## CABLE INTERNET SERVICE

**What is cable Internet service?** **Cable Internet service** is a means of distributing always-on broadband Internet access over the same infrastructure that offers cable television service. Local and national cable companies, such as Comcast, Cox, and Charter, offer cable Internet service for a monthly subscription. Of all Internet services, cable Internet currently offers the fastest access speeds.

**How does cable Internet service work?** The cable television system was originally designed for remote areas where TV broadcast signals could not be received in an acceptable manner with an antenna. These systems were called community antenna television, or CATV. The CATV concept was to install one or more large, expensive satellite dishes in a community, catch TV signals with these dishes, and then send the signals over a system of cables to individual homes.

The topology of a CATV system looks a lot like the physical topology for a computer network. And that is just what is formed when your cable TV company becomes your Internet provider. Your computer becomes part of a neighborhood LAN joined by wiring for the cable TV infrastructure.

**Are television and data signals carried over the same cable?** CATV coaxial and fiber optic cables have plenty of bandwidth to carry television signals for hundreds of channels in addition to digital data. CATV cables provide bandwidth for television signals, incoming data signals, and outgoing data signals (Figure 6-17).

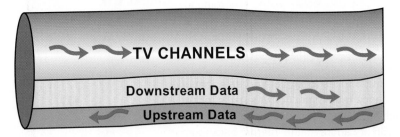

**How fast is cable Internet service?** Most cable Internet service is asymmetric, with upstream speeds considerably slower than downstream speeds to discourage subscribers from setting up public Web servers. A standard home service plan offers 6 Mbps (6000 Kbps) downstream and 384 Kbps upstream. Some premium plans offer speedier connections of 30 Mbps downstream and 2 Mbps upstream.

Cable signals are not particularly vulnerable to environmental interference, but data transport speeds are affected by subscriber use. The cable you share with your neighbors has a certain amount of bandwidth. As more and more neighbors use the service, it might seem to get slower and slower. As an analogy, consider the luggage conveyor belt in an airport, which moves at a constant speed. If you have three pieces of luggage and you are the only passenger on the plane, your bags arrive one right after another. However, if you just arrived on a full 747, your bags are intermixed with those of hundreds of other passengers, and it takes longer to collect them.

Your cable company's network carries packets at a constant speed. However, if many of your neighbors are sending and receiving packets at the same time, your packets seem to arrive more slowly. Cable Internet subscribers often find that their connection speed varies quite dramatically.

**FIGURE 6-17**

A CATV cable has enough bandwidth to support TV channels and data flowing downstream as well as data flowing upstream.

**Do I need special equipment for cable Internet service?** When you set up your computer for cable Internet service, you are essentially linking to the cable network's Ethernet-style LAN that connects a neighborhood of cable subscribers. The two requirements for this type of connection are circuitry to handle Ethernet protocols and a **cable modem**, which converts your computer's signal into one that can travel over the CATV network.

Most subscribers rent a cable modem from their cable company, and the rental fee is included in the monthly bill. Third-party cable modems manufactured by LinkSys, Motorola, DLink, and other companies can be purchased from electronic stores, but it is a good idea to check your cable company first to make sure the modem you select is compatible.

A cable modem can plug directly into a coaxial cable wall jack. If you need to connect your cable set-top box and cable modem to a single wall jack you can use a cable splitter as shown in Figure 6-18.

Cable wall jack

Television or set-top box

Cable splitter

Cable modem

**FIGURE 6-18**

If your home has only one CATV cable outlet, you need to use a splitter to link it to your cable modem and television. If you have multiple cable outlets, you can connect your cable modem directly to any one of them.

6

Most cable modems have USB and Ethernet ports, and you can use one or the other. Cable companies instruct subscribers to connect the modem directly to a computer. However, as you'll learn in the Internet Security section, the safest way to connect your computer to a cable modem is through a router.

**How secure are cable Internet connections?** In the early days of cable Internet service, some cable Internet subscribers were unpleasantly surprised when they happened to open Windows Network Neighborhood, only to be greeted with a list of their neighbors' computers! When you boot a PC, Windows automatically connects to available LANs and looks for shared files, folders, and printers on LAN workstations. Because cable Internet service uses LAN technology, computers in different households were treated as workstations on a shared LAN.

Today, most cable companies use DOCSIS-compliant cable modems that block crossover traffic between subscribers. **DOCSIS** (Data Over Cable Service Interface Specification) is a data transport technology that includes security filters. DOCSIS secures your computer from your neighbors, but it does not close up all the security holes that are opened when you use an always-on connection.

## SATELLITE INTERNET SERVICE

**What is satellite Internet service?** Most people are familiar with services that provide access to television programming over a personal satellite dish. Many companies that provide satellite TV also offer Internet access. **Satellite Internet service** is a means of distributing always-on, high-speed asymmetric Internet access by broadcasting signals to and from a personal satellite dish. In many rural areas, satellite Internet service is the only alternative to a dial-up connection.

**How does satellite Internet service work?** Satellite Internet service uses a geostationary satellite to transmit computer data directly to and from a satellite dish owned by an individual (Figure 6-19).

**FIGURE 6-19**

Satellite Internet services use geostationary satellites to transmit data between subscribers and ISPs.

Of all the Internet access services, satellite has the farthest range and ability to reach remote areas. Whereas ISDN and DSL services are limited to within several miles of a telephone company switching station, and cable Internet service is limited to areas where cable television is offered, satellite Internet service can be beamed to any customers whose property offers an unobstructed view of the orbiting satellite—in the U.S. that means an unobstructed view of the southern sky.

**How fast is satellite Internet service?** Satellite service typically averages 400–500 Kbps actual downstream speed but only 100–256 Kbps upstream. Satellite transmission and reception can be slowed or blocked by adverse weather conditions, such as rain and snow, which makes this type of data transport less reliable than wired Internet access services, such as cable and DSL.

Satellite data transport is subject to latency delays of one second or more, which occur as your data is routed between your computer and a satellite that orbits 22,200 miles above the Earth. Latency might not pose much of a problem for general Web surfing and downloading files, but it can become a showstopper for interactive gaming that requires quick reactions, and for Voice over IP.

As with cable Internet service, satellite data transport speeds might seem to decline when other users subscribe to the service because the satellite's bandwidth is shared among all users.

**TERMINOLOGY NOTE**

Communications satellites in geostationary orbits move in synchronization with the Earth's rotation and always appear to be in the same location of the sky.

**INFOWEBLINKS**

The **Satellite InfoWeb** dishes out lots of goodies about satellite Internet access—the technology, service providers, prices, and even reviews from disgruntled computer game players.

 CLICK TO CONNECT
www.course.com/np/concepts10/ch06

**Does satellite Internet service require special equipment?** A satellite dish and modem are the two pieces of equipment required for satellite Internet access. If you are already receiving satellite television and your service provider offers Internet services, you can most likely use your current satellite dish. Most consumer satellite dishes used in the northern hemisphere are fixed in one position and 18–31 inches (46–79 cm) in diameter, as shown in Figure 6-20.

**FIGURE 6-20**

Today's satellite dishes are small and can be easily mounted on roofs or exterior walls.

A **satellite modem** (Figure 6-21) is a device that modulates the data signals from a computer into a frequency band that can be carried to the satellite dish where it is converted to another frequency, amplified, and transmitted. The modem usually connects to the satellite dish using two coaxial cables: one to transmit and one to receive. The modem then can be connected to the Ethernet port of a computer, or for better security to an Ethernet port of a router.

Equipment and installation costs for satellite Internet service are higher than other Internet services. Some companies charge US$500 or more for a satellite dish, though the cost is often spread over a 2–3 year service contract.

**FIGURE 6-21**

A satellite modem looks similar to cable and DSL modems, but is designed for entirely different technology.

6

## FIXED WIRELESS SERVICE

**What is fixed wireless Internet service?** **Fixed wireless Internet service** (also called wireless broadband service) is designed to offer Internet access to homes and businesses by broadcasting data signals over areas large enough to cover most cities and outlying areas. Fixed wireless technologies are MAN (metropolitan area network) standards, in contrast to technologies such as Wi-Fi, which are LAN (local area network) standards. One of the most well-known fixed wireless standards is WiMAX, currently offered in the U.S. by companies such as Clearwire and in the UK by companies such as iAirWorks.

**What is WiMAX?** **WiMAX**, which stands for Worldwide Interoperability for Microwave Access, is an Ethernet-compatible network standard designated as IEEE 802.16. Its popularity is growing because it offers an alternative to wired technologies, such as DSL and cable Internet service, that require expensive infrastructures. WiMAX can be deployed in rural areas where cable service is not available and where customers are too far away from a telephone switching station for DSL service. In an urban environment, WiMAX can offer healthy competition to other Internet service providers.

**How does WiMAX work?** A WiMAX system transmits data to and from WiMAX antennas mounted on towers. A single tower can serve a large geographical area—up to 3,000 square miles (about 8,000 square KM). Towers can transmit data to subscribers, they can relay data to other towers using microwave links, and they can connect directly to the Internet backbone by cable. Within 3 miles/8 km of the tower, signals are strong enough to be picked up by subscribers on a non-line-of-sight device, similar to a Wi-Fi access point. Beyond that range, a line-of-sight antenna is required (Figure 6-22).

**What is the speed of WiMAX?** Under ideal conditions, WiMAX can transmit data at 70 Mbps. Actual speed, however, is affected by distance, weather, and usage. Current services claim speeds of 1.5–3 Mbps downstream. WiMAX can be distributed as symmetrical or asymmetrical service.

Fixed wireless technologies have less latency than satellite Internet service and can usually offer connection speeds suitable for online gaming, Voice over IP, and teleconferencing.

**What equipment do I need for WiMAX access?** Your wireless service provider typically supplies a wireless modem that you connect to your computer. The modem includes a transceiver to send and receive signals to a wireless point of access, usually located on a nearby communications tower. Subscribers on the outlying edges of the network's range might also require an antenna mounted on a window or roof, and line-of-sight range to the WiMAX tower.

### INFOWEBLINKS

The **WiMAX InfoWeb** has the latest information on this up-and-coming Internet access technology.

CLICK TO CONNECT
www.course.com/np/concepts10/ch06

**FIGURE 6-22**

A WiMAX tower broadcasts signals over a wide area. Subscribers close to the tower can use non-line-of-sight modems to pick up the signal.

## FIXED INTERNET CONNECTION ROUNDUP

**What's the best Internet connection for my PC?** The best Internet connection depends on your budget, what's available in your area, and what you do while connected. For fixed Internet access, cable Internet service is usually the first choice, when available. If cable Internet service is not available, or proves slower or less dependable than expected, the next choice would be DSL or fixed wireless service, if available.

If several fixed Internet services are offered in your area, the table in Figure 6-23 can help you evaluate their requirements, costs, advantages, and disadvantages.

**FIGURE 6-23**

Fixed Internet Access Options

| | Dial-up | ISDN | DSL | Cable | Satellite | WiMAX |
|---|---|---|---|---|---|---|
| **Downstream speed (max)** | 56 Kbps | 128 Kbps | 384 Kbps– 6 Mbps | 1.5–6 Mbps | 500 Kbps | 70 Mbps |
| **Upstream speed (max)** | 33 Kbps | 128 Kbps | 128 Kbps– 6 Mbps | 256–768 Kbps | 40–60 Kbps | 70 Mbps |
| **Downstream speed (actual)** | 44 Kbps | 128 Kbps | 2 Mbps | 3 Mbps | 400 Kbps | 1.5–3 Mbps |
| **Latency** | 100–200 ms | 10–30 ms | 10–20 ms | 10–20 ms | 1–3 seconds | 10–50 ms |
| **Short video (72 MB) download** | 4 hours | 78 minutes | 5 minutes | 3.2 minutes | 24 minutes | 6.4 minutes |
| **Requirements** | Telephone line, ISP, voiceband modem | Telephone line, ISDN service, ISDN terminal adapter | Computer located within 3 miles of local telephone switch; DSL modem | CATV service that provides Internet access; cable modem | Clear view of southern sky; satellite dish and modem | WiMAX modem, line-of-sight to WiMAX tower for distances > 3 miles |
| **Monthly fee** | $5–$25 | $50–$150 | $30–$200 | $20–$50 | $35–$80 | $0–$60 |
| **Installation cost** | $0 | $0–$200 | $0–$100 | $0–$50 | $200–$300 | $50–$150 |
| **Always-on** | N | N | Y | Y | Y | Y |

# QuickCheck

1. A _____ modem converts the signals from your computer into signals that can travel over telephone lines.

2. Always-on connections include dial-up, DSL, cable, and dedicated lines. True or false? _____

3. The two requirements for cable Internet service are circuitry to handle _____ protocols and a cable modem.

4. Satellite Internet service typically has a high _____ rate, which is unsuitable for some online gaming and Voice over IP.

5. _____ , which adheres to IEEE 802.16 standards, is one of the most promising fixed wireless Internet technologies.

▶ CHECK ANSWERS

# Portable and Mobile Internet Access

**WHEN YOU'RE ON THE GO** and away from your fixed Internet connection you are not necessarily cut off from your e-mail and other Internet activities. Portable and mobile Internet technologies can provide Internet access while you visit friends, commute to work or school, or take a vacation. In Section C, you'll find out what's available for portable and mobile access today and what's on the drawing board for the future.

## INTERNET TO GO

**What are the limitations of fixed Internet access?** Fixed Internet access through dial-up, cable, ISDN, DSL, satellite, and 802.16 WiMAX tether your computer to a tangle of cables and equipment, such as modems, satellite dishes, and antennas. It can be a hassle even to relocate your Internet modem to another room.

In the days when bulky desktop computers were the norm, a fixed Internet connection seemed sensible. Today, however, with the proliferation of sleek notebook computers, PDAs, and other portable computing appliances, Internet users are clamoring for the freedom to roam while accessing online information and services.

Suppose that you're on vacation and you want to download music for your iPod. What if you're visiting a friend across town and you want to get your e-mail? If you drop into your local video rental store with only your cell phone, can you access the Internet Movie Database to scan some reviews before you select a movie? If you're on a cross-country trip, would you be able to boot up your computer, access the MapQuest Web site, and give the driver directions to the nearest Cracker Barrel restaurant? (See Figure 6-24.)

**FIGURE 6-24**

Using mobile Internet access, you could find the location of the nearest roadside eatery.

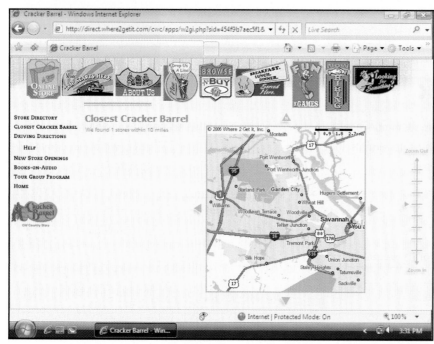

These scenarios are all possible, but not necessarily using a single Internet service provider, user account, or computer. Today's state-of-the-art is not an ideal "Internet anywhere" technology that allows you to use one Internet service and any digital device to tap into the global pool of Internet data from any location. Instead, Internet consumers have to contend with a hodgepodge of technologies, multiple accounts, and an unfortunate number of user fees for blanket Internet access.

Although the ideal Internet everywhere service has not yet arrived, looking at currently available portable and mobile Internet access options is worthwhile. Depending on your lifestyle, one or more of these options could be beneficial, productive, or just plain fun.

**What is portable Internet access?** Portable Internet access can be defined as the ability to easily move your Internet service from one location to another. It is portable in the sense that a hot plate is portable. It is light and compact enough to easily carry, even though it has to be plugged into an electrical outlet when you want to use it. Portable Internet access services include Wi-Fi, portable satellite, and portable wireless.

**What is mobile Internet access?** Mobile Internet access offers a continuous Internet connection as you are walking or riding in a bus, car, train, or plane. It is very similar in concept to cellular phone service that allows you to move freely within the coverage area as it seamlessly hands-off your signal from one tower to the next. Mobile Internet access includes Wi-Fi, mobile WiMAX, and cellular broadband service.

Let's take a look at some of the most popular and promising portable and mobile Internet access technologies.

## WI-FI HOTSPOTS

**How does Wi-Fi fit in with the Internet everywhere concept?** As you learned in the previous chapter, Wi-Fi is a wireless LAN technology. In addition to being popular for home networks, Wi-Fi is also used for public networks, operated by merchants, hotels, schools, and municipalities. If your computer is equipped for Wi-Fi, as are most of today's notebooks, you have a portable means of accessing the Internet by carrying your computer to any Wi-Fi hotspot (Figure 6-25).

**What is a Wi-Fi hotspot?** A **Wi-Fi hotspot** is an area in which the public can access a Wi-Fi network that offers Internet service. You can find hotspots in coffee shops, RV parks, hotels, community centers, and airports. Wi-Fi hotspot availability is currently limited, but expanding even in small towns and rural areas. Web sites such as *www.wi-fihotspotlist.com* help you find Wi-Fi hotspots in a specific city.

**How do Wi-Fi hotspots work?** In a typical scenario, you might take your notebook computer—equipped with a Wi-Fi card—to your local Starbucks cafe. You buy a cup of cappuccino, sit down in a comfortable chair, and switch on your computer. Windows networking utilities automatically sense a Wi-Fi network and establish a connection. You can then surf the Web, just as though you were at home using a connection supplied by your desktop ISP.

Some Wi-Fi hotspots offer free service; others require a service plan or one-time use fee. Companies that offer hotspot service plans include T-Mobile, Verizon, Sprint, and AT&T Wireless. Hotspot service plans are not interchangeable. You cannot, for example, access a T-Mobile hotspot if you have a Verizon Wi-Fi Access service plan. Access plans can be expensive, too.

**FIGURE 6-25**

Starbucks Wi-Fi hotspots offer wireless Internet access to customers with T-Mobile accounts.

Daily plans for 24 hours of access run US$4–$10. Monthly unlimited access costs about the same as basic cell phone service.

**Can I use hotspots for mobile Internet access?** Wi-Fi does not typically provide acceptable mobile Internet access because you can only remain connected within range of the network's hotspot. Wi-Fi hand-offs from one Wi-Fi network to another are clumsy and prone to packet loss, which is unacceptable for Voice over IP or streaming video applications. Although the IEEE has been working on standards for mobile Wi-Fi (sometimes called Mobile-Fi) protocols, new developments in WiMAX might make mobile enhancements to Wi-Fi unnecessary. The current model for using most Wi-Fi hotspots is that you enter the area of coverage, find a location with a strong signal, and remain there while accessing the Internet.

**How fast is hotspot access?** The speed of a hotspot is related to the speed of the wired line that connects it to the Internet. A hotspot that goes through a 1 Mbps DSL line will be slower than a hotspot that goes through a 6 Mbps cable Internet connection. Hotspot providers such as Verizon advertise peak speeds of 1.5 Mbps. Actual speed can vary depending on your distance from the access point, the number of people logged in, and interference from other networks.

**Is hotspot access secure?** Hotspots are as insecure as any wireless connection, so it is important for hotspot users to take steps to secure their computers with anti-virus software, firewalls, and encryption.

## PORTABLE AND MOBILE WIMAX

**What is portable WiMAX?** WiMAX can be used as a portable technology because Internet access is available to subscribers anywhere within a tower's coverage area. WiMAX subscribers who use non-line-of-sight modems with an integrated antenna (Figure 6-26) can easily move their Internet service by relocating their modems anywhere within the service provider's coverage area. One WiMAX service provider encourages its customers to "Just plug in and jump online anywhere within the service area."

WiMAX-equipped computers make portable Internet access even easier. Just as many notebook computers are equipped with Wi-Fi circuitry, manufacturers can also add WiMAX circuitry and antennas, eliminating the need for an external modem.

**What are the pros and cons of portable WiMAX?** The big bonus of portable WiMAX is that you use the same Internet service provider whether you are at home or on the road. You do not need supplemental service contracts or day passes as you do for Wi-Fi hotspots. On the downside, WiMAX is not yet in widespread use and therefore coverage is limited.

**What about mobile WiMAX?** Mobile WiMAX is an up-and-coming standard destined to be deployed by ISPs and cell phone carriers because it is designed to offer Internet access with seamless handoff from the coverage area or one tower to the coverage area of another tower. Mobile WiMAX could make it possible for you to deal with a single service provider for all your cell phone and Internet access needs.

**FIGURE 6-26**

WiMAX modems are easy to transport and can be plugged in anywhere within the coverage area of a WiMAX tower.

## PORTABLE SATELLITE SERVICE

**What if I travel to remote areas?** WiMAX and Wi-Fi hotspots provide coverage in cities and small towns, but do not typically extend far into sparsely populated areas. If you plan to remain in a single remote location, then fixed satellite Internet service is a good option. If, however, Internet access is required as you travel to various remote locations to hike, ski, or conduct research, then portable satellite technology is available (Figure 6-27).

**How does portable satellite technology work?** For portable satellite Internet service, a satellite dish is typically mounted on a vehicle. The disk is stowed while the vehicle is in motion, but can be quickly deployed when the vehicle stops.

Like a fixed satellite dish, a portable dish transmits signals to and receives signals from a geostationary satellite. If a fixed satellite dish moves out of alignment, signals can no longer be captured dependably. The challenge with mobile satellite service is to make sure the dish is correctly aimed from whatever location it is used.

Portable satellite systems have self-aiming hardware that automatically deploys the dish and rotates it until it locks onto the satellite signal (Figure 6-28).

**FIGURE 6-27**

Portable satellites are perfect for RVs and trucks, but remain a pricey technology.

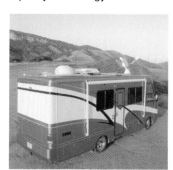

**FIGURE 6-28**

A vehicle-mounted satellite dish can be deployed from a control panel inside the vehicle.

CLICK TO START

**How fast is portable satellite service?** Portable satellite service providers advertise downstream speeds of 400–2000 Kbps and upstream speeds of 50–500 Kbps. Larger dishes offer faster speeds.

**What is the cost of portable satellite service?** Portable satellite service doesn't work with tight budgets. Hardware, which incudes the satellite dish, deployment mechanics, satellite modem, and interior control panel, can cost US$5,000–10,000. Hardware costs do not include installation, which has to be done by a professional according to FCC regulations. Monthly service fees range from US$100–300.

## CELLULAR DATA SERVICES

**How can I use my cell phone service to access the Internet?**
In many countries, including the U.S., cell phone coverage is extensive
and the technology is truly mobile; you can use cell phone service while
walking or in a moving vehicle. The handoff as you travel from one cell to
another is seamless. Using cell phone technology to access the Internet
offers mobility that is not yet possible with most of today's wired or wireless
computer network technologies. And though in the past cellular-based
Internet access was slower than dial-up, new technologies offer speeds
that are more competitive with other broadband offerings.

**How fast is cellular data transport?** Data transport rates depend on
the technology of the cellular system. Cellular technology is classified by
generation. First-generation (1G) technology is analog and offers few features beyond voice communications. Digital third-generation (3G)
technologies offered by today's cellular service providers offer higher
capacity for voice and data.

Within each generation are technology subcategories, such as CDMA,
GSM, and GPRS. You can see from Figure 6-29 that 2.5G technology offers
speeds equivalent to a 56 Kbps dial-up modem. 3G technologies have
speeds similar to satellite Internet service, and can potentially match DSL
speeds.

**FIGURE 6-29**

Cellular Network Technologies

| Generation | Service | Speed * | Features |
|---|---|---|---|
| 1G | APMS | N/A | Analog voice service<br>No data service |
| 2G | CDMA<br>PDC<br>GSM | 14.4 Kbps<br>9.6 Kbps<br>9.6–14.4 Kbps | Digital voice service<br>9.6 Kbps–14.4 Kbps speed<br>Enhanced calling features,<br>    such as caller ID<br>No always-on data connection |
| 2.5G | GPRS | 56–114 Kbps | Adds always-on data transfers<br>    at 171.2 Kbps to CDMA,<br>    TDMA, and GSM networks |
| 3G | UTMS<br>EDGE<br>EV-DO<br>HSUPA | 2 Mbps<br>384 Kbps<br>2.4 M<br>5.76 Mbps | Superior digital voice service<br>Broadband multimedia data<br>    services |

\* Maximum theoretical speed; actual speeds are slower

**Can I get to the Internet from any cell phone?** Most cellular service providers offer e-mail and Internet services. Basic phones can access a limited number of specially designed Web sites using WAP.

**What is WAP? WAP** (Wireless Access Protocol) is a communications protocol that provides Internet access from handheld devices, such as cell phones. WAP-enabled devices contain a microbrowser that displays simplified versions of popular Web sites, such as CNN, Google, Yahoo!, MSN, ESPN, UPS, FedEx, The Weather Channel, MapQuest, and Moviefone. WAP devices also include e-mail software formatted for small, low-resolution screens (Figure 6-30).

**Can I use a cell phone to access regular Web sites and use other Internet services?** Accessing the "real" Internet requires a different approach than offered by WAP. For the real Internet, cellular service providers offer data services, sometimes referred to as **mobile broadband**. Broadband access requires a fast connection, a data service subscription, and mobile broadband equipment.

**What are the fastest cellular technologies?** The fastest cellular technologies for Internet access are EDGE, EV-DO, and HSUPA.

**EDGE** (Enhanced Data rates for Global Evolution) is a 3G technology that works on GSM and GPRS cellular networks. EDGE can carry data at speeds up to 236 Kbps. Cingular, CellularOne, and T-Mobile are among the carriers in the U.S. that offer their subscribers EDGE technology for Internet access.

**EV-DO** (Evolution Data Optimized) is a 3G technology developed by Qualcomm and currently deployed by Alltel, Sprint, and Verizon in major U.S. markets. For mobile access, EV-DO offers average speeds of 400–700 Kbps, with peak speeds up to 2 Mbps.

**HSUPA** (High-speed Uplink Packet Access) is a 3.5G technology with theoretical maximum speeds in excess of 5 Mbps. Cingular is upgrading its EDGE technology to HSUPA in major markets.

Broadband speeds are not available in all of a cellular service provider's coverage area. Coverage maps can give you an idea of the service area, but actual coverage and speeds can vary. Where broadband coverage is not available, your device might operate at a much slower speed or might not have access to data services.

**What is a data service plan?** Most cellular service providers offer a data service plan for accessing the Internet. Prices for these plans fluctuate, but can range from $30 per month and up. Less expensive plans typically limit the amount of data you can send and receive, treating megabytes like minutes. Make sure you understand the terms of your service contract. Some service contracts prohibit users from streaming or downloading music, movies, or games; making Voice over IP phone calls; and using file-sharing networks.

**What equipment do I need for mobile broadband Internet access?** With a data service plan, there are four ways to take advantage of mobile broadband: using a PDA, using a mobile broadband card in a PC, using a mobile broadband-enabled computer, or using a cell phone as a modem for your desktop or notebook computer.

**FIGURE 6-30**

The advantage of WAP-enabled devices is their portability. The disadvantage is their small, low-res screens. Although various schemes for scrolling over a full-sized Web page have been tried, most WAP users stick to Web sites specially designed for small screen devices.

6

**How do I access the Internet with a PDA?** You can use a cellular-ready PDA, such as Palm Treo, Blackberry, HP iPAQ, or Dell Axim to directly access the Internet (Figure 6-31). These devices typically include browser and e-mail software.

You can use the PDA's QWERTY keyboard or stylus to manipulate on-screen icons for opening software, operating menus, and clicking links. Many of these devices use Windows Mobile OS, so the controls are similar to those on your desktop or notebook computer.

Although the screen on a PDA has much higher resolution than the screen on a basic WAP-enabled phone, it is not large enough to display most Internet services and Web pages at their normal size. To avoid excessive scrolling, you can use a service such as Skweezer (*www.skweezer.com*) to reformat Web pages to fit on your small PDA screen (Figure 6-32).

**FIGURE 6-31**

Many PDAs offer a large color screen and can connect to Wi-Fi hotspots and cellular data services to access the Internet.

**FIGURE 6-32**

Skweezer and similar utilities shrink and reformat Web pages so that they fit on small screens.

▶ CLICK TO START

Web page displayed on a computer screen

Web site displayed on a small screen using skweezer

**How do I access the Internet with a cellular wireless modem?** Most cellular service providers offer wireless modems compatible with EDGE, EV-DO, or HSUPA technology (Figure 6-33). The modem slides into the PC card slot of your notebook computer and is installed following the manufacturer's instructions.

After the card has been installed, you can use it to connect to the Internet and use your usual set of tools, including your Web browser and e-mail software. With a full-size screen, you'll have the "real" Internet experience.

**What is a mobile broadband-enabled computer?** Just as many notebook computers come with Wi-Fi circuitry for accessing wireless LANs and hotspots, some manufacturers offer notebook computers with built-in EDGE, EV-DO, or HSUPA circuitry for mobile broadband access. Although these configurations reduce installation hassles, they are not in demand because they limit consumers to one mobile broadband technology and its corresponding cellular service provider.

**How do I use a phone as a modem?** Some cell phones connect to your computer and act as a wireless modem to transmit data over the Internet. Data speed depends on the phone's technology. A GSM/GPRS phone transmits data at a much slower speed than an EDGE, EV-DO, or HSUPA phone.

To make the connection, obtain a data cable that's compatible with your phone from your cellular service provider or an electronics outlet. Follow the manufacturer's instructions for installing the cable and setting up a modem connection. When you want to access the Internet, plug your cellular phone into your computer (Figure 6-34) and connect through your mobile data service. As with other connection options for desktop and notebook computers, you can use your usual suite of Internet software.

**FIGURE 6-33**

A cellular wireless modem slides into a notebook computer's PC slot.

**FIGURE 6-34**

Using a data cable such as CellularOne's QuickLink, your cellular phone can become a modem for your notebook computer.

6

# QuickCheck

1. _____ Internet access can be defined as the ability to easily move your Internet service from one location to another.

2. A Wi-Fi _____ is an area in which the public can access a Wi-Fi network that offers Internet service.

3. Mobile _____ is an up-and-coming standard destined to be deployed by ISPs and cell phone carriers because it is designed to

offer Internet access with seamless handoff from the coverage area or one tower to the coverage area of another tower.

4. _____ is a protocol that provides Internet access from handheld devices with limited screen size and a cell phone-style keypad.

5. EV-DO, _____, and HSUPA are examples of mobile broadband Internet services.

CHECK ANSWERS

# Internet Services

**WHEN YOU HAVE** an Internet connection, you have access to a global data communications system. You know that protocols such as TCP/IP and UDP handle basic data transport, but additional protocols, sometimes referred to as application protocols, make possible a variety of useful Internet applications, such as real-time messaging, Voice over IP, grid computing, FTP, and file sharing. Section D explains how these applications work.

## REAL-TIME MESSAGING

**What is real-time messaging?** A networked-based **real-time messaging system** allows people to exchange short messages while they are online. One-on-one messaging is referred to as **instant messaging** (IM) and group communications are referred to as **chat**.

Everyday, millions of people use messaging systems, such as AOL Instant Messenger, Yahoo! Messenger, Google Talk, Apple iChat, and Windows Live Messenger, to communicate with friends, family, and coworkers. Some systems offer voice messaging options, so that participants can speak to each other using computer-based microphones. Video messaging is another option offered by some systems when both participants have computer-based cameras.

**How does real-time messaging work?** Most messaging is based on a client/server model that uses a server to handle communication packets between the participants (clients). When participants log on, they connect to the messaging server, which authenticates their user IDs and passwords. The server then sends back a list of participants or buddies. For a chat room, "participants" are those people who are currently logged into the discussion. For instant messaging, "buddies" are people in a participant's list of friends who are currently online.

Messages are typed into client software (Figure 6-35), which uses messaging protocols to break the message into packets and ship them to the server for distribution or directly to the recipient, depending on the system. Some protocols encrypt messages before they are transmitted. Messaging and chat protocols include IRC (Internet Relay Chat), MSNP (Mobile Status Notification Protocol), and Jabber.

**FIGURE 6-35**

IM client software displays a window for typing and viewing messages.

**How do I set up a messaging system?** Your first step is to select a service and get the client software. Messaging systems, such as Windows Live Messenger and Apple iChat, are packaged with computer operating systems and their client software might already be installed. Client software for other systems, such as AOL Instant Messenger, Yahoo! Messenger, and Google Talk, can be accessed by going to a Web site. When the client is installed, you can follow the configuration instructions to choose a nickname, "handle," or address, enter a buddy list, select chat rooms, and so on. Then you're ready to send messages and chat.

**Is messaging safe?** If you are using messaging services, you should take steps to protect your computer and your privacy. Instant messaging systems are vulnerable to instant message viruses and spyware hidden in files accessed by clicking a link in the message. To avoid these viruses, make sure your anti-virus software is active and up to date, use antispyware, and never open files or click links from someone you don't know (Figure 6-36). IM viruses take advantage of coding errors and vulnerabilities in instant messaging clients, so it is important to make sure you use the most recent version of the client and install updates as they become available.

**FIGURE 6-36**

Clicking an IM link to a file could activate a virus, worm, or spyware.

6

To protect your privacy, be careful about revealing personal information in chat rooms. Many chat room participants are not who they appear to be. Some people are just having fun with fantasy identities, but others are trying to con people by telling hard luck stories and faking illnesses. In a chat room, never reveal personal information, such as your full name, address, or phone number. Resist the temptation to meet face to face with chat room participants. When using IM, be aware that messages can be recorded by your buddies and forwarded to others. Messages can also be intercepted, so before discussing sensitive health and financial matters, check to see if your IM system encrypts messages.

## VOICE OVER IP

**What is Voice over IP?** As the Internet extended throughout the world, a cadre of IP telephony devotees began to spread the word about a technology called VoIP, which they claimed could make worldwide voice calling free, as in no monthly telephone or cellular phone bills. VoIP technology is finally here, but has not quite matched the hype.

**VoIP** (Voice over Internet Protocol) or Voice over IP, is a technology in which a broadband Internet connection is used to place telephone calls instead of the regular phone system. The earliest VoIP connections were computer-to-computer connections. Both the person initiating the call and the person receiving the call had to have computers with microphones and headsets or speakers. You could only call people who were using the same VoIP software and who happened to be online when you wanted to call them. These early VoIP systems worked more like instant messaging with voice than a traditional phone call.

You can still use VoIP to make calls from one computer to another, but today's VoIP systems allow you to use a standard telephone handset to make or receive calls. They also allow you to receive calls from regular telephones and to place calls to standard telephones.

**How do today's VoIP systems work?** Today's VoIP systems convert voice communications to data packets. An IP address is attached to each packet. If you are calling a friend with computer-based VoIP, for example, your friend's IP address will be attached to the packets. If you are calling a land line or other destination without its own IP address, your VoIP packets will carry an IP address of a service that can route your packets to their destination using land lines where necessary.

**How do I set up VoIP?** To set up a standard VoIP system, you can use an inexpensive ATA, IP phone, wireless IP phone, or USB phone.

An **ATA** (Analog Telephone Adapter) is a device that converts analog voice signals into digital data packets. An ATA connects a standard telephone to an Ethernet port on a LAN router or broadband modem.

An IP phone contains built-in analog to digital conversion and takes the place of a conventional handset. IP phones plug directly into a router's Ethernet port. A wireless IP phone sends Wi-Fi signals to a wireless router, so the handset can be used like a cordless phone.

A USB phone is a VoIP-enabled telephone that plugs into a computer's USB port. Figure 6-37 illustrates configurations for ATAs, IP phones, and USB phones.

If you plan to call land lines (rather than limiting your calls to other computers), you must sign up for VoIP service, such as Vonage or Skype. VoIP services charge a fixed monthly fee to handle the handoff between your Internet-based call data and local telephone companies. When you sign up for VoIP service, you are assigned a standard telephone number. You might be surprised to learn that you can choose the area code for your VoIP number, and it doesn't have to be an area code from your physical location.

**How do I use VoIP?** When you pick up your VoIP handset, you hear a dial-tone, just like with a regular phone. After you hear the dial tone, you can dial any phone, almost anywhere in the world just as you would from a regular phone.

**FIGURE 6-37**

Adding a VoIP handset to your computer system requires an ATA, an IP phone, or a USB phone.

**What are the advantages of Voice over IP?** VoIP service is still relatively new, but it already offers significant advantages over traditional phone service. For one monthly or annual fee, most VoIP services offer unlimited local and long distance calls in the U.S., Canada, and many other countries including most of Europe. That means no minute limitations, no roaming, no extra fees for long distance—not even for many international calls.

VoIP plans typically offer flexibility that regular phone service cannot match. Like a cell phone, your VoIP phone number moves with your IP phone or ATA. If you go away to school, you can continue to use your old number even though you may be in a different state or a different country.

VoIP plans typically offer flexibility that regular phone service cannot match. Like a cell phone, your VoIP phone number moves with your IP phone or ATA. If you go away to school, you can continue to use your old number even though you may be in a different state or a different country. You can even carry your VoIP service on a portable USB flash drive for use in any public computer with an Internet connection (Figure 6-38)

**FIGURE 6-38**

VoIP goes portable with a small set of earphones and software carried on a USB flash drive that can be plugged into any computer with Internet access.

Cell phones that offer Wi-Fi as well as cellular phone service can be used to make calls using your VoIP or cellular service. When you are within range of a Wi-Fi hotspot, the call is routed through the Internet as a VoIP call. If no hotspot is in range, the call is routed through the standard cellular service.

**What are the disadvantages of VoIP?** Like any technology, VoIP is not perfect. It does have disadvantages. The quality of VoIP calls can vary from good to very poor. If you have a fast Internet connection and if the packets flow freely over the Internet, the quality of the connection can be very good—basically as good as a telephone call using a land line. If your Internet connection is slow or if your packets encounter congestion, however, the quality of the connection can be very low, with clipped, almost unintelligible words.

VoIP service can let you down in an emergency. Like cordless phones, VoIP requires wall power. If the power goes out, you cannot use your VoIP phone. Since a VoIP number is not associated with a physical address, 911 systems cannot automatically direct emergency responders to your location in the event of an emergency. Most VoIP providers ask that you update your physical address when you move your VoIP phone so that 911 operators can find you in an emergency.

6

## GRID COMPUTING

**What is a grid computing system?** In the days when the Internet was really taking off, computer scientists noticed that thousands of computers connected to the Internet sit idle for hours while the people who own them are in meetings, talking on the telephone, sleeping, or otherwise occupied. If these idle processing cycles could be harnessed, they could supply a tremendous amount of computing power—perhaps as much as a supercomputer.

A **grid computing system** is a network of diverse computers, such as PCs, Macs, workstations, and servers, in which each computer contributes processing resources to solving a single problem. Computer grids generate massive processing power by using many off-the-shelf personal computers, which work together to achieve processing speeds that rival some of the world's top supercomputers. Grid computing systems can be public or private. Some grid systems use computers connected to the Internet as resources; others operate on private networks.

**How do grids work?** Grid management software divides computational problems into pieces that are farmed out to individual computers on the grid for processing. Each computer on the grid runs grid client software that contains the program necessary to process a piece of the problem. In this manner, complex calculations or tasks can be performed in parallel by using as many computers as are available on the grid. Results are sent back to the grid management software for consolidation. Figure 6-39 illustrates the basic architecture of a grid computing system.

**Where are grid systems used?** Because of their scalability, low cost, and high performance, grid computing systems play a central role in scientific high-performance computing. One of the most famous examples of a grid system is the SETI@home project. People who wish to donate their computers' idle processing cycles to the SETI@home project can download and install grid client software (Figure 16-40).

**FIGURE 6-39**

A grid computing system uses a diverse variety of computers as generic and equal resources.

A computer running grid management software farms out pieces of the problem to computers in the grid.

Computers in the grid run grid client software.

### INFOWEBLINKS

For more information about this fascinating use of grid computing, take a look at the **SETI@home InfoWeb**.

CLICK TO CONNECT

www.course.com/np/concepts10/ch06

**FIGURE 6-40**

SETI@home consists of a grid management system and millions of privately owned personal computers whose owners donate idle processing time to the project. The SETI@home grid management system receives and stores raw data from the Arecibo radio telescope in Puerto Rico, divides this data into small segments for analysis, and farms out each segment to one of the privately owned computers.

## What kinds of problems are best solved using grid systems?

Grid computing systems perform best on large, complex problems that can be divided into smaller problem segments, which can be processed in any sequence and at any time. One example of this type of problem is the process used to crack encryption algorithms, which are based on keys formed from very long numbers. The longer the number, the more keys are possible. For example, 56-bit encryption has many more possible keys than 12-bit encryption. Modern computerized encryption algorithms, which use 56-bit keys, were once thought to be unbreakable because the key can be any one of billions of numbers.

In 1997, a company called RSA Security Inc. set up a series of contests that awarded monetary prizes to the first person who could crack messages encrypted with a variety of common encryption algorithms. The contest caught the eye of a group of scientists who had an interest in encryption techniques and grid computing. The group, led by scientist Jeff Lawson, realized it would be possible to win the contest using simple brute force computing, which means trying every possible key. All that was needed was enough computer processing power to try all the different key combinations.

Lawson's group, Distributed.net, obtained the processing power by using a grid system. Group members created grid management software to divide keys into blocks and assign each block to one of the computers on the grid for processing. Each computer on the grid does the same thing—it starts with the first key in its block, checks it against the encrypted message to see if it's the correct key and, if unsuccessful, moves on to the next key. As more people donate their idle computer cycles to the project, the processing proceeds faster and faster. Using grid technology, Distributed.net cracked several encryption keys once thought to be unbreakable.

The first victory, RSA's RC5-56 challenge, was cracking a 56-bit code in 250 days. Over the course of the project, Distributed.net received donated cycles from more than 500,000 computers. The grid processed more than 34 quadrillion keys at a peak rate of 7 billion keys a second—the equivalent of 26,000 Pentium computers! In 2002, Distributed.net broke 64-bit encryption in 1,757 days with the help of 331,252 grid participants who tested 15,769,938,165,961,326,592 keys. Efforts to crack 72-bit encryption have been ongoing since 2002.

In addition to analyzing radio telescope signals and breaking codes, grid computing projects currently exist for applications such as studying global climate changes, predicting earthquakes, playing chess, and searching for new medicines (Figure 6-41). Sony is even considering a grid of Internet-connected PlayStation gaming consoles to enhance online game performance.

Not all computing tasks are suited to grid systems, however. Some problems cannot be divided into small processing segments for grid systems; other problems require extensive human interaction or highly specialized equipment.

**FIGURE 6-41**

Public Grid Computing Projects

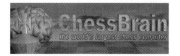

First distributed computing network to play online chess.

Study climate change in the 21st century and examine effects on food production, ecosystems, water resources, and energy demand.

Crack encryption algorithms.

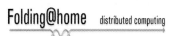

Protein folding research related to neurological diseases such as Alzheimer's and Parkinson's, and many cancers and cancer-related syndromes.

Collect data and design models to predict earthquakes.

**INFOWEBLINKS**

RSA Security Inc. continues to hold contests challenging people to break commonly used encryption algorithms. Think you can solve one? Find out more at the **Cracking Contests InfoWeb**.

**W** CLICK TO CONNECT

www.course.com/np/concepts10/ch06

6

## FTP

**What is FTP?** **FTP** (file transfer protocol) provides a way to transfer files from one computer to another over any TCP/IP network, such as a LAN or the Internet. The purpose of FTP is to make it easy to upload and download computer files without having to deal directly with the operating system or file management system of a remote computer. FTP also allows authorized remote users to change file names and delete files.

**Do I need to use FTP?** Many people use FTP without even knowing it. When you download an updated device driver from a technical support site, when you access a document in PDF format from a corporate Web site, or when you pull down an MP3 file from your favorite music site, FTP is in action although the mechanics of it are incorporated into other applications.

People who use FTP are often sharing large files stored on a file server in conjunction with a project. Files can be uploaded to the server by one participant and downloaded by others. An alternative to FTP, sending files as e-mail attachments, is not practical with very large files or for participants with slow Internet connections.

**How does FTP work?** An **FTP server** typically resides on a computer containing files that remote users might want to access. The server runs software that listens on ports 20 and 21 for requests coming in from other computers. When a request arrives, the server makes sure the user who made the request has rights to access the file. If the request is valid, the file is transferred over the Internet as a series of packets to the requesting computer, where it is saved in a designated location on a local storage device.

**How can I access FTP servers?** You can access FTP servers with FTP client software or with a browser. An **FTP client**, such as WSFTP, FTP Voyager, CuteFTP, or open-source FileZilla, offers an easy-to-use interface for accessing FTP servers. Convenient features allow you to save a list of server addresses and their corresponding user IDs and passwords, so you can connect to an FTP server with one click. FTP clients also allow you to download more than one file at a time and they can pick up where they left off if the transfer is interrupted by a glitch in your Internet connection (Figure 6-42).

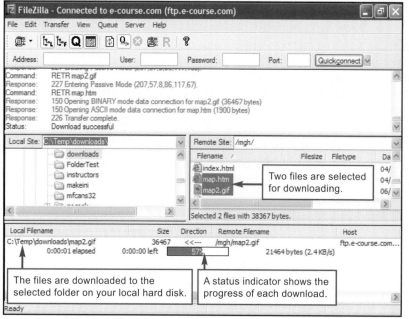

**FIGURE 6-42**

FTP clients such as FileZilla make it easy to upload and download files from an FTP server.

 CLICK TO START

Web browsers also allow you to access FTP servers as shown in Figure 6-43. Not every FTP server is accessible from a browser, and those that are might work only for downloading files, not uploading them. If you plan to work with FTP a lot, you should get FTP client software.

FIGURE 6-43

A browser can provide access to FTP downloads.

Enter the address of the FTP server on the browser's address bar. At an anonymous FTP server, the user ID and password would not be necessary.

Select the file you want to download.

When the download is complete, the safest procedure is to close the window and check the file with antivirus software before you run it.

FIGURE 6-43

A browser can provide access to FTP downloads.

▶ CLICK TO START

**Does FTP include security to prevent unauthorized access?** Some FTP sites require remote users to log in before accessing files. A login ID and password can be obtained from the FTP site operator. Access rights can be configured in various ways to allow or prevent remote users from changing file names, deleting files, uploading files, or downloading files.

**What is anonymous FTP?** **Anonymous FTP** can be accessed by logging in without a password by using the user ID "anonymous." Some anonymous sites request users to enter their e-mail addresses as a password, but rarely is that piece of information used for verification or tracking.

## FILE SHARING

**What is file sharing?** File sharing, sometimes called **P2P file sharing** uses peer-to-peer (P2P) protocols that allow users to obtain files from other users located anywhere on the Internet. In the late 1990s, file sharing burst onto the national scene when college students became aware of a technology called Napster that provided free access to hit songs.

File sharing originated on FTP-style servers, which held huge collections of popular music stored in digital MP3 files that could be easily downloaded and played on a computer or transferred to CD. Free distribution of music without the copyright holder's permission is illegal and file sharing server operators quickly encountered the legal ramifications of their computer's shady dealings.

To avoid legal hassles, file sharing technology evolved from thinly disguised client/server models to more distributed models that displaced legal responsibilities from a single operator of a central server to hundreds of

6

users who each might store and share a dozen or fewer songs. Rather than store the actual files on a server, Napster stored only a list of song titles, with pointers to privately-owned computers from which the files could be downloaded. After a legal challenge shut down Napster, a more decentralized technology called Gnutella emerged. One of the most recent popular file sharing technologies is called BitTorrent.

**What is BitTorrent? BitTorrent** is a file sharing protocol that distributes the role of file server across a collection of dispersed computers. BitTorrent is, in some sense, an offshoot of grid computing concepts, in which an ad-hoc collection of personal computers located anywhere on the Internet can cooperate to complete a task normally handled by monolithic servers or supercomputers.

A BitTorrent network is designed to reduce the bandwidth bottleneck that occurs when many people attempt to download the same very large file, such as a feature-length film, application software, or an interactive 3-D computer game.

With conventional uploading and downloading technology, simultaneous requests for large files can easily max out a central server's capacity. Such a bottleneck could, for example, pose a significant barrier to nationwide movie distribution over the Internet. Imagine the server capacity needed to handle simultaneous download requests on the release dates of big box office hits. BitTorrent technology eliminates the bottleneck by moving the workload from a single server to an ad-hoc collection of Internet-based personal computers.

**How does BitTorrent work?** Suppose that 100 computers request the film *Premonition* at about the same time. A server breaks the movie file into pieces and begins to download those pieces to the first computer that requested the movie. As more computers request the file, they become part of a "swarm" that uses peer-to-peer technology to exchange file pieces with each other. After the server has downloaded all the file pieces to the swarm, its job is complete and it can service other requests. The swarm continues to exchange file pieces until every computer in the swarm has the entire file (Figure 6-44).

**FIGURE 6-44**

BitTorrent protocols dissect files into small chunks that might reside on different computers. Source computers have received parts of a file from a server. They then distribute these parts to other computers in the swarm.

**How do I use BitTorrent?** BitTorrent client software is currently available from several Web sites. After installing the client, you can use it to download from any BitTorrent-enabled site simply by clicking the file you want. The BitTorrent client handles the entire file-swapping procedure. After getting the entire file, good etiquette requires clients to remain connected to the swarm so that they can "seed" (see BitTorrent Lingo box, Figure 6-45) file pieces to others.

**FIGURE 6-45**

BitTorrent Lingo

**Are BitTorrent and similar file swapping networks legal?** File swapping networks are often used to illegally distribute copyrighted material. Napster, the original music file sharing network was closed down by court order in 2001 because most of the freely shared music was distributed without the permission of copyright holders. The Napster name and logo are now used by Roxio for an online music store similar to iTunes. Although BitTorrent technology differs from the Napster model, BitTorrent networks are not immune to the consequences of copyright infringement. Several U.S. and European BitTorrent sites have been raided for ignoring copyright laws.

> **Swarm:** A group of computers temporarily networked to download a file.
>
> **Tracker:** Server software that helps establish a swarm of end-user computers.
>
> **Seed or seeder:** A computer that has downloaded an entire file and can upload pieces to other clients in a swarm.
>
> **Leech or leecher:** A computer in the process of obtaining file pieces from a swarm.
>
> **Chokers:** Clients that don't allow other clients to download file pieces.

Peer-to-peer file sharing networks and distributed technologies like BitTorrent have legitimate uses for distributing music, images, videos, and software with the approval of copyright holders. Peter Jackson's production diaries for King Kong have been posted for download using BitTorrent technology. Universal Studios and several independent film companies have released movie trailers with BitTorrent technology. The technology itself is not illegal; it is the use of the technology that is subject to legal scrutiny.

**Is BitTorrent safe?** Because BitTorrent files are assembled from little segments that come from a jumble of computers, they would seem on first thought to be bad candidates for distributing malware. Intelligent hackers would realize that their malicious code could easily be chopped up, too, and that pieces of it might not be delivered. And yet, BitTorrent files have become a source of adware and spyware. If you use BitTorrent make sure your computer is protected with a security software suite that offers good spyware protection.

# QuickCheck

**SECTION D**

1. One-on-one messaging is referred to as instant messaging (IM) and group communications are referred to as [_____].

2. You can use VoIP to call other computers because it is an Internet service, but you cannot use it to call land lines. True or false? [_____]

3. SETI@home is an example of [_____] computing, which generates massive processing power by using many off-the-shelf personal computers linked together by the Internet.

4. [_____] makes it easy to upload and download computer files without having to deal directly with the operating system or file management system of a remote computer.

5. [_____] is a peer-to-peer file sharing protocol that uses a "swarm" of computers to exchange chunks of data that can be eventually assembled into complete files.

 CHECK ANSWERS

# Internet Security

**WHEN COMPUTERS** are connected to a network, the risk of intrusion has to be taken seriously. When the connection is Internet-based, billions of people are just an IP address away from your computer and its valuable, personal, and confidential data. Section E explains the mechanics of an intrusion attempt, and offers some practical advice for securing your computer against unauthorized access.

## INTRUSION ATTEMPTS

**Should I worry about intrusions?** Suppose you live in a really dangerous neighborhood where gangs roam the streets, painting every available surface with graffiti and randomly attacking residents. A seemingly endless number of burglars creep from house to house looking for unlocked doors and windows, and occasionally trying to pick a lock or two. Punk kids rummage about looking for cars with keys in the ignition, unlocked doors, or loose hubcaps. Dark figures sift through your garbage cans searching for scraps of information that can be pieced together to steal your identity (Figure 6-46).

Unfortunately, this dangerous neighborhood has many similarities to the Internet where gangs of hackers deface Web sites, look for backdoors left open by network administrators, crack passwords to gain access to your data, and probe ports looking for ways to sneak bots into your computer. Your Internet connection puts you right in the middle of this dangerous neighborhood anytime you are connected—and with always-on connections like DSL and cable Internet service, that means any time your computer is turned on.

In the context of computers, an **intrusion** is any access to data or programs by hackers, criminals, or other unauthorized persons. As the result of an intrusion, data can be stolen or altered, system configurations can be changed to allow even more intrusions, and software can be surreptitiously installed and operated under the remote control of a hacker. Without any visible sign or warning, hackers can infiltrate your computer to obtain personal information or use your computer as a launching pad for attacks on other machines. Yes, you should worry about intrusions!

**How do hackers use the Internet to infiltrate my computer?** One of the most common ways of gaining unauthorized access to a network-based computer is by looking for open ports. Earlier in this chapter you learned that network services, such as the Web, FTP, and e-mail operate on ports. As an example, you learned that Web requests use port 80.

**FIGURE 6-46**

The Internet offers a wealth of useful tools and services, but it can be a dangerous neighborhood.

If a port is open and listening for requests—on any computer, even your own—a hacker can exploit it like an unlocked door to gain access to your computer. Hackers are continuously canvassing the Internet and probing ports to find their next victims.

A **port probe** (or port scan) is the use of automated software to locate computers that have open ports and are vulnerable to unauthorized access. Software called a port scanner goes to a randomly selected IP address and systematically checks for a response from each port. Open ports can then be further tested to gauge their suitability for exploitation.

You might scoff at your computer's vulnerability to port probes. After all, there are millions and millions of computers on the Internet and a limited number of hackers. The chances of your computer becoming a target would seem to be slim, but the opposite is true. Port scanning software can examine more than 30,000 computers per minute. If you use security software to monitor port probes on an unprotected computer, you would see probes within minutes of going online. According to researchers, the average "survival time" for an unprotected computer to remain uncompromised is only 9 minutes.

**How do I know if ports are open?** You can check your computer for open ports using software tools such as Steve Gibson's Shields Up! at *www.grc.com*. You can initiate an "innocent" port probe to discover vulnerabilities. A security report like the one in Figure 6-47 is your goal.

**FIGURE 6-47**

Your computer's ports are most secure if they don't even appear to exist when probed using a port scanner.

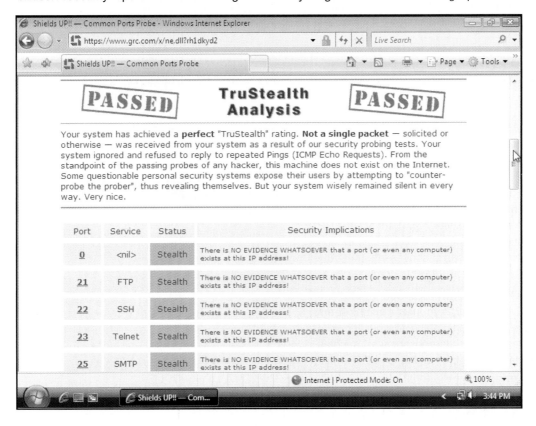

## SECURING PORTS

**How do I secure the ports on my computer?** One of the easiest steps to enhance your computer's security is to turn it off when you aren't using it. When your computer is turned off, its ports are inactive and they are not vulnerable to intrusions. Putting your computer into sleep mode or activating a screen saver is not sufficient protection. Your computer must be shut down and turned off.

FIGURE 6-48

To configure your computer for Automatic Updates, use Control Panel's System icon.

You should also keep your computer up-to-date with the latest operating system security patches and service packs. Operating systems are closely linked to port activity. Known vulnerabilities in Windows and Internet Explorer can be exploited to access ports or launch additional attacks once a port is breached. As Microsoft develops security patches, they are posted at Microsoft's Web site, *www.microsoft.com/security*. Check the site frequently to download the most recent patches.

You can also use Windows Automatic Updates to periodically check for patches. To configure Automatic Updates, go to Control Panel, select System, and select a setting from the Automatic Updates tab (Figure 6-48). When updates are available, you'll see the New Updates icon on the taskbar:

**What about firewall protection?** In the context of networking, a **firewall** is software or hardware designed to filter out suspicious packets attempting to enter or leave a computer. Firewall software helps keep your computer secure in several ways. It makes sure that incoming information was actually requested and is not an unauthorized intrusion. It blocks activity from suspicious IP addresses and—best of all—it reports intrusion attempts so that you can discover whether any hackers are trying to break into your computer.

You can use firewall software to open and close ports on your computer. Although it might seem safest to close all the ports, doing so would prevent you from accessing most Internet services, such as the Web, e-mail, instant messaging, and FTP. Most firewall software is preconfigured to block only unnecessarily open ports targeted by hackers.

Windows XP includes firewall software called Internet Connection Firewall (ICF) or Windows Firewall. To activate and configure it, use Control Panel's Windows Firewall option (Figure 6-49). Independently published firewall software includes Tiny Personal Firewall and BlackICE.

FIGURE 6-49

Windows includes a built-in firewall that can be activated to monitor intrusion attempts. Do not enable it, however, if your antivirus software firewall is activated.

**What other Windows security options should I use?** Sharing print-ers or files on a LAN or the Internet requires open ports so the data can be transferred to and from your computer. Those open ports can be a potential entryway for hackers. If your computer is not connected to a LAN or used for access to a public Wi-Fi network, you should deactivate file and printer sharing. Figure 6-50 demonstrates this procedure for Windows XP.

FIGURE 6-50

When you turn off file and printer sharing, your files and printer cannot be accessed by other network users.

When this box is not checked, file and printer sharing is deactivated.

## ROUTERS AND NAT

**How does a router affect security?** One of the most effective steps you can take to secure your computer from intrusions is to install a router. In the chapter on networking, you learned that a router can tie a LAN together and provide a portal to the Internet. Even if you have only one computer, however, a router can offer excellent security.

**How does a router work?** Routers are intended to work on LANs to monitor and direct packets being transported from one device to another. A router can also connect to the Internet through a DSL, cable, or satel-lite modem.

Routers are handy because they can screen IP addresses to keep locally addressed packets within the LAN so that they are delivered without traveling a cir-cuitous route over the Internet and back (Figure 6-51).

FIGURE 6-51

A router monitors the IP addresses of packets on a LAN. Packets with local addresses (green) are kept within the LAN. Packets with external addresses are routed out to the Internet.

Packets with external addresses go to the Internet

Router

Packets with local addresses remain within the LAN

LAN workstations

CLICK TO START

Your router has its own IP address, typically obtained from your Internet service provider's DHCP server. (Recall that a DHCP server assigns dynamic IP addresses to devices that request them.) It is also possible for your router to have a fixed IP address set up by you or an installer. The key point about your router's IP address is that it is routable. A **routable IP address** is one which can be accessed by packets on the Internet.

When you connect your computer to a router, and request an IP address, your *router* answers your request, not the ISP. Most routers are configured to assign private IP addresses. A **private IP address** is a non-routable IP address that can be used within a LAN, but not for Internet data transport. When the IP addressing scheme was devised, three ranges of addresses were reserved for internal or private use: 10.0.0.0–10.255.255.255, 172.16.0.0–172.31.255.255, and 192.168.0.0–192.168.255.255. If your computer has a private IP address it is essentially hidden from hackers.

**But how do packets with private IP addresses get out to the Internet?** Let's review the scenario. You have a router connected to an Internet device, such as a DSL or cable modem. The router has a routable IP address, visible to any device (and hackers) on the Internet. Your router isn't vulnerable to attacks because it doesn't contain any of your data. You've connected your computer to a router. Your computer has been assigned a private IP address.

**Network address translation** (NAT) is the process your router uses to keep track of packets and their corresponding private or public IP addresses. Jeff Tyson writing for *How Stuff Works* offers a useful analogy for how NAT works: "NAT is like the receptionist in a large office. Let's say you have left instructions with the receptionist not to forward any calls to you unless you request it. Later on, you call a potential client and leave a message for that client to call you back. You tell the receptionist that you are expecting a call from this client and to put her through. The client calls the main number to your office, which is the only number the client knows. When the client tells the receptionist that she is looking for you, the receptionist checks a lookup table that matches your name with your extension. The receptionist knows that you requested this call, and therefore forwards the caller to your extension."

A router and the receptionist perform essentially similar tasks. Your private IP address is like a private telephone extension in an office. Your router's public IP address is like the main switchboard number. Your router screens incoming packets and only lets one through to your private extension if you've requested it.

When you use the Internet, you initiate every valid transaction; you ask for a Web site, you ask to retrieve your mail, or you request a file from an FTP server. Only those requests that you initiate are valid. Suppose you want to download a file. You send a packet containing your request to the FTP server at 69.32.167.20. The packet goes to your router, which replaces your address with its own and makes an internal note that you initiated this FTP request. When the FTP server responds, it sends a packet addressed to the router. The router receives the packet, checks its internal note to see who made the original request, and then ships the FTP packet to your computer (Figure 6-52).

**FIGURE 6-52**

A router using NAT essentially cloaks your computer and makes it invisible from the Internet.

Internet-based
FTP server

To: 12.192.1.100
From: 69.32.167.20

To: 69.32.167.20
From: 12.192.1.100

Router
12.192.1.100

To: 69.32.167.20
From: 192.168.9.9

From: 69.32.167.20
To: 192.168.9.9

Your computer
192.168.9.9

## VIRTUAL PRIVATE NETWORKS

**Is it possible to secure connections for remote users?** Sales representatives and telecommuters often have to access corporate networks by using a remote connection from home or a customer's office. It is possible to secure these remote connections by setting up **virtual private network** (VPN) access to a remote access server in the corporate office.

**Who sets up VPNs?** On the corporate end, setting up a secure VPN is not a trivial task and it is typically handled by specialists in the corporation's information technology department.

**How do I access a VPN?** Access to a VPN is usually by invitation only. Employees who need to access a VPN are given the necessary instructions, addresses, and passwords to make connections. In general, a person initiates a VPN connection by connecting to an ISP as usual. After the connection is established, a second connection to the remote access server creates an encrypted channel for data transmission. Figure 6-53 illustrates how a VPN operates.

**How important is a VPN?** A VPN is typically a corporate solution, whereas the other security suggestions in this section can be implemented by individuals. To recap the most important security precautions, you should turn your computer off when not in use, make sure all your computer's unnecessary ports are closed, activate firewall software, turn off file and printer sharing, and install a router. Taking these precautions might not make your computer invincible, but they offer very strong protection against intruders who might steal your identity or hijack your computer for various shady activities.

FIGURE 6-53

Virtual Private Network

6

# QuickCheck

1. Hackers can use automated software to look for computers with open [＿＿＿＿＿] that are vulnerable to unauthorized access.

2. By downloading and applying operating system security [＿＿＿＿＿] and service packs, you can help to prevent unauthorized intrusions that exploit known operating system vulnerabilities.

3. [＿＿＿＿＿] software is designed to analyze incoming and outgoing packets to look

   for unusual activity that could be part of an intrusion.

4. One of the best defenses against intrusions is to use a(n) [＿＿＿＿＿] between your standalone or computer or LAN and your Internet connection device.

5. A(n) [＿＿＿＿＿] IP address is a non-routable IP address that can be used within a LAN, but not for Internet data transport.

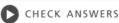 CHECK ANSWERS

# What's Happening to Free Speech?

**THE INTERNET** offers instant access to information across national and cultural borders, but along with helpful information the Internet hosts a disturbing amount of unsavory material. Militias and hate groups use Web sites to recruit new members and spread their views. Hundreds of pornographic sites make a business of selling lewd images and their come-ons can be accessed by anyone—even children. In chat rooms on innocent topics, the conversation can deteriorate into X-rated banter. Pedophile and bestiality sites that cater to warped sexual habits pop up in search engine lists. International terrorists use Web sites as recruiting tools and for boasting about suicide bombings. Criminals, terrorists, and hackers post guidebooks and tips on how to do all kinds of illegal activities, from making suitcase bombs to spreading computer viruses.

Some concerned netizens advocate cyber censorship to curtail irresponsible Web sites, blogs, discussion groups, and file sharing. Cyber censorship typically means blocking access to Web sites, but it can also mean closing sites and removing them from host servers. Censorship advocates are opposed by free speech supporters who believe that the right to free expression should be unshackled by any laws or regulations.

The controversy over censorship is not new. Guidelines from the pre-Internet era also shape the cyber-censorship-vs-free-speech debate.

In most cases, words are acceptable, whereas actions can be punishable. Writing a mystery novel that describes how the main character cultivates botulism and then uses it to poison one of the other characters is acceptable. Actually carrying out such an act would be against the law. This concept was applied to cyberspace when the U.S. Supreme Court upheld a law that pornography featuring real children was illegal, but ruled that child pornography featuring computer-generated children is not illegal because children were not harmed when it was created.

Cyberlaw is not yet totally consistent on the words vs. deeds precedent, however. In some cases, words are punishable. For example, the Digital Millennium Copyright Act makes it illegal to even disseminate information on defeating software, CD, and DVD copy restrictions.

A second censorship guideline hinges on local standards of morality. Local communities can apply their own standards to determine whether material is obscene. Therefore, a raunchy magazine that you might find on a supermarket newsstand in New York City might be limited to adult bookstore shelves in a conservative Tennessee community.

Local standards, however, are difficult to sort out on the Internet where a Web surfer in Tennessee can easily access Web sites, bulletin boards, and chat groups that originate from anywhere in the world. Judges upheld the conviction of two sysops whose California-based porn site distributed obscene material to individuals in Tennessee. The sysops claimed that the Internet required a more flexible definition of "community" to account for the Internet's global accessibility; otherwise Web sites would be forced to eliminate all materials objected to by anyone. Judges denied that claim, saying that technology could be used to filter out objectionable material based on age and location information provided by member registration data.

Underlying a group of decisions on cyber censorship, the U.S. Supreme Court seems to support the concept of cyberzones that limit net access to certain materials in a way similar to how the adult sections of street-corner newsstands restrict children from browsing through certain magazines. As now-retired Justice O'Connor explained, "Cyberspace is malleable. Thus, it is possible to construct barriers in cyberspace and use them to screen for identity, making cyberspace more like the physical world and, consequently, more amenable to zoning laws." As an example, AOL is trying to develop a family-friendly Internet portal by enforcing policies against offensive speech, but has been criticized by free-speech advocates for its policies. AOL responds that it is a private company and members who disagree with AOL terms of use are free to terminate their subscriptions.

In some countries, however, cyber citizens have no choice but to use a government-controlled ISP. In many countries, free speech is not a basic right conferred to all citizens. Many dictatorial regimes want their citizens to receive news from the outside world only after it has been screened by a government censor. Officials in more than 20 countries use sophisticated tools to block Web sites, filter e-mail, and censor discussion groups.

China has some of the most rigorous Internet censorship in the world. The "Great Firewall of China" as it is sometimes called, blocks Internet content by preventing IP addresses of objectionable sites from being routed through its gateways into China. The system also selectively engages in DNS poisoning, a technique that tricks a DNS server into believing it has received authentic information when, in reality, it has not. So Web surfers in China who attempt to access the Electronic Frontier Foundation's Web site that advocates free speech, might instead see a Chinese government site on social responsibility. In addition to blocking Web sites, the Chinese government filters e-mail, message boards, chat rooms, and blogs.

In Iran, government censors monitor political and news Web sites, and block access to many pornographic Web sites, anonymizer tools, sites with gay and lesbian content, politically sensitive sites, and women's rights sites. If you tried to access *Rolling*

*Stone* magazine's Web site from Saudi Arabia, you would find that access has been denied. The Saudi government claims it censors the Internet to preserve Islamic culture and heritage. That argument in many ways reflects the concept of cyberzones that conform to local standards of ethics and morality. Even free-speech activists at the OpenNet Initiative (ONI) seem to agree, "We do think that information should be free," states one ONI technician, "but we do need to find a balance for respect for sovereign states to preserve their own culture."

Despite such cultural sensitivity, technology giants, such as Microsoft, Yahoo!, and Cisco Systems have been criticized for providing foreign governments with tools for blocking culturally objectionable sites. Critics question whether companies in a free society should aid foreign governments' attempts to censor cyberspace.

For some people it is astonishing to realize that ideas such as liberty, equality, and women's rights would be subject to the same censorship attempts as pornography and hate speech. The solution to online censorship is still evolving as free speech comes into balance with cultural, ethical, and moral concerns in the global realm of cyberspace.

**INFOWEBLINKS**

You'll find more fascinating Internet myths and substantive articles about disinformation at the **Internet Censorship InfoWeb**.

W  CLICK TO CONNECT
www.course.com/np/concepts10/ch06

# What Do You Think?                                     ISSUE

1. Should governments be allowed to block access to Web sites based on local religions, politics, and customs?

   ○ Yes   ○ No   ○ Not sure

2. Do you believe that a privately-held Internet Service Provider like AOL has the right to censor the data posted on Web sites it hosts?

   ○ Yes   ○ No   ○ Not sure

3. Should companies like Microsoft, Yahoo!, and Cisco Systems provide blocking technology to foreign governments?

   ○ Yes   ○ No   ○ Not sure

4. Would you use filtering software that was preprogrammed to block pornographic and nuisance Web sites?

   ○ Yes   ○ No   ○ Not sure

   ▶ SAVE RESPONSES

# Banking

**FOR MOST OF HISTORY,** banks used low-tech methods to track one of the world's most cherished commodities—wealth. Checking accounts were in widespread use as early as 1550, when wealthy Dutch traders began depositing money with cashiers for safekeeping. The use of printed checks became popular in England in the late 18th century—so popular that banks found it difficult to process a steadily increasing stream of checks, including those drawn on accounts from other banks.

An unverified story that has become part of bank lore describes the origin of a solution to the check processing problem. As the story goes, a London bank messenger stopped for coffee and got to talking with a messenger from another bank. Realizing that they were delivering checks drawn on each other's banks, the two messengers decided to exchange checks there in the coffee house. This event evolved into a system of check clearinghouses where representatives from various banks met periodically to exchange checks and reconcile totals in cash. By 1839, British clearinghouses were annually processing in excess of £954 million of checks—equivalent to U.S. $250 billion in today's money.

Bank clearinghouses were described in an essay, *The Economy of Machinery and Manufactures*, written by Charles Babbage in 1832. He also included a reference to the "possibility of performing arithmetical calculations by machinery" along with a description of the Difference Engine, then under construction in his workshop.

This dream of automated check clearing did not, however, become reality until more than a century later when S. Clark Beise, senior vice president at Bank of America, contracted with Stanford Research Institute (SRI) to develop a computer system to automate check processing. SRI completed a prototype in 1955 that used mechanical sorting equipment to queue up each check and MICR technology to read check numbers. In 1959, the first ERMA (Electronic Recording Machine-Accounting) system went into service. With ERMA handling calculations, 9 employees could handle the job that once required 50 people. By 1966, 32 regional ERMA systems operated by Bank of America were processing more than 750 million checks per year. ERMA and similar check processing technologies quickly integrated with bank transaction processing systems to become the bedrock of today's banking technology.

Output from check sorting machines can be submitted to the Automated Clearing House (ACH) network, which offers a secure, batch-oriented data exchange system that can be accessed by financial institutions. On a daily basis, banks submit check data and receive a report of balances due to other banks. These balances can be reconciled by electronic funds transfer over the Federal Reserve's FedWire telecommunications network.

An upswing in check fraud during the 1960s made it increasingly difficult to cash checks at local merchants. As an alternative to trying to cash checks at banks and local merchants, automatic teller machines (ATMs) were first installed in the 1970s. A typical ATM connects to a bank's front-end processor—a computer that maintains account balances for in-network customers and monitors suspicious activity. The front-end processor is separated from the bank's main computer system for security.

Some ATMs exchange data with the front-end processor by using dedicated dial-up telephone lines. Other ATMs use always-on leased lines. Legacy protocols such as SNA and 3270 bisync, are being replaced by the standard Internet Protocol (IP) that can be routed through more affordable connections, such as cable, ISDN, DSL, or Internet VPN.

ATMs are expensive—about $50,000 to purchase a machine, install it, and operate it for one year. Banks have offset this cost by charging transaction fees and reducing the number of bank tellers. Once a promising entry-level occupation, bank tellers today earn less than $20,000 per year. Although tellers continue to accept deposits, process withdrawals, and cash payroll checks, they are increasingly pressed into customer service roles—opening new accounts, issuing ATM cards, resolving disputed transactions, and assisting customers who have lost bank cards or checkbooks. Despite this shift in job description, the number of bank teller jobs is expected to fall at least 10% by 2010.

ATMs offer access to bank services from convenient locations where customers shop, eat, and hang out with friends. The Internet takes banking convenience one step further and provides round-the-clock account access from customers' homes, schools, or work PCs. Today, most banks and credit unions offer some type of online banking (also called home banking, Internet banking, or electronic banking).

Basic online banking services allow customers to access checking account and bankcard activity, transfer funds between checking and savings accounts, view electronic images of checks and deposit slips, download and print monthly statements, and reorder checks. Customers can also pay bills online by scheduling payment dates and amounts. Many credit card and utility companies offer e-billing services that automatically forward electronic bills to customers' online banking accounts. For monthly fixed-amount bills, such as car loans, online banking offers automatic payment options that deduct funds from specified checking or savings accounts.

For managing assets more effectively, online banking sites also offer sophisticated tools, including account aggregation, stock quotes, rate alerts, and portfolio management programs. Most online banking sites are also compatible with personal finance software, such as Managing Your Money, QuickBooks, AOL BankNOW, and Microsoft Money, so that transaction data can be shuttled between customer's local computers and their online banking services.

A cadre of customer support personnel staff online help desks for customers with questions about online banking. Webmasters, computer security specialists, and network technicians are also part of banking's new job corps.

Online banking services are typically housed on a well-secured Web server, and customers are not allowed direct access to the computer system that actually processes transactions. Customer privacy is maintained by the use of passwords and connections that encrypt data as it is sent to and from customers' computers.

Successful banks are built on good business decisions. Bank managers are increasingly working with business intelligence tools to look for trends in customer behavior, analyze competing financial institutions, and examine current business practices. Tools for these activities include data warehouses that collect and organize data, data mining software that organizes and analyzes data in a meaningful way, and statistical tools that formulate comparisons and trendlines.

Today, banking depends on multilayered technologies that incorporate check processing equipment, transaction processing systems, business intelligence software, ACH networks, FedWire, ATM networks, the Internet, and Web servers. Many banking practices originated from batch check processing, and only gradually have banks begun to move to more modern online transaction processing (OLTP) systems that store scanned images of checks and instantly update accounts when a purchase is made or a bill is paid.

**INFOWEBLINKS**

For more information about this Computers in Context topic, check the **Computers and Banking InfoWeb.**

CLICK TO CONNECT

www.course.com/np/concepts10/ch06

6

# New Perspectives Labs

## On the BookOnCD

To access the New Perspectives labs for Chapter 6, start the BookOnCD, BookOnFlashDrive, or other NP10 BookOn product and then click the icon next to the lab title below.

### ▶ TRACKING PACKETS

#### IN THIS LAB YOU'LL LEARN:

- How Ping and Traceroute work
- How to use the Ping and Tracert utilities supplied by Windows
- How to interpret Ping and Tracert reports to determine the speed and reliability of your Internet connection
- How to access and use a graphical Traceroute utility
- How to find and use Web-based Ping and Traceroute utilities
- The advantages and disadvantages of Web-based Ping and Traceroute utilities
- How to access the Internet Traffic Report Web site and interpret its data and graphs
- How to use Internet traffic data, Ping, and Traceroute to pinpoint problems with your Internet connection

#### LAB ASSIGNMENTS

1. Start the interactive part of the lab. Make sure you've enabled Tracking if you want to save your QuickCheck results. Perform each lab step as directed, and answer all the lab QuickCheck questions. When you exit the lab, your answers are automatically graded and your results are displayed.

2. Use the Ping utility that's supplied by Windows to ping *www.abcnews.com*. Record the IP address for the ABC News site, plus the minimum, maximum, and average times. For each time, indicate whether it would be considered poor, average, or good.

3. Use the Tracert utility that's supplied by Windows to trace a packet between your computer and *www.excite.com*. Print the Traceroute report listing transmission times. Circle any pings on the report that indicate high latency.

4. Locate a Web-based Ping utility and use it to ping *www.gobledegok.com*. Indicate the address for the Web site where you found the Ping utility. Explain the ping results.

5. Connect to the Internet Traffic Report Web site, make a note of the date and time, and then answer the following questions:

   a. What is the traffic index for Asia?

   b. How does the index for Asia compare with the traffic index for North America?

   c. During the previous 24 hours in Europe, what was the period with the worst response time?

### ▶ SECURING YOUR CONNECTION

#### IN THIS LAB YOU'LL LEARN:

- How to use Windows utilities, online utilities, and firewall software to check the security of your Internet connection
- Why an unauthorized intruder might want to gain access to your computer
- The significance of communications ports as an intrusion risk factor
- How a Trojan horse can open up ports on your computer to provide intruders with full access to your computer system
- How to use the Windows Netstat utility to check your computer's open ports
- How to use an online utility to get a hacker's view of your computer
- Why Windows file and printer sharing can make your computer files vulnerable
- What features to look for in personal firewall software
- How to use firewall software, add packet filtering rules, and interpret firewall reports

#### LAB ASSIGNMENTS

1. Start the interactive part of the lab. Make sure you've enabled Tracking if you want to save your QuickCheck results. Perform each lab step as directed, and answer all the lab QuickCheck questions. When you exit the lab, your answers are automatically graded and your results are displayed.

2. Use the Netstat utility to scan any computer that you typically use. Write out the Netstat report or print it. To print the report, copy it to Paint or Word, and then print. Explain what the Netstat report tells you about that computer's security.

3. Connect to *grc.com* and access the Shields Up! tests. Test the shields and probe the ports for the same computer you used for Assignment 2. Explain the similarities and differences between the Shields Up! report and the Netstat report for this computer. Which report indicates more security risks? Why?

4. In the lab, you learned which dialog boxes to use for disabling Windows file and printer sharing, plus a technique for unbinding TCP from file and printer sharing. Without actually changing the settings, use the dialog boxes to determine whether file and printer sharing is active or disabled on your computer. Also, discover whether file and printer sharing is bound to TCP on your computer. Report your findings and indicate whether these settings are appropriate for network access and security.

# Key Terms

Make sure you understand all the boldfaced key terms presented in this chapter. If you're using the NP10 BookOnCD, BookOnFlashDrive, or other NP10 BookOn product, you can use this list of terms as an interactive study activity. First, try to define a term in your own words, and then click the term to compare your definition with the definition presented in the chapter.

Always-on connection, 307
Anonymous FTP, 337
Asymmetric Internet connection, 311
ATA, 332
BitTorrent, 338
Cable Internet service, 316
Cable modem, 317
Chat, 330
Dial-up connection, 312
DOCSIS, 317
Domain name, 307
Domain name server, 308
Domain Name System, 308
Downstream speed, 311
DSL, 314
DSL filter, 315
DSL modem, 315
Dynamic IP address, 306
EDGE, 327
EV-DO, 327
Firewall, 342
Fixed Internet access, 311
Fixed wireless Internet service, 320
FTP, 336

FTP client, 336
FTP server, 336
Grid computing system, 334
HSUPA, 327
ICANN, 309
Instant messaging, 330
Internet backbone, 303
Internet service provider, 303
Intrusion, 340
IP, 305
ISDN, 314
ISDN terminal adapter, 314
Latency, 309
Mobile broadband, 327
Mobile Internet access, 311
Modem, 304
Network access point, 303
Network address translation, 344
Network service provider, 303
P2P file sharing, 337
Ping, 310
Port, 308
Port probe, 341
Portable Internet access, 311
Private IP address, 344

Protocol suite, 305
Real-time messaging system, 330
Routable IP address, 344
Satellite Internet service, 318
Satellite modem, 319
Static IP address, 306
Symmetric Internet connection, 311
TCP, 305
TCP/IP, 305
Top-level domain, 307
Traceroute, 310
Upstream speed, 311
Virtual private network, 345
Voiceband modem, 312
VoIP, 332
WAP, 327
Wi-Fi hotspot, 323
WiMAX, 320

6

# Interactive Summary

To review important concepts from this chapter, fill in the blanks to best complete each sentence. When using the NP10 BookOnCD or other BookOn product, click the Check Answers buttons to automatically score your answers.

**SECTION A:** The Internet infrastructure is based on high capacity communications links called the Internet [_____], tied together at network [_____] points where data can cross over from one NSP's equipment to another's. An Internet [_____] provider offers Internet access to individuals, businesses, and smaller ISPs. The Internet uses several communications protocols, including [_____], which breaks a message or file into packets, and [_____], which is responsible for addressing packets. Every device on the Internet has an IP address, such as 204.127.128.1. [_____] IP addresses are permanently assigned to computers, whereas [_____] IP addresses are temporarily assigned by a DHCP server. Most high-speed Internet connections use [_____] technology, and even dynamic IP addresses might seem permanent because they don't change unless you turn off your modem or your ISP has an outage. A [_____] name server converts numeric IP addresses into familiar names, such as Travelocity.com. The speed of an Internet connection measured by utilities such as Ping and Traceroute refer to [_____], the elapsed time for data to make a round trip from point A to point B. The speed advertised by Internet service providers is a measure of the amount of data that travels between two points in a given amount of time. Many Internet connections are [_____], meaning the downstream speed is different than the upstream speed.

▶ CHECK ANSWERS

**SECTION B:** A [_____] connection is a fixed Internet connection that uses a [_____] modem and telephone lines to transport data between your computer and your ISP. Most modems use a standard called V.90 to provide a theoretical maximum speed of [_____] Kbps. Dial-up connections are asymmetrical; 44 Kbps is a typical [_____] speed for a 56 Kbps modem. [_____], the data rate drops to about 33 Kbps or less. [_____] is a fixed, symmetric Internet connection that moves data at speeds of 64 Kbps or 128 Kbps over ordinary telephone lines through a device called an ISDN terminal adapter, which sends digital signals. [_____] is a high-speed, digital, always-on, Internet access technology that runs over standard phone lines. [_____] Internet service is a means of distributing always-on broadband Internet access over the same infrastructure that offers cable television service. Satellite Internet service is a means of distributing always-on, high-speed asymmetric Internet access by broadcasting signals to and from a personal satellite [_____]. Fixed wireless Internet access technologies are [_____] area network standards, in contrast to technologies such as Wi-Fi, which are local area network standards. One of the most well-known fixed wireless standards is [_____], an Ethernet-compatible network standard designated as IEEE 802.16.

▶ CHECK ANSWERS

**SECTION C:** [_____] Internet access can be defined as the ability to easily move your Internet service from one location to another. [_____] Internet access offers a continuous Internet connection as you are walking or riding in a bus, car, train, or plane. Wi-Fi is an example of portable Internet access technology that allows public access to the Internet within the network's area of coverage, called a Wi-Fi [_____]. Portable WiMAX and portable satellite offer additional Internet access options in the portable category. Cellular phone service providers offer two ways to access the Internet. [_____] is a communications protocol that provides limited access to e-mail and Internet information from handheld devices with small screens and cell phone keypads. Mobile [_____] services using EV-DO, EDGE, and HSUPA technologies offer faster access using conventional browsers and e-mail clients.

▶ CHECK ANSWERS

## SECTION D:

A networked-based real-time [_____] system allows people to exchange short messages while they are online. One-on-one messaging is referred to as [_____] messaging and group communications are referred to as [_____]. Most messaging is based on a client/server model that uses a server to handle communication packets between the participants. Instant messaging systems are vulnerable to instant message viruses and [_____] distributed by marketing companies. IM malware is often hidden in files accessed by clicking a link in the message. Many chat room participants are not who they appear to be. In a chat room, never reveal personal information, and resist the temptation to meet face to face with chat room participants. Voice over Internet [_____] is a technology in which a broadband Internet connection is used to place telephone calls instead of the regular phone system. An [_____] is a device that converts analog voice signals into digital data packets. It connects a standard telephone to an Ethernet port on a LAN router or Broadband modem. An [_____] phone plugs into an Ethernet port, contains built-in analog to digital conversion, and takes the place of a conventional handset. A USB phone is a VoIP-enabled telephone that plugs into a computer's [_____] port. A grid computing system is a network of diverse computers, such as PCs, Macs, workstations, and servers, in which each computer contributes processing resources to solving a single problem. One of the most famous examples of a grid system is the SETI@home project, but grid technology has been used to crack codes, analyze earthquake data, and crunch numbers for medical research. File transfer [_____] provides a way to transfer files from one computer to another over any TCP/IP network, such as a LAN or the Internet. The purpose of FTP is to make it easy to upload and download computer files without having to deal directly with the [_____] system or file management system of a remote computer. [_____] file sharing uses peer-to-peer protocols that allow users to obtain files from other users located anywhere on the Internet. [_____] is an example of file sharing technology that links clients in a "swarm" for distributing files.

▶ CHECK ANSWERS

6

## SECTION E:

In the context of computers, an [_____] is any access to data or programs by hackers, criminals, or other unauthorized persons. As the result of an intrusion, data can be stolen or altered, system configurations can be changed to allow even more intrusions, and software can be surreptitiously installed and operated under the remote control of a hacker. One of the most common ways of gaining unauthorized access to a network-based computer is by looking for open [_____]. A port [_____] is the use of automated software to locate computers that have open ports and are vulnerable to unauthorized access. One of the easiest steps to enhance your computer's security is to turn it off when you aren't using it. You should also keep your computer up-to-date with the latest operating system security [_____] and service packs. You can also install [_____] software designed to filter out suspicious packets attempting to enter or leave a computer. One of the most effective steps you can take to secure your computer from intrusions is to install a [_____], which assigns private IP addresses to the computers it controls. The process a router uses to keep track of packets and their corresponding private or public IP addresses is called [_____] address translation. Corporations try to limit intrusions by setting up virtual [_____] networks that offer encrypted connections for access to a remote server.

▶ CHECK ANSWERS

# Interactive Situation Questions

Apply what you've learned to some typical computing situations. When using the NP10 BookOnCD, BookOnFlashDrive, or any other NP10 BookOn product, you can type your answers, and then use the Check Answers button to automatically score your responses.

1. You've just got cable Internet service. Your computer is connected to a router, which you connect to the cable modem. The instructions provided by the cable company tell you to make sure [_____] is activated so that you can get a dynamic IP address.

2. You're finally ready to get a high-speed Internet connection. Because the cable modem provided by your CATV company contains Ethernet circuitry, you can simply connect the modem to your computer's [_____] port (shown in the photo at right).

3. Your Internet access seems very slow one day. You might be able to use a networking utility called [_____] to discover the source of the slowdown.

4. Suppose that you decide to open a little Web store to sell handcrafted pottery. Your Web site will need a(n) [_____] IP address, and you'll want to register a(n) [_____] name.

5. Imagine that your computer contains a 56 Kbps modem that uses the V.90 standard. You can expect about 44 Kbps [_____] speed and about 33 Kbps as the maximum [_____] speed.

6. Suppose you have installed a cable modem on a standalone PC. To secure your computer, you should first use Control Panel's Network Connections icon to turn off

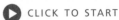

file and printer [_____] . You should also activate [_____] software to filter packets entering and leaving your computer.

7. Your friend, a film student, has created a 20 minute short film that she wants to distribute to friends. The file is much too large to be an e-mail attachment and she doesn't have access to a(n) [_____] server. You suggest that she try posting it at a [_____] P2P file sharing site where a swarm of computers can assist with the downloads.

8. You are going to be telecommuting two days a week, so your corporate information technology department has given you instructions to use the company [_____] private network.

▶ CHECK ANSWERS

# Interactive Practice Tests

Practice tests that consist of 10 multiple-choice, true/false, and fill-in-the-blank questions are available on both the NP10 BookOn products and the NP10 Web site. The questions are selected at random from a large test bank, so each time you take a test, you'll receive a different set of questions. Your tests are scored immediately, and you can print study guides that help you find the correct answers for any questions that you missed.

▶ CLICK TO START

# Study Tips

Study Tips help you to organize and consolidate the information in a unit by making lists, outlines, charts, and sketches. You can use paper and pencil or word processing software to complete most of the Study Tip activities.

1. Make sure you can use your own words to correctly answer each of the red focus questions that appear throughout the chapter.

2. Draw a conceptual diagram illustrating the Internet backbone, NAPs, NSPs, routers, and ISPs.

3. Draw a diagram to illustrate how computers on a LAN would access the Internet through a single DSL modem.

4. Explain the differences between static IP addresses, dynamic IP addresses, private IP addresses, and domain names.

5. Make sure that you can list the Internet access methods in which upstream transmission rates differ from downstream rates.

6. Study the Internet Access Options table in Figure 6-23. Add a statement for each column summarizing the strengths and weaknesses of each option.

7. List the options for mobile and portable Internet access and explain their strengths and weaknesses.

8. Explain the advantages of mobile broadband services compared to WAP service.

9. Create an outline to summarize the information in Section D about Internet services.

10. Make a list of security concerns that are related to Internet access.

11. Make a checklist of steps you can take to secure your computer from Internet-based intrusions.

12. Fill in the blanks on the concept map shown below to show the hierarchy of Internet access options.

6

# Concept Map

# Projects

 CRITICAL THINKING

"The Internet treats censorship like damage and routes around it."
Do you agree with this observation? Does it seem like the Internet—
similar to banned books, music, videos, and satellite dishes—has a
way of infiltrating even the most repressive societies? Does this ten-
dency make censorship more tolerable in the short run?

 GROUP PROJECT

Form a group with three or four other students and discuss the ways in
which you secure your Internet connections. Compose a summary
document that contains specific information about each group member's security and summarize the general level of security your group
has in place.

 CYBERCLASSROOM

Each member of your team should Ping Google and record results.
Exchange your results with other students in your team to find out who
has the fastest connection. How many members of the group have a
connection fast enough to play online interactive multiplayer games?
The member of your team with the fastest connection should summarize the team's data and submit it to your instructor.

 MULTIMEDIA PROJECT

The speed of your Internet connection can affect the download time for
media, such as photos and videos. Use Ping to find the speed of your
Internet connection, then experiment with viewing five different short
videos on news or entertainment Web sites. How does the performance of each video relate to the kind of Internet connection you have?
Compile your findings into a well-organized PowerPoint presentation.
Slide 1 should provide a brief description of your computer and
Internet connection. Slide 2 should include a screen shot of your Ping
statistics. Slides 3 through 7 should describe each of the videos you
viewed, including their addresses and your evaluation of the video
quality. The final slide should include your overall evaluation of the
quality and convenience of Web-based video. Follow your instructor's
guidelines for submitting and/or presenting your project.

 RESUME BUILDER

The Internet provides resources for career development. Think about
your ideal job and make a table that lists (in the first column) the top 10
qualifications and skills you'll need to be a successful applicant. In the
second column, indicate whether you currently possess each qualifica-
tion or skill. For those you need to develop in the future, indicate how
you plan to obtain them, for example from a college course, on-the-job
training, or self-paced study. Find out if you can develop any of these
skills and qualifications using online resources, such as online courses. Provide addresses for any Internet resources that you find.

 GLOBALIZATION

Worldwide, communications capabilities are growing at a rapid pace.
Nonetheless, there exists among countries a great disparity in communications capabilities. For this project, use library and Internet
resources to gather information about the communications options that
are available throughout the world. You should consider which technologies are available and the number of people who use each
technology. Your research can include any of the following: land-based
phones, cellular phones, premium phone services such as ISDN and
ADSL, Internet access, broadcast television, and cable television.
Once you have gathered these facts, consider how they might affect
the lifestyles, politics, and economies of various regions. Suppose that
you are organizing a high school debate about global communications
technology. As the organizer, you must devise a controversial question
on which the debate will be based. You should also write three "pro"
and "con" paragraphs just to make sure that both sides of the issue will
have substantial material to debate.

 ISSUE

The Issue section of this chapter addressed the controversy over censorship on the Internet. Free speech is in constant struggle with
individual rights and public safety. On the Web, some sites contain
pornography, bigotry, and terrorist rhetoric that many people would
rather not be public. One of the cornerstones of democracy, however,
is freedom of speech. Where do you draw the line when it comes to
censoring and filtering on the Internet? Explain your views, making
sure you consider questions such as: Do parents have the right to
monitor, screen, and filter their children's Web use? Are governments
ever justified in regulating what their citizens can access? Should anyone be responsible for policing the Internet? Incorporate your ideas in
a two-page summary and submit it to your instructor.

 COMPUTERS IN CONTEXT

The Computers in Context section of this chapter focused on banking
innovations and technology. The newest innovation to affect consumers is online banking. Although convenient, online banking has not
been enthusiastically adopted by many consumers because of security
concerns. For this project, research the services offered by online
banking, then research the risks. Summarize your findings in a short
paper. Connect to at least three banks that offer online banking services. Read through their promotional materials. Based on this material,
indicate which bank seems to offer the best and most secure online
banking services. Explain your choice in the last section of your paper.
Follow your instructor's guidelines to submit your work as a printed
document or by e-mail.

# On the Web

## STUDENT EDITION LABS

**W CLICK TO ACCESS THE NP10 WEB SITE**
or open your browser and connect to www.course.com/np/concepts10/ch06.
Lab results can be stored in the Universal Gradebook.

Work hands-on in structured simulations practicing important skills and concepts

### PROTECTING YOUR PRIVACY ONLINE

In the Protecting Your Privacy Online Student Edition Lab, you will learn the following topics and skills:

- How cookies work
- Deleting cookies using a browser
- Adjusting your cookie settings in Internet Explorer

### CONNECTING TO THE INTERNET

In the Connecting to the Internet Student Edition Lab, you will learn the following topics and skills:

- Establishing an Internet connection
- Connecting to the Internet using dial-up, DSL, cable, and wireless
- Installing ISP software
- Creating Internet connections manually

### GETTING THE MOST OUT OF THE INTERNET

In the Getting the Most out of the Internet Student Edition Lab, you will learn the following topics and skills:

- Keeping track of your favorite Web sites
- Customizing your browser
- Searching the Web
- Online job hunting
- Online travel reservations
- Building communities

### CHAPTER COURSECAST

Use your computer or iPod to hear a five-minute audio presentation of chapter highlights.

### FLASHCARD COURSECAST

Interact with audio flashcards to review key terms from the chapter.

### DETAILED OBJECTIVES

Make sure that you've achieved all the objectives for a chapter before it's time for your test!

### TEST YOURSELF

Review chapter material by taking these ten-question tests, then send your results to the Universal Gradebook.

### ONLINE GAMES

Have some fun while refreshing your memory about key concepts that might appear on the next test. You can even send your results to the Universal Gradebook!

### AND MORE!

At the NP10 Web site you'll also find TechBuzz, CNET videos, Extra Content, and InfoWebLinks.

6

# 7

# The Web and E-mail

## CHAPTER CONTENTS

## LEARNING OBJECTIVES

- Describe the roles that HTML, XHTML, HTTP, URLs, browsers, and Web servers play in bringing Web pages to your desktop
- Illustrate an example of an HTML tag
- List the names of at least four Web browsers
- Describe the purpose of helper applications, plug-ins, and players
- Describe the significance of a browser cache
- Explain why cookies are useful in an environment that is based on a stateless protocol, and provide some concrete examples of their use
- Identify at least three Web page authoring tools and discuss their advantages and disadvantages
- Identify the elements that typically form a Web page
- Explain how to test and post Web pages
- List some advantages and disadvantages of HTML scripts
- List and describe the elements of a search engine
- Demonstrate that you can use a search engine to locate information on the Web
- Create advanced search queries and correctly format citations for Web-based materials
- Discuss why e-commerce has become so popular with consumers and merchants
- List some threats to the security of credit card numbers and other sensitive data during e-commerce transactions
- Describe how the following e-commerce technologies work: shopping carts, SSL, one-time-use credit cards, electronic wallets, and person-to-person payment systems
- List the features that you would expect to find in a typical e-mail software package
- Explain how an e-mail system works and describe the difference between POP and Web-based e-mail
- List security precautions you can take to avoid cookie exploits, pharming, spam, and phishing

 **PRE-ASSESSMENT QUIZ**
Take the pre-assessment quiz to find out how much you know about the topics in this chapter.

**MULTIMEDIA and INTERACTIVE ELEMENTS**
When using the BookOnCD, BookOnFlashDrive, or other NP10 BookOn product, the ▶ icons are clickable to access multimedia resources.

BEFORE YOU READ ON, **TRY IT**

**WHAT'S MY BROWSER STATUS?**

Chapter 7 focuses on the World Wide Web, or "Web" for short. The most important software tool for accessing the Web is called a browser. To learn about the browser on your computer, do the following steps:

**1.** Make sure your computer is on and displaying the Windows desktop.

**2.** Which browser do you typically use to access the Web? _____
If you don't know, look for browser icons on your desktop. Popular browsers include Internet Explorer, Netscape Navigator, Firefox, and Opera.

**3.** What is the URL that your browser uses as your home page? _____
To find your browser's home page, start your browser. The home page is the first Web page displayed and the one displayed when you click the Home button.

**4.** What is the version number for the browser you are using? _____
To find your browser's version number, click Help and then click About. Your browser's version number should be displayed in a dialog box. After you write down the version number, close the dialog box.

**5.** Are you using the most recent version of your browser? _____

To find the most recent version for your browser, go to its Web site, for example *www.mozilla.org/products/firefox*, *www.microsoft.com/windows/ie*, *www.netscape.com*, or *www.opera.com*. You should be able to locate a download link that displays the latest version number. Unless you want to download the most recent version of your browser and have permission to do so, exit the download area and close your browser.

# Web Technology

**IN 1990,** a British scientist named Tim Berners-Lee developed specifications for URLs, HTML, and HTTP technologies designed to help researchers share information by creating access to a sort of "web" of electronic documents. Berners-Lee's free Web software appeared on the Internet in 1991, but the Web didn't take off until 1993 when Marc Andreessen and his colleagues at the University of Illinois created Mosaic, a graphical browser. Andreessen later formed his own company and produced a browser called Netscape, which put the Web into the hands of millions of Web surfers. In Section A, you'll peel back the layers of Web technologies to take a look at what happens behind your browser window.

## WEB BASICS

**What is the Web?** One of the Internet's most captivating attractions, the **Web** (short for World Wide Web) is a collection of document, image, video, and sound files that can be linked and accessed over the Internet using a protocol called HTTP.

The concept of interlinking documents to access them pre-dates the Web by almost half a century. In 1945, an engineer named Vannevar Bush described a microfilm-based machine called the Memex that linked associated information or ideas through "trails."

The idea of linked documents resurfaced in the mid-1960s when Harvard graduate Ted Nelson coined the term **hypertext** to describe a computer system that could store literary documents, link them according to logical relationships, and allow readers to comment and annotate what they read. Nelson sketched the diagram in Figure 7-1 to explain his idea of a computer-based "web" of "links."

**What is a Web site?** A **Web site** typically contains a collection of related information organized and formatted so it can be accessed using software called a browser. You are probably familiar with informational Web sites such as Wikipedia, Library of Congress, HowStuffWorks, CNN, ESPN, and CNET.

In addition to conventional sites that offer text-based information and news, Web sites also host a diverse array of activities. Web sites that host amateur video, photos, and music get lots of traffic. Online shopping is a popular Web-based activity. From tiny niche boutiques to the Amazon.com superstore and countless eBay auctions, you can find just about any merchandise or service on the Web.

Many Web sites offer tools for creating your own blog and viewing blogs created by others. Blogs have become a frequently referenced source of commentary on news and politics. The Web also hosts a thriving selection of podcasts. A **podcast** (sometimes called a Webcast) is an audio file that is distributed through downloads or the use of a feed, such as **RSS** (Really Simple Syndication) or **Atom**. You can subscribe to a feed to make sure you automatically receive new podcasts as they are produced.

**TERMINOLOGY NOTE**

Although the terms *Internet* and *Web* are sometimes used interchangeably, they are not the same. The Web is an interlinked collection of information; the Internet is a communications system used to transport that information from computers that store it to clients who want to view it.

**FIGURE 7-1**

Ted Nelson's early sketch of project Xanadu—a distant relative of the Web—used the terms "links" and "web."

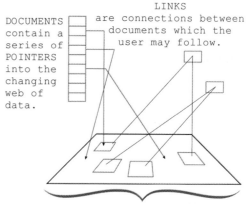

Expanding Tissue of Text, Data, and Graphics

Podcasting was originally used to distribute radio show episodes, but is now widely used to distribute news, sports, music, educational tutorials, and blogs. **Videocasting** is similar to podcasting, but with video instead of audio files.

Social networking sites, such as Facebook, Classmates, MySpace, and Bebo link people together whether they are just down the street or on the other side of the globe. Members post their own profiles and invite friends to join. You can find old friends or meet new ones by networking to friends of your friends.

The activities that take place at Web sites are under the control of Web servers. A **Web server** is an Internet-based computer that accepts requests from browsers. Servers collect the requested information and transmit it back in a format that the browser can display, usually in the form of a Web page.

**What is a Web page?** A **Web page** is the product or output of one or more Web-based files displayed in a format similar to a page in a book. Unlike book pages, however, Web pages can dynamically incorporate videos, sounds, and interactive elements.

A Web page can be based on a document stored as a file or it can be assembled on the fly from information stored in a database. For example, a course syllabus that you view on the Web is probably written with a word processor and stored as a document on a Web server, whereas the Web page you view about a newly released CD on Amazon.com is assembled from a database that contains the CD name, artist name, song titles, price, album cover art, and other product information.

**How do I access a Web page?** Your main tool for accessing Web pages is browser software, such as Microsoft Internet Explorer, open-source Mozilla Firefox, or Apple's Safari. A **Web browser** (usually simply referred to as a browser) is client software that displays Web page elements and handles links between pages. When using a browser, you can access a Web page by clicking a **hypertext link** (usually referred to simply as a link) or by typing a URL (Figure 7-2).

**What is a URL?** Every Web page has a unique address called a **URL** (Uniform Resource Locator, pronounced "You Are ELL"). For example, the URL for the Cable News Network (CNN) Web site is *http://www.cnn.com*. Most URLs begin with http:// to indicate the Web's standard communications protocol. When typing a URL, the http:// can usually be omitted, so *www.cnn.com* works just as well as *http://www.cnn.com*.

Most Web sites have a main page that acts as a doorway to the rest of the pages at the site. This main page is sometimes referred to as a home page, although this term can also refer to the page displayed by your browser each time it opens. The URL for a Web site's main page is usually short and to the point, like *www.cnn.com*.

**FIGURE 7-2**

Web page links can appear as underlined text, buttons, and graphics of varying size. When your pointer moves over a link, it changes from an arrow shape to a hand shape.

Web page URL

The Mardi Gras Hotel

| Home | Accommodations | Restaurants | Reservations |

Tucked away in a quiet corner of the Soulard district of St. Louis, you'll find the exclusive and very elegant Mardi Gras Hotel. Built in 1852, the hotel has operated continuously, serving visiting dignitaries, celebrities, and party-minded tourists. With its tranquil garden retreat, the hotel is just steps from the farmers market (map) and the second largest Mardi Gras parade in the United States.

Navigation links

Graphical link

Mardi Gras Calendar

Text link and hand-shaped pointer

7

The pages for a Web site are typically grouped into folders, which are reflected in the URL. For example, the CNN site might include weather information at *www.cnn.com/weather/* and entertainment information at *www.cnn.com/showbiz/*. The file name of a specific Web page always appears last in the URL. Web page file names usually have an .htm or .html extension, indicating that the page was created with Hypertext Markup Language. You'll learn more about HTML later in the chapter. Figure 7-3 identifies the parts of a URL.

**FIGURE 7-3**

The URL for a Web page indicates the computer on which it is stored, its location on the Web server, its file name, and its extension.

# http://www.cnn.com/showbiz/movies.htm

| Web protocol standard | Web server name | Folder name | Document name and file extension |

**What are the rules for correctly typing a URL?** A URL never contains spaces, even after a punctuation mark, so do not type any spaces within a URL. An underline symbol is sometimes used to give the appearance of a space between words, for example *www.detroit.com/top_10.html*.

Be sure to use the correct type of slash—always a forward slash (/)—and duplicate the URL's capitalization exactly. Some Web servers are case sensitive. On these servers, typing *www.cmu.edu/Info.html* (with an uppercase "I") will not locate the Web page that's stored on the Web server as *www.cmu.edu/info.html* (with a lowercase "i").

## HTML

**What is HTML?** HTML (Hypertext Markup Language) is a set of specifications for creating documents that a browser can display as a Web page. HTML is called a **markup language** because authors mark up documents by inserting special instructions, called **HTML tags**, that specify how the document should appear when displayed on a computer screen or printed.

Tim Berners-Lee developed the original HTML specifications in 1990. These specifications were revised several times by the World Wide Web Consortium (W3C), but many of the early revisions did not gain widespread acceptance. HTML 3.2, introduced in 1997, was the first widely adopted revision of the original HTML specifications. HTML version 4.0 was introduced in late 1997, and HTML 4.01 in 1999.

**XHTML** is the follow-up version to HTML 4. Rather than calling it HTML 5, the W3C preferred to name it XHTML 1.0 to reflect its extensibility. XHTML includes all HTML 4 tags, but it can be extended by adding customized tags. Today's Web operates according to XHTML standards, even though people commonly refer to the technology simply as HTML. Variations of HTML, such as **DHTML** (dynamic HTML) and **Ajax** (Asynchronous JavaScript and XML) offer tools and techniques for extending basic HTML and making Web pages more interactive, visually appealing, and media-rich.

**How do HTML tags work?** HTML tags are incorporated into an **HTML document**, which is similar to a word processing file, but has an .htm or .html extension. HTML tags, such as <hr /> and <b>, are enclosed in angle brackets and embedded in the document. These tags are instructions for the browser. When your browser displays a Web page on your computer screen, it does not show the tags or angle brackets. Instead, it attempts to follow the tags' instructions.

**INFOWEBLINKS**

The W3C is a worldwide organization that formulates standards for the Web. Learn more by connecting to the **W3C InfoWeb**.

 CLICK TO CONNECT
www.course.com/np/concepts10/ch07

**So HTML documents look a lot different from Web pages, right?** Exactly. An HTML document is like a screenplay, and your browser is like a director who makes a screenplay come to life by assembling cast members and making sure they deliver their lines correctly.

As the HTML "screenplay" unfolds, your browser follows the instructions in an HTML document to display lines of text on your computer screen in the right color, size, and position. If the screenplay calls for a graphic, your browser collects it from the Web server and displays it. Although the HTML screenplay exists as a permanent file, the Web page you see on your computer screen exists only for the duration of the "performance."

Technically speaking, you can distinguish HTML documents (the screenplay) from Web pages (the performance). However, in everyday conversation, the term *Web page* is often used for the HTML document as well as the Web page displayed on screen.

An HTML document is sometimes referred to as a source document because it is the source of the HTML tags used to construct a Web page. You can view the HTML source documents for most Web pages if you are curious about how they were constructed. Figure 7-4 illustrates the difference between an HTML source document and the Web page it produces.

**FIGURE 7-4**

An HTML document (top) contains text and HTML tags. Formatting tags are used to change font size, separate paragraphs, and add rules. Other tags add graphics and links to a page. The HTML document produces a Web page (bottom).

7

CLICK TO START

## HTTP

**How does HTTP work?** **HTTP** is a protocol that works with TCP/IP to get Web resources to your desktop. A Web resource can be defined as any chunk of data that has a URL, such as an HTML document, a graphic, or a sound file.

HTTP includes commands called *methods* that help your browser communicate with Web servers. GET is the most frequently used HTTP method. The GET method is typically used to retrieve the text and graphics files necessary for displaying a Web page. This method can also be used to pass a search query to a file server. HTTP transports your browser's request for a Web resource to a Web server. Next, it transports the Web server's response back to your browser.

An HTTP exchange takes place over a pair of sockets. A **socket** is an abstract concept that represents one end of a connection. Although a packet switching network doesn't actually make point-to-point connections between network nodes, many people find it handy to visualize network connections as a communication line with a doorway-like socket at each end. For HTTP, sockets usually are associated with port 80 on the client and server.

In an HTTP exchange, your browser opens a socket on your PC, connects to a similar open socket at the Web server, and issues a command, such as "send me an HTML document." The server receives the command, executes it, and sends a response back through the socket. The sockets are then closed until the browser is ready to issue another command. Figure 7-5 demonstrates the messages that flow between your browser and a Web server to retrieve an HTML document.

**FIGURE 7-5**

HTTP messages flow between a browser and a Web server.

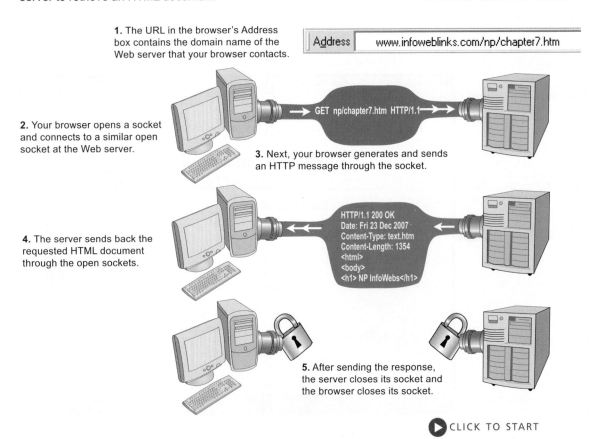

**1.** The URL in the browser's Address box contains the domain name of the Web server that your browser contacts.

Address   www.infoweblinks.com/np/chapter7.htm

**2.** Your browser opens a socket and connects to a similar open socket at the Web server.

GET np/chapter7.htm HTTP/1.1

**3.** Next, your browser generates and sends an HTTP message through the socket.

**4.** The server sends back the requested HTML document through the open sockets.

HTTP/1.1 200 OK
Date: Fri 23 Dec 2007
Content-Type: text.htm
Content-Length: 1354
<html>
<body>
<h1> NP InfoWebs</h1>

**5.** After sending the response, the server closes its socket and the browser closes its socket.

● CLICK TO START

**Is each Web page element retrieved separately?** Yes. HTTP is classified as a **stateless protocol**, which maintains no record of previous interactions and handles each request based entirely on information that comes with it.

HTTP generally allows only one request and response per session. As a result, your browser can request an HTML document during a session, but as soon as the document is sent, the session is closed, and the Web server forgets that your browser ever made a request. To make additional requests—for example, to request a graphic that's supposed to be displayed on a Web page—your browser must open another session. You can understand, then, that to assemble a complex Web page with several graphics, buttons, and sounds, your browser makes many HTTP requests to the Web server.

**What if an element cannot be found?** A Web server's response to a browser's request includes an **HTTP status code** that indicates whether the browser's request could be fulfilled. The status code 200 means that the request was fulfilled—the requested HTML document, graphic, or other resource was sent. Anyone who surfs the Web has encountered the "404 Not Found" message. Your browser displays this message when a Web server sends a 404 status code to indicate that the requested resource does not exist (Figure 7-6).

## WEB BROWSERS

**What are some of today's most popular browsers?** Today's most popular browsers include Microsoft Internet Explorer, Mozilla Firefox, Apple Safari, Netscape Navigator, and Opera. Figure 7-7 illustrates these popular programs.

Netscape Navigator was one of the first browsers with a graphical user interface. Published in December 1994, Netscape quickly became the most popular browser on Macintosh and PC platforms. Numerous revisions added pioneering features to enhance the overall browsing experience. Netscape is currently published by Netscape Communications and Weblogs, Inc., a subsidiary of AOL.

In 1998, Netscape source code became open source software, managed by an organization known as Mozilla. The organization's main product, a browser called Mozilla, was all but ignored by most computer owners. In 2004, however, a new version of Mozilla, dubbed Firefox, rapidly gained popularity because it offered effective security features.

Internet Explorer (IE) version 1.0 was published by Microsoft in August 1995. The program code for the original IE 1.0 browser was licensed from a Netscape spin-off called Spyglass, which provided IE with many of the same features as Netscape. Until IE 4.0 appeared in 1997, however, Microsoft's browser was unable to match Netscape's popularity. Today, IE has supplanted Netscape as the dominant browser for the PC platform. It is also available for Mac OS, Linux, and several versions of UNIX. AOL's browser is a slightly modified version of IE.

**FIGURE 7-6**

When a broken link points to a nonexistent HTML document, your browser typically produces a 404 Not Found error. When a broken link points to a nonexistent graphic or other non-HTML file, your browser usually displays one of the broken link icons, shown below.

**FIGURE 7-7**

Shown on this page, Netscape Navigator and Firefox.

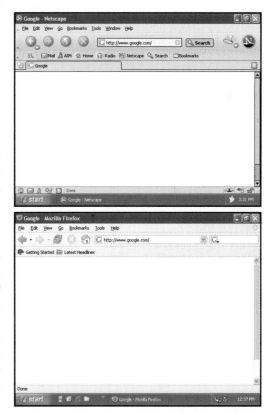

Before Firefox, Opera was one of the few alternatives to IE and Netscape. First published in December 1996, Opera began as a Norwegian phone company project to develop a small and fast browser for computers with meager memory and processing resources. Unlike IE and Netscape, which descended from Mosaic, Opera was written from scratch; as a result, it has some unique features, such as page zoom and a multidocument display. Versions of Opera are available for Windows, Linux, UNIX, and Mac OS.

Macintosh computers were preloaded with Netscape Navigator until 1997, when Microsoft Internet Explorer for Mac replaced it. In 2003, however, Apple introduced a new browser called Safari, which is now included with Macintosh computers. Safari has the distinction of being the first browser to pass the Acid2 test, which means that it follows W3C standards and can correctly display all complying Web pages.

**Should I upgrade my browser when new versions become available?** It is a good idea to upgrade when a new version of your browser appears. Because most browser updates are free, you can get up-to-date functionality simply by spending a few minutes downloading and installing an update.

The problem with using an old version of a browser is that some Web pages depend on new HTML features supported only by the latest browser versions. Without the latest upgrade, you might encounter errors when your browser tries to display a page, but cannot interpret some of the HTML. In other cases, your browser might display the Web page without errors, but you will not see all the intended effects.

Another important reason to upgrade is for increased security. As hackers discover and take advantage of security holes, browser publishers try to patch the holes. Upgrades usually contain patches for known security holes, although new features might sometimes open new holes.

**Why do I have to download software to view some Web pages?** Browsers were originally limited to displaying documents in HTML format and graphics files in GIF and JPEG formats. Today, browsers work with additional file formats. Some browsers, however, do not have built-in support for proprietary file formats commonly used on the Web to display video, animation, and other media.

If you click a link that leads to a file stored in a format your browser does not handle, you can usually download software necessary to read the file format. For example, to read a PDF file, you might be directed to the Adobe Web site to download Acrobat Reader software that handles PDF files. To display an animation, you might need Adobe's Flash software. The software your browser calls upon to read non-native file formats can take the form of a helper application, plug-in, or player.

**FIGURE 7-7 CONTINUED**

Shown on this page, Internet Explorer, Opera, and Safari.

**What is a helper application?** A **helper application** (sometimes called a browser add-on) is a program that extends a browser's ability to work with file formats. Most helper applications can be downloaded from the Web. The process of installing a helper application creates an association between the browser and a file format, such as PDF, SWF, or MOV. Whenever your browser encounters one of these file formats, it automatically runs the corresponding helper application, which in turn opens the file.

**Is a plug-in the same as a helper application?** A **plug-in** is a type of helper application, pioneered by Netscape developers, that can be activated from an <embed> tag inserted in an HTML document. For example, <embed src = "sample.swf"> instructs a browser to activate the plug-in that works with the SWF file format, which can in turn open the sample.swf file.

Recent versions of Internet Explorer, however, do not respond to the <embed> tag and, therefore, are not able to use Netscape-style plug-ins. Instead, IE uses ActiveX components, which are activated by the <object> tag. Aside from this technical distinction, today's helper applications and plug-ins are very similar from the user's perspective.

The current trend is to use the term **player** to refer to any helper application or plug-in that helps a browser display a particular file format. Figure 7-8 shows a list of players installed for use with Internet Explorer.

**What is a browser cache?** When your browser fetches pages and graphics to form a Web page, it stores that material on your computer in temporary files sometimes referred to as a **Web cache** or browser cache. These temporary files come in handy if you switch back and forth between pages or sites. Rather than fetch the entire page and all its graphics again, your browser can simply load them from the local cache. Files are deleted from the Web cache within days or weeks, depending on your browser's settings.

A potential problem with your Web cache is that it stores Web page elements from all the sites you've visited. If you use a public or lab computer, the Web page elements are stored there and can be viewed by others. To maintain your privacy, you might consider deleting these files periodically, adjusting browser settings to limit the time these files remain on your computer, or limiting the amount of space they can use on the hard disk.

**FIGURE 7-8**

You can usually find a list of players installed for use with your browser. If you use Internet Explorer, look for a Manage Add-ons option on the Tools menu. Your browser's list of players might include a PDF reader and spyware detectors used by your antivirus software.

 CLICK TO START

**INFOWEBLINKS**

For information about the most popular players, connect to the **Browser Players InfoWeb**.

 CLICK TO CONNECT
www.course.com/np/concepts10/ch07

## COOKIES

**What is a cookie?** A **cookie** (technically an HTTP cookie) is a small chunk of data generated by a Web server and stored in a text file on your computer's hard disk. Figure 7-9 contains an example.

ppkcookie1hellowww.quirksmode.org/1600182732736 0298117151147060128298 10307*

Cookies allow a Web site to store information on a client computer for later retrieval. Web sites use cookies to:

- Monitor your path through a site to keep track of the pages you viewed or the items you purchased.

- Gather information that allows a Web server to present ad banners targeted to products you previously purchased at that Web site.

- Collect personal information you type into a Web page form and retain it for the next time you visit the Web site.

**Why do Web sites need to use cookies?** In many respects, cookies are a fix for problems caused by HTTP's stateless protocol. Cookies are frequently used to remind a Web server who you are each time your browser makes a request.

Suppose that you use your browser to visit a popular online music store. You search for your favorite bands, listen to some sample tracks, and select a few CDs you want to purchase. After browsing through 20 or 30 pages, you eventually go to the checkout counter where you see a list of the CDs you selected. You fill out a form that requests your name, shipping address, and payment information.

Although you might have been browsing at the music site for 30 minutes or more, from the perspective of the site's server, that activity could just as well have been carried out by several people, each one spending only a few seconds at the site. Because HTTP is a stateless protocol, each time you connect to a different page, the server regards it as a new visit.

Cookies allow the music site's server to identify you so that your requests won't get mixed up with those of other people visiting the site. Cookies also enable the server to keep track of your activity and compile a list of your purchases.

**How do cookies work?** When your browser connects to a site that uses cookies, it receives an HTTP "Set-cookie" message from the Web server. This cookie message contains some information that your browser stores on your computer's hard disk. The cookie information can include a customer number, a shopping cart number, a part number, or any other data. In addition, the cookie usually contains the date the cookie expires and the domain name of the host that created the cookie. A server that creates a cookie can request it the next time you connect to one of its Web pages.

**How long do cookies stay on my computer?** A Web developer can program a cookie to time out after a designated period of time. When a cookie reaches the end of its predefined lifetime, your Web browser simply erases it. Some cookies have no expiration date or a date far into the future, so cookies tend to accumulate on your computer's hard disk.

**FIGURE 7-9**

When you look at the cookies stored on your computer, most of the information is unintelligible. This cookie is called ppkcookie, its value is "hello," and it was created at *www.quirksmode.org*. The cookie contains an expiration date, but it is encoded so you can't decipher it.

**INFOWEBLINKS**

At the **Cookies InfoWeb**, you'll find links to a collection of articles that focus on cookie technology, including how they affect security and privacy.

 CLICK TO CONNECT
www.course.com/np/concepts10/ch07

**Can I see the cookies stored on my computer?** You can view a list of the cookies stored on your computer, but first you must discover where they are stored. Netscape stores cookies in one large file called *Cookies.txt* on a PC or in *Magiccookie* on a Macintosh. IE stores each cookie in a separate file. Refer to your browser documentation to discover which folder holds your cookies. Figure 7-10 shows a list of cookies stored for Internet Explorer.

**FIGURE 7-10**

Internet Explorer typically stores cookies as individual files on your computer's hard disk. You can view a list of cookies stored on your computer. The information after the @ symbol usually indicates the domain name of the site that set the cookie.

## WEB PAGE AUTHORING

**What tools can I use to create Web pages?** Your ISP or school might offer space for you to store your own Web pages, which you can keep private or open for public access. You have several choices when it comes to Web page authoring tools. You can use a text editor, HTML conversion utilities, online Web authoring tools, or Web authoring software.

The most difficult—and some would say old-fashioned—way to create Web pages is to use a text editor such as Notepad to type the HTML tags along with the text that you want the browser to display on a Web page.

An **HTML conversion utility** adds HTML tags to a document, spreadsheet, or other text-based file to create an HTML document that can be displayed by a browser. For example, you can work with Microsoft Word to create a standard DOC file and then use the File menu's Save As Web Page option to convert the document into HTML format. Converting a document into HTML format sometimes produces an unusual result, however, because some of the features and formatting in your original document might not be possible within the world of HTML.

A third option for budding Web page authors is to use a set of online Web page authoring tools. These template-like tools are provided by some ISPs and other companies that host Web pages for individuals and businesses. Working with these tools is quite simple—you type, select, drag, and drop elements onto a Web page.

A fourth option for creating Web pages is a special category of software called Web authoring software, which provides tools specifically designed to enter and format Web page text, graphics, and links (Figure 7-11). Popular Web authoring products include Microsoft FrontPage and Adobe Dreamweaver.

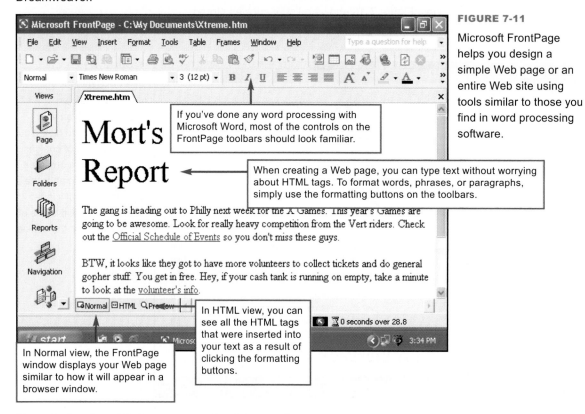

**FIGURE 7-11**

Microsoft FrontPage helps you design a simple Web page or an entire Web site using tools similar to those you find in word processing software.

**How do I get my Web pages on the Internet?** Creating a Web page is not the end of the publishing process. You also must test your pages, transfer them to a Web server, and test all your links, as explained by the steps in Figure 7-12.

**FIGURE 7-12**

Steps for Posting Web Pages

**1. Test each page locally.** When you complete the first draft of a Web page, you should test it to verify that every element is displayed correctly by any browsers that visitors to your Web page might use. You can accomplish this task without connecting to the Web. Simply open a browser, and then enter the local file name for the HTML document you created for your Web page. Repeat this process for any other browsers you expect visitors to use. One caution: Your hard disk drive is much faster than most Internet connections, so the text and graphics for your Web page are displayed faster during your local test than for someone viewing your page over the Internet.

**2. Transfer pages to a Web server.** Whether you're publishing a single page, a series of pages, or an entire Web site, you must put your pages on a Web server—a process called posting. To post Web page files manually you can use a file transfer utility, such as WSFTP. Web authoring software usually provides a menu option that automates the process of posting HTML documents and associated media files.

**3. Test all pages and links.** After you post your pages on a Web server, make sure you can access each page, and then test the links between your pages as well as any links to pages on other sites.

**4. Update your site to keep it current.** Periodically, you should review the information on your Web pages and verify that the links still connect to existing Web pages. You can easily change your pages and then test them offline before reposting them. You might encounter Under Construction signs at some Web sites, but they aren't usually necessary. You should handle your construction and revision work offline.

## HTML SCRIPTS

**Is it possible to add programs to a Web page?** Standard HTML provides a way to display text and graphics on a Web page and link to other Web pages, but because it isn't a programming language, HTML does not provide a way to perform complicated tasks or respond to user actions. A series of program instructions called an **HTML script** can be embedded directly into the text of an HTML document or in a file referenced from an HTML document. Scripts are not displayed by the browser; instead, they instruct the browser to perform specific actions or respond to specific user actions.

**How would a Web page author use a script?** Scripts allow Web pages to become more interactive and incorporate activities that would otherwise require a computer program. Scripts enable e-commerce sites to verify credit card information. They also make it possible to create interactive Web pages, that include fill-in forms. Scripts work with cookies to deliver custom Web pages, such as those Amazon.com generates each time you return to the site. Scripts don't replace normal HTML—they extend and enhance it.

As an example of scripting, consider what happens when you use online forms. **HTML forms** are used to collect user input for e-commerce orders, site registrations, opinion polls, and so on. The information you enter into an HTML form is held in the memory of your computer, where your browser creates temporary storage bins that correspond to the input field names designated by the form's HTML tags.

Your address, in the form shown in Figure 7-13, might be temporarily held in a memory location that's called Customer Address. When you click a Submit button, your browser gathers the data from memory and sends it to a specially designated script on an HTTP server, where it can be processed and stored.

**FIGURE 7-13**

HTML forms are typically used to collect payment and shipping information at the checkout counter of e-commerce Web sites.

**Do scripts run on my local computer or on a Web server?** Scripts can run on a client or a server. A **server-side script** consists of statements that run on a server. Server-side scripts accept data submitted by a form, process that data, and then generate a custom HTML document that is sent to the browser for display. These dynamically produced pages can often be identified because they contain question marks (?) in the URL displayed in the Address bar of your browser. Server-side scripts can be written using a variety of programming and scripting languages, such as Perl, C, C++, C#, and Java.

A **client-side script** consists of scripting statements that run on your local computer. The script is executed by the browser, which must have the capability to deal with the programming language used to write the script. Popular languages for client-side scripts include VBScript and JavaScript. Most of today's browsers can handle JavaScript, but only IE has the built-in capability to execute VBScript. Client-side scripts often take the form of Java applets or ActiveX controls.

**What's a Java applet?** A **Java applet** is an application written in the Java programming language. A programmer or Web page author places a reference to a Java applet in an HTML document using the <applet> HTML tag. When working with a Web page that contains an <applet> tag, your browser downloads the applet and executes its instructions. The applet is not installed on your computer, so it does not leave a permanent footprint.

You might wonder if a Java applet could contain a virus that would take up residence in your computer system or a worm that would spread over your network. Applets are fairly safe because they cannot open, modify, delete, or create files on your computer; they cannot make any network connections except to the originating site; and they cannot start other programs.

**What is an ActiveX control?** An **ActiveX control** is a compiled computer program that can be referenced from within an HTML document, downloaded, installed on your computer, and executed within the browser window. ActiveX controls can be used on the server side, too, but consumers typically encounter the client-side version when their browsers display a security warning and ask for permission to proceed with installation (Figure 7-14).

**FIGURE 7-14**

Web surfers who use Internet Explorer sometimes encounter the Security Warning dialog box for ActiveX components. If the component is supplied by a trusted source, then it should be safe to install it.

Programmers and Web page authors use programming languages such as C++ and Visual Basic to create ActiveX controls, which can be applied in a wide variety of ways to make Web pages interactive. ActiveX helps programmers provide the functionality many consumers expect after using full-featured applications, such as word processing, graphics, and entertainment software.

Most ActiveX controls are safe. However, an ActiveX control is a full-fledged program, which gives it the potential to include routines that alter or delete data on your computer's hard disk. ActiveX controls include digital certificates to increase their security. A **digital certificate** is an electronic attachment to a file that verifies the identity of its source (Figure 7-15).

**Is it easy to create Java applets and ActiveX controls?** Scripts are somewhat more difficult to write and test than HTML documents, so scripts are typically the domain of professional Web designers. A basic understanding of scripts, however, along with a grasp of HTML, HTTP, cookies, browsers, and hypertext, should give you a more complete understanding of how the Web works.

**FIGURE 7-15**

A digital certificate can be electronically attached to any ActiveX control the applicant creates. That control is then referred to as *signed*—it is as though the programmer signed his or her name to it. Theoretically, malicious programmers would not put their names on certificates that travel with an ActiveX control infected with a virus or worm.

# QuickCheck

1. When using a browser, you can access a Web page by clicking a hypertext _____ or by typing a URL.

2. When typing a URL, keep in mind that it can never contain a(n) _____ , even after a punctuation mark.

3. _____ software interprets and executes the special instructions embedded in HTML documents to display Web pages for you.

4. A(n) _____ application is a program that extends a browser's ability to work with files in a variety of formats.

5. Cookies were developed because HTTP is a(n) _____ protocol, so each time you connect to a different page, the Web server regards it as a new connection.

6. Some cookies can remain indefinitely on your computer's hard disk unless you manually delete them. True or false? _____

7. Because ActiveX controls are full-fledged programs that can alter, add, or delete data on your computer's hard disk, they include digital _____ for security purposes.

 CHECK ANSWERS

# Search Engines

THE WEB ENCOMPASSES hundreds of millions of pages stored on servers scattered all over the globe. To use this information, however, you have to find it. There is no rhyme or reason to the location of Web-based information; a particular fact you're trying to unearth could be located on an obscure server in Kazakhstan, or buried deep in the folder structure of a major e-commerce Web site. Modern Web surfers depend on search engines for help navigating the waves of information stored on the Web. In Section B you'll find out how Web search engines work, so that you can use them more efficiently.

## SEARCH ENGINE BASICS

**What is a Web search engine?** A **Web search engine** (usually referred to simply as a search engine) is a program designed to help people locate information on the Web by formulating simple keyword queries. In response to a query, the search engine displays results or "hits" as a list of relevant Web sites, accompanied by links to source pages and short excerpts containing the keywords (Figure 7-16).

**FIGURE 7-16**

A query for "mountain bike" returns a list of links to relevant sites.

Popular search engines are located at Web sites such as *www.google.com*, *www.msn.com*, *www.ask.com*, and *www.yahoo.com*. You might say that the search engines at these sites build the equivalent of a book index. Whereas a book index helps readers turn to a page on which they can find a particular word or concept, a search engine helps Web surfers link to pages that contain the information they seek. Unlike a book, however, the information on the Web is too vast to catalog manually, so search engine software does it autonomously.

**What is the difference between a search engine and a search engine site?** It is easy to think of *www.google.com* as a search engine, but to be precise it is a Web site that offers access to a search engine. Search engine sites often contain a variety of tools and services in addition to search engine access. For example, Google's Web site offers maps, calendars, e-mail, photo sharing, and blogs.

Google's search engine technology is used not only at the Google site, but also at search sites such as AOL and Netscape. Yahoo's search engine is used at search sites AltaVista and AlltheWeb. Ask.com uses Teoma search engine technology.

Many e-commerce, informational, and corporate sites offer query controls you can use to search the site or the entire Web. The sites that host these query controls typically link to major search engines or the sites that host them (Figure 7-17).

**FIGURE 7-17**

Many Web sites use search engine technology for searching within the site rather than searching the entire Web.

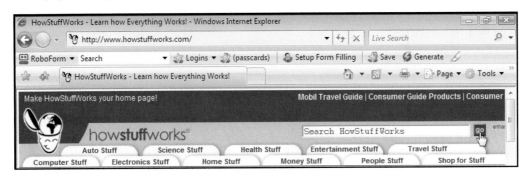

**How do search engines work?** A search engine contains four components: a Web crawler, an indexing utility, a database, and a query processor. The Web crawler combs the Web to gather data that's representative of the contents of Web pages. The indexer processes the information gathered by the crawler into a list of key words and URLs stored in a database. The query processor allows you to access the database by entering key terms, and then produces a list of Web pages that contain content relevant to your query. Let's take a look at each of these components to find out how they affect your ability to mine information from the Web.

**What is a Web crawler?** A **Web crawler** (also referred to as a Web spider) is a computer program that is automated to methodically visit Web sites. Web crawlers can be programmed to perform various activities as they visit sites, but in the context of search engines, Web crawlers download Web pages and submit them to an indexing utility for processing.

**How much of the Web does a Web crawler cover?** A Web crawler begins with a list of URLs to visit. After copying the material at a specified URL, the Web crawler looks for hypertext links and adds them to the list of URLs to visit. To cover the Web as efficiently as possible, a Web crawler can run multiple processes in parallel. Sophisticated algorithms keep processes from overlapping, getting stuck in loops, or trying to capture Web pages dynamically produced by server-side scripts.

High performance Web crawlers can visit hundreds of millions of Web pages a day. Those pages, however, are only a fraction of the Web. Researchers estimate that the most extensive search engines cover less than 20% of the Web. Each search engine seems to focus on a slightly different collection of Web sites. The same search entered into different search engines can produce different results, so it is sometimes worthwhile to try alternative search engines.

Web crawlers typically do not gather material from the invisible Web, which encompasses pages that require password protected logins and pages that are dynamically generated with server-side scripts. The potential volume of dynamically generated pages, such as all the possible pages that Amazon.com could generate from its inventory database, is just too great to feasibly index. To access information related to e-commerce merchandise or library catalogs, you might have to go directly to the merchant's or library's Web site and use its search tools.

**FIGURE 7-18**

A search engine's indexer looks for keywords on each page the Web crawler retrieves.

**How frequently do Web crawlers revisit sites?** When you query a search engine, you want the results to be up to date so that you don't waste time trying to link to pages that have changed or been deleted. Search engines use various algorithms to refresh their indexes.

The number of times a search engine's crawler visits a Web page varies, depending on several factors such as how often the page tends to change and its popularity. Obscure pages might be visited only once a month, whereas the pages at a news site would be visited daily.

**How do search engine indexers work?** A **search engine indexer** is software that pulls keywords from a Web page and stores them in a database. The purpose of the indexer is to make pages easy to find based on their contents. For example, a Web page at a classic comic book site might contain information and covers from old comics (Figure 7-18). Key words that might help catalog this page for future access include classic, comic, comic book, artwork, cover, gallery, super-hero, crime, romance, Marvel, and Weird Science.

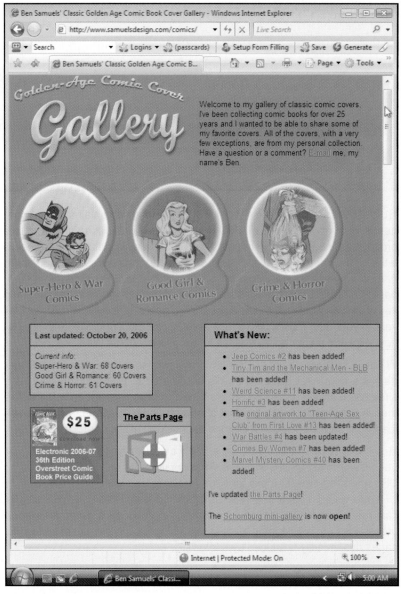

**Which Web sites are shown at the top of the results list?** A search engine's **query processor** looks for your search terms in the search engine's indexed database and returns a list of relevant Web sites. The order in which Web sites are listed in response to a search depends on relevancy criteria, such as key word matches and link popularity.

If a search is based on multiple keywords, pages that contain the most matching words are listed first. **Link popularity** is a measure of the quantity and quality of the links from one Web page to others. Pages with links to and from popular sites tend to get high relevancy ratings.

**Can a search engine be manipulated into giving a high ranking to a page?** Web sites can be added to a search engine index in several ways. Sites can automatically get discovered by a search engine's Web crawler, they can be submitted to a search engine by the Web masters who manage various Web sites, they can be submitted for a paid placement, or they can be submitted as banner or pop-up ads.

Most search engines make it easy to submit the URL for a Web site, so that Web masters don't have to wait for their sites to be discovered by a Web crawler. Manual submissions are added to the crawler's list of sites to visit and the site will eventually be indexed.

Some search engines accept paid placements, which are bumped to the top positions on the results list. Other search engines accept paid ads, but place them in a clearly marked area. For example, Google displays a column of ads related to the key words you enter for a search. Suppose you search for mountain bike trails. The main results list displays maps of mountain bike trails and reviews. An additional column of sponsored links are paid placements by merchants who have mountain-bike related products. Merchants are charged only if the ad is clicked (Figure 7-19).

**FIGURE 7-19**

Sponsored links on Google are paid placements that appear when users make queries using relevant keywords.

7

Disreputable Web site operators are constantly trying to devise schemes, such as manipulating meta keywords, to move their Web sites up to the top of search engine query results. A **meta keyword** is entered into a header section of a Web page when it is created and is supposed to describe the page contents.

**Keyword stuffing** is an unethical practice in which meta keywords are manipulated to gain high relevancy rankings. For example, a Web page author might include meta keywords such as "sex" (which happens to be the most frequently used search term) even though the term has little to do with the information on the page.

Socially responsible search engine sites take steps to foil practices that manipulate rankings and should make their policies on paid placements clear to users. When you use a search engine, read its About page to learn its placement policies and discover whether or not you can trust the search results to be unbiased.

## FORMULATING SEARCHES

**How do I formulate a basic search?** Most search engines work with keyword queries in which you enter one or more words, called **search terms**, related to the information you want to find. For example, if you're interested in Batman comics, you can simply type the obvious: "Batman" (Figure 7-20).

**TERMINOLOGY NOTE**

The words you enter for your search can be referred to as queries, search criteria, search terms, or keywords.

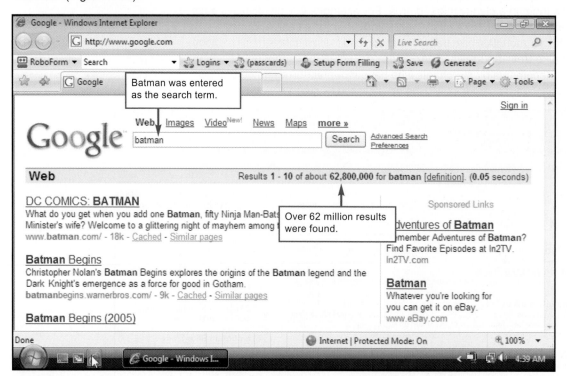

Narrowing a search can reduce the number of results and produce a more targeted list. For example, the query "first appearance Batman comic book" produces under a million entries and those listed first link to information about when Batman first appeared in the May 1939 issue of Detective Comics.

**FIGURE 7-20**

Simple queries sometimes produce an unmanageable number of results.

Searching is not a numbers game, however, because it is rare for a query to produce fewer than thousands of results. In fact, a game called Googlewhacking challenges you to type a two-word query that produces one and only one result. Try it! You need to choose two fairly unrelated words, but they cannot be totally unrelated or you'll get no results. You can view some googlewhacks at *www.googlewhack.com/tally.pl.*

When formulating queries, keep the simple guidelines from Figure 7-21 in mind.

FIGURE 7-21

Tips for Effective Queries

- Most search engines are not case sensitive, so you don't have to use the Shift key when entering proper names.

- Typically, search engines ignore common words, such as "and," "a," and "the," so don't bother to include them in your query.

- The top search engines use stemming technology that looks for plurals and other variations of the keywords you enter. For example, if you enter *diet*, the search engine also looks for pages with terms such as "diets," "dietary," and "dietician."

- To search for an exact phrase, enter it in quotes. For example, *"Dynamic Duo."*

- The asterisk (*) is sometimes referred to as a wildcard character. It allows a search engine to find pages with any derivation of a basic word. For example, the query *medic** would not only produce pages containing the word "medic," but also "medics," "medicine," "medical," "medication," and "medicinal."

- The NEAR operator tells a search engine that you want documents in which one of the keywords is located close to but not necessarily next to the other keyword. The query *library NEAR/15 congress* means that the words "library" and "congress" must appear within 15 words of each other. Successful searches could include documents containing phrases such as "Library of Congress" or "Congress funds special library research."

- When you enter multiple terms, the query processor assumes you want to see Web pages that include all your terms. Technically, the search engine inserts the Boolean operator "AND" between the keywords in your search. If you want to use other Boolean operators, however, you must enter them.

**What are Boolean operators?** A **Boolean operator** (sometimes called a search operator) is a word or symbol that describes a relationship between keywords and thereby helps you create a more focused query. They are called Boolean operators after George Boole, a 19th century English mathematician, who defined one of the first systems of logic. Figure 7-22 on the next page provides a quick overview of how to use Boolean operators when formulating searches.

7

**FIGURE 7-22**

Search Operators

| AND | When two search terms are joined by AND, both terms must appear on a Web page before it can be included in the search results. The query *railroad AND cars* will locate pages that contain both the words "railroad" and "cars." Your search results might include pages containing information about old railroad cars, about railroad car construction, and even about railroads that haul automobiles ("cars"). Some search engines use the plus symbol (+) instead of the word AND. |
|-----|------|
| OR | When two search terms are joined by OR, either one or both of the search words could appear on a page. Entering the query *railroad OR cars* produces information about railroad fares, railroad routes, railroad cars, automobile safety records, and even car ferries. |
| NOT | The keyword following NOT must not appear on any of the pages found by the search engine. Entering *railroad NOT cars* would tell the search engine to look for pages that include "railroad" but not the keyword "cars." In some search engines, the minus sign (-) can be used instead of the word NOT. |

**What is an advanced search?** Many search engines provide ways to make your searches more precise and obtain more useful results. You might be able to use advanced search options to limit your search to material written in a specific language or stored in a specific file format. You might be able to specify a date, eliminate results from adult sites, and stipulate whether to look for your search terms in the title, URL, or body of the Web page (Figure 7-23).

**Advanced Web Search**

**Find results** with **all** of the words   railroad          10 results ▼
with **any** of the words                      Google Search
with the **exact phrase**   Orient Express
**without** the words          American

**Occurrences**  Return results where my terms occur   anywhere in the page ▼
**Language**     Return pages written in                French ▼
**Domains**      Only ▼ return results from the site or domain
                                                       e.g. google.com, .org   *More info*
**SafeSearch**   ⦿ No filtering   ○ Filter using SafeSearch

**FIGURE 7-23**

Many search engines provide forms designed to simplify the search process. These forms are usually accessible by clicking an Advanced Search link, which often is located on the main page of the search engine Web site.

Some search engine sites offer separate searches for academic works, images, videos, news, e-commerce merchandise, and blogs. Look for links to these specialized searches at your favorite search engine sites.

In addition to using search engines, you can also find Web-based information using a **metasearch engine** that searches a series of other search engines and compiles the search results. Popular metasearch sites include *www.mamma.com*, *www.dogpile.com*, and *www.metagopher.com*.

**Do search engines keep records of my queries?** Considering that a major search engine can receive upward of 100 million queries every day, the surprising answer to this question is "yes." Search engines at major sites such as Google, AOL, MSN, and Yahoo! save massive numbers of searches made by site visitors. Although most search sites do not specify how long this information is retained, industry analysts believe that some sites retain it for at least 30 days, and perhaps at least one search engine site has retained every search ever made at the site.

Privacy advocates question the wisdom of search engines retaining queries. They find difficulty in identifying any beneficial uses for such data and fear that it is of potential benefit only to marketing companies. Although the privacy policies of major search sites claim to protect personal information, in 2006, AOL released a database of 20 million queries collected by its search engine. The database was released publicly and online, ostensibly to help academic researchers. A few months earlier, the U.S. Department of Justice requested query databases from all major search engines in conjunction with a crackdown on Internet child pornography. Some search engine operators complied, whereas others did not. Anyone who uses search engines should be aware that the content of their searches could become public.

**What kind of information does a search engine store?** Although your queries do not contain your name, you are assigned a unique ID number that is stored in a cookie on your computer. In addition to storing an ID number, search engines store the IP address from which the query was initiated, the date and time of the query, the search terms, and the URL for the Web site linked to from the results list (Figure 7-24).

**FIGURE 7-24**

A database of 20 million AOL queries is still available to the public. You can use it to get a glimpse of the wide range of human interests and also understand how valuable such data can be to marketers. For example, you can see that in a three month period over 18,000 queries contained the words "mountain bike." If you click user 1404131, you can see that he or she was also interested in Sony PSP products.

**What can I do to keep my searches confidential?** Your search-engine-assigned ID number is stored in a cookie and remains the same as long as the cookie remains on your computer. If you frequently delete your cookies as explained in Section E, a search engine's query database is unlikely to collect enough information to link back to you. You can block cookies from a specific search engine site, and that setting will force the search engine to assign a different ID number to you for each session. You can also download and use a cookie anonymizer that sets your Google ID number to 0. Scroogle, Tor, and other anonymizer sites act as relay stations to forward your searches to Google or other search engines without leaving a trail back to a cookie or IP address. These sites claim to delete all activity logs every day or two, but they are the subject of law enforcement scrutiny.

## CITING WEB-BASED SOURCE MATERIAL

**Can I copy text and graphics that I find on Web pages?** Most browsers provide a Copy command that allows you to copy a section of text from a Web page, which you can then paste into one of your own documents. To keep track of the source for each text section, you can highlight the Web page's URL in the Address box, use the Copy command, and then paste the URL into your document (Figure 7-25).

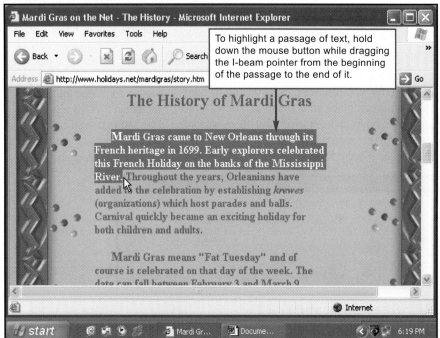

**FIGURE 7-25**
To copy a passage of text from a Web page, highlight the text, click the Edit menu, then select Copy. Next, switch to your own document and use the Paste option.
For a demonstration of this process, click the Start icon.

CLICK TO START

**How do I cite sources?** Information that identifies the source of a quotation or excerpted work is called a citation. Written documents, such as reports and projects, typically include footnotes, endnotes, or in-line citations formatted according to a standard style, such as those listed in Figure 7-26.

**FIGURE 7-26**
Various style manuals suggest different punctuation and formats for citations. Use the one recommended by your instructor or publisher.

**MLA Style**

Du Bois, W.E.B. "Of the Dawn of Freedom." The Souls of Black Folk. 1903. Project Bartleby. 27 Nov. 2000 <http://www.bartleby.com/114/>.

**APA Style**

Du Bois, W.E.B. (1903). Of the dawn of freedom. In The Souls of Black Folk. Retrieved November 27, 2007, from Project Bartleby Web site: http://www.bartleby.com/114/.

**Turabian Style**

Du Bois, W.E.B. 1906. Of the dawn of freedom. In The Souls of Black Folk. On-line. Available from Internet, http://www.bartleby.com/114/, accessed November 27, 2007.

**Chicago Style**

Du Bois, W.E.B. 1906. Of the dawn of freedom. In The Souls of Black Folk. http://www.bartleby.com/114/ (accessed November 27, 2007).

When compiling the citation for online sources, make sure you provide sufficient information to allow readers to locate your source. Also, include the date when you accessed the source and the full URL. According to APA style, a citation to a Web-based source should provide a document title or description; author name if available; the date of publication, update, or retrieval; and a URL.

**Do I need permission to use material?** In the United States, a fair use doctrine allows you limited use of copyrighted material for scholarship and review without obtaining permission. For scholarly reports and projects, for example, you can use a sentence or paragraph of text without obtaining permission if you include a citation to the original source. Photos and excerpts from music and videos can be used within the context of critique, but their use purely as decorative elements for a document would, in most cases, not be considered fair use.

Some Web sites clearly state allowable uses for material on the site. Look for a link to Terms of Use on the site. For example, the YouTube Web site contains a collection of videos submitted by amateurs and semi-professionals, who retain the copyright to their materials. The Terms of Use section of the site allows the public to access, use, reproduce, distribute, create derivatives, display, and perform user-submitted works. Even with such broad terms of use, however, it is essential to cite the original source of the material if you incorporate it in your own work.

**How do I get permission?** To obtain permission to use text, photos, music, videos, and other elements you find on the Web, contact the copyright holder by e-mail, explain what you want to use and how you plan to use it. You can usually find contact information on the Web site, if not for the copyright holder, at least for a Web master who can direct you to the copyright holder.

# QuickCheck

1. A Web [＿＿＿＿＿＿] is a computer program designed to methodically visit Web sites, fetch Web pages and submit them to an indexing utility for processing.

2. Keyword [＿＿＿＿＿＿] is an unethical practice in which meta keywords are manipulated to gain high relevancy rankings and move Web sites to the top of a search engine's results.

3. Most search engines are case sensitive, so you must make sure to capitalize the first letters of proper names and places. True or false? [＿＿＿＿]

4. "AND" is an example of a(n) [＿＿＿＿＿＿] operator, also referred to as a search operator.

5. Because of the massive number of searches initiated by visitors of Google, AOL, MSN, and Yahoo!, these search engine sites are unable to maintain records of their visitors' queries. True or false? [＿＿＿＿]

6. Information that identifies the source of a quotation, photo, video, music, or excerpted work is called a(n) [＿＿＿＿＿＿].

 CHECK ANSWERS

## SECTION C

# E-commerce

**ONE OF THE MOST POPULAR** activities on the Web is shopping. Online shopping has the same allure as catalogs—you can shop at your leisure, anonymously, and in your pajamas. But the economics of the Web provide opportunities that go beyond retail catalogs. The Internet was opened to commercial use in 1991. Since then, thousands of businesses have set up shop at Web sites. This section of the chapter focuses on e-commerce and the technologies a typical shopper might encounter on the Web.

### E-COMMERCE BASICS

**What is e-commerce?** Although the experts don't always agree on its definition, the term **e-commerce** typically refers to business transactions that are conducted electronically over a computer network. It encompasses all aspects of business and marketing processes enabled by Internet and Web technologies.

E-commerce wares include many kinds of physical products, digital products, and services. Physical products offered at e-commerce sites include such goods as clothing, shoes, skateboards, and cars. Most of these products can be shipped to buyers through the postal service or a parcel delivery service.

Increasingly, e-commerce goods include digital products, such as news, music, video, databases, software, and all types of knowledge-based items. The unique feature of these products is that they can be transformed into bits and delivered over the Web. Consumers can get them immediately upon completing their orders, and no one pays shipping costs.

E-commerce merchants also peddle services, such as online medical consultation, distance education, or custom sewing. Some of these services can be carried out by computers. Others require human agents. Services can be delivered electronically, as in the case of a distance education course, or they might produce some physical product, such as a custom-fit boat cover.

**What are the most common e-commerce business models?** Many e-commerce activities are classified as **B2C** (business-to-consumer) in which individual consumers purchase goods and services from online merchants. **C2C** (consumer-to-consumer) is another popular e-commerce model, in which consumers sell to each other at popular online auctions. **B2B** (business-to-business) e-commerce involves one enterprise buying goods or services from another enterprise. **B2G** (business-to-government) e-commerce aims to help businesses sell to governments. Figure 7-27 lists some popular B2C and C2C activities.

**Is e-commerce more profitable than off-line business?** E-commerce enhances traditional business models by offering efficiency and opportunities for automation, computerization, and digitization. As with a traditional brick and mortar business, profit in an e-commerce business is the difference between income and expenses.

**FIGURE 7-27**

B2C and C2C e-commerce offer consumers many types of goods and services.

Online storefronts sell a variety of goods, such as clothing, books, toys, music, food, sports gear, and electronics.

Online auctions provide consumers with a worldwide market for antiques, collectibles, and other new and used items.

Online schools offer credit and noncredit courses, tutorials, and even college degrees.

Online ticket and reservation systems provide concert and event tickets plus air, hotel, and car reservations.

Online information services sell subscriptions to news archives, databases, and online magazines.

One of the advantages of e-commerce is its ability to increase profit margins by cutting costs. For example, a typical catalog order placed over the phone costs the merchant US$2.50, whereas an online transaction costs about 35 cents. A hotel reservation made online costs the innkeeper 80% less than a booking by phone. A withdrawal or deposit costs a bank about a dollar when handled by a teller, about 25 cents on an ATM, and only a penny on the Web.

E-commerce merchants also gain income by hosting advertising space for marketers, who are creating increasingly hard-to-avoid styles of online advertisements, such as banner and pop-up ads. A **banner ad** is an advertisement, typically embedded at the top of a Web page. A **hover ad** overlays the content on a Web page, sometimes obscuring it until you click the ad or its timer expires and the ad disappears. A **pop-up ad**, such as the one in Figure 7-28, is an advertisement that appears in a separate window when you connect to a Web page. If you click a banner, hover, or pop-up ad, your browser connects directly to the advertiser's Web site, where you can find product information and make a purchase.

Banner, hover, and pop-up ads earn revenue for hosting merchants based on the **click-through rate**—the number of times that site visitors click the ad to connect to the advertiser's site. The hosting merchant is paid a small fee for each click through. Click-through rates have declined in recent years because most consumers simply ignore the ads or install **ad-blocking software** to prevent ads from appearing on their screens. Recent versions of Internet Explorer include a configurable feature to block pop-up ads.

**Who benefits from e-commerce?** Both merchants and consumers benefit from e-commerce because niche goods and small merchants can reach a global customer base. At online music shops and bookstores, for example, you can find obscure titles and alternative music that brick and mortar merchants haven't the space or inclination to stock.

Merchants are always looking for ways to attract customers. The Web and its search engines give small merchants without a budget for national advertising a way to be found by customers. When you're looking for hand-made chainmail, for example, you're unlikely to find it at your local WalMart, but chances are good that you can find a chainmail merchant on the Web.

**Is e-commerce popular worldwide?** North America accounts for about half of all e-commerce activity, and Western Europe and Asian Pacific regions account for most of the rest. The low volume of e-commerce activity in Africa, Eastern Europe, and Russia can be attributed to several factors, including lack of Internet access, language barriers, depressed economies, shipping limitations, and merchant policies.

Today's e-commerce model is aimed at English speakers with Internet access and a credit card. Although an increasing number of e-commerce Web sites offer language alternatives, many e-commerce sites have not been internationalized. In regions where electricity and telephone service are not available, Internet access is simply not possible (Figure 7-29). Many e-commerce merchants do not accept checks or cash and might not accept credit cards issued by non-U.S. banks. Even if cash payment is accepted, the price of goods remains beyond the budget of many people in developing countries.

**FIGURE 7-28**

Pop-up ads appear as separate windows.

7

**FIGURE 7-29**

In some regions of the world, e-commerce obstacles include language barriers, economic factors, and even lack of electrical service.

## ONLINE SHOPPING

**What makes online shopping so special?** E-commerce offers some unique advantages over brick-and-mortar stores and mail-order catalogs. Customers can easily search for specific merchandise. They can configure products online, see actual prices, and build an order over several days. Customers can easily compare prices between multiple vendors using Web sites such as BizRate, NexTag, and PriceGrabber.

**How does an e-commerce store work?** E-commerce seems simple from the perspective of a shopper who connects to an online store, browses the electronic catalog, selects merchandise, and then pays for it. The screentour in Figure 7-30 walks you through a typical shopping session.

**FIGURE 7-30**

In a typical shopping session, you connect to an online storefront and use navigation controls to browse through the merchant's catalog. As you browse, you can drop items into your electronic shopping cart. At the checkout counter, you enter the information necessary to pay for the items you selected.

CLICK TO START

Behind the scenes, an e-commerce site uses several technologies to display merchandise, keep track of shoppers' selections, collect payment data, attempt to protect customers' privacy, and prevent credit card numbers from falling into the wrong hands.

An e-commerce site's URL, such as *www.amazon.com*, acts as the entry to the online store. A Web page at this location—sometimes referred to as an electronic storefront—welcomes customers and provides links to various parts of the site. The goods and services for sale appear in a customer's browser window.

An e-commerce site usually includes some mechanism for customers to select merchandise and then pay for it. Customer orders might be processed manually in a small business. Most high-volume e-commerce businesses, however, use as much automation as possible; their order-processing systems automatically update inventories, and then print packing slips and mailing labels.

**What's an online shopping cart?** If you've done any shopping online, you've probably used an **online shopping cart**—a cyberspace version of the metal cart you wheel around a store and fill up with merchandise.

**How do shopping carts work?** As mentioned earlier, HTTP is a stateless protocol, which fulfills a single request for a Web resource and then immediately forgets about it. Under these circumstances, you might wonder how it is possible for an online retail store to remember the items you put in your shopping cart.

Most shopping carts work because they use cookies to store information about your activities on a Web site. Cookies work with shopping carts in one of two ways, depending on the e-commerce site. An e-commerce site might use cookies as a storage bin for all the items you load into your shopping cart, as shown in Figure 7-31.

**FIGURE 7-31**

Shopping cart items can be stored in a cookie.

**1.** When you click the Add to Cart button, the merchant's server sends a message to your browser to add that item number to the cookie, which is stored on your computer.

ITEM #B7655

**2.** When you check out, the server asks your browser for all the cookie data that pertains to your shopping cart items.

Cookies

**3.** Your browser sends those cookies along with a request for an order summary.

**Your order:**

1 Blender      $29.95

1 Wok          $38.49

**4.** The Web server uses the cookies to produce a Web page listing the items you want to purchase.

Some e-commerce sites use cookies simply as a way to uniquely identify each shopper. These sites generate a unique ID number that is stored along with your item selections in a server-side database (Figure 7-32).

**FIGURE 7-32**

Shopping cart items can be stored in a server-side database.

**Order for CART #2098-2**

1 Blender      B7655      $29.95

1 Wok          GJK4-31    $38.49

**4.** When you check out, your browser sends your shopping cart number to the server, which retrieves all your selections from the merchant's database.

**1.** When you connect to a merchant's site, the server assigns you a unique shopping cart ID number and sends it to your browser in a cookie.

**3.** The Web server stores this number and your merchandise selection in the merchant's server-side database.

**2.** When you select an item to purchase, your browser reads your shopping cart ID number from the cookie, and then sends this number to the merchant's Web server.

7

## ONLINE AUCTIONS

**What is an online auction?** Have you checked out eBay yet? If you're in a buying mood and looking for merchandise from tchotchkes to a new car, then you might turn first to an online auction, one of the hottest trends in online shopping. An **online auction** is the electronic equivalent to good old-fashioned yard sales, rummage sales, and auctions. Hosted by an Internet auction site, such as eBay, sellers post their merchandise or services and buyers bid for the posted items. The auction site does not own or hold the merchandise; rather, it merely facilitates the online bidding process and the transactions between buyers and sellers.

Online shoppers are attracted to online auctions for a number of reasons. Some merchandise can be obtained at bargain basement prices. Unique collectibles and memorabilia, which can be very difficult to find, are readily available for perusing and purchasing at auction. The greatest incentive, however, for participating in an online auction is perhaps the excitement of frenzied last-minute bidding to win an item you covet.

**What can I buy at an online auction?** You can expect to bid on new, used, closeout, overstock, or refurbished items at an online auction. Different types of services are also available. The merchandise covers a very broad spectrum of categories, such as antiques, collectibles, books and comics, coins, stamps, entertainment memorabilia, art, home and garden, cameras and camcorders, computers, cars and boats, sporting goods, apparel, jewelry, musical instruments, toys, and even theater tickets, special travel deals, and real estate (Figure 7-33).

The services up for auction are just as varied as the merchandise. For example, you can bid on tutoring lessons, printer repair, interior design, custom-made clothing, shopping assistance, printing and personalization, graphic design, and Web and computer services.

**What are the largest auction sites?** Originally founded in 1995 by Pierre Omidyar, eBay is by far the largest and most popular auction site. It is a virtual global marketplace that enables you to shop around the world. The number of confirmed registered users at eBay has risen year after year since it was founded, and had reached 180.6 million at the end of 2005.

Amazon Auctions, uBid, eBid, Bidz, and Overstock.com also offer a wide range of products and bargains. Bid4Assets.com differs from other auction sites because it also provides seized, surplus, and tax-foreclosed properties from federal, state, and local government agencies. AuctionBytes is a Web site that provides up-to-date information on the numerous online auction sites.

**How does an online auction work?** At an online auction site specially designed computer software takes the place of an auctioneer. Server databases store information about auction items, and customer ratings of sellers. Server-side scripts accept bids and notify winners.

**FIGURE 7-33**

eBay and other auction sites offer a huge variety of goods and services.

### Categories

Antiques
Art
Baby
Books
Business & Industrial
Cameras & Photo
Cars, Boats, Vehicles & Parts
Cell Phones
Clothing, Shoes & Accessories
Coins & Paper Money
Collectibles
Computers & Networking
Consumer Electronics
Crafts
Dolls & Bears
DVDs & Movies
Entertainment Memorabilia
Gift Certificates
Health & Beauty
Home & Garden
Jewelry & Watches
Music
Musical Instruments
Pottery & Glass
Real Estate
Specialty Services
Sporting Goods
Sports Mem, Cards & Fan Shop
Stamps
Tickets
Toys & Hobbies
Travel
Video Games
Everything Else
*All Categories*

## ONLINE PAYMENT

**How can I pay for merchandise from online shopping and auction sites?** The most popular ways to make online payments include submitting your credit card number directly to a merchant and using a third-party payment service such as PayPal. Online wallets and one-time-use credit card numbers offer additional online payment options.

**Is it safe to use my credit card online?** Online shoppers are justifiably worried that personal information and credit card numbers supplied in the course of an e-commerce transaction might be hijacked and used inappropriately. Many shoppers worry that hackers might use packet sniffers to intercept credit card numbers traveling over the Internet.

To protect your credit card from packet sniffers, you should engage in electronic transactions only over a secure connection. A **secure connection** encrypts the data transmitted between your computer and a Web site. Even if a hacker can capture the packets containing payment data, your encrypted credit card number is virtually useless for illicit purposes. Technologies that create secure connections include SSL, TLS, and S-HTTP.

**What are SSL and TLS?** **SSL** (Secure Sockets Layer) and its successor **TLS** (Transport Layer Security) are protocols that encrypt data traveling between a client computer and an HTTP server. This encryption protocol creates a secure connection using a specially designated port—typically port 443 rather than port 80, which is used for unsecured HTTP communication. Web pages that provide a secure connection start with *https:* instead of *http:*.

**What is S-HTTP?** **S-HTTP** (secure HTTP) is an extension of HTTP that simply encrypts the text of an HTTP message before it is sent. Although SSL and S-HTTP both use encryption techniques to securely transmit data, they are technically different. Whereas SSL creates a secure connection between a client and a server over which any amount of data can be sent securely, S-HTTP is simply designed to encrypt and then transmit an individual message.

**How do I know if a connection is secure?** Your browser helps you identify when you are using a secure connection. Figure 7-34 explains.

### TERMINOLOGY NOTE

Secure connections differ from secure Web sites. A secure connection encrypts the data transmitted between your computer and a Web site. A secure Web site, such as an online banking site, uses password security to prevent unauthorized access to pages on the site.

7

**FIGURE 7-34**

Secure connections are indicated by a dialog box, URL, and lock icon.

When a secure connection is about to be activated, your browser usually displays a dialog box.

While a secure connection is active, the URL begins with *https://* and the taskbar typically displays a padlock icon.

Lock icon in address bar.

**What is a person-to-person payment?** A **person-to-person payment** (sometimes called a P2P payment, an online payment, or a third-party payment) offers an alternative to credit cards. It can be used to pay for online auction items and to wire money over the Internet. The online service called PayPal, now owned by eBay, pioneered person-to-person payments. PayPal's model has since been copied by several other service providers.

**How does a person-to-person payment work?** The process begins when you open an account at a person-to-person payment service. Some services require you to deposit money in your account—just as though you were opening a bank account. Other services allow you to supply your credit card number or bank account number, which is billed or debited only as you make purchases. You receive a user ID and password that enable you to access your account to make purchases and deposit additional funds. Money can be sent to anyone who has an e-mail account, as shown in Figure 7-35.

**Is person-to-person payment safe?** The major advantage of person-to-person payments is that the payment service is the only entity that sees your credit card number—merchants, auction dealers, and other payment recipients never receive your credit card number and, therefore, can't misuse it or store it on an unsecured computer. Currently, however, the person-to-person payment industry is in its infancy, and companies are still scrambling to offer reliable, long-term service to customers. Consumer advocates recommend using these services with caution and keeping your account balances low.

**What is a one-time-use credit card?** Several credit card companies offer one-time-use credit card numbers, which allow consumers to make purchases while keeping their actual card numbers hidden.

A one-time-use credit card number works for a single online purchase. Your credit card company tracks the purchases you incur with one-time-use numbers and adds the charges to your monthly credit card statement. One-time-use numbers cannot be used twice, so even if a hacker steals the number, it will not be accepted for any online or offline purchases.

**What is an electronic wallet?** An **electronic wallet** (also called a digital wallet) is software that stores billing and shipping information, which can be submitted when finalizing an e-commerce purchase. Electronic wallets are especially handy during holiday shopping, when you're purchasing gifts at several online stores. Using an electronic wallet, you can check out with just a few clicks instead of entering all the details of your billing address and credit card number.

You can create an electronic wallet by subscribing at a wallet provider's site. Companies that offer electronic wallet services include Microsoft, Google, and Yahoo! The wallets are not interchangeable, however. For example if you have an electronic

**FIGURE 7-35**

Using a person-to-person payment service.

**1.** To use a person-to-person payment service, simply log in to your account, enter the recipient's e-mail address, and indicate the payment amount.

**2.** The recipient immediately receives an e-mail notification of your payment.

**3.** The recipient connects to the payment site to pick up the money by transferring the funds to his or her checking or payment account, requesting a check, or sending the funds to someone else.

**TERMINOLOGY NOTE**

In banking jargon, a one-time-use credit card number is called a controlled payment number. Banks and credit card companies offer this service under many different names, such as Citibank's Virtual Accounts and Discover Card's Deskshop.

wallet issued by Google, you can't use it at a Yahoo! merchant. After you create an electronic wallet, it pops up on your screen when you make a purchase at a participating merchant's site (Figure 7-36).

**FIGURE 7-36**

An electronic wallet can transfer your billing and shipping information to a participating site's e-commerce Web server when you check out.

CLICK TO START

7

**How safe is an electronic wallet?** Electronic wallets are protected by passwords and encrypted to prevent unauthorized use. Hackers can potentially snag your data by using Trojan horse technology to collect your wallet password, however, so don't get fooled into entering your electronic wallet password by a bogus e-mail message instructing you to update your account. Consumers should carefully study current security bulletins before trusting their data to electronic wallets.

# QuickCheck

SECTION C

1. An online auction is an example of C2C e-commerce. True or false? [_____]

2. A pop-up ad is an advertisement that appears in a separate window when you connect to a Web page. True or false? [_____]

3. One factor in the e-commerce economic model is ad revenue based on [_____] rates, the number of times that site visitors click an ad to connect to the advertiser's Web site.

4. Most online shopping carts work because they use [_____] to store information about your activities at a Web site.

5. Web sites that provide a secure connection display a padlock and start with sttp: instead of http:. True or false? [_____]

 CHECK ANSWERS

# E-mail

**THE INTERNET REALLY TOOK OFF** when people discovered electronic mail. More than 60 billion e-mail messages speed over the Internet each day. E-mail, which is derived from the term electronic mail, can refer to a single message or to the entire system of computers and software that transmits, receives, and stores electronic messages. In this section of the chapter, you get some background information about how e-mail works—in particular, the difference between Web-based e-mail and traditional client-based e-mail. E-mail labs at the end of the chapter provide hands-on overviews of how to read, compose, send, and reply to e-mail messages.

## E-MAIL OVERVIEW

**Who can use e-mail?** Any person with an e-mail account can send and receive e-mail. An **e-mail account** provides access to a storage area, or mailbox, supplied by an e-mail provider, such as an ISP. Each mailbox has a unique address, which typically consists of a user ID, an @ symbol, and the name of the computer that maintains the mailbox. For example, suppose that a university student named Dee Greene has an electronic mailbox on a computer called rutgers.edu. If her user ID is dee_greene, her e-mail address would be *dee_greene@rutgers.edu*.

**Exactly what is an e-mail message?** An **e-mail message** is a document that is composed on a computer and remains in digital, or electronic, form so that it can be transmitted to another computer. A **message header** includes the recipient's e-mail address and message subject. It might also contain the address of anyone who is receiving a copy of the message, and the name of any file attachments that accompany the message. The body of the e-mail contains your message. The message header and body are usually displayed in a form, as shown in Figure 7-37.

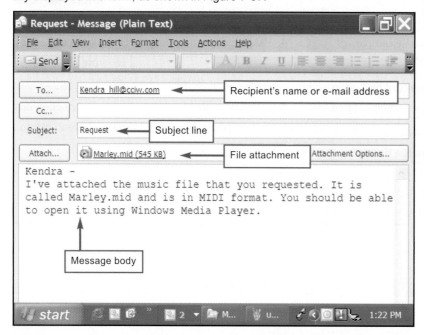

**FIGURE 7-37**

When you compose an e-mail message, you can begin by entering the address of one or more recipients and the subject of the message. You can also specify one or more files to attach to the message. The body of the e-mail message contains the message itself. When the message is sent, your e-mail software adds the date and your e-mail address to identify you as the sender.

**What can I do with basic e-mail?** Basic e-mail activities consist of writing, reading, replying to (Figure 7-38), and forwarding messages. Messages can be printed, kept for later reference, or deleted.

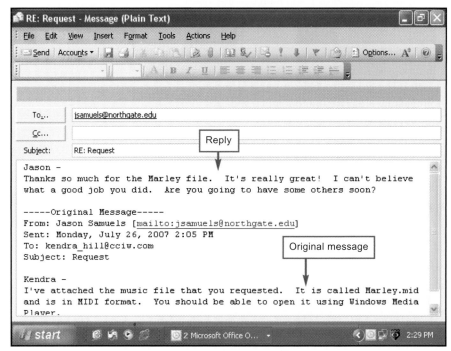

**FIGURE 7-38**

Your e-mail client's Reply button creates a new e-mail message and automatically addresses it to the person who sent the original message. Most e-mail systems also copy the text of the original message into the reply so that everyone has a complete transcript of the messages that were exchanged.

**How does forwarding work?** After you receive an e-mail message, you can use the Forward feature to pass it on to other people. You might, for example, forward a message that was sent to you but that should be handled by someone else. When you initiate the forwarding process, the original e-mail message is copied into a new message window, complete with the address of the original sender. You can then enter the address of the person to whom you are forwarding the message. You can also add a note about why you are passing the message along.

Some e-mail systems allow you to alter the text of the original message before you forward it. If you do so, include a note explaining your changes, especially if they alter the intent of the original message. You should not forward messages that were intended to be confidential. If you think that such a message needs to be shared with other people, obtain permission from the author of the original message.

**What's an e-mail attachment?** Originally, e-mail messages were stored in a plain and simple format called ASCII text. No fancy formatting was allowed—no variation in font type or color, no underlining or boldface, and, of course, no pictures or sounds. Although you cannot insert a digital photo or sound file into a plain ASCII e-mail message, you can send these kinds of files as e-mail attachments.

Any file that travels with an e-mail message is called an **e-mail attachment**. A conversion process called **MIME** (Multi-Purpose Internet Mail Extensions) provides a clever way of disguising digital photos, sounds, and other media as plain ASCII code that can travel over the Internet as e-mail attachments. An electronic message incorporated in the e-mail header provides your e-mail software with information that allows it to reconstruct the attachment into its original form.

Suppose you want to e-mail a photo to a friend who is working on a brochure for the Humane Society. The photo is stored in a file called PICT0011.JPG. You can address an e-mail message to your friend, write a short note ("I've attached a photo that might work for the brochure."), and then use the Insert file or Attachment menu option provided by your e-mail software to specify PICT0011.JPG. Your e-mail software converts PICT0011.JPG into MIME format and sends it along with your message.

When your friend receives the message, her e-mail software reconstitutes the file into the original photo. The way the attachment is displayed depends on your friend's e-mail software. The photo might appear at the end of the e-mail, or it could appear as an attachment icon that has to be double-clicked. With some e-mail systems, the attachment file might have to be downloaded separately and opened using the same software with which it was created. Figure 7-39 illustrates how to attach a photo when using Microsoft Outlook e-mail software.

**FIGURE 7-39**

An e-mail attachment typically is indicated by an icon in the message header section.

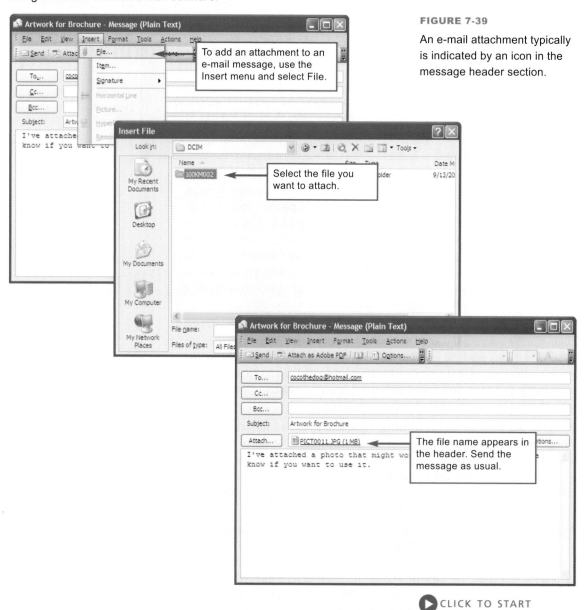

CLICK TO START

**How does HTML relate to e-mail?** Most e-mail software offers an HTML formatting option to create e-mail messages that contain graphics and lots of elaborate formatting that's just not possible with plain ASCII text.

By selecting your e-mail software's HTML option, you enter a world of colorful, bold, italic, and underlined text; fancy fonts; embedded graphics; and various font sizes. Your e-mail recipients must have HTML-compliant e-mail software. Otherwise, your message will be delivered as plain, unformatted ASCII text. You should also be aware that HTML formatted e-mail messages can distribute viruses and open security holes that leave your computer vulnerable to hackers. Figure 7-40 illustrates an e-mail message in HTML format.

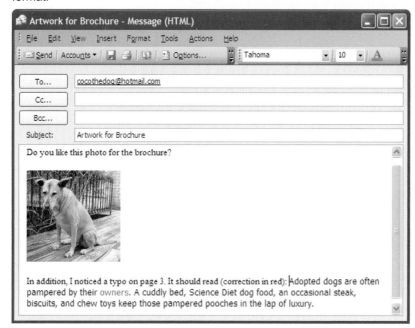

**FIGURE 7-40**

An e-mail message in HTML format can include graphics in addition to a variety of fonts and font colors.

**What other e-mail features are available?** In addition to attachments and HTML formatting, today's sophisticated e-mail systems typically offer features that help you perform the tasks listed in Figure 7-41.

**FIGURE 7-41**

E-mail features provide flexibility for sending and receiving messages.

- Maintain an address book and use it to select e-mail addresses instead of entering them every time you compose a message.
- Use the address book to send mail to a group that consists of several e-mail addresses.
- Send a carbon copy (Cc:) of a message to one or more recipients.
- Send a blind carbon copy (Bcc:), which hides the addresses in the Bcc: field from other recipients of the message.
- Assign a priority to a message—high priority is usually indicated by an exclamation point or red text.
- Find a particular message in your list of old mail.
- Enlarge text size for easier reading.
- Sort messages by date received, sender's name, subject, or priority.
- Refuse to accept messages that arrive from a particular e-mail address.
- Automate replies to messages that you receive while on vacation or when you will not be responding to e-mail messages for a few days.
- Automatically fetch mail at specified intervals.
- Check spelling before sending a message.

## NETIQUETTE

**Is e-mail different from other types of communication?** In some respects, e-mail is similar to an old-fashioned letter because its message is conveyed without benefit of the facial expressions, voice inflections, and body gestures that accompany face-to-face conversations. When composing a message, it is important to carefully consider your audience and the message you want to convey.

For example, you might have gotten into the habit of using text messaging shorthand to write messages such as "thnq 4 spking w me 2day. c u 2moro at 10." (Translation: Thank you for speaking with me today. See you tomorrow at 10:00.) Text messaging shorthand recently emerged as a quick and convenient way to communicate when using e-mail, instant messaging, and cell phone text messaging. Although text messaging shorthand works among your friends, it would not be appropriate in other situations, such as confirming the time for a job interview.

By understanding netiquette, you can avoid some of the pitfalls and problems of e-mail communications. **Netiquette** is online jargon for Internet etiquette. It is a series of customs or guidelines for maintaining civilized and effective communications in online discussions and e-mail exchanges.

- **Put a meaningful title on the subject line.** The subject line of your message should clearly describe the content of your e-mail message.

- **Use uppercase and lowercase letters.** An e-mail message that's typed in all uppercase means that you're shouting.

- **Check spelling.** Most e-mail software offers a Check Spelling command. Use it.

- **Be careful what you send.** E-mail is not private, nor is it secure. Treat your messages as though they are postcards that can be read by anyone. Remember that all laws governing copyright, slander, and discrimination apply to e-mail.

- **Be polite.** Avoid wording that could sound inflammatory or argumentative. If you would not say it face-to-face, don't say it in e-mail.

- **Be cautious when using sarcasm and humor.** The words in your e-mail arrive without facial expressions or voice intonations, so a sarcastic comment can easily be misinterpreted.

- **Use smileys and text messaging shorthand cautiously.** **Smileys** are symbols that represent emotions (Figure 7-42). They can help convey the intent behind your words. Smileys and text messaging shorthand should be used only in correspondence with people who understand them.

- **Use the Bcc function for group mailings.** By placing e-mail addresses for secondary recipients in the Bcc box, the recipients of your message won't have to scroll through a long list of addresses before reaching the meat of your message.

- **Don't send replies to "all recipients."** Use the Reply All command only when there is a very specific need for everyone listed in the To, Cc, and Bcc boxes to receive the message.

- **Don't send huge attachments.** Try to limit the size of attachments to 50 KB or less for recipients who have dial-up connections. If necessary, use a compression program, such as WinZip, to shrink the attachment.

- **Explain all attachments.** Attachments can harbor computer viruses. To determine whether an attachment is legitimate, your correspondents will want to know the file name of the attachment, what the attachment contains, and the name of the software you used to create it.

**INFOWEBLINKS**

You can read more about netiquette, smileys, and text messaging shorthand at the **Netiquette InfoWeb**.

 CLICK TO CONNECT
www.course.com/np/concepts10/ch07

**FIGURE 7-42**

Smileys, which are sometimes called emoticons, are clever symbols that can be added to e-mail messages to convey emotions and take the edge off potentially inflammatory remarks.

"Don't take offense."

"Just kidding!"

"I'm not happy about that."

"I'm perplexed."

"I'm amazed."

- **Stay alert for viruses.** Because viruses can tag along with e-mail attachments, don't open an attachment unless it was sent from a reliable source, its purpose is clearly explained in the body of the e-mail, and it was scanned using antivirus software.

- **Notify recipients of viruses.** If you discover that your computer sent out infected attachments, use antivirus software to remove the virus, and then notify anyone to whom you recently sent mail.

## E-MAIL TECHNOLOGY

**What is an e-mail system?** An **e-mail system** is the equipment and software that carries and manipulates e-mail messages. It includes computers and software called **e-mail servers** that sort, store, and route mail. An e-mail system also includes the personal computers that belong to individuals who send and receive mail. E-mail is based on **store-and-forward** technology—a communications method in which data that cannot be sent directly to its destination is temporarily stored until transmission is possible. This technology allows e-mail messages to be routed to a server and held until they are forwarded to the next server or to a personal mailbox.

Three types of e-mail systems are widely used today: POP, IMAP, and Web-based mail. **POP** (Post Office Protocol) temporarily stores new messages on an e-mail server. When you connect to your ISP and request your mail, it is downloaded from the e-mail server and stored on your computer. **IMAP** (Internet Messaging Access Protocol) is similar to POP, except that you have the option of downloading your mail or leaving it on the server. **Web-based e-mail** keeps your mail at a Web site, where it can be accessed using a standard Web browser (Figure 7-43).

7

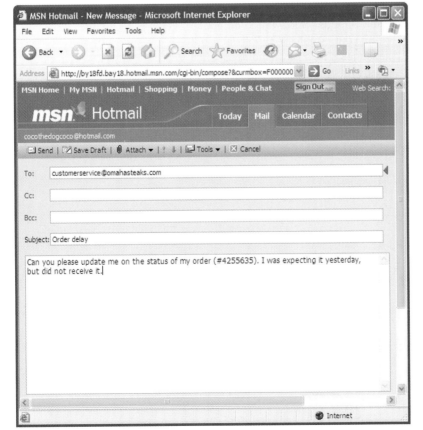

**FIGURE 7-43**

You can use a browser to access your Web-based e-mail account.

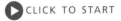
CLICK TO START

**How do I use Web-based e-mail?** Before you can use Web-based e-mail, you need an e-mail account with a Web-based e-mail provider. Popular Web-based e-mail services include Google's Gmail, MSN's Hotmail, and Yahoo's Yahoo! Mail.

To obtain a Web-based e-mail account, connect to the provider's Web site and enter the information required to obtain an e-mail address, a user ID, and a password. Armed with these identifiers, you can use a browser to connect to the e-mail Web site from any computer that has access to the Internet. At the Web site, you can write, read, reply to, and delete e-mail messages. Because most Web-based e-mail providers allocate a limited amount of space to each account, it is important to delete messages when you no longer need them. You don't want your electronic mailbox to overflow and cause some messages to be returned to the senders.

**How do POP and IMAP work?** Most people who use POP or IMAP e-mail have obtained an e-mail account from an ISP. POP mail accounts are more widely available. Such an account provides a mailbox on the ISP's **POP server**—a computer that stores your incoming messages until they can be transferred to your hard disk. Using POP requires **e-mail client software**, such as Microsoft Outlook, Mozilla Thunderbird (open source), or QUALCOMM Eudora. This client software, which is installed on your computer, provides an Inbox and an Outbox that allow you to work with your mail, even when your computer is not online.

An Inbox holds incoming messages. When you ask the e-mail server to deliver your mail, all your messages stored on the server are transferred to your computer, stored on your computer's disk drive, and listed as new mail in your Inbox. You can then disconnect from the Internet, if you like, to read and reply to the new mail at your leisure.

An Outbox temporarily holds messages you have composed and completed, but haven't transmitted over the Internet. Suppose you want to compose several e-mail messages. You can fire up your e-mail client software, but remain offline while you work on the messages. The ability to compose mail offline is especially useful if you access the Internet over a dial-up connection because the phone line isn't tied up while you compose mail. As you complete a message, it is stored on your computer and listed in the Outbox. When you go online, you can send all the mail being held in your Outbox. Outgoing mail is routed by an **SMTP server** (Simple Mail Transfer Protocol server) instead of a POP server, as Figure 7-44 illustrates.

**INFOWEBLINKS**

Many Web-based e-mail providers offer free accounts, though ads might get tacked onto messages. For descriptions and addresses of the most popular e-mail Web sites, hop over to the **Web-based E-mail InfoWeb**.

 CLICK TO CONNECT
www.course.com/np/concepts10/ch07

**INFOWEBLINKS**

What's the latest news about e-mail client software? You'll find descriptions, reviews, and links at the **E-mail Client Software InfoWeb**.

 CLICK TO CONNECT
www.course.com/np/concepts10/ch07

**FIGURE 7-44**

Outgoing mail can be stored in your Outbox until you connect to the Internet and send it. Incoming mail can be stored on a POP server until it is downloaded to the Inbox on your hard disk.

**Does e-mail client software work only for offline e-mail tasks?** No. Although you can use your e-mail client software to compose, read, and reply to messages while you're offline, you can also use it while you are online. In fact, this software often provides a setting that bypasses the Outbox and immediately sends messages out over the Internet.

**How does POP mail compare to Web-based e-mail?** Before answering this question, let's review the important distinctions between the two types of e-mail. First, POP mail requires you to install and use e-mail client software, whereas Web-based e-mail allows you to use a browser to work with your mail. Second, POP transfers messages to your computer's hard disk, whereas a Web-based e-mail system retains your messages on its server.

Both e-mail systems have similar features, allowing you to read, compose, reply to, delete, and forward e-mail messages; maintain an address book; and send attachments. Each system does, however, have unique advantages. In fact, many ISPs offer both POP and Web-based e-mail; POP for when customers are at their home computer, and Web mail for when they are traveling. You might consider using both.

- **Control.** POP mail gives you more control over your messages because they are transferred to your computer's hard disk, where you can control access to them. Web-based e-mail maintains your messages on its server, where you have less control over who can access them.

- **Security.** When messages are stored on your computer, a hard disk drive malfunction could wipe out all your correspondence (along with the rest of your files). A Web-based e-mail provider is rigorous about safeguarding its data, so your mail might be safer than if it was stored on your hard disk.

- **Travel.** The major advantage of Web-based e-mail is that you can access your messages from any computer connected to the Internet. Therefore, you can get your e-mail when you travel without taking your computer. In contrast, POP mail tools and data, such as your address book, e-mail software, and old mail are stored on your computer. To use your familiar POP mail tools on the road, you really have to carry your computer with you or store your e-mail files on a portable USB flash drive. Another solution is to temporarily forward your POP mail to a Web-based mail account that you can access from public computers.

# QuickCheck

**SECTION D**

1. In an e-mail address, the [_____] symbol separates the user ID from the name of the e-mail server.

2. E-mail attachments are typically converted using [_____] , which disguises media and other files as plain ASCII code. (Hint: Use the acronym.)

3. If you want an e-mail message to include various fonts, font colors, and graphics, you can use [_____] format for the message. (Hint: Use the acronym.)

4. Store-and-[_____] e-mail technology stores messages on an e-mail server until they are transmitted to an individual's computer.

5. For many client-based e-mail systems, a(n) [_____] server handles outgoing mail, and a(n) [_____] or IMAP server handles incoming mail. (Hint: Use acronyms.)

CHECK ANSWERS

# Web and E-mail Security

**THE WEB AND E-MAIL** abound with spam and scams engineered to monitor your online activities and collect confidential information, such as credit card numbers, passwords, and bank account numbers. You were introduced to spyware in an earlier chapter. Now you'll learn about specific spam and spyware exploits and find out how to minimize the risk they pose to computer security and your privacy.

## COOKIE EXPLOITS

**Can cookies be a security risk?** Cookies have built-in safeguards designed to reduce their abuse, but marketers, hackers, and pranksters have discovered loopholes that twist cookies to serve the dark side. One of the most prevalent cookie exploits involves ad-serving cookies, and Flash cookies are a newly emerging problem.

**What is an ad-serving cookie?** When you connect to a Web site, you expect it to store an innocuous cookie on your computer's hard disk. Some Web sites, however, feature banner ads supplied by third-party marketing firms. If you click the ad, this third party can surreptitiously create an **ad-serving cookie** and use it to track your activities at any site containing banner ads from that third party. The marketing firms that distribute ad-serving cookies claim that the data in their cookies is used simply to select and display ads that might interest you, but privacy advocates worry that shopper profiles can be compiled, sold, and used for unauthorized purposes. Figure 7-45 illustrates how third parties use ad-serving cookies.

**FIGURE 7-45**

Third-party ad-serving cookies make it possible to track your Internet activities across sites.

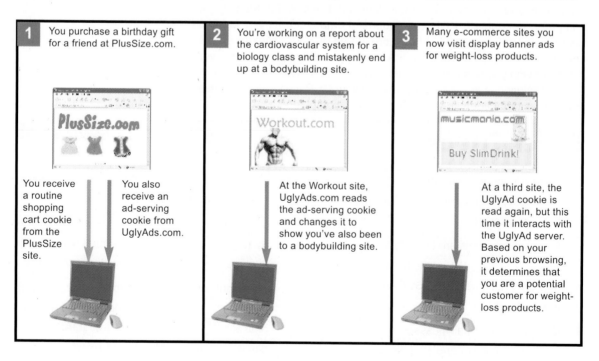

1. You purchase a birthday gift for a friend at PlusSize.com.

You receive a routine shopping cart cookie from the PlusSize site.

You also receive an ad-serving cookie from UglyAds.com.

2. You're working on a report about the cardiovascular system for a biology class and mistakenly end up at a bodybuilding site.

At the Workout site, UglyAds.com reads the ad-serving cookie and changes it to show you've also been to a bodybuilding site.

3. Many e-commerce sites you now visit display banner ads for weight-loss products.

At a third site, the UglyAd cookie is read again, but this time it interacts with the UglyAd server. Based on your previous browsing, it determines that you are a potential customer for weight-loss products.

**Can I turn off cookies to foil ad-serving exploits?** Most browsers include security settings that block cookies. Unfortunately, on many Web sites, cookies are the only mechanism available for tracking your activity or remembering your purchases. Cookies might also be required to join classes and chat groups.

If you disable cookies altogether, you might not be able to make online purchases, participate in online training classes, use Web-based mail, or register for premium services at search engine sites. In addition, you might have to manually enter your user ID and password every time you revisit a Web site. You won't be able to take advantage of targeted marketing, such as when a music Web site keeps track of your favorite band and notifies you when the band's new CDs are available.

Rather than block all cookies, you can block cookies from specific sites. For example, if you'd rather not have your favorite search engine compile and store your searches, you can block its cookies. Your browser might have a setting that blocks all third-party cookies to prevent ad-serving cookies from tracking your site visits (Figure 7-46).

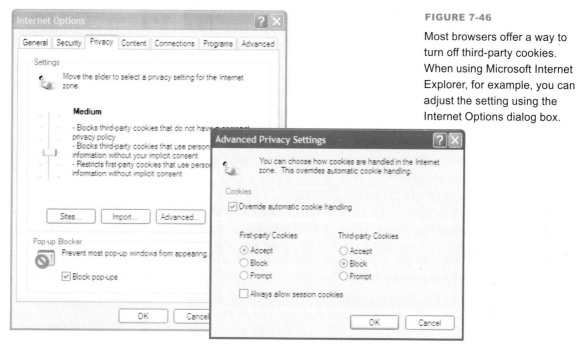

**FIGURE 7-46**

Most browsers offer a way to turn off third-party cookies. When using Microsoft Internet Explorer, for example, you can adjust the setting using the Internet Options dialog box.

**Does deleting cookies reduce risk?** Some privacy advocates suggest deleting cookies periodically, rather than blocking them. By deleting cookies, you can still interact with online shopping carts and take part in other activities that require cookies, but deleted third-party cookies won't be able to communicate with their handlers. The downside of deleting cookies is it might disrupt your attempts to opt out of various cookie schemes.

An opt-out function allows you to refuse to participate in an activity or promotion. Similar to the National Do Not Call list, several third-party advertising companies, such as DoubleClick and ZEDO, now provide users with an opt-out mechanism to disallow ad-serving cookies. The Network Advertising Initiative (NAI) offers a tool to opt out of the targeted advertising by NAI's member firms. In most cases, however, opting out creates an opt-out cookie and if you delete all the cookies on your computer the opt-out cookie will also be deleted and third-party cookies will again start to accumulate.

**What is a Flash Cookie?** A **Flash cookie**, also called a local shared object, is the Flash equivalent of a conventional Web cookie. Flash cookies are utilized and set by Adobe's Flash MX Player (previously distributed by Macromedia), which is installed on practically every computer to run movies, videos, and games. In the context of running Flash animations, Flash cookies can collect and store personal data, such as the user's name or the user's progress in a game.

Because so many computer users now delete or block conventional cookies, marketers are turning to Flash cookies for an alternative way to track and target consumers. United Virtualities (UV), an online marketing firm, developed the PIE (Persistent Identification Element) system, which essentially uses Flash cookies to track users even when they've deleted or aren't accepting conventional cookies.

**Can I avoid Flash Cookies?** You can manually delete Flash cookies from your computer after locating the #Shared Objects file in which they are stored. You can also visit the Adobe Flash Player Web site to adjust your computer's settings for Flash cookies. You can choose your options from the Settings Manager, which consists of several panels. The Website Privacy Settings panel lists all the Web sites that currently store information about you and allows you to set your preferences on a per site basis. A tutorial for using the Settings Manager is also provided by the Web site.

**What is a Web bug?** A **Web bug** or clear GIF is typically a 1x1 pixel graphic embedded in a Web page or e-mail message. It is almost invisible due to its size, and is designed to track who's reading the Web page or e-mail message. Web bugs on a Web page can generate third-party ad-serving cookies. Junk e-mail messages use Web bugs for monitoring the number of people who view the e-mail and use that data to determine the direction of marketing campaigns.

Unlike cookies that are generated when you click a banner ad, you don't have to click anything to receive a third-party cookie generated by a Web bug. When you view a Web bug infested page, an HTTP set-cookie request automatically goes to a third-party server, which can be the site of a marketer or hacker. The site can set a cookie on your computer for later retrieval, or log the IP address of your computer.

**Is there any way to avoid Web bugs?** A drastic solution is to turn off all the graphics displayed by your browser, but that step makes the Web much less interesting. Bugnosis and similar Web bug detectors work with your browser to test graphics on every Web page you visit and flag clear GIF images that might be used to set third-party cookies. Because clear GIFs are also used legitimately for alignment purposes on Web pages, however, it is difficult to determine if a clear GIF's purpose is to track your surfing habits. Web bug detectors are often included in antispyware.

**Antispyware** is a type of security software designed to identify and neutralize Web bugs, ad-serving cookies, and other spyware. Antispyware such as Spy Sweeper, Ad-Aware, Spybot Search & Destroy, Pest Control, and Microsoft Antispyware can offer some degree of protection against browser parasites and other Web-based nuisances (Figure 7-47). Avoid responding to or downloading spyware from pop-up ads, however. Those ads often lead to infected software or other malware.

**FIGURE 7-47**

Many computer owners use more than one antispyware utility if they suspect their computers are infested with spyware.

**Can I surf the Internet anonymously?** In addition to tracking cookies, Web sites can track IP addresses of computers that connect to their sites. IP addresses can sometimes be traced back to individuals, especially those who have fixed IP addresses or always-on connections that retain the same IP address for long periods of time. Individuals who prefer not to leave a trail of their Internet activities surf through an **anonymous proxy service**, which uses an intermediary, or proxy, server to relay Web page requests after masking the originating IP address (Figure 7-48).

Torpark and other anonymizer software allows you to browse through Web sites anonymously. It establishes an encrypted transport path from your computer to a Tor proxy server, which acts as a relay station to a destination site. Torpark can also be used as a portable application by storing it on a USB Flash drive that you plug into any Internet-enabled computer at school, at work, at the library, or other public Internet facility.

A trade-off to the anonymity offered by anonymous proxies is that they tend not to operate at the same speed as your regular browser. In addition, some Web sites and discussion groups block access from proxy servers because they have been used to spam the site or flood it with traffic. Also, anonymous proxies can be compromised by malicious third parties or monitored under court order, so anonymity is never assured.

## FAKE SITES

**What is a fake site?** A fake Web site looks legitimate, but has been created by a third party to be a very clever replica of a legitimate Web site, such as ebay.com or even the White House. Many fake Web sites are bogus storefronts designed exclusively for collecting credit card numbers from unwary shoppers. These sites might have the trappings of a real site. They might even offer a secure connection for transmitting your credit card number. When your data is received, however, it is stored in a database that belongs to a hacker, who can use the data for unauthorized transactions.

Some fake sites are not fake storefronts; rather, they are official-sounding sites, such as government agencies, that actually contain sexually explicit material. Other bogus sites simply present totally fabricated information or stories designed to fool the user. Fake sites are a key part of illegitimate pharming schemes.

**What is pharming?** **Pharming** is an exploit that redirects users to fake sites by "poisoning" a domain name server with a false IP address. As you know from the Internet chapter, a domain name server is responsible for converting a domain name, such as amazon.com, into an IP address. Pharming attacks take advantage of a loophole in the domain name system that under certain circumstances permits third parties to change a record in a domain name server's database. Hackers can attach the IP address of their own Web site to the URL of a legitimate site. Unwary Web surfers end up accessing a different Web site from the one they intended to visit. The redirection is invisible to most browsers, however, and therefore victims are fooled into believing they are at the correct Web site. Pharming is more surreptitious and tougher to detect than most other hacker schemes.

**FIGURE 7-48**

An anonymous proxy server relays your Web page requests after stripping off your IP address.

3. The Web site you want to visit receives your request for a Web page.

4. The Web page is sent to the proxy server.

Unencrypted HTTP from 333.333.333.333

Web page to 333.333.333.333

2. A proxy server decrypts your HTTP request and resends it using a proxy IP address.

5. The proxy server receives the Web page, encrypts it, and sends it to you.

Encrypted HTTP from 111.111.111.111

Encrypted Web page to 111.111.111.111

1. Anonymizer software on your computer provides a specially equipped browser that encrypts its requests.

6. Your computer receives the encrypted Web page, the anonymizer software unencrypts it, and your browser displays it.

Your computer at IP address 111.111.111.111

▶ CLICK TO START

**TERMINOLOGY NOTE**

Fake sites, URLs, and even e-mail addresses are often referred to as *spoofed* and the process of misdirection is called *spoofing*.

**How can I recognize a pharming attack?** To detect a possible pharming attack, you have to be alert to the appearance of Web sites you frequently visit. Be cautious about revealing sensitive information if the site has changed since your last visit. You might want to call the business or organization that operates the Web site to learn whether the Web site has undergone a valid facelift or if the site is a slightly flawed replica of the legitimate one. You can also make sure that you see the lock or key icon at the bottom of the browser when a site claims to be a secured site.

A bank that offers online services recently implemented the use of personal digital images to counteract pharming. Each user chooses an image that is supposed to appear when he or she logs on. If the secret image does not appear, the site is not the legitimate one. Anti-pharming tools are emerging in response to this growing security threat. Browser add-ons, such as Spoofstick, and new browser editions offer ways to compare the site you intend to view with the one that is actually displayed (Figure 7-49).

**FIGURE 7-49**

Antispoofing tools help to confirm that the site you're actually visiting is the one you intended to visit.

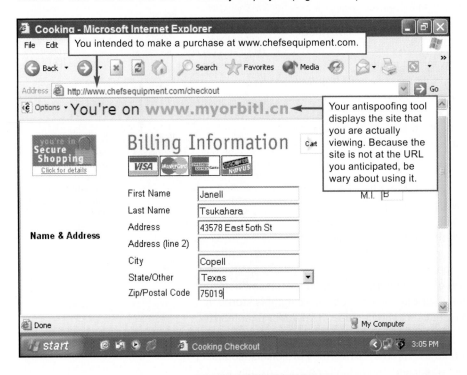

## SPAM

**What is spam?** One of e-mail's main disadvantages is **spam**—unwanted electronic junk mail about medical products, low-cost loans, and fake software upgrades that arrives in your online mailbox. Today's proliferation of spam is generated by marketing firms that harvest e-mail addresses from mailing lists, membership applications, and Web sites.

**Is spam dangerous?** In the past, spam flooding your Inbox with unsolicited and often pornographic messages was merely an annoyance. These days, however, spam has turned into another major hacking tool for cyber criminals. Spam sometimes contains Web bugs, viruses, worms, or keyloggers that can wreak havoc on your computer or steal personal information such as passwords. Spam can also be used for phishing scams, which are described later in this section. In addition to being an annoyance, spam can pose a danger to you and your computer.

**Can I avoid spam?** A **spam filter** is a type of utility software that captures unsolicited e-mail messages before they reach your inbox. It works by checking the text of e-mail headers and messages based on a series of rules. For example, a rule such as "Message header contains viagra, v1agra, or vi@gra" would help identify spam that's trying to hawk cheap pharmaceuticals.

Spam filters are available as standalone software, but often are included in security suites, such as Norton Internet Security and McAfee Security Center. Most spam filter software is shipped with a set of basic rules it uses to identify spam. The rules can be updated by downloads from the software publisher's Web site. Most spam filter software also allows end-users to create their own rules to target spam that gets through the standard filters (Figure 7-50).

**FIGURE 7-50**

Antispam software usually includes standard filters that block common spams, but you can create your own filters for spam that standard filters miss.

7

 CLICK TO START

Spam filters tend to slow down the process of downloading mail and they sometimes trash legitimate mail. Periodically, you should look in the junk e-mail folder used by your spam filters to retrieve any mail that's not junk.

In addition to using spam filters, you can avoid being a spam victim by following the guidelines in Figure 7-51.

**FIGURE 7-51**

Guidelines for Avoiding Spam

- Never reply to spam when you receive it.
- Don't click links in e-mail messages, even if it's an opt-out link.
- Give your e-mail address only to people from whom you want to receive e-mail. Be wary of providing your e-mail address at Web sites, entering it on application forms, or posting it in public places such as online discussion groups.
- Use a disposable e-mail address when you register for online sites. You can use this disposable address to get your confirmation number for online purchases you've made, but don't use it for regular e-mail correspondence.
- If your e-mail provider offers a way to report spam, use it.
- When spam gets out of hand, consider changing your e-mail account so that you have a different e-mail address.

**Can spam be blocked before it gets to my mailbox?** With millions of copies of some spam floating around the Internet, it would seem possible to identify and delete it before individuals have to contend with it. ISPs have stepped up their role in the fight against spam. For example, Hotmail, MSN, and RoadRunner actively participate in Return Path's Bonded Sender Program, which requires e-mail senders to post a bond to guarantee that the messages they send are not spam. A charge is made against the bond if enough end-users complain that they received spam from the bonded e-mail sender. Bonded e-mail senders have to go through a strict accreditation procedure.

To combat spam sent by hijacked botnet computers, **e-mail authentication** techniques, such as Sender ID and DomainKeys, verify that e-mail messages originate from the Internet domain from which they claim to have been sent. For example, if Bank of America e-mail messages are supposed to originate from mail.bankofamerica.net, an ISP that uses e-mail authentication will filter out messages that originate from spoofed addresses such as *www.bankofamerica.ru*. Google, Yahoo!, and Earthlink use authentication techniques to filter out e-mail with a forged origination address.

## PHISHING

**What is phishing?** **Phishing** is an e-mail based scam that's designed to persuade you to reveal confidential information such as your bank account number or Social Security number. Unlike pharming attacks, phishing scams require that you reply to the e-mail message or click an embedded Web site link for the scam to unfold.

If you've used e-mail for any length of time, you've probably encountered the granddaddy of all phishing scams, a letter from a Nigerian political refugee who wants to move a large sum of money to a bank in your country and needs a bank account (yours!) to stash it for a few days. Of course you'll get a percentage for your trouble. Don't even think about it. According to the FBI, several gullible individuals have been lured to foreign shores where they've been kidnapped and even killed.

More innocuous, but potentially damaging spam scams start with an e-mail message that appears to come from a legitimate organization such as a bank, an online payment service, an online store, or even your ISP. The message directs you to click a link to verify confidential data. The link connects you to a bogus site cleverly disguised to look very much like a legitimate Web site. There you are urged to enter your bank account number, PIN, password, credit card number, or other data.

**How do I avoid phishing scams?** If you don't want to become a phishing victim, be suspicious of e-mail messages that supposedly come from banks, ISPs, online payment services, operating system publishers, and online merchants. Even if the messages appear to be legitimate, do not click links in the messages, but instead go to the Web site using your browser and link to your account as you normally would. If your account needs updating, you should see instructions about how to proceed.

**What's the best defense against all the bad stuff on the Web and in e-mail?** First, understand that there is no perfect defense. Then understand that you should do all you can to safeguard your computer and your privacy. Use the list in Figure 7-52 as a starting point.

**FIGURE 7-52**

Guidelines for Secure and Private Web Surfing

7

1. Use antispyware utilities to clean up any spyware that might be on your computer.

2. Run antispyware continuously just as you do antivirus software.

3. Set your browser to reject third-party cookies.

4. Register to reject Flash cookies.

5. Install an antispoofing tool to help you identify fake Web sites.

6. Set up a disposable e-mail address and use it as necessary.

7. Do not click links in untrusted e-mail or pop-up ads, and never respond to e-mail offers, especially those that seem too good to be true.

# QuickCheck                                    SECTION E

1. An anonymous _____ service can prevent Web sites from tracking your activities on the Web.

2. Marketers are turning to _____ cookies as a backup mechanism for conventional cookies.

3. A Web _____ or clear GIF is typically a 1x1 pixel graphic embedded in a Web page or e-mail message.

4. _____ is an exploit that redirects users to fake sites by "poisoning" a domain name server with false information.

5. A type of utility software that captures unsolicited e-mail before it reaches your Inbox is called a spam _____.

6. For a pharming attack to take effect, you need to respond to an e-mail or click an embedded Web site link. True or false? _____

 CHECK ANSWERS

# Who's Reading Your E-mail?

**WHEN YOU DROP** an envelope into the corner mailbox, you probably expect it to arrive at its destination unopened, with its contents kept safe from prying eyes. When you make a phone call, you might assume that your conversation will proceed unmonitored by wiretaps or other listening devices. Can you also expect an e-mail message to be read only by the person to whom it is addressed?

In the United States, the Electronic Communications Privacy Act of 2000 prohibits the use of intercepted e-mail as evidence unless a judge approves a search warrant. That doesn't mean the government isn't reading your mail. Heightened security concerns after the September 11, 2001 terrorist attacks resulted in the rapid passage of the Patriot Act, which became law on October 26, 2001. In an effort to assist law enforcement officials, among its other provisions the Patriot Act relaxes the rules for obtaining and implementing search warrants and lowers the Fourth Amendment standard for obtaining a court order to compel an ISP to produce e-mail logs and addresses.

To eavesdrop on e-mail from suspected terrorists and other criminals, the FBI uses commercially available sniffing software, which scans through messages entering and leaving an ISP's e-mail system to find e-mail associated with a person who is under investigation. Privacy advocates are concerned because the sniffing software scans all messages that pass through an ISP, not just those messages sent to or received by a particular individual.

Although law enforcement agencies are required to obtain a court order before intercepting e-mail, no such restriction exists for employers who want to monitor employee e-mail. According to the American Management Association, 33% of U.S. businesses monitor employee e-mail. But this intentional eavesdropping is only one way in which the contents of your e-mail messages might become public. The recipient of your e-mail can forward it to one or more people—people you never intended for it to reach. Your e-mail messages could pop up on a technician's screen in the course of system maintenance, updates, or repairs.

Some Web-based e-mail providers—particularly those that make you look at ads in exchange for free accounts—collect information on how often you log in and might monitor your keystrokes to find out which ads and links you click. E-mail providers claim such information is used internally to deliver the best possible service, prevent fraud, and select the ads for products that you're most likely to buy. Also, keep in mind that e-mail messages—including those you delete from your own computer—can be stored on backups of your ISP's e-mail server.

You might wonder if such open access to your e-mail is legal. The answer in most cases is yes. Although the United States Omnibus Crime Control and Safe Streets Act of 1968 and the Electronic Communications Privacy Act of 1986 prohibit public and private employers from engaging in surreptitious surveillance of employee activity through the use of electronic devices, two exceptions to these privacy statutes exist. The first exception permits an employer to monitor e-mail if one party to the communication consents to the monitoring. An employer must inform employees of this policy before undertaking any monitoring. The second exception permits employers to monitor employees' e-mail if a legitimate business need exists, and the monitoring takes place within the business-owned e-mail system.

Employees generally have not been successful in defending their rights to e-mail privacy because courts have ruled that an employee's right to privacy does not outweigh a company's rights and interests. Courts seem to agree that because a company owns and maintains its e-mail system, it has the right to monitor the messages carried by the system.

Like employees of a business, students who use a school's e-mail system cannot be assured of e-mail privacy. When a CalTech student was accused of sexually harassing a female student by sending lewd e-mail to her and her boyfriend, investigators retrieved all the student's e-mail from the archives of the e-mail server. The student was expelled from the university even though he claimed that the e-mail had been spoofed to make it look as though he had sent it, when it had actually been sent by someone else.

Why would an employer want to know the contents of employee e-mail? Why would a school be concerned with the correspondence of its students? It is probably true that some organizations simply snoop on the off chance that important information might be discovered. Other organizations have more legitimate reasons for monitoring e-mail. An organization that owns an e-mail system can be held responsible for the consequences of actions related to the contents of e-mail messages on that system. For example, a school has a responsibility to protect students from harassment. If it fails to do so, it can be sued along with the author of the offending e-mail message. Organizations also recognize a need to protect themselves from false rumors and industrial espionage. For example, a business wants to know if an employee is supplying its competitor with information on product research and development.

Many schools and businesses have established e-mail privacy policies, which explain the conditions under which you can and cannot expect your e-mail to remain private. These policies are sometimes displayed when the computer boots or a new user logs in. Court decisions, however, seem to support the notion that because an organization owns and operates an e-mail system, the e-mail messages on that system are also the property of the organization. The individual who authors an e-mail message does not own all rights related to it. The company, school, or organization that supplies your e-mail account can, therefore, legally monitor your messages.

You should use your e-mail account with the expectation that some of your mail will be read from time to time. Think of your e-mail as a postcard, rather than a letter, and save your controversial comments for face-to-face conversations.

**INFOWEBLINKS**

You'll find lots more information about e-mail privacy (and lack of it) at the **E-mail Privacy InfoWeb**.

 CLICK TO CONNECT
www.course.com/np/concepts10/ch07

7

# What Do You Think?

ISSUE

1. Do you think most people believe that their e-mail is private?    ○ Yes  ○ No  ○ Not sure

2. Do you agree with CalTech's decision to expel the student who was accused of sending harassing e-mail to another student?    ○ Yes  ○ No  ○ Not sure

3. Should the laws be changed to make it illegal for employers to monitor e-mail without court approval?    ○ Yes  ○ No  ○ Not sure

4. Would you have different privacy expectations regarding an e-mail account at your place of work as opposed to an account you purchase from an e-mail service provider?    ○ Yes  ○ No  ○ Not sure

▶ SAVE RESPONSES

## COMPUTERS IN CONTEXT

# Fashion Industry

**FASHION IS BIG BUSINESS.** Worldwide, clothing sales generate more than $200 billion in revenue. Shoes, accessories, and jewelry bump the industry's revenue even higher. Competition is tough as designers, manufacturers, and retailers compete for customer dollars. In the fashion industry, trends change quickly. As the saying goes, "Today's style is tomorrow's markdown." Fashion industry players look for every competitive advantage. It is no surprise that technology plays a major role in this glitzy industry.

Fashion begins with designers, such as Miuccia Prada, John Galliano, and Ralph Lauren. Their runway extravaganzas set off fashion trends that eventually work their way to retail stores. Fashion runways went high-tech in 1999 when lingerie manufacturer Victoria's Secret produced a Webcast watched by over 1 million viewers. Bravo television's Project Runway show has been one of the top iPod downloads. Fashion podcasts and blogs abound on the Web, as do fashion sites packed with news about the latest trends.

Although runway fashions are typically conceived with a sketch and stitched by hand, designs are adapted for the ready-to-wear market by using computer-assisted design (CAD) tools, such as pattern-making software. Garments are constructed by sewing together sections of fabric that form arms, fronts, backs, collars, and so forth. The set of templates used to cut fabric sections is called a pattern. Pattern-making is a tricky 3D challenge because flat pieces of fabric eventually become garments shaped to conform to curved body contours. Pattern making software helps designers visualize how flat pieces fit together and drape when sewn. Once a master pattern is complete, pattern-making software automatically generates a set of patterns for each garment size.

Fashion requires fabric, and computers play a major role in fabric design and manufacturing. Computer software, such as ArahWeave, lets fabric designers experiment with colors, yarns, and weaves while viewing detailed, realistic on-screen samples. Fabric designs can be stored in a variety of formats for weaving machines. A few older mechanical weaving machines are controlled by punched cards. Digital fabric designs can be transferred to punched cards with a dedicated card punch machine. Most of today's weaving mills use computerized machinery that directly accepts digital input to control threads and patterns. Networks tie looms to CAD stations and to the Internet. Fabric designs can be stored in XML format, transmitted to a fabric manufacturer over the Internet, and used directly by computerized weaving machines.

Clothing production, warehousing, and shipping are also highly automated. Benetton's high-tech facility at Castrette, Italy can produce over 110 million garments per year. Its automated distribution center uses a workforce of only 24 people to handle 40,000 boxes of merchandise daily. Radio frequency identification (RFID) tags—sometimes called smart labels—can be attached to individual garments or to packing boxes as an important tool for controlling inventory.

RFID technology uses an inexpensive, tiny computer chip with built-in antenna and the capacity to store between 64 and 128 bits of data about a garment—its SKU number, size, model, dye lot, manufacturing date, and so on. Tags can be attached to a garment or its label. An RFID reader that can retrieve data from tags is used to track merchandise from the manufacturing plant through the distribution chain to the retailer. RFID tags are becoming popular for all types of merchandise. Businesses that use them can save time and money. For example, RFID tags can reduce the time it takes to do a physical inventory by a factor of 10. Privacy advocates, however, are worried because these tags remain active even after you bring your merchandise home. Could a thief circle your house with an RFID scanner to find out what's inside? Could a stalker follow your movements by tracking the RFID tag embedded in your sweater? After customers protested a plan to attach RFID tags to every sweater, Benetton currently uses the tags only on shipping cartons.

In response to competition from offshore companies, U.S. clothing manufacturers pioneered Quick Response (QR)—a business model for compressing supply chains to quickly obtain raw materials, such as fabric, yarn, buttons, and zippers. Sophisticated software tools, such as the Sourcing Simulator, simplify QR planning.

Online shopping has become routine, but one drawback of catalog and online ordering is the cost associated with restocking returned merchandise. Can an online customer find out how a garment will fit and look before ordering it? In 1998, Lands' End introduced My Virtual Model technology that allows shoppers to create a custom model of themselves by choosing from a variety of hair colors and styles, face shapes, and body types. The model can "try on" clothes to show online customers how they would look when wearing the garments.

More recently, Lands' End toured the country with a body-scanning device to collect actual measurements from thousands of customers. Body-scanning devices use cameras and lasers to capture approximately 300,000 data points that can be pieced together into a 3D image.

Body scanners are also helping the fashion industry by collecting research data. Sizing standards fell by the wayside when vanity sizing added an inch or two to a garment so that consumers can feel good about themselves by fitting into smaller sizes. In the U.S. clothing industry, a comprehensive study of body shapes and sizes can help standardize sizing and eliminate much of the trial and error involved in finding apparel that fits. Collecting data from body scans is part of this ongoing research effort.

No discussion of fashion and computers would be complete without highlighting wearable technology. Clothing that contains digital devices has made its way out of the laboratory and onto store shelves. For example, Burton Snowboards, electronic fabric manufacturer SOFTswitch, and Apple teamed up to create the limited-edition Burton Amp, a jacket with integrated iPod controls designed for snowboarders to control music from the sleeves of their jackets without fumbling with zippers, gloves, and small control buttons.

Another wearable, originally popular with secret service agents, is the SCOTTeVEST, a jacket with pockets for cell phone, PDA, MP3 player, and built-in wiring to connect these devices into a personal area network (PAN). Available as a jacket or vest and in men's and women's sizes, the jacket can now be purchased by civilians.

With a growing emphasis on the use of technology in fashion design and manufacturing, fashion degree programs at colleges and technical schools have added courses such as computer-aided fashion design, computer-based pattern drafting, pattern grading and computer-aided drafting, and wearable computers.

### INFOWEBLINKS

You'll find information related to this Computers in Context topic at the **Computers and Fashion InfoWeb**.

**W** CLICK TO CONNECT
www.course.com/np/concepts10/ch07

# New Perspectives Labs

## On the BookOnCD

To access the New Perspectives labs for Chapter 7, start the BookOnCD, BookOnFlashDrive, or other NP10 BookOn product and then click the icon next to the lab title below.

### ▶ BROWSER SECURITY SETTINGS

**IN THIS LAB YOU'LL LEARN:**

- How to adjust the security settings for Internet Explorer

- The significance of Internet, Local Intranet, Trusted, and Restricted security zones

- How to add sites to a security zone and adjust security zone settings

- Why ActiveX controls pose a potential security threat and how to adjust ActiveX control security settings

- Why downloads pose a potential security threat to your computer and how to activate the recommended download security settings

- Why Java applets pose a potential security threat to your computer

- The significance of Java permission levels

- How to activate the recommended Java security settings

**LAB ASSIGNMENTS**

1. Perform each lab step as directed, and answer all the lab QuickCheck questions.

2. Check the Internet zone security setting on the computer you typically use. Indicate whether the setting is High, Medium, Medium-low, Low, or Custom. Describe how this setting handles ActiveX controls, downloads, and Java applets.

3. On the computer you typically use, find out whether any Web sites are listed in the Trusted or Restricted zones. Would you make changes to the list of sites for these zones? Explain why or why not.

4. Activate the Prompt setting for the Download ActiveX controls security setting. After you have done so, use your browser to connect to *http://www.infoweblinks.com/np6/samples/active x.htm*, where you should encounter an ActiveX control security alert. Use your computer's Print Screen (PrtSc or PrtScrn) key to capture a screenshot of the warning. Paste the screenshot into Paint and then print it. Would you accept this ActiveX control? Why or why not?

### ▶ WORKING WITH COOKIES

**IN THIS LAB YOU'LL LEARN:**

- How Web servers use cookies

- Why cookies might pose a threat to your privacy

- How to locate cookies stored on your computer

- How to view the contents of a cookie

- How to delete a single cookie created by Internet Explorer

- How to delete all the cookies stored on your computer

- How to limit the space allocated to cookies created by Internet Explorer

- How to block cookies

- What a session cookie is

- How to set cookie prompts and use the cookie prompt dialog box

- How to take advantage of P3P and Compact Privacy Policies

- The differences between first-party and third-party cookies

- How to opt out of receiving third-party cookies

**LAB ASSIGNMENTS**

1. Perform each lab step as directed, and answer all the lab QuickCheck questions.

2. Use Windows Explorer to look at the cookies stored on your computer. Indicate how many cookies are currently stored. Examine the contents of one cookie, and indicate whether you think it poses a threat to your privacy.

3. Indicate the name and version of the browser you typically use. To find this information, open your browser, and then select the About option from the Help menu. Next, look at the cookie settings your browser provides. Describe how you would adjust these settings to produce a level of privacy protection that is right for your needs.

4. Adjust your browser settings so that you are prompted whenever a Web server attempts to send a cookie to your computer. Go to several of your favorite Web sites and watch for third-party cookies. When you receive a message from a third-party Web site, record the name of the third-party site and the contents of the cookie it is attempting to send. Finally, indicate whether you would accept such a cookie.

# Key Terms

Make sure you understand all the boldfaced key terms presented in this chapter. If you're using the NP10 BookOnCD, BookOnFlashDrive, or other NP10 BookOn product, you can use this list of terms as an interactive study activity. First, try to define a term in your own words, and then click the term to compare your definition with the definition presented in the chapter.

ActiveX control, 372
Ad-blocking software, 385
Ad-serving cookie, 400
Ajax, 362
Anonymous proxy service, 403
Antispyware, 402
Atom, 360
B2B, 384
B2C, 384
B2G, 384
Banner ad, 385
Boolean operator, 379
C2C, 384
Click-through rate, 385
Client-side script, 372
Cookie, 368
DHTML, 362
Digital certificate, 373
E-commerce, 384
E-mail account, 392
E-mail attachment, 393
E-mail authentication, 406
E-mail client software, 398
E-mail message, 392
E-mail servers, 397
E-mail system, 397
Electronic wallet, 390
Flash cookie, 402
Helper application, 367
Hover ad, 385
HTML, 362
HTML conversion utility, 369

HTML document, 362
HTML forms, 371
HTML script, 371
HTML tags, 362
HTTP, 364
HTTP status code, 365
Hypertext, 360
Hypertext link, 361
IMAP, 397
Java applet, 372
Keyword stuffing, 378
Link popularity, 377
Markup language, 362
Message header, 392
Meta keyword, 378
Metasearch engine, 380
MIME, 393
Netiquette, 396
Online auction, 388
Online shopping cart, 386
Person-to-person payment, 390
Pharming, 403
Phishing, 406
Player, 367
Plug-in, 367
Podcast, 360
POP, 397
POP server, 398
Pop-up ad, 385
Query processor, 377
RSS, 360
Search engine indexer, 376

Search terms, 378
Secure connection, 389
Server-side script, 371
S-HTTP, 389
Smileys, 396
SMTP server, 398
Socket, 364
Spam, 405
Spam filter, 405
SSL, 389
Stateless protocol, 365
Store-and-forward, 397
TLS, 389
URL, 361
Videocasting, 361
Web, 360
Web browser, 361
Web bug, 402
Web cache, 367
Web crawler, 375
Web page, 361
Web search engine, 374
Web server, 361
Web site, 360
Web-based e-mail, 397
XHTML, 362

7

# Interactive Summary

To review important concepts from this chapter, fill in the blanks to best complete each sentence. When using the NP10 BookOnCD or other BookOn product, click the Check Answers buttons to automatically score your answers.

**SECTION A:** The Web, one of the Internet's hottest attractions, is a collection of document, image, video, and sound files that can be linked and accessed over the Internet via the [ ] protocol. The Web is an interlinked collection of information; whereas the [ ] is the communications system used to transport Web information from computers that store it to client computers who request it. An Internet-based computer that stores and distributes Web files is called a Web [ ] . It can host one or more Web [ ] such as *www.wikipedia.com* or *www.myspace.com* containing HTML [ ] documents, which can be accessed and displayed using client

software called a Web [ ] . Each Web page has a unique address called a [ ] . [ ] markup language is a set of specifications for creating documents that a browser can display as a Web page. To create HTML documents, you can use a variety of Web authoring tools, such as a text [ ] , HTML conversion utility, online Web authoring tool, or Web authoring software. To enable your Web pages to perform tasks beyond what HTML can do, you can add programs by embedding a [ ] in your HTML document, or by coding a Java [ ] or [ ] control, which you can refer to in your document.

CHECK ANSWERS

**SECTION B:** To sift through massive amounts of information available on the Web and locate pertinent information about a topic, Web surfers utilize programs called search [ ] . These special programs have four major components. A Web [ ] , also called a Web spider, is automated to methodically visit Web sites and gather Web pages. A search engine [ ] culls keywords from the gathered pages and stores them in a [ ] . The search engine's query [ ] accepts one or

more words called search [ ] , looks them up in the database, and produces a list of relevant Web sites. There are a number of ways to narrow searches and produce more targeted results, such as using [ ] operators or putting exact phrases in [ ] . The order in which Web sites are returned in response to your query is dependent on relevancy criteria, such as keyword matches and [ ] popularity.

CHECK ANSWERS

**SECTION C:** Any business transaction that is conducted electronically over a computer network is typically referred to as a(n) [ ] transaction. The most common business models are business-to- [ ] , consumer-to-consumer, business-to- [ ] , and business-to-government. E-commerce merchants cut costs by taking advantage of efficiency and opportunities offered by [ ] , computerization, and digitization. They also increase their profits by providing space for third-party

[ ] ads and pop-up ads on their Web pages. Online stores use [ ] to track customers' online shopping carts. At an online [ ] site, sellers post their merchandise or services and consumers bid for the posted items. Online purchases can be paid for by submitting a credit card number directly to a merchant, using a person-to- [ ] payment service, submitting payment data using an electronic wallet, or making use of a one-time-use credit card number.

CHECK ANSWERS

**SECTION D:** E-mail, short for "electronic mail," can refer to a single electronic message or to the entire system of computers and software that transmits, receives, and stores digital e-mail messages. Any person with an e-mail [_____] can send and receive electronic mail. Basic e-mail activities include composing, reading, replying to, sending, forwarding, and deleting messages. More advanced activities include adding attachments and maintaining an address book. Most e-mail messages are created in a plain and simple format called [_____] text. It is also possible to create messages in [_____] format, which includes underlining, fancy fonts, colored text, and embedded graphics. An e-mail system consists of e-mail servers, which are accessible to e-mail account holders. Today, consumers can choose between three types of e-mail. [_____] mail holds your incoming mail on an e-mail server until you download it to your computer using e-mail [_____] software. [_____] mail gives you the option of downloading your mail or storing it on the e-mail server. [_____]-based mail allows you to use a browser as e-mail client software. E-mail has similarities with and differences from other forms of communications, but it is the differences that spawned a collection of online communications guidelines called [_____].

CHECK ANSWERS

7

**SECTION E:** When you surf the Web or work with your e-mail, you need to be aware of potential spyware exploits, such as [_____] cookies from third-parties. While browsers and marketing firms are now providing opt-out mechanisms to block third-party cookies, it is not as easy to turn off all kinds of cookies. [_____] cookies, also called local shared objects, are used as an alternative to conventional cookies, and most users are not aware of their existence. Web [_____], or clear GIFs, are practically invisible 1x1-pixel graphics embedded in a Web page or e-mail message, that can be used to set cookies for third-party Web sites. [_____] redirects users to fake sites by tampering with the information in a [_____] name server. While these attacks don't need any action on your part to be effective, [_____] scams require you to respond to an e-mail message or click an embedded link in your e-mail. [_____] is unsolicited e-mail that you can avoid by practicing safe e-mail techniques such as using a spam [_____]. You can also use a [_____] e-mail address to receive confirmation for online purchases without getting added to a spam mailing list. A safe bet for combating most forms of spyware is by using a type of security software called [_____].

CHECK ANSWERS

# Interactive Situation Questions

Apply what you've learned to some typical computing situations. When using the NP10 BookOnCD, BookOnFlashDrive, or any other NP10 BookOn product, you can type your answers, and then use the Check Answers button to automatically score your responses.

1. Suppose that you are about to check out at an online store, but you don't see any indication that your transaction data will be protected by a secure connection. It would be best, under these circumstances, to use PGP software to encrypt your shipping and billing data. True or false? _____

2. Your friend, who is a little computer phobic, is going to be creating his first Web page and asks you to recommend some software for the task. Which one requires the least knowledge of HTML tags: Notepad or Microsoft Word? _____

3. Suppose you visit a Web site that has eye-catching pages. You want to know how these pages were formatted, so you use one of the options on your browser's menu to take a look at the HTML _____ document.

4. Suppose you click a link at a Web site and get a message that the file cannot be displayed because it is in PDF format. To view the file, you need an updated version of your browser. True or false? _____

5. Suppose you're performing a local test of a Web page you created. All the page elements appear to be correctly positioned and formatted. You're also happy to discover that your large graphics files are displayed quite quickly by your browser. Can you expect similar performance after you post the page on a Web site? Yes or no? _____

6. You'd prefer not to have the search engine you use maintain accumulative records of your searches. You can block _____ from a specific search engine site, and that setting will force the search engine to assign a different ID number to you for each session.

7. You're getting ready for a week-long trip. You'd rather not take your computer, but you'll have access to public computers. Rather than use Web-based e-mail while you're away from home, you decide to use your familiar POP e-mail _____ software, by storing it and your e-mail files on a portable USB flash drive.

8. One of your relatives wants to try online shopping, but is suspicious that her credit card number might get stolen from a merchant's server by a hacker using a packet sniffer. Is it correct to tell her that she can best avoid these potential rip-offs by a secure connection, such as SSL? Yes or no? _____

9. Your inbox is getting more and more unsolicited messages with "fisd foos" in the header. You decide to generate a new rule for your security software's spam _____ to block those irritating messages.

10. You're looking through a list of cookies stored on your computer, but don't remember visiting sites such as bannerbank, hotlog, and ad.bb. You can assume that these cookies were created by _____ , such as ad-serving cookies.

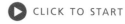 CHECK ANSWERS

# Interactive Practice Tests

Practice tests that consist of 10 multiple-choice, true/false, and fill-in-the-blank questions are available on both the NP10 BookOn products and the NP10 Web site. The questions are selected at random from a large test bank, so each time you take a test, you'll receive a different set of questions. Your tests are scored immediately, and you can print study guides that help you find the correct answers for any questions that you missed.

CLICK TO START

# Study Tips

Study Tips help you to organize and consolidate the information in a unit by making lists, outlines, charts, and sketches. You can use paper and pencil or word processing software to complete most of the Study Tip activities.

1. Make sure you can use your own words to correctly answer each of the red focus questions that appear throughout the chapter.

2. Draw a multi-panel cartoon that shows how a Web server and browser interact. Include the following terms: Web server, browser, HTTP, HTML, port, socket, HTML document, graphic file, and URL.

3. Make sure you can explain the relationship between an HTML source document and a Web page.

4. In your own words, explain what the term *stateless protocol* means, then describe how it relates to cookies.

5. Briefly sketch the evolution of Web browsers.

6. Describe the advantages and disadvantages of each type of Web page development tool discussed in this chapter.

7. Explain the purpose of HTML scripts and the differences between server-side scripts and client-side scripts.

8. Create a comic-strip like sequence of diagrams that illustrates how the following technologies interact: Web crawler, search engine database, indexer, query processor.

9. Use a search engine and Boolean operators to formulate a search for information about your favorite era in history. Can you make a more targeted search to find out what kind of slang was used during that time period?

10. List the four most commonly used styles of citation and make sure that you can correctly format a citation to a Web page using each style.

11. Explain two ways that shopping carts can work with cookies.

12. Outline what you've learned about online payment technologies.

13. List the advantages and disadvantages of HTML formatted mail.

14. Create a table that compares and contrasts POP mail with Web-based mail.

15. Make a list of security and privacy concerns discussed in this chapter. Describe each one and then describe procedures and technologies available to make your online experience more secure and private.

16. Fill in the blanks on the concept map below to show the hierarchy of Web technology concepts presented in this chapter.

7

# Concept Map

CHECK ANSWERS

# Projects

 CRITICAL THINKING

In this chapter you read about some of the pitfalls of shopping online. Reflect on what you read within the context of your own online usage habits. What aspects of your online activities could you change to become more secure, more private, or more efficient? What do you have to give up to get these benefits? Is it worth it to you? Incorporate your thoughts in a one-page summary. Follow your instructor's guidelines for submission.

 GROUP PROJECT

Brainstorm with a group of three to five students to come up with an idea for an e-business. For this project assign tasks from the list below and create a schedule for completing them. Compile your work into a single document for submission.
Tasks:

• Decide on a name for the business after finding an available URL.

• Design a Web site for the business. Mock up the Web site home page using Web authoring software or simply a graphics program, such as Paint.

• Locate at least five partner sites that might provide synergistic cross-marketing.

• Make a list of 10 keywords that can be used in your Web page header so customers can easily find your site when using a search engine.

• Find a site to host your online business and work up a spreadsheet showing monthly and annual hosting costs.

 CYBERCLASSROOM

Work with your team to create a blog on any topic. You can use the tools provided at any blogging site, such as *www.blogger.com*. Make sure that each person on the team posts at least one message to the blog. Send your instructor instructions for logging onto your blog. When all the blogs are up and running, your instructor might post the URLs so everyone in the class can judge whose blog is best.

 MULTIMEDIA PROJECT

Surf the Web to select a home page that needs improvement. Use the Print Screen key on your keyboard to take a screenshot of the original page. Paste the page into graphics software such as Paint and store it as Home Page Original [Your Name]. Use your graphics software to create an improved home page by following some of the tips and recommendations offered in the chapter. Save your makeover as Home Page Makeover [Your Name]. Make a list of the changes you made. Submit the original page, the makeover page, and list of changes to your instructor.

 RESUME BUILDER

Many companies have a Web site that provides information on their products and services. Use a search engine to locate a company in your career field. Suppose you are a recruiter for that company and you'll be attending a series of college career fairs. Create a one-page information flyer that you can hand out to prospective recruits. The flyer should include:

• The company name, URL, and physical location(s)

• A brief description of the company's mission, products, and services

• Instructions on how to submit a resume electronically

 GLOBALIZATION

Examine trends in global e-commerce, and submit your answers to the following questions.

• Which countries are the top players in the e-commerce market?

• How big is your country's share of the e-commerce pie, and is it increasing or decreasing?

• How does e-commerce affect developing countries?

• What are the advantages and disadvantages of a global market?

 ISSUE

The Issue section of this chapter focused on how much—or how little—privacy you can expect when using an e-mail account. For this project, write a two- to five-page paper about e-mail privacy based on information you gather from the Internet. To begin this project, consult the E-mail Privacy InfoWeb to get an in-depth overview of the issue. Next, determine the viewpoint you will present in your paper. You might, for example, decide to present the viewpoint of a student who believes that e-mail should be afforded the same privacy rights as a sealed letter. Or you might present the viewpoint of an employer who wants to explain why your company believes it is necessary to monitor employee e-mail. Whatever viewpoint you decide to present, make sure you can back it up with facts and references to authoritative articles and Web pages.

 COMPUTERS IN CONTEXT

The Computers in Context section of this chapter focused on computers in the fashion industry. For this report, create a visual timeline that traces a garment from the time it is conceived by a designer to the time it is placed on a designer's rack or store shelf. Indicate technologies that are used at various stages of this process. Make sure that you provide citations for your text and graphical sources.

# On the Web

## STUDENT EDITION LABS

**W CLICK TO ACCESS THE NP10 WEB SITE**
or open your browser and connect to www.course.com/np/concepts10/ch07.
Lab results can be stored in the Universal Gradebook.

### CREATING WEB PAGES

In the Creating Web Pages Student Edition Lab, you will learn the following topics and skills:

- Starting a Web page
- Formatting paragraphs and text on a Web page
- Using graphics and backgrounds on a Web page
- Linking to other Web pages
- Using tables on a Web page

### E-MAIL

In the E-Mail Student Edition Lab, you will learn the following e-mail skills:

- Composing, replying to, and printing e-mail messages
- E-mail organizational and management techniques such as moving messages to a folder and using an address book
- Signing up for and using Web-based e-mail to demonstrate your e-mail skills using your own e-mail account

### E-COMMERCE

In the E-Commerce Student Edition Lab, you will learn the following topics and skills:

- Paying with electronic cash
- Ensuring security in an e-commerce transaction
- Technical components of an e-commerce Web site
- Developing an e-commerce Web site

### WEB DESIGN PRINCIPLES

In the Web Design Principles Student Edition Lab, you will learn the following topics and skills:

- Designing the site structure
- Designing the site look and feel
- Designing for readability
- Using hypertext and images effectively

7

### CHAPTER COURSECAST

Use your computer or iPod to hear a five-minute audio presentation of chapter highlights.

### FLASHCARD COURSECAST

Interact with audio flashcards to review key terms from the chapter.

### DETAILED OBJECTIVES

Make sure that you've achieved all the objectives for a chapter before it's time for your test!

### TEST YOURSELF

Review chapter material by taking these ten-question tests, then send your results to the Universal Gradebook.

### ONLINE GAMES

Have some fun while refreshing your memory about key concepts that might appear on the next test. You can even send your results to the Universal Gradebook!

### AND MORE!

At the NP10 Web site you'll also find TechBuzz, CNET videos, Extra Content, and InfoWebLinks.

# 8

# Digital Media

## CHAPTER CONTENTS

## LEARNING OBJECTIVES

- Describe the formats used for digital music

- Explain how to download music files and transfer them to portable audio players

- Describe the advantages, disadvantages, and uses for digital media, such as bitmap graphics, vector graphics, 3-D graphics, 3-D animations, desktop video, digital audio, and MIDI music

- List the equipment and software that can be used to work with various types of digital media

- Identify digital media files by their file extensions

- Understand the advantages and disadvantages of using each type of digital media on the Web

- Explain how resolution, image size, color depth, and color palettes can be manipulated to adjust the file size of a bitmap graphic

- Recap key points about image compression

- Describe procedures required to convert bitmap graphics into vector graphics and vector graphics into bitmaps

- Explain how wireframes, rendering, and ray tracing apply to 3-D graphics

- Define the differences between digital video and 3-D animation

- Describe how to shoot, capture, edit, and process digital video

- Explain how window size, frame rate, and compression affect file size for a desktop video

- Summarize the process for creating DVD-Video

- List and define digital rights management technologies used to protect content that is broadcast, downloaded, or delivered on CDs and DVDs

- Provide at least two examples of time shifting, place shifting, and format shifting

 **PRE-ASSESSMENT QUIZ**

Take the pre-assessment quiz to find out how much you know about the topics in this chapter.

**MULTIMEDIA and INTERACTIVE ELEMENTS**
When using the BookOnCD, BookOnFlashDrive, or other NP10 BookOn product, the ▶ icons are clickable to access multimedia resources.

BEFORE YOU READ ON, **TRY IT**

## WHAT KINDS OF GRAPHICS, AUDIO, AND VIDEO FILES ARE ON MY COMPUTER?

You can use your computer to work with many types of media, such as photos, music, and videos. Your computer stores media that you've created and downloaded. It also stores images from Web sites you've recently visited. To discover what sort of media is stored on your computer, do the following steps:

**1.** Make sure your computer is turned on.

**2.** Click the Start button. If you're using Windows Vista, type **pictures** into the search box as shown below, and then press the Enter key.

If you are using Windows XP, click Search. The Search Results dialog box appears.

On the left side of the Search Results window, click the button for Pictures, Music, or Video.

Check the box for Pictures and Photos, then click the Search button. Your computer shows you a list of image files. If Windows displays a list of file names, but you'd rather see the images, click the View menu and select Thumbnails.

**3.** Repeat step 2 to search for Music and then again to search for video.

**4.** When you're finished looking at your media files, click the ⊠ button to close the Search Results dialog box.

## WEB SITE
Visit the NP10 Web site to access additional resources Ⓦ that accompany this chapter.

# Digital Sound

**COMPUTERS CAN RECORD,** store, and play back sounds, such as narrations, sound effects, and music. Swapping music files over the Internet is currently the most popular use of digital audio, but digital audio plays a key role in other very interesting applications. How would you like to quit messing with your computer keyboard and enter commands and documents simply by speaking into a microphone? Would you like to add music and sound effects to your Web pages? Maybe you'd like to pull tracks from your audio CDs and remaster them into your own collection of favorite songs. This section of the chapter covers a wide-ranging selection of digital audio concepts and technologies that you're likely to find handy for personal and professional use.

## DIGITAL AUDIO BASICS

**What is digital audio?** **Digital audio** is music, speech, and other sounds represented in binary format for use in digital devices. Sound is produced by the vibration of matter such as a violin string or a drum head. This vibration causes pressure changes in the surrounding air creating waves.

The smooth, continuous curve of a sound wave can be directly recorded on analog devices, such as records. To digitally record sound, samples of the sound wave are collected at periodic intervals and stored as numeric data. Figure 8-1 shows how a computer digitally samples a sound wave.

**FIGURE 8-1**

Sampling a Sound Wave

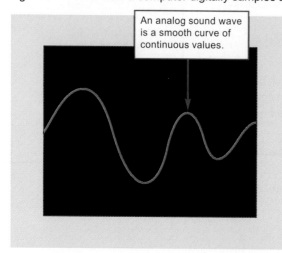

An analog sound wave is a smooth curve of continuous values.

To digitize a wave, it is sliced into vertical segments, called samples. For purposes of illustration, this one-second sound wave was sliced into 30 samples.

| Sample | Sample Height (Decimal) | Sample Height (Binary) |
|---|---|---|
| 1 | 130 | 10000010 |
| 2 | 140 | 1000110 |
| 3 | 160 | 10100000 |
| 4 | 175 | 10101111 |
| 5 | 185 | 10111001 |

The height of each sample is converted into a binary number and stored. The height of sample 3 is 160 (decimal), so it is stored as its binary equivalent—10100000.

**Does sampling rate affect sound quality?** **Sampling rate** refers to the number of times per second that a sound is measured during the recording process. It is expressed in hertz (Hz). One thousand samples per second is expressed as 1,000 Hz or 1 KHz (kilohertz). Higher sampling rates increase the quality of the sound recording but require more storage space than lower sampling rates.

The height of each sound sample can be saved as an 8-bit number for radio-quality recordings or a 16-bit number for high-fidelity recordings. The audio CDs you buy at your favorite music store are recorded at a sampling rate of 44.1 KHz, which means a sample of the sound is taken 44,100 times per second. Sixteen bits are used for each sample. To achieve stereo effects, you must take two of these 16-bit samples. Therefore, each sample requires 32 bits of storage space. When you sample stereo CD-quality music at 44.1 KHz, one minute of music requires about 10 MB of storage space. Forty-five minutes of music—the length of a typical album—require about 450 MB.

To conserve space, applications that do not require such high-quality sound use much lower sampling rates. Voice is often recorded with a sampling rate of 11 KHz (11,000 samples per second). This rate results in lower quality sound, but the file is about one-fourth the size of a file for the same sound recorded at 44.1 KHz. Figure 8-2 illustrates how sampling rate affects sound quality.

**FIGURE 8-2**

A higher sampling rate produces more true-to-life sound quality. Use your BookOnCD to compare the quality of these audio clips, which were digitized at different sampling rates. You'll have to listen carefully to notice the differences.

Low sampling rate: File size = 66 KB

▶ CLICK TO START

Medium sampling rate: File size = 124 KB

▶ CLICK TO START

High sampling rate: File size = 235 KB

▶ CLICK TO START

Regardless of sampling rate, digital audio file size can be reduced using audio compression techniques. **Audio compression** reduces the size of a sound file by removing bits that represent extraneous noise and sounds that are beyond the frequencies of normal hearing. In addition, general-purpose compression techniques explained later in the chapter can be applied to sound files. A compressed audio file requires less storage space than the uncompressed file and can be transmitted faster over a network. Popular portable music players typically work with compressed audio file formats.

**How does a computer produce digital audio?** Your computer's sound card is responsible for transforming the bits stored in an audio file into music, sound effects, and narrations. A **sound card** is a device that contains a variety of input and output jacks, plus audio-processing circuitry. A desktop computer's sound card is usually plugged into a PCI expansion slot inside the system unit. Alternatively, sound card circuitry might be built into the system board. Notebook computers rarely feature a separate sound card because manufacturers save space by incorporating sound circuitry into the system board.

8

A sound card is typically equipped to accept input from a microphone and send output to speakers or headphones. For processing digital audio files, a sound card contains a special type of circuitry called a **digital signal processor**, which performs three important tasks. It transforms digital bits into analog waves when you play back a digital audio file. It transforms analog waves into digital bits when you make a sound recording. It also handles compression and decompression, if necessary.

To play a digitally recorded sound, the bits from an audio file are transferred from disk to the microprocessor, which routes them to your computer's sound card. The digital signal processor handles any necessary decompression, and then transforms the data into analog wave signals. These signals are routed to the speakers and voilà! You have sound (Figure 8-3).

**FIGURE 8-3**

Most sound cards use a digital signal processor to convert bits into an analog signal.

The sound card receives data from the microprocessor.

The sound card's digital signal processor decompresses data and converts it to analog signals.

The sound card sends analog signals to speakers.

**How can I recognize a digital audio file?** You can recognize a digital audio file by looking at its file extension. Digital audio can be stored in a variety of file formats. The table in Figure 8-4 provides an overview of the most popular digital audio formats, including **AAC**, **AIFF**, **MP3**, **RealAudio**, **Wave**, and **WMA**.

**FIGURE 8-4**

Popular Digital Audio File Formats

| Audio Format | File Extension | Advantages | Disadvantages |
|---|---|---|---|
| **AAC (Advanced Audio Compression)** | .aac | Very good sound quality; compressed format, used on iTunes music download site | Files are copy protected and use is limited to approved devices |
| **AIFF (Audio Interchange Format)** | .aif | Excellent sound quality; supported in browsers without a plug-in | Audio data is stored in raw, uncompressed format, so files are very large |
| **MP3 (also called MPEG-1 Layer 3)** | .mp3 | Good sound quality even though the file is compressed; can be streamed over the Web | Requires a standalone player or browser plug-in |
| **RealAudio** | .ra, rx | High degree of compression produces small files; data can be streamed over the Web | Sound quality is not up to the standards of other formats; requires a player or plug-in |
| **Wave** | .wav | Good sound quality; supported in browsers without a plug-in | Audio data is stored in raw, uncompressed format, so files are very large |
| **WMA (Windows Media Audio)** | .wma | Compressed format, very good sound quality; used on music download sites | Files can be copy protected; requires Windows Media Player 9 or above |

**What type of software is required to record and play digital audio files?** To play an audio file on your computer, you must use audio or media player software. Player software tends to support several audio file formats. In the Windows environment, for example, you can use Windows Media Player to play Wave, AIF, and MP3 formats. Software that plays and records various audio file formats might be included with your computer's operating system, packaged with your sound card, or available on the Web.

Audio player software typically also includes features that help you organize and modify your audio files.The ability to create playlists is a useful feature, as are links to an online music store and options for transferring music files to a portable music player.

**Can I add digital audio files to my Web pages?** Yes. Digital audio files can be embedded into a Web page using an HTML tag, such as <embed src="daisy.wav"> or <bgsound src="imagine.wav">. WAV files are supported by most Web browsers, so it is a popular audio file format. Other audio formats can be delivered over the Web, but might require plug-ins.

Web-based digital audio is often delivered in streaming format to avoid lengthy delays while the entire audio file is downloaded. **Streaming audio** plays as its file is downloaded and provides the technology for real-time Internet radio broadcasts, podcasts, RSS feeds, and voice chat sessions.

## PORTABLE AUDIO PLAYERS

**How can I listen to my digital music collection when I'm away from my computer?** A **portable audio player** like the one in Figure 8-5 is a pocket-sized, battery-powered device that stores digital music. You can transfer a series of digital music tracks, called a playlist, from your computer's hard disk to your portable audio player and you'll have your personal collection of music wherever you go.

**Where can I get digital music?** Digital music is available from a wide variety of sources. At online music stores, such as iTunes Music Store, MusicMatch, Napster, MSN Music, Walmart Music Downloads, and Zune, individual songs can be downloaded for less than $1 each. The download price of an entire album is typically less than $10.

You can find free digital music, too. Famous performing artists and rock star wannabes post sample tracks from their CDs on Web sites. If fans like the music in these samples, they can purchase and download the entire song or CD.

You can also digitize music from your CD collection by using CD ripper software that converts CD-audio music into computer-friendly digital audio format.

**What are the most popular file formats for portable audio players?** The first generation of online music was distributed in MP3 format. MP3 is a compressed digital audio format that stores digitized music, vocals, and narrations in such a way that the sound quality is very good, but the file size remains relatively small—small enough to download from the Web. A CD track that requires 32 MB of storage space shrinks to approximately 3 MB in MP3 format.

Although MP3 remains a popular audio file format, newer standards offer better sound quality and compression. Apple is promoting the AAC format at its iTunes Music Store. Microsoft is promoting its WMA format at the Zune online music store.

8

**FIGURE 8-5**

Microsoft's Zune Portable Audio Player

**Can I play any digital music format on my portable audio player?** Some portable audio players support a variety of digital music formats, whereas others support only one format. For example, Sony's first digital audio Walkman supported only a proprietary ATRAC3plus format and required conversion for music downloaded in AAC or MP3 format. In contrast, Apple's iPod supports several digital music formats, including AAC, MP3, WAV, and AIFF. When purchasing a portable audio player, you should consider which music formats you are likely to use.

**What's all the buzz about the iPod?** Consumers demand convenience and prefer not to purchase two devices when a single device meets their needs. Market demand and technological innovation produce convergence, such as when PDAs gain Wi-Fi compatibility or when cell phones feature digital cameras.

As an example of convergence, take a portable audio player, outfit it with a screen, add a high-capacity mini hard disk, include personal organizer software, throw in a few games, and provide connections for an external microphone and memory card reader. What you get is the Apple iPod (Figure 8-6). Not only can you use it to store a huge collection of digital music, you can use the hard disk drive as a portable mass storage device for document, photo, and video files. You can use it as a voice recorder and as a personal organizer for storing contacts and appointments. The iPod's versatility has led at least one college to experiment with issuing them to all incoming students.

## MIDI MUSIC

**What is MIDI music?** Digital audio is a digital version of a real analog sound signal. In contrast, **synthesized sound** is an artificially created, or synthetic, sound. Synthesized sound can be classified as MIDI music or synthesized speech.

**MIDI** (Musical Instrument Digital Interface) specifies a standard way to store music data for synthesizers, electronic MIDI instruments, and computers. Unlike digital audio files, which contain digitized recordings of real sound passages, MIDI files contain instructions for creating the pitch, volume, and duration of notes that sound like various musical instruments.

MIDI is a music notation system that allows computers to communicate with music synthesizers. The computer encodes the music as a **MIDI sequence** and stores it as a file with a .mid, .cmf, or .rol file extension. A MIDI sequence is analogous to a player-piano roll that contains punched information indicating which musical notes to play. A MIDI sequence contains instructions specifying the pitch of a note, the point at which the note begins, the instrument that plays the note, the volume of the note, and the point at which the note ends.

Most computer sound cards are equipped to generate music from MIDI files, and many can capture music data from a MIDI instrument as well. A MIDI-capable sound card contains a **wavetable** (sometimes called a patch set), which is a set of prerecorded musical instrument sounds. The sound card accesses these sounds and plays them as instructed by the MIDI file. For example, if a sound card receives a MIDI instruction for a trumpet to play middle C, it accesses the trumpet's middle C patch and routes it to the speaker until it receives a MIDI instruction to stop the note.

**What are the advantages and disadvantages of MIDI?** MIDI files are much more compact than digital audio files. Depending on the exact

**FIGURE 8-6**

Apple's iPod portable audio player is also a handy mass storage device.

piece of music, three minutes of MIDI music might require only 10 KB of storage space, whereas the same piece of music stored in a high-quality, uncompressed digital audio file might require 30 MB of storage space.

One of the big disadvantages of MIDI is that it does not produce high-quality vocals. Another disadvantage is that it does not have the full resonance of real sound. Most musicians can easily identify MIDI recordings because they simply lack the tonal qualities of symphony-quality sound. You can compare the differences by using the Click to Start buttons in Figure 8-7.

**FIGURE 8-7**

MIDI music tends not to have the full resonance of digital audio. Use your BookOnCD to listen to these two sound clips and see if you can hear a difference.

▶ CLICK TO START

▶ CLICK TO START

**When would I use MIDI music?** MIDI is a good choice for adding background music to multimedia projects and Web pages. Using a procedure similar to that for digital audio files, you can add a link to a MIDI file by inserting a tag such as <embed src="sousa.mid"> within an HTML document. Most browsers include built-in support for MIDI music.

You can use music composition software, such as Finale, to create your own snappy tunes or get permission to use MIDI files you find on the Web. For composing your own MIDI music, you can input notes from a MIDI instrument directly to your computer. The input is typically handled by music composition software (Figure 8-8), which you can also use to edit notes and combine the parts for several instruments.

**8**

**FIGURE 8-8**

Music composition software provides tools for entering notes, specifying instruments, printing sheet music, and saving compositions in formats such as MIDI.

▶ CLICK TO START

## SPEECH RECOGNITION AND SYNTHESIS

**What's the difference between speech synthesis and speech recognition?** **Speech synthesis** is the process by which machines, such as computers, produce sound that resembles spoken words. **Speech recognition** (or voice recognition) refers to the ability of a machine to understand spoken words.

If you've dialed Directory Assistance lately to obtain a telephone number, you've probably encountered speech recognition and speech synthesis. An automated operator asks you to speak the name of the person whose telephone number you seek. The name you speak is collected by a speech recognition unit, which attempts to spell out the name and then look for it in a database. If it locates the name and telephone number, a synthesized voice speaks the telephone number.

The use of digital spectrographic analysis to identify human speakers is an emerging part of law enforcement and homeland security. Not only can digitized samples of voices be analyzed to confirm identity, but real-time voice print identification can be used to match speakers with known recordings of their voices.

**How does speech synthesis work?** A basic sound unit, such as "reh" or "gay" is called a **phoneme**. Most speech synthesizers string together phonemes to form words. For example, the phonemes "reh" and "gay" produce the word "reggae." A basic speech synthesizer consists of **text-to-speech software**, which generates sounds that are played through your computer's standard sound card. As an alternative, some speech synthesizers are special-purpose hardware devices.

Speech synthesis is a key technology in mobile communication, such as accessing your e-mail using a cell phone—a speech synthesizer reads your e-mail messages to you. A speech synthesizer can also read a computer screen aloud, which unlocks access to computers and the Internet for individuals with visual disabilities.

**How does speech recognition work?** On a personal computer, a speech recognition system typically collects words spoken into a microphone that's attached to the sound card. The sound card's digital signal processor transforms the analog sound of your voice into digital data. This data is then processed by speech recognition software.

Speech recognition software analyzes the sounds of your voice and converts them to phonemes. Next, the software analyzes the content of your speech. It compares the groups of phonemes to the words in a digital dictionary that lists phoneme combinations along with their corresponding English (or French, Spanish, and so on) words. When a match is found, the software displays the correctly spelled word on the screen.

Speech recognition software can be integrated with word processing software so that you can enter text simply by speaking into a microphone. Going beyond word processing, speech recognition can be used to activate Windows controls instead of using a mouse. Most speech recognition software also works with your browser, allowing you to voice surf the Web.

Microsoft Office includes speech recognition software you can activate by using the Speech icon in the Windows Control Panel. The first step in using Microsoft speech recognition is training the computer to recognize your speaking style. Training consists of reading a series of short text passages into a microphone attached to your computer. Figure 8-9 lists tips for successful voice recognition training.

**FIGURE 8-9**

Tips for Voice Recognition Training

- Speak at a consistent volume.
- Speak at a steady pace, without speeding up and slowing down.
- Speak naturally, without exaggerated pauses between words or syllables.
- Work in a quiet environment so that the computer hears your voice instead of the sounds around you.
- Use a good quality microphone and keep it in the same position.

You can train your computer by using the Voice Training Wizard, which displays paragraphs of text, waits for you to read them, and creates your personal speech profile (Figure 8-10).

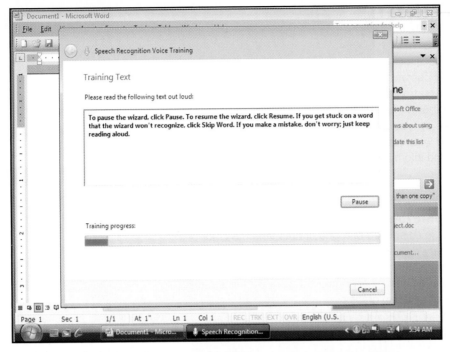

**FIGURE 8-10**

The Windows Voice Training Wizard displays short text passages. As you read each passage, the computer listens to the way you pronounce each word and stores it in your speech profile.

When training is complete, you can use Microsoft speech recognition to verbally issue commands in Windows and dictate text in Microsoft Word and Excel, plus any other Windows applications designed to support this feature.

8

# QuickCheck

SECTION A

1. _____ audio can deal with vocals, music, and narrations, whereas _____ music is primarily designed for instrumental sounds. (Hint: Use the acronym.)

2. The number of times per second that a sound wave is measured is referred to as the _____ rate.

3. The most popular digital audio formats for music downloads are MP3, WMA, and _____ . (Hint: Use the acronym.)

4. You can transfer digital music tracks, called a _____ , from your computer's hard disk to your portable audio player, and you'll have a great collection of music wherever you go.

5. Speech _____ software translates spoken words into text that appears on a computer screen or is stored in a file.

 CHECK ANSWERS

SECTION **B**

# Bitmap Graphics

**A DIGITAL CAMERA** seems easy to use. Point it, shoot the photo, and....what next? How do you transfer digital photos from camera to computer? How can you print them? How do you get them ready to become e-mail attachments? How do you prepare them for inclusion on Web pages? To understand the wide range of possibilities for digital photos, you'll need some background information about bitmap graphics—the topic for this section of the chapter.

## BITMAP BASICS

**What is a bitmap graphic?** A **bitmap graphic**, also called a raster graphic or simply a bitmap, is composed of a grid of dots, and the color of each dot is stored as a binary number. Think of a grid superimposed on a picture. The grid divides the picture into cells, called pixels. Each pixel is assigned a color, which is stored as a binary number. Figure 8-11 illustrates these basic characteristics of a bitmap graphic.

**TERMINOLOGY NOTE**

The term *pixel* is derived from *picture element*. It is the smallest element that can be manipulated by a computer display device or printer.

**FIGURE 8-11**

A bitmap graphic is divided into a grid of individually colored pixels. The color number for each pixel is stored in binary format.

**Where would I encounter bitmap graphics?** Bitmap graphics are typically used to create realistic images, such as photographs. You might also encounter bitmaps in the form of cartoons, images that appear in computer games, and rendered images produced by 3-D graphics software. When you use a digital camera or camera-enabled cell phone, your photos are stored as bitmaps. A scanner produces bitmaps. The photos you send or receive as e-mail attachments are bitmaps, as are most Web page graphics. Bitmap graphics formats include RAW, PNG, GIF, PCX, BMP, JPEG, and TIFF. Details about using these formats are presented later in this section.

**How do I create bitmap images?** You can create a bitmap graphic from scratch using the tools provided by graphics software—specifically a category of graphics software referred to as **paint software**. You might be familiar with paint software such as Adobe Photoshop, Jasc Paint Shop Pro, and Microsoft Paint (included with Windows). These programs have tools for freehand sketching, filling in shapes, adding realistic shading, and creating effects that look like oil paints, charcoal, or watercolors. If your freehand sketching talent maxes out with stick figures, you can also create bitmap graphics by using a scanner or digital camera.

## SCANNERS AND CAMERAS

**How do I convert a printed image into a bitmap?** When you have a printed image, such as a photograph, a page from a magazine, or a picture from a book, you can use a **scanner** to convert the printed image into a bitmap graphic. A scanner essentially divides an image into a fine grid of cells and assigns a digital value for the color of each cell. As the scan progresses, these values are transferred to your computer's hard disk and stored as a bitmap graphics file. Scanners, such as the one pictured in Figure 8-12, are inexpensive and easy to use.

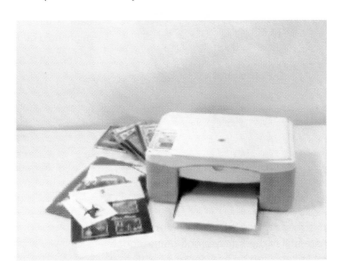

**INFOWEBLINKS**

For more information about scanning equipment, connect to the **Scanner Buyers Guide InfoWeb**.

 CLICK TO CONNECT
www.course.com/np/concepts10/ch08

**FIGURE 8-12**

To scan an image, turn on the scanner and start your scanner software. Place the image face down on the scanner glass, and then use the scanner software to initiate the scan. The scanned image is saved in RAM and can then be saved on your computer's hard disk.

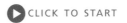 CLICK TO START

**When should I use a digital camera rather than a scanner?** Whereas a scanner is designed to digitize printed images, a **digital camera** digitizes real objects. Instead of taking a photo with a conventional camera, developing the film, and then digitizing it with a scanner, a digital camera, such as the one in Figure 8-13, takes a photo in digital format, which you can then transfer directly to your computer or print directly to a photo printer.

**INFOWEBLINKS**

You'll learn more about digital cameras and accessories at the **Digital Camera Buyers Guide InfoWeb**.

 CLICK TO CONNECT
www.course.com/np/concepts10/ch08

**FIGURE 8-13**

The controls for a digital camera are very similar to those for an analog, or film, camera. To take a photo, you simply point and shoot.

 CLICK TO START

8

**How does a digital camera store images?** Some digital cameras store photos on CDs, mini CDs, or microdrives, but the most popular digital camera storage is solid state memory cards. Like RAM, memory cards can be erased and reused. Unlike RAM, however, solid state storage holds data without consuming power, so it doesn't lose data when the camera is turned off. Figure 8-14 illustrates several digital camera storage options.

CompactFlash

xD-Picture cards

Memory stick

Secure Digital card

Microdrive

**FIGURE 8-14**

Storage options for digital cameras vary in capacity from 8 MB to 8 GB. The number of photos that can be stored depends on their resolution. High-resolution photos require more storage space than low-resolution photos. As few as two high-res photos might fit on a 32 MB card, whereas the same card might hold hundreds of low-res images.

**How can I get images out of the camera?** Digital cameras allow you to preview images while they are still in the camera and delete those you don't want. The photos you want to keep can be transferred directly to a properly equipped printer or transferred to your computer's hard disk. Depending on your camera, this transfer can be achieved in several ways:

● **Card readers.** A card reader is a small device designed to read data contained in a solid state memory card. Card readers can be connected to your computer's USB port, built into a computer system unit, or built into a photo-printer. To transfer photo data from a memory card, you remove it from the camera and insert it into the card reader, as shown in Figure 8-15.

● **Direct cable transfer.** If your computer and your camera have FireWire ports (also called IEEE-1394 ports), you can connect a cable between these two ports to transfer the photo data. You can use a similar transfer method if your computer and camera have USB ports or serial ports. A USB-2 or FireWire port provides good transfer speed. USB-1 ports are somewhat slower, and serial ports are quite slow.

● **Infrared port.** Some cameras can beam the data from your camera to your computer's infrared port. This method eliminates the need for a cable but is much slower than using a FireWire, USB, or serial port.

● **Media transfer.** If your camera stores data on CDs or similar optical media, you can simply remove the media from your camera and insert it into the appropriate drive of your computer.

● **Docking station.** Some camera manufacturers offer a camera docking station that connects to a computer by cable. A camera can be placed in the docking station to transfer photos to the computer's hard disk.

● **E-mail.** Cell phone photos can be transferred to a computer by e-mailing the photo to your e-mail account. The photo arrives as an attachment, which can be saved as a separate file.

**FIGURE 8-15**

A card reader transfers photo data from a memory card to your computer's hard disk.

Regardless of the technology you use, transferring photo data from your camera to your computer requires software, which might be supplied along with your camera, with your card reader, or by a standalone graphics software package, such as Adobe Photoshop. This software allows you to select a file format, specify a file name, and determine the location for each image file. You'll learn about your choices for file formats later in this section, but most cameras store photos in JPEG or TIFF formats.

After you store your digital photos on your computer's hard disk, you can modify them, send them as e-mail attachments, print them, post them on Web pages, or archive them onto a CD.

**What characteristics of a bitmap can I modify?** Because bitmap graphics are coded as a series of bits that represent pixels, you can use graphics software to modify or edit this type of graphic by changing individual pixels. You can retouch old photographs to eliminate creases, spots, and discoloration (Figure 8-16). You can modify photos to wipe out red eye or erase the "rabbit ears" that ruined an otherwise good family portrait. You can even design eye-catching new pictures with images you cut and paste from several photos or scanned images.

Whether you acquire an image from a digital camera or a scanner, bitmap graphics tend to require quite a bit of storage space. Although a large graphics file might provide the necessary data for a high-quality printout, these files take up space on your hard disk and can require lengthy transmission times that clog up mailboxes and make Web pages seem sluggish. The size of the file that holds a bitmap depends on its resolution and color depth. Read on to see how these factors affect file size and how you can alter them to create smaller graphics files, suitable for e-mail attachments and Web pages.

## IMAGE RESOLUTION

**How does resolution pertain to bitmap graphics?** The dimensions of the grid that forms a bitmap graphic are referred to as its resolution. The resolution of a graphic is usually expressed as the number of horizontal and vertical pixels it contains. For example, a small graphic for a Web page might have a resolution of 150 x 100 pixels—150 pixels across and 100 pixels high.

**How does resolution relate to image quality?** High-resolution graphics contain more data than low-resolution graphics. With more data, it is possible to display and print high-quality images that are sharper and clearer than images produced using less data. For example, a photograph of a cat taken with an inexpensive digital camera might produce a graphic with a resolution of 1600 x 1200, but a more expensive camera with 2272 x 1712 resolution contains more pixels and produces a higher-quality image.

Camera manufacturers sometimes express the resolution of digital cameras as megapixels. A **megapixel** is 1 million pixels. A camera with resolution of 1600 x 1200 has the capability of producing photos containing 1.9 megapixels (1600 multiplied by 1200). A camera with 2272 x 1712 resolution is technically 3.88 megapixels, but might be rounded off and called a 4.0 megapixel camera by its manufacturer.

**How does resolution relate to the file size of a graphic?** Each pixel in a bitmap graphic is stored as one or more bits. The more pixels in a bitmap, the more bits needed to store the file.

**FIGURE 8-16**

Bitmap graphics can be easily modified. Many graphics software products include wizards that help you retouch photographs.

Before

8

After

**How does resolution relate to the physical size of an image?**
A bitmap graphic is simply a collection of data. Unlike a printed photograph,
a bitmap has no fixed physical size. The size at which a bitmap is displayed
or printed depends on the density as well as the resolution (dimensions) of
the image grid.

Imagine that each bitmap image and its grid come on a surface that you can
stretch or shrink. As you stretch the surface, the grid maintains the same
number of horizontal and vertical cells, but each cell becomes larger and
the grid becomes less dense. As you shrink the surface, the grid becomes
smaller and more dense. The graphic retains the same resolution no matter
how much you stretch or shrink the graphic's physical size, as shown in
Figure 8-17.

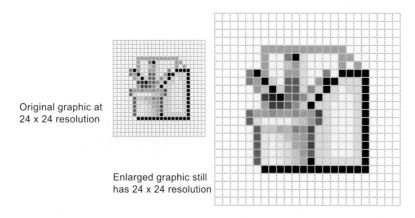

Original graphic at
24 x 24 resolution

Enlarged graphic still
has 24 x 24 resolution

**FIGURE 8-17**

When this bitmap graphic is
enlarged, it still retains its
original resolution—24 x 24.

This concept of stretching and shrinking without changing resolution is
important for understanding what happens when bitmaps are displayed
and printed. The denser the grid, the smaller the image will appear. The
density of an image grid can be expressed as dots per inch (dpi) for a
printer or scanner or as pixels per inch (ppi) on a monitor.

**How do I specify the size of a printed image?** Most graphics software allows you to specify the size at which an image is printed without
changing the resolution of the bitmap graphic. You'll get the highest print
quality if the resolution of the graphic meets or exceeds the printer's dpi. An
ink jet printer with a resolution of 1440 x 720 dpi produces a very dense
image grid. If each pixel of a 1600 x 1200 graphic was printed as a single
dot on this printer, the resulting image would be very high quality but just a
bit wider than 1 inch. You can specify a larger size for the printout, in which
case the printer must create additional data to fill the print grid. This
process can produce a fuzzy and blocky image if the printed image gets
very large.

As a general rule, when you incorporate an image in a desktop-published
document, or when you print photographs, you should work with high-
resolution bitmaps so that you can produce high-quality output. To
capture high-resolution bitmaps, use the highest resolution provided by
your digital camera. When scanning an image, choose a dpi setting on
your scanner that is at least as high as the dpi for the printout.

**How does a bitmap's resolution relate to what I see on the
screen?** In Chapter 2, you learned that you can set your computer monitor to a particular resolution, such as 1024 x 768. When you display a
bitmap graphic on the screen, each pixel of the graphic typically corresponds to one pixel on the screen. If the resolution of your graphic is

1024 x 768 and your monitor is set at 1024 x 768 resolution, the image appears to fill the screen. If you view a 4.0 megapixel image on the same monitor, the image is larger than the screen, and you have to scroll or change the zoom level to view it (Figure 8-18).

**Can I change a graphic's file size?** The resolution and corresponding file size of a graphic might not be right for your needs. For example, if you take a photo with a 4.0 megapixel camera, it is unsuitable for a Web page. Not only would it take a long time to download, but it would be larger than most screens. A 4.0 megapixel graphic is also not suitable for an e-mail attachment. Uploading and downloading such a large file—especially over a dial-up connection—would take much too long. Reducing the resolution of a bitmap can reduce its file size and on-screen display size. Most experts recommend that Web graphics not exceed 100 KB and that e-mail attachments not exceed 500 KB.

You can reduce the size of a bitmap by cropping it. **Cropping** refers to the process of selecting part of an image—just like cutting out a section of a photograph. Cropping decreases resolution and file size by reducing the number of pixels in a graphic. You can also reduce file size by removing pixels from the entire graphic; however, this process changes the image quality.

Bitmap graphics are **resolution dependent**, which means that the quality of the image depends on its resolution. If you reduce the resolution, the computer eliminates pixels from the image, reducing the size of the image grid. For example, if you reduce the resolution from 2160 x 1440 (3.1 megapixels) to 1080 x 720 (.8 megapixels), the image grid becomes a quarter of its original size. The file size is reduced by a similar amount. However, the computer threw away data with the pixels, which can reduce image quality.

If you attempt to enlarge a bitmap by increasing its resolution, your computer must somehow add pixels because no additional picture data exists. But what colors should these additional pixels become? Most graphics software uses a process called **pixel interpolation** to create new pixels by averaging the colors of nearby pixels. For some graphics, pixel interpolation results in an image that appears very similar to the original. Other images—particularly those with strong curved or diagonal lines—develop an undesirable **pixelated**, or "bitmappy," jagged appearance (Figure 8-19).

8

The figure above has a resolution of 130 x 130. The figure at right was enlarged to a resolution of 260 x 260, but it has a rough, pixelated appearance.

## COLOR DEPTH AND PALETTES

**What is color depth?** As you learned in Chapter 2, color depth is the number of colors available for use in an image. As the number of colors increases, image quality improves, but file size also increases. You can limit color depth to decrease the file size required for a graphic. To find out how this works, take a look at the storage requirements for various color depths. Then you can turn to the procedures for reducing color depth.

**How does color depth relate to file size?** To answer this question, go back to the old days of computing when monitors were simple monochrome devices. Each screen pixel could be either "on" or "off." A **monochrome bitmap** is displayed by manipulating the pattern of "off" and "on" pixels displayed on-screen. To store the data for a monochrome bitmap, an "on" pixel is represented by a 1 bit. An "off" pixel is represented by a 0 bit. Each row of the bitmap grid is stored as a series of 0s and 1s, as shown in Figure 8-20.

**FIGURE 8-20**

Each pixel in a monochrome bitmap graphic is stored as a bit.

**1.** This image originated as a black-and-white silhouette.

**2.** The computer divides the picture into a matrix.

**3.** If a cell is white, it is coded as a 1. If the cell is black, it is coded as a 0.

Monochrome bitmaps require very little storage space. Suppose you create a full-screen monochrome bitmap with your monitor's resolution set to 640 x 480. Your screen displays 307,200 pixels (that's 640 multiplied by 480). Each pixel is set to display a black dot or a white dot. When you store the graphic, each dot requires only one bit. Therefore, the number of bits required to represent a full-screen picture is the same as the number of pixels on the screen. At a resolution of 640 x 480, a full-screen graphic requires 307,200 bits of storage space. The number of bytes required to store the image is 307,200 divided by 8 (remember that there are eight bits in a byte). Your full-screen monochrome bitmap would, therefore, require only 38,400 bytes of storage space.

**But what about color?** Today's color monitors require a more complex storage scheme. Each screen pixel displays a color based on the intensity of red, green, and blue signals it receives. A pixel appears white if the red, green, and blue signals are set to maximum intensity. If red, green, and blue signals are equal but at a lower intensity, the pixel displays a shade of gray. If the red signal is set to maximum intensity, but the blue and green signals are off, the pixel appears in brilliant red. A pixel appears purple if it receives red and blue signals, and so forth.

Each red, green, and blue signal is assigned a value ranging from zero to 255. Zero represents the absence of color, and 255 represents the highest intensity level for that color. These values produce a maximum of 16.7 million colors. A graphic that uses this full range of colors is referred to as a **True Color bitmap** or a **24-bit bitmap**. You might be able to guess where the *24-bit* term comes from. The data for each pixel requires three bytes of storage space—eight bits for blue, eight bits for green, and eight bits for red—for a total of 24 bits. Although True Color bitmaps produce photographic-quality images, they also produce very large files. Because each pixel requires three bytes, a 3.1 megapixel True Color bitmap would require a 9.3 MB file!

You might occasionally encounter a **32-bit bitmap**. Just like a 24-bit bitmap, it displays 16.7 million colors. The extra bits are used to define special effects, such as the amount of transparency, for a pixel. These files are even larger than those containing 24-bit bitmaps. A 3.1 megapixel 32-bit bitmap would be about 10 MB.

Files containing full-screen 24-bit and 32-bit bitmaps are typically too large for Web pages because they require excessively long upload and download times. Earlier in the chapter, you learned that you can reduce a bitmap's file size by removing pixels. Another way to shrink a bitmap file is to reduce its color depth.

**How can I reduce color depth?** To reduce the color depth of a bitmap, you can use your graphics software to work with color palettes. A **color palette** (also called a color lookup table or color map) is the digital version of a kidney-shaped artist's palette that holds the selection of colors an artist uses for a particular painting. A digital color palette allows you to select a group of colors to use for a bitmap graphic.

The advantage of a palette is that if it contains only 256 colors, you can store the data for each pixel in 8 bits instead of 24 bits, which reduces the file to a third of the size required for a True Color bitmap.

**How does a color palette work?** A color palette is stored as a table within the header of a graphics file. Each palette contains a list of 256 color numbers. Each of these numbers is mapped to a 24-bit number that corresponds to the actual levels of red, green, and blue required to display the color. Figure 8-21 explains how this table works.

8

Pixels in the upper-left corner of an image

| Color Palette | |
|---|---|
| Index # | RGB Value |
| 0 | 000 000 000 |
| 1 | 060 000 255 |
| 2 | 020 167 167 |
| 3 | 120 060 060 |
| 4 | 180 060 060 |
| 5 | 255 000 000 |
| . | |
| . | |
| . | |
| 253 | 255 060 060 |
| 254 | 255 000 255 |
| 255 | 255 255 255 |

**FIGURE 8-21**

A color palette is a subset of all possible colors. Each color in the palette is numbered, and its number points to the full 24-bit RGB (red, green, blue) value stored in the graphics file header.

**How do I select a color palette?** Most graphics software offers a selection of ready-made palettes that you can choose by using the color palette or color picker tool. Ready-made palettes usually include a grayscale palette, a system palette, and a Web palette.

A **grayscale palette** uses shades of gray, or "gray scales," to display images that look similar to black-and-white photographs. Most grayscale palettes consist of 256 shades of gray. Figure 8-22 illustrates a grayscale palette and a grayscale bitmap graphic.

**FIGURE 8-22**

Grayscale bitmaps look like black-and-white photographs.

A **system palette** is the collection of colors the operating system uses for graphics that represent desktop icons and controls. Windows, for example, uses a system palette containing 20 permanent colors and 236 colors that can be changed, depending on the application.

A **Web palette** (also called a Web-safe palette or a browser palette) contains a standard set of colors used by Internet Web browsers. Because most browsers support this palette, it is typically regarded as a safe choice when preparing graphics for Internet distribution. Figure 8-23 shows the collection of colors used by system and Web palettes.

**FIGURE 8-23**

The Windows system palette and Web palette are usually provided by graphics software.

Your graphics software might offer additional palettes. They are likely to include a "woodsy" palette that works well for outdoor photographs, a pastel palette that works well with images filled with predominantly light colors, and a flesh-tone palette that's designed to work nicely for portraits.

## IMAGE COMPRESSION

**What is image compression?** **Image compression** refers to any technique that recodes the data in an image file so that it contains fewer bits. Smaller files produced as a result of image compression require less storage space and can be transmitted more rapidly than the larger, original files. Images can be compressed using lossless or lossy compression.

**What is the difference between lossless and lossy compression?** **Lossless compression** provides the means to compress a file and then reconstitute all the data into its original state. TIFF, PCX, and GIF graphics formats offer lossless compression. In contrast, **lossy compression** throws away some of the original data during the compression process. In theory, the human eye won't miss the lost information. JPEG files are compressed using lossy compression. Most lossy compression techniques have adjustable compression levels so that you can decide how much data you can afford to lose.

**How does lossless compression shrink a file without throwing away data?** Various techniques exist for lossless image compression. As a simple example, consider a type of lossless compression called run-length encoding. **Run-length encoding** (RLE) replaces a series of similarly colored pixels with a code that indicates the number of pixels and their colors. Suppose that a section of a picture has 167 consecutive white pixels, and each pixel is described by one byte of data, as in a 256-color bitmap image. RLE compresses this series of 167 bytes into as few as two bytes, as shown in Figure 8-24.

**FIGURE 8-24**

In an uncompressed file, each pixel of a 256-color bitmap requires one byte to indicate its color. For example, a white pixel might be coded 11111111. Run-length encoding compresses graphical data by recoding like-colored pixels when they appear in a series.

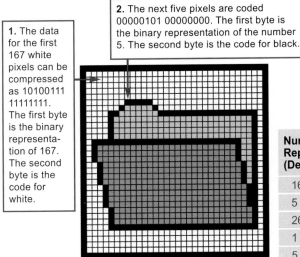

**1.** The data for the first 167 white pixels can be compressed as 10100111 11111111. The first byte is the binary representation of 167. The second byte is the code for white.

**2.** The next five pixels are coded 00000101 00000000. The first byte is the binary representation of the number 5. The second byte is the code for black.

**3.** With compression, the first nine rows of the graphic require only 30 bytes—the binary numbers in columns 2 and 4 of this table. The uncompressed graphic requires 288 bytes.

| Number of Repetitions (Decimal) | Number of Repetitions (Binary) | Pixel Color | Pixel Color (Binary) |
|---|---|---|---|
| 167 | 10100111 | White | 11111111 |
| 5 | 00000101 | Black | 00000000 |
| 26 | 00011010 | White | 11111111 |
| 1 | 00000001 | Black | 00000000 |
| 5 | 00000101 | Yellow | 10100000 |
| 1 | 00000001 | Black | 00000000 |
| 23 | 00010111 | White | 11111111 |
| 2 | 00000010 | Black | 00000000 |
| 7 | 00000111 | Yellow | 10100000 |
| 18 | 00010010 | Black | 00000000 |
| 5 | 00000101 | White | 11111111 |
| 1 | 00000001 | Black | 00000000 |
| 25 | 00011001 | Yellow | 10100000 |
| 1 | 00000001 | White | 11111111 |
| 1 | 00000001 | Black | 00000000 |

8

**What happens during lossy compression?** Lossy compression techniques discard some data from an image to shrink its file size. JPEG is a lossy version of run-length encoding that can be applied to images, such as photographs, that don't have large areas of solid color. A True Color photograph might not have any adjoining pixels of the same color. Applying RLE to such a photo would not result in any compression whatsoever. JPEG preprocesses an image by tweaking the colors in adjoining pixels so that they are the same color whenever possible. After this preprocessing is complete, run-length encoding can be applied with more success.

For many images, lossy compression results in only a minor reduction in the sharpness of the image. The reduction in quality can be unnoticeable in many circumstances. Figure 8-25 illustrates a section of a noncompressed image and a section of that same image after JPEG compression has been applied. Can you see the difference?

**FIGURE 8-25**

JPEG compression can slightly adjust the colors of adjacent pixels to make them the same. These like-colored pixels can then be compressed with RLE.

Non-compressed JPEG image

JPEG image with 35% compression

**How do I compress image files?** Some graphics file formats automatically compress file data. You can also compress files using a general-purpose file compression utility.

PCX, GIF, JPEG, PNG, and TIFF file formats support compression. Software that works with these file formats might allow you to select compression levels before saving a graphics file. For example, when saving an image in JPEG format, you might be given the option of selecting compression settings from 1 (worst quality) to 99 (best quality).

Some bitmap formats, such as BMP and RAW, do not support compression. If you want to compress these files before sending them as e-mail attachments, for example, you can do so manually using a file compression utility. A **file compression utility** uses lossless compression to shrink one or more files into a single new file. PKZIP and WinZip are popular shareware programs that compress and decompress files. You can compress any kind of file, including programs and data files, graphics and document files. BMP file sizes might shrink by as much as 70% when compressed. Files stored in formats such as PNG, GIF, and JPEG hardly shrink at all when you use compression utilities because they are already stored in compressed format.

Compressing files is sometimes called zipping, and decompressing files is sometimes called unzipping. Most file compression utilities not only zip single files, but can also zip several files into a single compressed file that can later be unzipped into the original separate files.

For example, suppose you want to send three files to your boss. The original files are called Technology.xls, Award.doc, and Insurance.bmp. You can zip all three files into a single compressed file called Report.zip (Figure 8-26). Simply attach this one file to an e-mail and send it to your boss. When Report.zip is unzipped, it produces the three original files.

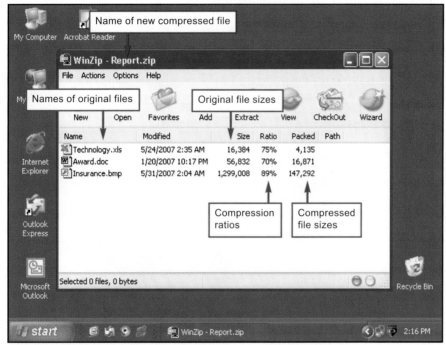

**FIGURE 8-26**

Popular file compression utilities, such as WinZip, zip one or more files into a new compressed file with a .zip extension.

● CLICK TO START

If you have not installed compression software such as PKZIP, you can use a feature of Windows XP to create compressed folders (Figure 8-27). Any files that you drag into a compressed folder are automatically compressed. You don't have to do anything special to open a file from a compressed folder. Simply double-click the file as usual, and Windows automatically decompresses the file before displaying its contents.

**FIGURE 8-27**

The Compressed Folder menu option creates a folder into which you can drag files you want to compress.

8

## BITMAP GRAPHICS FORMATS

**Are there different kinds of bitmap graphics?** Many graphics file formats exist, and most graphics software offers a choice of popular formats, such as BMP, RAW, PCX, TIFF, JPEG, GIF, and PNG.

**BMP**, pronounced "bee-em-pee" or "bump," is the native bitmap graphics file format of the Microsoft Windows environment. Microsoft Paint, included as part of Microsoft Windows, creates BMP graphics files. The BMP format supports True Color and can be used for a wide variety of graphics applications, such as photographs, illustrations, and graphs. BMP files are not compressed in any way, so this format typically creates very large files that are not suitable for e-mail attachments. BMP graphics are not supported by most browsers, so they are not used on the Web.

**FIGURE 8-28**

Digital cameras use a sensor array to capture an image. The sensor is packed with millions of light sensitive cells that record color and brightness for millions of points in the image grid.

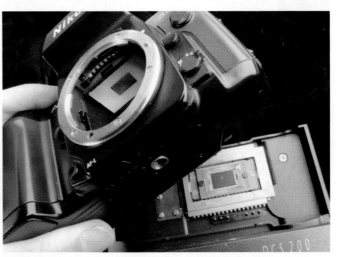

**RAW** image formats contain the unprocessed pixel data generated directly by a digital camera's sensor (Figure 8-28). Up to 12 bits of data can be stored for each of the red, blue, and green values for a pixel, so RAW files are very large. Cameras that offer a RAW format also supply proprietary software to convert RAW data to JPEG or TIFF.

**PCX** is one of the original personal computer bitmap graphics file formats. PCX graphics are usually 8-bit (256 colors) and are automatically compressed to reduce file size without any loss of image quality. Because it's not supported by browsers, PCX is not used on the Web.

**TIFF** (Tag Image File Format), or TIF, is a flexible and platform-independent graphics file format supported by most photo-editing software packages. Scanners and digital cameras commonly store bitmaps in TIFF format because it supports True Color and can be easily converted into other graphics file formats. TIFF is an excellent choice for desktop publishing projects, but it is not supported by most browsers.

**JPEG** (pronounced JAY peg), which stands for Joint Photographic Experts Group, is a graphics format with built-in compression that stores True Color bitmap data very efficiently in a small file. The JPEG format is popular for Web graphics and for photos attached to e-mail messages. When creating or converting an image in JPEG format, you can control the level of compression and the resulting file size. The compression process eliminates some image data, however, so highly compressed files suffer some quality deterioration.

**GIF** (pronounced GIF or JIFF), or Graphics Interchange Format, was specifically designed to create images that can be displayed on multiple platforms, such as PCs and Macs. GIF graphics are a very popular format for Web graphics, but they are limited to 256 colors. In addition, the compression algorithm that's built into the GIF format is patented by UniSys Corporation. Currently, UniSys allows individuals to freely use GIF graphics on Web sites, as long as those graphics are created by using graphics software that contains GIF routines licensed by UniSys. Although the GIF format is popular, some Web developers express concern about further restrictions or fees that UniSys might require in the future.

**PNG** (Portable Network Graphic), pronounced "ping," is a graphics format designed to improve on the GIF format. A PNG graphic can display up to 48-bit True Color (trillions of colors). Unlike JPEG, PNG compresses bitmap data without losing any data, so compressed images retain the same high quality as the originals. Unlike GIF, PNG is a public domain format without any restrictions on its use.

**How do I determine which graphics format to use?** Selecting the best graphics file format to use depends on what you intend to do with the image. Figure 8-29 summarizes popular uses for each format.

| Format | Use |
|--------|-----|
| BMP | Graphical elements, such as buttons and other controls used in computer programs |
| RAW | Used by professional and semi-professional photographers to manually adjust settings before images are stored in other formats |
| PCX | Older graphics format not used much today |
| TIFF | High-resolution scanned images and digital photos used in desktop publishing; high-quality digital photos reproduced on special photo printers |
| JPEG | Photographic or scanned images that might be used in a variety of applications, such as DTP or Web pages, where flexibility in file size is important |
| GIF | Popular format for Web graphics |
| PNG | An alternative to GIF for Web graphics |

**FIGURE 8-29**

Choosing a bitmap graphics format depends on how the image is used.

8

# QuickCheck

1. Images from a digital camera can be transferred to a computer by using a USB cable, serial cable, or [＿＿＿＿＿＿] cable.

2. A 3.5 megapixel digital camera captures images with a 2160 x 1440 [＿＿＿＿＿＿].

3. Bitmap graphics are resolution [＿＿＿＿＿＿], so that reducing the resolution also reduces the image quality.

4. A(n) [＿＿＿＿＿＿] palette produces images that resemble black and white photographs.

5. The [＿＿＿＿＿＿] format is a good choice for desktop publishing, but not for Web graphics. (Hint: Use the acronym.)

6. The most popular 256-color formats for Web graphics include [＿＿＿＿＿＿] and PNG. (Hint: Use the acronym.)

7. Unlike [＿＿＿＿＿＿] compression, [＿＿＿＿＿＿] compression shrinks a file without throwing away any data.

CHECK ANSWERS

# Vector and 3-D Graphics

**IF YOU'VE PLAYED** any computer games recently or watched an animated movie, you've seen the product of computer-generated 3-D animated graphics. To the uninformed, these photorealistic action characters might seem little more than fancy cartoons. After you understand the way they are created, however, you'll appreciate the incredible amount of computing power they require. This section begins with two-dimensional vector graphics. You'll find out how they differ from bitmaps and why you might want to use them. After covering the basics for two-dimensional graphics, the section progresses to static 3-D graphics and then to animated 3-D graphics.

## VECTOR GRAPHICS BASICS

**What is a vector graphic?** Unlike a bitmap graphic created by dividing an image into a grid of pixels, a **vector graphic** consists of a set of instructions for re-creating a picture. Instead of storing the color value for each pixel, a vector graphic file contains the instructions the computer needs to create the shape, size, position, and color for each object in an image. These instructions are similar to those a drafting teacher might give students: "Draw a 2-inch (or 112-pixel) circle. Locate this circle 1" down and 2" in from the right edge of the work area. Fill the circle with yellow." The Stonehenge image shown in Figure 8-30 was created as a vector graphic.

**FIGURE 8-30**

The parts of a vector graphic are created as separate objects. This image was created with a series of roughly rectangular objects for the stones and a circular object for the sun. The objects are layered and can be manipulated individually. This characteristic of vector graphics gives artists flexibility in arranging and editing image elements.

**How can I identify vector graphics?** It can be difficult to accurately identify a vector graphic just by looking at an on-screen image. One clue that an image might be a vector graphic is a flat, cartoon-like quality. Think of clip art images—they are typically stored as vector graphics. For a more definitive identification, however, you should check the file extension. Vector graphics files have file extensions such as .wmf, .dxt, .mgx, .eps, .pict, and .cgm.

**How do vector graphics compare with bitmap graphics?** Vector graphics are suitable for most line art, logos, simple illustrations, and diagrams that might be displayed and printed at various sizes. When compared to bitmaps, vector graphics have several advantages and a few disadvantages. You should take the following distinctions into account when deciding which type of graphic to use for a specific project.

● **Vector graphics resize better than bitmaps.** When you change the size of a vector graphic, the objects change proportionally and maintain their smooth edges. Whereas shapes in a bitmap graphic might appear to have jagged edges after they are enlarged, shapes in a vector graphic appear smooth at any size, as shown in Figure 8-31.

**FIGURE 8-31**

Unlike bitmaps, vector graphics can be resized without becoming pixelated and blurry.

Vector graphic at 200% (above) and 50% (left)

Bitmap graphic at 200% (above) and 50% (right)

● **Vector graphics usually require less storage space than bitmaps.** The storage space required for a vector graphic reflects the complexity of the image. Each instruction requires storage space, so the more lines, shapes, and fill patterns in the graphic, the more storage space it requires. The Stonehenge vector graphic used as an example in this chapter requires less than 4 KB of storage space. A True Color photograph of the same image requires 1,109 KB.

**8**

● **Vector graphics are not usually as realistic as bitmap images.** Most vector images tend to have a cartoon-like appearance instead of the realistic appearance you expect from a photograph. This cartoon-like characteristic of vector images results from the use of objects filled with blocks of color. Your options for shading and texturing objects are limited, which tends to give vector graphics a flat appearance.

● **It is easier to edit an object in a vector graphic than an object in a bitmap graphic.** In some ways, a vector graphic is like a collage of objects. Each object can be layered over other objects, but moved and edited independently. You can individually stretch, shrink, distort, color, move, or delete any object in a vector graphic. For example, if you delete some of the stones from the Stonehenge vector image, the background layers remain. In contrast, most bitmap graphics are constructed as a single layer of pixels. If you erase the pixels for some of the stones in the Stonehenge photograph, you'll create a hole of white pixels (Figure 8-32).

**FIGURE 8-32**

Vector graphic objects are layered, so it is easy to move and delete objects without disrupting the rest of the image. In contrast, deleting a shape from a bitmap image leaves a hole because the image is only one layer of pixels.

**What tools do I need to create vector graphics?** Neither scanners nor digital cameras produce vector graphics. Architects and engineers sometimes use a digitizing tablet to turn a paper-based line drawing into a vector graphic. A **digitizing tablet** (sometimes called a 2-D digitizer) is a device that provides a flat surface for a paper-based drawing and a pen or mouse-like puck that you can use to click the endpoints of each line on the drawing. The endpoints are converted into vectors and stored.

Usually, vector graphics are created from scratch with vector graphics software, referred to as **drawing software**. Popular drawing software includes Adobe Illustrator, Macromedia Freehand, and Corel Designer. Drawing software is sometimes packaged separately from the paint software used to produce bitmap graphics. In other cases, it is included with bitmap software as a graphics software suite.

Vector graphics software provides an array of drawing tools that you can use to create objects, position them, and fill them with colors or patterns. For example, you can use the filled circle tool to draw a circle filled with a solid color. You can create an irregular shape by connecting points to outline the shape. Figure 8-33 illustrates how to use drawing tools to create a vector graphic.

**INFOWEBLINKS**

To learn more about popular vector graphics software, you can connect to the **Vector Graphics Software InfoWeb**.

 CLICK TO CONNECT
www.course.com/np/concepts10/ch08

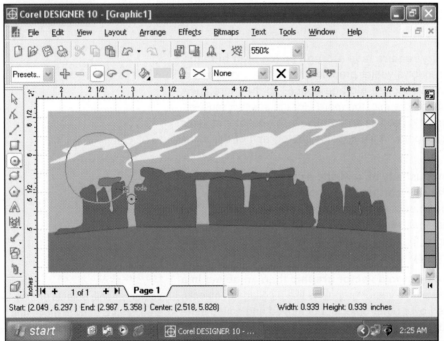

**FIGURE 8-33**

To draw a circle, select the filled circle tool, and then drag the mouse pointer to indicate the circle's location and size. A color palette allows you to select the circle color. After you create the circle object, you can move it and change its size or color. You can also create irregular shapes for objects, such as clouds, by connecting short line segments.

 CLICK TO START

The clouds are created as a series of short line segments and filled with color.

The stones are created as a series of short line segments and filled with black.

The background is a filled rectangle.

Vector graphics software helps you easily edit individual objects within a graphic by changing their sizes, shapes, positions, or colors. For example, the data for creating a circle for the sun is recorded as an instruction, such as CIRCLE 40 Y 200 150, which means create a circle with a 40-pixel radius, color it yellow, and place the center of the circle 200 pixels from the left of the screen and 150 pixels from the top of the screen. If you move the circle to the right side of the image, the instruction that the computer stores for the circle changes to something like CIRCLE 40 Y 500 150—500 pixels from the left instead of 200.

When filling a shape with color, your graphics software might provide tools for creating gradients. A **gradient** is a smooth blending of shades from one color to another or from light to dark. Gradients, as shown in Figure 8-34, can be used to create shading and three-dimensional effects.

Some vector graphics software provides tools that apply bitmapped textures to vector graphic objects, giving them a more realistic appearance. For example, you can create a vector drawing of a house, and then apply a brick-like texture derived from a bitmap photograph of real bricks. A graphic that contains both bitmap and vector data is called a **metafile**.

## VECTOR-TO-BITMAP CONVERSION

**Is it possible to convert a vector graphic into a bitmap?** A vector graphic can be converted quite easily into a bitmap graphic through a process called rasterizing. **Rasterization** works by superimposing a grid over a vector image and determining the color for each pixel. This process is typically carried out by graphics software, which allows you to specify the output size for the final bitmap image. On a PC, you can also rasterize a vector graphic by using the Print Screen key to take a screenshot of a vector image. It is important to rasterize images at the size you ultimately need. If you rasterize a vector image at a small size and then try to enlarge the resulting bitmap image, you will likely get a poor-quality pixelated image, such as the one in Figure 8-35.

After a vector graphic is converted to a bitmap, the resulting graphic no longer has the qualities of a vector graphic. For example, if you convert the Stonehenge vector graphic into a bitmap, the sun is no longer an object that you can easily move or assign a different color.

**How about converting a bitmap graphic into a vector graphic?** Converting a bitmap graphic into a vector graphic is more difficult than converting from a vector to a bitmap. To change a bitmap graphic into a vector graphic, you must use tracing software. **Tracing software** locates the edges of objects in a bitmap image and converts the resulting shapes into vector graphic objects.

Tracing software products, such as ImpressionX, work best on simple images and line drawings. They do not usually produce acceptable results when used on complex, detailed photos. Tracing capabilities are included in some general-purpose graphics software, but standalone tracing software offers more flexibility and usually produces better results.

**FIGURE 8-34**

Gradients can create the illusion of three dimensions, such as making this shape appear to be a tube.

**FIGURE 8-35**

When vector images are rasterized, they become bitmaps and can't be enlarged without becoming pixelated.

## VECTOR GRAPHICS ON THE WEB

**Do vector graphics work on the Web?** Web browsers were originally designed to support a limited number of graphics formats—GIF and
JPEG—and these formats were exclusively bitmaps. Built-in browser support for vector graphics has been slow, but plug-ins and players are
currently available for several of the most popular Web-based vector graphics formats.

**Which vector graphics formats can be used on the Web?** A
graphics format called **SVG** (Scalable Vector Graphics) is designed specifically for the Web (Figure 8-36). Graphics in SVG format are automatically
resized when displayed on different screens or when printed. SVG supports
gradients, drop shadows, multiple levels of transparency, and other effects,
along with portability to other platforms, such as handheld computers and
cellular phones. SVG graphic objects can include regular and irregular
shapes, images, and text, and they can be animated. You can add SVG
files to HTML and XML documents by using the <embed> tag.

**Flash** is another popular vector graphics format frequently used on the
Web. Adobe's Flash software creates vector graphics that are stored in
files with .swf extensions. Flash graphics can be static or animated. Flash
players are shipped with most browsers, and player updates can be
downloaded from the Adobe site.

Flash animations have advantages over other formats, such as animated
GIFs. An **animated GIF** is essentially a series of slightly different bitmap
images displayed in sequence to achieve animation effects. As a bitmap-
based format, GIF files are fairly large. Most Flash animations fit in compact
files and, therefore, can be transferred from a Web server to a browser
more rapidly than animated GIFs.

**What are the advantages of using vector graphics on the
Web?** Vector graphics have several advantages:

- **Consistent quality.** On Web pages, vector graphics appear with the
same consistent quality on all computer screens. This capability makes it
possible for browsers to adjust the size of an image on the fly to fit correctly
on a screen, regardless of its size or resolution. These adjustments don't
carry any penalty in terms of image quality—a large version of a vector
graphic displayed on a monitor set at 1024 x 768 resolution has the same
sharp detail and smooth curves as the original image sized to fit a smaller
screen set at 640 x 480 resolution. This flexibility is important for Web
pages that might be viewed at different resolutions on PCs, Macs, or other
platforms.

- **Searchable.** Another advantage is that any text contained in a vector
image is stored as actual text, not just a series of colored dots. This text
can be indexed by search engines so that it can be included in keyword
searches. For example, suppose a vector drawing was used to produce a
diagram describing the service box where your telephone line enters your
house. One of the components in this diagram is labeled "telephone test
jack." If you enter *telephone test jack* into a search engine, the service box
diagram will likely turn up in the list of search results.

- **Compact file size.** A third advantage of vector graphics on the Web is
their compact file sizes. A fairly complex graphic can be stored in a file that
is under 30 KB—that's kilobytes, not megabytes. These files require little
storage space and can be transmitted swiftly from a Web server to your
browser.

**FIGURE 8-36**

SVG graphics are typically
used on the Web for maps, ads,
organizational charts, and flow-
charts.

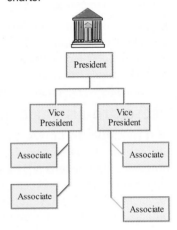

## INFOWEBLINKS

Connect to the **Web-based
Vector Graphics InfoWeb** for an
update on the latest vector graphics formats for the Web.

CLICK TO CONNECT
www.course.com/np/concepts10/ch08

## 3-D GRAPHICS

**How do vector graphics relate to 3-D graphics?** Like vector graphics, **3-D graphics** are stored as a set of instructions. For a 3-D graphic, however, the instructions contain the locations and lengths of lines that form a wireframe for a three-dimensional object. The **wireframe** acts in much the same way as the framework of a pop-up tent. Just as you would construct the framework for the tent, and then cover it with a nylon tent cover, a 3-D wireframe can be covered with surface texture and color to create a graphic of a 3-D object. The process of covering a wireframe with surface color and texture is called **rendering**. The rendering process, shown in Figure 8-37, outputs a bitmap image.

**FIGURE 8-37**

3-D graphics are based on a wireframe, which can be rendered into a bitmap image that looks three-dimensional.

For added realism, the rendering process can take into account the way that light shines on surfaces and creates shadows. The technique for adding light and shadows to a 3-D image is called **ray tracing**. Before an image is rendered, the artist selects a location for one or more light sources. The computer applies a complex mathematical algorithm to determine how the light source affects the color of each pixel in the final rendered image. This process can take time—hours for a complex image, even using today's most powerful personal computers. Figure 8-38 shows the image from the previous figure rendered with an additional light source and ray tracing.

**FIGURE 8-38**

Ray tracing adds realism to 3-D graphics by adding highlights and shadows that are produced by a light source.

8

**What tools do I need to create 3-D graphics?** 3-D graphics software runs on most personal computers, although some architects and engineers prefer to use high-end workstations. A fast processor, lots of RAM, and a fast graphics card with its own video RAM all speed up the rendering process. To create 3-D graphics, you need 3-D graphics software, such as AutoCad or Caligari trueSpace. This software has tools for drawing a wireframe and viewing it from any angle. It provides rendering and ray tracing tools, along with an assortment of surface textures that you can apply to individual objects. Figure 8-39 takes you on a tour of a popular 3-D graphics software package.

**FIGURE 8-39**

3-D graphics software provides tools for drawing a wireframe and then specifying colors and textures for rendering.

▶ CLICK TO START

**Is it possible to animate 3-D graphics?** 3-D graphics can be animated to produce special effects for movies or to create interactive, animated characters and environments for 3-D computer games. Animated special effects, such as massive battle scenes, are created by rendering a sequence of bitmaps, in which one or more objects are moved or otherwise changed between each rendering. In traditional hand-drawn animation, a chief artist draws the keyframes, and then a team of assistants creates each of the in-between images—24 of these images for each second of animation. For 3-D computer animation, the computer creates the in-between images by moving the object and rendering each necessary image. All the images are then combined into a single file, creating essentially a digital movie.

Graphics design companies such as Pixar Animation Studios and DreamWorks use 3-D animation techniques to produce animated feature films as well as special effects. The first full-length animated 3-D movie was *Toy Story*, released in 1995 by Walt Disney Studios and Pixar. Digitally animated films, such as *Cars*, *Ratatouille*, and *Shrek the Third*, illustrate the growing sophistication of 3-D animation.

**INFOWEBLINKS**

For additional resources about 3-D software (and shareware), rendering, ray tracing, and 3-D animated graphics, check out the **3-D Graphics InfoWeb**.

 CLICK TO CONNECT
www.course.com/np/concepts10/ch08

**Do game and movie animation require similar tools and techniques?** An important characteristic of special effects and animated films is that rendering can be accomplished during the production phase of the movie and incorporated into the final footage. In contrast, 3-D computer game animation happens in real time. Each frame that makes the image seem to move must be rendered while you are playing the game—a process that requires an incredible amount of computer power. To give you a handle on the immensity of the task, consider a game like Doom displayed on a computer monitor that's set at 1024 x 768 resolution (Figure 8-40). At this resolution, the screen contains 786,432 pixels (1024 multiplied by 768). If the game is presented in 32-bit color, each frame of the animation requires 25,165,824 bits (multiply 786,432 times 32).

Computer game designers believe that on-screen animation looks smoothest at 60 frames per second, which means your computer must handle 1,509,949,440—that's more than 1 billion—bits of information every second just to put the 3-D image onto the screen. In addition, the computer must process even more data to keep track of the movements of each player. To handle all this data, your computer's main processor gets help from a graphics processor located on your computer's graphics card. These graphics processors vary in their capabilities. For the fastest graphics capability, look for graphics cards billed as 3-D accelerators.

**Can I create my own animated 3-D graphics?** You can create 3-D animations on a standard PC or Mac with commercially available software, but professional 3-D software, such as Maya and Autodesk 3ds Max, is expensive and has a steep learning curve. If you want to dabble with 3-D animations before making an expensive software investment, you might try Curious Labs Poser, DAZ Bryce, or one of the shareware programs listed in the 3-D Graphics InfoWeb. Whether you use a commercial or shareware package, be prepared to spend lots of time with the manual before you are able to produce any original animations.

**FIGURE 8-40**

Classic computer games, such as Doom, established building blocks for animation technologies used to create today's fast-action, visually detailed computer games.

8

# QuickCheck

SECTION C

1. Unlike bitmaps, vector graphics can be enlarged without becoming pixelated. True or false? [        ]

2. Whereas the software used to work with bitmap graphics is often referred to as paint software, vector graphics software is usually referred to as [        ] software.

3. 3-D graphics are constructed based on a(n) [        ] that can be covered with surface texture and color.

4. The technique of adding light and shadows to a 3-D image is called ray [        ].

5. A vector graphic can be easily converted into a bitmap through a process called [        ].

6. Today, SVG and [        ] are the most popular vector graphics formats for the Web.

● CHECK ANSWERS

# Digital Video

**IN THE PREVIOUS SECTION,** you learned about GIF and Flash animations—popular options for adding motion to Web pages. You also learned about using animated 3-D graphics for movie special effects and computer games. Digital animation is typically created from scratch by an artist with the help of a computer. In contrast, digital video is based on footage of real objects filmed and then stored as bits. Digital video encompasses several technologies, including those that produce theater-quality DVD movies, desktop videos, Web-based videos, and PDA videos. In this section, you'll take a look at what you can do with affordable, easy-to-use desktop video tools. You'll also explore how to transfer digital videos onto DVD and then add interactive menus to access selected scenes and special features.

## DIGITAL VIDEO BASICS

**What is digital video?** A video is a series of still frames, like those in Figure 8-41, projected at a rate fast enough to fool the human eye into perceiving continuous motion. **Digital video** uses bits to store color and brightness data for each video frame. The process is similar to storing the data for a series of bitmap images in which the color for each pixel is represented by a binary number.

Unlike analog video, digital video retains image quality no matter how many times it is copied. Videos in digital format can be easily manipulated on a personal computer, putting the world of movie-making at your fingertips.

Footage for digital videos can be supplied by a video camera, videotape, television, DVD, or even a digital video recording device such as TiVo. You can shoot footage with a consumer-quality camcorder and use your personal computer to edit this footage into videos suitable for a variety of personal and professional uses, such as video wedding albums, product sales videos, training videos, video holiday greeting cards, documentaries for nonprofit organizations, and video scrapbooks. These videos can be stored on a hard disk or distributed on CDs, DVDs, videotapes, memory cards, or the Web.

Digital video is stored in a variety of file formats including ASF, AVI, MOV, MPEG-4, Ogg, and RealMedia. Later in the chapter, you'll learn about video file formats in more detail.

**Are there different kinds of digital videos?** Digital video is sometimes classified by its platform. The term **desktop video** refers to videos that are constructed and displayed using a personal computer. **Web-based video** is incorporated in Web pages and accessed with a browser. **DVD-Video** refers to a DVD format used for commercial DVDs that contain feature-length films. **PDA video** refers to small-format video designed to be viewed on a PDA or cell phone screen.

**FIGURE 8-41**

A video is composed of a series of bitmap graphics, each one called a frame.

**How do I create digital video?** To understand how you can create your own digital videos, you'll need information about four procedures summarized in Figure 8-42 and explained in the rest of this section.

1. **Produce video footage.** Select equipment for filming videos and use effective filming techniques.

2. **Transfer video footage to a computer.** Use a cable or a video capture card to move video footage from cameras, videotapes, television, and DVDs to your computer's hard disk.

3. **Edit video footage.** Use software to select video segments, arrange them into a video, and add a soundtrack.

4. **Store and play video.** Select digital video file formats for playback on desktop, Web, PDA, and DVD platforms.

**FIGURE 8-42**

Desktop video requires a few fairly simple steps.

## PRODUCING VIDEO FOOTAGE

**Is it necessary to use a digital video camera for filming digital video?** You can use a digital or an analog video camera to shoot video footage. As you might expect, a digital video camera stores footage as a series of bits. The video data can be stored on a tape in much the same way that computer data is stored on a backup tape. Video data can also be stored on 3" miniDVDs. Digital videotape formats include miniDV, DVCPro, and DVCam. MiniDV is the most popular and generally the format used by consumer digital video cameras.

You can also use an analog video camera to shoot footage that eventually becomes digital video. As with digital video cameras, the footage is stored on tape, but instead of storing bits, an analog video camera stores video signals as a continuous track of magnetic patterns. The three most popular analog video formats are Hi8, S-VHS, and VHS.

Another option for shooting video footage is a small, inexpensive **videoconferencing camera** (often called a Web cam or Web camera) that attaches directly to a computer (see Figure 8-43). These cameras capture a series of still photos, which are stored in digital format directly on your computer's hard disk. Web cameras typically produce rather low-quality video. These cameras are not usually battery powered and must remain tethered to your computer, which tends to limit your videos to "talking heads."

**What are the advantages of a digital video camera?** A digital video camera captures video data in digital format, which can then be transferred directly to a computer for editing. In addition, digital cameras generally produce higher quality video than analog or videoconferencing cameras. Images tend to be sharper and more colorful. A common

**8**

**FIGURE 8-43**

A Web camera sits on top of a computer monitor. It is designed mainly for "talking head" applications, such as online video chats and video conferences.

misconception is that because desktop, Web-based, and PDA videos are shown on a small computer screen at a fairly low resolution, a cheap camera won't make a difference. Just the opposite is true. The higher the quality of the original video, the better the final video will look.

**Does desktop video require special filming techniques?** When videos are processed and stored on a personal computer, some of the image data is eliminated to reduce the video file to a manageable size. Simpler videos tend to maintain better quality as they are edited, processed, and stored. Camera movements, fast actions, patterned clothing, and moving backgrounds all contribute to the complexity of a video and should be minimized. The techniques listed in Figure 8-44 can help you produce video footage that maintains good quality as it is edited and processed.

- Use a tripod to maintain a steady image.
- Move the camera slowly if it is necessary to pan from side to side.
- Zoom in and out slowly.
- Direct your subjects to move slowly, when possible.
- Position your shot to eliminate as much background detail and movement as possible.
- Ask the subjects of your video to wear solid-colored clothing, if possible.

**FIGURE 8-44**

Video Filming Tips

## VIDEO TRANSFER

**How do I transfer video footage to my computer?** Video footage can originate from a variety of sources, including video cameras, videotape, DVRs (digital video recorders), and even your TV. To digitally edit and process digital video, you must transfer the video footage from its source to your computer. After the footage is transferred and stored on a random-access device, such as your computer's hard disk, you can easily cut out unwanted footage, rearrange clips, and add a soundtrack.

The basic method for transferring video footage to your computer is to send the data over a cable that connects your video source to your computer (Figure 8-45). Analog video footage from TV, videotape, and analog video cameras must be converted into digital format before it is stored on your computer's hard disk. Video that originates as a digital signal usually can be transferred directly to your computer without conversion.

**How do I convert video from analog devices?** The process of converting analog video signals into digital format is referred to as **video capture** and requires a video capture device. Your computer's graphics card might include video capture capabilities. If not, you can purchase a separate video capture device that connects to your computer's USB port or a video capture card that plugs into one of your computer's PCI slots.

**FIGURE 8-45**

You can transfer video footage to a hard disk by connecting a cable between a video camera and a computer. When the transfer is complete, the cable can be disconnected.

Most video capture devices support a variety of analog video sources, such as cameras and VCRs. The trick is to find a cable with a connector at one end that plugs into the video output port of your analog video source and a plug at the other end that's compatible with your video capture device. Figure 8-46 illustrates the equipment necessary for capturing video from an analog camera.

### How do I transfer data from a digital camera to my computer?
The data from a digital camera typically requires no conversion, so it can be transferred directly to your computer's hard disk. Most digital cameras provide a USB or FireWire port for this purpose. Your computer needs a corresponding port to accept the cable from the camera.

### Can I capture video from a digital video recorder?
A **digital video recorder** (DVR), like those used with TiVo service, is a device that records television signals received by an antenna, through a cable, or from a satellite. Signals that originate from antenna or cable are converted from analog into digital format and stored on a built-in hard disk. Satellite signals, already in digital format, are converted or unscrambled as necessary before being stored. DVRs are controlled by customized operating systems, usually based on Linux.

It seems like it would be easy to transfer video files from this computer-like device to your personal computer for editing, but some DVRs store data in proprietary formats designed to discourage copying and distribution. These proprietary formats can make it difficult to convert DVR videos into formats that can be manipulated on a computer. Consumers, however, are demanding more compatibility between DVRs and computers. Until DVR manufacturers provide standard video formats, you can capture analog video direct from the TV using a video capture device.

### How do I control the transfer process?
Whether you transfer footage from an analog camera or a digital camera, you must use video capture software to control the transfer process. Video capture software allows you to start and stop the transfer, select a file format for storing your video footage, and specify the file name for each video clip. Video capture software is supplied with video editing software and with video capture devices.

Videos are easier to edit if you divide them into several files, each containing a one- or two-minute video clip. Some video capture software automatically creates clips by detecting frame changes, such as when you turn your camera off, pause, or switch to a new scene (Figure 8-47).

**FIGURE 8-46**

After it has been installed in your computer, a video capture card can be connected to an analog camera's video-out and audio-out ports.

**8**

**FIGURE 8-47**

Videos should be transferred as a series of short clips.

**What format should I use for video files?** For the best quality final product, experts recommend that you store video in a raw, non-compressed format for editing. After you trim out unwanted footage, arrange your clips, and add a soundtrack, you might want to convert your completed video into other formats for distribution. You learn more about distribution formats later in this section.

Most digital video cameras store data in DV format. Despite the use of real-time compression to filter out unnecessary data as you record with your camera, DV format contains lots of data. When transferred to your computer, a DV clip requires roughly 1 GB of storage per 5 minutes of video. If you have the disk capacity, you'll get the best quality video if you transfer all this data. If disk space is tight, however, you can whittle digital video down to a more manageable size by using your video capture software to decrease the video display size, reduce the frame rate, and compress file data.

- **Decrease video display size.** A smaller video window contains fewer pixels than a full-screen window and requires fewer bits to represent the data. Whereas a 720 x 480 video window contains 345,600 pixels, a 320 x 240 window contains only 76,800 pixels and fits in a file one-fourth the size. That's a big advantage. If you're creating Web-based videos designed to be displayed in a small window, or if you're designing video for handheld devices, consider decreasing the resolution at this stage of the process.

- **Reduce the frame rate. Frame rate** refers to the number of frames shown per second. Digital video cameras record 30 frames per second (fps). Feature films are typically projected at a rate of 24 frames per second. If you intend to output your digital videos to DVDs, you should maintain a high frame rate. Most desktop video, however, has a frame rate of only 15 fps. Reducing the frame rate tends to increase the blurriness of a video, especially for fast-action sequences. If your videos are destined for desktop, Web, or PDA playback, you can reduce the frame rate at this stage of the process because the finished video will be displayed at a lower frame rate.

- **Compress data.** Most video capture software offers a variety of compression options to reduce the size of video files. If storage space is a concern or if your videos are destined for the Web or a PDA, you might want to compress your video clips before you edit them.

## VIDEO EDITING

**Do I need special equipment for video editing?** Before camcorders went digital, editing a video consisted of recording segments from one videotape onto another tape. This process, called **linear editing**, required two VCRs at minimum. Professional video editors used expensive editing equipment, beyond the budget of most consumers.

Today's **nonlinear editing** simply requires a computer hard disk and video editing software. The advantage of nonlinear editing is that you can use a random-access device to easily edit and arrange video clips. Video editing requires lots of hard disk space, however, so before you begin an editing session, make sure your computer's hard disk has several gigabytes of available storage space. It is also a good idea to have at least 512 MB of RAM—professionals opt for at least 2 GB.

**How do I edit a video?** After your video footage is transferred to your computer and stored on the hard disk, you can begin to arrange your video clips by using video editing software, such as Adobe Premiere, Roxio VideoWave, Windows Movie Maker, or Ulead VideoStudio. Your completed

**INFOWEBLINKS**

The **Video Editing InfoWeb** contains tips about editing digital videos, updates on the latest consumer-level software, and links to the most popular digital video sites.

 CLICK TO CONNECT
www.course.com/np/concepts10/ch08

video consists of video tracks containing video segments and transitions, plus audio tracks containing voices and music. Most video editing software allows you to overlay a video track with several audio tracks. Figure 8-48 illustrates how to lay out video and audio tracks.

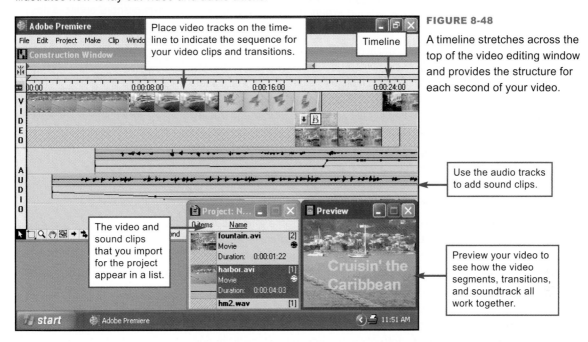

**FIGURE 8-48**

A timeline stretches across the top of the video editing window and provides the structure for each second of your video.

## VIDEO OUTPUT

**How does video footage become a digital video?** After you edit your video clips, arrange them on a timeline, and specify a soundtrack, your video editing software combines the data from all the video and audio files you selected into a single file, which is stored on your computer's hard disk as a digital video. You can think of the files that store your digital videos as containers because they can hold video and audio streams. Digital video file formats are sometimes referred to as **container formats** because they are essentially a receptacle for the elements of a video. Figure 8-49 describes some popular video container formats—**AVI**, **QuickTime Movie**, **MPEG**, **RealMedia**, **ASF**, **Flash Video**, and **VOB**.

**FIGURE 8-49**

Popular Digital Video Formats

| Format | Extension | Platform | Description and Use |
|---|---|---|---|
| **AVI (Audio Video Interleave)** | .avi | PC | Often the format for storing digital clips from video cameras; used for desktop video on the PC platform |
| **QuickTime Movie** | .mov | PC, Mac, UNIX, Linux | One of the most popular formats for desktop and streaming Web videos |
| **MPEG (Moving Pictures Experts Group)** | .mpg or .mpeg | PC, Mac, UNIX, Linux | Versions include MPEG1, MPEG2, and MPEG4; used for desktop video, PDA video, and streaming Web video |
| **RealMedia** | .rm | PC, Mac, UNIX, Linux | Produced by RealNetworks, a popular format for streaming Web videos |
| **ASF (Advanced Systems Format)** | .asf or .wmv | PC | Container format for Microsoft's Windows Media Video (WMV) desktop, PDA, and streaming video |
| **Flash Video** | .flv | PC, Mac | Popular for Web-based video; requires Adobe Flash Player |
| **VOB (Video Object)** | .vob | Standalone DVD players, PCs, Macs, Linux | Industry-standard format for standalone DVD players |

**Which compression techniques should I use?** Suppose you decide to store your video in an AVI container file for desktop viewing. You can compress the video stream using various codecs. A **codec** (compressor/ decompressor) is the software that compresses a video stream when a video is stored and decompresses the file when the video is played. Popular codecs include MPEG, Indeo, Cinepak, DivX, and Windows Media Video.

Each codec uses a unique compression algorithm and allows you to specify the compression ratio. A compression ratio indicates the ratio of compressed data to uncompressed data. A video file with a high compression ratio, such as 35:1 has more compression, a smaller file size, and lower image quality than a file with a lower compression ratio, such a 5:1.

It is important to understand that the codec used to compress a video also must be used to decompress the video when it is played. Videos intended for a widespread audience should use one of the codecs included in popular video players, such as QuickTime or Windows Media Player.

Video compression can be achieved by decreasing the frame rate, reducing the frame size, or using techniques similar to JPEG to compress the data stored for each frame. Temporal compression techniques can also be used to eliminate data that doesn't change from frame to frame.

**Temporal compression** is a technique that can be applied to video footage to eliminate redundant or unnecessary data between frames. For example, if you are working with a video of a "talking head," the background image is likely to contain lots of redundant information that doesn't change from one frame to the next.

As the temporal compression algorithm begins to analyze frames, the first frame becomes a **key frame** that contains all the data. Key frames are stored at preset intervals or whenever a cut, wipe, or transition changes the scene. As the compression algorithm analyzes subsequent frames in the video, it stores only the data that is different from data in the key frame.

The videos in Figure 8-50 illustrate the differences in image quality and file size that result from using various compression ratios and frame rates.

**FIGURE 8-50**

Different compression ratios and frame rates can have a remarkable effect on video quality and file size.

Uncompressed video

Compression ratio: 35:1
Frame rate: 3
File size: 35 KB

 CLICK TO START

Compression ratio: 14:1
Frame rate: 10
File size: 76 KB

 CLICK TO START

Compression ratio: 3:1
Frame rate: 15
File size: 353 KB

 CLICK TO START

## DESKTOP, PDA, AND WEB VIDEO

**How are desktop videos used?** Desktop videos are usually displayed on a computer screen with popular video player software, such as the RealMedia player, Windows Media Player, or Apple's QuickTime player. Desktop videos are typically stored on hard disk or CD, and they are sometimes sent as e-mail attachments.

**Can I view movies on my PDA?** Some PDAs and smartphones can be configured to play digital videos (Figure 8-51), including movie trailers, TV shows, and even feature-length movies. The device requires video or multimedia player software, such as Pocket TV or Windows Media Player, and storage capacity for the video file—usually on a solid-state memory card. Videos specially optimized for handheld devices can be downloaded from Web sites to your computer, then transferred to handheld storage and played. Popular formats for handheld video include MPEG and WMV.

**How do Web-based videos work?** A video for a Web page is stored on a Web server in a file. Usually, a link for the video file appears on the Web page. When you click the link, the Web server transmits a copy of the video file to your computer. If you have the correct video player installed on your computer, the video appears on your computer screen.

The transfer of a digital video file from the Web to your computer can happen in one of two ways, depending on the video format. In one case, your computer waits until it receives the entire video file before starting to play it. For large video files, you might wait several minutes or more before the video starts. An alternative method, called **streaming video**, sends a small segment of the video to your computer and begins to play it. While this first segment plays, the Web server sends the next part of the file to your computer, and so on, until the video ends. With streaming video technology, your computer essentially plays the video while it continues to receive it.

**How do I post a video to YouTube or a similar file-sharing site?** YouTube is a video-sharing Web site which encourages members to upload, view, and rate video clips. YouTube and similar sites typically accept most popular video file formats directly from digital cameras, camcorders, and cell phones. Usually, however, you would edit the video first and save it in a standard video container format such as AVI, QuickTime MOV, or MPEG. YouTube automatically converts all submitted files into Flash Video format. Most sites have a length and file limitation, so you should check those before you finalize your video.

**How do I add a video to my own Web pages?** You can add two styles of video to your Web pages. The first style, called external video, simply displays a link to a video file. An HTML tag, such as <a href="ducks.avi"> 1.5 MB AVI Video </a>, indicates the file that contains the video (ducks.avi) and the text for the link (1.5 MB AVI Video). When the link is clicked, the video file is downloaded, and the video player is opened and displayed as a separate window in which the video appears.

A second style of Web video uses the <embed> tag to create an internal video, also referred to as an in-place video. Instead of opening a separate window for the video player, an internal video plays within the Web page. Figure 8-52 on the next page illustrates external and internal Web page videos.

**FIGURE 8-51**

You can watch digital videos on some PDAs and cell phones.

8

**INFOWEBLINKS**

The **Video Players InfoWeb** provides lots of handy information about Microsoft Media Player, QuickTime, and other video player software.

CLICK TO CONNECT
www.course.com/np/concepts10/ch08

**FIGURE 8-52**

An external Web video (below) displays the player as a separate window. An internal, or in-place, video (left) displays the clip as though it were part of the Web page.

Internal Web video plays in place.

External Web video displays video in a separate window.

**How does Internet connection speed affect Web videos?** Although it is possible to play streaming videos over a dial-up connection, it is truly an unsatisfying experience. New compression techniques are able to jam more video data into a smaller package, but with a dial-up connection images tend to be fuzzy and motion is often jerky.

High-speed Internet connections provide much more bandwidth for streaming video. Videos designed to be transmitted over high-speed connections can play in a larger video window, use less compression, and display better image quality. Until everyone has a high-speed connection, however, many Web sites provide one video file that's optimized for dial-up connections and a better quality video file that's optimized for high-speed connections.

**What are the best formats for Web videos?** Today's most popular Web video formats include MPEG4, MOV, ASF, and RM. All these formats offer streaming video and allow developers to adjust compression levels to produce file sizes optimized for dial-up or broadband connections.

## DVD-VIDEO

**Can I incorporate my digital videos onto DVDs with interactive menus like commercial movies?** Suppose you've used video editing software to create a really spectacular video of your class reunion. You can package your completed video footage into a professional-style DVD that can be played on computer DVD drives (if your computer is equipped with DVD player software) or standalone DVD players. It can include interactive menus with options, such as Play Video, Select a Scene, and Special Features, that viewers can select using their DVD remote controls.

**What equipment do I need?** To create video DVDs, you need a writable DVD drive (sometimes called a DVD burner) plus software that includes tools for DVD menu creation and writing data onto a DVD-Video—

a process sometimes called burning. These tools are offered by DVD authoring software, such as Adobe Encore, Sonic MyDVD, Nero, and Ulead DVD MovieFactory. Many video editing software packages and suites also include tools for creating DVD menus and burning projects onto DVDs.

**What's the process for making a video DVD?** To create a video DVD, you usually begin by selecting one or more completed videos that include soundtracks, transitions, titles, special effects, and so on. You then use DVD authoring software to design menus and buttons that viewers can use to navigate to specific parts of your video. To complete the project, you can test your project and then burn it to DVD.

**What are my options for creating interactive DVD menus?** A DVD menu is a screen that provides viewers with navigation tools to start a video, skip to specific scenes, play special features, and link to other menus. A typical DVD menu consists of a decorative background and option buttons that viewers can select using their DVD players' remote control. Static backgrounds are simply bitmap images, such as a frame from the video or an abstract design. Motion backgrounds display animations or video segments.

Option buttons can be a variety of shapes and sizes. They typically change appearance when selected. For example, when a viewer selects the Play button, it might light up or an icon might appear next to it.

Some DVD authoring software offers a selection of predesigned menu and button templates that you can easily incorporate with your videos. Your software might also provide the option to create your own backgrounds and buttons using graphics software, such as Adobe Photoshop or Microsoft Paint. Figure 8-53 illustrates a DVD menu being created using a simple DVD authoring software package.

**8**

**FIGURE 8-53**

Sonic's MyDVD software offers a selection of backgrounds and button styles for creating DVD menus.

**Are menus easy to create?** Yes, they just require a little advance planning. As you design the menu flow, remember that you want to provide viewers with a way to return to the main menu from each submenu. You might also want viewers to return to the main menu after viewing individual clips. If a submenu offers options for outtakes or other special features, you should provide a way for viewers to return to the submenu when the special feature ends. To help visualize the way your menus will work you can draw a diagram similar to the one in Figure 8-54.

**FIGURE 8-54**

Sketching a diagram of the menus for your DVD can help you envision how viewers will navigate to selected scenes and special features.

**How do I output my video to DVD?** To create a DVD that can be viewed on a standalone DVD player, you have to output your video in DVD-Video format, which requires video encoded with MPEG2 and stored in VOB (video object) files. Your DVD authoring software can generate MPEG2-encoded video clips and menus, store them in VOB files, and lay them out on a DVD according to industry standards.

Most DVD authoring software can accomplish the MPEG encoding on the fly as it burns the DVD. This process takes time, however, so if you are burning more than one copy, or if you want to test your menu structure before burning the video onto a DVD, you might want to consider creating a DVD image.

**What's a DVD image?** A **DVD image** (sometimes called a DVD volume) is essentially a prototype of your DVD, but it is stored on your computer's hard disk. If you have space to store a DVD image, it is a good idea to make one before burning a DVD. You can use a DVD image for testing. You can also use the image to burn multiple DVDs without waiting for your software to prepare the files for each burn.

**Can I simply copy a desktop video to a DVD using Windows Explorer or My Computer?** Desktop videos are typically stored in AVI or MOV format and most standalone DVD players are not equipped to handle those formats. So, although you can use Windows Explorer to copy MOV and AVI files to a DVD and distribute them, these files can be viewed on most computers, but not on all DVD players.

Even copying files stored in MPEG format might not produce a DVD that works in a standalone player. The DVD-Video format specification requires a specific layout for data on the DVD surface. The method you use to copy computer data files does not produce the required layout, so most DVD players will not be able to play the video.

**How do I test my DVD image?** Your DVD is ready for production and distribution if the video quality looks good and the menus work correctly. Use the tips listed below to test your DVD on your computer before you burn a DVD.

- Test each button to make sure it links to the correct clip.

- Play each clip to the end and make sure it returns to the correct menu when completed.

- Watch the video carefully and look for any poor quality segments with distracting artifacts, such as blurs or halos. Artifacts can sometimes be removed by revisiting your MPEG coding options.

- Listen to the soundtrack to make sure the audio is clear, smooth, and synchronized with the video.

**Does it make a difference if I use recordable or rewritable DVDs?** Commercial DVD movies are stamped onto DVD-ROM disks during the manufacturing process—something you can't do with your computer's DVD drive. Your computer can burn data on DVD-R, DVD+R, or DVD-RW disks. Because the DVD industry has not achieved a single media standard, some standalone DVD players—particularly those manufactured before 2004—are not able to read one or more of these disk types. DVD+R and DVD-R seem to be compatible with the widest variety of DVD players, whereas DVD-RWs seem to be the least compatible. Before you distribute your DVDs make sure you test them in a standalone DVD player.

> **TERMINOLOGY NOTE**
>
> In the world of video production, an artifact is any visible degradation in the image quality, such as shimmering where contrasting colors meet or backgrounds that become wavy during fast pans or zooms.

**8**

# QuickCheck

**SECTION D**

1. _____ video refers to digital videos constructed and displayed using a personal computer.

2. The process of converting analog video signals into digital format is referred to as video _____.

3. The size of a video file can be reduced by three techniques: shrinking the size of the video window, reducing the _____ rate, and compressing the video data.

4. Compressing a video at a ratio of 35:1 produces higher quality than compressing it at a 5:1 ratio. True or false? _____

5. PDA videos are stored in MP3 files, similar to those used on portable audio players. True or false? _____

6. Some Web pages feature _____ video, which sends a small segment of the video to your computer and begins to play it. While this first segment plays, the Web server sends the next part of the file to your computer, and so on, until the video ends.

7. DVD-Video requires files in _____ format.

 CHECK ANSWERS

SECTION E

# Digital Rights Management

**THE SECURITY SECTIONS** of earlier chapters looked at security from the user perspective. In contrast, the security section for this chapter examines the techniques used by content providers to protect digital media from unlicensed duplication and use. Pirating music and movies is a multi-billion dollar worldwide activity that is increasingly controlled by organized crime. Legitimate content providers are taking steps to reduce piracy by prosecuting digital pirates and using digital rights management technologies to deter duplication. Unfortunately, technical measures taken to reduce illicit duplication can be inconvenient for legitimate users. In this section, you'll learn about DRM technologies you may have already encountered and some that are likely to affect your ability to use digital media in the future.

## DRM BASICS

**What is DRM?** **Digital rights management** (DRM) is a collection of techniques used by copyright holders to limit access and use of digital content. Because DRM is primarily used to protect products of the entertainment industry, in the context of DRM, **digital content** (or simply content) usually refers to movies, music, e-books, and computer games.

Digital content is accessed by means of a player. Keep in mind that the term *player* can refer to a hardware device or software. Software players include familiar media players, such as iTunes, Windows Media Player, and QuickTime. Hardware players include standalone devices such as CD players, VCRs, DVD players, and portable music players. Computer devices, such as CD, DVD, and Blu-ray drives, are also considered players, though they require software to play back content.

Every hardware device and software program that interacts with digital content poses a potential vulnerability that can be exploited by pirates. Software that encrypts content can be cracked, signals that travel from one device to another can be intercepted, and when all else fails, the **analog hole** allows pirates to capture content by using a microphone to record songs as they are output to speakers or using a camcorder to film movies as they are projected in a movie theater.

In response to the creativity and sheer stubbornness of digital pirates, modern DRM systems include layers of protection, with the goal of controlling content from its distribution point through to its playback (Figure 8-55).

**FIGURE 8-55**

The threat of legal penalties has not been enough to discourage digital piracy, so copyright holders are working on increasingly sophisticated ways to prevent illegal copying.

The unauthorized reproduction or distribution of this copyrighted work is illegal. Criminal copyright infringement, including infringement without monetary gain, is investigated by the FBI and is punishable by up to 5 years in federal prison and a fine of $250,000.

**How does DRM affect my use of digital media?** The average consumer uses a variety of electronic devices to play digital content. Many of these devices offer convenient time and place shifting, but DRM technologies can curtail their use.

**Time shifting** is the process of recording a broadcast, such as a television show, so that it can be played back at a more convenient time. **Place shifting** allows media that originates in one place to be accessed from another place without changing the device on which it is stored (Figure 8-56). Place shifting is often achieved using computer networks, as when you view a cable television broadcast sent from your Wi-Fi equipped set-top box to your Wi-Fi equipped notebook.

**Format shifting** is the process of converting media files from a format suitable to one device to a format suitable for a different kind of device. A common use of format shifting is ripping audio tracks from a CD and converting them into MP3 format for playback on a portable audio device, such as an iPod.

**Is DRM effective?** DRM has not lived up to the expectation of copyright holders and it has disappointed consumers by curtailing their options for using content they have legitimately purchased. Digital piracy continues to run rampant and hackers stubbornly continue to devise work-arounds to defeat DRM. There is evidence that the incidence of casual copying has decreased, but some of this casual copying might actually be legitimate, fair use. The Issue section of this chapter looks at the relationship between DRM technologies and the concept of fair use.

To judge whether DRM technologies are effective and to gauge their effect on consumers, it is helpful to take a more detailed look at the evolution of DRM technologies from their first applications for scrambling cable television signals to more recent applications designed to protect online delivery of digital content.

## SIGNAL SCRAMBLING AND DIGITAL WATERMARKS

**What is signal scrambling?** **Signal scrambling** is a term commonly used for obscuring cable or satellite television images until they are unscrambled by a set-top box or other authorized mechanism. The first scrambling systems were based on various proprietary algorithms that transmitted unsynchronized video signals designed to be resynchronized by a set-top box. With the advent of digital content, scrambling was implemented by encrypting the digital bits of the signal.

It is technically possible to build a device to descramble signals, but it is illegal to use one. For the most part, consumers accept signal scrambling technology with the understanding that once signals are received and unscrambled, they can be recorded for later viewing. DRM technologies such as digital watermarks, however, can limit the use of unscrambled content.

**What is a digital watermark?** A **digital watermark** is a pattern of bits inserted at various places in an image or a content stream that can be used to track, identify, verify, and control content use. Watermarks, such as broadcast flags, are usually imperceptible to viewers or listeners, but can be picked up by compliant devices.

A **broadcast flag** is a set of bits inserted into the data stream of digital television or radio programs that specifies how the stream can and cannot be used. Broadcast flags can prohibit a program from being unencrypted or

FIGURE 8-56

A Slingbox is a place-shifting device that redirects video content from a cable box, satellite receiver, or digital video recorder to a remote computer over a LAN or the Internet.

8

copied. They can limit copies to low resolution, such as by reducing high-definition video to the resolution of a standard television. In addition, broadcast flags can prevent fast forwarding past commercials.

Broadcast flags are intended to combat indiscriminate use of digital video recorders, such as TiVos. In the United States, many HDTVs are equipped to recognize broadcast flags, but the number of consumers who own HDTVs is not high, making it unlikely for broadcast flags to be widely used in the near future. Nevertheless, consumers should be aware that future implementations of broadcast flags are possible and can affect use of digital media.

## CD COPY PROTECTION

**How does digital rights management affect music and other media distributed on CDs?** Compact disc (CD) technology was introduced in 1982. It was originally developed for storing digital audio and is still a primary distribution method for recorded music. CDs adhere to a standardized format commonly called the Red Book, which implements DRM with a data bit that can be set to "no-copy." The Red Book no-copy bit is easy to defeat, so the recording industry has attempted to use more robust DRM technologies, such as copy protection.

**What is copy protection?** **Copy protection** refers to technologies designed to prohibit consumers from copying content. CDs with copy protection cannot be duplicated and music that is ripped to another format does not play back correctly. Copy protection technologies include Copy Control, CDS (Cactus Data Shield), and XCP (Extended Copy Protection).

**How does CD copy protection work?** Most CD copy protection technologies rely on two techniques: multiple sessions and corrupted data. A copy protected CD with multiple sessions is essentially divided into two parts called sessions. The first session contains an audio stream of recorded music that has been intentionally corrupted. The second session contains a computer program that can essentially reverse the corruption.

The audio stream is corrupted by replacing certain frames (about 1/75th of a second of music) with data, rather than sound. Dedicated CD players simply skip the data, but computer CD drives tend to play the data frames, resulting in loud pops and other audio glitches. On some drives, the CD seems to pause every few seconds while the drive attempts to make sense of the data. Ripping and pirating the corrupted audio tracks is pointless because they don't play back correctly. To filter out the corrupted data, your computer requires specialized software. This software is stored as the CD's data session and is installed the first time that you use the CD (Figure 8-57).

> **TERMINOLOGY NOTE**
>
> Some consumer advocates take issue with the term *copy protection* because it has connotations biased toward the recording industry that is trying to protect content, rather than to the consumer who is prevented from using the material freely. More consumer-oriented terms include *copy prevention* and *copy control*.

**FIGURE 8-57**

Copy protected CDs contain a software program that strips out intentionally corrupted data.

Copy protected CD contains music and computer software

The corrupted audio stream makes popping sounds

Software is installed on hard drive the first time CD is accessed

Software filters out intentionally corrupted data

**How do I know if a CD is copy protected?** Some distributors, such as Amazon.com, do their best to identify copy protected CDs in product descriptions. The existence of a data session and intentionally corrupted audio on copy protected CDs does not adhere to the Red Book standard for audio CDs, so the official CDDA logo is missing on the CD packaging. Most copy protected CDs also carry warnings that they might not function on some equipment, such as car CD players.

**How prevalent is CD copy protection?** Copy protected CDs have become much less common since the 2005 Sony BMG rootkit incident. Several Sony BMG CDs were copy protected by software that limited duplication to three copies. The copy protection software was surreptitiously installed and once installed used a rootkit to conceal itself. Not only was the software installed without user consent, once installed, the software made consumers' computers more open to Internet viruses. The copy protection software had no uninstall routine and if users deleted the files, their CD drives no longer worked. After a high-profile rash of negative publicity, the CDs were recalled and music publishers quietly began to abandon copy protection.

## DVD DRM

**Do DVDs and CDs use similar DRM?** The first DVD players were introduced in 1996 primarily as a distribution medium for mainstream movies. Based on prior experience with CD and VHS piracy, technologies to discourage piracy were built into the DVD standard from its inception.

Unlike CD DRM, protection for DVD content did not have to be tacked onto the distribution media as corrupted data and rootkits. DRM designed for DVDs could take advantage of more sophisticated technologies both on disks and on players. The major DRM technologies for DVDs include copy generation management, analog output protection, and CSS. These technologies can be implemented individually or together to provide layers of protection.

**What is copy generation management?** **Copy generation management** is a digital watermark that specifies the number of times a content stream can be duplicated. Compliant players recognize the watermark and abide by it. With the watermark set to no copy, for example, a video stream cannot be copied to other compliant devices. If a content stream carries a one-copy-only watermark, compliant devices can make a copy, but will change the watermark to no-copies-allowed. As a result, second generation copies cannot be used to make additional copies (Figure 8-58).

**FIGURE 8-58**

Watermarks are read by devices that comply with the limitations embedded in the content stream.

Original DVD with one-copy-only watermark

Compliant DVD burner

DVD copy now contains do-not-copy watermark

Compliant DVD burner will not copy the DVD

**What is an analog protection system?** An **analog protection system** is any DRM technology that interjects signals into the video stream to prevent analog output from being copied. As used in the context of protecting DVDs, an analog protection system places signals within the content stream that disrupt playback on VCRs by making the image appear dim or scrambled. The intended use of this technology is to prevent DVD video streams from being output to videotape, then being converted back into digital format.

**What is CSS? CSS** (Content Scramble System) is a digital rights management technology designed to encrypt and control the use of content stored on DVDs. It is intended to render DVD copies nonfunctional and enforces additional restrictions, such as region coding. CSS is the most well-known DRM technology for DVDs.

**How does CSS work?** CSS technology is a type of authentication-and-encryption DRM technology built into standalone DVD players and computer DVD players/burners. A key aspect of CSS is the use of authentication keys that allow a DVD disk and player to prove to each other that they are legitimately licensed to use CSS. Only after authentication can the encrypted video stream be decoded.

DVD players are manufactured with a built-in set of CSS keys. When a DVD is inserted, the player runs through every key until one unlocks the disc. Once this disc key is known, the player uses it to retrieve a title key from the disc. The title key allows the player to unscramble the DVD video stream (Figure 8-59).

Title key ➝ **1.** DVD Player decrypts title key using one of 400 pre-programmed keys

Key to decrypt content stream

DVD protected by CSS

**2.** The title key contains a unique key to decrypt the data stream

DVD Player

**FIGURE 8-59**

In addition to limiting playback to compliant devices, CSS prevents DVDs from being successfully duplicated by end-users using standard copy utilities. Decryption keys are stored on a hidden area of the DVD which is not copied to the new DVD during duplication.

**What is a region code?** The CSS authentication process includes checking region codes. A DVD **region code** specifies a geographical area of legitimate use for DVD disks and players. For example, the United States, Canada, Bermuda, and U.S. territories make up region 1. DVD players are sold according to region, so in Canada consumers purchase region 1 DVD players, while consumers in India purchase players for region 5. A DVD player will play only DVDs encoded for its region. Region codes allow the film industry to charge higher prices in some countries than others without worrying about cheaper versions affecting sales in more expensive regions.

**Has CSS been cracked?** Soon after CSS appeared, hackers were able to crack it. **DeCSS** is the most well-known software for decrypting DVD content that is protected by CSS. New DRM technologies, such as RipGuard, have emerged as replacements for CSS, but most of these have also been cracked. Although DeCSS and other tools for bypassing DVD protection are widely available on the Internet, their distribution and use is illegal in the United States or other countries with similar copyright laws or treaties.

**What about copy protection for Blu-ray and HD-DVDs?** Like earlier DVD standards, Blu-ray and HD-DVD incorporate layers of DRM technologies, but they use AACS instead of CSS for authorization and encryption. **AACS** (Advanced Access Content System) is a DRM technology designed to encrypt and protect content on optical disks. Additional DRM layers include BD+ and BD ROM Mark.

**How does AACS work?** Like CSS, AACS works with an encrypted content stream. AACS, however, uses a much stronger encryption key, which makes it quite difficult for hackers to break the encryption using brute force methods. Another difference between the two methods is that CSS uses a shared set of encryption keys, and all devices of a specific model use the same key. In contrast, AACS compliant devices each contain their own unique set of keys and these keys can be revoked if a player is found to be compromised. The concept of **authorization and revocation** can be applied to hardware devices and software players to give licensing bodies the means to keep non-complying players off the market and deny further access to complying devices that have become compromised (Figure 8-60).

**FIGURE 8-60**

AACS depends on authentication and revocation built into devices and content.

In addition to encryption, AACS protects content with two types of digital watermarks, a theatrical mark and a consumer mark. The theatrical mark is inserted into the soundtrack of films actually shown in theaters. If a home player detects this watermark, playback stops because the disk is suspected to be one created using an illicitly borrowed professional reel of the film. The second AACS watermark is inserted into legitimate DVDs sold to consumers. If the mark is not detected on a DVD that is supposed to have it, playback will terminate.

**Do video disc DRM technologies make my computer less secure?** DVD publishers can use DRM to prevent consumers from making a copy of a DVD in case the original is damaged, force viewers to watch the ubiquitous FBI warning, and prohibit viewers from fast-forwarding through commercials. Using DRM in such a manner annoys consumers, but does not threaten the security of their computers. So far, the technologies used to protect video disc content have not opened security holes that are widely exploited by hackers.

## DRM FOR DIGITAL DOWNLOADS

**Can DRM protect downloaded files?** As you have learned so far, DRM technologies can be applied to broadcasts and to content distributed on physical storage media, such as CDs and DVDs. DRM also plays a role in controlling the use of downloaded audio, video, and e-book files.

Free file-sharing sites popular in the 1990s had a devastating effect on the recording industry. Free sites still exist, but the recording industry is waging war against site operators and users. In addition to legal recourse, the recording industry reportedly pays private firms to seed file-sharing networks with fake versions of popular copyrighted songs, so that it is difficult to find genuine versions. After litigation shut down many free sites, a new crop of legitimate sites offered to pay royalties by charging customers for downloads.

Many consumers seem content to pay a dollar or less to download a song from a legitimate online music store, so iTunes, Zune, and others do a booming business. Part of the agreement between the recording industry and online music stores is that music downloads have to be distributed in a way that prevents unauthorized copying and sharing. Apple uses a DRM technology called **FairPlay** to control music downloaded from the iTunes store. Microsoft supplies DRM technologies for several online music stores, including Zune.

**How does FairPlay work?** FairPlay packages iTunes in a standard MP4 container format as described in Figure 8-61.

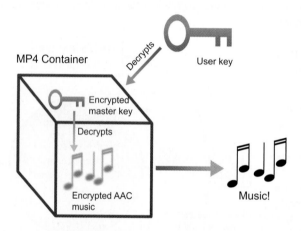

**FIGURE 8-61**

The MP4 container holds an encrypted AAC audio stream and a master key used to decrypt the audio. The master key is also encrypted, so before you can play iTunes music, you need a so-called user key that decrypts the master key. Each time you purchase an iTunes track, a unique user key is generated for your computer. The user key is stored on your computer so that you can decrypt the master key, which is then used to decrypt the track before you can play it.

 CLICK TO START

FairPlay user keys are tied to specific computers, which are authorized to play the track. You can authorize other computers to play the songs you've purchased and you can deauthorize a computer, for example, before you send it for repair or sell it. Changes in authorization require a connection to the iTunes store where a database stores customer accounts, authorized machine identifiers, a list of purchased tracks, and user keys.

User accounts add a dimension to DRM technology that is not possible with standalone CD and DVD players. Your keys open only your copy of downloaded content and may allow illicit copies of songs or players to be traced back to their source. This concept, sometimes referred to as **DRM individualization**, has become a key component of digital rights management for downloaded content.

iTunes software is stored on subscriber computers and can be updated by Apple as necessary to plug vulnerabilities in its DRM. Subscribers are forced to install new versions of the iTunes software before they can continue to purchase content from the iTunes store.

The iTunes EULA prohibits subscribers from attempting to "circumvent or modify any security technology or software" and Apple's policy is to aggressively prosecute anyone who develops or distributes software to bypass its DRM.

**How does Windows Media DRM work? Windows Media DRM** was developed by Microsoft to provide secure digital content delivery over networks. Its purpose is similar to FairPlay—to make sure that digital music and movies can be used only by consumers who purchase them legitimately—but the two DRM technologies differ slightly. Like FairPlay, Windows Media DRM encrypts the content stream. The key is stored in an encrypted license, which unlike FairPlay is distributed separately. The digital media file contains an encrypted link to the license.

Files protected by Windows Media DRM can be distributed from a Web site, on a CD, or as an e-mail attachment. If you receive one of these files from a friend and try to access it, you will be prompted to get a license. This process of sharing files but forcing users to pay for licenses before accessing content is sometimes referred to as **super distribution**.

Files protected by Windows Media DRM can be accessed only when using a compliant hardware or software player. Before producing a compliant player, companies must be authorized by Microsoft. Authorization can be revoked from players that become compromised. Windows Media DRM is designed to be updatable. It has been cracked several times, but in every case quick updates from Microsoft have patched the vulnerabilities.

**What about movie download sites?** Movie download technology at legitimate online stores such as CinemaNow, Vongo, AOL Video, and MovieLink has lagged behind music downloads. Movie files are huge and take time to download—about 30 minutes for a low resolution version or more than an hour for DVD quality. Lengthy downloads are not only inconvenient for users, but also create a burden on servers that subsequently limits availability. In addition, movie download sites tend to have a somewhat skimpy selection, a factor that can be attributed in part to the reluctance of copyright holders to release content on a platform that seems so inherently easy for pirating.

DRM technologies such as watermarks and copy generation management are used in various ways to limit how you can use movies you've downloaded. At some movie download stores, content viewing is limited to your computer screen. At other sites, you are allowed to burn a limited number of DVDs. DRM can also limit the length of time you are allowed to view a movie. Often the limit is 24 hours, but some sites offer a 30-day or unlimited viewing window. Most movie download sites require a monthly subscription fee, so before you subscribe, carefully examine the Terms of Use and FAQs to become familiar with download and copy policies.

# QuickCheck

1. _____ shifting is the process of recording a broadcast, such as a television show, so that it can be played back at a more convenient time.

2. A digital _____ inserted into an audio or video stream is imperceptible to users, but can be read by complying devices.

3. When first accessing a copy _____ audio CD, software is installed on your computer that essentially reverses the intentionally corrupted data inserted into the audio track.

4. _____ is the primary technology used to protect DVDs, but it was cracked soon after it was introduced. (Hint: Use the acronym.)

5. A key aspect of protecting content downloaded from online music and video stores is the concept of DRM _____ that ties decryption keys to a user account.

6. Microsoft DRM allows _____ distribution, a process whereby consumers can share protected files with friends, who are required to obtain their own license for accessing the content.

 CHECK ANSWERS

# What Happened to Fair Use?

**SUPPOSE YOU PURCHASE** a music CD of your favorite recording group. Now you want to transfer the file to your computer, rip the best tracks, and transfer them to your portable audio player. But wait! That CD is copy protected and your computer CD drive won't read it. You purchased the disk. Can't you listen to the music on any device you choose? The answer depends on a concept called fair use.

Fair use is the right to use portions of copyrighted material without the permission of the copyright holder for purposes such as review, criticism, or parody. Under certain circumstances, fair use is also a successful defense for practices, such as time shifting, in which whole works are copied for limited personal use.

Exactly what does or does not constitute fair use, however, is only sketched out in copyright law. The precise nature of fair use is shaped by a somewhat amorphous cloud of court decisions covering situations and devices as disparate as player piano rolls, printer toner cartridges, video tape recorders, and file-sharing networks.

As one of the original time-shifting technologies, VCRs made it possible to set a recording time to capture movies and shows broadcast on television or cable channels. Digital video recorders, such as TiVo, make time shifting possible by saving content to a digital storage device, such as a hard disk.

The legal precedent for time shifting is the landmark 1984 Betamax case in which Universal Studios attempted to hold Sony Corp. of America liable for copyright infringement by people who used video recorders to tape movies from their televisions. The

U.S. Supreme court sided with Sony and concluded that some instances of time shifting were not illegal.

The court's decision, however, was based on a definition of time-shifting as "the practice of recording a program to view it once at a later time." Note the word "once." The Betamax case did not offer legal precedent for copying and saving content for viewing multiple times. The Supreme Court was also influenced by testimony from copyright holders, such as the host of the well-known children's show *Mister Rogers' Neigborhood*, who welcomed the practice of time shifting. At the time, some TV guides even listed shows that networks permitted viewers to copy.

The proliferation of computer networks and streaming media has made place shifting a reality. You can, for example, view a cable television broadcast sent from your Wi-Fi equipped set-top box in your living room to your Wi-Fi equipped notebook out on the deck. The network, however, is transmitting a copy of the broadcast, a use of copyrighted work that is not explicitly allowed by copyright law in most countries. Therefore, unless a user agreement extends the basic rights granted by copyright law, place shifting would be considered to be a questionable practice.

So how about format shifting? Surely, it must be legal to rip tracks from a CD that you own, save them as an MP3 file, and play them on your iPod.

Many consumers believe that format shifting is a legal type of adaptation. That is true for computer software. According to section 117 of the United States Code "it is not an infringement for the owner of a copy of a computer program to make or authorize the making of another copy or adaptation."

It might seem that digital content is similar to computer programs because both are in digital formats that can be manipulated by computers. The courts, however, do not agree that the two are the same, so consumers do not have a right to format-shift movies and music. Copyright holders can, however, allow format shifting for specific works if they choose to do so.

It is interesting to consider the basis for the widely held belief that once a song or video has been purchased, consumers have a right to use it in any manner they please short of redistributing it for profit. Precedents for this belief exist in the music and publishing industries.

Although it is not well known, until 1971 no U.S. law protected recorded music. Sheet music and the underlying composition could be copyrighted, but a particular artist's performance was not. So-called "record pirates" could freely copy, say, an Elvis Presley recording without violating U.S. Federal law until an amendment to the copyright law was passed in 1971.

A statement accompanying the 1971 amendment seemed to approve of copying music for personal use: "Specifically, it is not the intention of Congress to restrain the home recording, from broadcasts or from tapes or records, of recorded performances, where the home recording is for private use and with no purpose of reproducing or otherwise capitalizing commercially on it."

Consumers are also familiar with copyright restrictions on printed books and have an expectation that digital media can be legally used in parallel ways. Readers expect to be able to carry a book with them to any location, read it at any time they like, use any type of reading light or reading glasses, loan the book to friends, and sell the book when they have finished using it. No wonder consumers are peeved when e-book vendors and other digital content providers use DRM technology to limit how much of an e-book can be viewed, whether the text can be printed or shared, and how long it can be viewed.

Although it is convenient to focus on the "once I buy it I can use it as I like" rationale, we tend to ignore situations in which our expectations about content use are more limited. For example, we do not expect that after attending a Widespread Panic concert, we are entitled to a free DVD or video of the performance. If we pay to see a movie at a theater, we don't then expect not to pay for the DVD or soundtrack CD when they are released.

From rock concerts to theaters, consumers are familiar with the idea that different venues and formats might require separate payments. Digital rights management technologies simply enforce this idea in practice.

Advocates of DRM even contend that it broadens the scope of what consumers can do with digital content because EULAs often provide consumers with more flexibility than today's copyright laws.

Circumventing DRM is possible and it would seem okay to do so for legitimate reasons, such as making backup or archival copies. However, the Digital Millennium Copyright Act makes it illegal to circumvent any technological measure that controls access to a work.

The current status of DRM seems to conflict with consumer fair-use expectations for manipulating and copying music, video, and other digital content. DRM technologies are still evolving, however, as are copyright laws. The Digital Millennium Copyright Act undergoes a formal review every three years, and a bill is circulating in Congress to revise the DMCA ban on circumventing DRM protection for noninfringing activities. Let's see whether the future produces a shift in the balance between fair use, digital rights management, and copyright law.

8

**INFOWEBLINKS**

You'll find information related to this controversy at the **Digital Rights Management InfoWeb**.

 CLICK TO CONNECT
www.course.com/np/concepts10/ch08

## What Do You Think?

ISSUE

1. Have you had trouble using software, music CDs, or movie DVDs because of copy protection?

    ○ Yes   ○ No   ○ Not sure

2. In your opinion, do sites like the iTunes Music Store provide consumers with enough flexibility for copying files and creating playlists?

    ○ Yes   ○ No   ○ Not sure

3. Do you think digital rights management technologies are justified because of the high rate of piracy?

    ○ Yes   ○ No   ○ Not sure

▶ SAVE RESPONSES

## COMPUTERS IN CONTEXT

# Film

**IN 1895,** eager Parisians crowded into a busy café to watch the first public presentation of an exciting new invention—the Cinematograph. The 10-minute film, mostly scenes of everyday life, was a smashing success and ushered in the motion picture era. Early films were short, grainy, grayscale, and silent, but technology quickly improved. In the New York debut of *The Jazz Singer* (1927), Al Jolson spoke the first words in a feature film, "Wait a minute, wait a minute. You ain't heard nothin' yet!" The audience rose to its feet, applauding wildly. In 1935, RKO studios released *Becky Sharp*, the first feature-length movie filmed from beginning to end in Technicolor—a real milestone for the film industry.

Even before "talkies" and Technicolor, filmmakers sought ways to escape the bounds of reality through special effects. As early as 1925, directors such as Willis O'Brien used stop-motion photography to animate dinosaurs, giant gorillas, and sword-wielding skeletons. Special-effects technologies—miniatures, blue screens, puppets, claymation, and composite shots—were used with varying degrees of skill over the next 50 years. Films such as Stanley Kubrick's masterpiece, *2001: A Space Odyssey* (1968), and George Lucas's original *Star Wars* (1977) stretched these technologies to their limits, but audiences demanded even more spectacular, yet "realistic," effects.

In 1982, Disney released *TRON*, a movie about a computer programmer who becomes trapped in the depths of a computer where programs are human-like creatures that serve every whim of an evil Master Control Program. The movie included the first primi-

tive attempts at computer-generated footage—30 minutes of computer-generated imagery (CGI) created by two Cray XMP supercomputers.

CGI uses rendering techniques to create a 3-D scene from a 2-D image, a camera angle, and a light source. Sophisticated algorithms determine how textures, colors, and shadows appear in the rendered scene. Camera angles can be changed at will, and fantastic effects can be created by bending or stretching the image, manipulating light, creating textures, and adding movement to the scene.

Rendered scenes can be set in motion with computer animation techniques. Manual animation requires a painstaking process called in-betweening, in which an artist draws a series of incrementally different images to produce the illusion of movement. Computers can easily generate in-between images and free up human animators for more challenging work.

A captivating animation special effect called morphing was first seen on the big screen in James Cameron's *Abyss* (1989) and later used in *Terminator 2* (1991) and other movies. Like in-betweening, morphing starts out with animators defining the morph's start and end points—for example, in *Terminator 2*, the liquid metal face of the T-1000 robot and actor Robert Patrick's face. The start and end points are rendered into digital images, and then the computer generates all the in-between images. Human animators tweak the images by inserting small discrepancies for a touch of less-than-perfect realism in the final image.

Although the process might sound simple, morphing complex objects realistically and believably takes a tremendous amount of time and computer power. The five-minute morphing sequence in *Terminator 2* took special-effects company Industrial Light and Magic a year to create.

Memorable computer-generated scenes from 2002 blockbusters include the breathtaking aerial scenes in *Spiderman*, a furry blue monster called Sully careening downhill in *Monsters, Inc.*, and the endless army of Uruk-hai marching down the valley toward Helm's Deep in *The Two Towers*. Spiderman's acrobatic swing through Manhattan was generated with three professional rendering products: Maya, Houdini, and RenderMan. The Uruk-hai were created with MASSIVE, a custom program that gave each computer-generated warrior a unique sequence of actions. To individually animate each of Sully's 2,320,413 blue hairs, animators developed software called Fizt, a dynamic simulator.

Rendering, morphing, and other special-effects processing require sophisticated computer systems. Pixar Inc., the company that provided the technology behind *Toy Story*, *Shrek*, *Monsters, Inc.*, and many other feature-length animated films, uses a cluster of computers dubbed the "RenderFarm." A movie such as *Toy Story* took more than 800,000 computer hours to produce using the RenderFarm. That might seem like a long time, but if Pixar animators had attempted to use a single-processor computer, it would have taken 43 years to finish the job!

Other CGI variations are being used for increasingly sophisticated effects. Special-effects guru John Gaeta developed bullet time and image-based rendering for *The Matrix* (1999). They have been used for stunning visual effects in movies such as *The Matrix: Reloaded* (2003), *The Matrix: Revolutions* (2003), and *Hero* (2002/2004). Bullet time produces reality-defying action sequences that slow time to a tantalizing crawl and then crank it back up to normal speed as the camera pivots rapidly around the scene. The effect requires a computer to meticulously trigger a circular array of more than 100 still cameras in sequence. Image-based rendering generates a digital image based on photos of objects, scenes, or people. The 2-D photos can be digitally manipulated to create 3-D objects, eliminating the need for conventional CGI's computationally intensive 3-D wireframes and ray tracing.

Films, such as *Sky Captain And The World Of Tomorrow* (2004) and *Sin City* (2005), took green screen special effects to a new level. Filmed entirely indoors on a sound stage, these movies used a tech-

nique called compositing that layers two or more video clips over each other and merges them into one image. Actors were filmed against a green background screen. During post-production, video editing software removed the background and layered in scenery created with CGI or from real footage on location.

*Sin City* is also notable as one of the first fully digital live action motion pictures. It was filmed in full color with high-definition digital cameras. The footage was converted to black and white and then color was reintroduced digitally with the use of a DLP Cinema projector.

Sophisticated animation and rendering techniques now come close to producing realistic human figures. Animations were once clearly two-dimensional and far from lifelike, but CGI renderings are becoming more difficult to distinguish from real actors. What might happen in the future is the subject of *Simone* (2002), starring Al Pacino as a washed-up director who is given a hard disk containing code for a computer-generated movie star. Pacino uses her as the leading lady in a string of hits, all the while keeping her identity secret. According to reviewer Leigh Johnson, it becomes clear that Simone, a computer-generated image, is more authentic than the people watching her. It is one of the film's main themes, expressed by Pacino's character: "Our ability to manufacture fraud now exceeds our ability to detect it."

The implications of computer-generated actors are just emerging. Not only do they blur the line between reality and fiction, but they also raise puzzling questions for actors and their agents, directors, and programmers. Is it possible to create CGI doubles for long-dead actors, such as Marilyn Monroe and James Dean? If so, who controls their use and profits from their work? Can aging actors sign contracts for use of their "young" CGI counterparts? Would it be legal and ethical for programmers to create and market virtual characters based on real actors or a compilation of the best traits of popular stars? As is often the case, new technologies present issues along with their benefits—issues you might want to consider the next time you watch a movie.

**INFOWEBLINKS**

To find more information on this topic, visit the **Computers and Film InfoWeb**.

CLICK TO CONNECT
www.course.com/np/concepts10/ch08

8

# New Perspectives Labs

## On the BookOnCD

To access the New Perspectives labs for Chapter 8, start the BookOnCD, BookOnFlashDrive, or other NP10 BookOn product and then click the icon next to the lab title below.

▶ **WORKING WITH BITMAP GRAPHICS**

### IN THIS LAB YOU'LL LEARN:

- How to identify common bitmap graphics file extensions
- How to capture an image from the Web
- How to find the properties of a graphic
- How to eliminate red eye and manipulate brightness, contrast, and sharpness of photos
- How to make a photo look "old"
- How to select a palette and apply a dithering technique
- How to prepare graphics for the Web and e-mail attachments
- The effects of lossy compression

### LAB ASSIGNMENTS

1. Start the interactive part of the lab. Make sure you've enabled Tracking if you want to save your QuickCheck results. Perform each lab step as directed, and answer all the lab QuickCheck questions. When you exit the lab, your answers are automatically graded and your results are displayed.

2. Use the Start button to access the Programs menu for the computer you typically use. Make a list of the available bitmap graphics software.

3. Capture a photographic image from a digital camera, scanner, or Web page. Save it as "MyGraphic." Open the image using any available graphics software. Use this software to discover the properties of the graphic. Indicate the source of the graphic, and then describe its file format, file size, resolution, and color depth.

4. Prepare this graphics file to send to a friend as an e-mail attachment that is smaller than 200 KB. Describe the steps that were required.

5. Suppose you want to post this image on a Web page. Make the necessary adjustments to file size and color depth. Describe the resulting graphic in terms of its resolution, color depth, palette, and dithering.

▶ **VIDEO EDITING**

### IN THIS LAB YOU'LL LEARN:

- How to identify and use the basic tools provided by video editing software
- How to select clips for a video and arrange them on the timeline
- How to add transitions
- What sound formats are acceptable for video sound clips
- How to select sound clips for a video and arrange them on the timeline
- How to preview a video
- How to identify popular video formats and codecs
- How characteristics such as frame rate, frame size, sound sampling, and codecs affect file size
- How to specify a codec and other video attributes
- How to find out which video players are installed on a computer
- How to find the properties of a Web-based video
- The differences between streaming and non-streaming video formats

### LAB ASSIGNMENTS

1. Start the interactive part of the lab. Perform each lab step as directed, and answer all the lab QuickCheck questions.

2. Use the Control Panel's Add or Remove Programs icon to make a list of the video players available on your computer.

3. Locate a video clip on the Web and indicate the URL of the Web page on which it can be found. Describe the video's properties, including file size and format.

4. Play the video you located for Lab Assignment #3. Describe the video's visual and sound qualities, and discuss how they relate to your Internet connection speed. Also, describe the length and content of the video, the use of transitions or special effects (if any), and the use of sound tracks. If you could edit this video yourself, what changes would you make to produce a more effective video?

# Key Terms

Make sure you understand all the boldfaced key terms presented in this chapter. If you're using the NP10 BookOnCD, BookOnFlashDrive, or other NP10 BookOn product, you can use this list of terms as an interactive study activity. First, try to define a term in your own words, and then click the term to compare your definition with the definition presented in the chapter.

24-bit bitmap, 437
32-bit bitmap, 437
3-D graphics, 449
AAC, 424
AACS, 469
AIFF, 424
Analog hole, 464
Analog protection system, 468
Animated GIF, 448
ASF, 457
Audio compression, 423
Authorization and revocation, 469
AVI, 457
Bitmap graphic, 430
BMP, 442
Broadcast flag, 465
Codec, 458
Color palette, 437
Container formats, 457
Copy generation management, 467
Copy protection, 466
Cropping, 435
CSS, 468
DeCSS, 468
Desktop video, 452
Digital audio, 422
Digital camera, 431
Digital content, 464
Digital rights management, 464
Digital signal processor, 424
Digital video, 452
Digital video recorder, 455
Digital watermark, 465
Digitizing tablet, 446
Drawing software, 446
DRM individualization, 470
DVD image, 462

DVD-Video, 452
FairPlay, 470
File compression utility, 440
Flash, 448
Flash Video, 457
Format shifting, 465
Frame rate, 456
GIF, 442
Gradient, 447
Grayscale palette, 438
Image compression, 439
JPEG, 442
Key frame, 458
Linear editing, 456
Lossless compression, 439
Lossy compression, 439
Megapixel, 433
Metafile, 447
MIDI, 426
MIDI sequence, 426
Monochrome bitmap, 436
MP3, 424
MPEG, 457
Nonlinear editing, 456
Paint software, 430
PCX, 442
PDA video, 452
Phoneme, 428
Pixel interpolation, 435
Pixelated, 435
Place shifting, 465
PNG, 443
Portable audio player, 425
QuickTime Movie, 457
Rasterization, 447
RAW, 442
Ray tracing, 449

RealAudio, 424
RealMedia, 457
Region code, 468
Rendering, 449
Resolution dependent, 435
Run-length encoding, 439
Sampling rate, 423
Scanner, 431
Signal scrambling, 465
Sound card, 423
Speech recognition, 428
Speech synthesis, 428
Streaming audio, 425
Streaming video, 459
Super distribution, 471
SVG, 448
Synthesized sound, 426
System palette, 438
Temporal compression, 458
Text-to-speech software, 428
TIFF, 442
Time shifting, 465
Tracing software, 447
True Color bitmap, 437
Vector graphic, 444
Video capture, 454
Videoconferencing camera, 453
VOB, 457
Wave, 424
Wavetable, 426
Web palette, 438
Web-based video, 452
Windows Media DRM, 470
Wireframe, 449
WMA, 424

8

# Interactive Summary

To review important concepts from this chapter, fill in the blanks to best complete each sentence. When using the NP10 BookOnCD or other BookOn product, click the Check Answers buttons to automatically score your answers.

**SECTION A:** Music, voice, and sound effects can all be recorded and digitally stored as [＿＿＿＿] audio. To digitally record sound, [＿＿＿＿] of the sound are collected at periodic intervals and stored as numeric data. High-quality sound is usually sampled at 44.1 [＿＿＿＿], and each stereo sample requires 32 bits of storage space. To conserve space, radio-quality recordings of speaking voices are often recorded at lower sampling rates. A computer's [＿＿＿＿] card is responsible for transforming the bits stored in an audio file into music, sound effects, and narrations. It contains digital [＿＿＿＿] processing circuitry that transforms bits into analog sound, records analog sounds as digital bits, and handles audio compression. Digital audio file formats include Wave, Audio Interchange Format, RealAudio, AAC, WMA, and MP3. Most portable audio players work with digital audio formats, such as [＿＿＿＿], used by the iTunes Music Store.

MIDI music is [＿＿＿＿] sound that is artificially created. Unlike digital audio sound files, which contain digitized recordings of real sound passages, MIDI files contain [＿＿＿＿] for creating the pitch, volume, and duration of notes made by musical instruments. MIDI files are typically much smaller than digital audio files for similar musical passages, so they are ideal for Web pages. However, MIDI music tends to lack the full resonance of symphony-quality sound that can be achieved with digital audio. Speech [＿＿＿＿] is the process by which machines, such as computers, produce sound that resembles spoken words. Speech [＿＿＿＿] refers to the ability of machines to "understand" spoken words.

▶ CHECK ANSWERS

**SECTION B:** A [＿＿＿＿] graphic is composed of a grid of dots, and the color of each dot is stored as a binary number. Both scanners and cameras produce images in bitmap format. The dimensions of the grid that forms a bitmap graphic is referred to as its [＿＿＿＿]. High-resolution graphics typically produce better image quality than low-resolution graphics, but require more storage space. It is possible to change the resolution and/or the file size of a bitmap graphic, but because bitmaps are resolution [＿＿＿＿], these changes can reduce image quality. For example, enlarging a bitmap requires your computer to fill in missing pixels, which often results in a jagged or [＿＿＿＿] image. As a general rule, images that you intend to print should remain at full size and resolution. When sending bitmap files as e-mail attachments, they can be [＿＿＿＿] in size or resolution to produce a file that is less than 500 KB.

Color [＿＿＿＿] refers to the number of colors available for use in an image. For example, a bitmap graphic composed of 256 colors requires only [＿＿＿＿] bits to store the data for each pixel, whereas 24 bits are required for each pixel in a [＿＿＿＿] Color graphic. Grayscale, system, and Web palettes use eight bits to represent each pixel. Image [＿＿＿＿] shrinks the size of a graphics file. [＿＿＿＿] compression permanently removes data, but [＿＿＿＿] compression shrinks files without removing any data. Popular bitmap graphics formats include BMP, PCX, TIFF, GIF, JPEG, RAW, and PNG. Of these formats, GIF, JPEG, and PNG are supported by most Web browsers.

▶ CHECK ANSWERS

**SECTION C:** Unlike a bitmap graphic, created by superimposing a grid of pixels over an image, a [＿＿＿＿＿] graphic consists of a set of instructions for creating a picture. These graphics are created by using a type of graphics software called [＿＿＿＿＿] software. They are stored as a collection of [＿＿＿＿＿] and their corresponding sizes, colors, and positions. You can identify these graphics by their flat cartoon-like appearance and their file extensions: .wmf, .dxt, .mgx, .eps, .pict, and .cgm. A vector graphic can be converted into a bitmap by a process called [＿＿＿＿＿]. Once converted, however, the resulting graphic loses the object-editing qualities it had in its vector state. Two vector graphics formats, [＿＿＿＿＿] and Flash, are popular for Web-based graphics. 3-D graphics are stored as a set of instructions that contain the locations and lengths of lines that form a [＿＿＿＿＿] for a 3-D object. These lines form a framework that can be covered by colored, patterned, and textured surfaces. This process, called [＿＿＿＿＿], produces a bitmap image of the 3-D object. [＿＿＿＿＿] tracing adds highlights and shadows to the image. 3-D graphics can be animated to produce special effects for movies and animated characters for 3-D computer games.

▶ CHECK ANSWERS

**SECTION D:** Videos that are constructed and played on a personal computer are called [＿＿＿＿＿] videos. Video footage is typically stored on a computer's [＿＿＿＿＿] disk for editing, and then it can be transferred to CDs, DVDs, or videotape. A video is composed of a series of bitmap graphics. Each one is called a [＿＿＿＿＿]. Popular desktop video file [＿＿＿＿＿] include AVI, QuickTime, MPEG, RealMedia, WMV, ASF, and VOB. When video footage is filmed using an analog camera, it can be converted into digital format by a video [＿＿＿＿＿] device. Footage from a digital video camera requires no conversion and can be streamed directly from camera to computer through a serial, [＿＿＿＿＿], or USB port. Raw video footage contains a huge amount of data. The size of a video file can be reduced by three techniques: shrinking the size of the video window, reducing the [＿＿＿＿＿] rate, and [＿＿＿＿＿] the video data. A [＿＿＿＿＿] is the software or hardware that compresses and decompresses files, such as graphics and videos. Videos can be added to Web pages by using techniques such as [＿＿＿＿＿] video, which transmits the first segment of a video, begins to play it, and then continues to transfer additional segments. Digital videos can be transferred to DVDs, which use files in the [＿＿＿＿＿] format.

▶ CHECK ANSWERS

**SECTION E:** Digital [＿＿＿＿＿] management is a collection of techniques used by copyright holders to limit access to and use of digital content. DRM technologies can limit or prevent convenient [＿＿＿＿＿], place, and format shifting. A digital [＿＿＿＿＿] is a DRM technology that is inserted into the content stream in such a way that it is imperceptible to users, but can be recognized by complying devices. Copy [＿＿＿＿＿] DRM for CDs depends on intentionally [＿＿＿＿＿] data and CD-based software. The major DRM technology to protect DVD content called [＿＿＿＿＿] was cracked shortly after it was introduced. A more sophisticated DRM technology called [＿＿＿＿＿] is used on Blu-ray and HD-DVD. The concept of authorization and [＿＿＿＿＿] can be applied to hardware devices and software players to give licensing bodies the means to keep non-complying players off the market and deny further access to complying devices that have become compromised. Content downloaded from online music and video stores is heavily protected by DRM technologies, such as Apple's [＿＿＿＿＿] and Microsoft's Windows Media DRM.

▶ CHECK ANSWERS

8

# Interactive Situation Questions

Apply what you've learned to some typical computing situations. When using the NP10 BookOnCD, BookOnFlashDrive, or any other NP10 BookOn product, you can type your answers, and then use the Check Answers button to automatically score your responses.

1. Suppose you are creating an English-as-a-Second-Language Web page and you want to add links to sound files that pronounce English phrases. Would it be better to store the files in Wave or MIDI format? [          ]

2. Imagine that you're a musician and you are asked to synthesize some music for the opening screen of a Web site. For this project, you would most likely work with [          ] music.

3. Suppose you visit a Web site that allows you to enter sentences, and then it reads the sentences back to you. The site even gives you a choice of a female or male voice. You assume that this site uses speech [          ] technology.

4. You have an old photograph that you want to incorporate in a brochure for your antiques business. To convert the photo into digital format, you use a(n) [          ].

5. Imagine that you are preparing a series of bitmap graphics for a Web site. To decrease the download time for each graphic, you can remove pixels or reduce the color [          ].

6. You've taken a photo with a high resolution digital camera and you want to send it as an e-mail attachment. You decide to use PKZIP to [          ] the image into a more manageable size.

7. Suppose you are designing a logo for a client. You know the design will undergo several revisions, and you understand

that the logo will be used at various sizes. You decide it would be best to use drawing software to create the logo as a(n) [          ] graphic.

8. After you finish arranging video clips and adding a soundtrack, you can select a video file format and a compression technique. For example, you might store the video in AVI container format and use the Cinepak [          ] to compress the file.

9. After purchasing a CD of your favorite rock group you try to rip one of the tracks to your computer and convert it to MP3 format. When you play the file on your computer, you notice loud pops in the audio that indicate that the CD was probably copy [          ].

10. You receive an e-mail attachment from a friend containing a music video from the Zune site. Accessing the file after paying for your own license is an example of [          ] distribution.

 CHECK ANSWERS

# Interactive Practice Tests

Practice tests that consist of 10 multiple-choice, true/false, and fill-in-the-blank questions are available on both the NP10 BookOn products and the NP10 Web site. The questions are selected at random from a large test bank, so each time you take a test, you'll receive a different set of questions. Your tests are scored immediately, and you can print study guides that help you find the correct answers for any questions that you missed.

 CLICK TO START

# Study Tips

Study Tips help you to organize and consolidate the information in a unit by making lists, outlines, charts, and sketches. You can use paper and pencil or word processing software to complete most of the Study Tip activities.

1. Make sure you can use your own words to correctly answer each of the red focus questions that appear throughout the chapter.

2. Make a list of 10 digital audio applications and indicate whether each one would use Wave or MIDI.

3. Make a list of the file extensions that were mentioned in this chapter and group them according to digital media type: bitmap graphic, vector graphic, digital video, digital audio, and MIDI. Circle any formats that are used on the Web.

4. Make a list of the software mentioned in this chapter, indicating the type of task that it helps you accomplish.

5. Describe the devices that transfer photos from a digital camera to a computer.

6. Describe how resolution and color depth contribute to the size of a graphics file.

7. Summarize how you would prepare bitmap graphics for the following uses: e-mail attachment, Web page, desktop publishing, and printed photo.

8. Explain how a computer monitor displays color, and how that relates to the way it stores a color palette.

9. Explain how the concept of layering relates to your ability to modify a vector graphic.

10. Make a list of the advantages and disadvantages of bitmaps and vector graphics.

11. Make a series of quick sketches that illustrates the evolution of a 3-D graphic from wireframe to rendered image, and to ray-traced image.

12. Explain the different procedures required to transfer analog or digital video from camera to computer.

13. Define the differences between linear and non-linear editing.

14. List three ways in which you can reduce the file size of a desktop video.

15. Explain how streaming audio and video work, and contrast them to non-streaming technology.

16. Use your own words to make a list of the steps required to burn video onto a DVD that can be viewed on standalone DVD players.

17. In your own words describe each type of compression mentioned in the chapter.

18. Explain how specific DRM technologies are used to prevent consumers from a) recording television broadcasts, b) making a copy of a music CD, c) ripping tracks from a music CD, d) copying a DVD movie, and e) watching a movie captured on TiVo and streamed over a network to a PC.

19. Fill in the blanks on the concept map shown below to show the hierarchy of digital media described in this chapter.

8

# Concept Map

CHECK ANSWERS

# Projects

 ## CRITICAL THINKING

Copyright laws are changing as digital sound, image, and video technologies evolve and become easier to use. Although the courts seem to clearly hold that it is illegal to copy media for profit, they are not as clear about the acceptability of modifications. For example, video editing software makes it relatively simple for people to clip out parts of movies they find to be objectionable for themselves or their children. Should it be legal to do so for personal use? What if an organization wanted to rent out such edited copies? What if DVD players and movies were set up so that the devices would edit and display the revised version on the fly? After you consider your own opinion, you might check the Web to see the latest information about this issue.

 ## GROUP PROJECT

Work with a group of four students to research Web-based music download sites. Create one PowerPoint slide for each site. The slide should give a basic overview of the site, including its name, URL, price, pros, and cons. For the final slide in the presentation, create a table comparing the features and prices of each site.

 ## CYBERCLASSROOM

Each person on your team should e-mail a photo in JPEG format to the other members of the group. The photo can be one you've taken or one you find on the Web. If you get your photo from the Web, make sure there are no prohibitions for using it for a personal project and keep track of the Web site so you have a record of your source. When you receive the photos from your teammates, be creative and use Photoshop or similar photo editing software to create a composite image that contains elements from all the photos. Submit your original photo and your composite photo to your instructor.

 ## MULTIMEDIA PROJECT

Use Windows Sound Recorder or similar software to record your own 15-second radio ad for your favorite music or video download service. Submit the text of your script along with the .wav file containing your ad.

 ## RESUME BUILDER

Artists routinely create a portfolio containing examples of their best work. How can you apply the portfolio concept to your job search? Suppose you've decided to create a multimedia portfolio that showcases your talents. Describe what you'd like your portfolio to contain, indicating which of the items you currently have and which you'd like to create and add in the future. Also, describe the format for each item: photo, document, scan, audio, or video. Finally, describe whether you envision delivering your portfolio on CD or the Web, and then discuss the advantages and limitations of your choice.

 ## GLOBALIZATION

The United States has been accused of exporting its culture and values through films and television. Sometimes referred to as Coca Colonization, the mass exportation of American culture is expected to increase as more and more people have access to the Internet. But is digital distribution a two-way street? What can you find out about the *importation* of cultures to the United States (or your country)? Incorporate your findings into a two-page paper. Make sure you cite specific examples and offer your ideas on how technology aids or discourages cross cultural interchanges. Include a list of references on a third page.

 ## ISSUE

The Issue section of this chapter focused on digital rights controversies, such as your rights to share music files, copy DVD movies, or use software to break copy protection. To begin the project, consult the Digital Rights Management InfoWeb and link to the recommended Web sites to get an in-depth overview of the issues. With this background, work with a partner and select a digital rights controversy that seems interesting. Use the Web to research the controversy. Collaborate with your partner to write a dialog between two people who are arguing both sides of the issue.

 ## COMPUTERS IN CONTEXT

The Computers in Context section of this chapter focused on digital special effects technology used in recent films. For this project, conduct your own exploration of the special effects that have appeared in your favorite movies. To begin the project, browse through the material presented in the Computers and Film InfoWeb on page 475. Look for information about specific movies using Web sites such as the Internet movie database (*www.imdb.com*). Many movies also have dedicated Web sites that you can find using a search engine. To complete the project, select one of your favorite movies and write a two- to four-page movie review that focuses on how its special effects contribute to the movie's overall quality.

# On the Web

## STUDENT EDITION LABS

**W CLICK TO ACCESS THE NP10 WEB SITE**
or open your browser and connect to www.course.com/np/concepts10/ch08. Lab results can be stored in the Universal Gradebook.

Work hands-on in structured simulations practicing important skills and concepts

## WORKING WITH GRAPHICS

In the Working with Graphics Student Edition Lab, you will learn the following topics and skills:

- Downloading images from the Web
- Enhancing an image with filters and manipulating brightness, contrast, and sharpness
- Incorporating type in an image and working with layers
- Cropping vs. resizing and reducing file size
- Creating Web graphics

## WORKING WITH VIDEO

In the Working with Video Student Edition Lab, you will learn the following topics and skills:

- Viewing digital video
- Importing and working with clips
- Using the storyboard
- Adding transitions and including audio
- Saving the video

## WORKING WITH AUDIO

In the Working with Audio Student Edition Lab, you will learn the following topics and skills:

- Audio file formats and extensions
- Importing and downloading audio files
- Burning audio CDs
- Including audio files on a Web site

8

## CHAPTER COURSECAST

Use your computer or iPod to hear a five-minute audio presentation of chapter highlights.

## FLASHCARD COURSECAST

Interact with audio flashcards to review key terms from the chapter.

## DETAILED OBJECTIVES

Make sure that you've achieved all the objectives for a chapter before it's time for your test!

## TEST YOURSELF

Review chapter material by taking these ten-question tests, then send your results to the Universal Gradebook.

## ONLINE GAMES

Have some fun while refreshing your memory about key concepts that might appear on the next test. You can even send your results to the Universal Gradebook!

## AND MORE!

At the NP10 Web site you'll also find TechBuzz, CNET videos, Extra Content, and InfoWebLinks.

# QUICK CHECK ANSWERS

## ORIENTATION

**QuickCheck A**
1. unit
2. Start
3. False
4. Backspace
5. menu

**QuickCheck B**
1. Save
2. browser
3. search
4. @
5. account

**QuickCheck C**
1. False
2. security
3. Spyware
4. spam

**QuickCheck D**
1. Annotation
2. False
3. labs
4. Tracking

**QuickCheck E**
1. True
2. home
3. Overview
4. Labs

## CHAPTER 1

**QuickCheck A**
1. Internet
2. networks
3. Cyberspace
4. digitization
5. convergence

**QuickCheck B**
1. output
2. False
3. stored
4. supercomputer
5. microcontroller

**QuickCheck C**
1. digital
2. binary
3a. ASCII
3b. binary
4. gigabyte
5. integrated

**QuickCheck D**
1. source
2. object
3. operands
4. arithmetic
5. control

**QuickCheck E**
1. authentication
2. independent
3. keylogger
4. True
5. password

## CHAPTER 2

**QuickCheck A**
1. peripheral
2. desktop
3. tablet computers
4. media
5. compatible

**QuickCheck B**
1. clock
2. processor
3. bus
4. core
5. volatile
6. virtual
7. EEPROM

**QuickCheck C**
1. Access
2a. direct
2b. sequential
3. density
4. head
5. crashes
6. lands
7. True
8. state

**QuickCheck D**
1. pointing
2. refresh
3. resolution
4. duplex
5. slots
6. USB

**QuickCheck E**
1. Slot
2. surge
3. battery
4. death
5. Safe

## CHAPTER 3

**QuickCheck A**
1. system
2. productivity
3. groupware
4. utility
5. driver

**QuickCheck B**
1. document
2. False
3. spreadsheet
4. Database
5. ripper
6. DVD

**QuickCheck C**
1. suite
2. requirements
3. False
4. Public
5. concurrent
6. Open

**QuickCheck D**
1. executable
2. local
3. True
4. Portable
5. patch

**QuickCheck E**
1. blended
2. viruses
3. worm
4. rootkit
5. quarantines

## CHAPTER 4

**QuickCheck A**
1. resources
2. memory, RAM
3. kernel
4. bootstrap
5. interface

**QuickCheck B**
1. False
2. backward
3. dual
4. virtual
5. fork
6. Linux
7. True

**QuickCheck C**
1. conventions
2. True
3. C:
4. subdirectories
5. folders
6. size
7. header
8. native

**QuickCheck D**
1. Save
2. metaphor, model
3. Explorer
4a. tracks
4b. sectors
5. shredder

**QuickCheck E**
1. Registry
2. folder
3. external
4. incremental
5. recovery

## CHAPTER 5

**QuickCheck A**
1. interface
2. False
3. protocols
4a. packet
4b. circuit
5. IP

**QuickCheck B**
1. Ethernet
2. True
3. 100
4. hub
5. router

**QuickCheck C**
1. Wi-Fi
2. Bluetooth
3. ad-hoc
4. infrastructure
5. SSID

**QuickCheck D**
1. resources
2. root
3. driver
4. file
5. application

**QuickCheck E**
1a. WEP
1b. WPA2
2. Symmetric
3. Public
4. PGP

## CHAPTER 6

**QuickCheck A**
1. backbone
2. ISP
3a. TCP
3b. IP
4a. static
4b. dynamic
5. domain
6. .edu
7. True

**QuickCheck B**
1. voiceband
2. False
3. Ethernet
4. latency
5. WiMAX

**QuickCheck C**
1. Portable
2. hotspot
3. WiMAX
4. WAP
5. EDGE

**QuickCheck D**
1. chat
2. False
3. grid
4. FTP
5. BitTorrent

**QuickCheck E**
1. ports
2. patches
3. Firewall
4. router
5. private

## CHAPTER 7

**QuickCheck A**
1. link
2. space
3. browser
4. helper
5. stateless
6. True
7. certificates

**QuickCheck B**
1. crawler or spider
2. stuffing
3. False
4. Boolean
5. False
6. citation

**QuickCheck C**
1. True
2. True
3. clickthrough
4. cookies
5. False

**QuickCheck D**
1. @
2. MIME
3. HTML
4. forward
5a. SMTP
5b. POP

**QuickCheck E**
1. proxy
2. Flash
3. bug
4. Pharming
5. filter
6. False

## CHAPTER 8

**QuickCheck A**
1a. MP3, MP4, WMA
1b. MIDI
2. sampling
3. AAC
4. playlist
5. recognition

**QuickCheck B**
1. FireWire, IEEE 1394
2. resolution
3. dependent
4. grayscale
5. TIFF
6. GIF
7a. Lossy
7b. lossless

**QuickCheck C**
1. True
2. drawing
3. wireframe
4. tracing
5. rasterization
6. SWF, Flash

**QuickCheck D**
1. Desktop
2. capture
3. frame
4. False
5. False
6. streaming
7. VOB, Video Object

**QuickCheck E**
1. Time
2. watermark
3. protected
4. CSS
5. individualization
6. super

# CREDITS

Figure 5-20, Courtesy of Linksys

Figure 5-25, Courtesy of Dell Inc

Figure 5-27, Courtesy of Bluetooth SIG

Figure 5-28, Courtesy of Motorola

Figure 5-27b, Courtesy of Nokia

Figure 5-30, Courtesy of D-Link Systems

Figure 5-33a, Courtesy of Nokia

Figure 5-33c, Courtesy of NETGEAR, Inc.

Figure 5-39, © Steve Chenn/CORBIS

Figure 5-40a, Courtesy of Sonos, Inc.

Figure 5-40b, Courtesy of D-Link Systems

Figure 5-40c, Courtesy of Toshiba America Information Systems

Figure 5-44b, Courtesy of Intel Corporation

Figure 5-48, AP Images

Figure 5-54, © A. Ramey/Photo Edit— all rights reserved.

Issue-5a, Courtesy of Ken Pau and Stone Creek Coffee Company

Issue-5b, Courtesy of Rob Flickenger
(http://www.oreillynet.com/pub/wlg/448)

CinC-5a, Photography courtesy of the University of Illinois at
Urbana-Champaign Archives

CinC-5b, © Tom Stewart/CORBIS

Figure 6-01, Computer History Museum

Figure 6-06, Courtesy of DNSstuff.com

Figure 6-14, Courtesy of Zyxel

Figure 6-16a, Courtesy of 2Wire.com

Figure 6-16b, Courtesy of Zoom Technologies

Figure 6-20, © Siri Stafford/Getty Images

Figure 6-20, © Bryce Kroll /iStockphoto.com

Figure 6-20, © Jonathan Ling/iStockphoto.com

Figure 6-21, Courtesy of Hughes Network Systems, LLC

Figure 6-22, Courtesy of Intel Corporation

Figure 6-24, Cracker Barrel Old Country Store, Inc.

Figure 6-25, Royalty-Free/CORBIS

Figure 6-26, Siemens Press Photo

Figure 6-27, Courtesy of Ground Control

Figure 6-28, Courtesy of Ground Control

Figure 6-31, Opera Software ASA

Figure 6-33, Courtesy of Kyocera-Wireless

Figure 6-34, photo BenQ Mobile

Figure 6-36, Courtesy of Microsoft Corporation

Figure 6-38, AP Images

Figure 6-40, SETI@home

Figure 6-41 a, Courtesy of Chessbrain.net

Figure 6-41 b, Courtesy of www.climateprediction.net

Figure 6-41 c, Courtesy of distributed.net

Figure 6-41 d, Courtesy of Vijay Pande, Folding@Home, and
Standord University http://folding.stanford.edu

Figure 6-41 e, Courtesy of NASA/JPL-Caltech

Figure 6-46, © Paul Edmondson/Getty Images

Figure 6-47, Courtesy of Gibson Research Corporation

Issue-6b, © Steve Allen/Getty Images

CinC-6a, © H.F. Davis/ Getty Images

CinC-6b, © Royalty-Free/CORBIS

Figure 7-01, Courtesy of Ted Nelson, Project Xanadu

Figure 7-18, Courtesy of Ben Samuels

Figure 7-27a, Eric Bean/Getty Images

Figure 7-27b, Don Farrall/Getty Images

Figure 7-27c, Ryan McVay/Getty Images

Figure 7-27d, © S.T. Yiap / Alamy

Figure 7-27e, © Comstock Images / Alamy

Figure 7-29, © Nicholas DeVore/Getty Images

Figure 7-47a, Courtesy of Webroot Software

Figure 7-47b, Courtesy of Computer Associates

Figure 7-47c, Courtesy of Zone Alarm

Issue-7a, © Ron Chapple/Getty Images

Issue-7b, © Dennis MacDonald/PhotoEdit

CinC-7a, Courtesy of ArahWeave www.arahne.si and fabric
courtesy of MTT Maribor

CinC-7b, Courtesy of Scott Jordan of SCOTTeVEST

Figure 8-05, Courtesy of Microsoft Corporation

Figure 8-06, Courtesy of Apple Computer, Inc.

Figure 8-09, © Photodisc/Getty Images

Figure 8-14a, Courtesy of SanDisk Corporation

Figure 8-14b, Courtesy of SanDisk Corporation

Figure 8-14c, Courtesy of SanDisk Corporation

Figure 8-14d, Courtesy of SanDisk Corporation

Figure 8-14e, Courtesy of Hitachi Global Storage Technologies

Figure 8-28, Courtesy of Learning Technology Services, University
of Wisconsin-Stout

Figure 8-40, © Rodolfo Arpia / Alamy

Figure 8-43, © Corbis Premium Collection / Alamy

Figure 8-54, © Getty Images

Figure 8-56, Courtesy of Sling Media, Inc.

Issue-8a, Victor Spinelli/www.photomilennium.com

CinC-8a, © Peter DaSilva/CORBIS SYGMA

CinC-8b, © CORBIS/SYGMA

# GLOSSARY

**24-bit bitmap** A True Color graphic, which requires 24 bits for each pixel, used for photographic-quality images that can include any of 16.7 million colors. 437

**3-D graphics** A type of digital graphics format that displays a three-dimensional image on a two-dimensional space. 449

**3-D graphics software** The software used to create three-dimensional wireframe objects, then render them into images. 137

**32-bit bitmap** A graphical image which requires 32 bits for each pixel. 437

**AAC** (Advanced Audio Compression) A file format that provides highly compressed audio files with very little loss of sound quality and is promoted by Apple on its iTunes Web site. 424

**AACS** (Advanced Access Content System) A digital rights management system that uses encryption to restrict access and copying content from optical media. 469

**Absolute reference** In a worksheet formula, cell references (usually preceded by a $ symbol) that cannot change as a result of a move or copy operation. 132

**Access time** The estimated time for a storage device to locate data on a disk, usually measured in milliseconds. 77

**Accounting software** A category of software that includes accounting, money management, and tax preparation software. 142

**ActiveX control** A set of commands and components that can be used by programmers to add interactive features to Web pages. 372

**Ad-blocking software** A type of software that prevents ads from appearing on your computer screen. 385

**Ad-serving cookie** A cookie installed by a marketing firm to track user activities on Web sites containing their ads. 400

**AES** (Advanced Encryption Standard) An encryption standard that uses three separate key sizes and is based on the Rijndael encryption algorithm. 285

**AGP** (Accelerated Graphics Port) A type of interface, or slot, that provides a high-speed pathway for advanced graphics. 96

**AIFF** (Audio Interchange File Format) An audio file format developed by Apple that is popular for cross-platform use. 424

**Ajax** An approach to developing interactive Web sites that uses tools such as JavaScript and XML. 362

**ALU** (Arithmetic Logic Unit) The part of the CPU that performs arithmetic and logical operations on the numbers stored in its registers. 31

**Always-on connection** In the context of Internet access, a permanent connection, as opposed to a connection that is established and dropped as needed. 307

**Analog data** Data that is measured or represented on a continuously varying scale, such as a dimmer switch or a watch with a sweep second hand. 22

**Analog hole** Any device or technique that allows digital content to be copied legally or illegally from an analog device. 464

**Analog protection system** (APS) A DVD copy prevention technology developed by Macromedia that scrambles data copied to video tape. 468

**Animated GIF** A type of GIF image that displays a sequence of frames to create the appearance of continuous motion. 448

**Anonymizer tools** Software and/or hardware that cloaks the origination of an e-mail or Web page request. 10

**Anonymous FTP** A type of FTP access that requires no account on a server, but rather can be accessed using "anonymous" as the user ID. 337

**Anonymous proxy service** A server on the Internet that can be used to forward Web requests after cloaking the originating address for users who want to surf anonymously. 403

**Antispyware** Software that blocks spyware from entering a computer. 402

**Antivirus software** A computer program used to scan a computer's memory and disks to identify, isolate, and eliminate viruses. 167

**Application server** A computer on a network that is dedicated to running applications and delivering applications to client computers. 249

**Application software** Computer programs that help you perform a specific task such as word processing. Also called application programs, applications, or programs. 16

**ASCII** (American Standard Code for Information Interchange) A code that represents characters as a series of 1s and 0s. Most computers use ASCII code to represent text, making it possible to transfer data between computers. 24

**ASF** (Advanced System Format) Microsoft's proprietary container format for streaming digital multimedia; typically holds WMV and WMA files. 457

**Asymmetric Internet connection** Any connection to the Internet in which the upstream speed differs from the downstream speed. 311

**ATA** (Analog Telephone Adapter) A device used with VoIP systems to convert analog voice signals from a standard telephone into digital data. 332

**Atom** A syndicated data feed technology for the Web similar to RSS. 360

**Audio compression** Techniques used to reduce the size of files that contain audio data. 423

**Audio editing software** A program that enables users to create and edit digital voice and music recordings. 139

**Audio encoding software** A computer program designed to convert sound files into a digital sound format, such as MP3 or AAC. 139

**Authentication protocol** Passwords, user IDS, and biometric measures used to verify a person's identity. 34

**Authorization and revocation** A component of digital rights management that can be used to disable compromised players. 469

**Automatic recalculation** A feature found in spreadsheet software that automatically recalculates every formula after a user makes a change to any cell. 132

**AVI** (Audio Video Interleave) A video file format, developed by Microsoft, that was once the most common format for desktop video on the PC. 457

**B2B** (Business-to-Business) An e-commerce exchange of products, services, or information between businesses. 384

**B2C** (Business-to-Consumer) An e-commerce exchange of products, services, or information between businesses and consumers. 384

**B2G** (Business-to-Government) An e-commerce exchange of products, services, or information between businesses and governments. 384

**Backup** A duplicate copy of a file, disk, or tape. Also refers to a Windows utility that allows you to create and restore backups. 222

**Backup software** A set of utility programs that performs a variety of backup related tasks, such as helping users select files for backup. 226

**Backward compatibility** The ability to work with products designed for prior generations of the product. 198

**Bandwidth** The data transmission capacity of a communications channel. Digital signals are measured in bits per second, analog signals in Hertz. 251

**Banner ad** A type of advertisement typically embedded at the top of a Web page. 385

**Benchmarks** A set of tests used to measure computer hardware or software performance. 69

**Binary number system** A method for representing numbers using only two digits, 0 and 1. Contrast to the decimal number system, which uses ten digits: 0, 1, 2, 3, 4, 5, 6, 7, 8, and 9. 23

**Biometrics** The use of physical attributes such as a fingerprint to verify a person's identity. 34

**Bit** The smallest unit of information handled by a computer. A bit is one of two values, either a 0 or a 1. Eight bits comprise a byte, which can represent a letter or number. 23

**Bitmap graphic** An image, such as a digital photo, that is stored as a grid work of colored dots. 430

**BitTorrent** A peer-to-peer technology in which pieces of files are distributed to and from a collection of networked computers; used for distributing music and movies over the Internet. 338

**Blended threat** A combination of more than one type of malicious program. 162

**Blogs** (WeB LOG) A publicly-accessible personal journal posted on the Web. Blogs often reflect the personality of the author and are typically updated daily. 6

**Blu-ray DVD** A high-capacity DVD that holds up to 25 GB per layer; also called Blu-ray Discs or BDs. 81

**Blue screen of death** An error condition in which a PC "freezes" and displays a blue screen; usually turning the computer off and turning it on again clears the error. 103

**Bluetooth** A wireless technology used in conjunction with standard Ethernet networks that allows data transfer rates between 200 and 700 Kbps up to a maximum range of 35 feet. 267

**BMP** The native bitmap graphic file format of the Microsoft Windows OS. 442

**Boolean operator** A logical search operator such as AND, OR, and NOT that helps form complex queries. 379

**Boot disk** A floppy disk or CD that contains the files needed for the boot process. 228

**Boot process** The sequence of events that occurs within a computer system between the time the user starts the computer and the time it is ready to process commands. 192

**Bootstrap program** A program stored in ROM that loads and initializes the operating system on a computer. 192

**Bot** An intelligent agent that autonomously executes commands behind the scenes. Sometimes used to refer to a remote access Trojan horse that infects computers. 164

**Botnet** A group of bots under the remote control of a botmaster, used to distribute spam and Denial of Service attacks. 164

**Bridge** A device that connects two similar networks by simply transferring data without regard to the network format. 250

**Broadband** A term used to refer to communications channels that have high bandwidth. 251

**Broadcast flag** A status flag inserted into the data stream of digital television to indicate whether it can be copied. 465

**Brute force attack** A method of breaking encryption code by trying all possible encryption keys. 37

**BSD license** (Berkeley Software Distribution) An open source software license patterned on a license originally used by the University of California. 150

**Bulletin boards** One of the original communications and social network technologies used on the Internet. 6

**Bus topology** A network arranged on a common backbone that connects all the network devices. If the backbone fails the network becomes unusable. 250

**Button** An onscreen graphical control that can be clicked to initiate an action or command. 190

**Byte** An 8-bit unit of data that represents a single character. 26

**C2C** (Consumer-to-Consumer) An e-commerce exchange of products, services, or information between consumers; for example online auctions. 384

**Cable Internet service** A type of Internet connection offered to subscribers by cable television companies. 316

**Cable modem** A communications device that can be used to connect a computer to the Internet via the cable TV infrastructure. 317

**Cache** Special high-speed memory that gives the CPU rapid access to data that would otherwise be accessed from disk. Also called RAM cache or cache memory. 68

**CAD software** (Computer-Aided Design software) A program designed to draw 3-D graphics for architecture and engineering tasks. 138

**Capacitors** Electronic circuit components that store an electrical charge; in RAM, a charged capacitor represents an "on" bit, and a discharged one represents an "off" bit. 72

**Card reader** A device that can be used to read and record data on solid stage storage devices, such as flash memory cards. 84

**Case sensitive** A condition in which uppercase letters are not equivalent to their lowercase counterparts. 35

**CD** (Compact Disc) An optical storage medium used to store digital information. CD-ROMs are read only. CD-R and CD-RWs can be used to record data. 81

**CD drive** An optical drive that can work with one or more CD formats, such as CD-ROM, CD-R, or CD-RW. 81

**CD ripper software** Software that converts the music on an audio CD to a WAV file. 139

**CD-DA** (Compact Disc Digital Audio) The format for commercial music CDs, typically recorded by the manufacturer. 82

**CD-R** (Compact Disc Recordable) CD-R is a type of optical disk technology that allows the user to record data once on a disc. 83

**CD-ROM** (Compact Disc Read-Only Memory) The read-only data format that is stamped onto a CD, usually by the manufacturer. 83

**CD-RW** (Compact Disc ReWritable) CD-RW is a type of optical disk technology that allows the user to write data onto a CD, then change that data much like on a floppy or hard disk. 83

**Cell** In spreadsheet terminology, the intersection of a column and a row. In cellular communications, a limited geographical area surrounding a cellular phone tower. 130

**Cell references** The column letter and row number that designate the location of a worksheet cell. For example, the cell reference C5 refers to a cell in column C, row 5. 131

**Central processing unit** (CPU) The main processing unit in a computer, consisting of circuitry that executes instructions to process data. 15

**Character data** Letters, symbols, or numerals that will not be used in arithmetic operations (name, social security number, etc.). 24

**Chat** Interactive real-time person-to-person communication over a network. 330

**Chat groups** A discussion in which a group of people communicates online simultaneously. 6

**Ciphertext** An encrypted message. 285

**Circuit switching** The method used by the telephone network to temporarily connect one telephone with another for the duration of a call. 253

**CISC** (Complex Instruction Set Computer) A general-purpose microprocessor chip designed to handle a wider array of instructions than a RISC chip. 69

**Click-through rate** The number of times Web site visitors click an ad to connect to an advertiser's site. 385

**Client** A computer or software that requests information from another computer or server. 18

**Client-side script** Scripting statements embedded in an HTML document that are executed by a client's browser. 372

**Client/server mode** A network where processing is split between workstations (clients) and the server. 249

**Clip art** Graphics designed to be inserted into documents, Web pages, and worksheets, usually available in CD-ROM or Web-based collections. 129

**Cluster** (1) A group of sectors on a storage medium that, when accessed as a group, speeds up data access. (2) A group of two or more devices connected together to share processing, storage, input, or output tasks. 219

**Codec** Short for COmpressor/ DECompressor, a hardware or software routine that compresses and decompresses digital graphics, sound, and video files. 458

**Color depth** The number of bits that determines the range of possible colors that can be assigned to each pixel. For example, an 8-bit color depth can create 256 colors. 91

**Color palette** The selection of colors used in a graphic. 437

**Command-line interface** A style of user interface which requires users to type commands, rather than use a mouse to manipulate on-screen controls. 189

**Commercial software** Copyrighted computer applications sold to consumers for profit. 149

**Communications channel** Any pathway between the sender and receiver; channel may refer to a physical medium or a frequency. 251

**Communications protocol** A set of rules that ensures the orderly and accurate transmission and reception of data. 252

**Compiler** Software that translates a program written in a high-level language into low-level instructions before the program is executed. 30

**Compute-intensive** Refers to any task, problem, or product that is able to handle massive amounts of data and complex mathematical calculations. 19

**Computer** A device that accepts input, processes data, stores data, and produces output according to a stored program. 14

**Computer network** A collection of computers and related devices, connected in a way that allows them to share data, hardware, and software. 7

**Computer program** A detailed set of instructions that tells a computer how to solve a problem or carry out a task. 15

**Computer virus** A program designed to attach itself to a file, reproduce, and spread from one file to another, destroying data, displaying an irritating message, or otherwise disrupting computer operations. 163

**Computer worm** A software program designed to enter a computer system, usually a network, through security "holes" and then replicate itself. 163

**Computer-aided music software** Software used to generate unique musical compositions with a simplified set of tools, such as tempo, key, and style. 139

**Concurrent-use license** Legal permission for an organization to use a certain number of copies of a software program at the same time. 147

**Container formats** File formats, typically for storing sound and video, that contain one or more types of data that is compressed using standard codecs. 457

**Control unit** The part of the microprocessor that directs and coordinates processing. 31

**Convergence** In the context of technology, the melding of digital devices into a single platform that handles a diverse array of digital content, such as cell phones also playing digital music and displaying digital video. 8

**Cookie** A message sent from a Web server to a browser and stored on a user's hard disk, usually containing information about the user. 368

**Copy generation management** A digital rights management technology that controls the number of times that a CD, DVD, or tape can be recopied. 467

**Copy protection** Any digital rights management technology designed to prevent duplication of digital content; also referred to as copy prevention or copy restriction. 466

**Copyright** A form of legal protection that grants certain exclusive rights to the author of a program or the owner of the copyright. 146

**Copyright notice** A line such as "Copyright 2007 by ACME CO" that identifies a copyright holder. 147

**CPU** (Central Processing Unit) The main processing circuitry within a computer or chip that contains the ALU, control unit, and registers. 15

**Cropping** The process of selecting and removing part of an image. 435

**CRT** (Cathode Ray Tube) A display technology that uses a large vacuum tube, similar to that used in television sets. 90

**Cryptographic algorithm** A specific procedure for encrypting and decrypting data. 285

**Cryptographic key** A specific word, number, or phrase that must be used to encrypt or decrypt data. 285

**CSMA/CD** (Carrier Sense Multiple Access with Collision Detection) A method of responding to an attempt by two devices to use a data channel simultaneously. Used by Ethernet networks. 259

**CSS** (1) (Content Scramble System) A DRM technology designed to prevent unauthorized duplication of DVDs. (2) (Cascading Style Sheets) A Web technology for specifying Web page styles. 468

**Custom Recovery CD** A CD that can be used to reboot a computer after a hard disk failure and can be used to begin restoring programs to it. 231

**Cyberspace** A term coined by William Gibson and now used to refer to information and other resources offered in virtual "worlds" based on computer networks and the Internet. 7

**Data** In the context of computing and data management, data refers to the symbols that a computer uses to represent facts and ideas. 15

**Data bus** An electronic pathway or circuit that connects the electronic components (such as the processor and RAM) on a computer's motherboard. 95

**Data fork** An element of the Macintosh file system that comprises the part of the file that contains the text, audio, or video data; contrast with resource fork. 200

**Data representation** The use of electronic signals, marks, or binary digits to represent character, numeric, visual, or audio data. 22

**Data transfer rate** The amount of data that a storage device can move from a storage medium to computer memory in one time unit, such as one second. 77

**Database** A collection of information that might be stored in more than one file or in more than one record type. 134, 610

**Database software** Software designed for entering, finding, organizing, updating, and reporting information stored in a database. 134

**Decryption** The process of converting ciphertext into plaintext. 285

**DeCSS** A program that defeats the CSS copy protection and allows users to copy DVDs. 468

**Defragmentation utility** A software tool used to rearrange the files on a disk so that they are stored in contiguous clusters. 221

**Demoware** Commercial software that is distributed free, but expires after a certain time limit and then requires users to pay to continue using it. 149

**Desktop** A term used to refer to the main screen of a graphical user interface that can hold objects such as folders and widgets. 189

**Desktop computer** A computer that is small enough to fit on a desk and built around a single microprocessor chip. 58

**Desktop operating system** An operating system specifically designed for use on personal computers, such as Windows Me or Mac OSX. 188

**Desktop publishing software** (DTP) Software used to create high-quality output suitable for commercial printing. DTP software provides precise control over layout. 125

**Desktop video** Videos stored in digital format on a PC's hard disk or CD. 452

**Desktop widget** An interactive program that is represented on the desktop by an information-rich graphic, such as a clock or graph. 123

**Device driver** A type of system software that provides the computer with the means to control a peripheral device. 124

**DHCP** (Dynamic Host Configuration Protocol) A set of rules that allow network client computers to find and use the Internet address that corresponds to a domain name. 255

**DHTML** (Dynamic HTML) A collection of technologies such as HTML and JavaScript used to create animated and interactive Web pages. 362

**Dial-up connection** A connection that uses a phone line to establish a temporary Internet connection. 312

**Dialog box** An element of graphical user interfaces that appears in a window and requests information, such as command parameters, from a user. 191

**Dictionary attack** A method of discovering a password by trying every word in an electronic dictionary. 36

**Differential backup** A copy of all the files that changed since the last full backup of a disk. 227

**Digital audio** Music or voice that has been digitized into files using sampling techniques; sometimes referred to as waveform audio. 422

**Digital camera** A camera that takes and stores a digital image instead of recording onto film. 431

**Digital certificate** A security method that identifies the author of an ActiveX control. A computer programmer can "sign" a digital certificate after being approved. 373

**Digital content** A term popularized in the content of multimedia that refers to digital music, video, text, and images. 464

**Digital data** Text, numbers, graphics, or sound represented by discrete digits, such as 1s and 0s. 22

**Digital divide** A gap between those who have access to digital technologies and those who do not. 12

**Digital revolution** A set of significant changes brought about by computers and other digital devices during the second half of the 20th Century. 4

**Digital rights management** (DRM) A set of techniques and technologies designed to discourage and prevent unauthorized duplication of digital content. 464

**Digital signal processor** Circuitry that is used to process, record, and playback audio files. 424

**Digital video** A series of still frames stored sequentially in digital format by assigning values to each pixel in a frame. 452

**Digital video recorder** (DVR) A time-shifting device, such as a TiVo, that captures television and cable TV programs then stores them on a built-in hard disk for later viewing. 455

**Digital watermark** A digital rights management technology that inserts a hidden signal into multimedia content as an identifying marker that can be tracked or verified. 465

**Digitization** To convert non-digital information or media to a digital format through the use of a scanner, sampler, or other input device. 7

**Digitizing tablet** A device that provides a flat surface for a paper-based drawing and a "pen" used to create hand-drawn vector drawings. 446

**Directory** In the context of computer file management, a list of files contained on a computer storage device. 206

**Disk partition** An area of a hard disk created by dividing a large hard disk into several smaller virtual ones, such as when using two operating systems on a single computer. 205

**Distribution media** One or more floppy disks, CDs, or DVDs that contain programs and data, which can be installed on a hard disk. 146

**DOCSIS** (Data Over Cable Services Interface Specification) A security technology used for filtering packets and maintaining customer privacy on cable Internet services. 317

**Document production software** Computer programs that assist the user in composing, editing, designing, and printing documents. 125

**Domain name** Short for "fully qualified domain name;" an identifying name by which host computers on the Internet are familiarly known (for example, "cocacola.com"). 307

**Domain name server** A computer that hosts the domain name system database. 308

**Domain Name System** (DNS) A large database of unique IP addresses that correspond with domain names. 308

**DOS** (Disk Operating System) The operating system software shipped with the first IBM PCs, then used on millions of computers until the introduction of Microsoft Windows. 202

**DOS boot disk** A floppy disk or CD that contains boot sectors and can be used to boot a computer without accessing the hard disk, such as when a hard disk has failed. 228

**Dot matrix printer** A printer that creates characters and graphics by striking an inked ribbon with small wires called "pins," generating a fine pattern of dots. 92

**Dot pitch** The diagonal distance between colored dots on a display screen. Measured in millimeters, dot pitch helps to determine the quality of an image displayed on a monitor. 90

**Double layer DVD** A DVD that essentially stacks data in two different layers on the disk surface to store 8.5 GB, twice the capacity of a standard DVD. 81

**Download** The process of transferring a copy of a file from a remote computer to a local computer's storage device. 8

**Downstream speed** The rate at which transmitted data flows from a host or server to a local computer (Contrast with upstream speed). 311

**Drawing software** Programs that are used to create vector graphics with lines, shapes, and colors, such as logos or diagrams. 137, 446

**Drive bays** Areas within a computer system unit that can accommodate additional storage devices. 86

**Drive mapping** A process of assigning a drive letter to a storage device located on a different network workstation. 276

**DRM individualization** A digital rights management concept that ties access to digital content to individual subscribers, whose access can be tracked, if necessary. 470

**DSL** (Digital Subscriber Line) A high-speed Internet connection that uses existing telephone lines, requiring close proximity to a switching station. 314

**DSL filters** Devices that are commonly used to prevent interference from analog devices, such as telephones, that use the same line as DSL devices. 315

**DSL modem** A device that sends and receives digital data to and from computers over telephone lines. 315

**Dual boot** A computer that contains more than one operating system and can boot into either one. 199

**Dual core processor** A single integrated circuit containing circuitry for two microprocessors. 69

**Duplex printer** A printer that prints on both sides of the paper in a single pass. 93

**Duty cycle** A measurement of how many pages a printer is able to produce per day or month. 93

**DVD** (Digital Video Disc or Digital Versatile Disk) An optical storage medium similar in appearance and technology to a CD but with higher storage capacity. 81

**DVD authoring software** Computer programs that offer tools for creating DVD menus and transferring digital video onto DVDs that can be played in a computer or standalone DVD player. 140

**DVD drive** An optical storage device that reads data from CDs and DVDs. 81

**DVD image** A series of files containing the data needed for a video DVD. The image is typically stored on a hard disk for testing before the image is transferred or "burned" to the DVD. 462

**DVD+R** (Digital Versatile Disk Recordable) A DVD data format that, similar to CD-R, allows recording data but not changing data on a DVD. 83

**DVD+RW** (Digital Versatile Disk ReWritable) A DVD technology that allows recording and changing data on DVDs. 83

**DVD-R** (Digital Versatile Disk Recordable) A DVD data format that, similar to CD-R, allows writing data but not changing data on a DVD. 83

**DVD-ROM** A DVD disk that contains data that has been permanently stamped on the disk surface. 83

**DVD-RW** A DVD technology similar to DVD+RW that allows recording and changing data on DVDs. 83

**DVD-video** A DVD format used for commercial movies shipped on DVDs. 82, 452

**Dynamic IP address** A temporarily assigned IP address usually provided by an ISP. 306

**E-commerce** Short for electronic commerce, it is the business of buying and selling products online. 384

**E-mail** Messages that are transmitted between computers over a communications network. Short for electronic mail. 6

**E-mail account** A service that provides users with an e-mail address and a mailbox. 392

**E-mail attachment** A separate file that is transmitted along with an e-mail message. 393

**E-mail authentication** A technology designed to defeat spam by checking to make sure that messages originate from valid addresses. 406

**E-mail client software** Software that is installed on a client computer and has access to e-mail servers on a network. This software is used to compose, send, and read e-mail messages. 398

**E-mail message** A computer file containing a letter or memo that is transmitted electronically via a communications network. 392

**E-mail servers** A computer that uses special software to store and send e-mail messages over the Internet. 397

**E-mail system** The collection of computers and software that works together to provide e-mail services. 397

**Ear training software** Software used by musicians to develop tuning skills, recognize keys, and develop musical skills. 139

**EBCDIC** (Extended Binary-Coded Decimal Interchange Code) A method by which digital computers, usually mainframes, represent character data. 25

**EDGE** (Enhanced Data Rates for GSM Evolution) A cell phone technology that offers faster data transport than basic GSM service. 327

**Educational software** Software used to develop and practice skills. 140

**EEPROM** (Electrically Erasable Programmable Read-Only Memory) A type of non-volatile storage typically used in personal computers to store boot and BIOS data. 74

**Electronic wallet** Software that stores personal information used during e-commerce transactions. 390

**Encryption** The process of scrambling or hiding information so that it cannot be understood without the key necessary to change it back into its original form. 285

**Ethernet** A type of network in which network nodes are connected by coaxial cable or twisted-pair wire; the most popular network architecture, it typically transmits data at 10 or 100 megabits per second. 258

**Ethernet adapter** A type of network interface card designed to support Ethernet protocols. 261

**EULA** (End User License Agreement) A type of software license that appears on the computer screen when software is being installed and prompts the user to accept or decline. 148

**EV-DO** (Evolution-Data Optimized) A technology used by cell phone companies to offer faster data transport than basic CDMA service. 327

**Executable file** A file, usually with an .exe extension, containing instructions that tell a computer how to perform a specific task. 152

**Expansion bus** The segment of the data bus that transports data between RAM and peripheral devices. 95

**Expansion card** A circuit board that is plugged into a slot on a computer motherboard to add extra functions, devices, or ports. 95

**Expansion port** A socket into which the user plugs a cable from a peripheral device, allowing data to pass between the computer and the peripheral device. 96

**Expansion slot** A socket or "slot" on a PC motherboard designed to hold a circuit board called an expansion card. 95

**Extended ASCII** Similar to ASCII but with 8-bit character representation instead of 7-bit, allowing for an additional 128 characters. 24

**FairPlay** A digital rights management technology used to protect content distributed at the iPod store. 470

**Fast Ethernet** A type of Ethernet that operates at 100 Mbps. 259

**FAT32** A file system used by Microsoft Windows 95, 98, and Me operating systems to keep track of the name and location of files on a hard disk. 219

**Field** The smallest meaningful unit of information contained in a data file. 134, 615

**File** A named collection of data (such as a computer program, document, or graphic) that exists on a storage medium, such as a hard disk or CD. 15

**File Allocation Table** (FAT) A special file that is used by some operating systems to store the physical location of all the files on a storage medium, such as a hard disk or floppy disk. 219

**File compression utility** A type of data compression software that shrinks one or more files into a single occupying less storage space than the files did separately. 440

**File date** The date that a file was created or last modified. 206

**File extension** A set of letters and/or numbers added to the end of a file name that helps to identify the file contents or file type. 204

**File format** The method of organization used to encode and store data in a computer. Text formats include DOC and TXT. Graphics formats include BMP, TIFF, GIF, and PCX. 207

**File header** Hidden information inserted at the beginning of a file to identify its properties, such as the software that can open it. 207

**File management utilities** Software, such as Windows Explorer, that helps users locate, rename, move, copy, and delete files. 214

**File server** A network computer that is dedicated to storing and distributing files to network clients. 249

**File shredder software** Software designed to overwrite sectors of a disk with a random series of 1's and 0's to ensure deletion of data. 220

**File size** The physical size of a file on a storage medium, usually measured in kilobytes (KB). 206

**File specification** A combination of the drive letter, subdirectory, file name, and extension that identifies a file (such as, A:.doc). Also called a "path." 206

**File system** A method that is used by an operating system to keep files organized. 219

**File-naming conventions** A set of rules, established by the operating system, that must be followed to create a valid file name. 204

**Firewall** Software or hardware designed to analyze and control incoming and outgoing packets on a network, used to enhance security by filtering out potential intrusion attempts. 342

**Fixed Internet access** Any Internet access service designed to be used from a fixed, non-portable location, i.e., dial-up, ISDN, DSL, and cable Internet service. 311

**Fixed wireless Internet service** High-speed, wide area Internet service alternative to cable and DSL that transmits data wirelessly using RF signals. 320

**Flash** A file format developed by Macromedia that has become popular for animations on Web pages. 448

**Flash cookie** A cookie-like object that is created and used by the Adobe Flash player; also referred to as a local shared object. 402

**Flash video** A popular video file format developed by Adobe systems and used for Web-based video at sites such as YouTube. 457

**Floppy disk** A removable magnetic storage medium, typically 3.5" in size, with a capacity of 1.44 MB. 80

**Folder** The subdirectories, or subdivisions of a directory, that can contain files or other folders. 206

**Font** A typeface or style of lettering, such as Arial, Times New Roman, and Gothic. 127

**Footer** Text that appears in the bottom margin of each page of a document. 128

**Form factor** The configuration of a computer's system unit; examples include, tower, mini-tower, pizza box, and cube. 58

**Format** (1) Specified properties for setting a document's appearance. (2) File type, i.e. BMP format. 127

**Format shifting** The process of converting media into a different file format to use it on a device other than the original one. 465

**Formatting** The process of dividing a disk into sectors so that it can be used to store information. 218

**Formatting utilities** Software usually included in an operating system that assists with formatting disks. 219

**Formula** In spreadsheet terminology, a combination of numbers and symbols that tells the computer how to use the contents of cells in calculations. 131

**Fragmented files** Files stored in scattered, noncontiguous clusters on a disk. 221

**Frame rate** Refers to the number of frames displayed per second in a video or film. 456

**Frames** An outline or boundary, frequently defining a box. For document production software, a pre-defined area into which text or graphics may be placed. 129

**Freeware** Copyrighted software that is given away by the author or copyright owner. 150

**Front side bus** (FSB) The data bus that carries signals between the CPU and RAM, disks, or expansion slots. 68

**FTP** (File Transfer Protocol) A set of rules for uploading and downloading files between a client computer and a remote server. 336

**FTP client** The computer or software that is used to access an FTP server and transfer files to it or from it. 336

**FTP server** A computer that stores and distributes files to remote client computers. 336

**Full backup** A copy of all the files for a specified backup job. 226

**Fully justified** The horizontal alignment of text where the text terminates exactly at both margins of the document. 128

**Function** In spreadsheet software, a built-in formula for making a calculation. In programming, a section of code that manipulates data, but is not included in the main sequential execution path of a program. 131, 696

**Gateway** A network device that connects two dissimilar networks even if the networks use different protocols. 251

**GIF** (Graphics Interchange Format) A bitmap graphics file format, popularized by CompuServe, for use on the Web. 442

**Gigabit** (Gb or Gbit) Approximately one billion bits, exactly 1,024 megabits. 26

**Gigabit Ethernet** An Ethernet standard that carries data at speeds up to 1 Gbps. 259

**Gigabyte** (GB) Approximately one billion bytes; exactly 1,024 megabytes (1,073,741,824 bytes). 26

**Gigahertz** (GHz) A measure of frequency equivalent to one billion cycles per second. 67

**Globalization** A group of social, economic, political, and technological interdependencies linking people and institutions from all areas of the world. 12

**GPL** (General Public License) A software license often used for freeware that insures it will be distributed freely whether in its original form or as a derivative work. 151

**Gradient** A smooth blending of shades of different colors, from light to dark. 447

**Grammar checker** A feature of word processing software that coaches the user on correct sentence structure and word usage. 127

**Graphical user interface** (GUI) A type of user interface that features on-screen objects, such as menus and icons, manipulated by a mouse. 189

**Graphics** Any picture, photograph, or image that can be manipulated or viewed on a computer. 137

**Graphics card** A circuit board inserted into a computer to handle the display of text, graphics, animation, and videos. Also called a "video card." 91

**Graphics processing unit** (GPU) A microprocessor dedicated to rendering and displaying graphics on personal computers, workstations, and videogame consoles. 91

**Graphics software** Computer programs for creating, editing, and manipulating images; types include paint software and drawing software. 137

**Grayscale palette** Digital images that are displayed in shades of gray, black, and white. 438

**Grid computing system** A network of diverse computers in which each computer is treated as a generic and equal processing resource. 334

**Groupware** Software that enables multiple users to collaborate on a project, usually through a pool of data that can be shared by members of the workgroup. 121

**Handheld computer** A small, pocket-sized computer that is designed to run on its own power supply and provide users with basic applications. 19

**Handshaking** A process where a protocol helps two network devices communicate. 252

**Hard disk controller** A circuit board in a hard drive that positions the disk and read-write heads to locate data. 79

**Hard disk drive** A computer storage device that contains a large-capacity rigid storage surface sealed inside a drive case. Typically used as the primary storage device in personal computers. 78

**Hard disk platter** The component of a hard disk drive on which data is stored. It is a flat, rigid disk made of aluminum or glass and coated with a magnetic oxide. 78

**Hash value** A number produced by a hash function to create a unique digital "fingerprint" that can be used to allow or deny access to a software application. 157

**HD-DVD** A high-density DVD that stores up to 15 GB in a single layer or 30 GB in dual layers. 81

**Head crash** A collision between the read-write head and the surface of the hard disk platter, resulting in damage to some of the data on the disk. 80

**Header** Text that is placed in the top margin of each page of a document. 128

**Helper application** An external program that is used to display content retrieved using a Web browser. 367

**Home computer system** A personal computer designed for use with mainstream computer applications such as Web browsing, e-mail, music downloads, and productivity software. 60

**HomePNA** A network technology that uses a building's existing phone lines to connect nodes. 257

**Horizontal market software** Any computer program that can be used by many different kinds of businesses (for example, an accounting program). 142

**Hover ad** An advertisement, created using interactive Web tools such as DHTML, that appears on top of Web pages sometimes obscuring parts of them. 385

**HSUPA** (High Speed Uplink Packet Access) A data transmission standard used by cell phone companies for high-speed data transport. 327

**HTML** (Hypertext Markup Language) A standardized format used to specify the layout for Web pages. 362

**HTML conversion utility** Utility software that converts documents, spreadsheets, and databases into HTML files that can be posted on the Web. 369

**HTML document** A plain text or ASCII document with embedded HTML tags that dictate formatting and are interpreted by a browser. 362

**HTML forms** An HTML document containing blank boxes that prompt users to enter information that can be sent to a Web server. Commonly used for e-commerce transactions. 371

**HTML script** A series of instructions embedded directly into the text of an HTML document or a file referenced from an HTML document. 371

**HTML tags** A set of instructions, such as <B>, inserted into an HTML document to provide formatting and display information to a Web browser. 362

**HTTP** (Hypertext Transfer Protocol) The communications protocol used to transmit Web pages. HTTP:// is an identifier that appears at the beginning of Web URLs (for example, http://www.fooyong.com). 364

**HTTP status code** A code used by Web servers to report the status of a browser's request. The HTTP status code 404 means document not found. 365

**Hyper-Threading technology** A feature of microprocessors that allows a single processor to simulate the operation of two processors. 69

**Hypertext** A way of organizing a collection of documents by assigning an address to each and providing a way to link from one address to another. 360

**Hypertext link** Also referred to simply as a "link", an underlined word or phrase on a Web page that when clicked, takes you to a designated URL. 361

**Hypertransport** A computer bus technology that increases the speed at which data is transported to a microprocessor. 68

**ICANN** (Internet Corporation for Assigned Names and Numbers) A global organization that coordinates the management of the Internet's domain name system, IP addresses, and protocol parameters. 309

**Icon** A graphical object, such as those that represent programs or folders on a computer desktop. 189

**Identity theft** An illegal practice in which a criminal obtains enough information to masquerade as someone. 36

**Image compression** Any technique that is used to reduce the size of a file that holds a graphic. 439

**IMAP** (Internet Messaging Access Protocol) A protocol similar to POP that is used to retrieve e-mail messages from an e-mail server, but offers additional features, such as choosing which e-mails to download from the server. 397

**Incremental backup** A backup that contains files that changed since the last backup. 227

**Infrared light** A transmission technology that uses a frequency range just below the visible light spectrum to transport data. 265

**Ink jet printer** A non-impact printer that creates characters or graphics by spraying liquid ink onto paper or other media. 92

**Input** As a noun, "input" means the information that is conveyed to a computer. As a verb, "input" means to enter data into a computer. 15

**Instant messaging** A private chat in which users can communicate with each other in real time using electronically transmitted text messages. 330

**Instruction cycle** The steps followed by a computer to process a single instruction; fetch, interpret, execute, then increment the instruction pointer. 32

**Instruction set** The collection of instructions that a CPU is designed to process. 30

**Integrated circuit** (IC) A thin slice of silicon crystal containing microscopic circuit elements such as transistors, wires, capacitors, and resistors; also called chips and microchips. 27

**Intellectual property** A legal concept that refers to ownership of intangible information, such as ideas. 11

**Internet** The worldwide communication infrastructure that links computer networks using TCP/IP protocol. 6

**Internet backbone** The major communications links that form the core of the Internet. 303

**Internet service provider** (ISP) A company that provides Internet access to businesses, organizations, and individuals. 303

**Interpreter** A program that converts high-level instructions in a computer program into machine language instructions, one instruction at a time. 30

**Intrusion** In the context of computer security, the unauthorized access to a computer system. 340

**IP** (Internet Protocol) One of the main protocols of TCP/IP; responsible for addressing packets so that they can be routed to their destinations. 305

**IP address** Unique identifying numbers assigned to each computer connected to the Internet. 255

**ISA** (Industry Standard Architecture) A standard for moving data on the expansion bus. Can refer to a type of slot, a bus, or a peripheral device. An older technology, it is rapidly being replaced by PCI architecture. 96

**ISDN** (Integrated Services Digital Network) A telephone company service that transports data digitally over dial-up or dedicated lines. 314

**ISDN terminal adapter** A device that connects a computer to a telephone jack and translates the data into a signal that can travel over an ISDN connection. 314

**Java applet** Small programs that add processing and interactive capabilities to Web pages. 372

**Joystick** An input device that looks like a small version of a car's stick shift. Popular with gamers, moving the stick moves objects on the screen. 89

**JPEG** (Joint Photographic Experts Group) A format that uses lossy compression to store bitmap images. JPEG (pronounced JAY-peg) files have a .jpg extension. 442

**Kernel** The core module of an operating system that typically manages memory, processes, tasks, and storage devices. 192

**Key frame** Frames at intervals in a digital video clip that contain all data for that frame. The rest of the frames in the video contain only the information that is different from the preceding key frame. 458

**Keylogger** A program, sometimes part of a Trojan Horse, that records a person's keystrokes, saves them, and then sends them to a system administrator or remote hacker. 163

**Keyword stuffing** An unpopular practice of including a huge variety of keywords in the header of an HTML document in the hopes that a search engine will display it even when the content of the page is not relevant to the search. 378

**Kilobit** (Kbit or Kb) 1024 bits. 26

**Kilobyte** (KB) Approximately 1,000 bytes; exactly 1,024 bytes. 26

**Label** In the context of spreadsheets, any text used to describe data. 130

**LAN** (Local Area Network) An interconnected group of computers and peripherals located within a relatively limited area, such as a building or campus. 247

**LAN jacking** Unauthorized access to a wireless network; also called war driving. 282

**LAN party** An assembly of computer users and their computers for the purpose of creating a temporary local area network for gaming. 280

**Lands** Non-pitted surface areas on a CD that represent digital data. (See also Pits.) 81

**Laser printer** A printer that uses laser-based technology, similar to that used by photocopiers, to produce text and graphics. 92

**Latency** The elapsed time it takes for a packet of data to arrive at its destination. 309

**LCD** (Liquid Crystal Display) Technology used for flat panel computer screens typically found on notebook computers. 90

**Leading** Also called line spacing, the vertical spacing between lines of text. 128

**Level 1 cache** (L1 cache) Cache memory built into a microprocessor chip. L1 cache typically can be read in one clock cycle. 68

**Level 2 cache** (L2 cache) Cache memory that is located in a chip separate from the microprocessor chip. 68

**Line spacing** Also called leading, the vertical spacing between lines of text. (See leading.) 128

**Linear editing** A video editing technique involving recording segments of video from one tape to another. 456

**Link popularity** A metric used by some search engines to rank the sites that are relevant to a query. 377

**Linux** An operating system that is a derivative of UNIX, available as freeware, and widely used for servers though it is also used on personal computers and workstations. 201

**Linux distribution** Usually a download that includes the Linux operating system, a Linux desktop, and other Linux utilities. 201

**Linux platform** A computer that is running the Linux operating system. 64

**Local application** Software designed to be installed on and run from a hard disk. 154

**Logical storage models** Any visual or conceptual aid that helps a computer user visualize a file storage system. Also called a storage metaphor. 215

**Lossless compression** A compression technique that is able to reconstitute all of the data in the original file, hence "lossless" means that this compression technique does not lose data. 439

**Lossy compression** Any data compression technique in which some of the data is sacrificed to obtain more compression. 439

**MAC address** (Media Access Control) A unique identifier similar to a serial number assigned to networking equipment at time of manufacture. 254

**Mac OS** The operating system software designed for use on Apple Macintosh computers. 197

**Mac platform** A family or category of Macintosh-compatible personal computers designed and manufactured by Apple Computers. 64

**Machine code** Program instructions written in binary code that the computer can execute directly. 30

**Machine language** A low-level language written in binary code that the computer can execute directly. 30

**Magnetic storage** A technology for recording data onto disks or tape by magnetizing particles of an oxide-based surface coating. 78

**Mail merge** A feature of document production software that automates the process of producing customized documents, such as letters and advertising flyers. 129

**Mainframe computer** A large, fast, and expensive computer generally used by businesses or government agencies to provide centralized storage, processing, and management for large amounts of data. 18

**Malicious software** Any program or set of program instructions, such as a virus, worm, or Trojan horse, designed to surreptitiously enter a computer and disrupt its normal operations. 162

**Malware** (Malicious software) Programs such as viruses, worms, and bots designed to disrupt computer operations. 162

**MAN** (Metropolitan Area Network) A public, high-speed network that can transmit voice and data within a range of 50 miles. 247

**Markup language** A language that provides text and graphics formatting through the use of tags. Examples of markup languages include HTML, XML, SGML. 362

**Mass-mailing worm** A worm that sends itself to every e-mail address in the address book of an infected computer. 163

**Master File Table** An index file used in NTFS storage systems to maintain a list of clusters and keep track of their contents. 219

**Mathematical modeling software** Software for visualizing and solving a wide range of math, science, and engineering problems. 133

**Mathematical operators** Symbols such as + - / * that represent specific mathematical functions in a formula. 131

**Media Center PC** A personal computer system designed to be a home entertainment hub; a computer system that includes Microsoft Windows Media Center operating system. 60

**Megabit** (Mb or Mbit) 1,048,576 bits. 26

**Megabyte** (MB) Approximately one million bytes; exactly 1,048,576 bytes. 26

**Megahertz** (MHz) A measure of frequency equivalent to 1 million cycles per second. 67

**Megapixel** One million pixels; expresses the resolution and quality of an image; usually used in reference to digital cameras. 433

**Memory** The computer circuitry that holds data waiting to be processed. 15

**Memory leak** An undesirable state in which an operating system does not correctly allocate memory for programs causing parts of one program to overwrite parts of others and malfunction. 187

**Menu** In the context of user interfaces, a list of commands or options often displayed as a list. 190

**Menu bar** A standard component of most graphical user interfaces that is displayed as a strip of clickable options, that in turn display a list of commands. 190

**Mesh topology** A network arranged in such a way that each device is connected to many other devices. Data traveling on a mesh network can take any of several possible paths. 250

**Message header** The section of an e-mail file that contains address, subject, and file attachment information. 392

**Meta keyword** A word that is included in the header of an HTML document in order to describe the document's contents. 378

**Metafile** In the context of graphics, a file that contains both vector and bitmap data. 447

**Metasearch engine** A search engine that searches other search engines. 380

**Microcontroller** A special purpose microprocessor that is built into the device it controls. 20

**Microprocessor** An integrated circuit that contains the circuitry for processing data. It is a single-chip version of the central processing unit (CPU) found in all computers. 15

**Microprocessor clock** A timing signal that sets the pace for executing instructions in a microprocessor. 67

**Microsoft Windows** An operating system, developed by Microsoft Corporation, that provides a graphical interface. Versions include Windows 3.1, Windows 95, 98, Me, NT, 2000, XP, and Vista. 194

**Microwaves** Electromagnetic waves with a frequency of at least 1 gigahertz; one type of channel for transmitting data over communications networks. 265

**MIDI** (Musical Instrument Digital Interface) A standardized way in which sound and music are encoded and transmitted between digital devices that play music. 426

**MIDI sequence** Digitally encoded MIDI music stored on a digital device, such as a computer or MIDI instrument. 426

**MIDI sequencing software** Software that uses a standardized way of transmitting encoded music or sounds for controlling musical devices, such as a keyboard or sound card. 139

**MIME** (Multi-purpose Internet Mail Extensions) A standard for formatting non-ASCII messages so that they can be sent over the Internet, typically as e-mail messages. 393

**MIMO** (Multiple Input Multiple Output) A wireless communications device that uses an array of antennas to transmit data over more than one channel. 268

**Mobile broadband** High bandwidth wireless technology that was developed for sending digital data over cell phone systems. 327

**Mobile Internet access** Any service that allows subscribers to access the Internet while on the go. 311

**Mod** In the context of personal computers, a customized or "modified" system unit typically jazzed up with lights, chrome, and decals. 65

**Modem** A device that modulates and demodulates a signal, typically used to send data from a computer to the Internet over telephone, cable television, or satellite networks. 304

**Money management software** Software used to track monetary transactions and investments. 133

**Monochrome bitmap** A bitmap image that contains only the colors black and white. 436

**Mouse** An input device that allows the user to manipulate objects on the screen by clicking, dragging, and dropping. 88

**MP3** A file format that provides highly compressed audio files with very little loss of sound quality. 424

**MPEG** (Moving Pictures Experts Group) A family of highly compressed container file formats and codecs for digital multimedia; MPEG-1, MPEG-2, and MPEG-4. 457

**Multiple-user license** Legal permission for more than one person to use a particular software package. 147

**Multiprocessing** The ability of a computer or operating system to support dual core processors or multiple processors. 186

**Multitasking** The ability of a computer, processor, or operating system to run more than one program, job, or task at the same time. 186

**Multithreading** A technology that allows multiple parts or threads from a program to run simultaneously. 186

**Multiuser operating system** An operating system that allows a single computer to deal with simultaneous processing requests from multiple users. 187

**NAN** (Neighborhood Area Network) A network with a range of a few blocks, such as a Wi-Fi hotspot offered by a coffee shop or neighborhood free Wi-Fi organization. 246

**Nanosecond** A unit of time representing 1 billionth of a second. 73

**Narrowband** A term that refers to communications channels that have low bandwidth. 251

**Native file format** A file format that is unique to a program or group of programs and has a unique file extension. 209

**Natural language query** A query formulated in human language, as opposed to an artificially constructed language such as machine language. 136

**Netiquette** (Internet etiquette) A set of guidelines for posting messages and e-mails in a civil, concise way. 396

**Network access point** (NAP) An Internet node that links together different network service providers so that data can be transferred from one service provider to the other. 303

**Network Address Translation (NAT)** A security technique that allows a LAN to use one type of IP address for intra-network data and another type of address for data traveling to and from the Internet. 344

**Network attached storage** (NAS) Storage devices that are designed to be attached directly to a network, rather than to a workstation or server. 248

**Network device** Any device, such as a gateway, hub, or router, that is used to broadcast network data, boost signals, or route data to its destination. 248

**Network hub** A network device that connects several nodes of a local area network. 261

**Network interface card** Circuitry, often on an expansion card mounted inside a computer, that transmits and receives data on a local area network. Also called a NIC, network card, or network adapter. 248

**Network operating system** System software designed to control the flow of data, maintain security, and keep track of accounts on a network. 187

**Network router** A device found at each intersection on the Internet backbone that examines the IP address of incoming data, and forwards the data towards its destination. 261

**Network service provider** (NSP) A company that maintains a series of nationwide Internet links. 303

**Network switch** A network device that sends data to a specific address instead of broadcasting it over an entire network. 261

**Networked peripheral** A peripheral device that contains circuitry that allows it to be directly connected to a network, rather than connecting to a computer that transfers data to a network. 248

**Node** In a network, a connection point; in a hierarchical database, a segment or record type. 248

**Non-executing zip file** A type of compressed file that has to be unzipped manually to extract the file or files contained within it. 157

**Non-volatile** Any electronic component that does not require a constant supply of power to hold data. 84

**Nonlinear editing** A digital video editing technique that requires a personal computer and video editing software. 456

**Notation software** Software used to help musicians compose, edit, and print their compositions. 139

**Notebook computer** A small, lightweight, portable computer that usually runs on batteries. Sometimes called a laptop. 59

**NTFS** (New Technology File System) A file system used by Microsoft Windows NT, 2000, and XP operating systems to keep track of the name and location of files on a hard disk. 219

**Numeric data** Numbers that represent quantities and can be used in arithmetic operations. 23

**Object code** The low-level instructions that result from compiling source code. 30

**Octet** One of four sections of an IP address. 255

**Online auction** A consumer-to-consumer form of e-commerce in which merchandise and services are sold to the highest bidder. eBay is a popular example. 388

**Online shopping cart** A feature of e-commerce sites that stores information about items selected for purchase often by creating a cookie on a shopper's computer. 386

**Online social networks** Web sites that provide ways for people to communicate and socialize. MySpace is a popular example. 6

**Op code** Short for operation code, an op code is an assembly language command word that designates an operation, such as add (ADD), compare (CMP), or jump (JMP). 31

**Open source** An approach to developing and licensing software in which source code remains public so it can be improved and freely distributed. 12

**Open source software** Software that includes its source code, allowing programmers to modify and improve it. 150

**Operand** The part of an instruction that specifies the data, or the address of the data, on which the operation is to be performed. 31

**Operating system** The software that controls the computer's use of its hardware resources, such as memory and disk storage space. Also called OS. 16, 184

**Optical storage** A technology that records data as light and dark spots on a CD, DVD, or other optical media. 81

**Output** The results produced by a computer (for example, reports, graphs, and music). 15

**Overclocking** Forcing a computer component, such as a microprocessor, to run at a higher speed than intended by the manufacturer. 70

**P2P file sharing** A practice in which individuals can obtain music, video, and other types of files from other users on a network; sometimes the files are shared without authorization from the copyright holder. 337

**Packet** A small unit of data transmitted over a network. 253

**Packet switching** A technology used by data communications networks, such as the Internet, where a message is divided into smaller units called "packets" for transmission. 253

**Page layout** The physical positions of elements on a document page such as headers, footers, page numbering, and graphics. 128

**Paint software** Software that creates and manipulates bitmap graphics. 137, 430

**Palm OS** A popular type of operating system produced by PalmSource specifically for handheld computers. 202

**PAN** (Personal Area Network) An interconnected group of personal digital devices located within a range of about 30 feet. 246

**Paragraph alignment** The horizontal position (left, right, justified, centered, for example) of the text in a document. 128

**Paragraph style** A specification for the format of a paragraph, which includes the alignment of text within the margins and line spacing. 128

**Parallel processing** The simultaneous use of more than one processor to execute a program. 69

**Password** A special set of symbols used to restrict access to a user's computer or network. 35

**Password manager** Software that keeps track of sites at which a user has registered and the password that corresponds to each site. 40

**Path** A file's location specified by the drive on which it is stored and the hierarchy of folders in which it is stored. (See File specification.) 206

**Payroll software** A type of horizontal market software used to maintain payroll records. 142

**PC card** (Personal Computer Memory Card International Association or PCMCIA card) A credit card-sized circuit board used to connect a modem, memory, network card, or storage device to a notebook computer. 96

**PC platform** A family of personal computers that use Windows software and contain Intel-compatible microprocessors. 64

**PC slot** (Personal Computer Memory Card International Association or PCMCIA slot) An external expansion slot typically found on notebook computers. 96

**PCI** (Peripheral Component Interconnect) A method for transporting data on the expansion bus. Can refer to type of data bus, expansion slot, or transport method used by a peripheral device. 96

**PCX** The PC Paintbrush file format that incorporates a compression algorithm. 442

**PDA** (Personal Digital Assistant) A computer that is smaller and more portable than a notebook computer (also called a palm-top or handheld computer). 19

**PDA video** Digital video formatted for viewing on a PDA or other handheld device. 452

**Peer-to-peer mode** A method of using a network in which workstations act as both file servers and clients. 249

**Peripheral device** A component or equipment, such as a printer, that expands a computer's input, output, or storage capabilities. 56

**Person-to-person payment** A method of e-commerce payment that uses an intermediary or third party such as PayPal to handle payment between a buyer and seller. 390

**Personal computer** A microcomputer designed for use by an individual user for applications such as Web browsing and word processing. 17

**Personal finance software** Software geared toward individual finances that helps track bank account balances, credit card payments, investments, and bills. 133

**PGP** (Pretty Good Privacy) A popular program used to encrypt and decrypt files and e-mail messages. 287

**Pharming** An exploit that redirects users to fake Web sites. 403

**Phishing** An e-mail based scam that's designed to fool users into revealing confidential information. 37, 406

**Phoneme** A unit of sound that is a basic component of words and is produced by speech synthesizers. 428

**Photo editing software** The software used to edit, enhance, retouch, and manipulate digital photographs. 137

**Physical storage model** A representation of data as it is physically stored. 218

**Physical topology** The actual layout of network devices, wires, and cables. 250

**Piconet** A network formed by Bluetooth devices. 267

**Ping** (Packet INternet Grouper) A command on a TCP/IP network that sends a test packet to a specified IP address and waits for a reply. 310

**Pipelining** A technology that allows a processor to begin executing an instruction before completing the previous instruction. 69

**Pits** Spots on a CD that are "burned" onto an optical storage medium to represent digital data. 81

**Pixel interpolation** A process that is used by graphics software to average the color of adjacent pixels in an image, usually when the image is enlarged. 435

**Pixelated** Describes the effect of increasing the size and thus decreasing the quality of an image. 435

**Pixels** Short for picture element, a pixel is the smallest unit in a graphic image. Computer display devices use a matrix of pixels to display text and graphics. 90

**Place shifting** The practice of accessing media from a remote location, such as over a network. 465

**Plaintext** An original, un-encrypted message. 285

**Plasma screen** A compact, lightweight, flat panel computer display that uses a technology similar to that of neon lights. 90

**Player** Standalone software, helper applications, and plug-ins, that work with one or more file formats, such as MP3, MIDI, or AAC. 367

**Plug and Play** The ability of a computer to automatically recognize and adjust the system configuration for a newly added device. 96

**Plug-in** A software module that adds a specific feature to a system. In the context of browsers, a plug-in adds the ability to play files referenced from the EMBED tag. 367

**PNG** (Portable Network Graphics) A type of graphics file format similar to but newer than GIF or JPEG. 443

**Podcast** An audio file that is distributed over the Internet through downloads or the use of an RSS feed or Atom. 360

**Point size** A unit of measure (1/72 of an inch) used to specify the height of characters in a font. 127

**Pointing device** An input device such as a mouse, trackball, pointing stick, or trackpad, that allows users to manipulate an on-screen pointer and other screen-based graphical controls. 88

**Pointing stick** A mouse-substitute input device that looks like the tip of an eraser embedded in the keyboard of a notebook computer. 89

**POP** (Post Office Protocol) A standard for retrieving e-mail messages from an e-mail server. 397

**POP server** A computer that receives and stores e-mail data until retrieved by the e-mail account holder. 398

**Pop-up ad** A type of advertisement that usually appears in a separate window when you enter a Web site. 385

**Port** In the context of computer networks, a virtual device that sets up one or more connections over which data can flow. 308

**Port probe** An exploit used by hackers to locate computer ports that can be used for surreptitious access. 341

**Portable audio player** A digital device designed to store and play digital music; also called MP3 player. 425

**Portable computer** Any type of computer, such as a notebook computer, that runs on batteries and is designed to be carried from one location to another. 59

**Portable Internet access** Any type of Internet service, such as portable satellite, that can be moved from one place to another. 311

**Portable media players** Small, lightweight, battery-powered devices designed to store and play audio, video, or image files stored in such formats as MP3 and AAC. 20

**Portable software** Software designed to be stored on a flash drive or CD, and that does not require installation before it is used. 158

**PostScript** A printer language, developed by Adobe Systems, which uses a special set of commands to control page layout, fonts, and graphics. 94

**Power surge** A spike in electrical voltage that has the potential to damage electronic equipment such as computers. 99

**Powerline network** A network that uses a building's existing power line cables to connect nodes; also called HomePlug, HPLC, or HomePLC. 258

**Presentation software** Software that provides tools to combine text, graphics, graphs, animation, and sound into a series of electronic "slides" that can be output on a projector, or as overhead transparencies, paper copies, or 35-millimeter slides. 138

**Print server** A device that controls a cluster of printers by distributing jobs that arrive in its print queue—a list of documents that require printing. 249

**Printer Control Language** (PCL) A standard for formatting codes embedded within a document that specify how a printer should format each page. 94

**Private IP address** An IP address that cannot be routed over the Internet. 344

**Processing** The manipulation of data by a computer's microprocessor or central processing unit. 15

**Product activation** The process of becoming a registered user of a software product; the process might include entering a validation code to unlock the software. 157

**Productivity software** Software that helps people work more efficiently; traditionally word processing, spreadsheet, presentation, e-mail, and database software. 121

**Programming language** A set of keywords and grammar (syntax) that allows a programmer to write instructions that a computer can execute. 29, 676

**Project management software** Software specifically designed as a tool for planning, scheduling, and tracking projects and their costs. 142, 571

**Proprietary software** Software that carries restrictions on its use that are delineated by copyright, patents, or license agreements. 149

**Protocol suite** A group of protocols, such as TCP and IP, that work together. 305

**Public domain software** Software that is available for public use without restriction except that it cannot be copyrighted. 149

**Public key encryption** (PKE) An encryption method that uses a pair of keys, a public key (known to everyone) that encrypts the message, and a private key (known only to the recipient) that decrypts it. 286

**Quarantined file** A file suspected to be infected with a virus that antivirus software moves to a special folder to prevent accidental access to it. 169

**Query** A search specification that prompts the computer to look for particular records in a file. 136

**Query by example** (QBE) A type of database interface in which the user fills in a field with an example of the type of information that she is seeking. 136

**Query language** A set of command words that can be used to direct the computer to create databases, locate information, sort records, and change the data in those records. 136

**Query processor** The component of a search engine that examines keywords entered by users and fetches results that match the query. 377

**QuickTime Movie** A video and animation file format developed by Apple Computer that can also be run on PCs. QuickTime files have a .mov extension. 457

**RAM** (Random Access Memory) Computer memory circuitry that holds data, program instructions, and the operating system while the computer is on. 71

**Random access** The ability of a storage device (such as a disk drive) to go directly to a specific storage location without having to search sequentially from a beginning location. 77

**Rasterization** The process of superimposing a grid over a vector image and determining the color depth for each pixel. 447

**RAW** In the context of digital graphics, a file that contains unprocessed image data directly from a digital camera's sensors. 442

**Ray tracing** A technique by which light and shadows are added to a 3-D image. 449

**Read-only technology** Storage media that can only be read from, but not recorded on. 82

**Read-write head** The mechanism in a disk drive that magnetizes particles on the storage disk surface to write data, or senses the bits that are present to read data. 78

**Readability formula** A feature found in some word processing software that can estimate the reading level of a written document. 127

**Real-time messaging system** Technologies, such as instant messaging and chat that allow people to exchange messages when they are online. 330

**RealAudio** An audio file format developed by Real Networks especially for streaming audio data over the Web. 424

**RealMedia** A video file format developed by Real Networks that is popular for streaming Web videos. 457

**Record** In the context of database management, a record is the fields of data that pertain to a single entity in a database. 134, 615

**Recordable technology** The devices and standards that allow computers to write data permanently on CDs and DVDs, but does not allow that data to be changed once it has been recorded. 82

**Recovery disk** A CD that contains all the operating system files and application software files necessary to restore a computer to its original state. 230

**Reference software** Software that contains a large database of information with tools for sorting, viewing, and accessing specific topics. 141

**Refresh rate** The speed at which a computer monitor is rewritten, measured in Hertz. Faster refresh rates reduce flickering. 90

**Region code** A signal added to commercial DVDs that limits playback to devices that have a corresponding region code. 468

**Registers** A sort of "scratch pad" area of the microprocessor into which data or instructions are moved so that they can be processed. 31

**Relative reference** In a worksheet, a cell reference that can change if cells change position as a result of a move or copy operation. 132

**Remote access Trojan** (RAT) A type of Trojan horse malware that allows remote hackers to transmit files to victims' computers. 163

**Rendering** In graphics software, the process of creating a 3-D solid image by covering a wireframe drawing and applying computer-generated highlights and shadows. 449

**Reserved words** Special words used as commands in some operating systems that may not be used in file names. 205

**Resolution** The density of the grid used to display or print text and graphics; the greater the horizontal and vertical density, the higher the resolution. 91

**Resolution dependent** Graphics, such as bitmaps, in which the quality of the image is dependent on the number of pixels comprising the image. 435

**Resource** A component, either hardware or software, that is available for use by a computer's processor. 185

**Resource fork** A storage characteristic of Mac OS that creates a file containing a description of the data stored in an accompanying raw data file. 200

**Restore point** Data stored about the state of files and the operating system at a given point in time, then used to roll back the computer system to that state. 225

**Rewritable technology** The devices and standards that allow users to write data on a storage medium and then change that data. 82

**RF signals** (Radio Frequency Signals) Data that is broadcast and received via radio waves with a transceiver. 265

**Ring topology** A network in which all devices are connected in a circle with each device having exactly two neighbors. 250

**RISC** (Reduced Instruction Set Computer) A microprocessor designed for rapid and efficient processing of a small set of simple instructions. 69

**RJ45 connector** A square plastic cable connector that resembles an oversized telephone connector, and is used to connect Ethernet devices. 262

**ROM** (Read-Only Memory) Refers to one or more integrated circuits that contain permanent instructions that the computer uses during the boot process. 73

**ROM BIOS** A small set of basic input/output system instructions stored in ROM. 74

**Root directory** The main directory of a disk. 206

**Rootkit** Software that conceals running processes; used by hackers to disguise security breaches and breakins. 165

**Routable IP address** A network address that can be routed over the Internet; contrast to private IP address. 344

**RSS** (Really Simple Syndication) Delivers files called "feeds" from Websites to subscribers. 360

**Run-length encoding** A graphics file compression technique that looks for patterns of bytes and replaces them with messages that describe the patterns. 439

**S-HTTP** (Secure HTTP) A method of encrypting data transmitted between a computer and a Web server by encrypting individual packets of data as they are transmitted. 389

**Safe Mode** A menu option that appears when Windows is unable to complete the boot sequence. By entering Safe Mode, a user can gracefully shut down the computer, then try to reboot it. 105

**Sampling rate** The number of times per second a sound is measured during the recording process. 423

**Satellite Internet service** A high-speed Internet service that uses a geosynchronous or low-earth orbit satellite to send data directly to satellite dishes owned by individuals. 318

**Satellite modem** A device that connects a computer to a satellite for purposes of accessing the Internet. 319

**Scanner** A device that converts a printed image into a bitmap graphic. 431

**Search and Replace** A feature of document production software that allows the user to automatically locate all instances of a particular word or phrase and substitute another word or phrase. 127

**Search engine indexer** The component of a search engine that reviews the Web pages brought back by a crawler and creates pointers to them so that they can be quickly accessed. 376

**Search terms** The words entered into a search engine or database to form a query. 378

**Sectors** Subdivisions of the tracks on a storage medium that provide storage areas for data. 218

**Secure connection** An internet connection that encrypts data transmitted between your computer and a Web site. 389

**Security software** Any software package that is designed to protect computers from destructive software and unauthorized intrusions. 162

**Security suite** A software suite containing modules to protect computers against viruses, worms, intrusions, spyware, and other threats. 166

**Self-executing zip file** A type of compressed file that can be run to unzip the file or files contained within it. 157

**Self-installing executable file** A program that automatically unzips and then initiates its setup program. 157

**Semiconducting materials** (Semiconductors) Substances, such as silicon or germanium, that can act either as a conductor or insulator. Used in the manufacture of computer chips. 27

**Sequential access** A characteristic of data storage, usually on computer tape, that requires a device to read or write data one record after another, starting at the beginning of the medium. 77

**Serial processing** Processing of data one instruction at a time, completing one instruction before beginning another. 69

**Server** A computer or software on a network that supplies the network with data and storage. 18

**Server-side script** Scripting statements that are executed by a Web server in response to client data. 371

**Service pack** A collection of patches designed to correct bugs and/or add features to an existing software program. 159

**Setup program** A program module supplied with a software package for the purpose of installing the software. 154

**Shared resources** On a network, resources such as hardware, software, and data, made available for authorized users to share. 274

**Shareware** Copyrighted software marketed under a license that allows users to use the software for a trial period and then send in a registration fee if they wish to continue to use it. 149

**Shrink-wrap license** A legal agreement printed on computer software packaging, which becomes binding when the package is opened. 147

**Signal scrambling** A technique that encrypts or otherwise disrupts broadcast signals so that they have to be unscrambled before they are sensible. 465

**Single-user license** Legal permission for one person to use a particular software package. 147

**Single-user operating system** A type of operating system that is designed for one user at a time using one set of input devices. 187

**Site license** Legal permission for software to be used on any and all computers at a specific location (for example, within a corporate building or on a university campus). 147

**Smart phone** A handheld device that integrates the functions of a mobile phone, PDA, portable music player, or other digital device. 20

**Smileys** Text-based symbols used to express emotion. 396

**SMTP server** (Simple Mail Transfer Protocol Server) A computer used to send e-mail across a network or the Internet. 398

**Sniffing** In the context of computer hacking, a technique that uses packet sniffer software to capture packets as they are sent over a network. 37

**Socket** A communication path between 2 remote programs. 364

**Software** The instructions that direct a computer to perform a task, interact with a user, or process data. 15

**Software installation** The process by which programs and data are copied to the hard disk of a computer system and otherwise prepared for access and use. 153

**Software license** A legal contract that defines the ways in which a user may use a computer program. 147

**Software patch** A section of software code designed to modify an existing program to fix a specific error or add a feature. 159

**Software Suite** A collection of individual applications sold as one package. 144

**Solid state storage** A technology that records data and stores it in a microscopic grid of cells on a nonvolatile, erasable, low-power chip. 84

**Sound card** A circuit board that gives the computer the ability to accept audio input from a microphone, play sound files stored on disks and CD-ROMs, and produce audio output through speakers or headphones. 423

**Source code** Computer instructions written in a high-level language. 29

**Spam** Unsolicited e-mail typically sent as a bulk or mass-mailing and often used for fraudulent or deceptive marketing. 405

**Spam filter** Software that identifies unsolicited and unwanted e-mail messages and blocks them from the recipient's inbox. 405

**Speech recognition** The process by which computers recognize voice patterns and words, then convert them to digital data. 428

**Speech synthesis** The process by which computers produce sound that resembles spoken words. 428

**Spelling checker** A feature of document production software that checks each word in a document against an electronic dictionary of correctly spelled words, then presents a list of alternatives for possible misspellings. 126

**Spelling dictionary** A data module that is used by a spelling checker as a list of correctly spelled words. 126

**Spreadsheet** A numerical model or representation of a real situation, presented in the form of a table. 130

**Spreadsheet software** Software for creating electronic worksheets that hold data in cells and perform calculations based on that data. 130

**Spyware** Any software that covertly gathers user information without the user's knowledge, usually for advertising purposes. 164

**SSID** (Service Set IDentifier) A code that identifies a wireless network and is attached to every packet that travels on that network. 272

**SSL** (Secure Sockets Layer) A security protocol that uses encryption to establish a secure connection between a computer and a Web server. 389

**Star topology** A network configured with a central connection point or hub for all workstations and peripherals. 250

**Stateless protocol** A protocol, such as HTTP, that allows one request and response per session. 365

**Static IP address** A permanently assigned and unique IP address, used by hosts or servers. 306

**Statistical software** Software for analyzing large sets of data to discover patterns and relationships within them. 133

**Storage** The area in a computer where data is retained on a permanent basis. 15

**Storage density** The closeness of the particles on a disk surface. As density increases, the particles are packed more tightly together and are usually smaller. 77

**Storage device** A mechanical apparatus that records data to and retrieves data from a storage medium. 76

**Storage medium** The physical material used to store computer data, such as a floppy disk, a hard disk, or a CD-ROM. 76

**Store-and-forward** A technology used by communications networks in which an e-mail message is temporarily held in storage on a server until it is requested by a client computer. 397

**Stored program** A set of instructions that resides on a storage device, such as a hard drive, and can be loaded into computer memory and executed. 16

**Streaming audio** An audio file format that allows the audio clip to begin before the file is entirely downloaded. 425

**Streaming video** An Internet video technology that sends a small segment of a video file to a user's computer and begins to play it while the next segment is being sent. 459

**Strong encryption** Encryption that is difficult to decrypt or "break" without the encryption key. 285

**Style** A feature in many desktop publishing and word processing programs that allows the user to apply numerous format settings with a single command. 128

**Subdirectory** A directory found under the root directory. 206

**Submenu** A user interface element that emerges after a menu is selected to offer additional options. 191

**Super distribution** A concept incorporated into Microsoft DRM that allows users to share protected media with others who can access it after they obtain their own license for it. 471

**Supercomputer** The fastest and most expensive type of computer, capable of processing trillions of instructions per second. 18

**Surge strip** A device that filters out electrical spikes that could damage computer equipment. 100

**SVG** (Scalable Vector Graphics) A graphics format designed specifically for Web display that automatically re-sizes when displayed on different screens. 448

**SVGA** (Super Video Graphics Array) SVGA typically refers to 800 x 600 resolution. 91

**SXGA** (Super eXtended Graphics Array) A screen resolution of 1280 x 1024. 91

**Symbian OS** An operating system typically used on mobile phones and open to programming by third-party developers. 203

**Symmetric Internet connection** Any connection to the Internet in which the upstream speed is the same as the downstream speed. 311

**Symmetric key encryption** An encryption key that is used for both encryption and decryption of messages. 286

**Synthesized sound** Artificially created sound, usually found in MIDI music or synthesized speech. 426

**System board** The main circuit board in a computer which houses chips and other electronic components. 28

**System palette** A selection of colors that are used by an operating system to display graphic elements. 438

**System software** Computer programs, such as an operating system or utility software, that help the computer carry out essential operating tasks. 16

**System unit** The case or box that contains the computer's power supply, storage devices, main circuit board, processor, and memory. 57

**Table** (1) An arrangement of data in a grid of rows and columns. (2) In a relational database, a collection of record types with their data. 129, 618

**Tablet computer** A small, portable computer with a touch-sensitive screen that can be used as a writing or drawing pad. 59

**Tape drive** A device that stores data on magnetic tape. 80

**Taskbar** A graphical user interface element usually displayed near the bottom of the screen to help users launch and monitor applications. 190

**Tax preparation software** Personal finance software that is specifically designed to assist with tax preparation. 133

**TCP** (Transmission Control Protocol) The protocol within TCP/IP that is responsible for establishing a data connection between two hosts and breaking data into packets. 305

**TCP/IP** (Transmission Control Protocol/Internet Protocol) The primary protocol suite for transmitting messages over the Internet. 305

**Temporal compression** A data compression scheme that, when applied to video or audio data, eliminates unnecessary data between video frames or audio samples. 458

**Text-to-speech software** Software that generates speech based on written text that is played back through a computer's sound card. 428

**Thesaurus** A feature of documentation software that provides synonyms. 127

**TIFF** (Tag Image File Format) A bitmap image file format with .tif extension that automatically compresses the file data. 442

**Time shifting** The practice of recording digital content for later playback. 465

**TLS** (Transport Layer Security) An update of the Secure Sockets Layer (SSL) protocol for encrypting data before it is transmitted over a network. 389

**Toolbar** A component of graphical user interfaces that displays icons representing tools, commands, and other options. 190

**Top-level domain** A major domain category into which groups of computers on the Internet are divided, such as com, edu, gov, int, mil, net, and org. 307

**Touch screen** A display device that accepts input from being touched with a stylus or fingertip. 89

**Traceroute** A network utility that records a packet's path, number of hops, and the time it takes for the packet to make each hop. 310

**Tracing software** Software that locates the edges of objects in a bitmap graphic and converts the resulting shape into a vector graphic. 447

**Trackball** An input device that looks like an upside down mouse. The user rolls the ball to move the on-screen pointer. 89

**Trackpad** A touch-sensitive surface on which you slide your fingers to move the on-screen pointer. 89

**Tracks** A series of concentric or spiral storage areas created on a storage medium during the formatting process. 218

**Transceiver** A combination of a transmitter and a receiver used to send and receive data in the form of radio frequencies. 265

**Tree topology** Multiple star networks connected into a bus configuration by a backbone. 250

**Trojan horse** A computer program that appears to perform one function while actually doing something else, such as inserting a virus into a computer system or stealing a password. 163

**True Color bitmap** A color image with a color depth of 24 bits or 32 bits. Each pixel in a true color image can be displayed using any of 16.7 million different colors. 437

**U3 drive** A specially formatted USB flash drive that autoplays when inserted and requires special U3 versions of application software. 85

**Ultra-mobile PC** (UMPC) A small form-factor PC with a touch-sensitive screen. 59

**Unicode** A 16-bit character-representation code that can represent more than 65,000 characters. 25

**Uninstall routine** A program that removes software files, references, and registry entries from a computer's hard disk. 160

**UNIX** A multi-user, multitasking server operating system developed by AT&T Bell Laboratories in 1969. 201

**Unzipped** Refers to files that have been uncompressed. 156

**UPS** (Uninterruptible Power Supply) A battery-backed device designed to provide power to a computer during blackouts, brownouts, or other electrical disruptions. 100

**Upstream speed** The rate at which data is transmitted from your home computer to the Internet. 311

**URL** (Uniform Resource Locator) The address of a Web page. 361

**USB** (Universal Serial Bus) A high-speed bus commonly used for connecting peripheral devices to computers. 94

**USB flash drive** A portable solid state storage device nicknamed "pen drive" or "keychain drive" that plugs directly into a computer's USB port. 85

**User ID** A combination of letters and numbers that serves as a user's "call sign" or identification. Also referred to as a user name. 34

**User interface** The software and hardware that enable people to interact with computers. 189

**Utility software** A type of system software provided by the operating system or third-party vendors that specializes in tasks such as system maintenance, security, or file management. 122

**UXGA** (Ultra eXtended Graphics Array) A screen resolution of 1600 x 1200. 91

**Value** A number used in a calculation. 130

**Vector graphic** An image generated from descriptions that specify the position, length, and direction in which lines and shapes are drawn. 444

**Vertical market software** Computer programs designed to meet the needs of a specific market segment or industry, such as medical record-keeping software for use in hospitals. 142

**VGA** (Video Graphics Array) A screen resolution of 640 x 480. 91

**Video capture** The process of converting analog video signals into digital data stored on a hard drive. 454

**Video editing software** Software that provides tools for capturing and editing video from a camcorder. 140

**Videocasting** Online delivery of a video clip as an Atom or RSS feed; also referred to as a video podcasting or vodcasting. 361

**Videoconferencing camera** (Also called a Web camera.) An inexpensive digital camera that attaches directly to a computer and creates a video by capturing a series of still images. 453

**Videogame console** A computer specifically designed for playing games using a television screen and game controllers. 17

**Viewable image size** (vis) A measurement of the maximum image size that can be displayed on a monitor screen. 90

**Viewing angle width** The angle at which you can clearly see the screen image from the side. 90

**Virtual machine** Software that creates an operating environment that emulates another computer platform; as an example, Parallels Desktop creates a virtual PC on an Intel Macintosh computer. 199

**Virtual memory** A computer's use of hard disk storage to simulate RAM. 72

**Virtual private network** (VPN) A network connection that typically carries encrypted data over the Internet to and from a remote access server. 345

**Virus definitions** A group of virus signatures used by antivirus software to identify and block viruses and other malware. 168

**Virus hoax** A message, usually e-mail, that makes claims about a virus problem that doesn't actually exist. 166

**Virus signature** The unique computer code contained in a virus that security software uses to identify it. 167

**VOB** (Video OBject) An industry-standard video format for standalone DVD players. 457

**Voiceband modem** The type of modem typically used to connect a computer to a telephone line. 312

**VoIP** (Voice over Internet Protocol) Hardware, software, and protocols used to make telephone-style calls over the Internet. Also referred to as Internet telephony. 332

**Volatile** A term that describes data (usually in RAM), which can exist only with a constant supply of power. 72

**WAN** (Wide Area Network) An interconnected group of computers and peripherals that covers a large geographical area, such as multiple branches of a corporation. 247

**WAP** (Wireless Access Protocol) A communications protocol that provides Internet access for handheld devices. 327

**War chalking** The practice of locating Wi-Fi networks and identifying them for public access, often by writing the SSID with chalk on a nearby sidewalk. 283

**Wave** An audio file format with .wav extension that was Windows original "native" sound format. 424

**Wavetable** A set of pre-recorded musical instrument sounds in MIDI format. 426

**Weak encryption** Encryption that is relatively easy or simple to decrypt without the encryption key. 285

**Web** Short for World Wide Web. An Internet service that links documents and information from computers located worldwide, using the HTTP protocol. 7, 60

**Web applications** Applications software that is accessed and used from within a browser. 158

**Web authoring software** Computer programs for designing and developing customized Web pages that can be published electronically on the Internet. 125

**Web Browser** A program that communicates with a Web server and displays Web pages. 361

**Web bug** A small graphic on a Web page that installs cookies designed to track your online activities. Also known as a Clear GIF. 402

**Web cache** A collection of Web pages and associated graphics that have been accessed and are temporarily stored locally to speed up subsequent access to them. 367

**Web crawler** The component of a search engine that autonomously visits Web sites collecting Web page data that will be indexed and available for searching. 375

**Web page** Information displayed by a Web browser that's produced from an HTML document or generated on the fly from data in a database. 361

**Web palette** A standard selection of colors that all Internet browsers can display. 438

**Web search engine** A program that uses keywords to find information on the Internet and returns a list of links to relevant documents. 374

**Web server** A computer that listens for queries from Web browsers and transmits HTML documents over the Internet. 361

**Web site** A Web address that holds a collection of information identified by a common domain name, such as www.cnn.com. 360

**Web-based e-mail** An e-mail system that allows users to access e-mail messages using a browser. 397

**Web-based video** Digital video designed to be accessed using a browser and played on a computer. 452

**WEP** (Wired Equivalent Privacy) An encryption algorithm used to protect data on Wi-Fi networks. 283

**What-if analysis** The process of setting up a model in a spreadsheet and experimenting to see what happens when different values are entered. 130

**Wi-Fi** An Ethernet-compatible wireless network that uses 802.11 a, b, g, and n standards. 268

**Wi-Fi card** A type of network interface card that includes a transmitter and a receiver using Wi-Fi protocols. 269

**Wi-Fi hotspot** The geographical area in which you can connect to a Wi-Fi signal, such as a Wi-Fi equipped campus or coffeehouse. 323

**WiMAX** Fixed wireless Internet service based on Ethernet protocols with range of 30 miles and transmission speed of 70 Mbps. 320

**Window** An element of graphical user interfaces that is rectangular in shape and displays the controls for a program or a dialog box. 189

**Windows Explorer** A file management utility included with most Windows operating systems that helps users manage their files. 216

**Windows Media DRM** Microsoft's digital rights management technology. 470

**Windows Mobile OS** An operating system designed by Microsoft for hand-held computers. 203

**Windows Registry** A crucial set of data files maintained by the operating system that contains the settings needed by a computer to correctly use any hardware and software that has been installed. 154

**Wired network** A network that uses cables or wires to transmit data from one network device to another. 256

**Wireframe** A representation of a 3-D object using separate lines, which resemble wire, to create a model. 449

**Wireless access point** A network device that connects several devices of a local area network by broadcasting signals to any device with compatible Wi-Fi cards. 270

**Wireless ad hoc network** A wireless network in which devices broadcast directly to each other instead of to a central access point. 270

**Wireless encryption** A security measure for wireless networks that scrambles data transmitted between network devices. 283

**Wireless infrastructure network** A wireless network in which devices communicate through a central access point. 270

**Wireless network** Networks that use radio or infrared signals (instead of cables) to transmit data from one network device to another. 265

**Wireless network key** The encryption key used to encrypt and decrypt data that travels over a wireless network protected by WEP, WPA, or WPA2. 284

**Wireless router** A network device that contains circuitry for a wireless access point and routing data to the Internet. 270

**WMA** (Windows Media Audio) A file format with .wma extension that is promoted by Microsoft and provides highly compressed audio files with very little loss of sound quality. 424

**Word processing software** Computer programs that assist the user in producing documents, such as reports, letters, papers, and manuscripts. 125

**Word size** The number of bits that a CPU can manipulate at one time, which is dependent on the size of the registers in the CPU, and the number of data lines in the bus. 68

**Worksheet** A computerized, or electronic, spreadsheet. 130

**Workstation** (1) A computer connected to a local area network. (2) A powerful desktop computer designed for specific tasks. 17

**WPA** (Wi-Fi Protected Access) A method for encrypting data transmitted over wireless networks. 283

**WPA2** (Wi-Fi Protected Access 2) The second generation of WPA encryption for data transmitted over wireless networks. 283

**WUXGA** (Widescreen Ultra eXtended Graphics Array) A display resolution of 1920 X 1200 pixels. 91

**XGA** Extended Graphics Array or XGA usually refers to 1024 x 768 resolution. 91

**XHTML** The follow-up version to HTML 4. 362

**Zipped** Refers to one or more files that have been compressed. 156

**Zombie** A computer that has been compromised by malware that allows it to be controlled by a remote user. 164

# INDEX